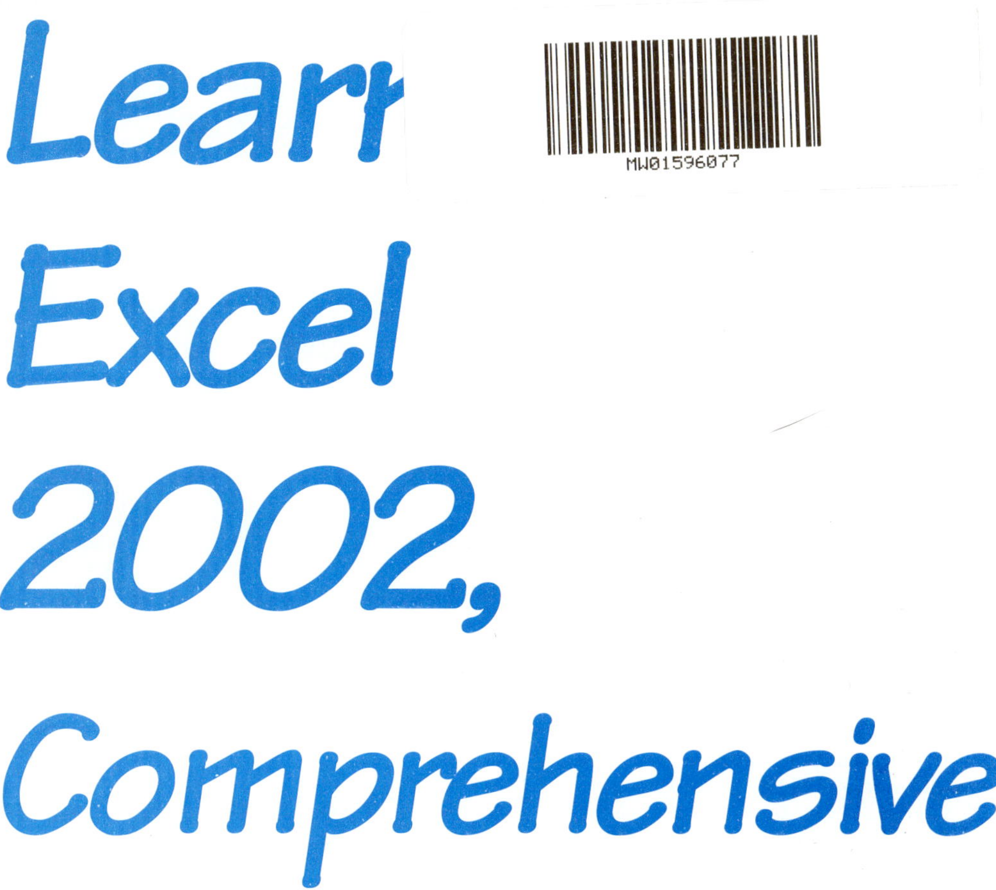

# *Learn Excel 2002, Comprehensive*

John Preston
Sally Preston
Robert L. Ferrett

Prentice Hall

Upper Saddle River, New Jersey 07458

**Acquisitions Editor:** Melissa Whitaker-Oliver
**VP Publisher:** Natalie Anderson
**Assistant Editor:** Melissa Edwards
**Editorial Assistant:** Mary Ann Broadnax
**Development Editor:** Joyce Nielson
**Media Project Manager:** Cathleen Profitko
**Marketing Manager:** Emily Knight
**Marketing Assistant:** Scott Patterson
**Manager, Production:** Gail Steier de Acevedo
**Project Manager:** Lynne Breitfeller
**Associate Director, Manufacturing:** Vincent Scelta
**Manufacturing Buyer:** Lynne Breitfeller
**Design Manager:** Pat Smythe
**Interior & Cover Design:** Judy Allen
**Full-Service Project Management & Composition:** Pre-Press Co., Inc.
**Printer/Binder:** RR Donnelley & Sons Company
**Cover Printer:** Phoenix Color Corp.

10 9 8 7 6 5 4 3 2 1
ISBN 0-13-009724-1

# Learn Excel 2002, *Comprehensive*

SERIES EDITORS **John Preston, Sally Preston, Robert L. Ferrett**

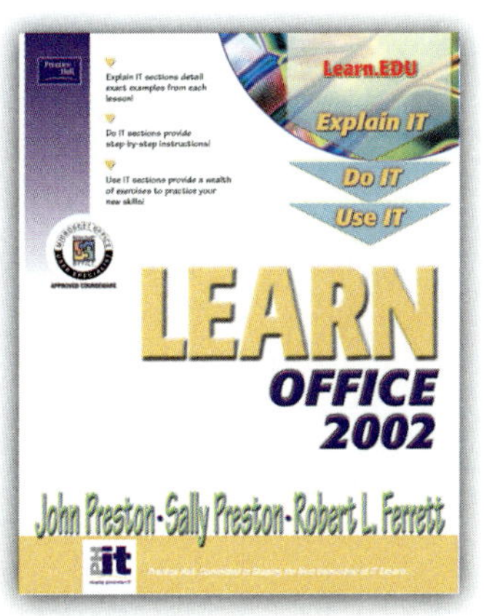

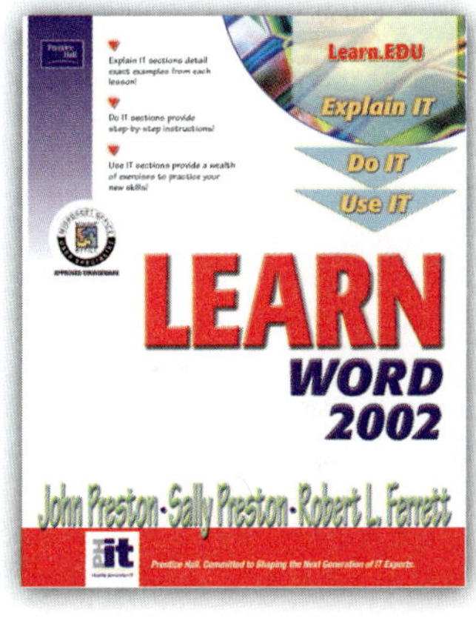

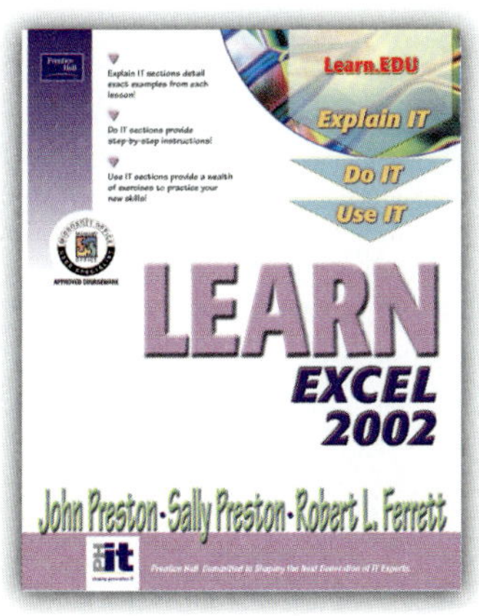

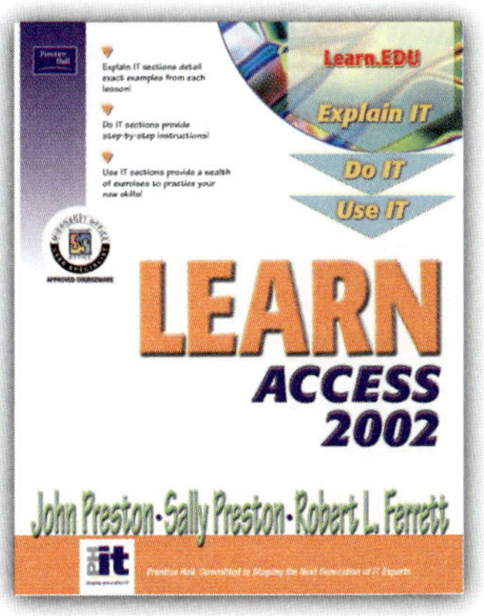

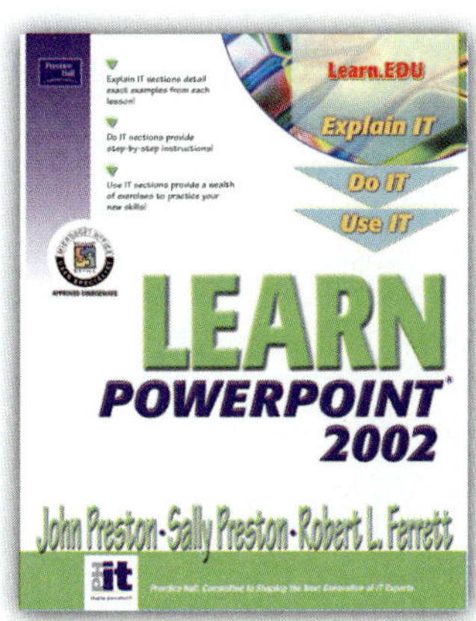

**John Preston** is an associate professor at Eastern Michigan University in the College of Technology, where he teaches microcomputer application courses at both the undergraduate and graduate levels. He has been teaching, writing, and designing computer training courses since the advent of PCs, and he has authored and co-authored over 40 books on Microsoft Word, Excel, Access, and PowerPoint. He is a series editor for the *Learn 97, Learn 2000,* and *Learn XP* books. Two books on Microsoft Access he co-authored with Robert Ferrett have been translated into Greek and Chinese. He has received grants from the Detroit Edison Institute and the Department of Energy to develop Web sites for energy education and alternative fuels, and has also developed one of the first Internet-based microcomputer applications courses at an accredited university. He has a B.S. in physics, mathematics, and education from the University of Michigan, and an M.S. in physics education from Eastern Michigan University. His doctoral studies are in instructional technology at Wayne State University.

**Sally Preston** is president of Preston & Associates, which provides software consulting and training. She teaches computing in a variety of settings, which provides her with ample opportunity to observe how people learn, what works best, and what challenges are present when learning a new software program. This diverse experience provides a complimentary set of information, which is blended into the *Learn* series books. Sally has been a co-author on the *Learn* series since its inception. In addition, she has authored books for the *Essentials* and *Microsoft Office User Specialist (MOUS) Essentials* series. Sally has an MBA from Eastern Michigan University and graduated magna cum laude. When Sally is away from her computer, she is often found planting flowers in her garden.

**Robert L. Ferrett** is the director of the Center for Instructional Computing at Eastern Michigan University, where he provides computer training and support to faculty. He has authored or co-authored more than 40 books on Access, PowerPoint, Excel, Publisher, WordPerfect, and Word, and he was the editor of the *1994 ACM SIGUCCS Conference Proceedings.* He has been designing, developing, and delivering computer workshops for nearly two decades, and is a series editor for the *Learn 97, Learn 2000,* and *Learn XP* books. He has a B.A. in psychology, an M.S. in geography, and an M.S. in interdisciplinary technology from Eastern Michigan University. His doctoral studies are in instructional technology at Wayne State University. As a sidelight, Bob teaches a four-week Computers and Genealogy class and has written books on genealogy and local history.

**APPROVED COURSEWARE**

# WHAT DOES THIS LOGO MEAN?

It means this courseware has been approved by the Microsoft® Office User Specialist Program to be among the finest available for learning *Excel 2002*. It also means that upon completion of this courseware, you may be prepared to become a Microsoft Office User Specialist.

# WHAT IS A MICROSOFT OFFICE USER SPECIALIST?

A Microsoft Office User Specialist is an individual who has certified his or her skills in one or more of the Microsoft Office desktop applications of Microsoft Word, Microsoft Excel, Microsoft PowerPoint®, Microsoft Outlook®, Microsoft Access, or in Microsoft Project. The Microsoft Office User Specialist Program typically offers certification exams at the "Core" and "Expert" skill levels.[1] The Microsoft Office User Specialist Program is the only Microsoft approved program in the world for certifying proficiency in Microsoft Office desktop applications and Microsoft Project. This certification can be a valuable asset in any job search or career advancement.

# MORE INFORMATION:

To learn more about becoming a Microsoft Office User Specialist, visit www.mous.net

To purchase a Microsoft Office User Specialist certification exam, visit www.DesktopIQ.com

To learn about other Microsoft Office User Specialist approved courseware from Prentice Hall, visit  http://www.prenhall.com/phit/mous_frame.html

---

[1]The availability of Microsoft Office User Specialist certification exams varies by application, application version and language. Visit www.mous.net for exam availability.

Microsoft, the Microsoft Office User Specialist Logo, PowerPoint and Outlook are either registered trademarks or trademarks of Microsoft Corporation in the United States and/or other countries.

# Contents

## PHILOSOPHY OF THE *LEARN* SERIES

The Preston-Ferrett *Learn* series is designed for students who want to master the core or expert competencies of particular software in an efficient and effective manner. We use the rubric EDU to organize the text into sections labeled "Explain It," "Do It," and "Use It." The books use extensive visual cues to provide immediate feedback to the students. Each step is accompanied by a figure displaying the result of doing that step. Highlights and callouts identify key screen elements. Steps are divided into paragraphs that give specific directions and paragraphs that explain the results of those actions. Special fonts and colors are used to identify the objects of actions and what the student should type. Deeper understanding is provided in asides called "In Depth." Places where students are likely to go astray are identified by asides labeled "Caution." The series uses visual elements, such as buttons and icons, to make it easier for beginners to learn the software. However, it recognizes that students who need to use the software at work are interested in speed. Asides called "Quick Tip" give directions on how to use keyboard shortcuts to accomplish tasks that are likely to be common in the workplace.

The exercises at the end of each lesson promote increasing levels of abstraction similar to those described in Bloom's taxonomy. The "Comprehension" exercises test students' knowledge of the facts and their ability to recognize relationships and visual elements. The "Reinforcement" exercises provide the opportunity to apply these new skills to a different assignment with less-detailed instructions. "Challenge" exercises require students to learn a new skill that is related to the skills covered in the lesson. "On Your Own" provides students with guidelines for applying the newly acquired skills to a unique project of their own. The guidelines specify general requirements to give the student and the instructor a common ground for evaluation but otherwise allow for creativity and innovation. Books in this series give beginners very detailed step-by-step instruction while providing challenging options for more advanced learners.

## STRUCTURE OF A *LEARN* SERIES BOOK

Each of the books in the *Learn* series is structured the same and contains elements that explain what is expected, how to do the tasks, and how to transfer this knowledge into daily use. The elements—"Explain It," "Do It," and "Use It" —are described in detail below.

### Explain It
Students are provided with a cognitive map of the lesson where they see a list of the tasks, an introduction, and a visual summary.

**Introduction**
The EDU design relates to the lessons.

Each lesson has an introduction that describes the contents of the lesson to provide an overview of how the tasks are related to a larger concept that is identified by the title of the lesson.

**Visual Summary**

A visual summary displays the expected results of performing the tasks. Callouts are used to show the student and the instructor where to look in each file to identify the results of following the instructions correctly.

## Do It

Once students are oriented to the objective of the lesson and are aware of the expected outcome, they proceed with the task. Tasks begin with an explanation of the relevance of the tasks and are followed by step-by-step, illustrated instructions on how to "Do It."

**Why would I do this?**

The authors draw upon their experience in education, business, government, and personal growth to explain how this task is relevant to the student's life. Students are motivated to learn when they can relate the task to practical applications in their lives.

**Step-by-step instruction**

Instructions are provided in a step-by-step format. Explanations follow each instruction and are set off in a new italicized paragraph.

**Figures**

Each step has an accompanying figure that is placed next to it. Each figure provides a visual reinforcement of the step that has just been completed. Buttons, menu choices, and other screen elements used in the task are highlighted or identified.

**Special Notes**

Three recurring note boxes are found in the Preston-Ferrett *Learn* series:

An area where trouble may be encountered, along with instructions on how to avoid or recover from these mistakes.

A detailed look at a topic or procedure, or another way of doing it.

A faster or more efficient way of achieving a desired end.

## Use It

The end-of-lesson material, "Use It," consists of four elements: "Comprehension"; "Reinforcement"; "Challenge"; and "On Your Own." Students are guided through increasing levels of abstraction until they can apply the skills of the lesson to a completely new situation in the "On Your Own" exercise.

> **"Comprehension":** These exercises are designed to check the student's memory and understanding of the basic concepts in the lesson. Next to each exercise is a notation that references the task number in the lesson where the topic is covered. The student is encouraged to review the task referenced if he or she is uncertain of the correct answer. The "Comprehension" section contains the following three elements:

*"True/False":* True/false questions test the understanding of the new material in the lesson.

*"Matching":* Matching questions are included to check the student's familiarity with concepts and procedures introduced in the lesson.

*"Visual Identification":* A captured screen or screens is used to gauge the student's familiarity with various screen elements introduced in the lesson.

**"Reinforcement":** These exercises, that provide practice in the skills introduced in the tasks, generally follow the sequence of the tasks in the lesson. Since each exercise is usually built on the previous exercise, it is a good idea to do them in the order in which they are presented.

**"Challenge":** These exercises test students' abilities to apply skills to new situations with less-detailed instructions. Students are challenged to expand their skills set by using commands similar to those they've already learned.

**"On Your Own":** This exercise is designed to provide students with an opportunity to apply what they have learned to a situation of their choice. Guidelines are provided to give students and the instructor an idea of what is expected.

## Glossary

New words or concepts are printed in italics and emphasized with color the first time they are encountered. Definitions of these words or phrases are provided in the text where they occur and are also included in the glossary at the back of the book.

## MOUS Certification

Students may wish to become certified by taking the Microsoft Office User Specialist (MOUS) Core or Expert examinations in Excel. Learn Excel 2002 Comprehensive addresses all the topics required for Core and Expert level certification. Learn books that cover the certification topics in Word 2002, PowerPoint 2002, and Access 2002 are also available. For more information about MOUS certification, visit our website at www.prenhall.com/learn.

## Learn Themes

Personal note from the authors to the student: Microsoft Office is a tool that we have used in our professional and personal lives for many years. This experience helps us explain how each lesson in this book relates to practical use. Between the three of us, our interests range across a broad spectrum of activities. We have chosen four themes throughout the *Learn* series that are based on our personal use of Microsoft Office. We hope that one or more of these themes will be of interest to you as well.

**Business:** Sally's financial experience and Bob's personal experience in pool and spa sales provide the background for the exercises dealing with business. We use a fictional company named Armstrong Pool, Spa, and Sauna Company to illustrate the use of Microsoft Office XP in a business setting. Armstrong is a regional company that was founded in 1957 in Ypsilanti, Michigan. They have expanded to eight locations in Michigan, Indiana, and Ohio, and have sales of around $10 million a year. Armstrong has been trying to improve the communication between their locations and has recently installed Microsoft Office XP. You will see how a company can use Office XP to communicate with customers, manage finances, organize data, and make presentations.

**Travel:** All three of us love to travel, so we created the fictional Alumni Travel Club, which is an organization that provides travel packages to the alumni of a local college. This theme illustrates how an organization can benefit from the use of Microsoft Office XP. The pictures used for this theme were taken by either Bob or John.

**Social Science:** Bob's personal interest in genealogy and historical research provides the background for several lessons. Bob's family is from Alcona County, which is a small rural community in northern lower Michigan. Immigrants from Canada, England, Germany, and other predominantly European countries settled there in the late 1800s. Bob Ferrett and his brother Don gathered data from U.S. government census records for that period of time and have published a book on the subject. This information provides interesting clues about the life of people in a rural community before the 20th century and gives us insight into how much the role of women has changed. You will see how Microsoft Office XP applications can be used to explain, tabulate, record, and illustrate research data for a social science project.

John teaches several classes on the Internet and has written papers on how this new form of communication affects the way we learn. These documents are used in the *Learn Word 2002* chapters where you practice formatting long documents.

**Science/Environment:** John's physics background and interest in energy and the environment are the source of material for several documents and presentations. Every summer he teaches a class on utility power generation to junior high school science teachers.

Bob collaborates on weather-related research and has published articles on the risks associated with tornadoes and lightning. We have included a database of all the tornadoes in the United States from 1950 to 1995 so that users of this book can learn how to use Access and Excel to answer real research questions using a real database with over 38,000 records. We enjoy the excitement of doing this type of research with the tools found in Office and hope to share this excitement with our readers.

# SUPPLEMENTS PACKAGE

There are lots of supplements available for both students and teachers. Let's take a look at these now.

### Student Supplements

**Companion Web site (www.prenhall.com/learn):** Includes student data files as well as test questions that allow students to test their knowledge of the material and get instant assessment.

### Instructor Supplements

**Instructor's Resource CD-ROM:** Includes Instructor's Manual, Test Manager, PowerPoint presentations, and the data and solution files for all four applications, which are available for downloading.

# TRADEMARK ACKNOWLEDGEMENTS

All terms mentioned in this book that are known to be trademarks or service marks have been appropriately capitalized. Prentice Hall cannot attest to the accuracy of this information. Use of a term in this book should not be regarded as affecting the validity of any trademark or service mark.

# ACKNOWLEDGEMENTS

We would like to acknowledge the efforts of the finest team of editing professionals, with whom we have had the pleasure of working. We have worked with editors from four other publishing firms, and none have done as thorough and professional a job as the people who have labored diligently on this series.

Our acquisitions editor, Melissa Whitaker-Oliver, has done an outstanding job of coordinating the efforts of a diverse team, spread across the country, working around the clock in an all-electronic environment.

Other team members include:

Melissa Edwards – Assistant Editor
Mary Ann Broadax – Editorial Assistant
Cathi Profitko – Media Project Manager
Lynne Breitfeller – Project Manager, Pearson
Gail Steier – Manager, Production
Pat Smythe – Design Manager
Jen Carley – Project Manager, Pre-Press

The authors wish to acknowledge the contributions of students at Eastern Michigan University. These students, most of whom are in the Technical Writing Degree Program, worked under the instruction and guidance of Professor Nancy Allen to ensure the accuracy of the final product. The students who participated in this project are:

Tom Barthel
Carrie Bartkowiak
Sandy Becker
Maureen Cousino
Lisa DeLibero
Julie Gibson
Candice Havener
Bill Inman
Jyoti Lal
Jill Money
Ines Perrone
Matt Phillips
Brian Rahn
Darcey Schafer
Jeri Vickerman
Tracy Williams
Christine Zito

# Learn.EDU Features

Books in the *Learn 2002* series follow the Learn.EDU philosophy: Explain It, Do It, and then Use It.

## *E*xplain It

**EXPLAIN IT sections begin each Lesson. Students learn up front what will be covered in a Lesson and what they can expect to learn from it.**

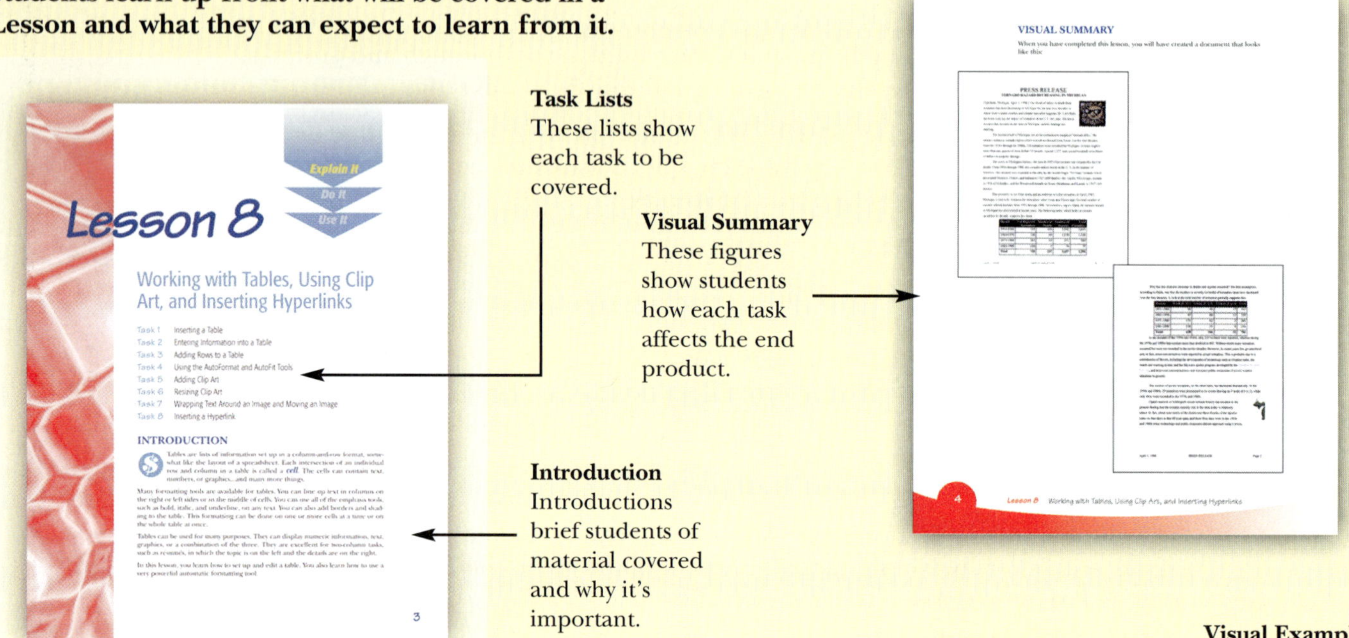

**Task Lists**
These lists show each task to be covered.

**Visual Summary**
These figures show students how each task affects the end product.

**Introduction**
Introductions brief students of material covered and why it's important.

**Visual Examples**
Numerous screen captures show how the student's own screen should look.

## *D*o It

**DO IT sections contain numbered steps that walk students through each task, allowing them to do the work themselves along with the instruction.**

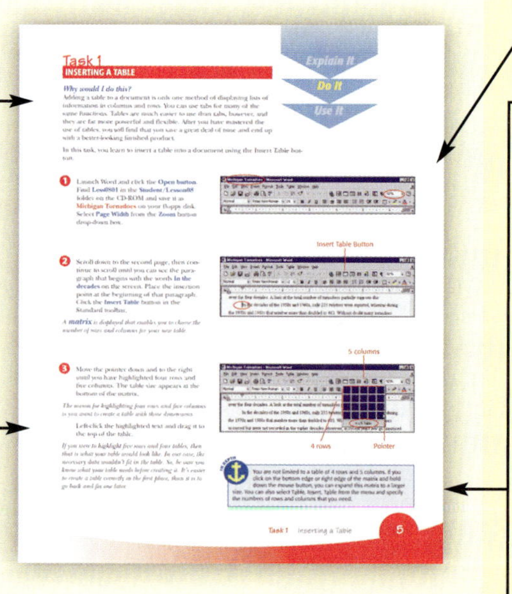

**Why would I do this?**
These sections explain the relevance to the student of each concept covered.

**Numbered Steps**
Students are guided through each task in a step-by-step format with explanations in italics.

**Quick Tip**
A faster or more efficient way of doing something.

**In Depth**
A detailed look at a topic or procedure, or another way of doing something.

**Caution**
Troubleshooting tips that point out common pitfalls.

# *U*se It

USE IT sections give the student opportunities to evaluate and practice skills learned in the Lessons, furthering their knowledge, comprehension, and understanding of the topics.

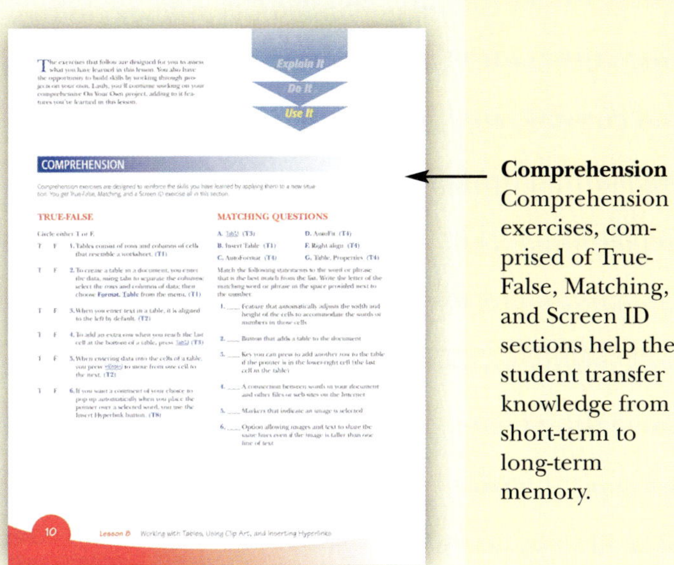

## Reinforcement

These exercises provide practice in skills introduced in the tasks.

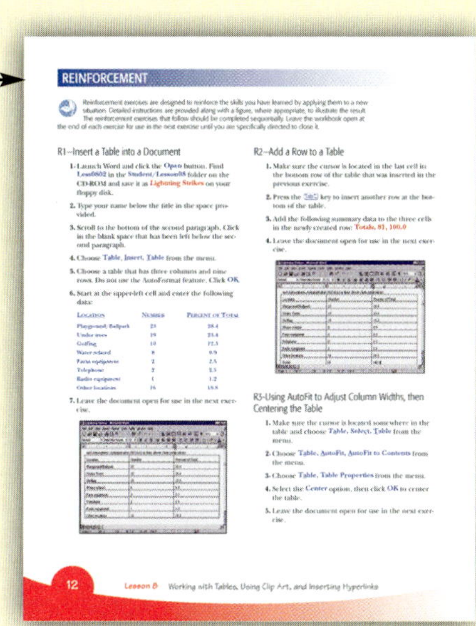

## Comprehension

Comprehension exercises, comprised of True-False, Matching, and Screen ID sections help the student transfer knowledge from short-term to long-term memory.

## Challenge

The exercises test the student's ability to apply their skills to new situations with less-detailed instructions.

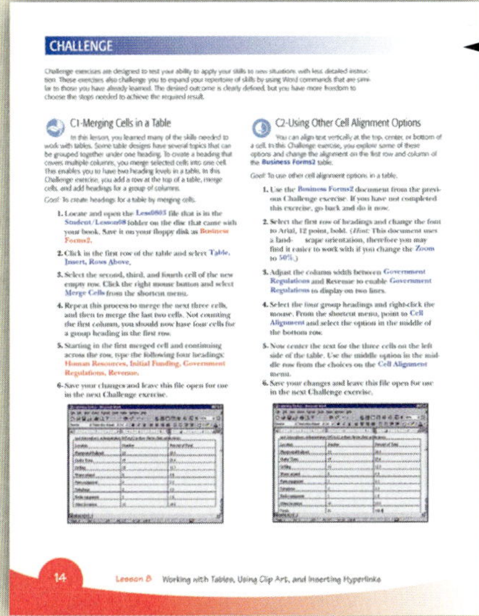

## On Your Own

Students are provided with guidelines on how to apply the skills acquired to a project of their choice.

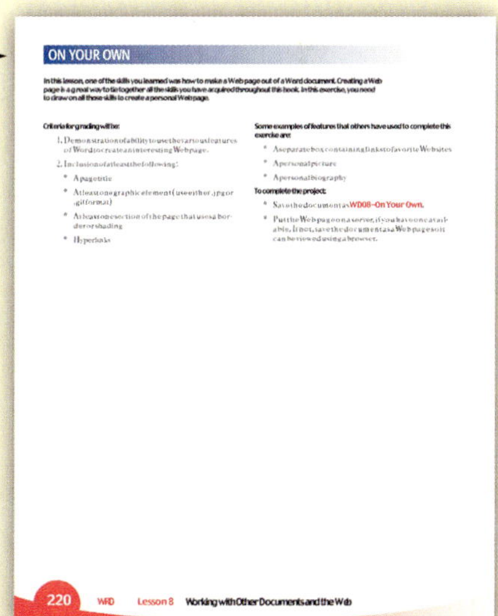

# Using Common Elements in Office



## INTRODUCTION

Many of the techniques and procedures you use in one Microsoft Office application will work in most or all of the other applications. (Note: The term *application* refers to one of the parts of the Office suite, such as Word or Excel. In this book, it is used synonymously with the word *program*). For example, you use the same procedures to activate a menu in Word as you do in Excel and PowerPoint. The toolbars are also used in the same way, and some of the more common buttons (Print, Copy, Paste, Undo, and several others) that you learn about in the following lessons are exactly the same in every application.

There are also differences between the applications. No two have exactly the same menu options, although all have many similarities. Some buttons are common to many of the programs, but are missing from one or two others. Some features are available in several programs, but absent from others. For example, Word, PowerPoint, and Excel have a feature that enables people who are collaborating on a document to write screen comments to each other. You cannot attach comments in Access, however.

One of the main strengths of the Microsoft Office suite is the consistency of the programs and the way they work together. A chart created in Excel can easily be inserted into a Word document or a PowerPoint presentation. An outline in Word can be used as the backbone of a PowerPoint presentation. A table of information in Access can be sent to Excel for numerical analysis.

Another strength of the Office suite is the capability to save files in a format that can be read on the World Wide Web. You can create a Web page using many of the programs. You can even create a Web slideshow using PowerPoint, and you can publish Access data files that can be read, searched, and sorted by people all over the world.

In this lesson, you will look at some of the features common to all (or nearly all) of the Microsoft Office applications.

## VISUAL SUMMARY

By the time you have completed this lesson, you will have worked with a document that looks like this:

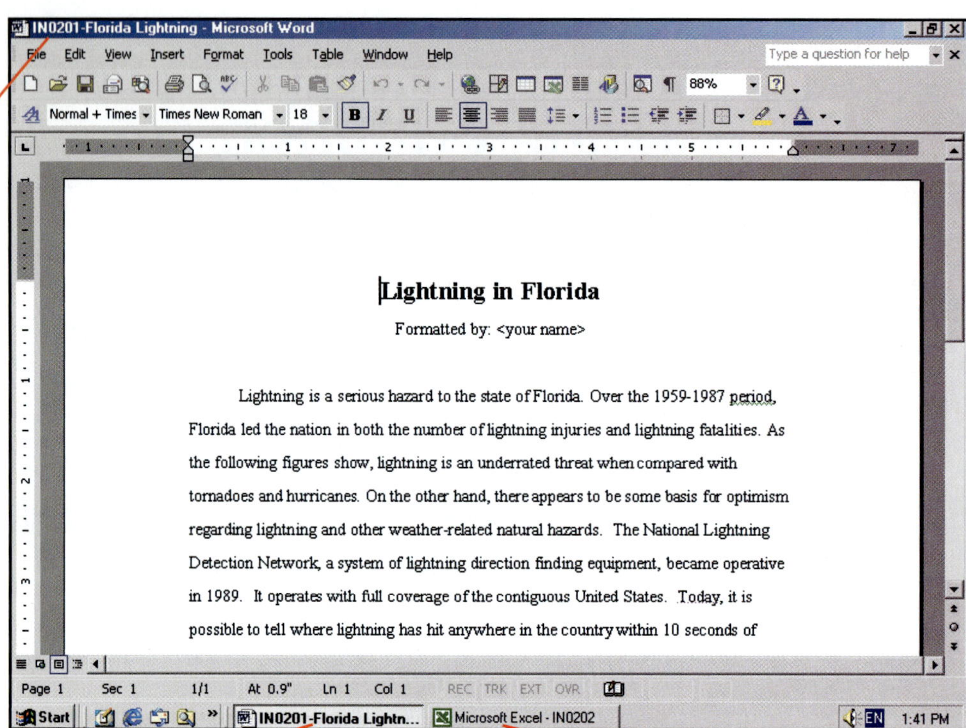

# Task 1
## STARTING AND EXITING AN OFFICE APPLICATION

### Why would I do this?

To work in one of the Microsoft Office applications, it first needs to be opened. Starting an application is also referred to as launching the program. This is usually done using the *Start button* on the taskbar. The Start button provides an easy way to open programs and utilities, activate Windows Help, move quickly to recently used documents, and even shut down your computer. All Office applications can be started in the same way. The exit procedure is also consistent for all Office applications.

In this task, you start and exit Microsoft Word.

**1** Click the **Start** button and move to the **Programs** option.

*A submenu displays. It doesn't matter if Windows Explorer or any other program is open. You can launch any Office application with one or more programs open.*

**CAUTION**

The Microsoft Word option might not be available in the Programs submenu. If not, look for a Microsoft Office option that has another submenu.

If the Start button does not activate the Start menu, it probably means that you are working in a lab in which security software has been installed. In this case, you will probably need to use a shortcut on the desktop to open programs. Check with the lab manager for further instructions.

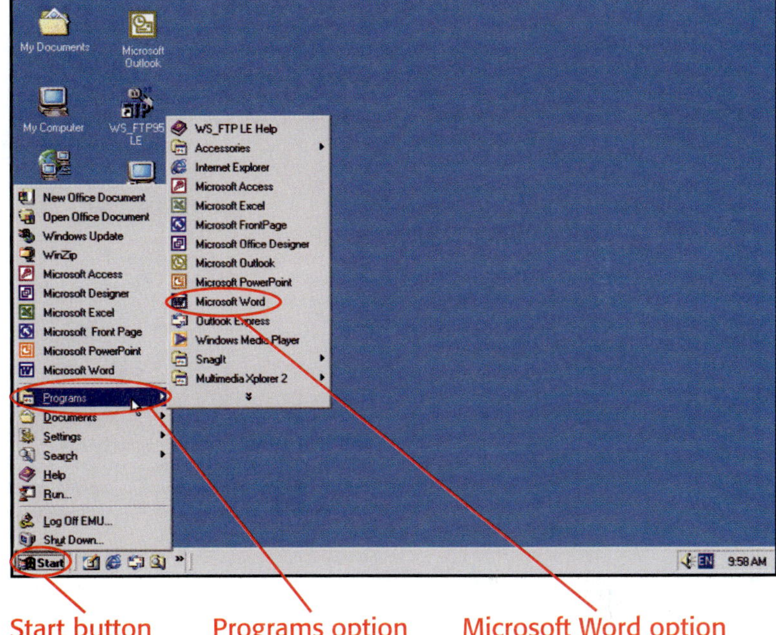

**2** Select **Microsoft Word** from the submenu.

*The Microsoft Word window opens to a new document. The document is given a default name, such as Document1. The document name is displayed in both the title bar and the taskbar at the bottom of the screen. A task pane also appears on the right side of the screen, displaying recently edited documents and program options. This feature can be turned on and off by selecting View, Task Pane from the menu.*

Default name in the title bar

Work area

Recently edited documents

Task pane

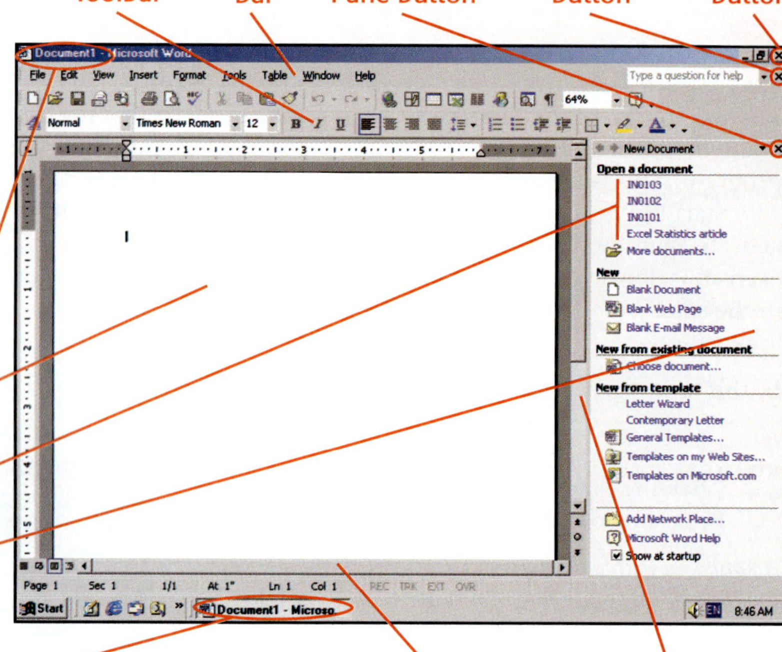


**IN DEPTH**

You may have only one toolbar displayed instead of the two that are shown in the figure. This issue is addressed in Task 4. Your work area may also look different. There are several different views you can choose when working in Word, and the one that is displayed is the last one that was used on that machine. Finally, the rulers may also be turned off.

In some of the applications, such as Access and PowerPoint, you will have to answer questions before you get to the window in which you will enter information. In Word and Excel, however, a blank document (or worksheet) is displayed as soon as the program is started.

**CAUTION**

You may not see the default document name in the taskbar if the taskbar is hidden. If the taskbar is hidden, move your pointer to the bottom of the screen. The taskbar will pop up. If you want to display or hide the taskbar, right-click in an open area of the taskbar and select Properties from the shortcut menu. Click the Auto hide check box to turn the Auto hide feature on or off. The taskbar will be displayed in the figures through the end of this lesson, and then hidden for the rest of the book. This gives you the maximum viewing area for the figures.

**3** If the window is not maximized, click the **Maximize** button in the title bar.

*The Maximize button is the middle button on the right end of the title bar. When the window is maximized, the Maximize button changes to a Restore button. Maximizing the work area will give you the largest area in which to work.*

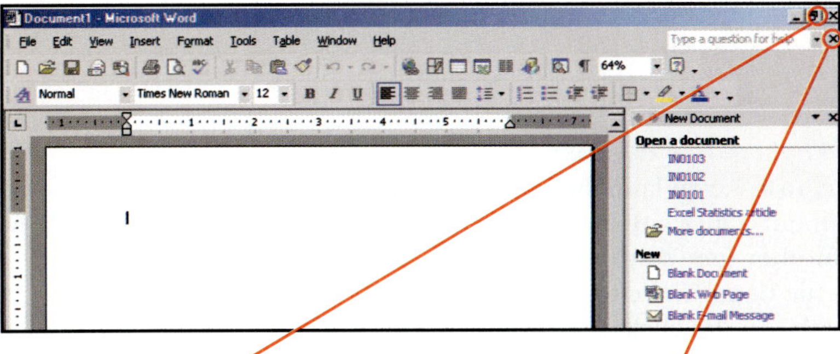



**4** Click the **Close Window** button on the right edge of the menu bar.

*The Close Window button is just below the Close button in the title bar. The document closes, leaving the Microsoft Word window open.*

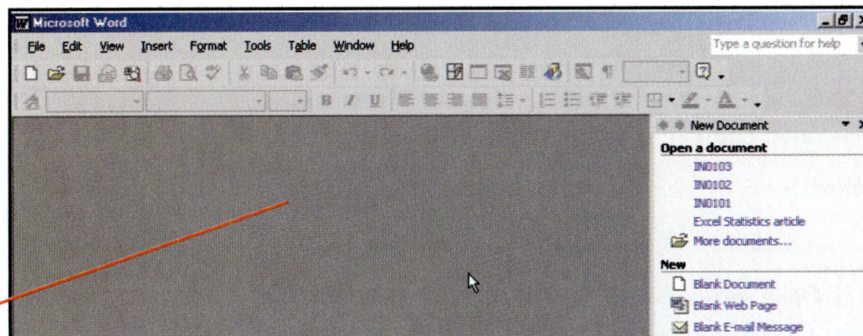



**5** Click the **Close** button in the upper-right corner of the Microsoft Word window.

*This closes Microsoft Word and takes you back to the screen you saw just before you opened Word.*

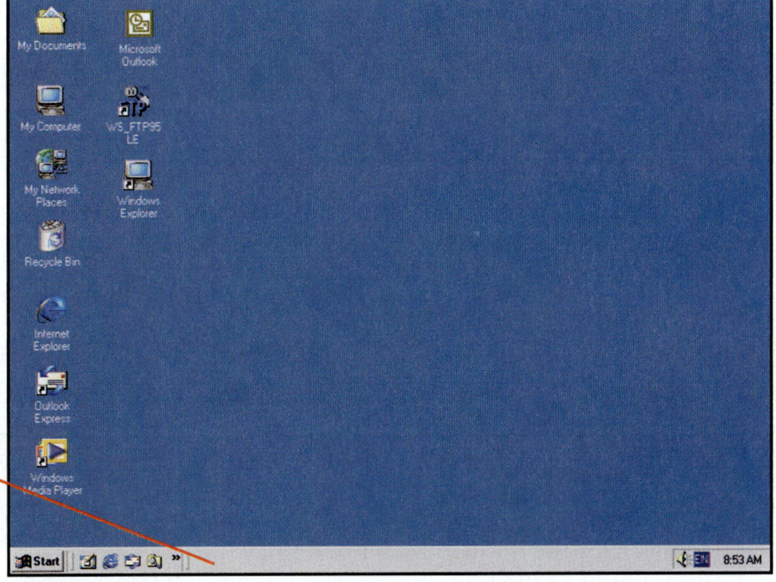



**IN DEPTH**

There are several ways to start an Office application. The most common is to use the Start menu, where you can get to the program using the Programs option. You can also add Office application shortcuts to the top of the Start menu or to the desktop. Use Windows Help if you would like to use one of these shortcut methods. In this book, you will be instructed to start the application. It is up to you which method you use.

# Task 2
## OPENING AND SAVING AN EXISTING DOCUMENT WITH A NEW NAME

### Why would I do this?

In Task 1, you launched Microsoft Word, which automatically opened a blank document. Once a document is created and saved to a disk, you may want to open it at another time so you can edit it or print it. After you have given an active document a file name and chosen a storage location, you will be able to save the file quickly with just the click of a button.

In this task, you use the Open dialog box to copy a file from its storage location (which may be a hard drive, a network drive, a Web site, or a CD-ROM disc) to your floppy disk. You then open the document, save it with a new name, make a change, and save the change. This is the document you will be using for the rest of this lesson.

**1** Click the **Start** button, choose **Programs**, and then select **Microsoft Word**.

*Word opens to a blank document.*

   Click the **Open** button on the toolbar.

*The Open dialog box displays. The files contained in your Open dialog box are likely to be different than the ones shown in the figure.*

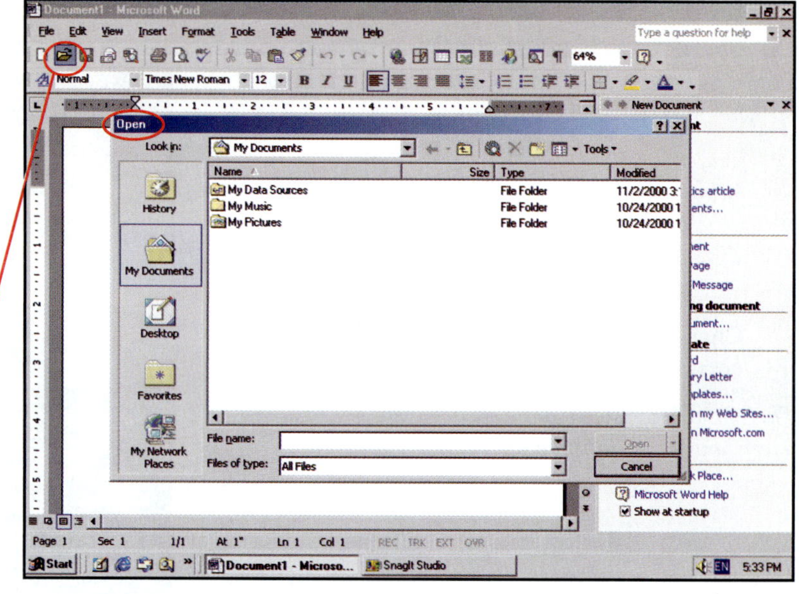


**2** Click the down arrow at the end of the **Look in** box, and select the location of the student files from the list.

*The folders (in this case on a CD-ROM disc) are displayed.*

   Double-click the **Student** folder to display the contents of the folder.

*The files you see will not be exactly the same as those shown in the figure.*

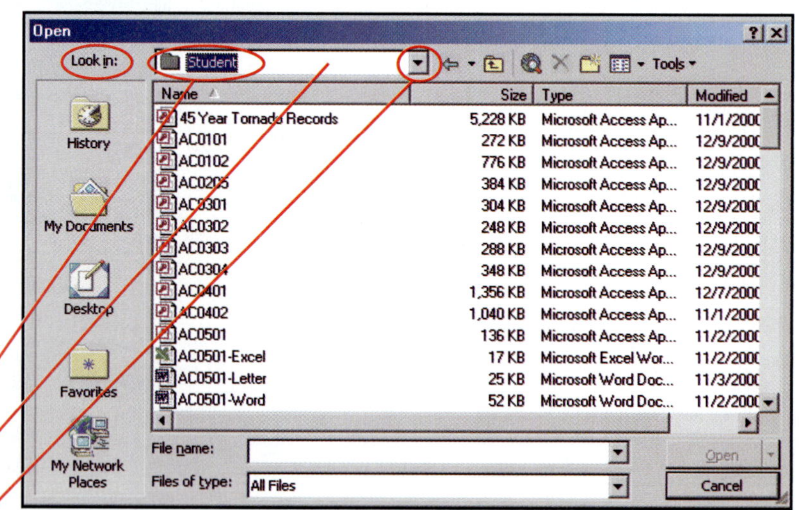

**3** Use the vertical scroll bar to scroll down. Select **IN0201** and click the **Open** button.

*If you are using a file from a CD-ROM, it will be in a read-only format that does not allow you to modify it. This may also be true of files downloaded from a network server. Before you can begin to use this file, you need to save it with a new name. In the example that follows, a floppy disk is used.*

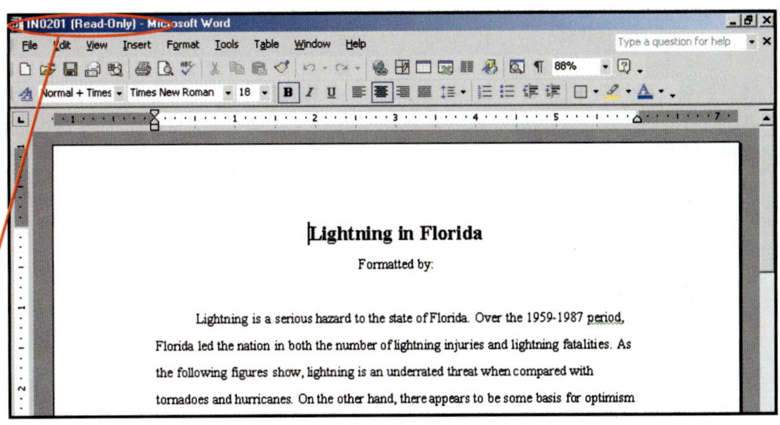


Title bar indicates whether the file is read-only

**4** Click the **File** option in the menu bar, move the mouse pointer down the options that are displayed, and click **Save As**.

*The Save As dialog box opens showing a list of Word files in the Student folder. The Open dialog box and the Save As dialog box are very similar except one is used to open files, and the other is used to save files. To save this file, you need to choose a location for the file and a new file name. For this example, use a formatted floppy disk. If you don't have one available, use a folder on a hard drive or a network drive. (Note: You will learn more about using menus in Task 4.)*

With your formatted floppy disk in the **A** drive, click the down arrow at the end of the **Save in** box and select **3½ Floppy (A:)**.

*The contents of the disk in the A drive are displayed.*

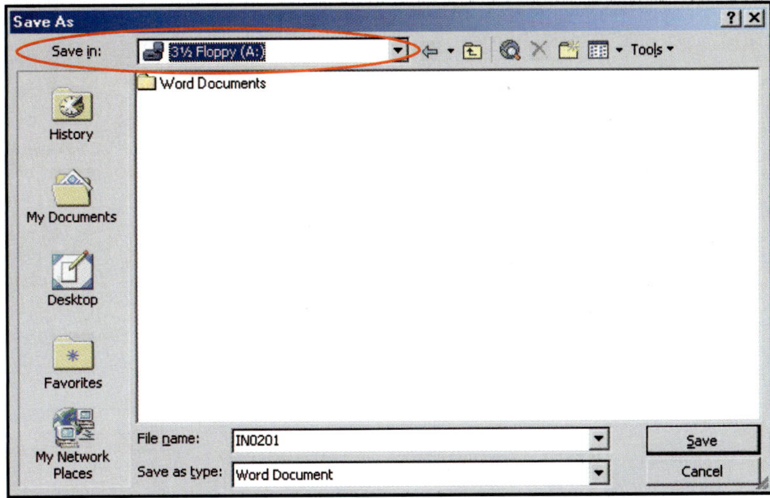


**5** Click-and-drag across the name in the **File name** box, and then type **IN0201-Florida Lightning**.

*The new file name replaces the old one.*

IN DEPTH

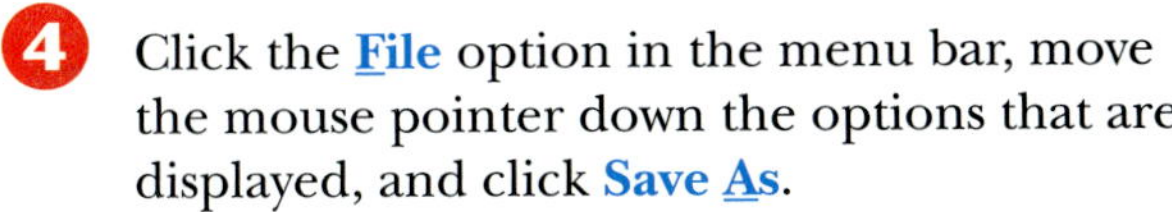 If you want to create a new folder to store your new file, you can click the Create New Folder button on the toolbar. The New Folder dialog box will ask you to type a folder name, and then creates the new folder when you click OK.

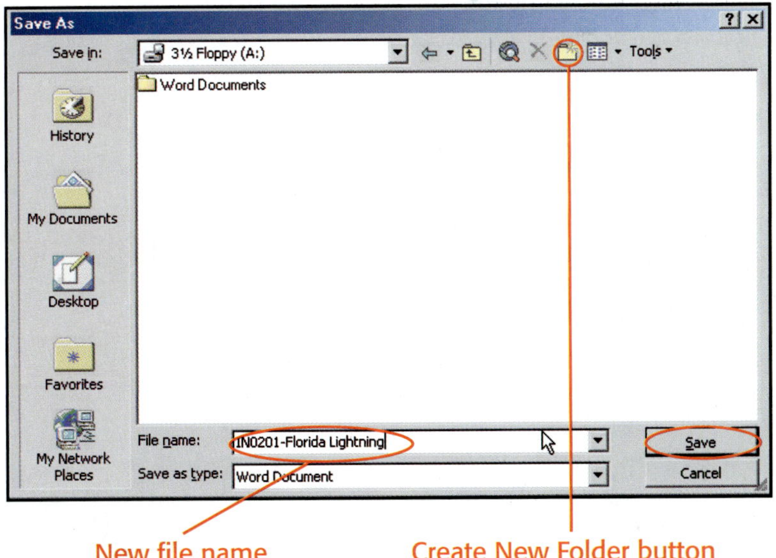


New file name                    Create New Folder button

**6** Click the **Save** button.

*The file is saved with the new name on your floppy disk, and the title bar no longer indicates it is a read-only file.*

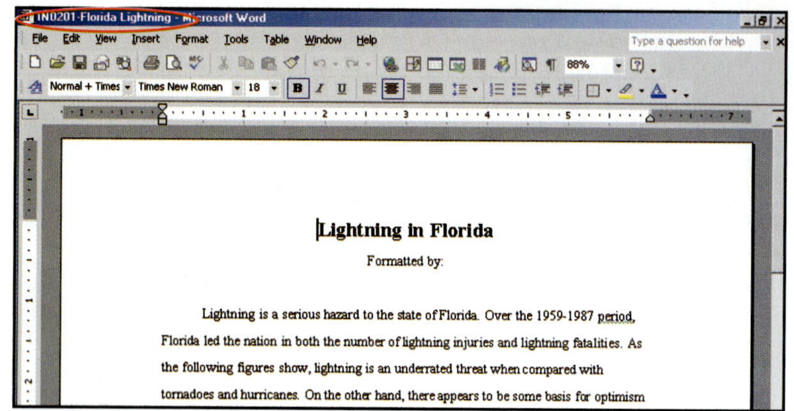



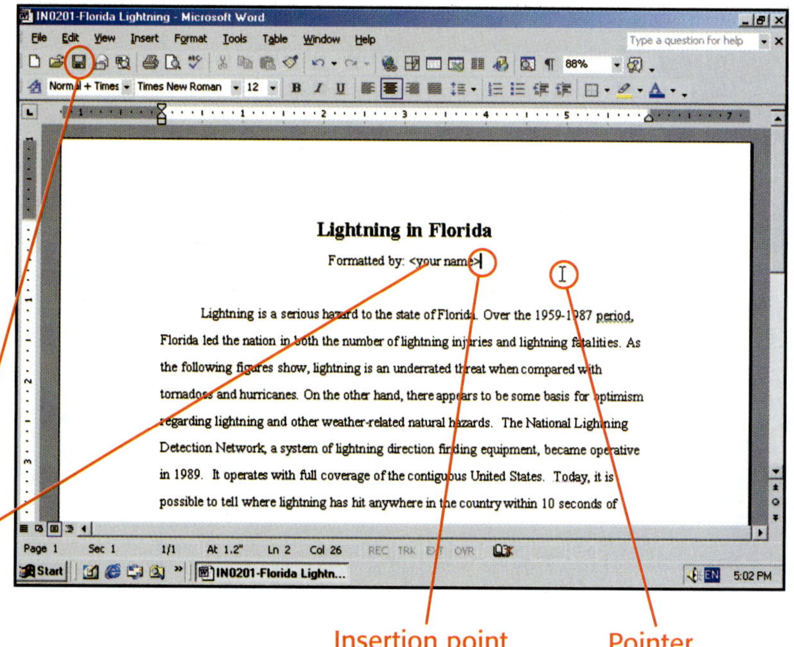



When using a floppy disk to save your work, make sure that the disk has enough room for your file before you save it. Always keep an extra disk handy. If you try to save your work and get an error message that the disk is full, click OK. Replace the floppy disk with one that has enough room and use the File, Save As procedure to select the new disk. If you do not have another disk available and are using a lab computer, you can right-click on one or more unneeded files in the Save As dialog box and select Delete from the shortcut menu. This will free up space to save your current document. If all else fails, save your work to the My Documents folder on the lab hard drive and go get another disk!

**7** Click the pointer to the right of **Formatted by:** and type your name.

*The pointer is now in the form of an I-bar. When you position the I-bar pointer and click with the left mouse button, a flashing vertical line is inserted. This is known as the **insertion point**. When you start typing, the text will appear at the insertion point, not at the pointer location. This is true in all Office programs.*

    Click the **Save** button on the toolbar.

*The changes you just made to the document are saved. Leave the document open for the next task.*

Once you have the document saved on your floppy disk, there is a quick method to open it in the future. Open Windows Explorer or my Computer, find the file, and double-click it. The application that created the file (in this case Word) is launched automatically and the document opens.

# Task 3



### Why would I do this?

There will be times when you need to have two or more applications open at the
same time. For example, you may be working on a Word document, but occasionally need to refer to data in a database or calculations in a spreadsheet. Also, you
might want to copy a chart from Excel into a PowerPoint presentation. You can
open one application, get the information you want, close it, and then open
another application. It is much easier, however, to open multiple documents at
the same time. To do this, you need to know how to effectively use the taskbar.

In this task, you learn how to keep several documents open at the same time and
how to move from one to the other.

**1** With the **IN0201-Florida Lightning** document open from Task 2, click the **Start** button, choose **Programs**, and then select
**Microsoft Excel**.

*Microsoft Excel opens and a blank worksheet displays.
The toolbars might be displayed in either one or two
lines.*

   Click the **Open** button on the toolbar.

*The Open dialog box displays. The files and folders
contained in your Open dialog box are likely to be different than the ones shown in the figure.*

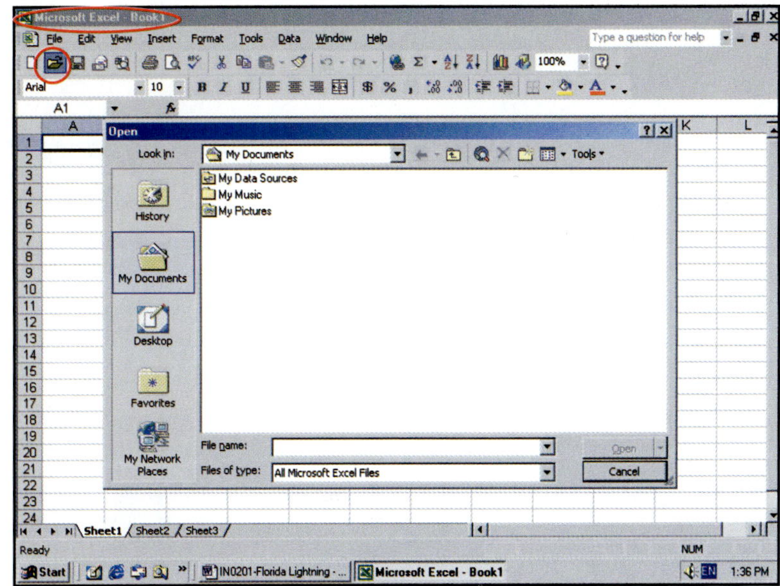

**2** Select the location of your student files.

*The Student folder displays.*

   Double-click the **Student** folder to display
the contents of the folder.

*The files you see will not be exactly the same as those
shown in the figure.*

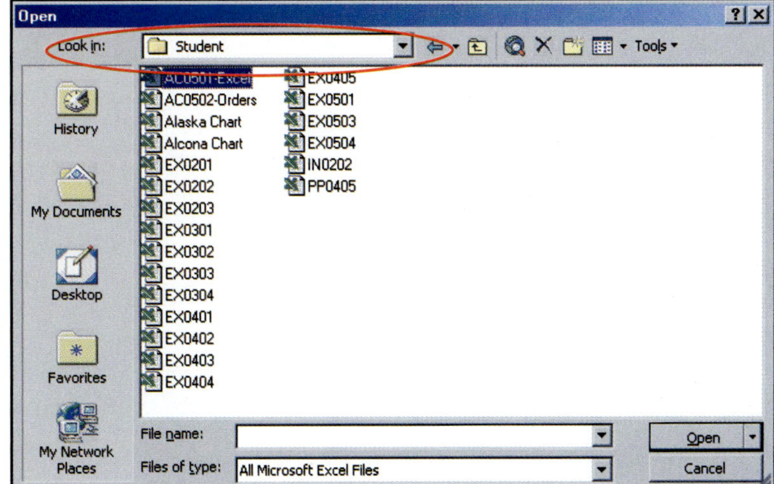

**3**    Select **IN0202** and click the **Open** button.

*The file opens. Because you will not be making any changes to this file, you do not need to make any modifications if it opens as a read-only file.*

     Examine the taskbar.

*Notice that you now have two open documents created by two different applications, even though only one is displayed.*

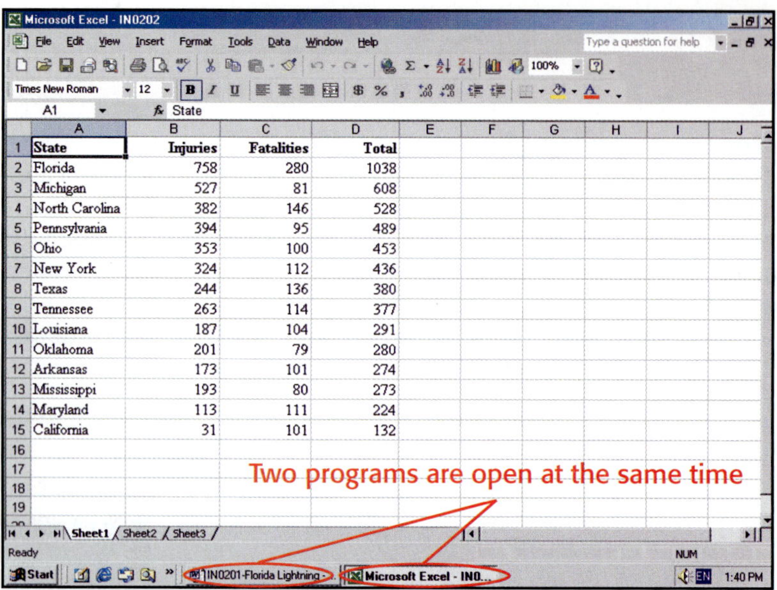


**4**    Click the **Microsoft Word** button on the taskbar.

*You return to the Word document, leaving the Excel document open and conveniently available.*

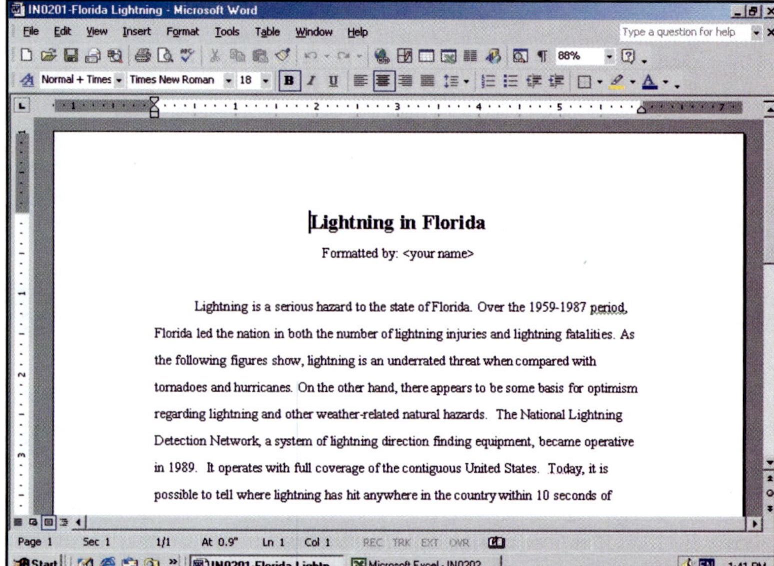

**5** Click the **Microsoft Excel** button on the taskbar, and then click the **Close** button in the upper-right corner of the Excel title bar.

*Excel closes, and the screen reverts to the most recently open window, in this case the Word document. There is only one open document shown in the taskbar.*

Leave the IN0201-Florida Lightning document open for the next task.

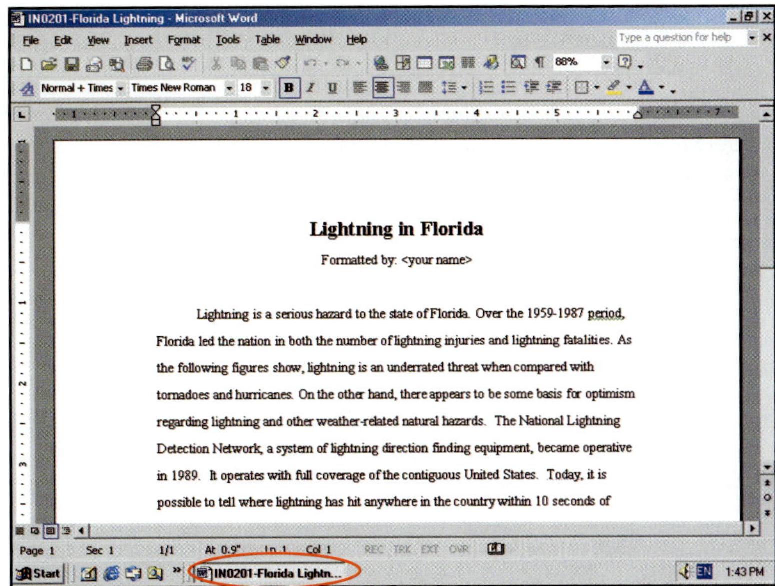

# Task 4

## USING MENUS AND TOOLBARS

### Why would I do this?

You have already used both menus and toolbars in the introductory tasks of this book. For example, you used the File menu option in Task 2 to save a document using a different name. On occasion, you have also been asked to click buttons in a toolbar. The toolbars and menu bar have features that you will need to know to understand the way Microsoft Office works. (Note: The Standard and Formatting toolbars are shown on one line for this task.)

In this task, you learn how to use the menu bar and how to use and modify a toolbar.

**1** With the **IN0201-Florida Lightning** document open, click the **Tools** option in the menu bar.

*A fairly short drop-down menu displays. The options shown are the most commonly used Tools options and the ones most recently used on your computer. There are other Tools options that are not visible yet. The look of the menu displayed on your computer will depend on which options have been used recently.*

The Tools drop-down menu

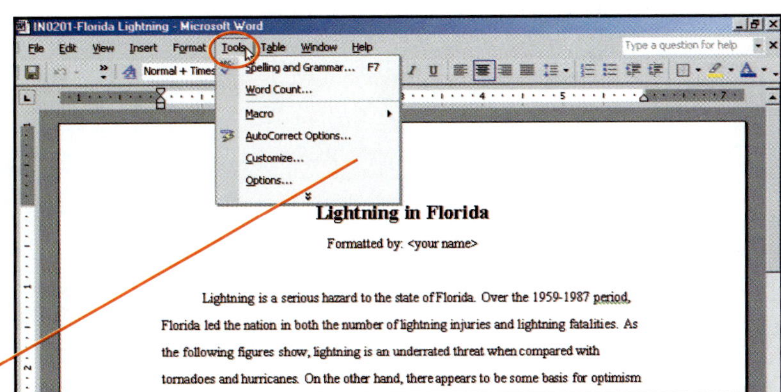

The letter that is underlined in the menu option refers to a keyboard shortcut for that option. An alternative way to activate the menu is to press and hold Alt and press the underlined letter, which activates the drop-down menu. You can press Alt+T, for example, to activate the Tools menu. You can then use the up and down arrows to move to menu choices and press Enter to select a command.

**2** Leave the pointer on the **Tools** menu option for a couple of seconds.

*The Tools drop-down menu expands. The options with the light gray background on the left are the commands that were visible in the unexpanded drop-down menu. Those with a dark gray background on the left are less commonly-used commands. This feature enables you to choose from the most commonly-used commands in a short menu, but adds other options to be used when necessary. If you use one of these other options on a regular basis, it will appear in the short drop-down menu.*

*Notice that some of the commands in the Tools menu have arrows on the right side. This means that there is a submenu for that menu option.*

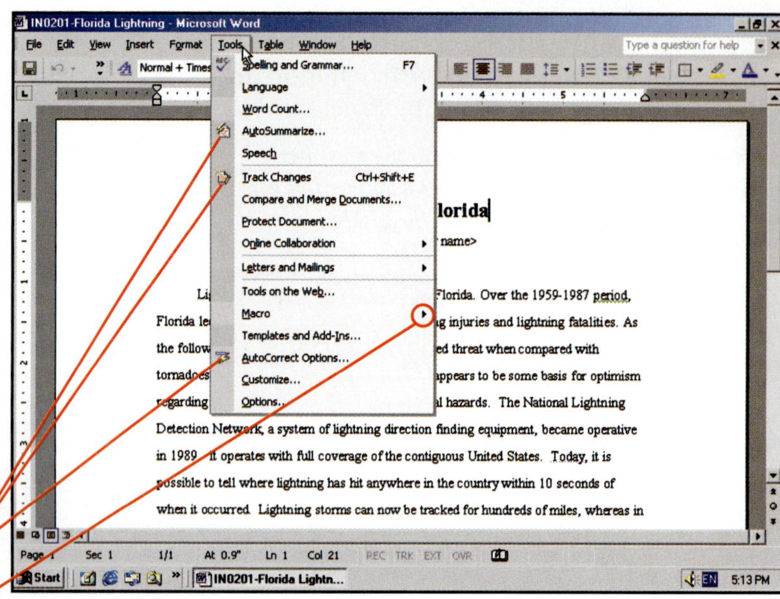

Items on the short version of the menu

Arrow indicates a submenu

**3** Move the pointer anywhere in the document and click.

*When you have a menu open and want to close it, clicking outside the menu will turn it off. You can also press* Esc *to turn off a menu.*

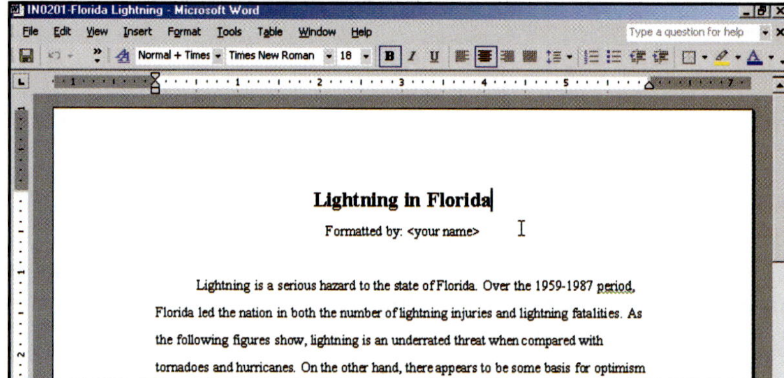

**4** Click **View** from the menu and move the pointer down to the **Toolbars** option.

*A submenu displays showing the toolbars that are available. The ones that are displayed on the screen have check marks to the left. There is also a Customize option at the bottom of the submenu.*

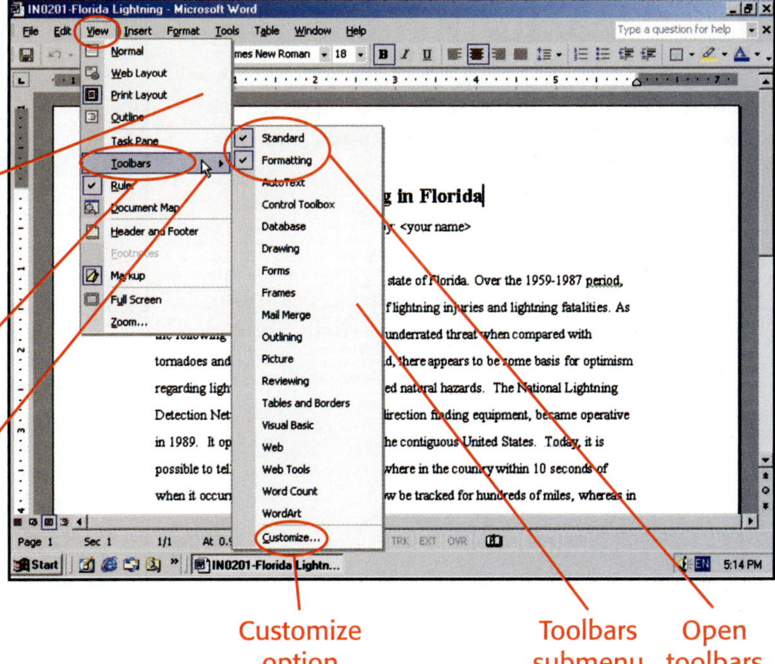


View drop-down menu

Toolbars option

Pointer

Customize option

Toolbars submenu

Open toolbars



**IN DEPTH**

Both the Standard and Formatting toolbars are on the same line in the figure. This is the default toolbar setting for several Office programs, including Word, Excel, and PowerPoint. You can stretch or shrink each toolbar by clicking the double vertical bars at the left end of the toolbar and holding down the mouse button, and dragging to the left or right. The problem with using a single line for the two most commonly-used toolbars is that you probably don't recognize each of the buttons or remember where they are located. It is much easier to use these two toolbars on separate lines so you can see all of the buttons.

If your screen shows the toolbars on separate lines, follow the rest of these steps to familiarize yourself with the procedure for turning this option on and off.

**5** Move the pointer to the **Toolbars** submenu and select **Customize**.

*The Customize dialog box displays. This dialog box consists of three tabs—Toolbars, Commands, and Options.*

Tabs used to access different pages of the dialog box

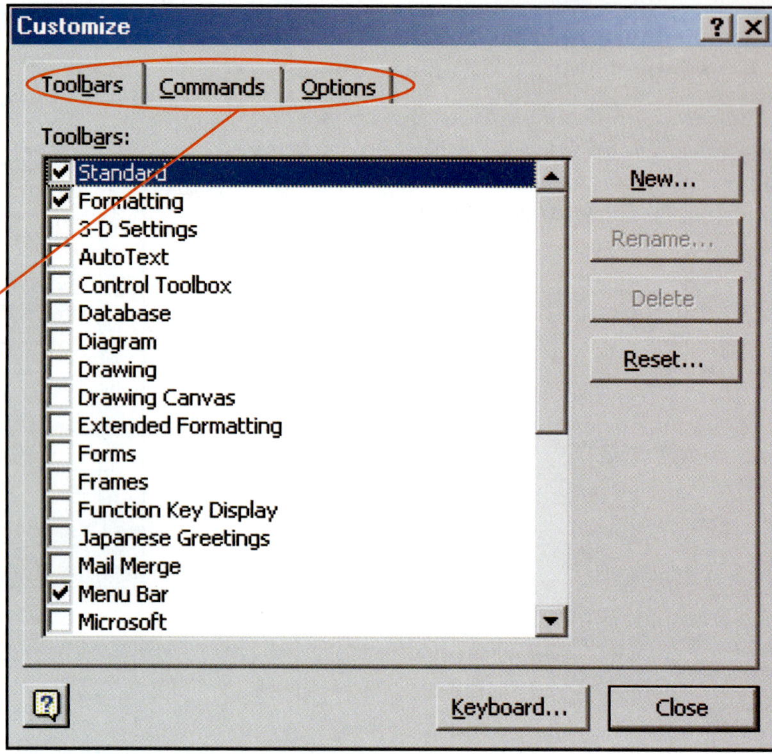

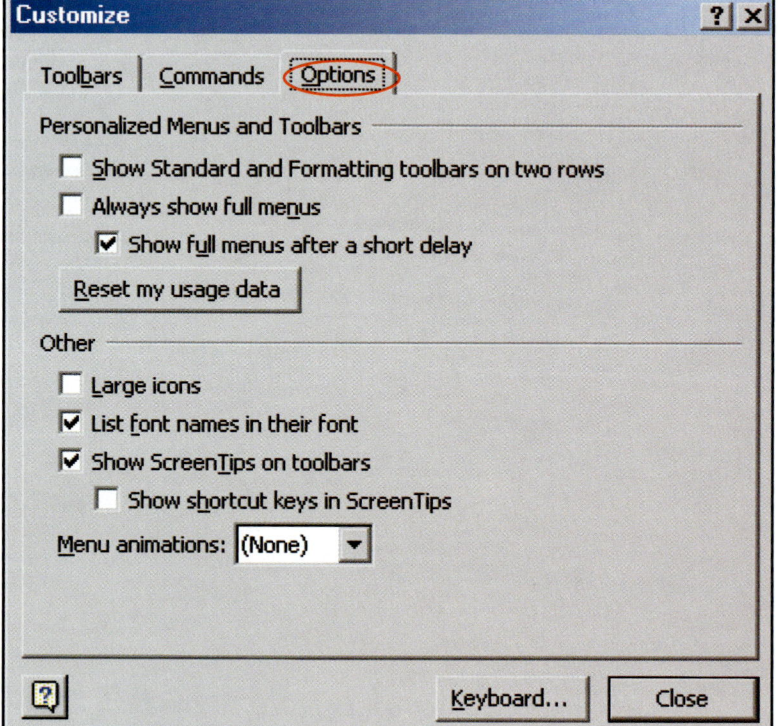

**6** Click the **Options** tab to bring it to the fore-front, if necessary.

*The various toolbar options are shown.*

**7** Click the check box to turn on the **Show Standard and Formatting toolbars on two rows** option, if necessary.

*This causes the Standard and Formatting toolbars to display on separate rows. The second toolbar decreases your work area slightly, but the convenience of seeing all of the buttons more than makes up for a smaller work area. All of the figures in this book show the double toolbars when appropriate.*

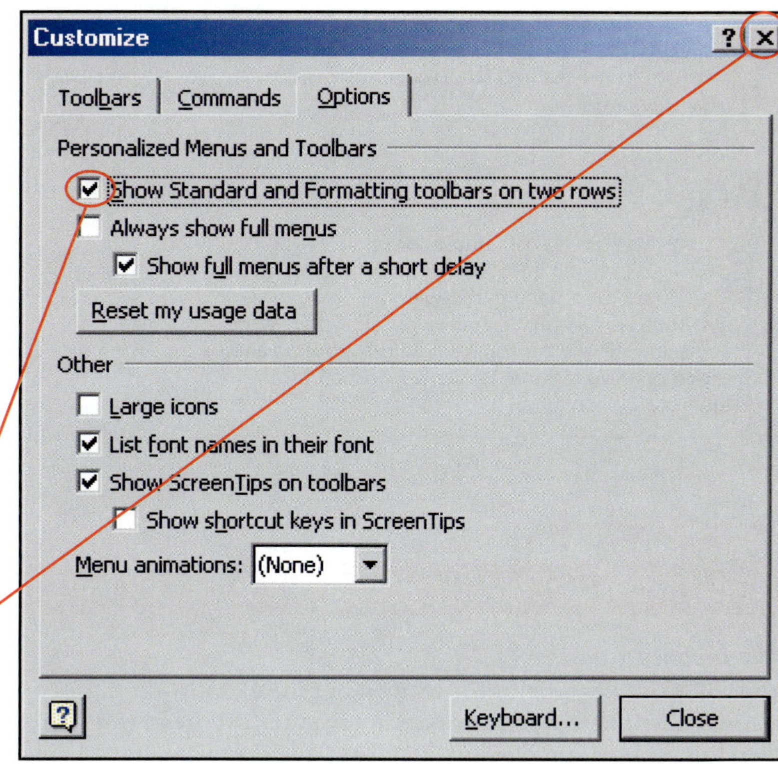


The toolbars will be displayed on two rows

Close button

**8** Click the **Close** button in the dialog box to close it.

*Notice that you now have two rows of toolbars. Also, notice that some buttons on the toolbar have arrows on the right side, which are referred to as down arrows or list arrows.*

Click the down arrow on the **Font Size** button on the Formatting toolbar and release the mouse button.

*A drop-down list displays, showing some of the available font sizes. There is also a vertical scroll bar to the right of the drop-down list. Try scrolling up and down to see the different font sizes available to use.*

Standard toolbar    Formatting toolbar

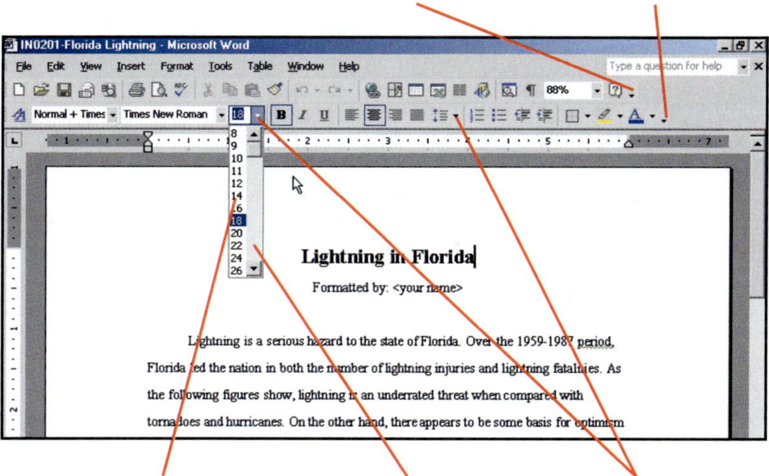


Font Size drop-down list    Scroll bar    List (down) arrows

**QUICK TIP**

If you are using an operating system newer than Windows 95, you can grab the bar on the left edge of the Formatting toolbar and move it up to the Standard toolbar row or down to a row of its own if both toolbars are in one row. If you are using Windows Me or Windows 2000, you can also move back and forth between one row and two rows by clicking the down arrow at the right end of either the Standard or Formatting toolbars and selecting Show Buttons on One Row or Show Buttons on Two Rows from the drop-down list.

**9** Click anywhere in the document to close the Font Size list. Leave the document open for the next task.

> You can add or remove toolbars by right-clicking on any toolbar. This activates a shortcut menu that displays all of the available toolbars and the Customize option. Scroll down and select the toolbar you want to turn on or off and click it once. To test this, try turning on the Drawing toolbar and then turn it back off.

# Task 5

## PRINTING A DOCUMENT USING THE TOOLBAR BUTTON AND THE MENU

### Why would I do this?

You will print documents for many different reasons—as draft copies for proofing, as final documents and handouts, or even for overhead transparencies. There are two different printing levels with most Office applications. The easiest way to print is to simply click the Print button. This sends a complete document to the printer. The problem with using the Print button is that it gives you little control over the process. You can also print using the <u>P</u>rint command from the <u>F</u>ile menu. This gives you much more control and enables you to print specific pages or ranges of information. It also enables you to specify a printer and set the page layout.

In this task, you print the document you've been working on in this lesson using both the Print button and the menu command.

**1** With the **IN0201-Florida Lightning** document still active, make sure your printer is turned on, and then click the **Print** button on the Standard toolbar.

*The entire document is sent to the printer.*

Print button

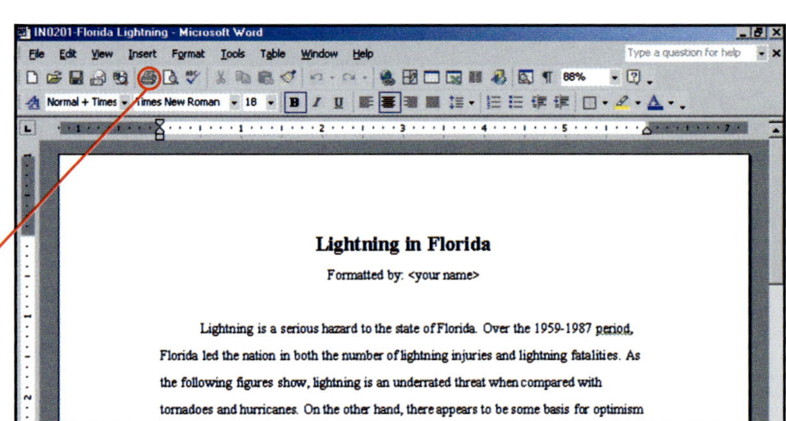




> If the document does not print, it could mean that your printer is not turned on or is not connected properly. Check your connections and try again. If this does not work, you will need to make sure the correct printer is chosen in the Print dialog box, which you open in step 2. If there are several printers available, ask your instructor or lab administrator which printer you should use.

**2** Choose **File**, **Print** from the menu.

*The Print dialog box displays. This dialog box enables you to choose a printer, specify the number of copies to be printed, select specific pages to print, and choose from several other important options.*

Click here to select another printer

Current page option

Enter pages to print

Specify the number of copies

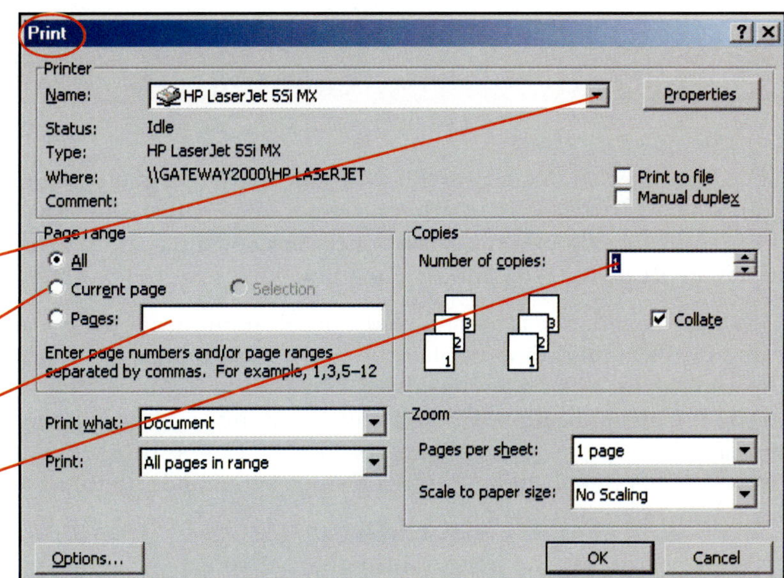

**3** Click the **Current page** option in the **Page range** section.

*The page you print may not be the page showing on the screen. The program will print whichever page contains the insertion point.*

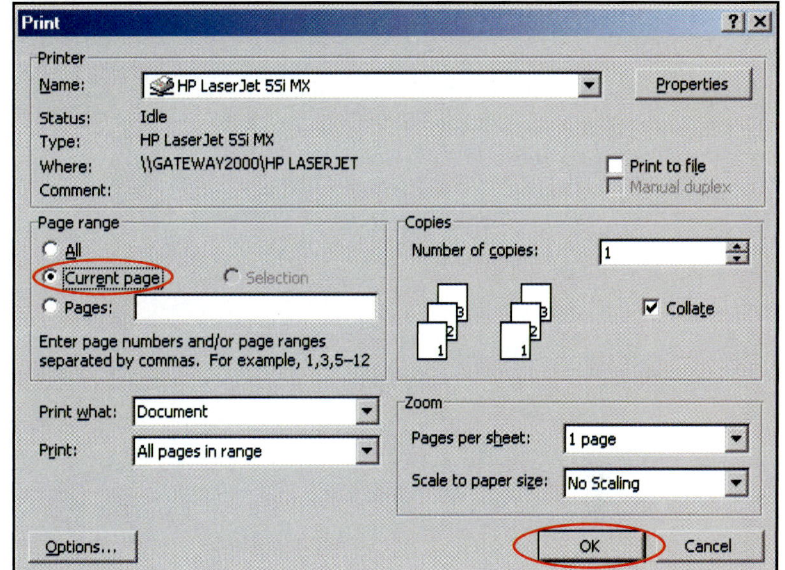

**4** Click **OK** to print the current page.

*The dialog box closes and the page containing the insertion point is printed. Leave the document open for the next task.*

# Task 6


## Why would I do this?

There are several ways to get help with your questions in any of the Office programs. The ***Office Assistant*** is a program that enables you to ask questions in sentence form. When you ask the Office Assistant a question, a series of related topics are displayed. You choose one of the topics to get further information.

The help that you see is specific to the application that you are using. If you are using several applications at once, be sure to access Microsoft Help from within the application where you need help. The Help program enables you to learn as you use an application. You will find that using an Office application is an ongoing learning process, and Microsoft Help can be an integral part of that process. Sometimes when you use a Help program, it is useful to print the topic for future reference.

In this task, you use the Office Assistant to get Help.

**1** Select **Help**, **Show the Office Assistant** from the menu.

*The Office Assistant displays on the screen. You can move it by dragging it to a new location. You can also activate the Office Assistant by clicking the **Microsoft Word Help** button on the Standard toolbar. (Note: The name of this button changes depending on which application is running.)*

Office Assistant

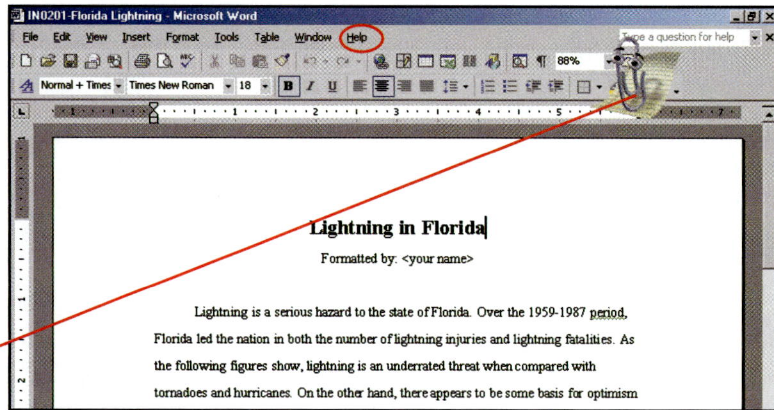


**IN DEPTH**

Occasionally, when you are typing a document or trying to perform a procedure, the Office Assistant will appear, even though you haven't selected it. Don't worry—the Office Assistant is just trying to be helpful. Read through the comment, and if it looks like it might be helpful, follow the on-screen instructions. If you do not want this Help, you can simply close the Help window. If you do not like these hints appearing on your screen, click the Office Assistant **Options** button and turn off the check boxes in the **Show tips about** section of the Options page.

**2** To get help on a topic, click once on the Office Assistant.

*A small dialog box displays, asking you what you would like to do.*

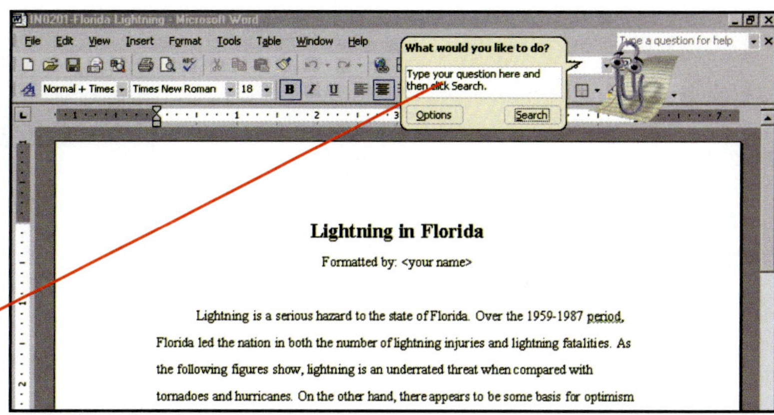

Type your question here

**3** In the box, type **How do I center text**.

*The Office Assistant looks for keywords in your question and tries to suggest answers. Notice that you do not have to add a question mark to your question.*

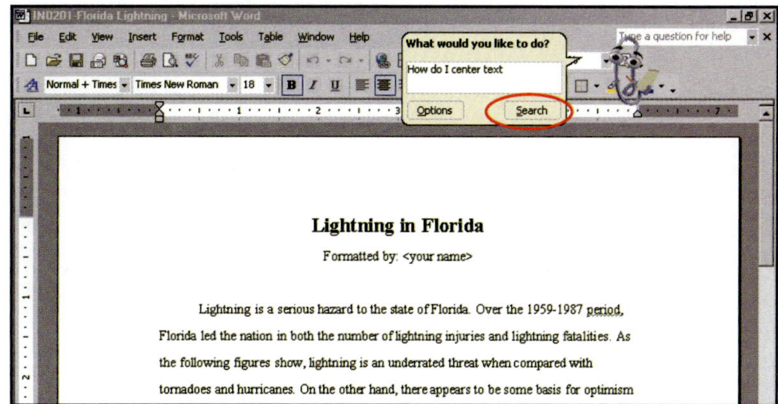

**QUICK TIP**

If you start to use the Office Assistant and change your mind, you can remove the dialog box from the screen by clicking anywhere in the document outside of the dialog box.

**4** Click the **Search** button.

*The Office Assistant looks for topics that match the keywords it found in your question. Topics that have the most matches are listed first. Other possible matches are displayed if you click the **See more** button.*

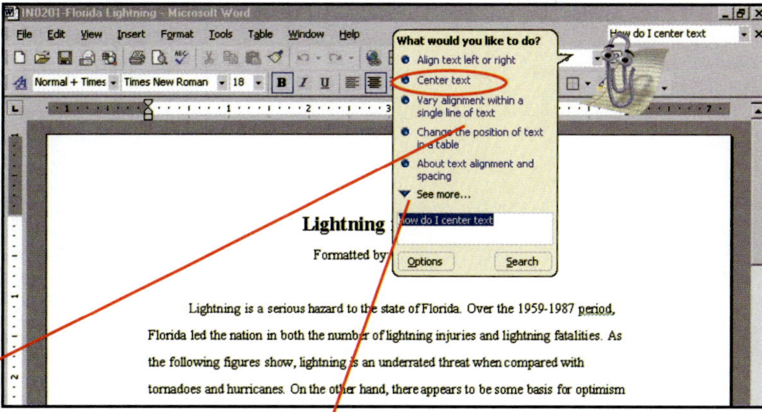

A list of possible topics is displayed

See more button

**5** Click the button for the **Center text** topic.

*A Help window displays and covers part of your document. Notice that some of the text is in blue. This means that more help is available if you click the blue word or phrase. You can use the vertical scroll bar to move down the Help window. (Note: If your Help pane is wider than the one shown, you can skip step 6.)*

Show button

A Help window explains the topic you select

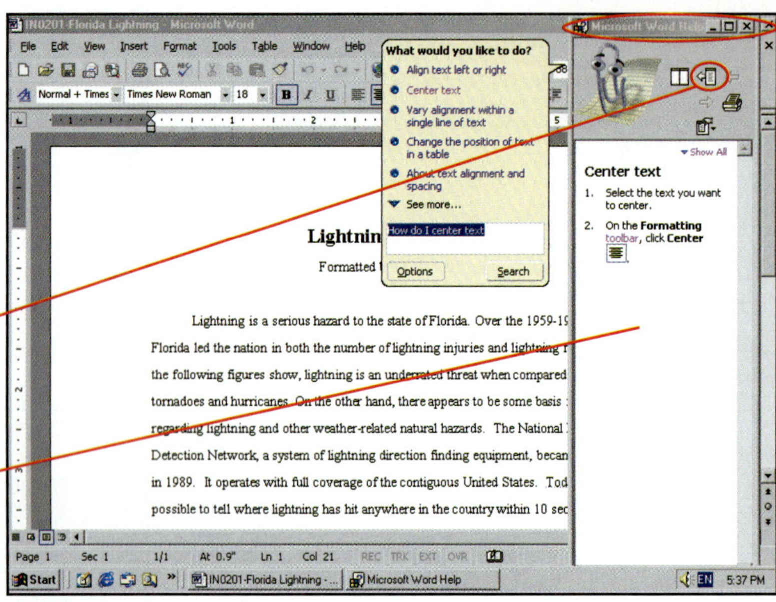

**6** Click the **Show** button, if necessary.

*The Help window expands to include different types of help. The text box in the Index tab may be used to enter a word and see if it matches a predefined topic, whereas the Contents tab lists chapters and topics. The Answer Wizard tab works just like the Office Assistant—you type in a question, and the wizard displays a list of related topics. To move between these features, simply click the tabs at the top of the window. The Show button changes to the Hide button. If you click the Hide button, the additional Help area is removed from the screen.*

Hide button

Tabs for different Help options

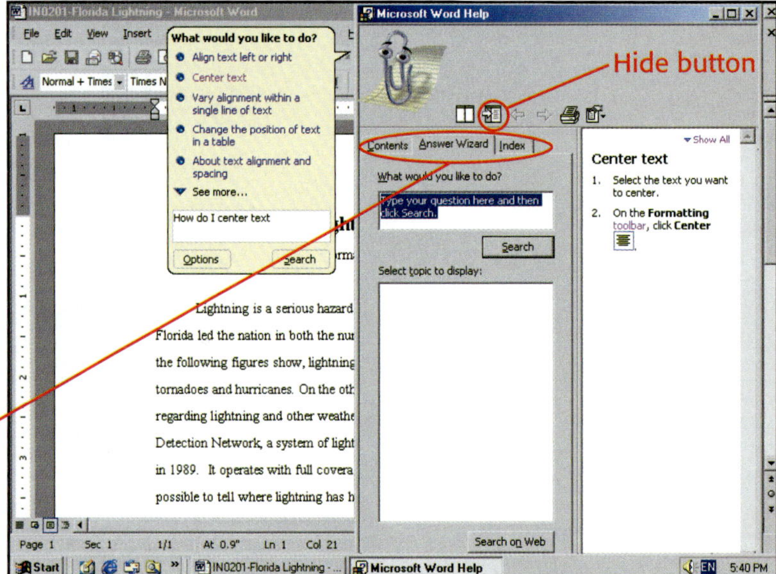

**7** Click the **Contents** tab and double-click **Document Fundamentals**.

*A number of topics are displayed. To get help, keep double-clicking on the appropriate topics until you see a group of icons with question marks. You can single-click these topics and read the Help topic, or follow the links for more help.*

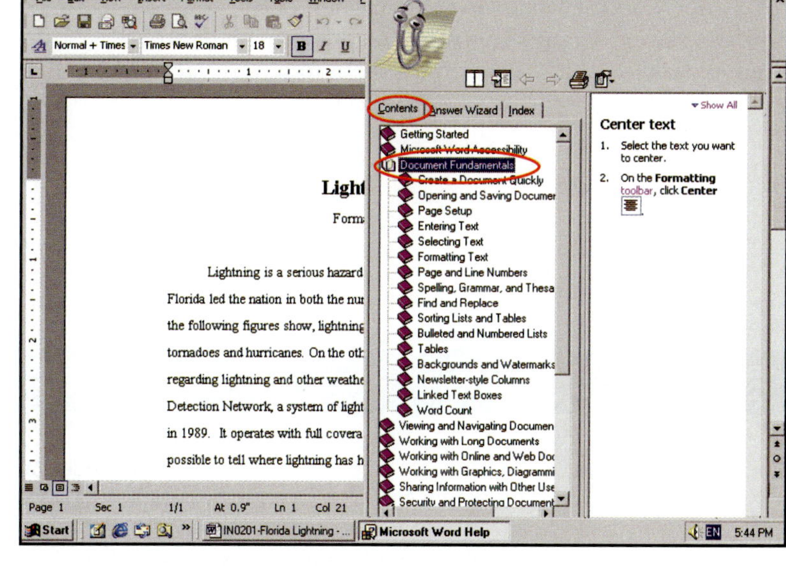

**8** Click the **Close** button to close the Help window.

*The Help window closes, and the Office Assistant remains on your screen.*

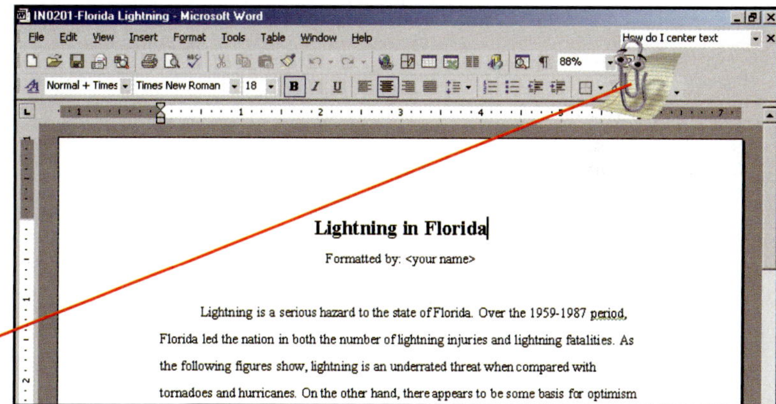


**9** Right-click on the Office Assistant and choose **Hide** from the shortcut menu.

*The Office Assistant is removed from the screen.*

Click the **Close Window** button to close the document, and then click the **Close** button to exit Word.

---

**IN DEPTH**

Some people do not like to have the Office Assistant on the screen at all. If you open an application and see it on your screen, you can hide the Office Assistant by choosing Help, Hide the Office Assistant. To turn it off completely, click once on the Office Assistant and click the Options button. Click the check box for the Use the Office Assistant option at the top of the dialog box.

The exercises that follow are designed for you to review and use what you have learned in this lesson. You also have the opportunity to practice your skills and then expand on them by applying them to new situations.

## COMPREHENSION

Comprehension exercises are designed to check your memory and understanding of the basic concepts in this lesson. You distinguish between true and false statements, identify new screen elements, and match terms with related statements. If you are uncertain of the correct answer, refer to the task number following each item (for example, T4 refers to Task 4), and review that task until you are confident you can provide a correct response.

## TRUE-FALSE

Circle either T or F.

T   F   **1.** To start an Office program, you need to close any other Office program that is running at the time. **(T3)**

T   F   **2.** You can activate the menu by pressing Ctrl. **(T4)**

T   F   **3.** One way to turn toolbars on or off is to right-click anywhere in the toolbar area and click on one of the toolbar choices. **(T4)**

T   F   **4.** Using **File**, **Print** from the menu gives you more control over printing than using the **Print** button. **(T5)**

T   F   **5.** You can type in questions in sentence form when you use the Office Assistant. **(T5)**

T   F   **6.** When you see blue text in a Help window, it means that more help is available by clicking on the text. **(T6)**

## MATCHING QUESTIONS

**A.** **Open** button      **D.** **Hide** button

**B.** **Show** button      **E.** Right-click, select **Hide**

**C.** Double-click the file name      **F.** **Save** button

Match the following statements to the word or phrase that is the best match from the list. Write the letter of the matching word or phrase in the space provided next to the number.

1. ____ Button used in the Help window to access Contents and Index features **(T6)**

2. ____ Button used in the Help window so you can no longer see the Contents and Index features **(T6)**

3. ____ Button used to locate and open an existing file **(T2)**

4. ____ Button used to preserve the changes you have made to a document **(T2)**

5. ____ Procedure to remove the Office Assistant from your screen **(T6)**

6. ____ Opens a file from within Windows Explorer **(T2)**

# IDENTIFYING PARTS
# OF THE SCREEN

Refer to the figure and identify the numbered parts of
the screen. Write the letter of the correct label in the
space next to the number.

1. _______________

2. _______________

3. _______________

4. _______________

5. _______________

6. _______________

7. _______________

8. _______________

9. _______________

10. _______________

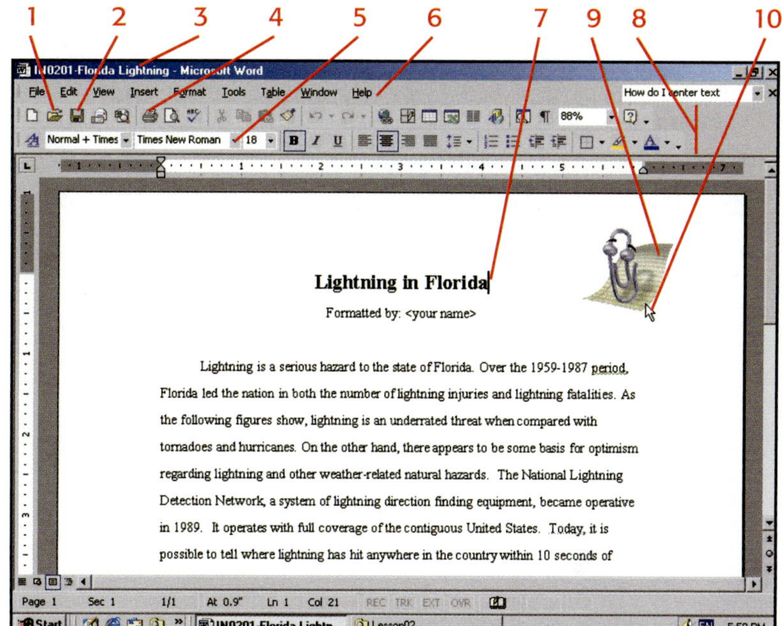



A. Office Assistant  (T6)

B. File name  (T2)

C. Used to open drop-down list  (T4)

D. Menu bar  (T4)

E. Toolbars  (T4)

F. Insertion point  (T2)

G. **Save** button  (T2)

H. **Open** button  (T3)

I. **Print** button  (T5)

J. Pointer  (T4)

# Lesson 1

## Learning the Basics of Excel

Task 1   Navigating a Workbook
Task 2   Selecting Individual Cells
Task 3   Entering Text and Numbers into Cells
Task 4   Fixing Simple Typing Errors
Task 5   Summing a Column of Numbers
Task 6   Saving a Workbook, Printing and Closing a Worksheet

### INTRODUCTION

Spreadsheets are used for a variety of information that benefits from being displayed in a grid of columns and rows. Traditionally, spreadsheets have been used for financial information, but they can also be used for schedules, inventories, simple lists, and other information.

This lesson is designed to provide you with the basic skills that you need to create a simple spreadsheet, print it, and save it. In Excel, spreadsheets are called worksheets. A workbook may contain several worksheets.

In this lesson, you learn the basic skills necessary to create and print a useful worksheet. You will create a worksheet showing the May sales for the Armstrong Pool, Spa, and Sauna Company.

# VISUAL SUMMARY

When you have completed this lesson, you will have created a worksheet that looks like this:

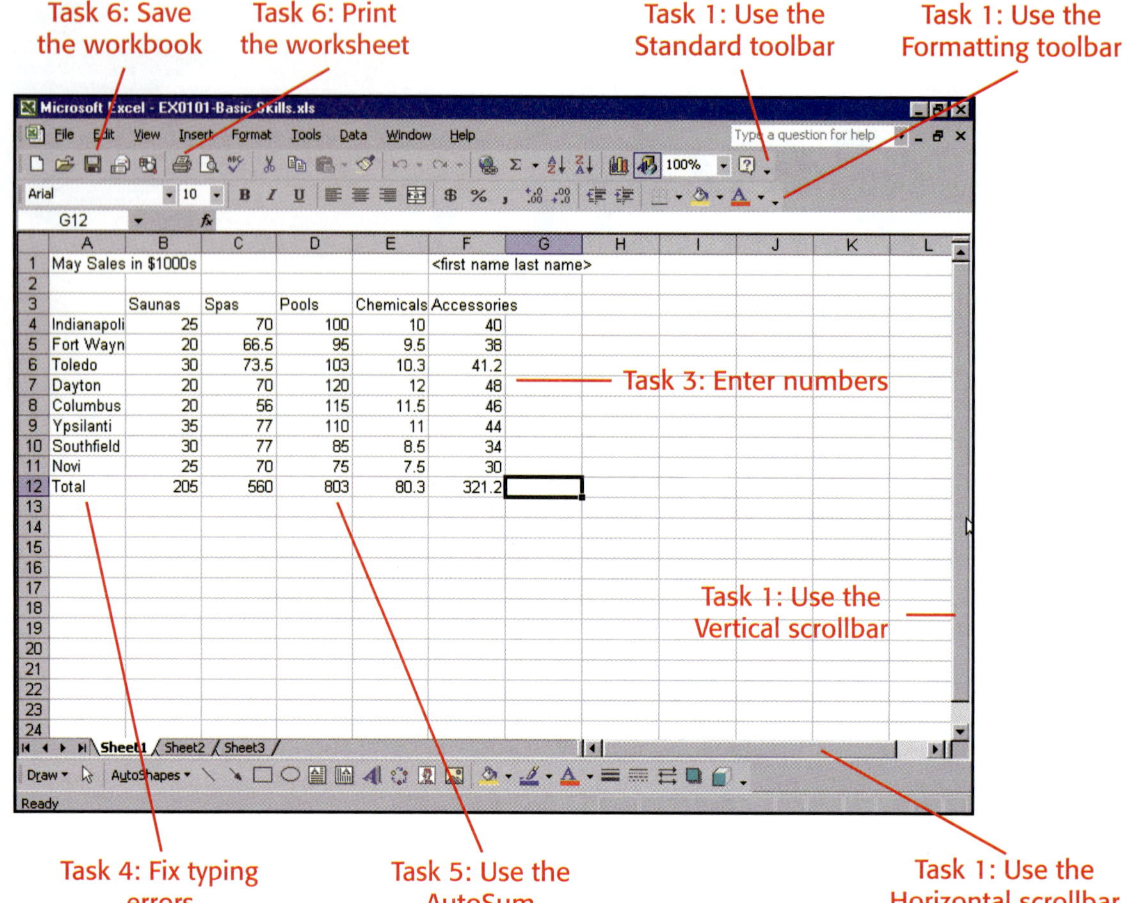

# Task 1
## NAVIGATING A WORKBOOK



### Why would I do this?

To understand how to use Excel, you first need to have a basic under-standing of how Excel is structured. An Excel file is a *workbook* that consists of several *worksheets* identified by tabs at the bottom of the window. Each of these worksheets is divided into rows and columns; their intersections form a grid of cells. There are many more rows and columns available than will show in the window. To work in Excel, you need to know how to navigate in a worksheet to see different rows and columns.

In this task, you will learn how to select a *sheet* and scroll it to display additional rows and columns.

**1** Start Excel.

*The program displays a set of three empty worksheets by default. The sheets are designated with tabs near the bottom of the window.*

> Move the pointer to the tab labeled **Sheet2** at the bottom of the window. Click on the tab.

*A second empty sheet is displayed.*

> Click the **Sheet1** tab to return to the default sheet. Notice the *task pane* on the right side of the screen.

*The task pane is used for various functions such as opening previously created workbooks or creating new workbooks from existing ones. The workbooks and tem-plates displayed on your screen will differ from those shown in the figure.*

> If the task pane is not displayed on your screen, you can display it by choosing **View, Task Pane** from the menu.



A feature introduced in Office 2000 places the two most com-monly used toolbars, **Standard** and **Formatting**, on the same line. The buttons showing on that line change depending on recent use. To provide a consistent set of instructional images, we have disabled this feature. If the toolbars on your screen do not match the figures shown, see the introduction to this book for a description of how to disable this feature.

**2** Click the **Close** button on the task pane to close it.

*The task pane closes, and the worksheet window expands to display more columns.*

Click once on the down arrow at the bottom of the *vertical scrollbar*.

*Row 1 disappears, and a previously hidden row appears at the bottom of the screen. The vertical scrollbar may be used to scroll through the rows of the worksheet.*

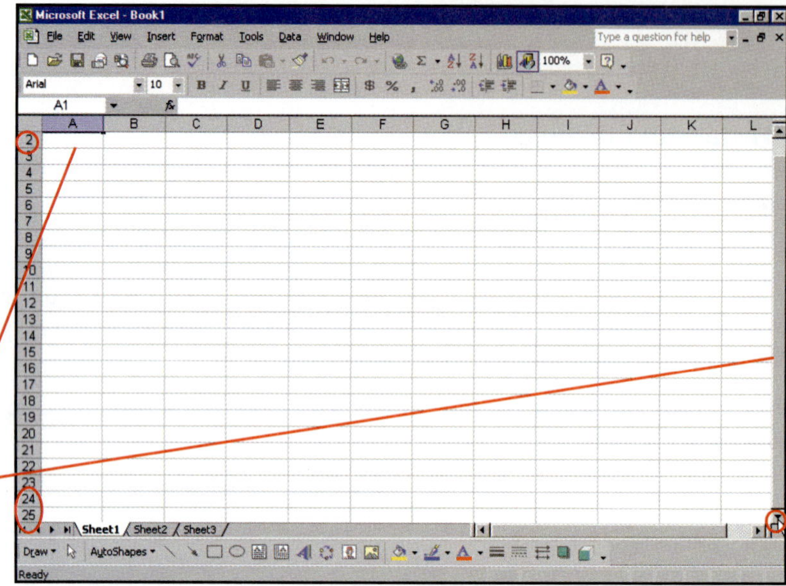


**3** Click the same down arrow and hold down the mouse button.

*The rows will scroll by rapidly.*

Release the mouse button. Click the up arrow at the top of the vertical scrollbar and hold down the button until row 1 appears. Release the button.

Click once on the right arrow on the *horizontal scrollbar*.

*Column A will scroll off the screen, and the next column to the right will appear.*

**4** Click once on the left arrow on the horizontal scrollbar.

*The sheet scrolls to the right and column A will reappear.*

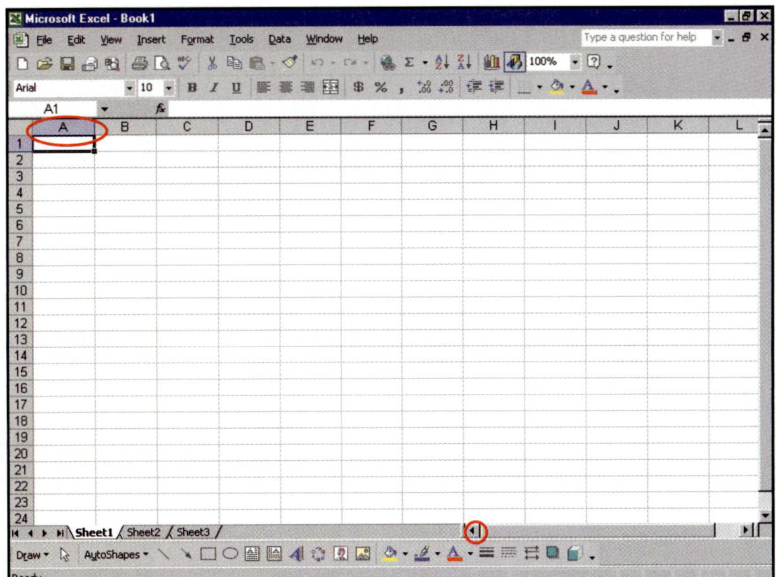

# Task 2

## SELECTING INDIVIDUAL CELLS

### Why would I do this?

You must select a *cell* before you can enter text, numbers, or formulas. A cell is a bounded area that is identified by a column letter and a row number. If a cell is selected, it will have a dark border around it. Selecting cells is one of the most commonly used procedures in Excel and there are several ways to do this.

In this task, you learn how to select cells using the mouse, Tab↹, ↵Enter, and the arrow keys.

**1** Use the mouse to move the pointer to the cell that is in column **B** and row **2** (this cell is referred to as cell B2).

*Notice that the cell selection does not move with the pointer.*

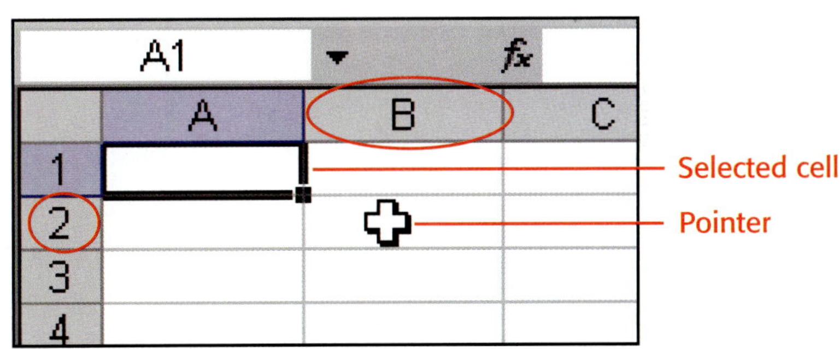

Moving the pointer to a cell does not select it. If you start typing without actually moving the selection, your text or number will be placed in whatever cell is currently selected.

**2**    Click the left mouse button.

*Notice that the border of the cell on which you clicked changes to a darker line. The **column heading** and **row heading** are highlighted, and the address of the cell (B2) appears in the Name box.*

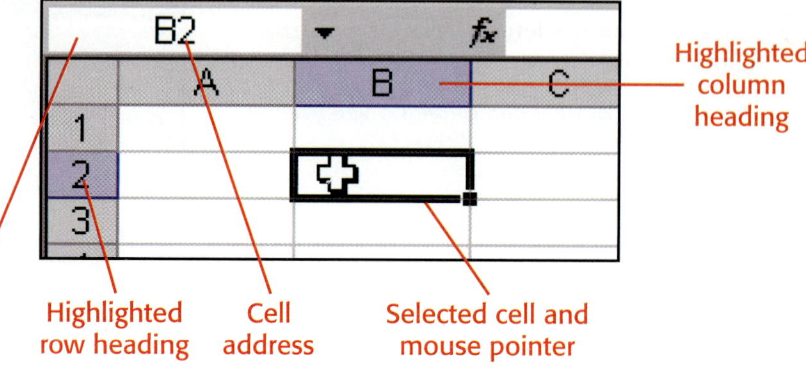


**3**    Press the up arrow on your keyboard once.

*Notice that the selection moves to cell B1.*

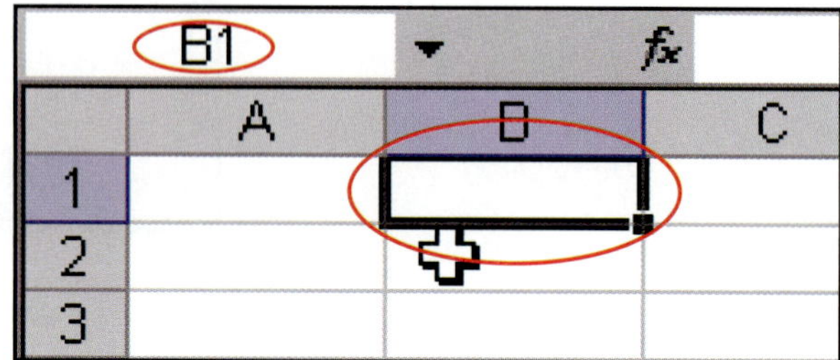


**4**    Press ⏎Enter.

*The selection moves downward one row to cell B2. This method of moving the selection is useful when you are entering columns of numbers.*

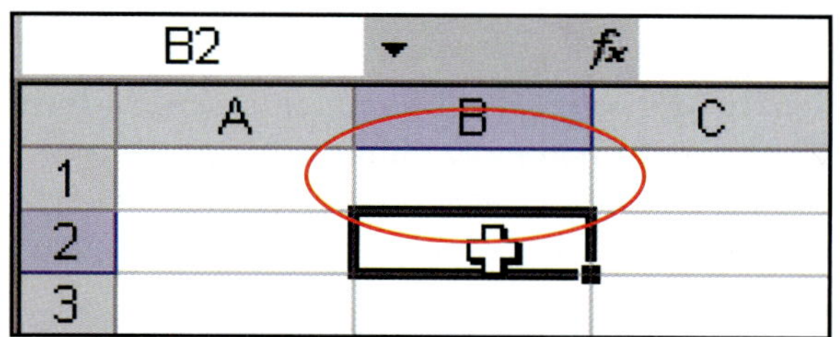


**5**    Press Tab three times.

*The selection begins at cell B2 and moves one cell to the right each time you press this key. This method is useful when you are typing a series of numbers in a row of cells.*

     Press ⏎Enter.

*This time the selection moves to cell B3. When you enter numbers in a row of cells using Tab, ⏎Enter will return to the start of the next row of cells.*

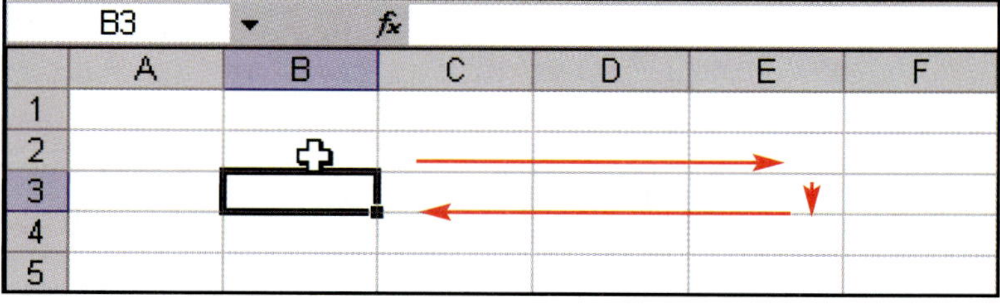

**6** Press `Tab` three times.

*The selection moves three cells to the right.*

Hold `Shift` and press `Tab`.

*The selection moves one cell to the left.*

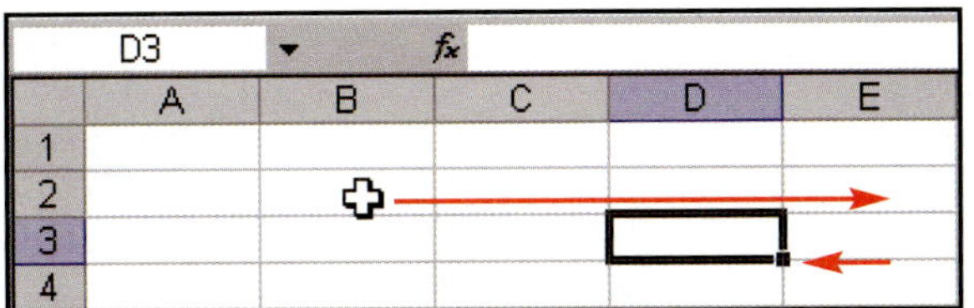

Notice that most `Tab` keys have two arrows on the key to indicate that it can be used to move the selection to the left or right depending on whether or not the `Shift` key is also pressed.

# Task 3
## ENTERING TEXT AND NUMBERS INTO CELLS

### Why would I do this?

Before you start to enter words and numbers into a worksheet, it is a good idea to plan for the future. It is easier to copy formulas, chart data, and transfer tables of data into Word or Access if the data and its labels are organized correctly. If you plan to gather the same data each week or quarter, consider using a separate, identical worksheet for each time period. Place labels in cells at the top of a column or at the left of a row of data. Do not use empty cells or cells with dashes to separate sections of a table. Visual cues such as these should be signaled with borders or shading. Summaries are most useful if they are presented on their own sheet the same way that year-end summaries of quarterly data are treated.

Text is entered into cells to provide labels and other information for users of the sheet. Numbers are used in calculations and formulas. Usually, a cell contains text or numbers, but not both. Once the numbers have been entered into the cells, you can manipulate the numbers, perform calculations, and use the numbers to visually portray a trend by creating a chart. If numbers are used as labels or mixed with text, as in a street address, they are treated as text.

In this task, you learn how to enter text and numbers into cells.

**1** Move the pointer to cell **A1** and click the left mouse button to select the cell.

**2** Type the phrase **Sales in May in $1000s** and press ↵Enter.

*The selection moves to cell A2.*

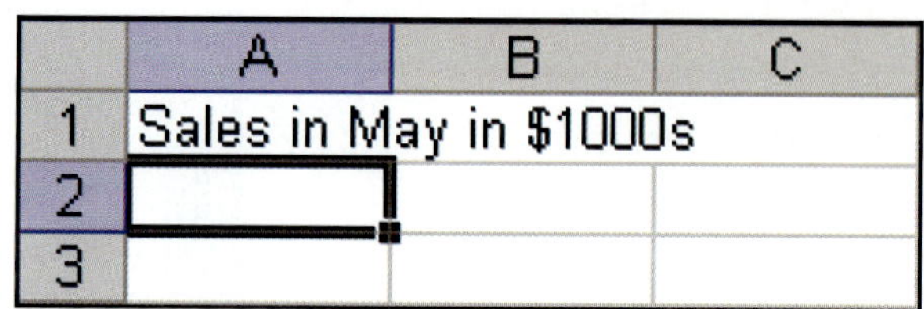



**3** Select cell **A3**.

*This will be the upper-left corner of the table of data. It is left blank. You will enter the table one row at a time by using Tab⇄ to move across and ↵Enter to begin the second row.*

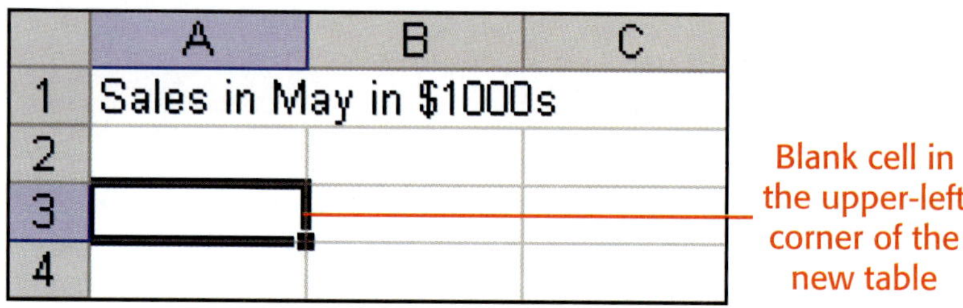

Blank cell in the upper-left corner of the new table

**4** Press Tab⇄.

*This moves the selection to cell B3.*

Type **Saunas** and press Tab⇄.

*The first column heading is now in cell B3.*

**5** Type **Spas** and press Tab⇄. Repeat this process to enter **Pools** and **Chemicals** in cells D3 and E3.

*If the word is wider than the cell, do not be concerned at this time. You will learn how to adjust column widths in a later task.*

Type **Accessories** in cell **F3**, then press ↵Enter instead of Tab⇄.

*The selection automatically returns to cell A4 to start the next row.*

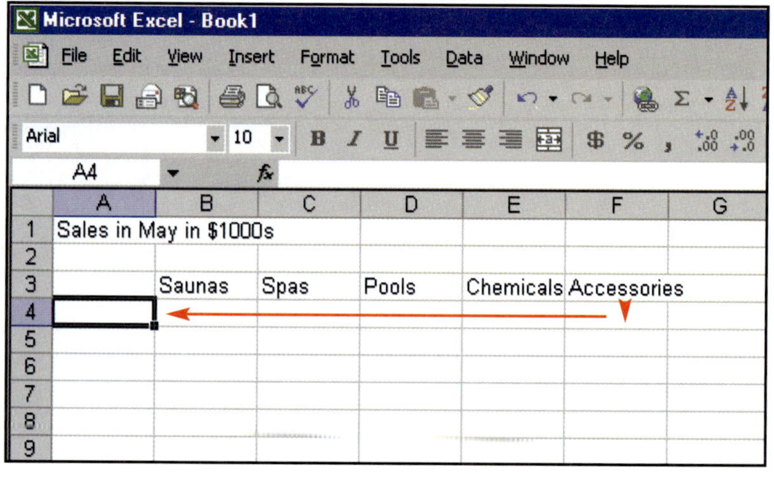

**6** Type **Indianapolis** in cell **A4** and press Tab.

Refer to the figure and use this method to fill out the table with the following sales figures for May:

|  | Saunas | Spas | Pools | Chemicals | Accessories |
|---|---|---|---|---|---|
| Indianapolis | 25 | 70 | 100 | 10 | 40 |
| Fort Wayne | 20 | 66.5 | 95 | 9.5 | 38 |
| Toledo | 30 | 73.5 | 103 | 10.3 | 41.2 |
| Dayton | 20 | 70 | 120 | 12 | 48 |
| Columbus | 20 | 56 | 115 | 11.5 | 46 |
| Ypsilanti | 35 | 77 | 110 | 11 | 44 |
| Southfield | 30 | 77 | 85 | 8.5 | 34 |
| Novi | 25 | 70 | 75 | 7.5 | 30 |

|  | A | B | C | D | E | F |
|---|---|---|---|---|---|---|
| 1 | Sales in May in $1000s |  |  |  |  |  |
| 2 |  |  |  |  |  |  |
| 3 |  | Saunas | Spas | Pools | Chemicals | Accessories |
| 4 | Indianapoli | 25 | 70 | 100 | 10 | 40 |
| 5 | Fort Wayn | 20 | 66.5 | 95 | 9.5 | 38 |
| 6 | Toledo | 30 | 73.5 | 103 | 10.3 | 41.2 |
| 7 | Dayton | 20 | 70 | 120 | 12 | 48 |
| 8 | Columbus | 20 | 56 | 115 | 11.5 | 46 |
| 9 | Ypsilanti | 35 | 77 | 110 | 11 | 44 |
| 10 | Southfield | 30 | 77 | 85 | 8.5 | 34 |
| 11 | Novi | 25 | 70 | 75 | 7.5 | 30 |
| 12 |  |  |  |  |  |  |
| 13 |  |  |  |  |  |  |

**CAUTION**

When you use Tab to enter values in adjacent cells, Excel remembers the starting point of the series and returns to that column when you press Enter. Interrupting the pattern, for instance to correct an error, sets a new starting point. Therefore, if you make mistakes entering the text or the numbers, leave them for now. You will learn how to fix mistakes in the next task.

**7** Select cell **F1** and type your last name. Press Enter.

*If your name is too long to fit in the cell, enter it anyway. You will learn how to deal with this formatting problem in a later lesson.*

|  | A | B | C | D | E | F | G |
|---|---|---|---|---|---|---|---|
| 1 | Sales in May in $1000s |  |  |  |  | <last name> |  |
| 2 |  |  |  |  |  |  |  |
| 3 |  | Saunas | Spas | Pools | Chemicals | Accessories |  |
| 4 | Indianapoli | 25 | 70 | 100 | 10 | 40 |  |
| 5 | Fort Wayn | 20 | 66.5 | 95 | 9.5 | 38 |  |
| 6 | Toledo | 30 | 73.5 | 103 | 10.3 | 41.2 |  |
| 7 | Dayton | 20 | 70 | 120 | 12 | 48 |  |
| 8 | Columbus | 20 | 56 | 115 | 11.5 | 46 |  |
| 9 | Ypsilanti | 35 | 77 | 110 | 11 | 44 |  |
| 10 | Southfield | 30 | 77 | 85 | 8.5 | 34 |  |
| 11 | Novi | 25 | 70 | 75 | 7.5 | 30 |  |
| 12 |  |  |  |  |  |  |  |

Type your own name

# Task 4

## FIXING SIMPLE TYPING ERRORS

### Why would I do this?

It is possible to make mistakes when entering data. Also, information may change and need to be adjusted. The power of using an electronic spreadsheet is in the ability to easily change information and have formulas recalculated automatically.

In this task, you learn how to edit the contents of the cells.

**1** Select cell **A12** and type the incorrectly spelled word **Totle** in the cell. Do not press the ⏎Enter or Tab⇥ key yet.

*Notice that a vertical line marks the position where text is entered. This line is called the **insertion point**.*

|  | | | | | |
|---|---|---|---|---|---|
| 1 | Sales in May in $1000s | | | | <last name> |
| 2 | | | | | |
| 3 | | Saunas | Spas | Pools | Chemicals Accessories |
| 4 | Indianapoli | 25 | 70 | 100 | 10 | 40 |
| 5 | Fort Wayn | 20 | 66.5 | 95 | 9.5 | 38 |
| 6 | Toledo | 30 | 73.5 | 103 | 10.3 | 41.2 |
| 7 | Dayton | 20 | 70 | 120 | 12 | 48 |
| 8 | Columbus | 20 | 56 | 115 | 11.5 | 46 |
| 9 | Ypsilanti | 35 | 77 | 110 | 11 | 44 |
| 10 | Southfield | 30 | 77 | 85 | 8.5 | 34 |
| 11 | Novi | 25 | 70 | 75 | 7.5 | 30 |
| 12 | Totle | | | | |
| 13 | | | | | |

**The vertical line is the insertion point**

**2** Press ⬅Backspace twice.

*The insertion point moves to the left, erasing the last two letters.*

| | A | B | C | D | E | F |
|---|---|---|---|---|---|---|
| 1 | Sales in May in $1000s | | | | | <last name> |
| 2 | | | | | | |
| 3 | | Saunas | Spas | Pools | | Chemicals Accessories |
| 4 | Indianapoli | 25 | 70 | 100 | 10 | 40 |
| 5 | Fort Wayn | 20 | 66.5 | 95 | 9.5 | 38 |
| 6 | Toledo | 30 | 73.5 | 103 | 10.3 | 41.2 |
| 7 | Dayton | 20 | 70 | 120 | 12 | 48 |
| 8 | Columbus | 20 | 56 | 115 | 11.5 | 46 |
| 9 | Ypsilanti | 35 | 77 | 110 | 11 | 44 |
| 10 | Southfield | 30 | 77 | 85 | 8.5 | 34 |
| 11 | Novi | 25 | 70 | 75 | 7.5 | 30 |
| 12 | Tot | | | | | |
| 13 | | | | | | |

**IN DEPTH**

You can move the insertion point within the text by using the right and left arrow keys on the keyboard. ⬅Backspace deletes characters to the left of the insertion point, and Del deletes characters to the right of the insertion point.

**3** Type **al** and press Tab⇥.

| | A | B | C | D | E | F | G |
|---|---|---|---|---|---|---|---|
| 1 | Sales in May in $1000s | | | | | <last name> | |
| 2 | | | | | | | |
| 3 | | Saunas | Spas | Pools | | Chemicals Accessories | |
| 4 | Indianapoli | 25 | 70 | 100 | 10 | 40 | |
| 5 | Fort Wayn | 20 | 66.5 | 95 | 9.5 | 38 | |
| 6 | Toledo | 30 | 73.5 | 103 | 10.3 | 41.2 | |
| 7 | Dayton | 20 | 70 | 120 | 12 | 48 | |
| 8 | Columbus | 20 | 56 | 115 | 11.5 | 46 | |
| 9 | Ypsilanti | 35 | 77 | 110 | 11 | 44 | |
| 10 | Southfield | 30 | 77 | 85 | 8.5 | 34 | |
| 11 | Novi | 25 | 70 | 75 | 7.5 | 30 | |
| 12 | Total | | | | | | |
| 13 | | | | | | | |

**4** To replace an entire entry, just type over it. Select cell **A1**, type **May Sales in $1000s** and press ⏎Enter.

*The previous entry is replaced.*

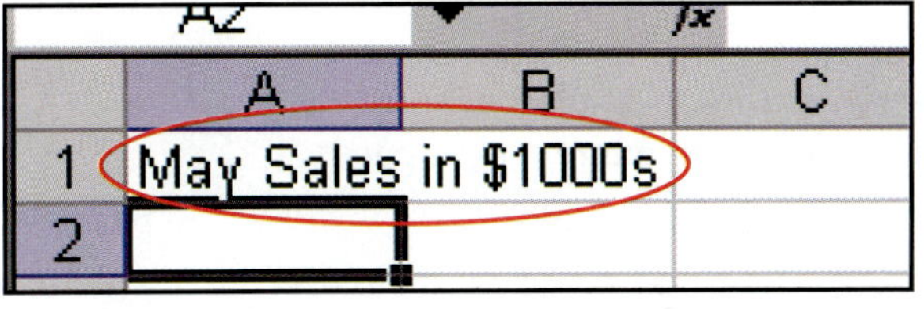

**5** Click the **Undo** button on the Standard toolbar.

*The Undo button reverses the previous action.*

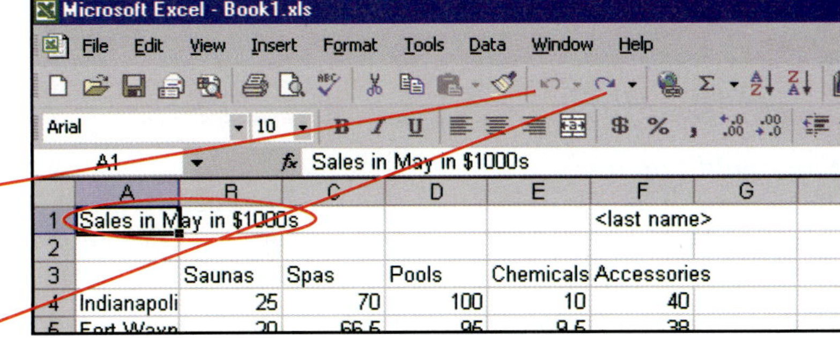



**6** Click the **Redo** button.

*The cell changes back to **May Sales in $1000s**.*

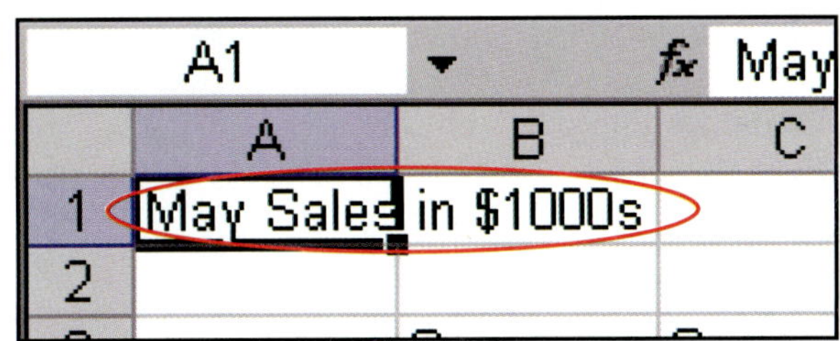

**CAUTION**

If you are using the feature that places the Standard and Formatting toolbars on the same line, you may not see the Redo button if it has not been used recently. If that is the case, locate the Toolbar Options button for the Standard toolbar and click on it to display the rest of the buttons on the Standard toolbar. Do not use the Toolbar Options button at the far right. That one refers to the additional buttons on the Formatting toolbar.

**7** Move the pointer to cell **F1**. Double-click the left mouse button to place the insertion point in the text within the cell.

*Double-clicking on a cell allows you to edit the contents of a cell.*

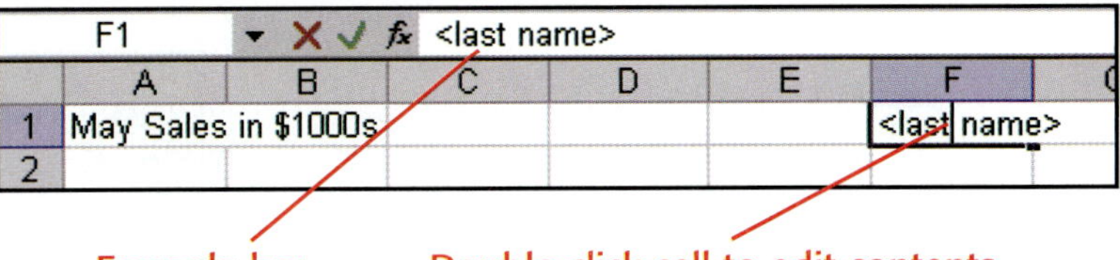



**CAUTION**

You may have trouble double-clicking. The most common problem with double-clicking is caused by moving the mouse slightly between clicks. Rest the heel of your hand on the table so the mouse is less likely to roll. This may take a little practice. If double-clicking is frustrating you, click the cell once and the contents will appear in the **Formula bar**. Click once on the text in the Formula bar and edit it.

**8** Use the left arrow on the keyboard to position the insertion point to the left of your last name. Type your first name and a space.

Press ↵Enter to finish.

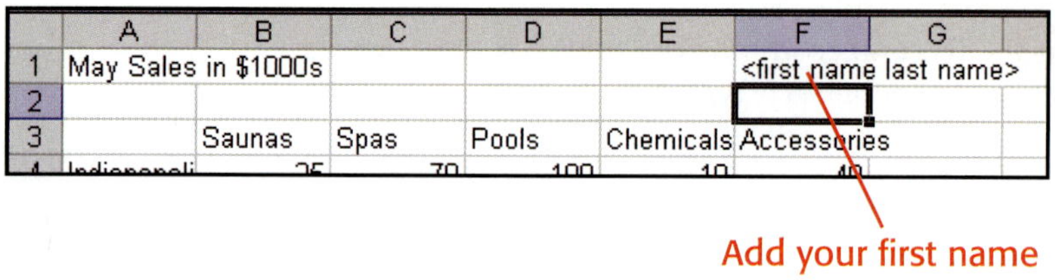

|   | A | B | C | D | E | F | G |
|---|---|---|---|---|---|---|---|
| 1 | May Sales in $1000s | | | | | <first name last name> | |
| 2 | | | | | | | |
| 3 | | Saunas | Spas | | Pools | Chemicals | Accessories |
| 4 | Indianapoli | 25 | 70 | | 100 | 10 | 40 |



# Task 5
## SUMMING A COLUMN OF NUMBERS

### Why would I do this?

The purpose of most worksheets is to make *calculations* based on the data you have entered. The simplest and most commonly used calculation is the sum calculation. It is used so often, in fact, that Excel has a built-in AutoSum button.

In this task, you learn how to sum columns of numbers using AutoSum.

**1** Select cell **B12**.

Click the **AutoSum** button located in the Standard toolbar.

*Several things happen. A formula, =SUM(B4:B11), appears in cell B12 and in the Formula bar. Also, a moving dashed line called a* **marquee** *surrounds the group of cells being summed.*

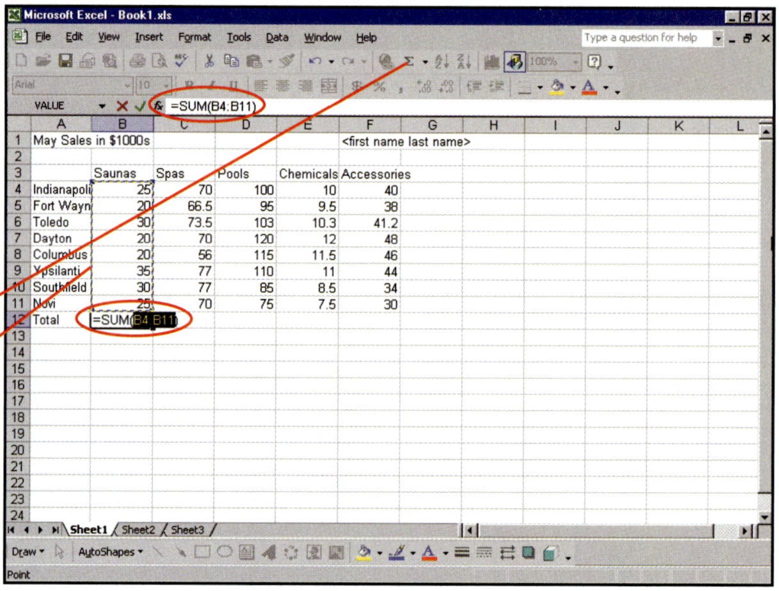

**IN DEPTH**

The program will guess which range of cells you wish to include in the formula. If the guess is incorrect, you may click-and-drag to select a different range of cells.

**2** Press Tab to accept the formula and enter the result into the cell.

*The sum is the total number of sauna sales in the various locations.*

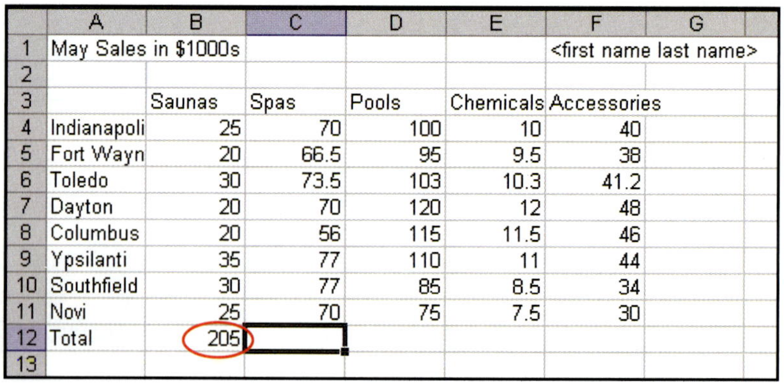

**IN DEPTH**

Excel guesses which group of numbers you want to sum. If it is not the correct group, you can edit the formula just as you edit text. In the formula above, B4:B11 refers to all of the cells in a rectangle that starts with B4 and ends with B11. If you wanted to add up a different range of cells, you would edit the formula and put in different cell addresses. You will learn more about such formulas in later lessons.

|   | A | B | C | D | E | F | G |
|---|---|---|---|---|---|---|---|
| 1 | May Sales in $1000s | | | | | <first name last name> | |
| 2 | | | | | | | |
| 3 | | Saunas | Spas | Pools | | Chemicals | Accessories |
| 4 | Indianapoli | 25 | 70 | 100 | | 10 | 40 |
| 5 | Fort Wayn | 20 | 66.5 | 95 | | 9.5 | 38 |
| 6 | Toledo | 30 | 73.5 | 103 | | 10.3 | 41.2 |
| 7 | Dayton | 20 | 70 | 120 | | 12 | 48 |
| 8 | Columbus | 20 | 56 | 115 | | 11.5 | 46 |
| 9 | Ypsilanti | 35 | 77 | 110 | | 11 | 44 |
| 10 | Southfield | 30 | 77 | 85 | | 8.5 | 34 |
| 11 | Novi | 25 | 70 | 75 | | 7.5 | 30 |
| 12 | Total | 205 | | | | | |
| 13 | | | | | | | |

**3** Repeat this process for each of the remaining columns.

*The formula may be accepted by using* ↵Enter *or* Tab.

| | A | B | C | D | E | F | G |
|---|---|---|---|---|---|---|---|
| 1 | May Sales in $1000s | | | | | <first name last name> | |
| 2 | | | | | | | |
| 3 | | Saunas | Spas | Pools | Chemicals | Accessories | |
| 4 | Indianapoli | 25 | 70 | 100 | 10 | 40 | |
| 5 | Fort Wayn | 20 | 66.5 | 95 | 9.5 | 38 | |
| 6 | Toledo | 30 | 73.5 | 103 | 10.3 | 41.2 | |
| 7 | Dayton | 20 | 70 | 120 | 12 | 48 | |
| 8 | Columbus | 20 | 56 | 115 | 11.5 | 46 | |
| 9 | Ypsilanti | 35 | 77 | 110 | 11 | 44 | |
| 10 | Southfield | 30 | 77 | 85 | 8.5 | 34 | |
| 11 | Novi | 25 | 70 | 75 | 7.5 | 30 | |
| 12 | Total | 205 | 560 | 803 | 80.3 | 321.2 | |
| 13 | | | | | | | |
| 14 | | | | | | | |

# Task 6

## SAVING A WORKBOOK, PRINTING AND CLOSING A WORKSHEET

### Why would I do this?

A computer has a short-term memory that forgets what it was doing when the power is turned off or interrupted. In order to record your spreadsheet for later use, you will need to make a more permanent copy of it. One way to do this is to save a copy magnetically on a disk.

Even in an age of digital communications, there are still advantages to recording data on paper. A paper copy is lightweight, portable, and compatible with older storage systems. It is often easier to review several pages of data simultaneously and share the information with others who do not have a computer.

In this task, you will learn how to print a worksheet and save the workbook on disk. In addition, you will learn how to close a workbook and exit Excel.

**1** Click the **Save** button on the Standard toolbar.

*The Save As dialog box appears with a suggested file-name already highlighted in the File name box.*

**IN DEPTH**

The conventions of this book assume that the file extensions for *registered programs* have been hidden. If this is not the case in your computer setup, you will see an .xls extension added to your Excel filenames. File extensions can be turned on or off in Windows Explorer under View, Folder Options.

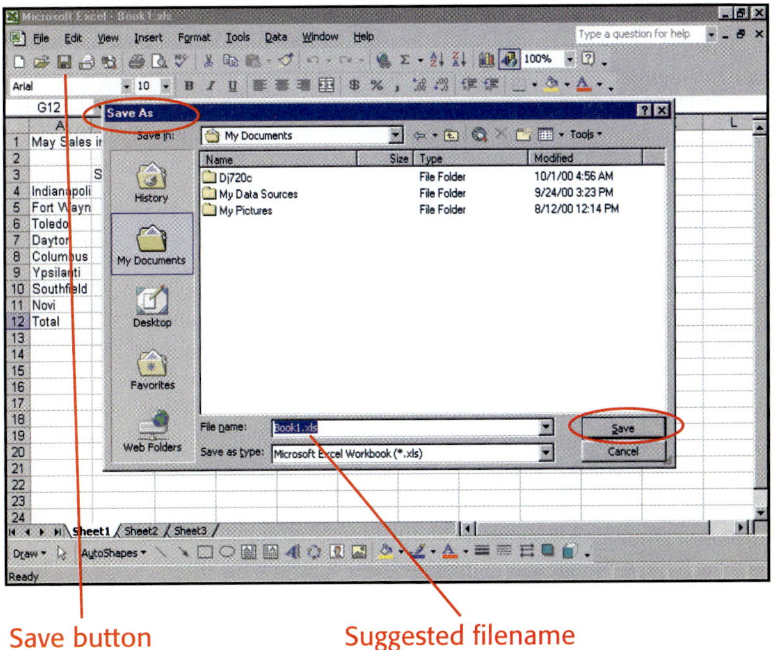

**2** Type **EX0101-Basic Skills**. Do not press `↵Enter` yet.

*This action replaces the highlighted text in the File name box.*

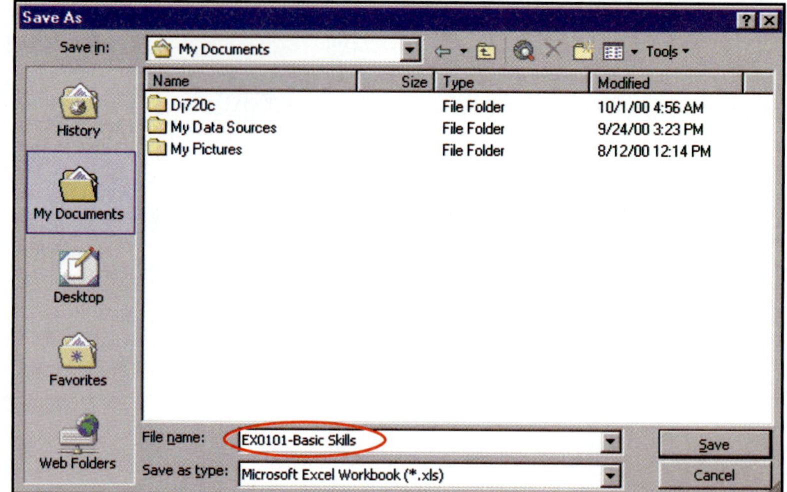

**CAUTION**

A dialog box has buttons in it that you can click on to produce certain actions. Often, one of the buttons is indicated as the default choice by a darker and thicker border. In this case, the Save button is the default. If you press the `↵Enter` key after typing in the name of the file, it will save the file in whatever folder or disk is currently selected. If you do this by mistake, click File, Save As. This will open the Save As dialog box, and you can now select the folder where this file should be saved.

**3** Place a 3½" floppy disk in drive A.

*Ask your instructor for assistance if necessary.*

Click the down arrow at the right side of the **Save in** box.

*A diagram of your computer's disk drives will appear.*

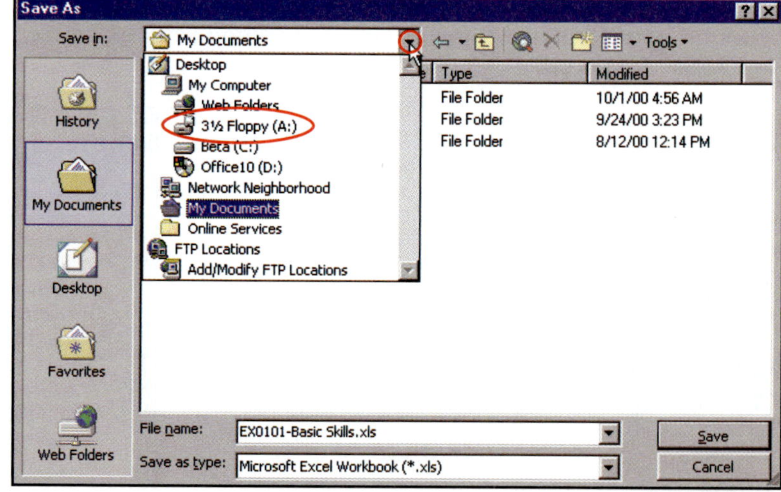

**4**  Click the **3½" Floppy (A:)** drive.

*If your class is using another disk drive, follow your instructor's directions.*

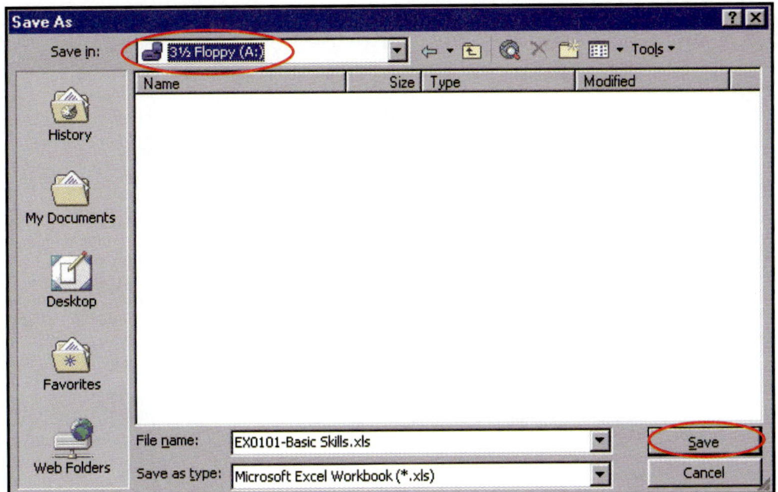

**5**  Click the **Create New Folder** button.

*The New Folder dialog box is displayed.*

Type **Excel Exercises** in the **Name** box.

*A new folder will be created on the floppy disk.*

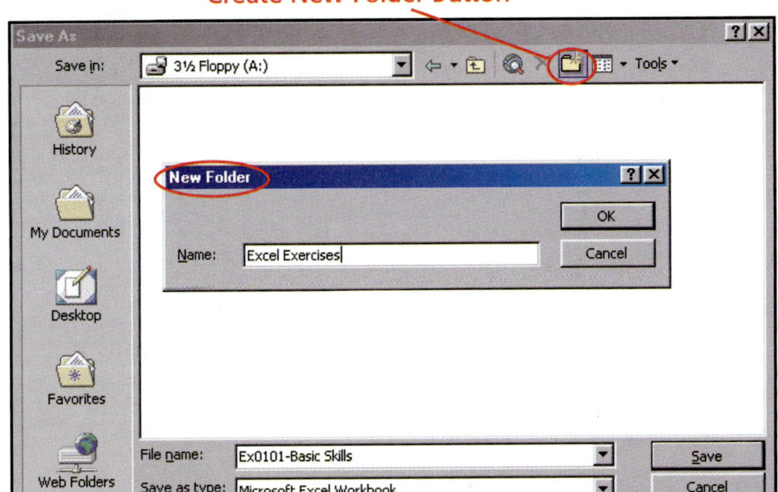


**6**  Click **OK**.

*The folder is created on the floppy disk, and its name is displayed in the Save in box.*

Click **Save**.

*A copy of the workbook is saved on your floppy disk in the new folder. The pointer turns into an hourglass while the file is being saved, and an indicator displays in the status bar.*

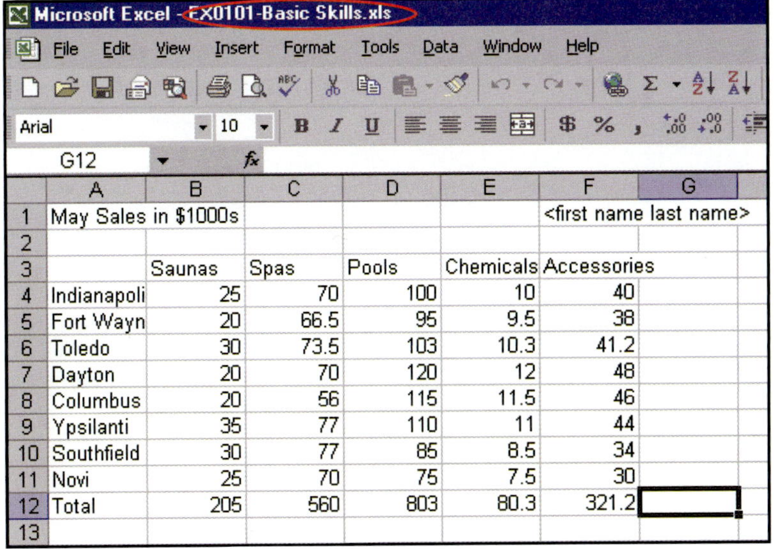

**7** Check to make sure that your printer is connected and turned on.

Click the **Print** button on the Standard toolbar.

*The current worksheet is sent to the printer.*

Move the pointer onto the **Close Window** button on the menu bar.

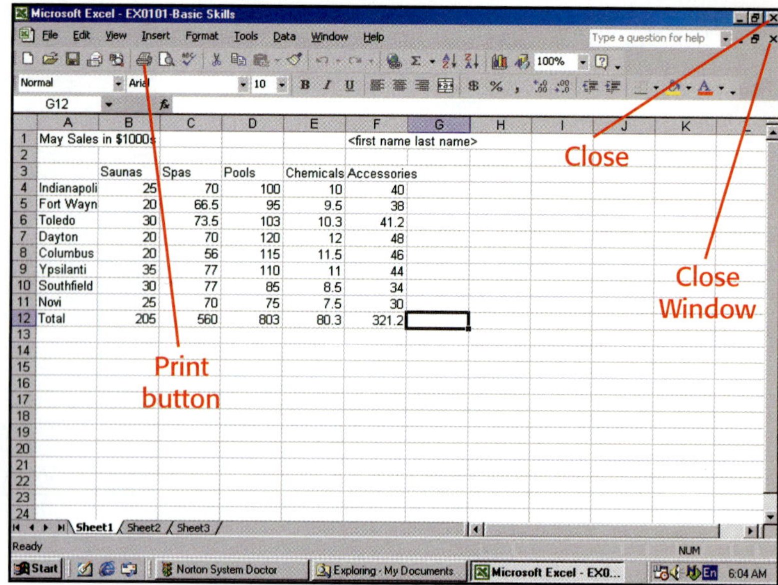


CAUTION

If you click the **Close** button on the title bar, the Excel program will close along with any open workbooks. This is not a big problem since you will not lose your work. Simply launch Excel again if you had intended to leave it open.

**8** Click the **Close Window** button on the menu bar.

*The workbook closes, but Excel stays open. If you have made any changes to the workbook since the last time it was saved, you will be prompted to save it.*

Click the **Close** button on the Excel title bar.

*The Excel program closes.*

The exercises that follow are designed for you to review and use what you have learned in this lesson. You also have the opportunity to practice your skills and then expand on them by applying them to new situations.

## COMPREHENSION

Comprehension exercises are designed to check your memory and understanding of the basic concepts in this lesson. You distinguish between true and false statements, identify new screen elements, and match terms with related statements. If you are uncertain of the correct answer, refer to the task number following each item (for example, T4 refers to Task 4), and review that task until you are confident you can provide a correct response.

### TRUE-FALSE

Circle either T or F.

T   F   **1.** A workbook and a worksheet are the same thing. The words may be used interchangeably. **(T1)**

T   F   **2.** The vertical scrollbar and its arrows can be used to rapidly scroll through the sheet or to scroll one row at a time. **(T1)**

T   F   **3.** A cell in column C and row 2 would be referred to as cell 2C. **(T2)**

T   F   **4.** A selected cell has a darker border than the other cells. **(T2)**

T   F   **5.** When you press ⏎Enter, the selection will always move to the cell below it. This is a basic feature of Excel that cannot be changed. **(T3)**

T   F   **6.** Clicking on the AutoSum button will place a formula in the currently selected cell that will automatically add up the nearest row or column of numbers. **(T5)**

### MATCHING QUESTIONS

**A.** D3

**B.** Button with an X in it

**C.** ⏎Enter

**D.** Save

**E.** AutoSum button

**F.** Tab↹

Match the following statements to the word or phrase that is the best match from the list. Write the letter of the matching word or phrase in the space provided next to the number.

**1.** _____ Automatically adds up the numbers in nearby cells **(T5)**

**2.** _____ May be the Close button or the Close Window button **(T6)**

**3.** _____ Button that looks like a 3½" floppy disk **(T6)**

**4.** _____ The cell in row 3, column D **(T2)**

**5.** _____ May be used to finish the process of placing a number or text into a cell and move downward to the next cell **(T2)**

**6.** _____ May be used to move the selection to the right **(T2)**

Refer to the figure and identify the numbered parts of
the screen. Write the letter of the correct label in the
space next to the number.

1. ________________

2. ________________

3. ________________

4. ________________

5. ________________

6. ________________

7. ________________

8. ________________

9. ________________

10. ________________

11. ________________

12. ________________

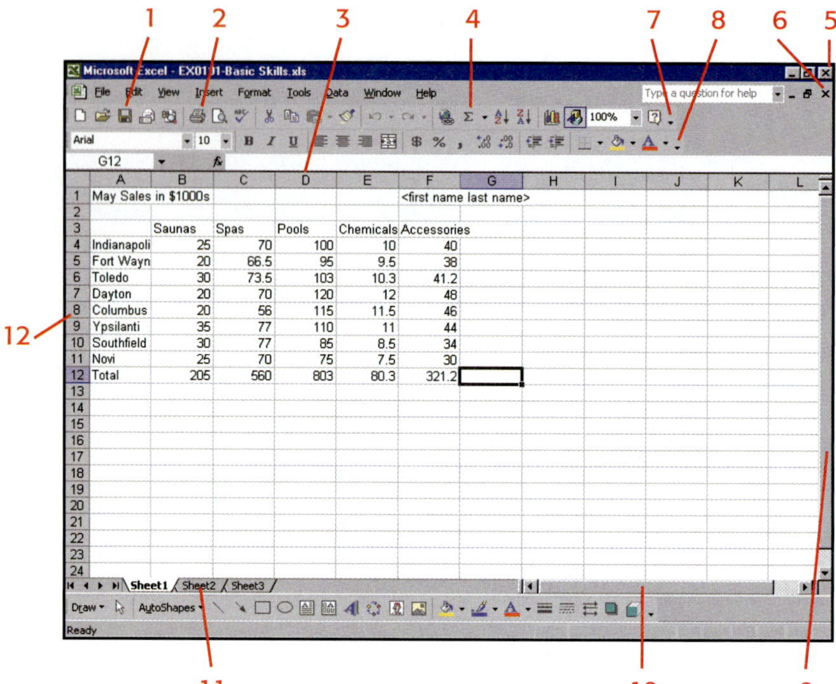

A. Tabs to identify sheets  **(T1)**

B. Column heading  **(T2)**

C. Row heading  **(T2)**

D. Vertical scrollbar  **(T1)**

E. Horizontal scrollbar  **(T1)**

F. Save button  **(T6)**

G. Print button  **(T6)**

H. Close button for Excel  **(T6)**

I. Close Window button for the workbook  **(T6)**

J. AutoSum button  **(T5)**

K. Standard toolbar  **(T1)**

L. Formatting toolbar  **(T1)**

Reinforcement exercises are designed to reinforce the skills you have learned by applying them to new situations. Detailed instructions are provided along with a figure, where appropriate, to illustrate the result. The reinforcement exercises that follow should be completed sequentially. Leave the file open at the end of each exercise for use in the next exercise until you are specifically directed to close it.

In these exercises you create a worksheet for the utitlity bills for the Armstrong Pool, Spa, and Sauna Company stores.

## R1–Creating a Worksheet to Show Utility Bills

1. Launch Excel and enter **January** in cell **A1**.

2. Enter your name in cell **F1**.

3. Select cell **A3** and press ⇥. Enter the following data in the cells as shown in the figure:

| | GAS | WATER | ELECTRIC | PHONE |
|---|---|---|---|---|
| **Indianapolis** | 165 | 55 | 250 | 120 |
| **Fort Wayne** | 100 | 35 | 225 | 67 |
| **Toledo** | 150 | 45 | 215 | 125 |
| **Dayton** | 125 | 60 | 185 | 150 |
| **Columbus** | 150 | 75 | 170 | 85 |
| **Ypsilanti** | 220 | 85 | 285 | 300 |
| **Southfield** | 118 | 55 | 125 | 110 |
| **Novi** | 125 | 45 | 156 | 130 |

4. Use the **AutoSum** button at the bottom of each column.

5. Click the **Print** button to print the worksheet.

6. Save the workbook on your disk. Use **EX0102-Reinforcement** for its name. Leave the workbook open for use in the next exercise.

| | A | B | C | D | E | F | G |
|---|---|---|---|---|---|---|---|
| 1 | January | | | | | <student name> | |
| 2 | | | | | | | |
| 3 | | Gas | Water | Electric | Phone | | |
| 4 | Indianapo | 165 | 55 | 250 | 120 | | |
| 5 | Fort Wayr | 100 | 35 | 225 | 67 | | |
| 6 | Toledo | 150 | 45 | 215 | 125 | | |
| 7 | Dayton | 125 | 60 | 185 | 150 | | |
| 8 | Columbus | 150 | 75 | 170 | 85 | | |
| 9 | Ypsilanti | 220 | 85 | 285 | 300 | | |
| 10 | Southfield | 118 | 55 | 125 | 110 | | |
| 11 | Novi | 125 | 45 | 156 | 130 | | |
| 12 | | 1153 | 455 | 1611 | 1087 | | |
| 13 | | | | | | | |

## R2–Entering Data in Another Sheet

1. Click the **Sheet2** tab to select the second sheet of the **EX0102-Reinforcement** workbook.

2. Enter **February** in cell **A1**.

3. Place your name in cell **E1**.

4. Enter the following text and numbers as shown in the figure:

| | GAS | WATER | ELECTRIC | PHONE |
|---|---|---|---|---|
| **Indianapolis** | 175 | 55 | 230 | 110 |
| **Fort Wayne** | 120 | 30 | 245 | 90 |
| **Toledo** | 160 | 40 | 225 | 135 |
| **Dayton** | 155 | 65 | 195 | 140 |
| **Columbus** | 170 | 70 | 190 | 95 |
| **Ypsilanti** | 190 | 80 | 305 | 290 |
| **Southfield** | 98 | 65 | 145 | 120 |
| **Novi** | 105 | 50 | 170 | 110 |

5. Use the **AutoSum** button to calculate the sum of each column of numbers.

6. Print the sheet. Click the **Save** button on the Standard toolbar to save your changes. (You will not need to give it a name again. It will automatically update the existing file on your disk.) Leave the workbook open for use in the next exercise.

| | A | B | C | D | E | F |
|---|---|---|---|---|---|---|
| 1 | February | | | | <student name> | |
| 2 | | | | | | |
| 3 | | Gas | Water | Electric | Phone | |
| 4 | Indianapo | 175 | 55 | 230 | 110 | |
| 5 | Fort Wayr | 120 | 30 | 245 | 90 | |
| 6 | Toledo | 160 | 40 | 225 | 135 | |
| 7 | Dayton | 155 | 65 | 195 | 140 | |
| 8 | Columbus | 170 | 70 | 190 | 95 | |
| 9 | Ypsilanti | 190 | 80 | 305 | 290 | |
| 10 | Southfield | 98 | 65 | 145 | 120 | |
| 11 | Novi | 105 | 50 | 170 | 110 | |
| 12 | | 1173 | 455 | 1705 | 1090 | |
| 13 | | | | | | |

## R3—Editing a Worksheet

1. Click the **Sheet1** tab to select Sheet1.

2. Edit cell **B4** to read **2400** and press ↵Enter. (If you have used the AutoSum button correctly, the sum of column B will be automatically updated.)

3. Click the **Save** button to save the change.

4. Print **Sheet1**. Leave the workbook open for the next exercise.

| | A | B | C | D | E | F | G |
|---|---|---|---|---|---|---|---|
| 1 | January | | | | | <student name> | |
| 2 | | | | | | | |
| 3 | | Gas | Water | Electric | Phone | | |
| 4 | Indianapo | 2400 | 55 | 250 | 120 | | |
| 5 | Fort Way | 100 | 35 | 225 | 67 | | |
| 6 | Toledo | 150 | 45 | 215 | 125 | | |
| 7 | Dayton | 125 | 60 | 185 | 150 | | |
| 8 | Columbus | 150 | 75 | 170 | 85 | | |
| 9 | Ypsilanti | 220 | 85 | 285 | 300 | | |
| 10 | Southfield | 118 | 55 | 125 | 110 | | |
| 11 | Novi | 125 | 45 | 156 | 130 | | |
| 12 | | 3388 | 455 | 1611 | 1087 | | |
| 13 | | | | | | | |

## R4—Closing and Exiting Excel

1. Click the **Close Window** button to close the workbook. (If you have any unsaved work, the program will always prompt you to save your changes before it closes the workbook.)

2. Click the **Close** button to close the Excel program.

Challenge exercises are designed to test your ability to apply your skills to new situations with less-detailed instructions. These exercises also challenge you to expand your repertoire of skills by using commands that are similar to those you have already learned. The desired outcome is clearly defined, but you have more freedom to choose the steps needed to achieve the required result.

The following exercises use separate sheets in the same workbook. The exercises are not sequential and do not depend on each other.

## C1—Calculating Trip Expenses

Your boss tells you to prepare for a short trip to Chicago and provide a detailed estimate of the cost.

*Goal:* Create a worksheet to itemize the expenses of a two-day trip to Chicago.

1. Launch Excel. Select **Sheet1**, if necessary, and place your name in cell **A1**.

2. Type the following expense categories in column **A** in cells **A3** through **A6**: **Air Fare**, **Rental Car**, **Hotel for Two Nights**, and **Food**.

3. Enter dollar values for these expenses in column **B** in cells **B3** through **B6**. Estimate the values, they do not have to be exact.

4. Use the **AutoSum** button in cell **B7** to add up the expenses.

|   | A | B |
|---|---|---|
| 1 | <Your Name> | |
| 2 | | |
| 3 | Air Fare | 110 |
| 4 | Rental Car | 85 |
| 5 | Hotel for T\| | 185 |
| 6 | Food | 80 |
| 7 | | 460 |
| 8 | | |

5. Save the workbook as **EX0103-Challenge**.

6. Print **Sheet1** if your instructor requires printouts. Leave this file open for use in the next Challenge exercise.

## C2—Summarizing the Expenses of Conducting a Survey

Social scientists often write grant proposals in which they must estimate the cost of a project.

*Goal:* Create a worksheet to summarize the cost of preparing and conducting a survey.

Use the workbook **EX0103-Challenge**, which was created in the previous exercise. If you did not do exercise C1, start Excel and use a blank workbook.

1. Select **Sheet2** and place your name in cell **A1**.

2. Type the following expense categories in cells **A3** through A8: **Writing**, **Validating**, **Printing**, **Telephone**, **Callers**, and **Analysis**.

|   | A | B |
|---|---|---|
| 1 | <Your Name> | |
| 2 | | |
| 3 | Writing | 1500 |
| 4 | Validating | 3000 |
| 5 | Printing | 150 |
| 6 | Telephone | 300 |
| 7 | Callers | 1000 |
| 8 | Analysis | 500 |
| 9 | | 6450 |

3. Enter dollar values for these expenses in cells **B3** through **B8**. Estimate the values; they do not have to be exact.

4. Use the **AutoSum** button in cell **B9** to add up the expenses.

5. Save the workbook. Name it **EX0103-Challenge**, if necessary.

6. Print **Sheet2** if your instructor requires printouts. Leave this file open for use in the next Challenge exercise.

 ## C3—Tracking the Operating Costs of Alternative Fuel Vehicles

Schools and cities across the nation are using alternative fuel vehicles. In this exercise you track the consumption of bifuel automobiles that use compressed natural gas (CNG) or gasoline.

*Goal:* Create a worksheet to summarize the cost of fuel for a fleet of five bifuel vehicles.

Use the workbook **EX0103-Challenge**, which was created in the first challenge exercise. If you did not do exercise C1, start Excel and use a blank workbook.

1. Select **Sheet3** and place your name in cell **A1**. Select **A2** and type **September**.

2. Type the following column headings in cells **A4** through **C4**: **License**, **CNG**, and **Gasoline**.

|   | A | B | C | D |
|---|---|---|---|---|
| 1 | <Your Name> | | | |
| 2 | September | | | |
| 3 | | | | |
| 4 | License | CNG | Gasoline | |
| 5 | 35AGFI | 85 | 15 | |
| 6 | 3698FA | 60 | 30 | |
| 7 | ACF345 | 120 | 50 | |
| 8 | D90CFJ | 35 | 65 | |
| 9 | Total | 300 | 160 | 460 |
| 10 | | | | |

3. Refer to the figure and the table below to fill out the fuel consumption. Units used for CNG are equivalent in energy to one gallon of gasoline.

| LICENSE | CNG | GASOLINE |
|---|---|---|
| 35AGFI | 85 | 15 |
| 3698FA | 60 | 30 |
| ACF345 | 120 | 50 |
| D90CFJ | 35 | 65 |

4. Use the **AutoSum** button in cells **B9** and **C9** to add up each type of fuel used.

5. Use the AutoSum function in cell **D9** to calculate a grand total.

6. Save the workbook. Name it **EX0103-Challenge**, if necessary.

7. Print **Sheet3** if your instructor requires printouts. Close the workbook. Close Excel.

## C4—Using Prewritten Spreadsheet Templates

When you use the menu option for opening a new workbook, you have the opportunity to create a new workbook that is based upon one of several prewritten workbook templates that have been set up to accomplish specific tasks.

*Goal:* Modify a prewritten workbook.

1. Start Excel. Choose **View**, **task pane** and choose **General Templates** from the **New from template** section.

2. Click the **Spreadsheet Solutions** tab, choose **Expense Statement**, and click **OK**.

3. Fill in the worksheet with numbers of your choosing. Add your name.

4. Save the workbook as **EX0104-Expense Statement**.

5. Print the worksheet if your instructor requires it. Close the workbook.

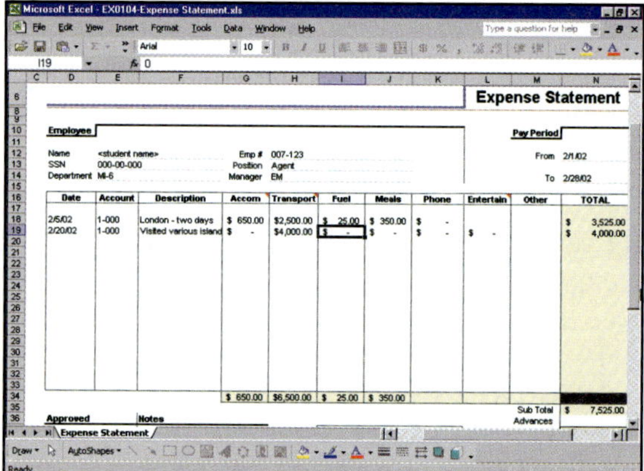

 **EXC** **Lesson 1** Learning the Basics of Excel

 Create a worksheet to balance your checkbook. Criteria for grading will be:

**1.** Demonstration of mastery of Excel skills that were taught in this lesson.

Some examples of features that students have learned to use in previous classes to enhance their personal checkbook worksheet are:

- Entering text and numbers in separate cells

- Using negative numbers for checks and withdrawals and positive numbers for deposits

- Using the summation formula to add up the deposits, checks, and withdrawals to determine the balance

- Including a column for the date of the transaction

- Including a column for check number

- Including a column for a description of the deposit, withdrawal, or check

- Placing the description column last, so long text entries have room to overlap cells to the right

- Using the first row to show the starting balance

**2.** Identify yourself. Place your name in a cell that is clearly visible.

**3.** To complete the project Save your file on your own disk. Name it **EX0105-Checkbook**.

- Check with your instructor to determine if the project should be submitted in electronic or printed form. If necessary, print out a copy of the worksheet to hand in.

# Lesson 2

## Formatting the Worksheet

Task 1    Selecting Groups of Cells
Task 2    Formatting Large Numbers, Currency, Decimal Places, and Dates
Task 3    Adjusting Columns and Cells for Long Text or Numbers
Task 4    Aligning Text in a Cell
Task 5    Changing the Font, Size, and Emphasis of Text
Task 6    Adding Lines, Borders, Colors, and Shading

## INTRODUCTION

 A variety of formatting techniques can be used to improve the appearance of a worksheet. Formatting your worksheet can also make it easier to read. This is especially important for worksheets that are used by others.

In this lesson, you learn how to work with existing worksheets to improve their appearance, make them easier to read, and give them a professional look. You will be working with the utility bills for the branch locations of the Armstrong Pool, Spa, and Sauna Company, the company you worked with in Lesson 1.

# VISUAL SUMMARY

When you have completed this entire lesson, you will have a worksheet that looks like this:

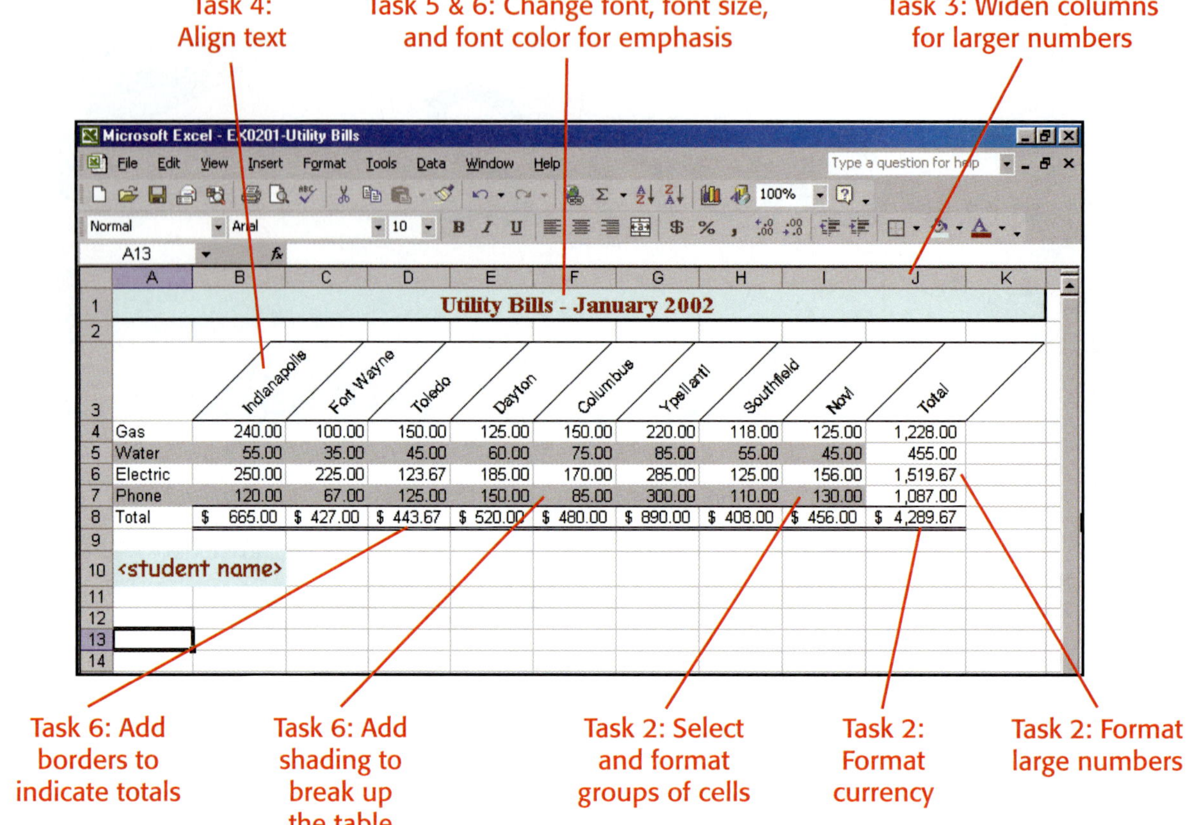

# Task 1
## SELECTING GROUPS OF CELLS

### Why would I do this?

To change the formatting of a cell, it must be selected. It is common to want to change the formatting of groups of cells, so it is preferable to select the entire group and format all of them at the same time. You can select the entire sheet, an entire row or column, a rectangle of cells, or unconnected groups of cells. By selecting the entire group of cells, you help ensure that the same formatting is applied to all of them.

In this task, you learn different techniques for selecting a group of cells.

**1** Launch Excel and click the **Open** button.

*The Open dialog box is displayed.*

Click the down arrow next to the **Look in** box, find **EX0201** in the **Student** folder, and open it.

*This worksheet summarizes the Armstrong Pool, Spa, and Sauna Company utility bills by city.*

Save the file as **EX0201-Utility Bills** on your floppy disk.

*The new file name appears in the title bar.*

Click the **Select All** button in the upper-left corner of the sheet.

*The entire worksheet is selected.*

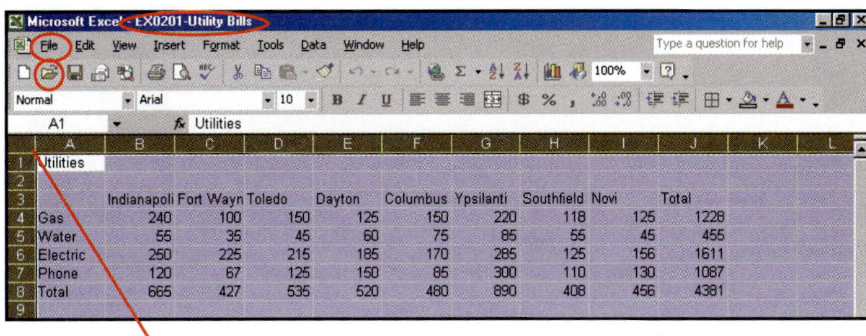

Select All button

**2** Click the heading of column **J**.

*The entire column of totals is selected.*

**CAUTION**

All of the cells in the row, including those that are not visible, are selected. Be careful when you select an entire sheet, row, or column. You may make unwanted changes to cells that are not on the screen.

**3** Click the header for row **5**.

*The entire row pertaining to water bills is selected.
Notice that the first cell of the group is always the
opposite highlight of the rest of the selected cells. This
indicates that it is the active cell and its contents are
displayed in the formula bar. It is still one of the
selected group.*

**4** Position the pointer over cell **B4**. Click-and-
drag a rectangular selection area to cell **I7**
and then release the mouse button.

*This selects the actual bills.*

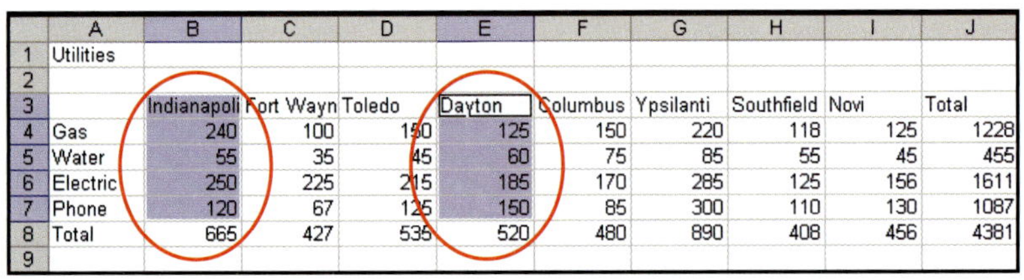

The letters **I** and **O** may be easily confused with numbers, especially if the text font is Arial. Cell I7 refers to the cell in column I
and row 7.

**5** Select cells **B3** through **B7** and release the
mouse button.

*Selecting two groups of cells that are not next to each
other is a two-step process.*

Hold down Ctrl and select cells **E3** through
**E7**. Release the mouse button and Ctrl.

*Both sets of cells are selected. This is a useful skill that
can be applied in a later lesson when you chart content
of cells that are not next to each other.*

**6** Click cell **B1** to select it. Use the vertical
scrollbar to scroll down so that you can see
cell **B60**.

Hold down ✦Shift and click cell **B60**.

*This selects all of the cells between **B1** and **B60**.*

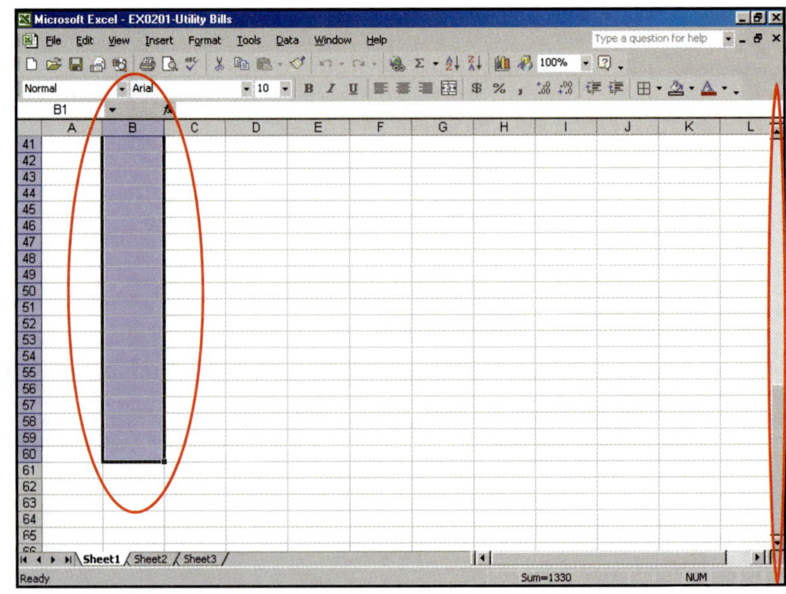

**7** Scroll back to the top of the sheet.

*This method is useful when selecting a group of cells that are so far apart that you have to use the scrollbar to find the other end of the group.*



# Task 2

## FORMATTING LARGE NUMBERS, CURRENCY, DECIMAL PLACES, AND DATES

### Why would I do this?

Most numbers greater than 999 should have commas inserted to make them easier to read. In some cases, numbers represent money and should have commas and dollar signs. Many numbers have decimal components and you have to decide how many decimal places to display. Excel allows you to format numbers the way you want them to be displayed. You also need to know how to handle dates.

In this task, you learn how to apply different types of numerical formats.

**1** Select the cells from **B4** through **J7** and click the **Comma Style** button.

*Notice the totals in column J are displayed with comma where needed and two decimal places are displayed by default.*

**Comma Style button**

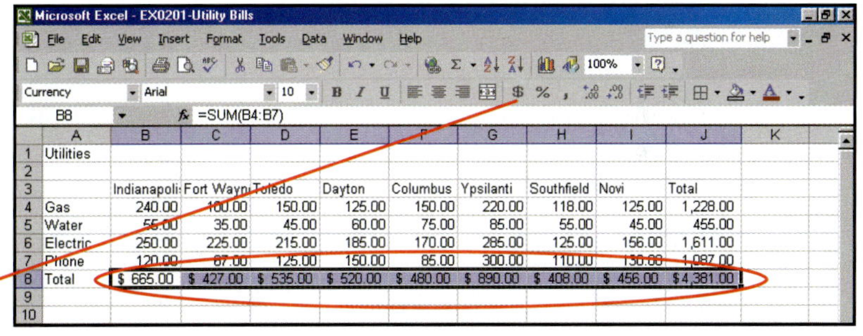

**2** Select cells from **B8** through **J8** and click the **Currency Style** button.

*A dollar sign is added to the left side of the cell, and commas are inserted in numbers that are greater than 999. Leave this range selected for the next step.*

**Currency Style button**

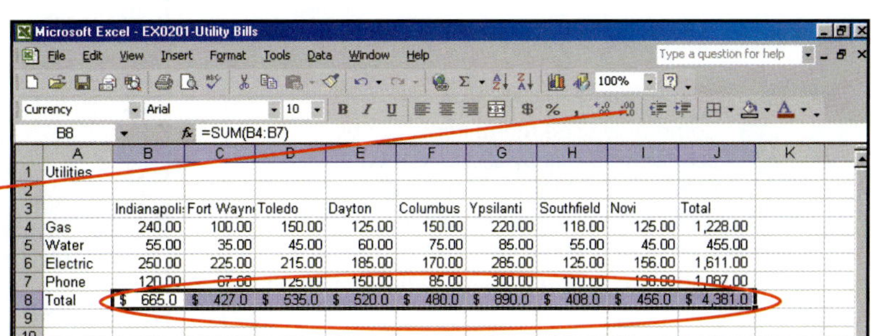

**3** Click once on the **Decrease Decimal** button.

*Notice that the numbers are displayed with one less decimal place.*

**Decrease Decimal button**

**4** Click the **Increase Decimal** button once.

*The cells display two decimal places.*

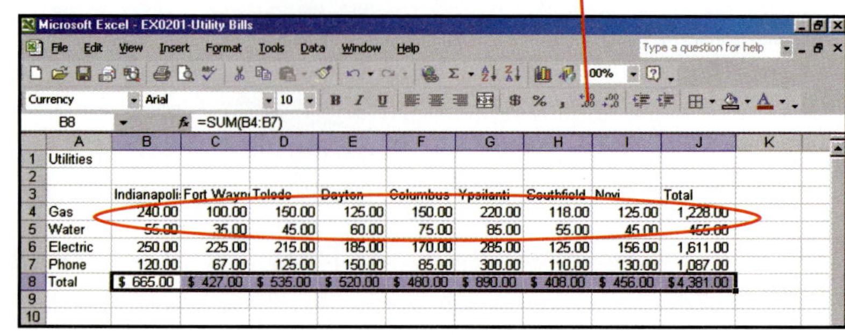

**CAUTION**

Rounding the display does not change the actual number in the cell or any cell that depends upon it. If you use the Decrease Decimal button to change the display so that it does not show all of the decimal places, cells containing totals or other values calculated using those numbers may appear to be incorrect.

**5** Select cell **A15**, type **1/30/02**, and press **↵Enter**.

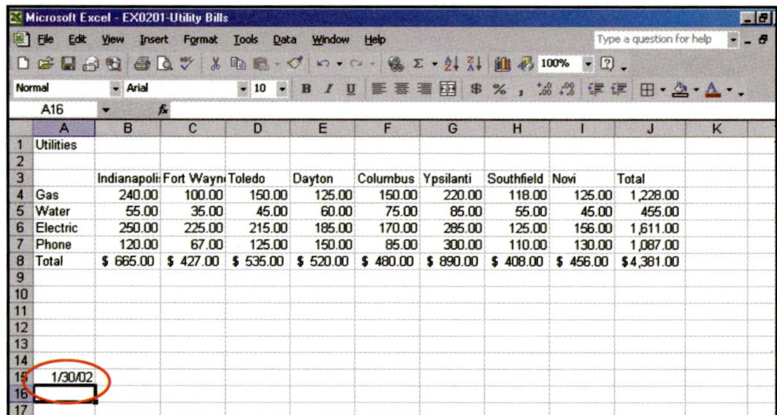

**6** Select cell **A15** again. Choose **Format** from the menu, and then choose **Cells**.

*The Format Cells dialog box is displayed.*

Click the **Number** tab if necessary.

Click **Date** in the **Category** box if necessary. Scroll down the list of options and click the example **Mar-01** in the **Type** box.

*This selection will display the month and year.*

**QUICK TIP**

Commonly used menu items can be accessed quickly by clicking on an object using the right mouse button. A shortcut menu opens containing options that are relevant to the object. At step 6, you could have right-clicked cell A15 and chosen Format Cells from the shortcut menu.

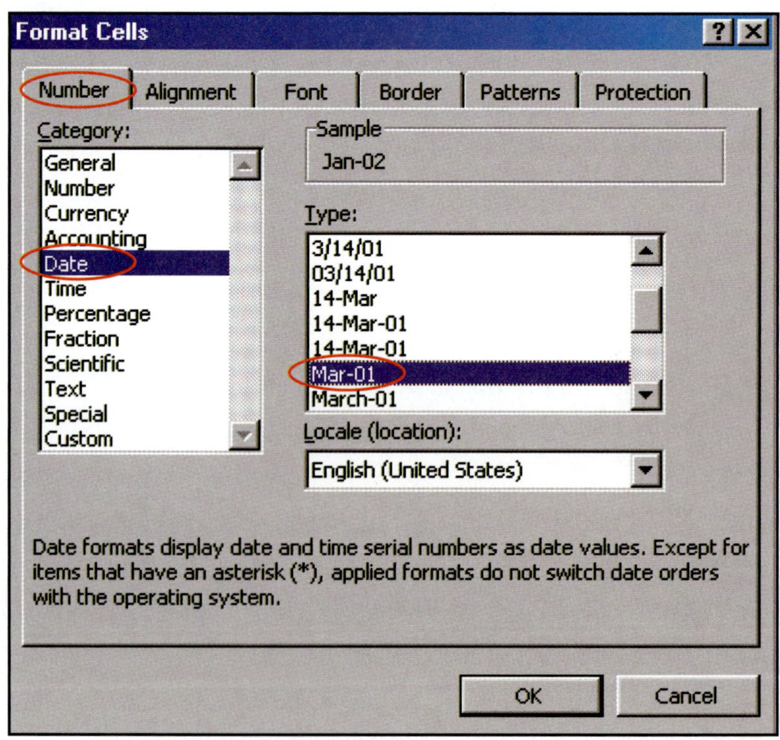

 **7** Click **OK**.

*The date now shows just the month and year. Notice that the actual content of the cell is displayed in the formula bar and that the program converted 02 to 2002.*

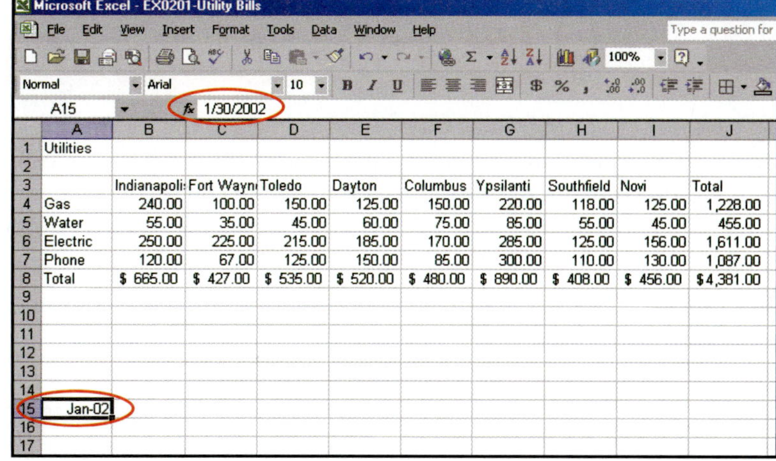

**8** With cell **A15** still selected, choose **Edit**, **Clear**, **Formats** from the menu.

*The number 37286 appears.*

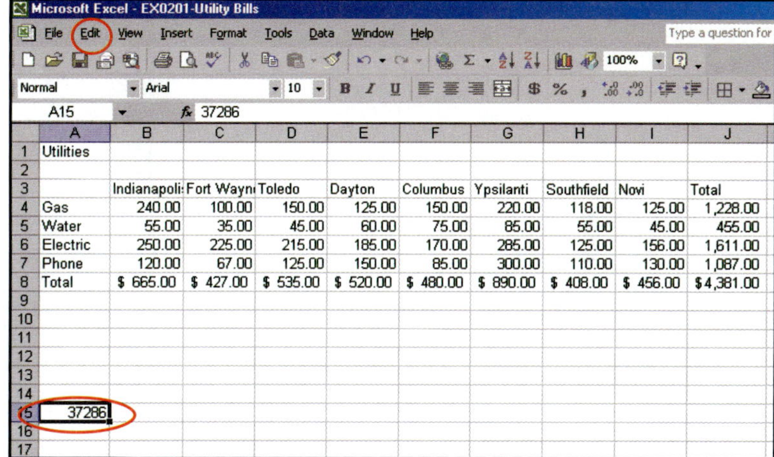

**IN DEPTH**

Excel thinks of dates in terms of the number of days from a fixed date in the past. When you remove the formatting from the cell, it displays the number that it is actually using. This makes it possible to subtract one date from another to determine the number of days between two dates. The number that Excel uses for the date is the number of days since the year 1900—that is what is displayed when you remove all the formatting.

**9** With cell **A15** selected, choose **Edit**, **Clear**, **All**.

*The date is removed as well as the formatting.*

# Task 3
## ADJUSTING COLUMNS AND CELLS FOR LONG TEXT OR NUMBERS

### Why would I do this?

Text and numbers entered into a cell are often longer than the cell width. If the cell to the right contains an entry, the text in the left cell is cut off. If a number is too long to fit conveniently, but has fewer than eleven digits, Excel displays a string of # signs.

In this task, you learn how to change column widths to accommodate entries and center titles across several columns.

**1**  Select cell **B3**.

*Notice that city's name is cut off. You can see the full name in the formula bar.*

Complete city name

**2**  Move the pointer to the line that separates the headings for columns **B** and **C**.

*The mouse pointer turns into a double-sided black arrow.*

**3**  Double-click.

*The width of the column automatically adjusts to fit the longest word in any of the cells in column B.*

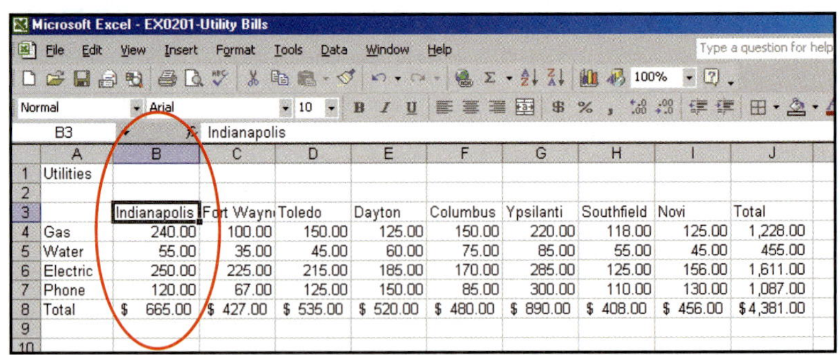

IN DEPTH

You can adjust the width of a column or the height of a row by clicking and dragging the boundary between two headings. If you click-and-drag across several headings to select them together, you can adjust the width or height of all of them at the same time.

**4** Select cell **A1** and type **Utility Bills - January 2002**. Press Enter.

*Notice that the text overlaps the cells to the right because they are empty. If cell B1 had any content, the display of cell A1 would be cut off.*

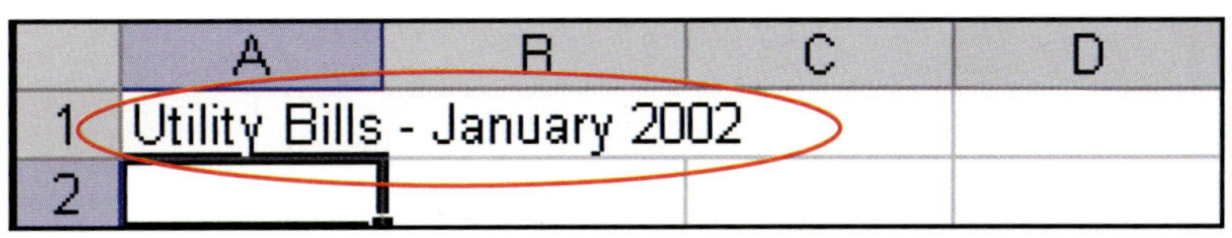

**5** Select cells **A1** through **K1**. Click the **Merge and Center** button.

*The selected cells display the text as if they were one cell, and the long title is centered. The text is centered across one more column than necessary to accommodate a change in the orientation of the cells that will be made in a later task.*

Merge and Center button

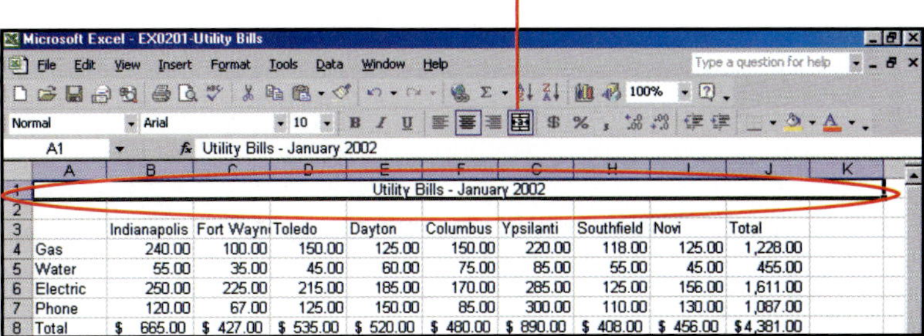

IN DEPTH

To split cells that have been merged, select the cell and choose Format, Cells. Click the Alignment tab, and deselect the Merge cells box.

**6** Select cell **D6**, type **7000**, and then press Enter.

*Notice that the size of the totals in cells D8 and J8 exceeds the available cell space. A series of # signs is displayed in each.*

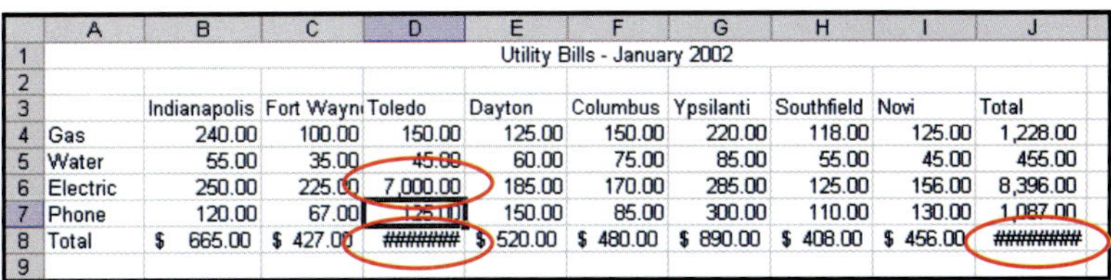

**7** Double-click the line between the headings for columns **J** and **K**.

*The width of column J adjusts to display the larger number.*

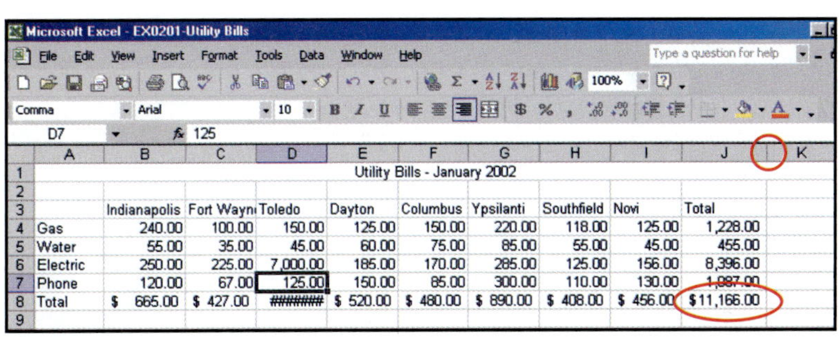

**8** Select cell **D6**, type **123.67**, and then press Enter.

*The entry is replaced with a more realistic number. Notice that column J did not revert to its narrower width.*

Click the **Save** button to save the changes made up to this point.

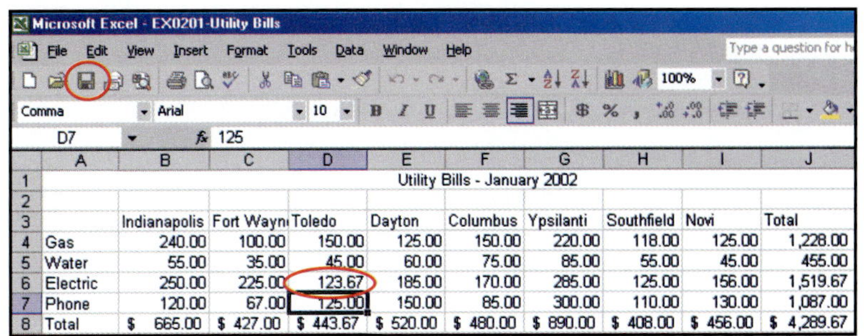

# Task 4
## ALIGNING TEXT IN A CELL

### Why would I do this?

If text is used to label a row or column, you may find that it looks better if the text is centered in or aligned with the right side of the cell. If the text used as a column label is much longer than the numbers in the column, you may want to increase the height of the row and wrap the text in the cell. Another way to handle long column labels is to slant the cells at an angle.

In this task, you learn how to wrap text onto several lines within a cell and align long text labels.

**1** Select cells **B3** through **J3**. Choose **Format, Cells**.

*The Format Cells dialog box appears.*

Click the **Alignment** tab, if it is not already selected.

*This dialog box may be used to control the alignment of text and numbers within cells.*

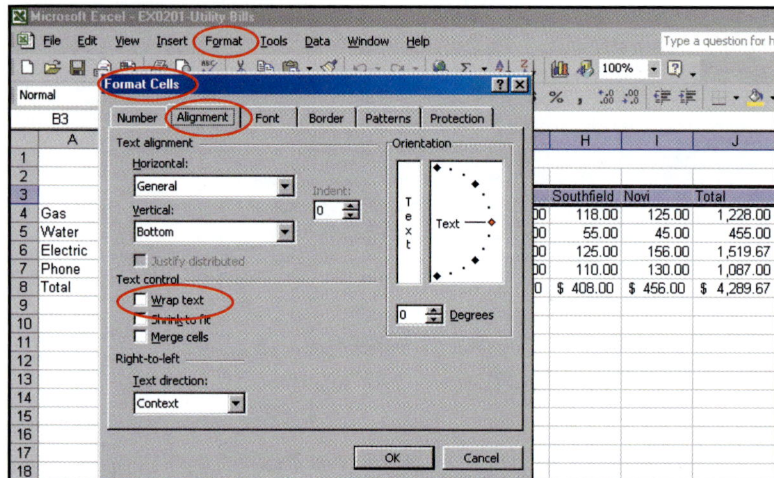

**2** Click the **Wrap text** check box. Click **OK**.

*The height of the row increases and the text wraps within the cells just as if it were a word processing document. In this example, the text in cell C3 wrapped to a second line.*

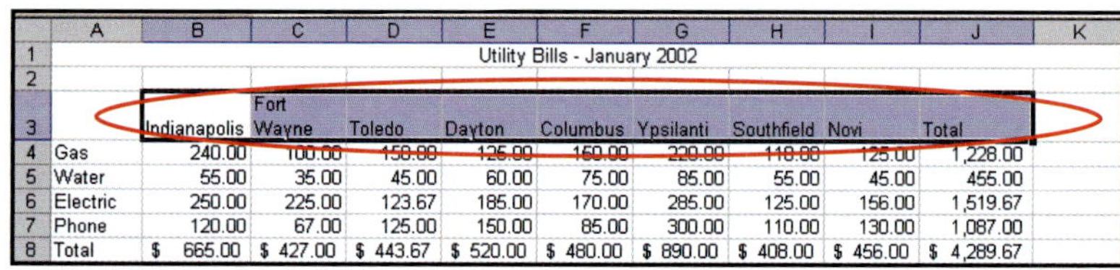



Excel's word wrapping feature does not have an automatic hyphenation feature and is not as smart as a word processor when it comes to estimating where to break words. Check your work when you use the Wrap text feature.

**3** Click the **Undo** button to remove the **Wrap text** feature.

*There is another way to handle this type of column label.*

Make sure that cells **B3** to **J3** are still selected and choose **Format**, **Cells** from the menu.

*The Format Cells dialog box appears.*

B3 to J3 still selected

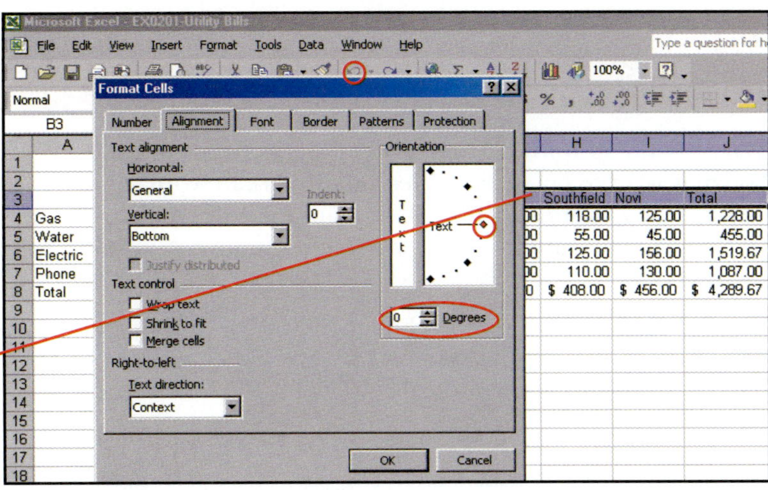

**4** Click-and-drag the small red diamond in the **Orientation** window upward until the **Degrees** box reads **45**.

*This will align the text at a 45-degree angle in the cell.*

You can also type the angle in the <u>D</u>egrees box or use the small arrows in the <u>D</u>egrees box to change the angle.

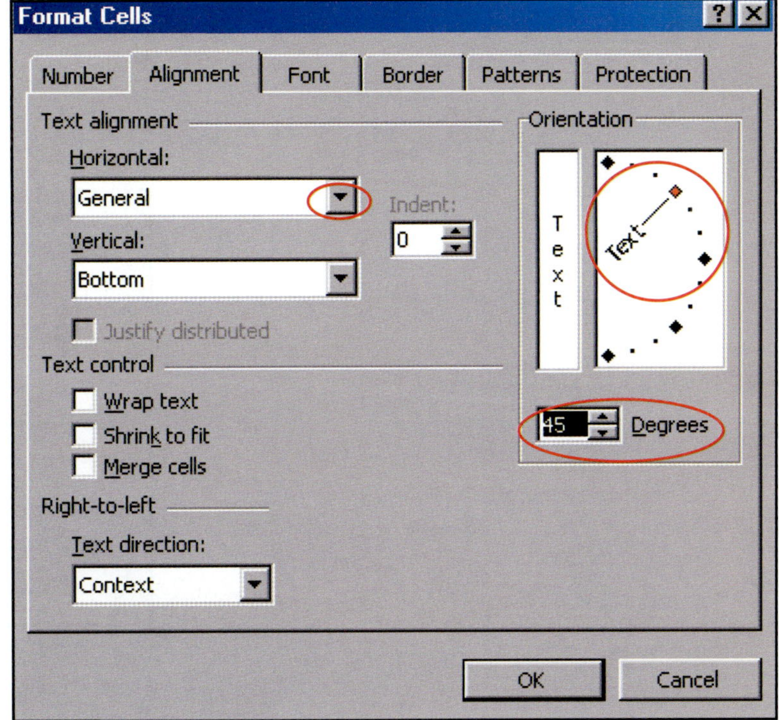

**5** Click the down arrow next to the **Horizontal** box. Click **Center**.

*This centers the text in the cell.*

Click **OK**.

*The text in cells B3 to J3 is displayed at an angle.*

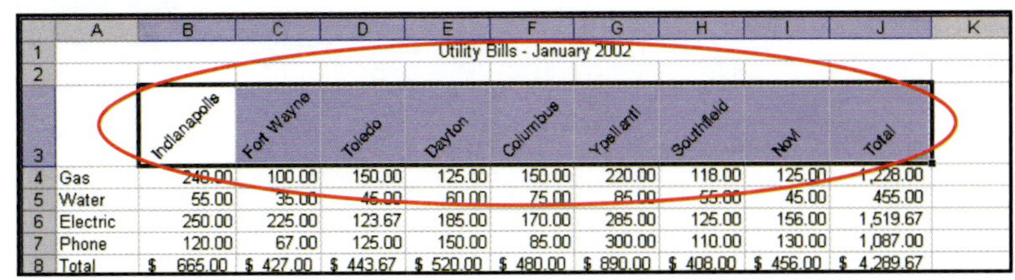

A faster way to change horizontal alignment is to use one of the three buttons on the Formatting toolbar: Align Left, Center, or Align Right.

## CHANGING THE FONT, SIZE, AND EMPHASIS OF TEXT

### Why would I do this?

You may want to emphasize titles and important words by making them larger and by using a different *font*. This helps improve the overall appearance of your worksheet. You can draw attention to key numbers by adding emphasis to those numbers.

In this task, you learn how to change the *point size* of a title and change a font from Arial to Times New Roman. You also add emphasis by using boldface or italicized versions of the font.

**1** Click anywhere on the title in the first row to select it. Click the down arrow next to the **Font** box. Scroll down and click **Times New Roman**.

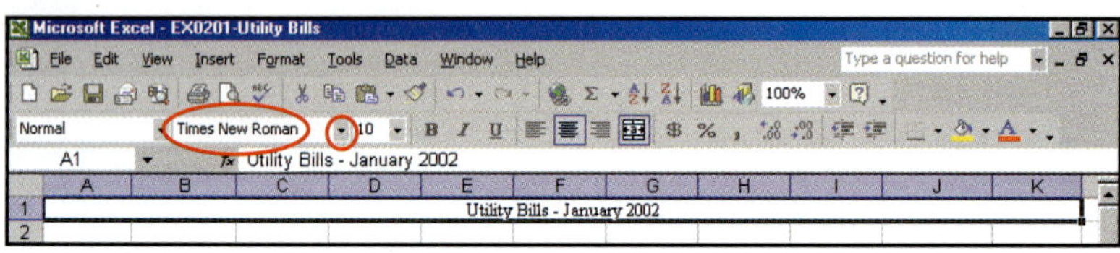

*The font of the title changes, and the height of the row increases to accomodate the larger text.*

**2** Click the down arrow next to the **Font Size** box. Click **14**.

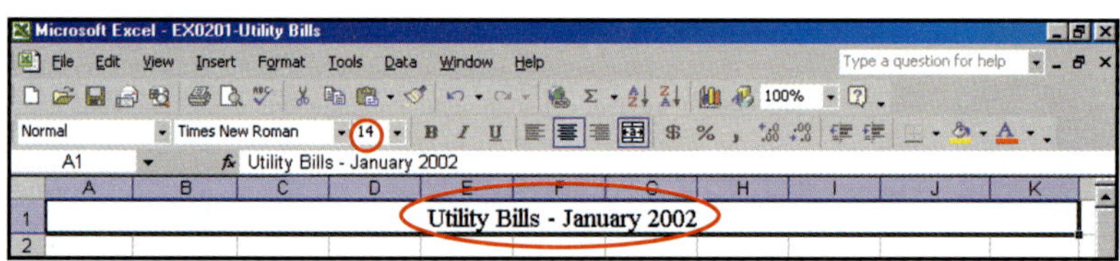

*The title changes to 14 points.*

**3** Click the **Bold** button.

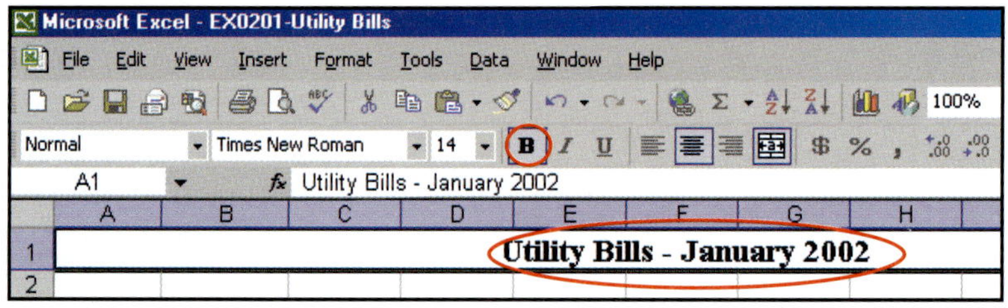

*The font, size, and emphasis have been changed to make the title stand out.*

In addition to Bold, you also can change the emphasis of text or numbers by using the Underline or Italic buttons. Simply select the cells you want to change and click the appropriate button on the Formatting toolbar. Numerous other options may be found by using Format, Cells, and selecting the Font tab.

# Task 6
## ADDING LINES, BORDERS, COLORS, AND SHADING

### Why would I do this?

Borders help emphasize important data, and also separate titles, subtotals, and totals. Colors and shading add emphasis and impact. They help draw the reader's attention and make the data easier to read.

In this task, you learn how to add borders and shading to various parts of the worksheet.

**1** Make sure that the title is still selected from the previous task. Click the down arrow next to the **Borders** button.

*A menu of borders is displayed.*

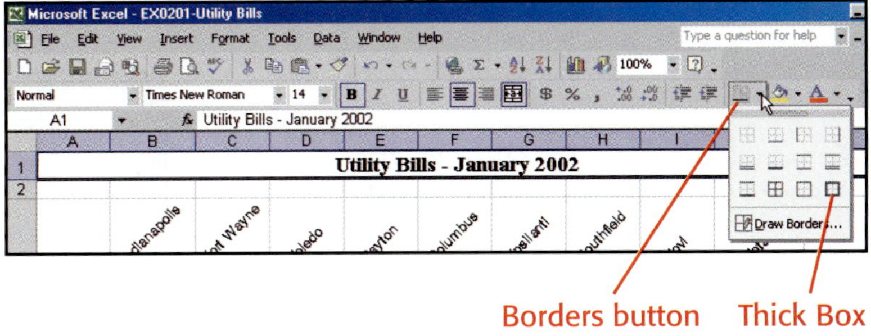



**2** Click the **Thick Box Border** option at the right side of the bottom row.

Select cells **B3** to **J3**.

Click the down arrow next to the **Borders** button.

*The border that you select from the menu will be applied to the selected cells.*

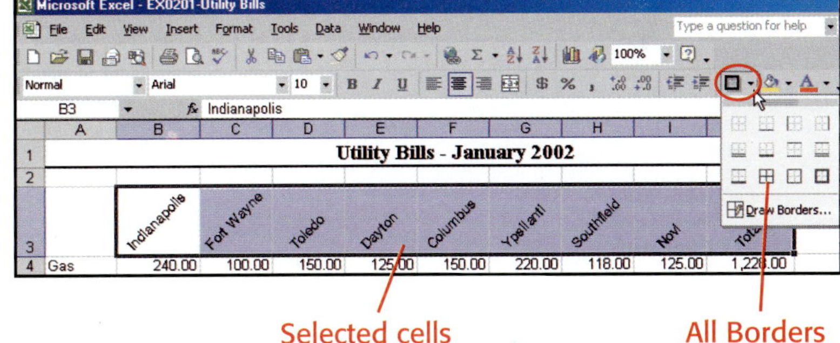



**3** Click the **All Borders** option that is the second box from the left in the bottom row.

*Borders are applied to all sides of the selected cells. Notice that the title in row 1 now appears to be centered due to the width of the angled headings.*

Select cells **B8** through **J8**. Click the down arrow next to the **Borders** button.

*The total of a column of numbers is usually indicated by a single top border and a double bottom border.*

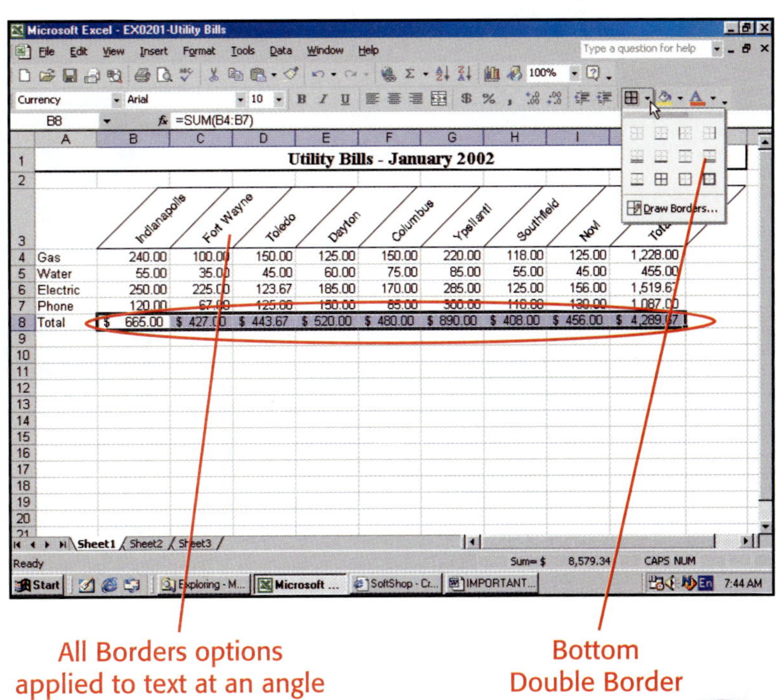

**4** Click the **Top and Double Bottom Border** option that is fourth from the left in the second row.

*The border is applied to indicate the totals.*

Select cells **A5** through **I5** and cells **A7** through **I7** (remember to use Ctrl to select the second group of cells). Click the down arrow next to the **Fill Color** button.

*It is easier to follow rows of data if some of the rows are shaded.*

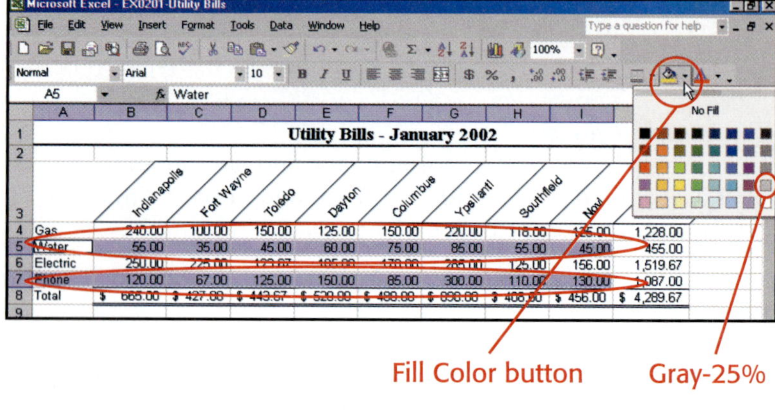


**5** Click the **Gray-25%** button.

*The selected cells are shaded. (To see the gray, deselect the shaded cells by clicking in any other cell.)*

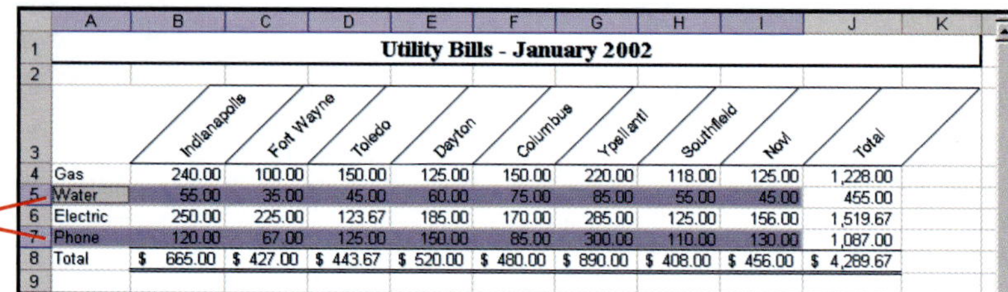

If you are unsure of the name of a color, allow the pointer to remain stationary on one of the colors for a few seconds and a ScreenTip displays the name.

**6** Select the title again. Click the down arrow next to the **Fill Color** button and click the **Light Turquoise** option.

*This changes the background (fill color) to a light turquoise color on the screen.*

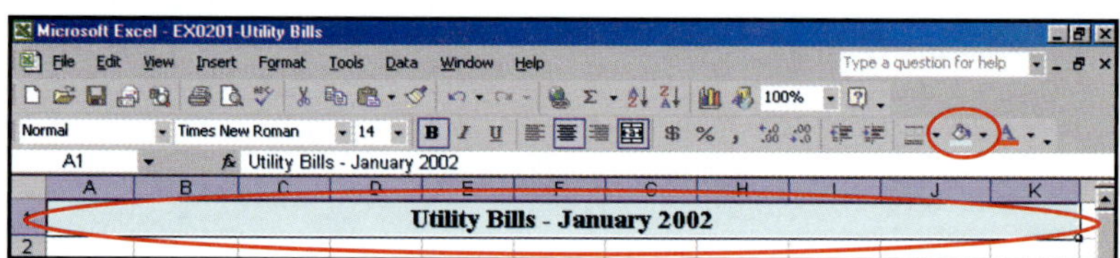



If you do not have a color printer, the program assigns different shades of gray to different colors. If you pick two colors for your text and background that are assigned to the same shade of gray, the printout is unreadable.

**7** With the title still selected, click the down arrow next to the **Font Color** button.

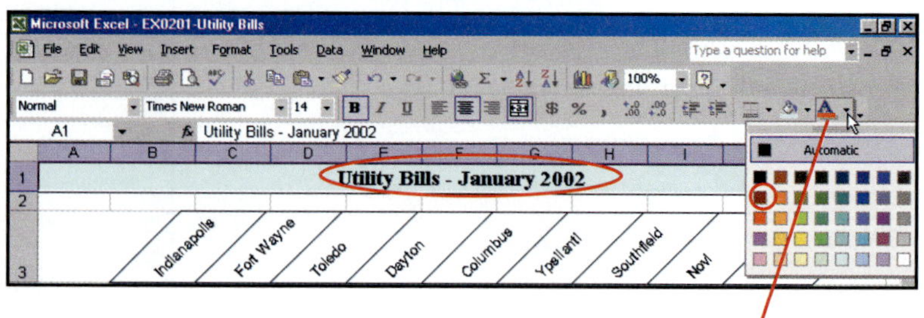

**8** Click the **Dark Red** option.

Select cell **A10,** type your name, and then press ↵Enter. Change the font, font size, border, background color, and font color in cell **A10** to something you like. Merge across two or more cells if your name exceeds the current column width.

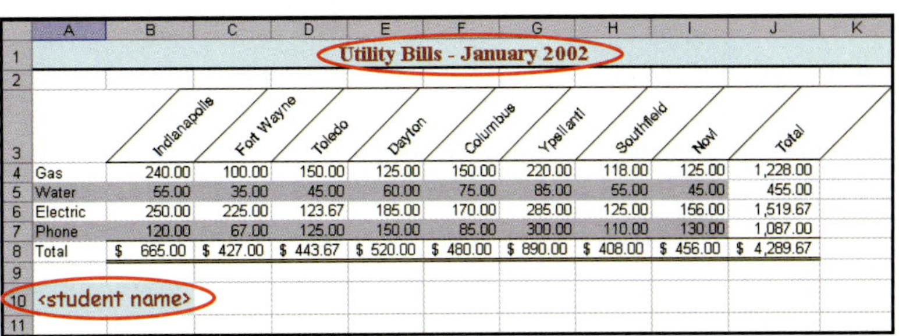



**QUICK TIP**

The Font Color, Fill Color, and Borders buttons on the Formatting toolbar display the most recent choice. If you want to use the type of emphasis that is displayed on the button, you can apply it by clicking once on the button without using the drop-down menu.

**9** Click the **Print** button to print a copy of the worksheet.

Click the **Close Window** button to close the workbook.

*A dialog box warns you that you have not saved the changes that you have made.*

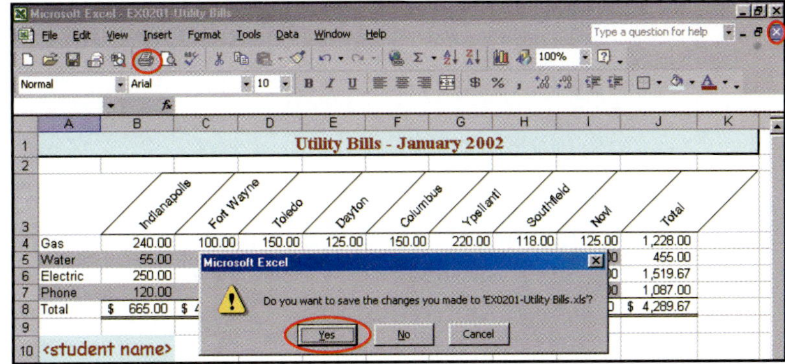



**10** Click **Yes**.

*The workbook closes, leaving the Excel program active.*

The exercises that follow are designed for you to review and use what you have learned in this lesson. You also have the opportunity to practice your skills and then expand on them by applying them to new situations.

## COMPREHENSION

Comprehension exercises are designed to check your memory and understanding of the basic concepts in this lesson. You distinguish between true and false statements, identify new screen elements, and match terms with related statements. If you are uncertain of the correct answer, refer to the task number following each item (for example, T4 refers to Task 4), and review that task until you are confident you can provide a correct response.

### TRUE-FALSE

Circle either T or F.

T   F   **1.** If a number is too long to fit in a cell, it will extend into the cell to the right. **(T3)**

T   F   **2.** You can select all of the cells in a row by clicking on the row heading. **(T1)**

T   F   **3.** One way to handle long labels is to use the **Wrap text** option. **(T4)**

T   F   **4.** A 16-point character is larger than an 8-point character. **(T5)**

T   F   **5.** If you have a printer with only one color of ink, it does not matter what colors you choose for text and background. **(T6)**

T   F   **6.** It is possible to print long column labels at an angle. **(T4)**

### MATCHING QUESTIONS

**A.** Move pointer to the line between column headings and double-click

**B.** `Ctrl`

**C.** Click-and-drag the line between column headings

**D.** Wrap text

**E.** Merge and Center

**F.** Thick box

Match the following statements to the word or phrase that is the best match from the list. Write the letter of the matching word or phrase in the space provided next to the number.

**1.** _____ Text that is used as a title may occupy several cells using this feature **(T3)**

**2.** _____ Used to select a group of cells that is not touching the first group **(T1)**

**3.** _____ Method used to automatically adjust the width of a column to accommodate the widest cell entry **(T3)**

**4.** _____ Method used to manually change the width of a column **(T3)**

**5.** _____ Setting that forces long text entries to fit within the available column width by increasing the row height and displaying the text on several lines within the cell **(T4)**

**6.** _____ A border style **(T6)**

# IDENTIFYING PARTS OF
# THE EXCEL SCREEN

Refer to the figure and identify the numbered parts of
the screen. Write the letter of the correct label in the
space next to the number.

1. ______________

2. ______________

3. ______________

4. ______________

5. ______________

6. ______________

7. ______________

8. ______________

9. ______________

10. ______________

11. ______________

12. ______________

13. ______________

14. ______________

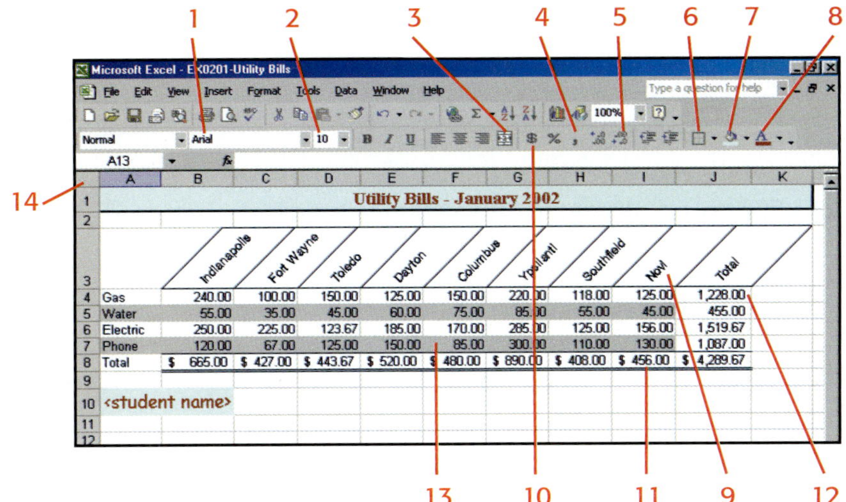


A. Text aligned at an angle  **(T4)**

B. Cells displaying a gray fill color  **(T6)**

C. **Select All** button  **(T1)**

D. Example of **Comma Style**  **(T2)**

E. **Currency Style** button  **(T2)**

F. **Comma Style** button  **(T2)**

G. **Decrease Decimal** button  **(T2)**

H. **Merge and Center** button  **(T3)**

I. **Borders** button  **(T6)**

J. Font Size  **(T5)**

K. Font name  **(T5)**

L. **Fill Color** button  **(T6)**

M. **Font Color** button  **(T6)**

N. Cell with a top and double bottom border  **(T6)**

Reinforcement exercises are designed to reinforce the skills you have learned by applying them to a new situation. Detailed instructions are provided along with a figure, where appropriate, to illustrate the result. The reinforcement exercises that follow should be completed sequentially. Leave the workbook open at the end of each exercise for use in the next exercise until you are specifically directed to close it.

Open **EX0202** and save it as **EX0202-Reinforcement** on your disk for use in the following exercises.

You have been asked to compare two types of office cubicle dividers that are of different heights. A weighted average comparison method is used in your department to make such decisions, but the worksheet doesn't look good enough to distribute to members of the committee. Change the formatting as described in these exercises.

## R1—Applying Formats to an Existing Worksheet

Format Sheet1 to match the figure. See the following steps for more detail.

1. Select **Sheet1,** if necessary.

2. Enter your name in cell **A19.**

3. Use the **Merge and Center** feature to center the main title across columns **A** through **F.** Center the subtitle **Four Feet High** across **C2** and **D2** and the subtitle **Six Feet High** across cells **E2** and **F2.**

4. Center and wrap the text in cells **B3** through **F3.**

5. Center data in all cells from **B4** through **F13.**

6. Select cells **C4** through **C13** and **E4** through **E13.** Choose a fill color of **Gray-25%.**

7. Select cells **A1, A4, A7, A11, A14, A15,** and **A16.** Make them **Bold.**

8. Select **D15** and **F15** and format the numbers to display currency with no decimals.

9. Select **D16** and **F16** and format the numbers to display only three decimal places.

10. Adjust the width of column **A** to display the full contents of cell **A16**, print the sheet, and save the workbook.

## R2—Adding Border Lines and Colors

Add border lines and colors to match the figure. See the steps below for more information.

1. Select **Sheet2.** Enter your name in cell **F19.**

2. Place a **Thick Box** border around the title and the two ratio numbers in cells **D15** and **F15.**

3. Add a **Bottom Border** to cells **A3** through **F3, A6** through **F6,** and **A10** through **F10.**

4. Add a **Bottom Double Border** to the bottom of cells **D12** and **F12.**

5. Change the **Fill Color** of the title to **Turquoise** and change the **Font Color** to **Dark Red.**

6. Change the orientation of the column labels in cells **B2** through **F2** to a **45-degree** angle. Select the **All Borders** option that shows all lines. (Your text may wrap differently than is shown in the figure.)

7. Save the workbook. Leave the workbook open for use in the next exercise.

| | A | B | C | D | E | F |
|---|---|---|---|---|---|---|
| 1 | | Comparison of Office Dividers | | | | |
| 2 | | | Four Feet High | | Six Feet High | |
| 3 | Characteristics | Weight For Relative Importance | Rating On Individual Characteristics | Weighted Rating | Rating On Individual Characteristics | Weighted Rating |
| 4 | **Cost-Related** | | | | | |
| 5 | Initial Cost | 9 | 5 | 45 | 7 | 63 |
| 6 | Maintenance Cost | 8 | 1 | 8 | 6 | 48 |
| 7 | **Physical Attributes** | | | | | |
| 8 | Sound Transmission | 3 | 1 | 3 | 10 | 30 |
| 9 | Durability | 10 | 3 | 30 | 3 | 30 |
| 10 | Movability | 5 | 4 | 20 | 6 | 30 |
| 11 | **Other Benefits** | | | | | |
| 12 | Appearance | 10 | 6 | 60 | 9 | 90 |
| 13 | Privacy | 2 | 6 | 12 | 4 | 8 |
| 14 | Total (Weighted Values) | | | 178 | | 299 |
| 15 | **Actual cost** | | | $ 17,000 | | $ 20,000 |
| 16 | **Ratio of Value Points to Cost** | | | 0.010 | | 0.015 |
| 17 | | | | | | |
| 18 | | | | | | |
| 19 | <student name> | | | | | |

| | A | B | C | D | E | F | G |
|---|---|---|---|---|---|---|---|
| 1 | | Comparison of Office Dividers | | | | | |
| 2 | Characteristics | Weight For Relative Importance | Rating On Individual Characteristics - All Metal | Weighted Rating | Rating On Individual Characteristics - Metal and Glass | Weighted Rating | |
| 3 | **Cost-Related** | | | | | | |
| 4 | Initial Cost | 9 | 5 | 45 | 7 | 63 | |
| 5 | Maintenance Cost | 8 | 1 | 8 | 6 | 48 | |
| 6 | **Physical Attributes** | | | | | | |
| 7 | Sound Transmission | 3 | 1 | 3 | 10 | 30 | |
| 8 | Durability | 10 | 3 | 30 | 3 | 30 | |
| 9 | Movability | 5 | 4 | 20 | 6 | 30 | |
| 10 | **Other Benefits** | | | | | | |
| 11 | Appearance | 10 | 6 | 60 | 9 | 90 | |
| 12 | Privacy | 2 | 6 | 12 | 4 | 8 | |
| 13 | **Total (Weighted Values)** | | | 178 | | 299 | |
| 14 | **Actual cost** | | | $17,000 | | $20,000 | |
| 15 | **Ratio of Value Points to Cost** | | | 0.010 | | 0.015 | |
| 16 | | | | | | | |
| 17 | | | | | | | |
| 18 | | | | | | | |
| 19 | | | | | | <student name> | |

# R3—Formatting a Worksheet

Format the sheet to match the figure. Make sure you change font size and style, merge and center, center text, fill color, align text, and add borders. Remember to adjust the columns to fit to the data. See the steps below for further details.

1. Select **Sheet3**. Enter your name in cell **A17**.

2. Merge and center the title in cell **A1** across cells **A1** through **L1**. Change its font to **Times New Roman, 16** point, and make it **Bold**.

3. Select cells **A2** through **L2**. Format the cells to wrap text, centered, and display the text at a **45-degree** angle. Use the **All Borders** option (The text will not fit correctly.)

4. Drag the boundary between rows **2** and **3** to adjust the height. Select the column headers, **A** through **L**, and double-click on one of the boundaries between column headings to adjust all of the widths at once.

5. Apply a **Gray-25%** fill color to the cells **D2** through **D15**, **J2** through **J15**, and **L2** through **L15**.

6. Format cells **B4** through **B15** as currency.

7. Save and close the workbook.

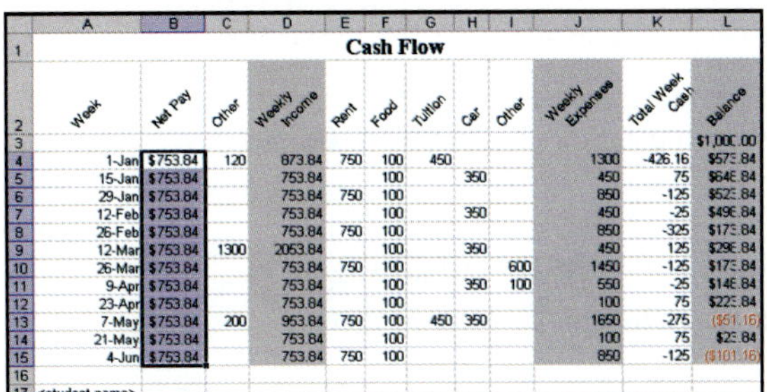

| Week | Net Pay | Other | Weekly Income | Rent | Food | Tuition | Car | Other | Weekly Expenses | Total Week Cash | Balance |
|---|---|---|---|---|---|---|---|---|---|---|---|
|  |  |  |  |  |  |  |  |  |  |  | $1,000.00 |
| 1-Jan | $753.84 | 120 | 873.84 | 750 | 100 | 450 |  |  | 1300 | -426.16 | $573.84 |
| 15-Jan | $753.84 |  | 753.84 |  | 100 |  | 350 |  | 450 | 75 | $648.84 |
| 29-Jan | $753.84 |  | 753.84 | 750 | 100 |  |  |  | 850 | -125 | $523.84 |
| 12-Feb | $753.84 |  | 753.84 |  | 100 |  | 350 |  | 450 | -25 | $498.84 |
| 26-Feb | $753.84 |  | 753.84 | 750 | 100 |  |  |  | 850 | -325 | $173.84 |
| 12-Mar | $753.84 | 1300 | 2053.84 |  | 100 |  | 350 |  | 450 | 125 | $298.84 |
| 26-Mar | $753.84 |  | 753.84 | 750 | 100 |  |  | 600 | 1450 | -125 | $173.84 |
| 9-Apr | $753.84 |  | 753.84 |  | 100 |  | 350 | 100 | 550 | -25 | $148.84 |
| 23-Apr | $753.84 |  | 753.84 |  | 100 |  |  |  | 100 | 75 | $223.84 |
| 7-May | $753.84 | 200 | 953.84 | 750 | 100 | 450 | 350 |  | 1650 | -275 | ($51.16) |
| 21-May | $753.84 |  | 753.84 |  | 100 |  |  |  | 100 | 75 | $23.84 |
| 4-Jun | $753.84 |  | 753.84 | 750 | 100 |  |  |  | 850 | -125 | ($101.16) |

<student name>

Challenge exercises are designed to test your ability to apply your skills to new situations with less detailed instruction. These exercises also challenge you to expand your repertoire of skills by using commands that are similar to those you have already learned. The desired outcome is clearly defined, but you have more freedom to choose the steps needed to achieve the required result.

The following exercises use separate sheets in the same workbook. The exercises are not sequential and do not depend on each other. Open **EX0203** and save it on your floppy disk as **EX0203-Challenge**.

## C1—Using Formatting to Indicate Organization

If a table of data is to be distributed to other people, it is useful to use formatting tools so they can understand how the table is organized. In this example, several people in the office have been asked to evaluate and compare two room divider systems using a weighted scale.

*Goal:* Format the table to make it easier to identify the organization of the numbers.

Use the following guidelines:

1. Select **Sheet1**.

2. Center the text in cells **B2** through **F2**.

3. Use **Tools**, **Options**, **View** tab, **Gridlines** to turn off the gridlines on the screen.

4. Use **Borders** to add the lines shown.

| | A | B<br>Weight For<br>Relative<br>Importance | C<br>Rating On<br>Individual<br>Characteristics -<br>All Metal | D<br>Weighted<br>Rating | E<br>Rating On<br>Individual<br>Characteristics<br>- Metal and<br>Glass | F<br>Weighted<br>Rating |
|---|---|---|---|---|---|---|
| 1 | Comparison of Office Dividers | | | | | |
| 2 | Characteristics | | | | | |
| 3 | **Cost-Related** | | | | | |
| 4 | Initial Cost | 9 | 5 | 45 | 7 | 63 |
| 5 | Maintenance Cost | 8 | 1 | 8 | 6 | 48 |
| 6 | **Physical Attributes** | | | | | |
| 7 | Sound Transmission | 3 | 1 | 3 | 10 | 30 |
| 8 | Durability | 10 | 3 | 30 | 3 | 30 |
| 9 | Movability | 5 | 4 | 20 | 6 | 30 |
| 10 | **Other Benefits** | | | | | |
| 11 | Appearance | 10 | 6 | 60 | 9 | 90 |
| 12 | Privacy | 2 | 6 | 12 | 4 | 8 |
| 13 | **Total (Weighted Values)** | | | 178 | | 299 |
| 14 | **Actual cost** | | | $17,000 | | $20,000 |
| 15 | **Ratio of Value Points to Cost** | | | 0.010 | | 0.015 |

5. Save the workbook. Leave this file open for use in the next Challenge exercise.

## C2—Aligning Text Displayed at an Angle

When you display a column heading at a 45-degree angle, it is unclear which direction is indicated by the horizontal or vertical controls. You can determine how to align the text through a little trial-and-error.

*Goal:* Change the column headings to align at a 45-degree angle and add a border. Adjust the height of the row so that the text wraps as shown.

1. Select **Sheet2**. Select cells **B2** through **F2** and align the text at 45 degrees.

2. Use the **All Borders** option that looks like a window with four panes.

3. Drag the line between row headings 2 and 3 to adjust the height of the row so that none of the text wraps to more than two lines and no words are wrapped incorrectly.

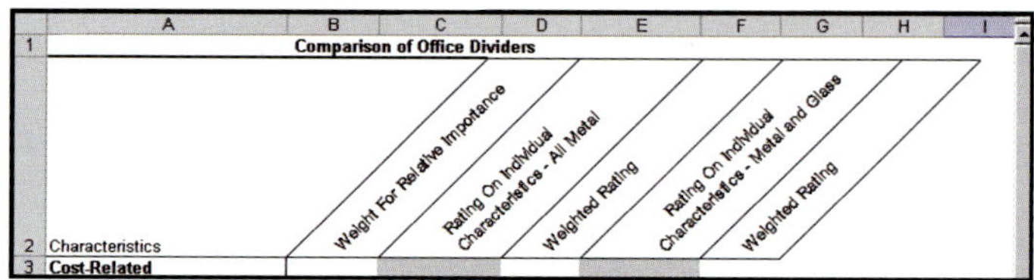


4. Save the workbook.

## C3–Working with Two-Digit Dates

Representing the year in a date with only two digits creates problems because the computer is forced to guess the century in which it belongs. If you are using Excel to compute the age of elderly people, you may get incorrect answers if you subtract their birth dates from today's date.

*Goal:* Determine how to work with the century assumptions built into Excel 2002 so that you know when you must use four digits to represent the year in a date.

1. Select **Sheet3**. Place your name in cell **A1**. Enter today's date in cell **C3** (use the month/day/year format).

2. In cell **B3**, type a date of birth from the 1920s such as **5/20/27**. Notice that the calculation in cell D3 displays a negative number because it assumed you meant 2027 rather than 1927.

3. Type the date in cell **B3** again, but specify the year **1927**, using four digits. The formula in cell **D3** displays a positive number because the date in **B3** is earlier than today's date.

4. Try dates with different two-digit years in cell **B3** to determine which years are assumed to be from the 1900s and which years are assumed to be from the 2000s.

5. Write a directive in cell **A6** that instructs users when to use four digits for the year when entering numbers into Excel worksheets.

6. Widen column **A** to about four times its current width and format the text in cell **A6** to wrap.

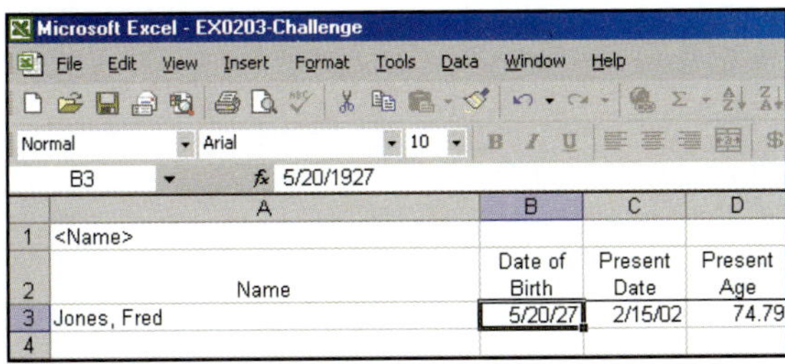

## C4–Protecting Cells from Unintentional Change

The problem with using a lot of volunteers on a project is that there is little time to train them and the turnover is high. It is important to be able to prevent accidental mistakes.

The formula in cell D3 will be lost if someone accidentally enters a value in the cell. Similarly, you do not want others to change the column headings or message you have chosen. To prevent users from overwriting formulas or making unauthorized changes, you can limit the cells they can write in by unlocking particular cells and then protecting the rest of the sheet.

*Goal:* Unlock cells B3 and C3, and then protect the rest of the sheet so that users can only change values in cells B3 and C3.

Use the following guidelines:

1. Select **Sheet3**, if necessary. Select cells **B3** and **C3**. Choose **Format**, **Cells**, and the **Protection** tab. Deselect **L**ocked and click OK.

2. Choose **Tools**, **Protection**, **Protect Sheet** to protect the sheet. Do not use a password. Click OK.

3. Try to make changes to any other part of the sheet and observe the error message.

4. Save the changes you have made. (You are going to use this workbook, Sheet 4, in the next exercise)

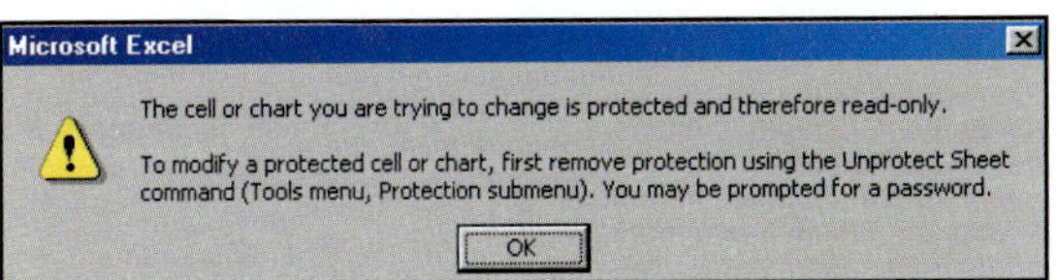

## C5—Splitting Merged Cells and Moving Cells Using Click-and-Drag

Merged cells make good table titles and prevent truncation of the display when text is added to adjacent cells. The merged cells can cause problems when you are trying to work with one of the columns that is included in a merged cell. It is occasionally necessary to remove the merge-and-center formatting from a set of cells.

It is also useful to be able to move the contents of a cell more quickly than using the cut and paste options.

*Goal:* Remove the **Merge cells** format from the cells that contain the student name, and then move the name to another location using the click-and-drag method.

Use the following guidelines:

1. Select **Sheet4**. Click cell **A1** and enter your first and last name.

2. Select cell **A1** then choose **Format**, **Cells**, and the **Alignment** tab. Deselect <u>M</u>erge cells. Click **OK**.

3. Confirm that cell **A1** is still selected. Move the mouse pointer onto the edge of the cell where it turns into a four-headed pointer.

4. Click-and-drag the selected cell to **G5** and release the mouse button.

5. Save the changes you have made.

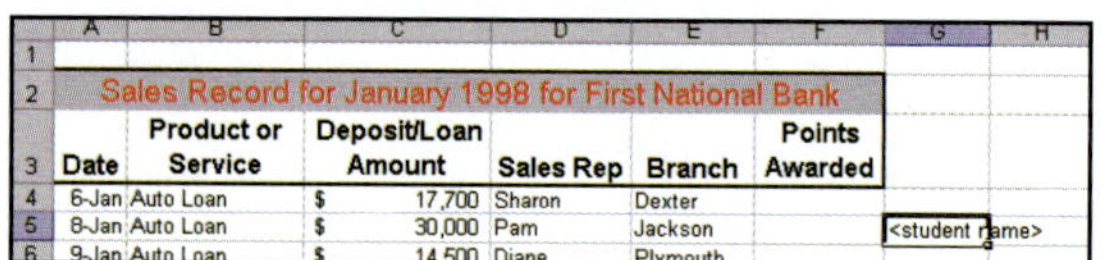

| | | A | B | C | D | E | F | G | H |
|---|---|---|---|---|---|---|---|---|---|
| 1 | | | | | | | | | |
| 2 | | | Sales Record for January 1998 for First National Bank | | | | | | |
| 3 | Date | | Product or Service | Deposit/Loan Amount | | Sales Rep | Branch | Points Awarded | |
| 4 | 6-Jan | Auto Loan | $ | 17,700 | Sharon | Dexter | | | |
| 5 | 8-Jan | Auto Loan | $ | 30,000 | Pam | Jackson | | <student name> | |
| 6 | 9-Jan | Auto Loan | $ | 14,500 | Diane | Plymouth | | | |



## C6—Filtering a List

Many people use Excel as a database to record information about events, purchases, or transactions because they are not familiar with Access. Excel can perform basic sorting and filtering to help people find information.

The filter feature of Excel places a small down arrow at the top of each column of the table. The list box associated with the down arrow displays one of each type of data in the column. When you choose an item from the list, the table is displayed with rows that match the chosen item.

*Goal:* Filter the table of sales to show those made by the Jackson branch.

Use the following guidelines:

1. Select **Sheet4**, if necessary. Click on one of the branch names in column **E**. (You may select any cell of the contiguous data in the table.)

2. Choose **Data**, **Filter**, **AutoFilter**.

3. Click the down arrow at the top of the **Branch** column. Choose **Jackson** from the list.

4. Save the changes you have made. Close the workbook and close Excel.

| | A | B | C | D | E | F | G | H |
|---|---|---|---|---|---|---|---|---|
| 1 | | | | | | | | |
| 2 | Sales Record for January 1998 for First National Bank | | | | | | | |
| 3 | Date | Product or Service | Deposit/Loan Amount | Sales Rep | Branch | Points Awarded | | |
| 5 | 8-Jan | Auto Loan | $ 30,000 | Pam | Jackson | | <student name> | |
| 9 | 23-Jan | Auto Loan | $ 17,750 | Rhonda | Jackson | | | |
| 11 | 30-Jan | Auto Loan | $ 25,000 | Pam | Jackson | | | |
| 12 | 6-Jan | Certificate | $ 30,000 | Pam | Jackson | | | |
| 18 | 22-Jan | Certificate | $ 25,000 | Pam | Jackson | | | |
| 20 | 28-Jan | Certificate | $ 15,000 | Rhonda | Jackson | | | |
| 21 | 30-Jan | Certificate | $ 15,600 | Pam | Jackson | | | |
| 36 | 9-Jan | Mortgage | $ 125,000 | Rhonda | Jackson | | | |
| 38 | 27-Jan | Mortgage | $ 165,000 | Pam | Jackson | | | |
| 43 | 16-Jan | Savings | $ 4,000 | Pam | Jackson | | | |
| 45 | 21-Jan | Savings | $ 2,500 | Pam | Jackson | | | |

Create a worksheet to track expenses for a wedding, a holiday party, or some other event that would involve expenses from various sources. Format the worksheet to take advantage of the skills you have learned. Criteria for grading will be:

**1.** Demonstration of mastery of Excel skills that were taught in this lesson.

Some examples of features that students have learned to use in previous classes to enhance their expense worksheet are:

- Formatting currency to two decimal places

- Adjusting the width of columns or wrapping the text within cells to avoid overlap of adjacent cells by long text entries

- Using font size appropriately to identify column headings and titles

- Using color to emphasize an important aspect of the sheet

- Using borders to separate the sheet into sections

**2.** Identify yourself. Place your name in a cell that is clearly visible.

**3.** To complete the project:

- Save your file on your own disk. Name it **EX0204-Event**.

- Check with your instructor to determine if the project should be submitted in electronic or printed form. If necessary, print out a copy of the worksheet to hand in.

# Lesson 3

## Using Formulas



### INTRODUCTION

Excel is at your command, whether you need to do basic arithmetic or advanced statistics. Once you set up a worksheet, you can change the numbers many times to see how those changes affect the "bottom line."

In this lesson, you work on three worksheets. The first worksheet shows you how to perform basic math calculations using Excel. The next worksheet shows you how to use the Fill function with a formula and how to use absolute and relative cell references. In the third worksheet, you learn how to use the Insert Function dialog box to calculate a monthly payment on a car or house loan. You also calculate the total amount you will pay for the loan.

# VISUAL SUMMARY

By the time you have completed this entire lesson, you will have created three worksheets that look like these:

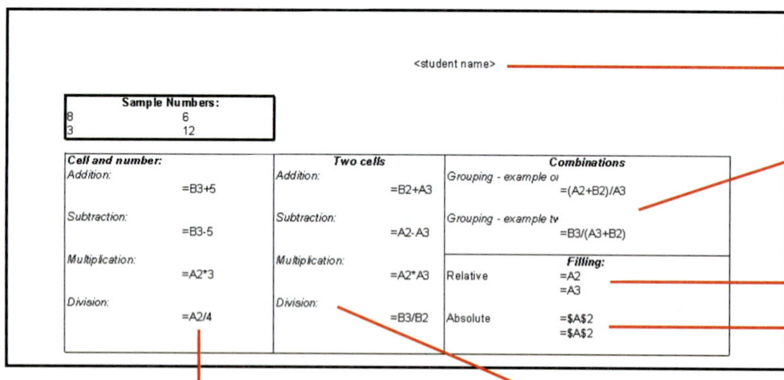


Task 4: Add your name to the custom header

Task 3: Combine formulas with operations

Task 4: Fill formulas with relative references

Task 4: Fill formulas with absolute references

Task 1: Add formulas with one cell reference

Task 2: Add formulas with two cell references

| | D12 | | $f_x$ =D11*$B$2 | | | |
|---|---|---|---|---|---|---|
| | A | B | C | D | E | F |
| 1 | | | *Calculation of Sales Commission* | | | |
| 2 | Commission rate: | 5% | | | | |
| 3 | | | | | | |
| 4 | | Dave | Eric | Sally | Natasha | Siri |
| 5 | Monday | 2,500 | 2,000 | 600 | 800 | 1,900 |
| 6 | Tuesday | 1,500 | 1,800 | 3,000 | 700 | 2,500 |
| 7 | Wednesday | 600 | 1,400 | 2,000 | 550 | 2,000 |
| 8 | Thursday | 1,900 | 1,500 | 1,900 | 3,000 | 900 |
| 9 | Friday | 1,000 | 1,900 | 1,400 | 700 | 800 |
| 10 | Saturday | 1,000 | 500 | 900 | 2,000 | 2,000 |
| 11 | | 8,500 | 9,100 | 9,800 | 7,750 | 10,100 |
| 12 | | $ 425.00 | $ 455.00 | $ 490.00 | $ 387.50 | $ 505.00 |

Task 4: Fill formulas with relative references

Task 4: Fill formulas with a mix of relative and absolute references

| | B6 | | $f_x$ =PMT(B3,B5,B1) | |
|---|---|---|---|---|
| | A | B | C | |
| 1 | Loan Amount (pv): | $ 10,000 | | |
| 2 | Annual Interest | 7.50% | | |
| 3 | Monthly Interest (rate) | 0.625% | | |
| 4 | Years to Pay Back | 3 | | |
| 5 | Number of Payments (nper) | 36 | | |
| 6 | Monthly Payment | ($311.06) | | |
| 7 | Total of All Payments | $ (11,198.24) | | |

Task 5: Use basic formulas

Task 6: Use a financial formula

# Task 1

## ADDING, SUBTRACTING, MULTIPLYING, AND DIVIDING USING CELL REFERENCES AND NUMBERS



### Why would I do this?

Worksheets have been used in paper form for years as a means of keeping track of financial data. The value of using an electronic worksheet program such as Excel is its ability to quickly make mathematical calculations. Before the era of computers, people were employed to calculate rows and columns of numbers for use in navigational charts or other types of computational charts. The job title for the people who performed these calculations was Computer. In today's world, electronic computers keep track of financial data and perform mathematical computations. Computers are faster and more accurate than people for these kinds of tasks.

When you use Excel to perform a mathematical operation, it needs to be done in a way that is similar to ordinary math, but with a few special rules. For example, all formulas must begin with an equal sign (=), and you use cell references or names in the formulas.

In this task, you practice applying the basic formula rules in Excel. The sheet you produce serves as a convenient reference for later use.

**1** Open **EX0301** from the **Student** folder. Save it as **EX0301-Math** on your disk.

In the **Basic Operations** sheet, select cell **B7** and type **=B3+5** in the cell.

*This formula adds the contents of cell B3 and the number 5.*

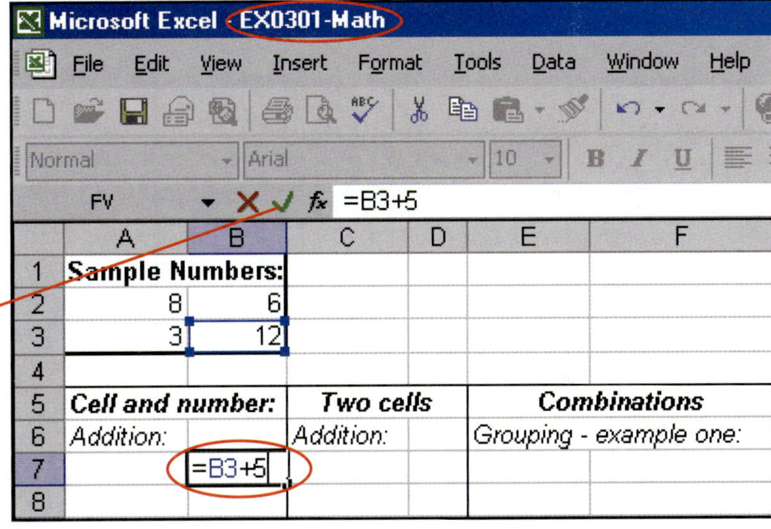



Enter button on the formula bar

**2** Click the **Enter** button on the formula bar.

*Notice that cell B3 contains the number 12, and that cell B7 displays the result of adding 5 to the contents of B3.*

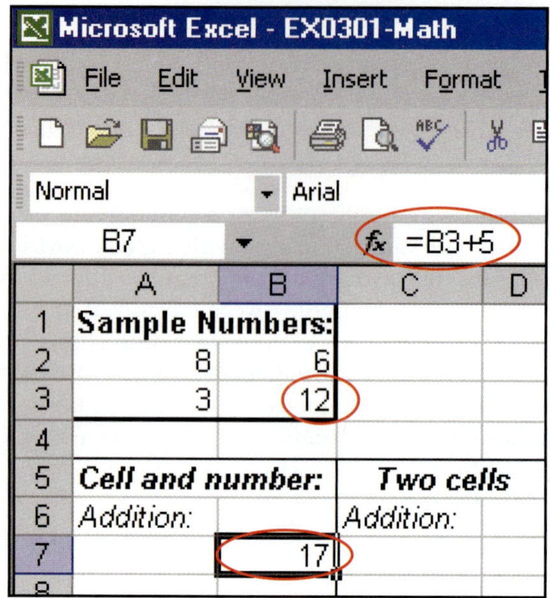


**IN DEPTH**

You can enter a formula by pressing (⏎Enter) or (Tab⇥); however, the selection moves to another cell, and you have to move the selection back if you want to see the formula in the formula bar. If you click the Enter button on the formula bar, the selection does not move to another cell.

**3** Select cell **B10** and type **=B3-5**.

*Determine what you think the answer should be before you proceed. In this case, you subtract 5 from the contents of cell B3.*

Click the **Enter** button on the formula bar.

*If you anticipated a different answer, take the time to figure out why.*

**4** Select cell **B13**, type **=A2*3**, determine what you think the answer should be, and then click the **Enter** button on the formula bar.

*Excel uses the asterisk to indicate multiplication.*

**5** Select cell **B16**, type **=A2/4,** anticipate the answer, and then click the **Enter** button on the formula bar.

*Excel uses the slash to indicate division.*

**CAUTION**

There are two slash keys. The forward slash (/) is used to indicate division in Excel formulas. If you use the backslash (\) by mistake, Excel displays #NAME? to indicate that it does not recognize your entry as a formula, but thinks it is a misspelled cell reference.

| B16 | | ▼ | | $f_x$ =A2/4 | |
|---|---|---|---|---|---|
| | A | B | C | D |
| 1 | Sample Numbers: | | | |
| 2 | 8 | 6 | | |
| 3 | 3 | 12 | | |
| 4 | | | | |
| 5 | Cell and number: | | Two cells | |
| 6 | Addition: | | Addition: | |
| 7 | | 17 | | |
| 8 | | | | |
| 9 | Subtraction: | | Subtraction: | |
| 10 | | 7 | | |
| 11 | | | | |
| 12 | Multiplication: | | Multiplication: | |
| 13 | | 24 | | |
| 14 | | | | |
| 15 | Division: | | Division: | |
| 16 | | 2 | | |
| 17 | | | | |

# Task 2
## USING FORMULAS WITH MORE THAN ONE CELL REFERENCE

### Why would I do this?
When writing a *formula*, an equation used to calculate values in a cell, it is common to refer to numbers entered in more than one cell on your worksheet. For example, if you want to know the profit for your business, you subtract expenses from income. If you want to know the percent increase in sales, you use numbers entered for two different sales periods to make that calculation.

In this task, you learn to use numbers from more than one cell to make calculations.

**1** Select cell **D7**, type **=A2+A3**, estimate the answer, and then click the **Enter** button on the formula bar.

*In this case, the formula adds the numbers in cells A2 and A3.*

**QUICK TIP**

After typing an equal sign to begin the formula, you can point to a cell and click to enter its name in the formula. You can then type the math symbol you want to use before you point and click on the next cell you want in the formula. When this method is used, a marquee outlines the cell that has been selected. This method is preferable if you are writing a formula and the cell you want is off the screen where you cannot see the cell reference.

| D7 | | ▼ | | $f_x$ =A2+A3 | |
|---|---|---|---|---|---|
| | A | B | C | D | |
| 1 | Sample Numbers: | | | | |
| 2 | 8 | 6 | | | |
| 3 | 3 | 12 | | | |
| 4 | | | | | |
| 5 | Cell and number: | | Two cells | | |
| 6 | Addition: | | Addition: | | Gro |
| 7 | | 17 | | 11 | |
| 8 | | | | | |

**2** Select cell **D10**, type **=A2-A3,** estimate the answer, and then click the **Enter** button on the formula bar.

*This formula tells the program to take the number in cell A2 and subtract the number in cell A3.*

**3** Select cell **D13**, type **=A2*A3**, determine what the answer should be if the numbers in these cells were multiplied together, and then click the **Enter** button on the formula bar.

*In this case, you told the program to multiply the number in cell A2 by the number in cell A3.*

**4** Select cell **D16**, type **=B3/B2,** estimate the answer, and then click the **Enter** button on the formula bar.

*In this case, you told the program to take the number in cell B3 and divide by the number in cell B2.*

QUICK TIP

If you make a mistake and want to start over, click the Cancel button next to the Enter button on the formula bar.

**5** Double-click on cell **D7**.

*The formula is displayed in the cell and in the formula bar. The cell references, in the formula and the cells to which they refer, change to matching colors. An insertion mark is placed in the formula.*



**6** Use the Backspace and Del keys to edit the formula the way you would edit ordinary text. Change it to **=B2+A3**.

Click the **Enter** button on the formula bar to finish the change.



# Task 3
## COMBINING OPERATIONS AND FILLING CELLS WITH FORMULAS

### Why would I do this?

You may want to add the contents of several cells together and then divide by the contents of another cell. To do this, use parentheses to group operations together to make sure they are done first.

If the same formula is to be used in several cells, it may be filled into those cells using the *fill handle*. The fill handle is a small box at the lower-right corner of a selected cell that can be used to fill in a series of cells. Sometimes you want cell references to change to adapt to the new position they are in; for example, you may have a formula that totals the cells above it and wish to copy this formula across several cells. In each case, you want the formula to add up the column of cells directly above the formula. This is called a *relative reference*. In other cases, you want the cell reference to always refer to a specific cell. This is called an *absolute reference*.

In this task, you will learn how to group operations in a formula and how to fill cells with formulas using relative and absolute cell references.

**1** Select cell **F7**, and then type **=(A2+B2)/A3**. Estimate what the result should be if you add the contents of cells A2 and B2 and then divide by the number in cell A3 (it is not a whole number). Click the **Enter** button on the formula bar to confirm your estimate.

*Notice that the numbers in cells A2 and B2 (8 and 6) are added first and then divided by the number in cell A3 (3).*

| F7 | | | fx =(A2+B2)/A3 | | |
|---|---|---|---|---|---|
| **A** | **B** | **C** | **D** | **E** | **F** |
| **Sample Numbers:** | | | | | |
| 8 | 6 | | | | |
| 3 | 12 | | | | |
| | | | | | |
| **Cell and number:** | | **Two cells** | | **Combinations** | |
| *Addition:* | | *Addition:* | | *Grouping - example one:* | |
| | 17 | | 9 | | 4.666666667 |
| | | | | | |

**2** Select cell **F10**, and then type **=B3/(A3+B2)**. Estimate what the answer will be if the number in cell B3 is divided by the sum of the numbers in cells A3 and B2. Click the **Enter** button on the formula bar to confirm your estimate.

| F10 | | | fx =B3/(A3+B2) | | |
|---|---|---|---|---|---|
| **A** | **B** | **C** | **D** | **E** | **F** |
| **Sample Numbers:** | | | | | |
| 8 | 6 | | | | |
| 3 | 12 | | | | |
| | | | | | |
| **Cell and number:** | | **Two cells** | | **Combinations** | |
| *Addition:* | | *Addition:* | | *Grouping - example one:* | |
| | 17 | | 9 | | 4.666666667 |
| | | | | | |
| *Subtraction:* | | *Subtraction:* | | *Grouping - example two:* | |
| | 7 | | 5 | | 1.333333333 |
| | | | | | |

**3** Select cell **F13**.

*Look at the formula in the formula bar. It shows that the formula simply equals the value of cell A2.*

| F13 | | | fx =A2 | | |
|---|---|---|---|---|---|
| **A** | **B** | **C** | **D** | **E** | **F** |
| **Sample Numbers:** | | | | | |
| 8 | 6 | | | | |
| 3 | 12 | | | | |
| | | | | | |
| **Cell and number:** | | **Two cells** | | **Combinations** | |
| *Addition:* | | *Addition:* | | *Grouping - example one:* | |
| | 17 | | 9 | | 4.666666667 |
| | | | | | |
| *Subtraction:* | | *Subtraction:* | | *Grouping - example two:* | |
| | 7 | | 5 | | 1.333333333 |
| | | | | | |
| *Multiplication:* | | *Multiplication:* | | **Filling:** | |
| | 24 | | 24 | Relative | 8 |
| | | | | | |

**4** Click-and-drag the fill handle down to cell **F14**. Release the mouse button.

*Notice that cell F14 displays the number 3, which is the value in cell A3.*



The Auto Fill Options button that appears next to the fill handle may be used to choose options for how to fill a selection. For example, you could choose to fill the formatting rather than the numbers or text.

| F13 | | fx =A2 | | | |
|---|---|---|---|---|---|
| **A** | **B** | **C** | **D** | **E** | **F** |
| 1 | **Sample Numbers:** | | | | |
| 2 | 8 | 6 | | | |
| 3 | 3 | 12 | | | |
| 4 | | | | | |
| 5 | *Cell and number:* | | *Two cells* | | *Combinations* |
| 6 | *Addition:* | | *Addition:* | | *Grouping - example one:* |
| 7 | | 17 | | 9 | | 4.666666667 |
| 8 | | | | | |
| 9 | *Subtraction:* | | *Subtraction:* | | *Grouping - example two:* |
| 10 | | 7 | | 5 | | 1.333333333 |
| 11 | | | | | |
| 12 | *Multiplication:* | | *Multiplication:* | | ***Filling:*** |
| 13 | | 24 | | 24 | Relative | 8 |
| 14 | | | | | | 3 |
| 15 | *Division:* | | *Division:* | | |
| 16 | | 2 | | 2 | Absolute | 8 |

Fill handle    Auto Fill Options

**5** Select cell **F14**.

*Notice that the formula equals the value in cell A3. The formulas in cells F13 and F14 both refer to a cell that is eleven rows up and five columns to the left.*

| F14 | | fx =A3 | | | |
|---|---|---|---|---|---|
| **A** | **B** | **C** | **D** | **E** | **F** |
| 1 | **Sample Numbers:** | | | | |
| 2 | 8 | 6 | | | |
| 3 | 3 | 12 | | | |
| 4 | | | | | |
| 5 | *Cell and number:* | | *Two cells* | | *Combinations* |
| 6 | *Addition:* | | *Addition:* | | *Grouping - example one:* |
| 7 | | 17 | | 9 | | 4.666666667 |
| 8 | | | | | |
| 9 | *Subtraction:* | | *Subtraction:* | | *Grouping - example two:* |
| 10 | | 7 | | 5 | | 1.333333333 |
| 11 | | | | | |
| 12 | *Multiplication:* | | *Multiplication:* | | ***Filling:*** |
| 13 | | 24 | | 24 | Relative | 8 |
| 14 | | | | | | 3 |
| 15 | *Division:* | | *Division:* | | |
| 16 | | 2 | | 2 | Absolute | 8 |



When you fill a formula from one cell to another, Excel uses a relative cell reference. In this example, Excel used A3 to fill cell F14. Cell F14 is one position below F13, and cell A3 is one position below A2. Excel uses the relative position of the cell that is being referenced to determine the location of the next value to place in the new cell. This is the default method that Excel uses to fill a formula from one cell to another.

**6** Select cell **F16**. Look at the formula in the formula bar.

*In this case, a $ has been placed to the left of the column and row identifiers to indicate that the cell reference will not change when it is copied.*

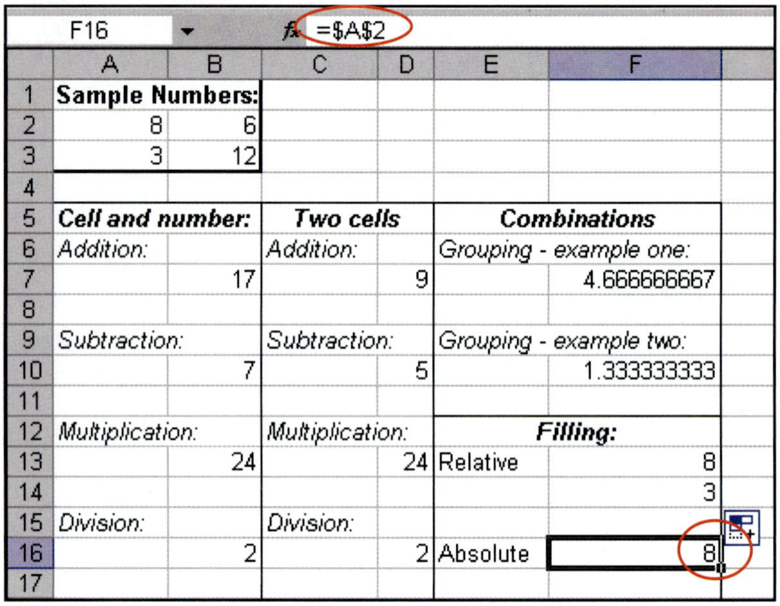

**7** Use the fill handle to fill this formula into cell **F17**.

*Notice that F17 also displays the contents of cell A2.*

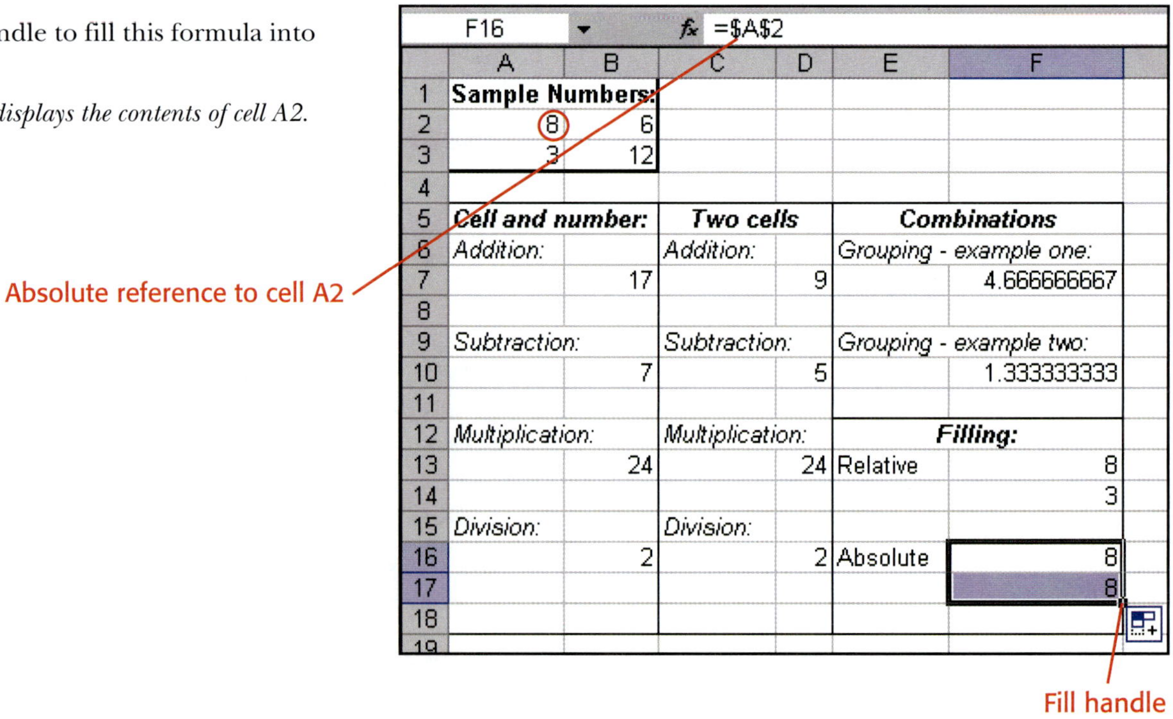

Absolute reference to cell A2

Fill handle

**8** Select cell **F17**. Look at the formula in the formula bar.

*Notice that it did not change when the formula was filled into the cell. This type of cell reference (with the $ sign) is called an absolute reference. Use an absolute reference when you want to ensure that the formula always refers to a specific cell.*

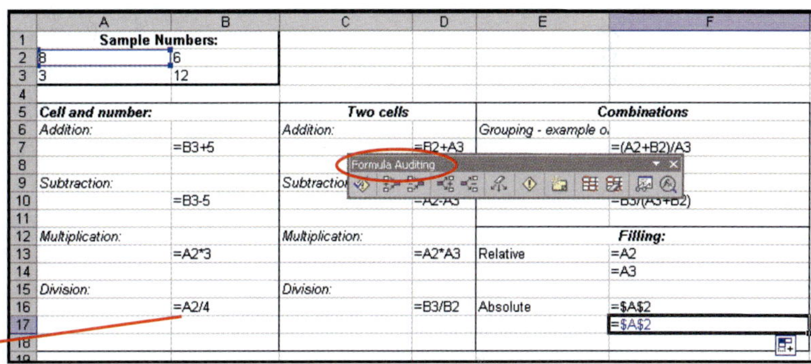

**9** Press `Ctrl`+` ` ` (the accent grave mark found on the key to the left of the 1 key).

*The formulas for each cell and the Formula Auditing toolbar are displayed.*

Cells display formulas

**10** Choose **File**, **Page Setup**, **Header/Footer** tab, **Custom Header**. Add your name to the custom header **Center section**. Click **OK**.

Click **Print** to print the worksheet. Check the printer destination, and then click **OK**.

*The printed worksheet displays a record of the formulas in your worksheet.*

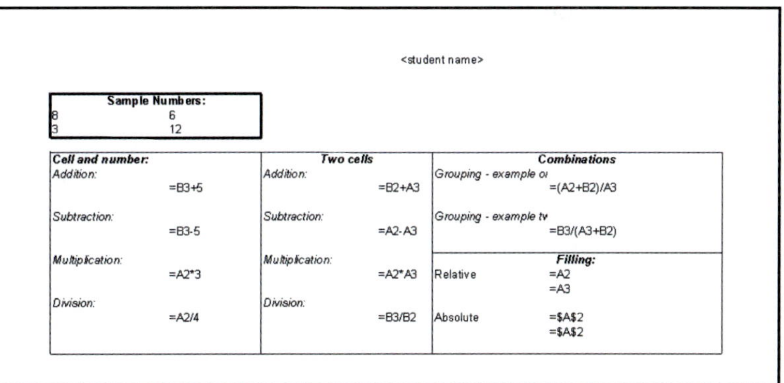

**11** Press ⌃Ctrl⌄+⌃`⌄ to return the worksheet to the Normal view, showing the formula results.

Click the **Save** button to save your workbook.

# Task 4



## FILLING CELLS WITH RELATIVE AND ABSOLUTE FORMULAS

### Why would I do this?

The ability to fill formulas into adjacent cells greatly increases the speed at which a worksheet can be created. Formulas or text can be filled into adjacent cells. The formulas are automatically revised to reflect the new locations.

In this task, you learn how to fill cells using formulas that include both relative and absolute references.

**1** Click the **Commission** tab to switch to the **Commission** sheet and select cell **B11**, if necessary.

*Notice that it contains a formula that adds the contents of cells B5 through B10, which are directly above B11.*

**IN DEPTH**

Two cell references separated by a colon, such as B5:B10, indicate a rectangular-shaped group of cells where the two cells are at opposite corners of the block of cells.

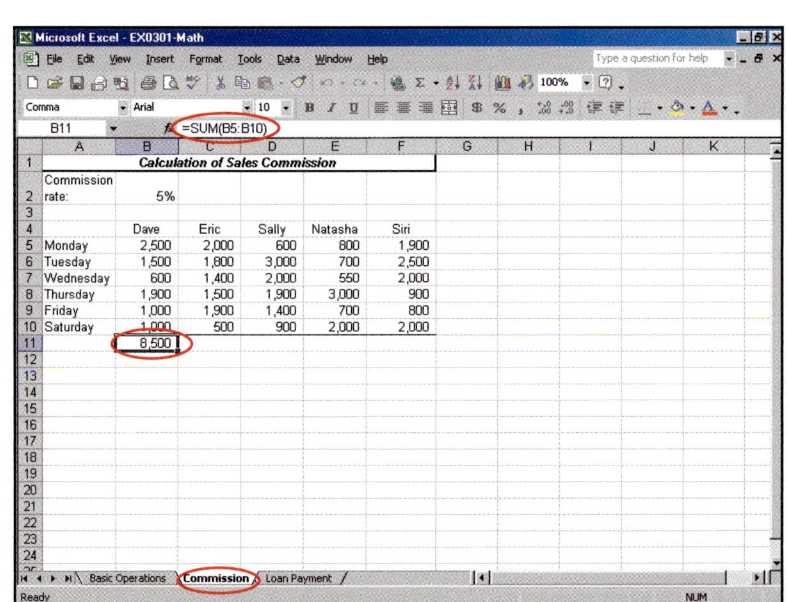

**2** Drag the fill handle to the right to cell **F11** and release the mouse button.

*The formula is filled into cells C11 through F11.*

| B11 | | *fx* =SUM(B5:B10) | | | |
|---|---|---|---|---|---|
| | A | B | C | D | E | F |

| | A | B | C | D | E | F |
|---|---|---|---|---|---|---|
| 1 | | *Calculation of Sales Commission* | | | | |
| 2 | Commission rate: | 5% | | | | |
| 3 | | | | | | |
| 4 | | Dave | Eric | Sally | Natasha | Siri |
| 5 | Monday | 2,500 | 2,000 | 600 | 800 | 1,900 |
| 6 | Tuesday | 1,500 | 1,800 | 3,000 | 700 | 2,500 |
| 7 | Wednesday | 600 | 1,400 | 2,000 | 550 | 2,000 |
| 8 | Thursday | 1,900 | 1,500 | 1,900 | 3,000 | 900 |
| 9 | Friday | 1,000 | 1,900 | 1,400 | 700 | 800 |
| 10 | Saturday | 1,000 | 500 | 900 | 2,000 | 2,000 |
| 11 | | 8,500 | 9,100 | 9,800 | 7,750 | 10,100 |
| 12 | | | | | | |

Fill handle

**3** Click on cell **D11**.

*You see that the formula changed to add the six cells in the column directly above cell D11. This shows how the use of the fill handle results in a relative reference.*

| D11 | | *fx* =SUM(D5:D10) | | | |
|---|---|---|---|---|---|

| | A | B | C | D | E | F |
|---|---|---|---|---|---|---|
| 1 | | *Calculation of Sales Commission* | | | | |
| 2 | Commission rate: | 5% | | | | |
| 3 | | | | | | |
| 4 | | Dave | Eric | Sally | Natasha | Siri |
| 5 | Monday | 2,500 | 2,000 | 600 | 800 | 1,900 |
| 6 | Tuesday | 1,500 | 1,800 | 3,000 | 700 | 2,500 |
| 7 | Wednesday | 600 | 1,400 | 2,000 | 550 | 2,000 |
| 8 | Thursday | 1,900 | 1,500 | 1,900 | 3,000 | 900 |
| 9 | Friday | 1,000 | 1,900 | 1,400 | 700 | 800 |
| 10 | Saturday | 1,000 | 500 | 900 | 2,000 | 2,000 |
| 11 | | 8,500 | 9,100 | 9,800 | 7,750 | 10,100 |

**4** Select cell **B12** and type **=B11*$B$2**, then click the **Enter** button on the formula bar.

*This formula multiplies the sum of Dave's sales in cell B11 by the commission rate in cell B2. The reference to B11 is relative, and the reference to B2 is absolute.*

Absolute reference to cell B2

| B12 | | *fx* =B11*$B$2 | | | |
|---|---|---|---|---|---|

| | A | B | C | D | E | F |
|---|---|---|---|---|---|---|
| 1 | | *Calculation of Sales Commission* | | | | |
| 2 | Commission rate: | 5% | | | | |
| 3 | | | | | | |
| 4 | | Dave | Eric | Sally | Natasha | Siri |
| 5 | Monday | 2,500 | 2,000 | 600 | 800 | 1,900 |
| 6 | Tuesday | 1,500 | 1,800 | 3,000 | 700 | 2,500 |
| 7 | Wednesday | 600 | 1,400 | 2,000 | 550 | 2,000 |
| 8 | Thursday | 1,900 | 1,500 | 1,900 | 3,000 | 900 |
| 9 | Friday | 1,000 | 1,900 | 1,400 | 700 | 800 |
| 10 | Saturday | 1,000 | 500 | 900 | 2,000 | 2,000 |
| 11 | | 8,500 | 9,100 | 9,800 | 7,750 | 10,100 |
| 12 | | $ 425.00 | | | | |
| 13 | | | | | | |

**5** Drag the fill handle to the right to cell **F12** and release the mouse button.

*The formula is filled into cells C12 through F12.*

| B12 | | $f_x$ =B11*$B$2 | | | |
|---|---|---|---|---|---|
| | A | B | C | D | E | F |

| | A | B | C | D | E | F |
|---|---|---|---|---|---|---|
| 1 | | *Calculation of Sales Commission* | | | | |
| 2 | Commission rate: | 5% | | | | |
| 3 | | | | | | |
| 4 | | Dave | Eric | Sally | Natasha | Siri |
| 5 | Monday | 2,500 | 2,000 | 600 | 800 | 1,900 |
| 6 | Tuesday | 1,500 | 1,800 | 3,000 | 700 | 2,500 |
| 7 | Wednesday | 600 | 1,400 | 2,000 | 550 | 2,000 |
| 8 | Thursday | 1,900 | 1,500 | 1,900 | 3,000 | 900 |
| 9 | Friday | 1,000 | 1,900 | 1,400 | 700 | 800 |
| 10 | Saturday | 1,000 | 500 | 900 | 2,000 | 2,000 |
| 11 | | 8,500 | 9,100 | 9,800 | 7,750 | 10,100 |
| 12 | | $ 425.00 | $ 455.00 | $ 490.00 | $ 387.50 | $ 505.00 |
| 13 | | | | | | |
| 14 | | | | | | |

**6** Click on cell **D12** and look at the formula bar.

*The relative reference changed so that it refers to the sum of Sally's sales in cell D11, but the absolute reference to the commission rate in cell B2 did not change.*

Relative cell reference changed

Absolute cell reference did not change

| D12 | | $f_x$ =D11*$B$2 | | | |
|---|---|---|---|---|---|
| | A | B | C | D | E | F |

| | A | B | C | D | E | F |
|---|---|---|---|---|---|---|
| 1 | | *Calculation of Sales Commission* | | | | |
| 2 | Commission rate: | 5% | | | | |
| 3 | | | | | | |
| 4 | | Dave | Eric | Sally | Natasha | Siri |
| 5 | Monday | 2,500 | 2,000 | 600 | 800 | 1,900 |
| 6 | Tuesday | 1,500 | 1,800 | 3,000 | 700 | 2,500 |
| 7 | Wednesday | 600 | 1,400 | 2,000 | 550 | 2,000 |
| 8 | Thursday | 1,900 | 1,500 | 1,900 | 3,000 | 900 |
| 9 | Friday | 1,000 | 1,900 | 1,400 | 700 | 800 |
| 10 | Saturday | 1,000 | 500 | 900 | 2,000 | 2,000 |
| 11 | | 8,500 | 9,100 | 9,800 | 7,750 | 10,100 |
| 12 | | $ 425.00 | $ 455.00 | $ 490.00 | $ 387.50 | $ 505.00 |

**7** Choose **File**, **Page Setup**, **Header/Footer** tab, **Custom Header**. Add your name to the custom header **Left section**. Click **OK**.

*Click Print to print the worksheet. Check the printer destination, and then click OK.*

Save the workbook and leave it open for use in the next task.

<student name>

| | | *Calculation of Sales Commission* | | | | |
|---|---|---|---|---|---|---|
| Commission rate: | | 5% | | | | |
| | Dave | Eric | Sally | Natasha | Siri |
| Monday | 2,500 | 2,000 | 600 | 800 | 1,900 |
| Tuesday | 1,500 | 1,800 | 3,000 | 700 | 2,500 |
| Wednesday | 600 | 1,400 | 2,000 | 550 | 2,000 |
| Thursday | 1,900 | 1,500 | 1,900 | 3,000 | 900 |
| Friday | 1,000 | 1,900 | 1,400 | 700 | 800 |
| Saturday | 1,000 | 500 | 900 | 2,000 | 2,000 |
| | 8,500 | 9,100 | 9,800 | 7,750 | 10,100 |
| | $ 425.00 | $ 455.00 | $ 490.00 | $ 387.50 | $ 505.00 |

# Task 5

## APPLYING BASIC FORMULAS TO A LOAN REPAYMENT

### *Why would I do this?*

When you borrow money for a car or a house, the loan repayment is based on several factors, such as interest rate, time to repay, and the loan amount. With Excel, you can set up a worksheet to calculate your monthly payments based on these factors, then change the value of the factors to match whatever loan terms you are quoted by a bank or other lender.

In this task, you learn how to set up a worksheet to calculate total monthly payments.

**1** Click on the **Loan Payment** tab to switch to the **Loan Payment** sheet.

*Notice that column A is used for labels and column B is used for formulas.*

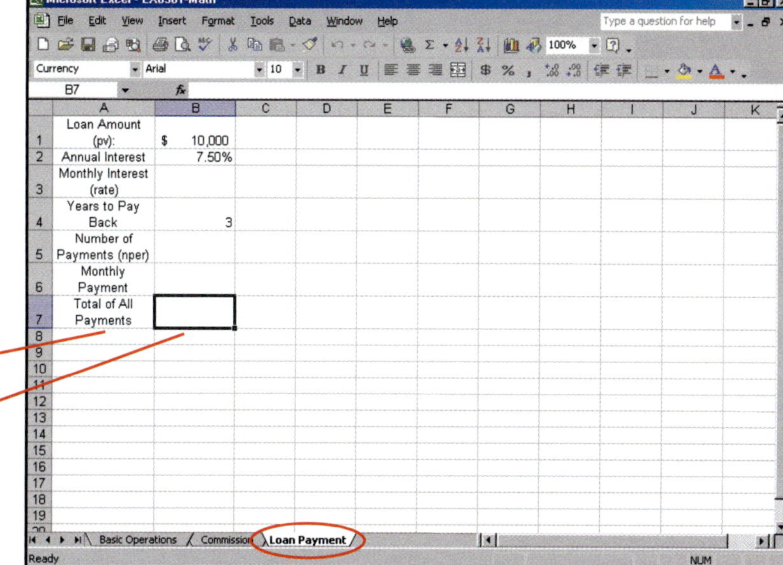


**2** Select cell **B3**, type **=B2/12**, and click the **Enter** button on the formula bar.

*This formula takes the annual interest rate in cell B2 and divides by 12 to calculate the monthly interest rate.*

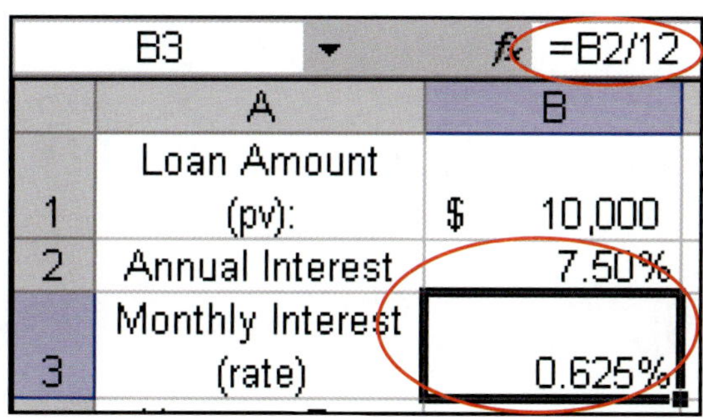


**IN DEPTH**

To calculate the monthly payment, the formula requires the number of months and the interest rate per month. Most loan interest rates are given as an Annual Percentage Rate, or **APR**. If the payment is made every month, the formula needs to use one-twelfth of the annual interest rate to calculate the interest cost per month.

**3** Select cell **B5**, type **=B4*12**, and then click the **Enter** button on the formula bar.

*This formula calculates the number of months over which the loan is repaid.*



| | A | B |
|---|---|---|
| 1 | Loan Amount (pv): | $ 10,000 |
| 2 | Annual Interest | 7.50% |
| 3 | Monthly Interest (rate) | 0.625% |
| 4 | Years to Pay Back | 3 |
| 5 | Number of Payments (nper) | 36 |
| | Monthly | |

**4** Select cell **B7**, type **=B5*B6**, and then click the **Enter** button on the formula bar.

*This formula multiplies the number of payments in cell B5 times the amount of the payment in B6. In this case, no number is displayed in the cell because cell B6 is still empty, and cell B7 has been formatted to show a dollar sign and a dash when the value is zero.*

Leave the workbook open for the next task.



| | A | B |
|---|---|---|
| 1 | Loan Amount (pv): | $ 10,000 |
| 2 | Annual Interest | 7.50% |
| 3 | Monthly Interest (rate) | 0.625% |
| 4 | Years to Pay Back | 3 |
| 5 | Number of Payments (nper) | 36 |
| 6 | Monthly Payment | |
| 7 | Total of All Payments | $ - |

# Task 6

## USING BUILT-IN FINANCIAL FORMULAS

### Why would I do this?

When you take out a loan, you usually rely on someone else to tell you how much the payment will be. In order to shop around for the best rate or terms, it is helpful to see the effect of different loan terms that may be quoted to you. In the previous task, the factors used to calculate a loan were outlined.

In this task, you learn how to use one of Excel's built-in financial formulas to calculate the monthly payment.

**1** Select cell **B6**. Choose **Insert**, **Function** from the menu.

*The Insert Function dialog box opens.*

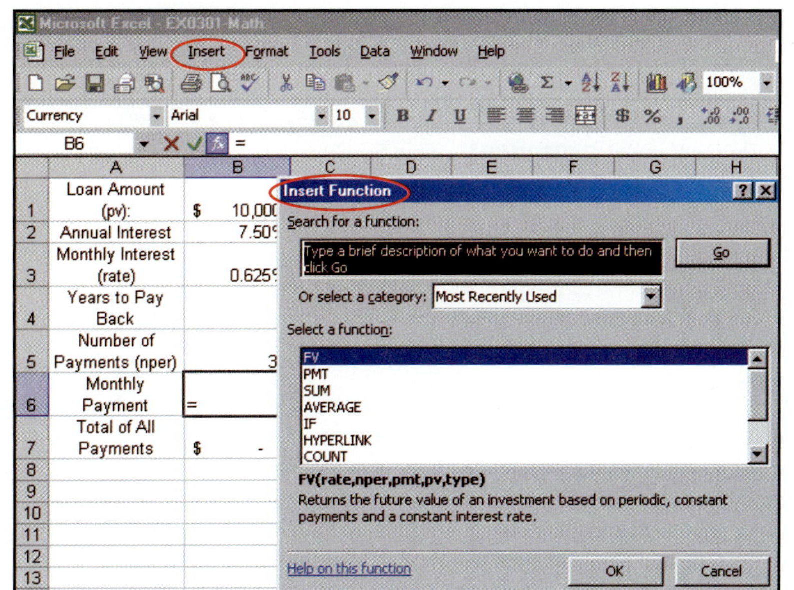

The default category, Most Recently Used, displays a list of recently used functions in the box below. This list is different for each computer because it is based on recent use.

**2** Click the down arrow to the right of the Or select a <u>c</u>ategory box.

*Categories of formulas are displayed.*

    Click **Financial**.

*A list of built-in financial formulas appears in the **Select a functio<u>n</u>** box.*

**3** Scroll down and click on the **PMT** function.

*The name of the function, the values it requires, and a brief description of the function's use are displayed. The values are called* **arguments**. *This function is used to calculate loan payments.*

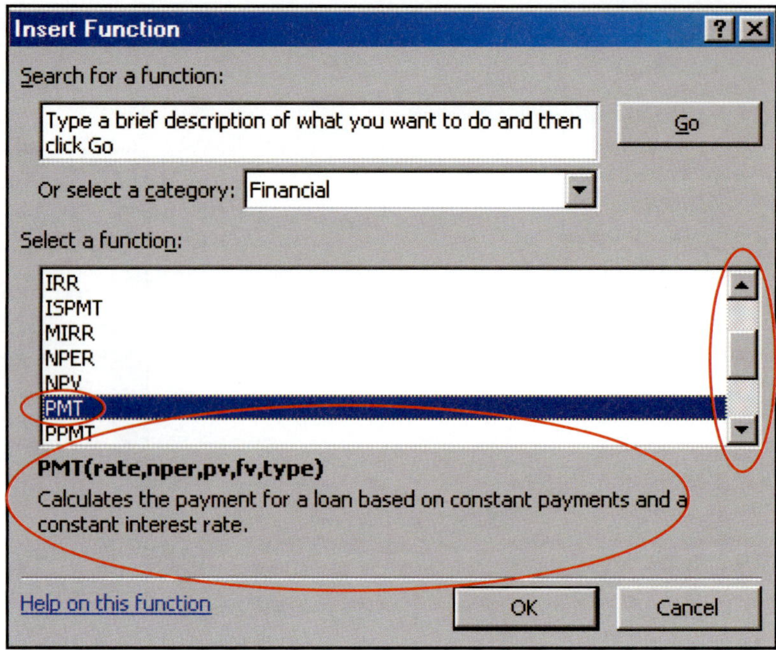

**4** Click **OK**.

*A wizard dialog box opens. You use the wizard to identify the cells that contain values, or arguments, that the PMT function requires. The first three arguments are required, and their names are in boldface type. The last two are optional, and their names are in normal type.*

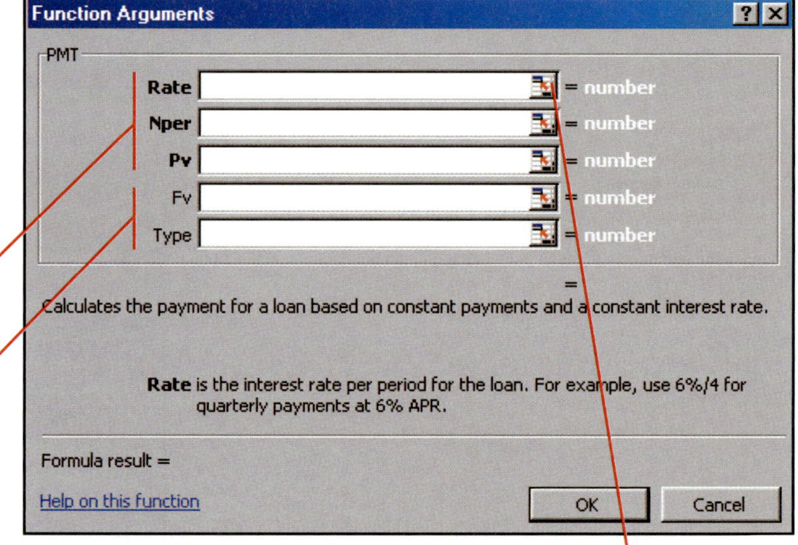


IN DEPTH

Wizards usually consist of a series of questions that guide you through the creation of a formula or a chart. Wizards are used in Excel to help with a number of different processes. These include a Help Wizard known as the Office Assistant, a Chart Wizard used for creating charts, and the wizards in Insert Function that help create complex formulas such as a payment formula. When you are working on a formula, you can click the equal sign on the formula bar to open the Formula Palette, which displays current information about the formula you are using.

**5** Click the **Collapse Dialog Box** button at the right end of the **Rate** box.

*The dialog box collapses to a single input box to make it easier to view the worksheet.*

**QUICK TIP**

You can move back and forth between the worksheet and the dialog box. It is not necessary to collapse the dialog box if you can see the numbers you want to use.

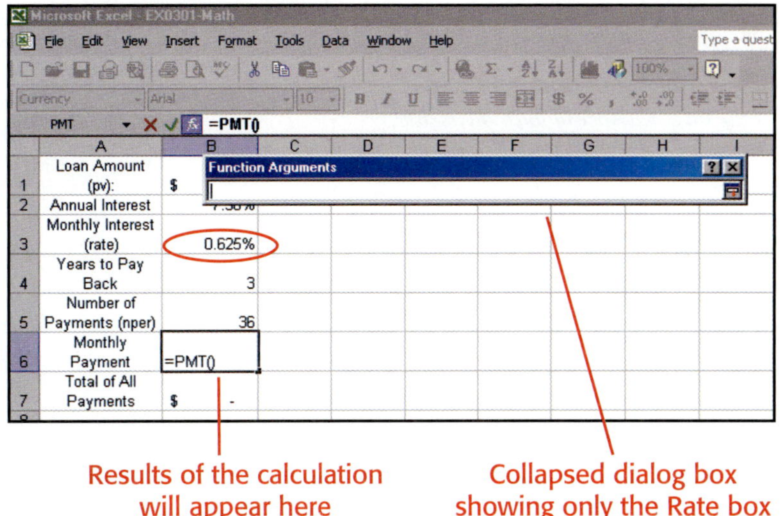

Results of the calculation will appear here

Collapsed dialog box showing only the Rate box

**IN DEPTH**

If the collapsed dialog box obscures the range of cells that you want to select, drag it to another location.

**6** Click cell **B3**.

*This cell reference is entered into the formula as the first argument.*

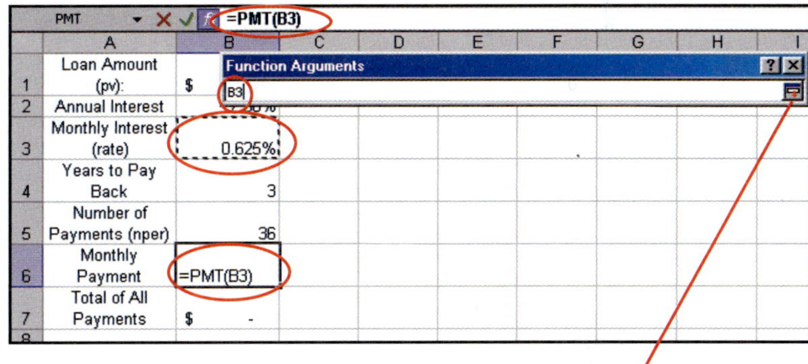

Expand Dialog Box button

**7** Click the **Expand Dialog Box** button.

*This action restores the dialog box. The cell reference is displayed in the Rate box.*

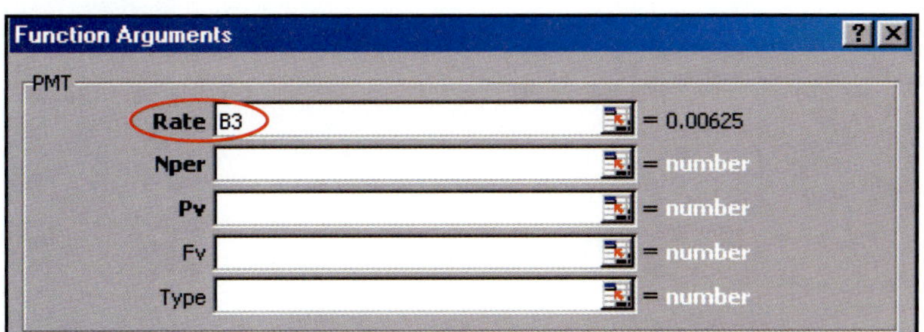

**8** Press `Tab` to move to the **Nper** box.

*The message at the bottom of the box explains that this is the total number of loan payments.*

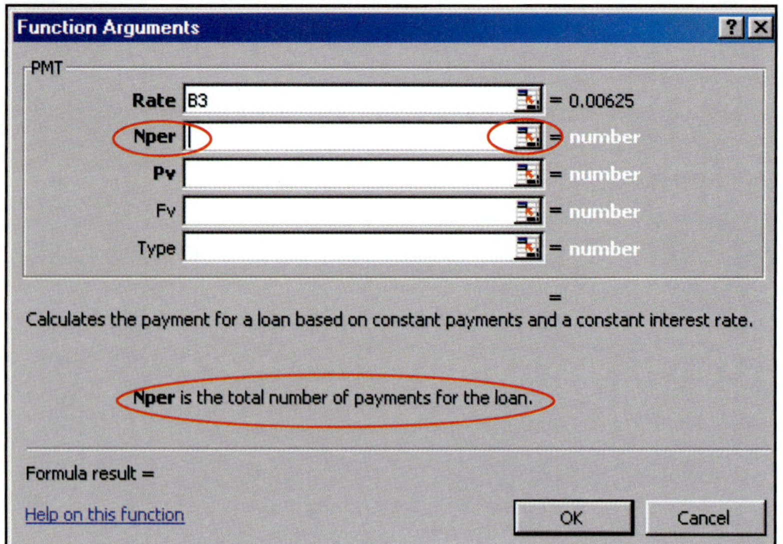

**9** Click the **Collapse Dialog Box** button at the right side of the **Nper** box, click on cell **B5**, and then click the **Expand Dialog Box** button.

*The reference to cell B5 is added as the second argument to the formula.*

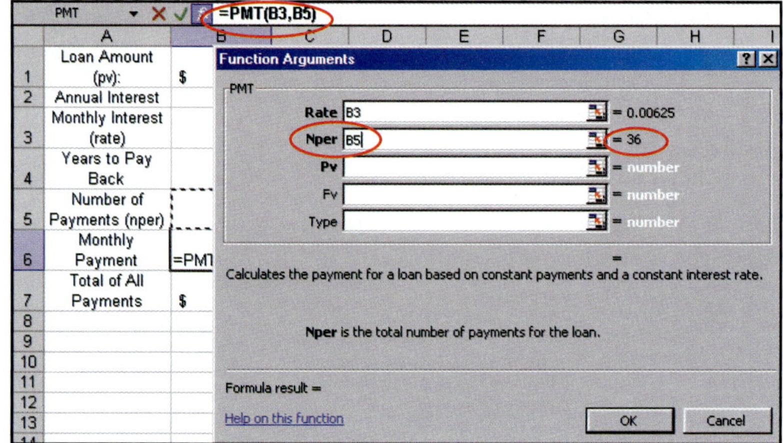

**10** Press `Tab` to move to the **Pv** box.

*This argument is used to identify the present value of the loan or the amount you want to borrow.*

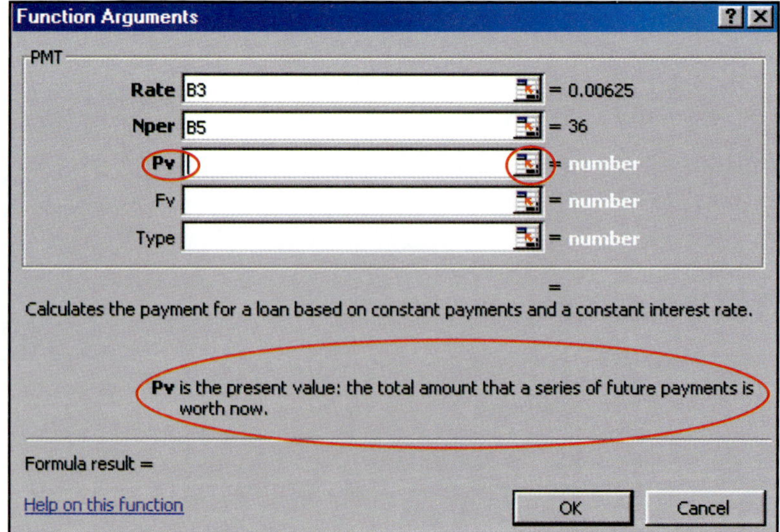

**11** Click the **Collapse Dialog Box** button, click on cell **B1**, and click the **Expand Dialog Box** button.

*The reference to cell B1 is added as the third argument to the formula. The formula now has enough information to calculate the payment. The result is displayed at the bottom of the dialog box.*

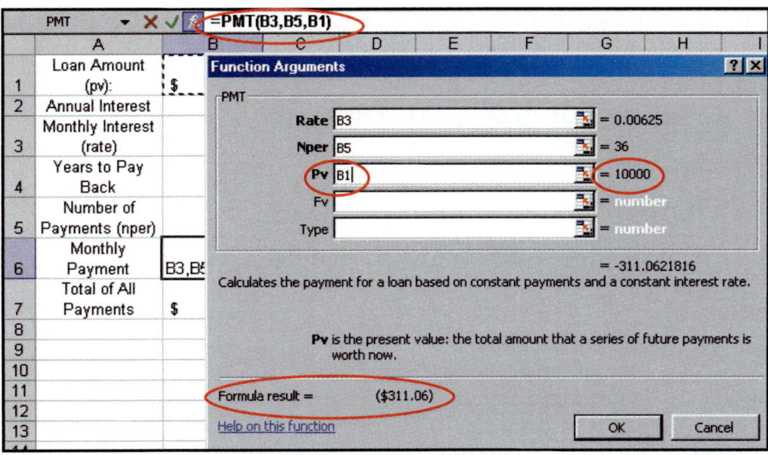

**12** Click **OK**.

*The calculated payment is displayed. The currency format that has been chosen for this cell displays negative numbers in red, enclosed by parentheses. (If the loan amount is entered as a positive number, the payment is negative.) Notice that cell B7 now shows the total amount of all payments.*

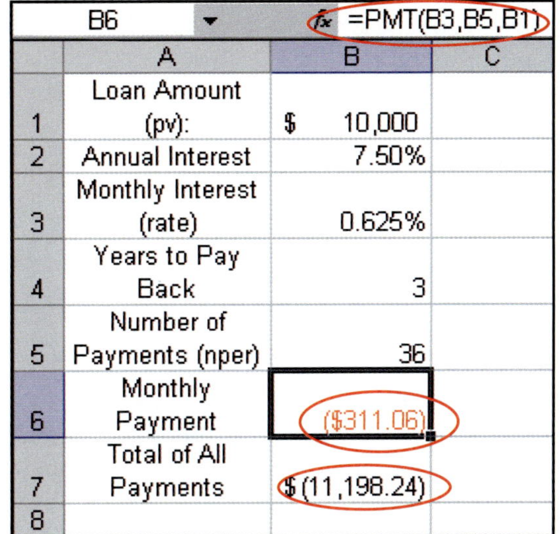

**13** Click the **Save** button on the toolbar, and then close the workbook.

The exercises that follow are designed for you to review and use what you have learned in this lesson. You also have the opportunity to practice your skills and then expand on them by applying them to new situations.

## COMPREHENSION

Comprehension exercises are designed to check your memory and understanding of the basic concepts in this lesson. You distinguish between true and false statements, identify new screen elements, and match terms with related statements. If you are uncertain of the correct answer, refer to the task number following each item (for example, T4 refers to Task 4), and review that task until you are confident you can provide a correct response.

### TRUE-FALSE

Circle either T or F.

T  F  **1.** You can only use one cell reference in a formula.  **(T2)**

T  F  **2.** When you use the fill handle to copy a formula that sums a column, Excel assumes an absolute reference to the numbers in the original column.  **(T3)**

T  F  **3.** To designate a cell reference as absolute, place a $ to the left of both the column and row identifiers.  **(T4)**

T  F  **4.** The loan payment formula uses an annual interest rate and the number of years of the loan to calculate the monthly payment amount.  **(T5)**

T  F  **5.** A relative reference is a cell reference that will change when the formula is copied, moved, or filled.  **(T4)**

T  F  **6.** A quick way to format a cell to display currency is to use dollar signs in the name of the cell.  **(T3)**

### MATCHING QUESTIONS

**A.** Arguments          **D.** $B$3

**B.** ✓                 **E.** /

**C.** Accent grave       **F.** =

Match the following statements to the word or phrase that is the best match from the list. Write the letter of the matching word or phrase in the space provided next to the number.

**1.** ____ Symbol used to represent division  **(T1)**

**2.** ____ Term used for numbers or words that are used by a function to perform a calculation or operation  **(T6)**

**3.** ____ **Enter** button on the formula bar  **(T1)**

**4.** ____ Used to begin every formula  **(T1)**

**5.** ____ Name of the character that is used with the Ctrl key to reveal the formulas in the cells (it resembles an apostrophe)  **(T3)**

**6.** ____ An example of an absolute cell reference  **(T4)**

# IDENTIFYING PARTS OF THE EXCEL SCREEN

Refer to the figure and identify the numbered parts of the screen. Write the letter of the correct label in the space next to the number.

1. _______________

2. _______________

3. _______________

4. _______________

5. _______________

6. _______________

7. _______________

8. _______________

9. _______________

10. _______________

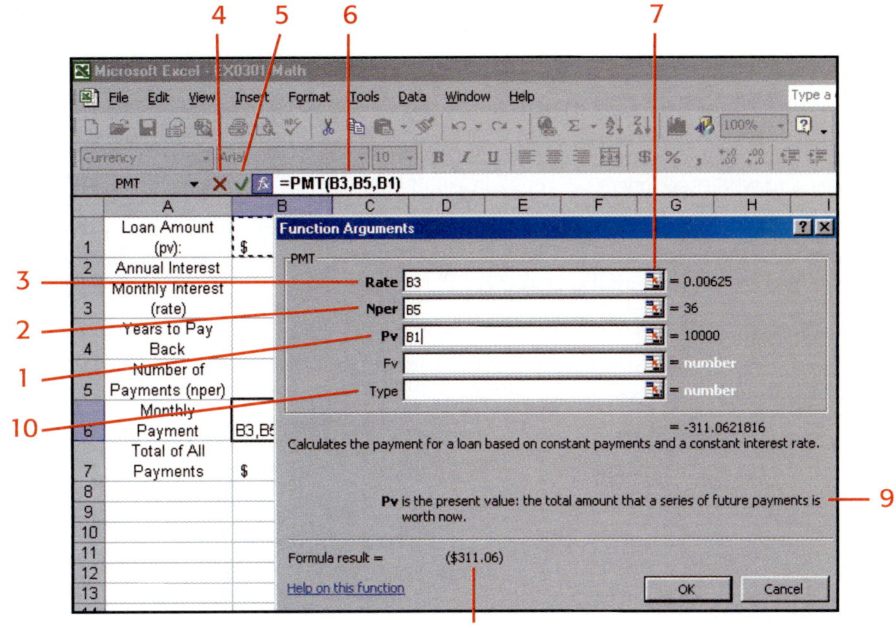

A. Optional argument  **(T6)**

B. **Enter** button  **(T1)**

C. Projected payment amount  **(T6)**

D. Interest rate per loan period  **(T6)**

E. Amount of money that is borrowed  **(T6)**

F. Number of payments in a loan  **(T6)**

G. **Collapse Dialog Box** button  **(T6)**

H. Formula with arguments  **(T6)**

I. Description of the selected argument  **(T6)**

J. **Cancel** button  **(T2)**

Reinforcement exercises are designed to reinforce the skills you have learned by applying them to new situations. Detailed instructions are provided along with a figure, where appropriate, to illustrate the result. The reinforcement exercises that follow should be completed sequentially. Leave the file open at the end of each exercise for use in the next exercise until you are specifically directed to close it.

Open **EX0302** and save it as **EX0302-Reinforcement** on your floppy disk for use in the following exercises.

## R1—Using Basic Excel Formulas

Worksheets are very useful when calculating retail prices for items purchased at wholesale prices.

Modify the **Patio Furniture** worksheet to match the figure. See the steps below for more detail. (The sheet zoom is set at 80 percent to provide a full view of the worksheet.)

1. Click the **Patio Furniture** sheet tab, if necessary. Select cell **D3** and enter **=B3*C3** to calculate the total cost of each item.

2. Use the fill handle to copy the formula in **D3** to cells **D4** through **D9**. Format the values in cells **D3** through **D9** to be currency with no decimals. Reduce the column width as shown in the figure.

3. Select cell **F3** and enter **=B3*E3** to calculate the retail values.

4. Use the fill handle to copy the formula in **F3** to cells **F4** through **F9**. Format the values in cells **F3** through **F9** as currency with no decimals. Reduce the column width as shown in the figure.

5. Use the **AutoSum** button to place a SUM function in cells **D10** and **F10** to add the numbers in the column above.

6. To calculate the percent markup, select cell **G3** and enter **=(E3-C3)/C3**. Fill the formula to cells **G4** through **G9**. Format the values in this column as percentages with no decimals (use the **Percent Style** button on the Formatting toolbar).

7. To calculate the percent contribution, select cell **H3** and enter **=F3/$F$10**. Fill the formula to the other cells in the column. Format the values in this column as percentages with two decimals.

8. Place a top and double bottom border on cells **D10**, **F10**, and **H10**. Sum the column in cell **H10**.

9. Choose **File**, **Page Setup**, **Header/Footer** tab, **Custom Header**. Add your name to the custom header **Left section**. Click **OK**.

10. Click the **Page** tab and choose **Landscape** orientation. Click **Print Preview** and print the sheet if your instructor requires it.

11. Close Print Preview and use `Ctrl`+`` ` `` to display the formulas. Narrow the columns and wrap the column headings so the worksheet will print on one page (see figure). Print the sheet showing the formulas.

12. Change the worksheet back to show the values rather than the formulas and save the workbook. Leave the workbook open for use in the next exercise.

|  | A | B | C | D | E | F | G | H |
|---|---|---|---|---|---|---|---|---|
| 1 | Patio Furniture Division | | | | | | | |
| 2 | Inventory | Quantity | Average Cost | Total Cost | Retail Price | Retail Value | Percent Mark Up | Percent Contribution |
| 3 | Table Umbrellas | 2000 | $ 22.70 | $ 45,400 | $ 45.00 | $ 90,000 | 98% | 10.31% |
| 4 | Patio Chairs | 5000 | $ 35.00 | $ 175,000 | $ 65.00 | $ 325,000 | 86% | 37.23% |
| 5 | Patio Tables | 1000 | $ 48.00 | $ 48,000 | $ 120.00 | $ 120,000 | 150% | 13.75% |
| 6 | Side Tables | 2000 | $ 19.25 | $ 38,500 | $ 33.00 | $ 66,000 | 71% | 7.56% |
| 7 | Grills | 1500 | $ 38.50 | $ 57,750 | $ 89.00 | $ 133,500 | 131% | 15.29% |
| 8 | Citronella Torches | 5000 | $ 2.50 | $ 12,500 | $ 12.50 | $ 62,500 | 400% | 7.16% |
| 9 | Lounge Chairs | 3450 | $ 5.00 | $ 17,250 | $ 22.00 | $ 75,900 | 340% | 8.70% |
| 10 | | | | $ 394,400 | | $ 872,900 | | 100.00% |

## R2—Using Absolute and Relative References

Tracking employee salaries and taxes can be done using a worksheet.

Modify the **Computer Support** worksheet to match the figure. See the steps below for more detail.

1. Select the **Computer Support** sheet, select cell **B5**, and enter **=B3*$B$15**. Use the fill handle to copy the formula to the right to cell **G5**. With the cells still selected, use the **Comma Style** button to format the cells, if needed, then decrease the decimals to show no decimals.

2. Select cell **B6** and enter **=B3*.20**. Use the fill handle to copy the formula to the right to cell **G6**. Format row **6** the same as row **5**.

3. Select cell **B7** and enter **=B3*$B$16**. Use the fill handle to copy the formula to the right to cell **G7**. Format row **7** the same as rows **5** and **6**.

4. Select cell **B8**. Write a formula that will multiply the salaries by an absolute reference to the Medicare tax percent (refer to the **Fixed Percentages** table in the figure). Use the fill handle to copy the formula to the right to cells **C8** through **G8**. Use the same format for these cells.

5. Add a double bottom border to the figures in row **8** and sum the deductibles in each column in row **9**. Notice that the empty cell in row **4** prevents the AutoSum function from accidentally selecting the salaries in row **3**.

6. Calculate the net salary figures by writing a formula in cell **B11** that takes the salaries for the month and subtracts the deductibles for the month. Copy the formula to cells **C11** through **G11**.

7. Check the results of your formulas against the figure to be sure they are working properly. Change the state tax to **6%**. (Type **.06** or **6%**, not just the number 6.) The worksheet is recalculated.

8. Choose **File**, **Page Setup**, **Header/Footer** tab, **Custom Header**. Add your name to the custom header **Left section**. Click **OK**.

9. Change the page orientation to **Landscape**. Save and print your work.

| | A | B | C | D | E | F | G |
|---|---|---|---|---|---|---|---|
| 1 | Computer Technical Support Inc. | | | | | | |
| 2 | | January | February | March | April | May | June |
| 3 | Salaries | $2,584,625 | $2,001,489 | $2,657,881 | $2,600,579 | $2,701,544 | $2,675,255 |
| 4 | Deductibles: | | | | | | |
| 5 | Social Security Tax | 160,247 | 124,092 | 164,789 | 161,236 | 167,496 | 165,866 |
| 6 | Federal Income Tax | 516,925 | 400,298 | 531,576 | 520,116 | 540,309 | 535,051 |
| 7 | State Income Tax | 118,893 | 92,068 | 122,263 | 119,627 | 124,271 | 123,062 |
| 8 | Medicare Tax | 38,769 | 30,022 | 39,868 | 39,009 | 40,523 | 40,129 |
| 9 | Total Deductibles | 834,834 | 646,481 | 858,496 | 839,987 | 872,599 | 864,107 |
| 10 | | | | | | | |
| 11 | Net Salaries | $1,749,791 | $1,355,008 | $1,799,385 | $1,760,592 | $1,828,945 | $1,811,148 |
| 12 | | | | | | | |
| 13 | *Fixed Percentages* | | | | | | |
| 14 | Medicare Tax | 1.50% | | | | | |
| 15 | Social Security Tax | 6.20% | | | | | |
| 16 | State Tax | 4.60% | | | | | |

## R3—Calculating a House Payment and Amortization Schedule for a Five-Year Balloon Mortgage

In this exercise, you use the PMT function to calculate a house payment. Then you use Excel's ability to copy relative and absolute cell references to calculate a list of payments and balances for each month. You also learn how to use this table of payments to determine how much you would need to refinance if you select a common form of loan known as a five-year balloon mortgage.

Modify the **Mortgage** worksheet to match the figure. See the steps below for more detail.

1. Select the **Mortgage** sheet. Select cell **B5** and write a formula to determine the monthly interest rate. Format it as a percent showing three decimal places.

2. Select cell **B7** and write a formula to determine the number of monthly payments over the term of the loan.

3. Select cell **B8** and use **Insert**, **Function** to insert the financial payment formula, PMT, for the mortgage. Select the appropriate arguments for the formula.

4. Select cells **D5** and **D6**. Use the fill handle to fill the date column for five years. The last date should be **1/1/07** in row **64**.

5. Select cells **E6** through **G6**. Drag these three cells to the bottom of the date column to complete the amortization schedule. Look in cell **G64**. If you need to refinance the home loan in five years, you will need to borrow **$118,559.67** (and pay closing costs again).

6. Change the Annual Percentage Rate (APR) to **8%**.

7. Add your name to the sheet header. Save the workbook and close it.

| | A | B | C | D | E | F | G |
|---|---|---|---|---|---|---|---|
| 1 | Mortgage for 1602 Stoney Creek Drive | | | | | | |
| 2 | | | | | | | |
| 3 | Loan Amount | $ 125,000 | | Date | Payment | Interest Paid | Balance |
| 4 | Annual Percentage Rate (APR) | 8.00% | | | | | $ 125,000.00 |
| 5 | Monthly Interest Rate | 0.667% | | 2/1/02 | -917.21 | $ 833.33 | $ 124,916.13 |
| 6 | Number of Years | 30 | | 3/1/02 | -917.21 | $ 832.77 | $ 124,831.70 |
| 7 | No. of Monthly Payments | 360 | | 4/1/02 | -917.21 | $ 832.21 | $ 124,746.70 |
| 8 | Payment | ($917.21) | | 5/1/02 | -917.21 | $ 831.64 | $ 124,661.14 |
| 9 | | | | 6/1/02 | -917.21 | $ 831.07 | $ 124,575.01 |
| 10 | | | | 7/1/02 | -917.21 | $ 830.50 | $ 124,488.30 |

Challenge exercises are designed to test your ability to apply your skills to new situations with less-detailed instructions. These exercises also challenge you to expand your repertoire of skills by using commands that are similar to those you have already learned. The desired outcome is clearly defined, but you have more freedom to choose the steps needed to achieve the required result.

Challenge exercises C1 through C5 use different worksheets in the workbook **EX0303-Challenge**. Open **EX0303** from the **Student** folder on your CD-ROM disc and save it as **EX0303-Challenge** on your floppy disk.

### C1—Using Goal Seek to Find an Interest Rate

Sometimes you know what the answer needs to be, but you do not know how to get there. If you have a worksheet set up to calculate an answer based on one or more cells, you can use an Excel tool named Goal Seek that will try different numbers in the cell you select until the answer in another cell matches the value you set.

*Goal:* Use the Goal Seek tool to determine the annual interest rate that would produce a monthly payment of $600 if the loan amount and payment period remain unchanged.

Use the following guidelines:

1. In the **EX0303-Challenge** workbook, select the **Goal Seek (1)** sheet tab.

2. Select **Tools**, **Goal Seek** from the menu.

3. Use the Goal Seek dialog box to set cell **B6** to **600** by changing the annual interest rate in cell **B2**. The resulting Annual Interest Rate is approximately **7.02%**. (The display is limited to two decimal places, but the actual calculated answer is much more precise.)

4. Save the workbook and leave it open for use in the next exercise.

|   | A | B | |
|---|---|---|---|
| 1 | Loan Amount | $ | 90,000 |
| 2 | Annual Interest Rate | | 7.02% |
| 3 | Monthly rate | | 0.585% |
| 4 | Years | | 30 |
| 5 | Months | | 360 |
| 6 | Payment | $ | 600.00 |

### C2—Using Goal Seek to Determine the Largest Loan Amount

When you buy a car, you may know how much you can afford to pay each month and you may know the interest rate that is charged for a car loan, but you do not know how much you can afford to borrow under those conditions. You can use Goal Seek to find out.

*Goal:* Determine how big a loan you can afford (Loan Amount) on a five-year car loan at an Annual Interest Rate of 8.5 percent if the most you can afford for a monthly car payment is $350.

Use the following guidelines:

1. In the **EX0303-Challenge** workbook, select the **Goal Seek (2)** sheet tab.

2. Use **Goal Seek** to find out what loan amount will yield a payment of **$350**. The sheet is protected so that you do not accidentally overwrite the formulas. The answers shown in the figure are rounded, but the actual values computed by the program are not.

3. Save the workbook. Leave the workbook open for use in the next exercise.

|   | A | B | |
|---|---|---|---|
| 1 | Loan Amount | $ | 17,059 |
| 2 | Annual Interest Rate | | 8.50% |
| 3 | Monthly rate | | 0.708% |
| 4 | Years | | 5 |
| 5 | Months | | 60 |
| 6 | Payment | $ | 350.00 |

 ## C3—Calculating Percentage Increases or Decreases

Prices are often determined by marking up a wholesale price by a certain percentage. When those items go on sale, the price is reduced by a certain percentage.

In this exercise, you will see how formulas are used to increase or decrease a price by a given percentage. In general, if you want to increase a value by 40 percent, you multiply the value by (1+40%). If you want to decrease the price by 20 percent, you multiply by (1-20%). An example is provided to show how a merchant starts with a wholesale price for a pair of boots, increases the price by 40 percent to get the retail price, decreases the retail price by 20 percent for a sale, and then figures out the gross profit and percent profit.

*Goal:* Calculate percentage increases and decreases.

1. In the **EX0303-Challenge** workbook, select the **Percent** sheet.

2. Look at the formula in cell **C2**. Notice how the retail price for the boots was calculated by multiplying the wholesale price in cell **B2** by **(1+40%)**.

3. Enter a similar formula in cell **C3** that calculates a retail price for gloves at a **50%** increase over the wholesale price.

4. Observe the formula in cell **D2** to see how the sale price for boots was determined by multiplying the retail price by **(1-20%)**.

5. Enter a similar formula in cell **D3** to calculate the sale price for gloves if their price is reduced by **30%**.

6. Fill the formulas in cells **E2** and **F2** into cells **E3** and **F3**, respectively. The percent profit on the gloves will be **5%** if you have written the formulas correctly.

7. Enter similar formulas for the hats. Use an increase of **120%** to determine the retail price and then determine the sale price for a **50%** off sale. Fill the gross profit and percent profit formulas into cells **E4** and **F4**.

8. Check your work. All three items should have a positive profit. Save the workbook. Leave the workbook open for use in the next exercise.

| | A | B | C | D | E | F |
|---|---|---|---|---|---|---|
| | Item | Wholesale price | Retail Price | Sale Price | Gross Profit | Percent Profit |
| 2 | Boots | $ 22.35 | $ 31.29 | $ 25.03 | $ 2.68 | 12% |
| 3 | Gloves | $ 12.35 | $ 18.53 | $ 12.97 | $ 0.62 | 5% |
| 4 | Hats | $ 18.20 | $ 40.04 | $ 20.02 | $ 1.82 | 10% |

 ## C4—Using Statistical Functions: Average, Median, Minimum, Maximum, and Standard Deviation

When we describe a set of numbers, such as the income of a certain group, we often use terms such as average or median. We can use Excel to compute these numbers and see how they describe a set of numbers. Average and median are two ways of describing where the "center" of a set of numbers is. They do not describe whether the numbers are all close to that central number or if they vary greatly. The statistic that describes this type of variation is the standard deviation. It is also useful to know the greatest and least values to see how far from the "center" the numbers can vary.

In this exercise, you look at the monthly rainfall in Buffalo and Seattle. The average for both is about the same, but looking at just one statistic does not tell the whole story.

*Goal:* Use Excel's statistical functions to compare the average, median, minimum, maximum, and standard deviation of rainfall.

1. In the **EX0303-Challenge** workbook, select the **Stats** sheet. Notice that both cities have almost the same total annual rainfall. Look at the rainfall for each month of the year—it is apparent that the rainfall in Seattle varies much more from month to month.

2. Insert the **AVERAGE** function in cell **B16** (it is one of the Statistics functions, as are all of the remaining functions you enter in this exercise).

3. The median of a set of numbers is the value that has as many values above it as below it. Insert the **MEDIAN** function in cell **B17**. Make sure the range of cells is restricted to **B3** through **B14**.

4. To see how much the numbers vary from the average, find the standard deviation of the rainfall. Use the **STDEVP** function in cell **B18**. If you add or subtract this amount from the average, the resulting range will contain roughly two-thirds of the values. The larger the standard deviation, the more the values differ from the average. Use cells **B3** through **B14** in the **STDEVP** formula; do not include the total in cell **B15**.

5. Insert the **MAX** and **MIN** functions in cells **B19** and **B20** respectively to determine the maximum and minimum rainfall. Make sure they both refer to cells **B3** through **B14**.

6. Select the five formulas in cells **B16** through **B20**. Use the fill handle to copy the formulas into the cells in column **C**.

7. Format the formulas in cells **B16** through **C20** to show one decimal place. Notice how the Total, Average, and Median are almost the same for the rainfall in the two cities. The difference is not apparent until you look at the other three statistics.

8. Save the workbook and leave it open for use in the next exercise.

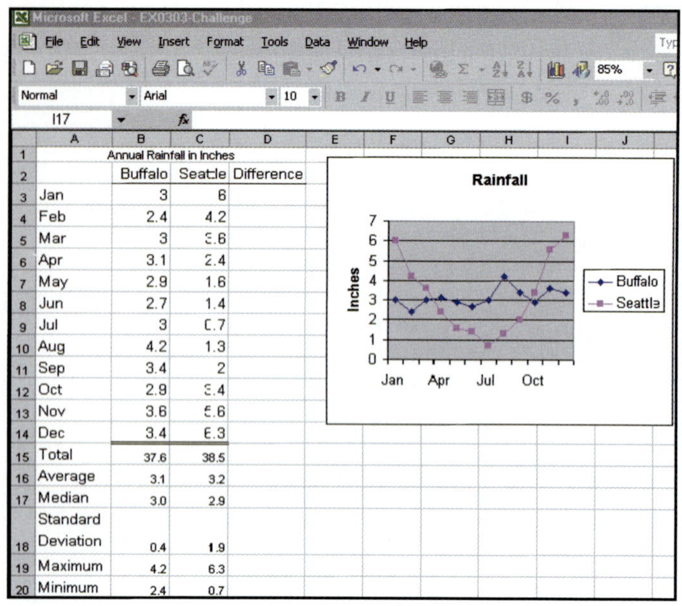

| | A | B | C | D |
|---|---|---|---|---|
| 1 | | Annual Rainfall in Inches | | |
| 2 | | Buffalo | Seattle | Difference |
| 3 | Jan | 3 | 6 | Higher |
| 4 | Feb | 2.4 | 4.2 | Higher |
| 5 | Mar | 3 | 3.6 | Higher |
| 6 | Apr | 3.1 | 2.4 | Lower |
| 7 | May | 2.9 | 1.6 | Lower |
| 8 | Jun | 2.7 | 1.4 | Lower |
| 9 | Jul | 3 | 0.7 | Lower |
| 10 | Aug | 4.2 | 1.3 | Lower |
| 11 | Sep | 3.4 | 2 | Lower |
| 12 | Oct | 2.9 | 3.4 | Higher |
| 13 | Nov | 3.6 | 5.6 | Higher |
| 14 | Dec | 3.4 | 6.3 | Higher |

## C5—Using the IF Logical Function

A difference between two sets of numbers may be apparent to the person who uses them but may not stand out to others. You can use a logical statement to test a given condition and then take action based on the result.

In this exercise, you look at the monthly rainfall in Buffalo and Seattle, compare them, and display the term **Higher** if the rainfall in Seattle is higher than Buffalo or **Lower** if it is lower.

*Goal:* Use Excel's logical IF function to display one of two words based on a comparison of rainfall.

1. In the **EX0303-Challenge** workbook, select the **Stats** sheet. Look at the rainfall for each month of the year—it is apparent that the rainfall in Seattle varies much more from month to month.

2. Select cell **D3** and insert the logical function, **IF**.

3. Type **C3>B3** in the **Logical_test** box.

4. Press Tab to move to the **Value_if_true** box and type **"Higher"** (include the quotation marks).

5. Press Tab to move to the **Value_if_false** box and type **"Lower"**. Click **OK**.

6. Use the fill handle to copy this formula into cells **D4** through **D14**. The resulting **IF** formulas indicate that the rainfall amounts in Seattle exceed those in Buffalo during the months of October through March, whereas Buffalo's numbers are higher from April through September.

7. Save the workbook and close it.

## C6—Locating Data in a Table Using VLOOKUP

Challenge exercises C6 through C8 use different worksheets in the workbook **EX0304-Challenge**. Open **EX0304** from the **Student** folder on your CD-ROM disc and save it as **EX0304-Challenge** on your floppy disk.

If you are providing a quotation for a job, the price often depends on the cost of parts and labor. These costs vary depending on the item and the quantity purchased. It can be very time consuming to look up information in tables to include in your calculations. Excel has two functions that are designed to look up values in a table, column, or array. These are called **VLOOKUP** and **HLOOKUP**. VLOOKUP is used to look up values in a vertical column and HLOOKUP is used to look up values in a horizontal row. In this exercise, you will learn how to use the VLOOKUP function.

*Goal:* Use the VLOOKUP function to find and retrieve a value from a table for use in a formula.

To use the VLOOKUP function to find the correct value in a table and use it in a calculation, follow these steps:

1. Select the **Lookup** sheet, if necessary.

2. Use Help to find the description of the **VLOOKUP** function. Read the description and examine the example in cell **C4**. There are three arguments included in this formula. The first defines the value that is looked up in a table. The second argument defines the table or range of cells that should be examined. The third is the column that should be used to locate the matching value. Each column in

the defined table is identified with a number, 1, 2, 3, etc. (Note: The values in the first column of a table that is used with this function must be sorted in increasing order, as shown in column E of this example.)

3. Test the function in cell **C4** by changing values in cells **A4** and **B4**. Use one of the codes from column **1** of the **Quantity Charge** table for cell **A4** and either a **2** or **3** for cell **B4**. The number in cell **B4** indicates whether column **2** or **3** of the Quantity Charge table should be used to look up the value that matches the code in cell **A4**.

4. Find the **Multi-Color Charge** table. Insert the **VLOOKUP** function from the list of **Lookup & Reference** functions into cell **C18** and select the arguments so that it will find the correct charge for additional shirt colors and display it in cell **C18**.

5. Test the function by trying different numbers in cells **A18** and **B18**. Your sheet will differ from the example shown if you use different numbers when you test it.

6. Save the workbook and leave it open for use in the next exercise.

| | A | B | C | D | E | F | G |
|---|---|---|---|---|---|---|---|
| 1 | | | Shirt Price Calculaton | | | | |
| 2 | Charge per Shirt Based on Style and Quantity Ordered | | | | | Quantity Charge | |
| 3 | Enter Code | Enter 2 or 3 | Calculated Price | | Column 1 | Column 2 | Column 3 |
| 4 | SS11 | 2 | 34.95 | | Style Code | Small Order | Large Order |
| 5 | | | | | GS100 | 15.95 | 14.75 |
| 6 | | | | | GS5/5 | 13.95 | 12.25 |
| 7 | | | | | GSH100 | 23.95 | 22.75 |
| 8 | | | | | GSH5/5 | 21.95 | 20.25 |
| 9 | | | | | SS11 | 34.95 | 32.95 |
| 10 | | | | | SS7 | 14.95 | 13.4 |
| 11 | | | | | SS9 | 19.95 | 15.5 |
| 12 | | | | | SSHD | 15.95 | 14.9 |
| 13 | | | | | TS100 | 8.95 | 6.7 |
| 14 | | | | | TS5/5 | 6.95 | 5.6 |
| 15 | | | | | | | |
| 16 | Extra Charge for Multiple Colors | | | | Multi Color Charge | | |
| 17 | # of Shirts | Enter 2 or 3 | Color Charge | | # of Shirts Ordered | Column 2 One Color | Column 3 Two or More |
| 18 | 15 | 2 | 0.95 | | 1 | 0 | 2.65 |
| 19 | | | | | 12 | 0.95 | 2.55 |
| 20 | Total Charge per shirt | $ | 35.90 | | 24 | 0.8 | 2.25 |
| 21 | | | | | 48 | 0.75 | 1.15 |
| 22 | | | | | 96 | 0.65 | 0.9 |
| 23 | | | | | 144 | 0.55 | 0.8 |
| 24 | | | | | 201 | 0.5 | 0.65 |
| 25 | | | | | 501 | 0.3 | 0.6 |
| 26 | | | | | 1000 | 0.2 | 0.55 |



## C7—Creating a Frequency Distribution

This exercise requires the Analysis ToolPak Add-in. Look under the **Tools** menu to determine if you have the **Data Analysis** option. If not, select **Tools**, **Add-Ins**, **Analysis ToolPak**. If you plan to do the Solver exercise, C8, select the Solver Add-in. You may need your Office 2002 CD-ROM disc, or ask your lab administrator to install these features.

If you are trying to determine how many of each kind of number you have in a group, you want to know the frequency distribution. For example, 25 people have answered a question that has five possible answers numbered 1 through 5, and you would like to know how many people chose each answer.

Excel provides two options for determining the frequency distribution. There is a Frequency function that can be found by using the **Insert**, **Function** menu option. The other is part of the Histogram tool in the Analysis ToolPak. The Histogram tool is much easier.

*Goal:* Learn how to use the Histogram tool to determine the number of people answering each option for a question.

1. In the **EX0304-Challenge** workbook, select the **Frequency** sheet.

2. Search for Help on the **Histogram** analysis tool.

3. Look at the example analysis that was done on the first question.

4. Use the Histogram analysis tool to produce a similar analysis of the second question. Use cells **B12** through **X12** as the input range, cells **T5** through **T9** as the bin range, and select cell **Y14** as the output cell that will be used as the upper-left corner of the output range.

5. Save the workbook and leave it open for use in the next exercise.

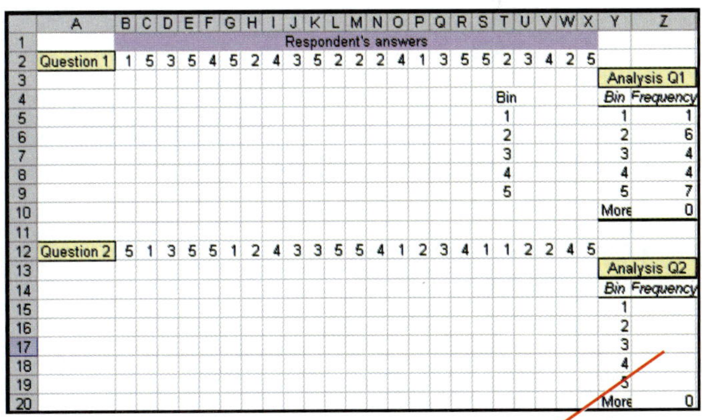

| | A | B | C | D | E | F | G | H | I | J | K | L | M | N | O | P | Q | R | S | T | U | V | W | X | Y | Z |
|---|---|---|---|---|---|---|---|---|---|---|---|---|---|---|---|---|---|---|---|---|---|---|---|---|---|---|
| 1 | | Respondent's answers | | | | | | | | | | | | | | | | | | | | | | | | |
| 2 | Question 1 | 1 | 5 | 3 | 5 | 4 | 5 | 2 | 4 | 3 | 5 | 2 | 2 | 2 | 4 | 1 | 3 | 5 | 5 | 2 | 3 | 4 | 2 | 5 | | |
| 3 | | | | | | | | | | | | | | | | | | | | | | | | | Analysis Q1 | |
| 4 | | | | | | | | | | | | | | | | | | | | Bin | | | | | Bin | Frequency |
| 5 | | | | | | | | | | | | | | | | | | | | 1 | | | | | 1 | 1 |
| 6 | | | | | | | | | | | | | | | | | | | | 2 | | | | | 2 | 6 |
| 7 | | | | | | | | | | | | | | | | | | | | 3 | | | | | 3 | 4 |
| 8 | | | | | | | | | | | | | | | | | | | | 4 | | | | | 4 | 4 |
| 9 | | | | | | | | | | | | | | | | | | | | 5 | | | | | 5 | 7 |
| 10 | | | | | | | | | | | | | | | | | | | | | | | | | More | 0 |
| 11 | | | | | | | | | | | | | | | | | | | | | | | | | | |
| 12 | Question 2 | 5 | 1 | 3 | 5 | 5 | 1 | 2 | 4 | 3 | 3 | 5 | 5 | 4 | 1 | 2 | 3 | 4 | 1 | 1 | 2 | 2 | 4 | 5 | | |
| 13 | | | | | | | | | | | | | | | | | | | | | | | | | Analysis Q2 | |
| 14 | | | | | | | | | | | | | | | | | | | | | | | | | Bin | Frequency |
| 15 | | | | | | | | | | | | | | | | | | | | | | | | | 1 | |
| 16 | | | | | | | | | | | | | | | | | | | | | | | | | 2 | |
| 17 | | | | | | | | | | | | | | | | | | | | | | | | | 3 | |
| 18 | | | | | | | | | | | | | | | | | | | | | | | | | 4 | |
| 19 | | | | | | | | | | | | | | | | | | | | | | | | | 5 | |
| 20 | | | | | | | | | | | | | | | | | | | | | | | | | More | 0 |

Results to be determined by the student

## C8—Using the Solver Add-in

This exercise requires the Solver Add-in. Look under the **Tools** menu to determine if you have the **Solver** option. If not, select **Tools**, **Add-Ins**, **Solver Add-in**. You may need your Office 2002 CD-ROM disc, or ask your lab administrator to install these features.

Solver is similar to Goal Seek, but it has more options. It can change more than one input cell, and you can specify constraints on several cells. You can have it determine the inputs to produce a match, a maximum, or a minimum value.

A classic physics problem is to determine how high a projectile will go if it is shot straight up at a given initial speed. The formula is $H = -16T^2 + ST$. This formula can be written in Excel as $= -16*$ (*time cell reference*)$\wedge 2 +$(*speed cell reference*)$*$(*time cell reference*). In the example sheet used for this exercise, the formula is $= -16*B3\wedge 2 + B4*B3$. There are two ways to solve this problem. You could use differential calculus to find the derivative, set it equal to zero, solve for T, and then plug the value of T into the original formula. A second way would be to try increasing values of time in the formula until the value of the height stopped increasing and started decreasing. In order to solve for the time down to the nearest tenth of a second, you would have to do the formula many times.

The Solver works by trying different values in the formula, subject to the constraints you have imposed, until the target cell matches the value you have chosen or is a maximum or minimum if you have selected either of those options.

*Goal:* Use the Solver tool to find the maximum height to which a projectile will rise given an initial speed of 2,000 feet per second.

1. In the **EX0304-Challenge** workbook, select the **Solver** sheet

2. Search for Help on guidelines for using the Solver.

3. Use the Solver to determine the **Maximum** value for the formula in cell **B5** by changing the time values in cell **B3**.

4. Keep the Solver solution if it is between 50 and 100. The answer calculated by the program will be more accurate than the value displayed in the cell due to rounding of the display.

5. Save the workbook and leave it open for use in the next exercise.

| | A | B |
|---|---|---|
| 1 | Find Maximum Height of a projectile | |
| 2 | | |
| 3 | Time in seconds | 62.5 |
| 4 | Initial speed in feet/sec | 2,000 |
| 5 | Height | 62,500 |

Time to maximum height rounded to one decimal place

Maximum height

## C9—Using Date Functions to Determine Present Age

You can use Excel to calculate the difference between a fixed date and today's date. This may be useful for determining retirement benefits or simply recognizing birthdays in a retirement home.

*Goal:* Use the NOW() function to determine a person's present age.

1. In the **EX0304-Challenge** workbook, select the **Dates** sheet.

2. Enter a birth date such as **5/21/47** in cell **B3**.

3. Insert the **Date & Time** function, **NOW**, into cell **B4**.

4. Enter a formula into cell **B5** that will subtract the value in cell **B3** from the value in cell **B4**.

5. Select cell **B5** and click the **Comma Style** formatting button on the toolbar (to the right of the Percent Style formatting button). The number of days between the two dates is displayed in cell **B5**.

6. Select cell **B6** and enter a formula that will divide the contents of cell **B5** by **365.25**. Cell **B6** will display the difference in years. Format cell **B6** to display one decimal place.

7. Save the workbook and leave it open for use in the next exercise.

| | A | B |
|---|---|---|
| 1 | Use Date Functions | |
| 2 | | |
| 3 | Your Birth Date | 5/21/47 |
| 4 | Today's date | 11/24/00 19:36 |
| 5 | Days old | 19546.82 |
| 6 | Years old | 53.5 |

# C10—Using Named Cells in Formulas

Formulas that refer to cells by their column and row labels are short and compact but may be difficult to understand. It is possible to give cells names that reflect the meaning of their contents and then use those names in formulas.

*Goal:* Give names to the total cost and total retail values in cells D10 and F10 and then use these names in a formula to determine the gross profit.

1. In the **EX0304-Challenge** workbook, select the **Named Cells** sheet.

2. Select cell **D10**. Click in the **Name** box on the formula toolbar and type **Total_Cost**. Be sure to type the underscore character. Excel does not accept blanks in the cell names.

3. Select cell **F10**. Click in the **Name** box on the formula toolbar and type **Retail_Value**. Be sure to type the underscore character.

4. Select cell **E13** and type **=Retail_Value − Total_Cost**.

5. Save the workbook and close it.

| E13 | | $f_x$ =Retail_Value - Total_Cost | | | | | | |
|---|---|---|---|---|---|---|---|---|
| | A | B | C | D | E | F | G | H |
| 1 | | | | Patio Furniture Division | | | | |
| 2 | Inventory | Quantity | Average Cost | Total Cost | Retail Price | Retail Value | Percent Mark Up | Percent Contribution |
| 3 | Table Umbrellas | 2000 | $ 22.70 | $ 45,400 | $ 45.00 | $ 90,000 | 98.2% | 10.31% |
| 4 | Patio Chairs | 5000 | $ 35.00 | $ 175,000 | $ 65.00 | $ 325,000 | 85.7% | 37.23% |
| 5 | Patio Tables | 1000 | $ 48.00 | $ 48,000 | $ 120.00 | $ 120,000 | 150.0% | 13.75% |
| 6 | Side Tables | 2000 | $ 19.25 | $ 38,500 | $ 33.00 | $ 66,000 | 71.4% | 7.56% |
| 7 | Grills | 1500 | $ 38.50 | $ 57,750 | $ 89.00 | $ 133,500 | 131.2% | 15.29% |
| 8 | Citronella Torches | 5000 | $ 2.50 | $ 12,500 | $ 12.50 | $ 62,500 | 400.0% | 7.16% |
| 9 | Lounge Chairs | 3450 | $ 5.00 | $ 17,250 | $ 22.00 | $ 75,900 | 340.0% | 8.70% |
| 10 | | | | $ 394,400 | | $ 872,900 | | 100.00% |
| 11 | | | | | | | | |
| 12 | | | | | | | | |
| 13 | | | | Gross Profit | 478500 | | | |
| 14 | | | | | | | | |

If you want to have an income of your own when you retire, you need to save or invest money each year that will accumulate interest and result in a sizeable balance that you can draw from during your retirement. The FV function may be used to calculate the future value of a series of equal deposits in an interest earning account.

Set up a worksheet that calculates the future value of a series of deposits that you might make into a savings or investment account for your retirement. Criteria for grading will be:

1. Demonstration of the use of the FV financial function.

Some examples of features that students have learned to use in previous classes to enhance their personal retirement worksheet are:

- The rate of interest, the years to retirement, and monthly investment are in separate cells, and any formulas that use them refer to those cells so that these assumptions may be changed and all the dependant cells will be recalculated automatically

- The formula uses one month as a basis for calculation to show how much the student must save per month

- The monthly interest rate is calculated from the annual interest rate, and the number of months is calculated from the years to retirement

- All dollar amounts are formatted with zero decimal places

- A negative number is used for the investment amount to make the future value positive

2. Identify yourself. Place your name in a cell that is clearly visible.

3. To complete the project:

- Save your file on your own disk. Name it **EX0305-Retire**.

- Check with your instructor to determine if the project should be submitted in electronic or printed form. If necessary, print out a copy of the worksheet to hand in.

# Lesson 4

## Understanding the Numbers Using a Chart

Task 1    Creating a Chart to Show a Trend
Task 2    Creating a Chart to Show Contributions to a Whole
Task 3    Creating a Chart to Make Comparisons
Task 4    Editing the Elements of a Chart and Adding a Callout
Task 5    Printing a Chart

### INTRODUCTION

 People process information in several different ways. Most of us recognize trends more readily if a line or a series of columns of differing heights represents them. We also recognize how one member of a group compares to the others if they are represented by slices of a pie chart.

This lesson is designed to provide you with the basic skills you need to create a variety of *charts* to represent your numerical data graphically. Excel's *Chart Wizard* guides you through the necessary steps. You will be working with store data from the Armstrong Pool, Spa, and Sauna Co.

# VISUAL SUMMARY

By the time you have completed this entire lesson, you will have created a worksheet containing a data table and three charts that look like these:

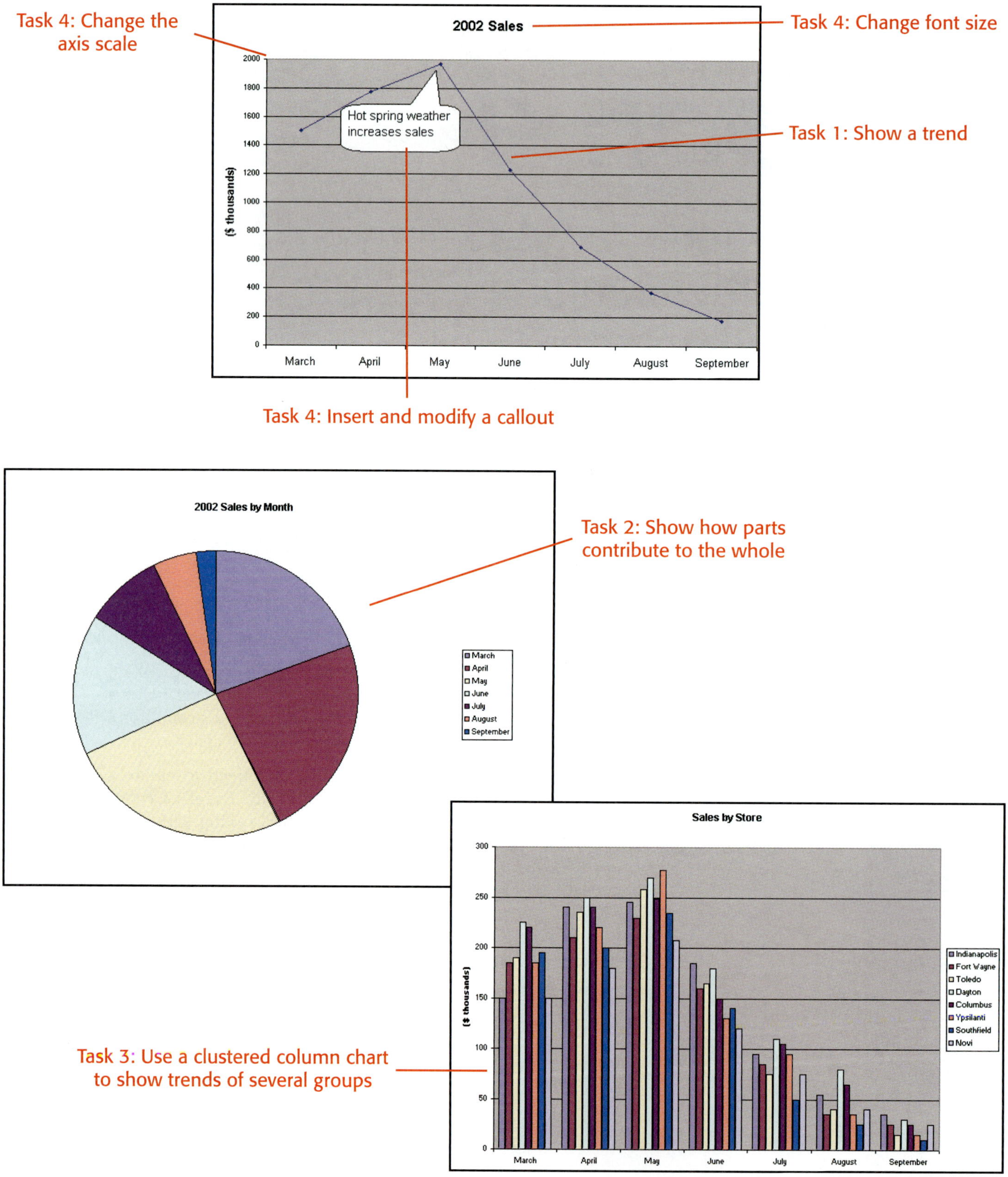

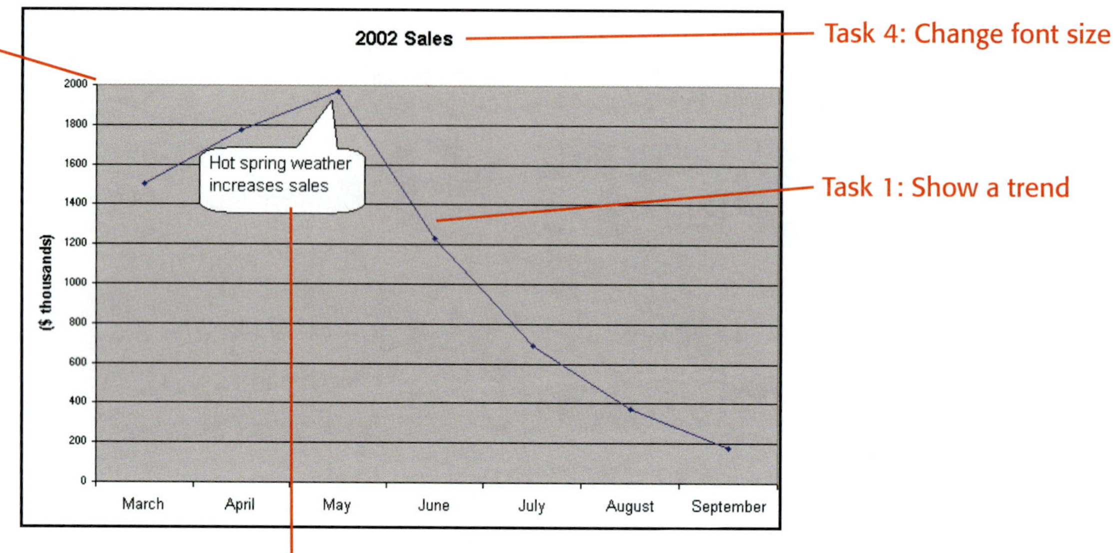

# Task 1

## CREATING A CHART TO SHOW A TREND

### Why would I do this?

It is sometimes easier to analyze numbers when looking at a visual representation. A picture or *chart* helps, and some chart types are better than others for specific purposes. For instance, when you want to show a trend (change over time), a *line chart* is usually most effective.

In this task, you learn how to create a line chart to show the trend in sales for the Armstrong firm.

**1** Open **EX0401** from the **Student** folder. Save it as **EX0401-Sales**.

*The new title appears in the title bar.*

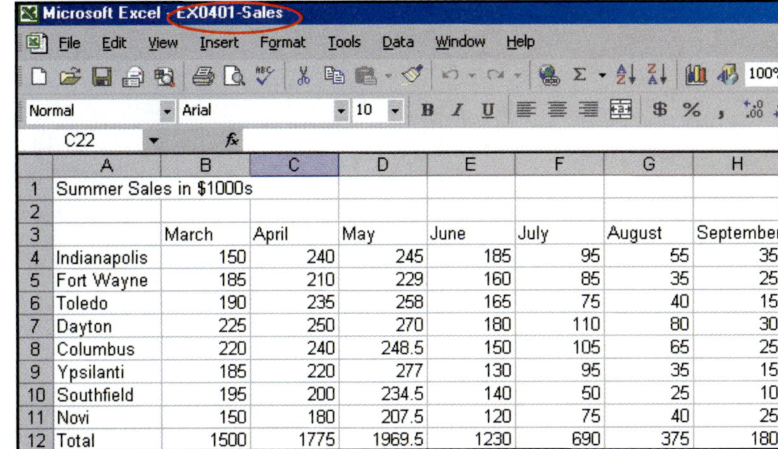

**2** Move the pointer to cell **A3**. Click-and-drag to select cells **A3** through **H3**, and then release the mouse button.

Hold down ⟨Ctrl⟩ and select cells **A12** through **H12**.

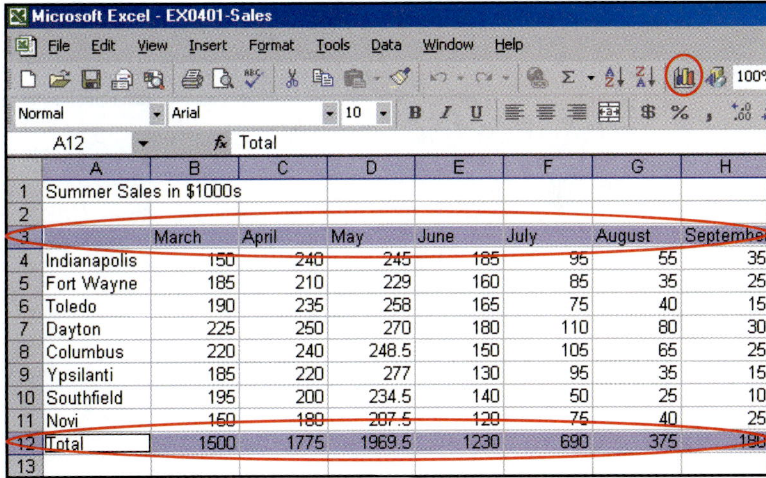

**3** Click the **Chart Wizard** button.

*The first Chart Wizard dialog box is displayed.*

Click **Line** in the **Chart type** area.

*Notice that the default **Chart sub-type** is a line with data markers. Each chart type has several variations that you can use to display the data.*

Default Chart sub-type

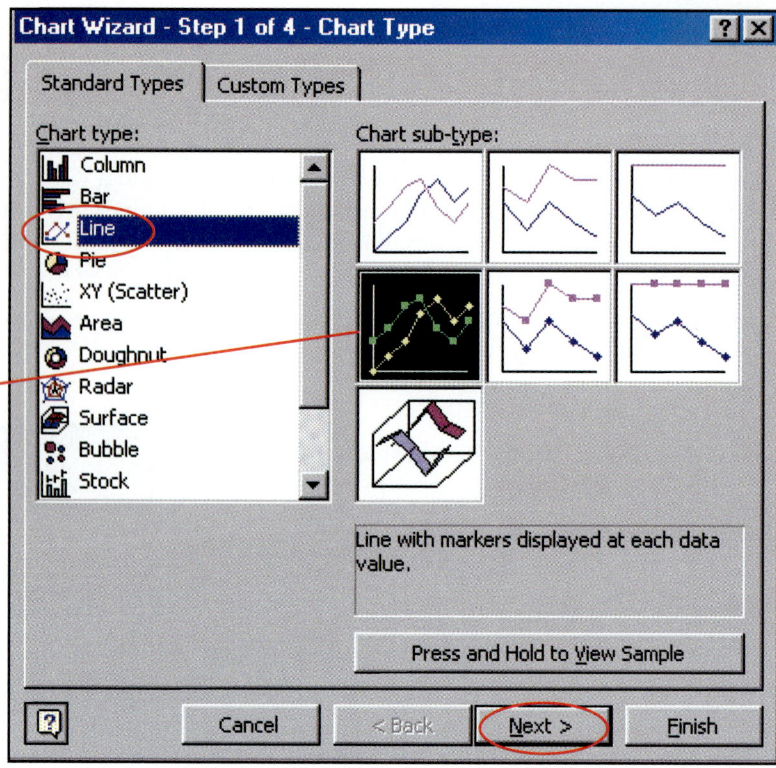


**4** Click **Next**.

*The second Chart Wizard dialog box is displayed. Make sure Rows is selected from the **Series in** area.*

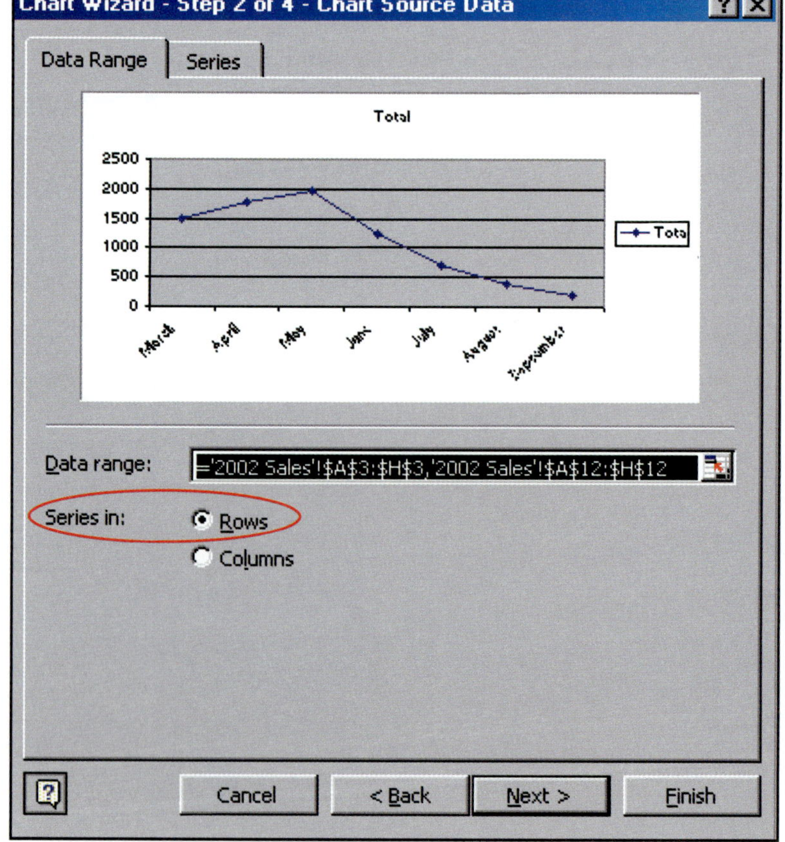

**5** Click **Next**.

*The third Chart Wizard dialog box is displayed.*

Click the **Titles** tab, if necessary. Replace the default title in the **Chart title** box with **2002 Sales**. Type **($ thousands)** in the **Value (Y) axis** box.

Legend

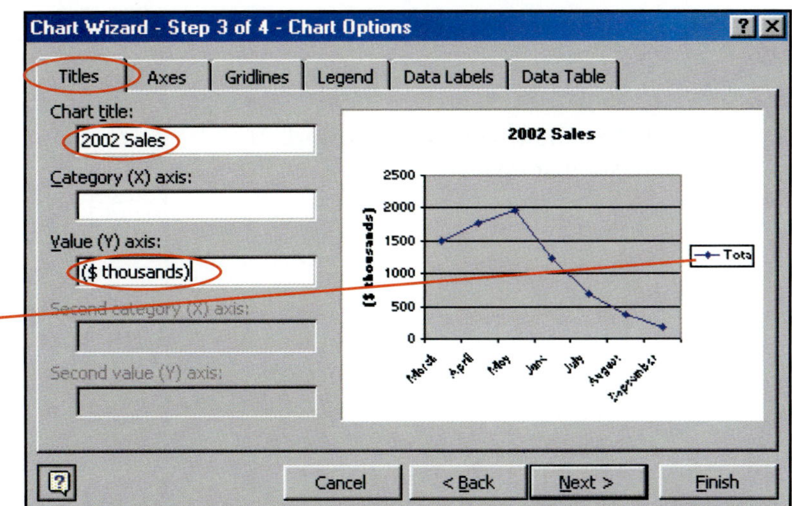

**6** Click the **Legend** tab.

*A legend is a list that identifies a pattern or color used in an Excel chart.*

Click the **Show legend** box to turn the legend off.

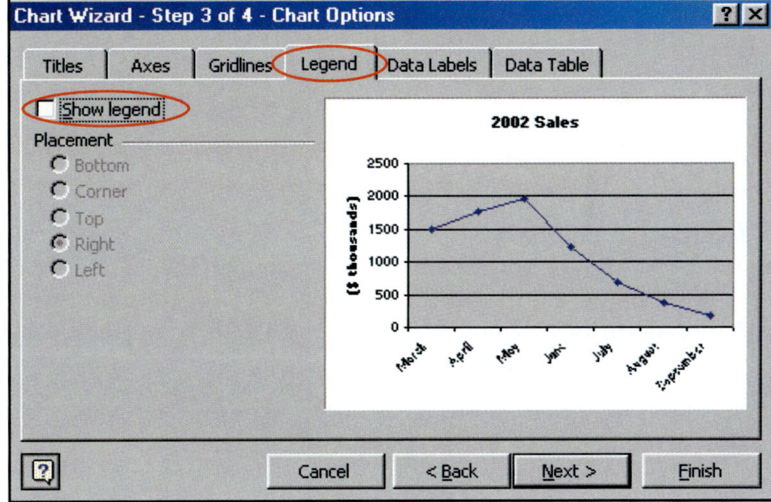

IN DEPTH

The first three Chart Wizard dialog boxes contain multiple tabs. These tabs let you control such things as the chart scale, whether to show vertical or horizontal gridlines, and how to label the data points.

**7** Click **Next**.

*The fourth Chart Wizard dialog box is displayed.*

Click **As new sheet** to select it and type **2002 Sales Chart** in the adjacent box.

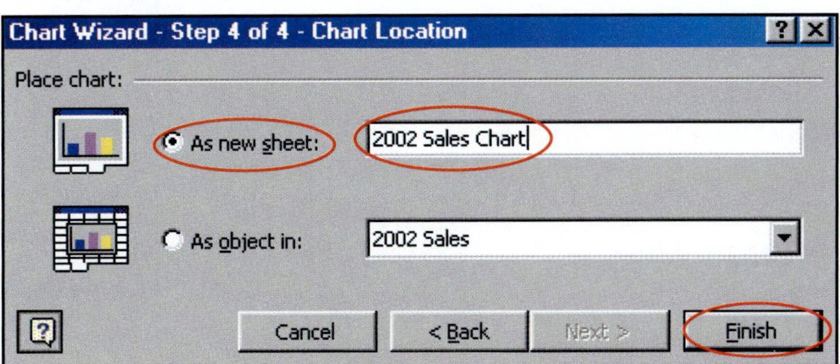

8 Click **Finish**.

*The chart is shown full-size on its own sheet.*

Click the **Save** button to save your work. If the Chart toolbar appears, close it.

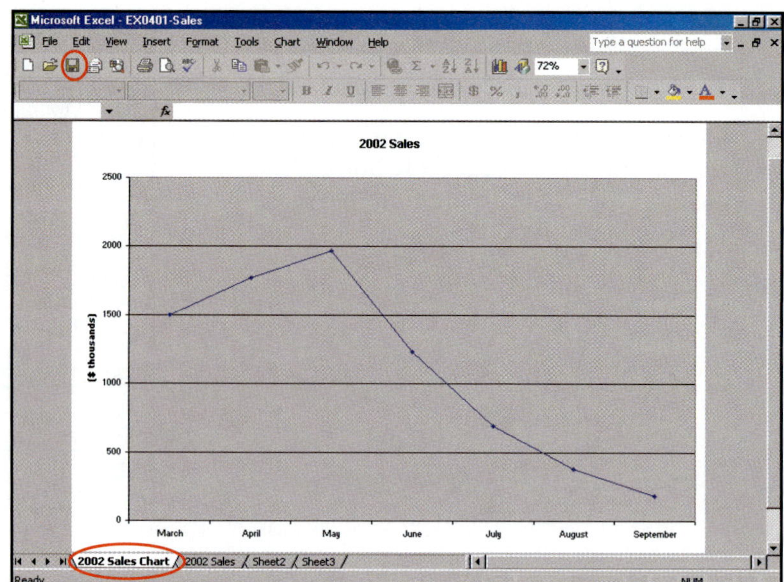

# Task 2

## CREATING A CHART TO SHOW CONTRIBUTIONS TO A WHOLE

### Why would I do this?

In the previous task, you took a set of data and created a line chart to show a trend over time. You may find that it is often beneficial to graphically represent the contribution of various elements to the whole. The best way to illustrate parts of a whole is to use a *pie chart*.

In this task, you learn how to create a pie chart that shows the contribution each region made to the total sales amount for the year.

1 Click the **2002 Sales** sheet tab. If necessary, select cells **A3** through **H3**. Hold down Ctrl and select cells **A12** through **H12** if necessary.

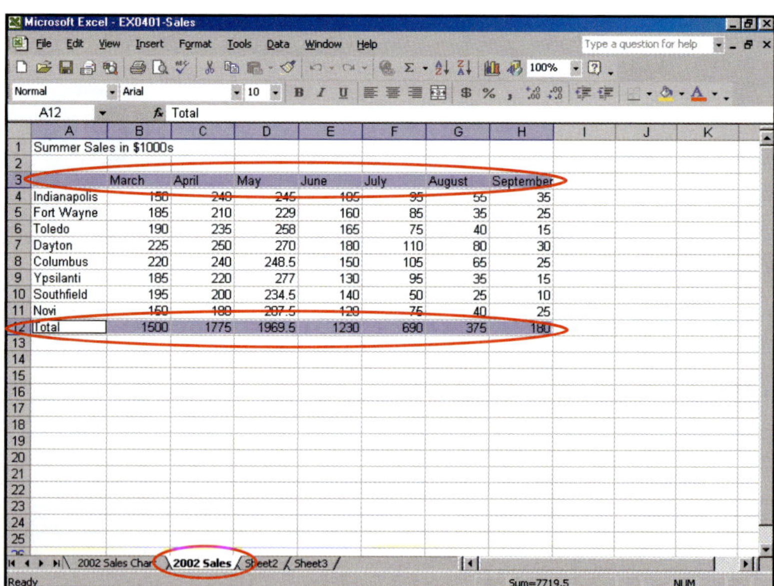

**2** Click the **Chart Wizard** button.

*The first Chart Wizard dialog box is displayed.*

Click **Pie** in the **Chart type** area and select **Pie**, the default chart sub-type, in the **Chart sub-type** area.

Description of sub-type

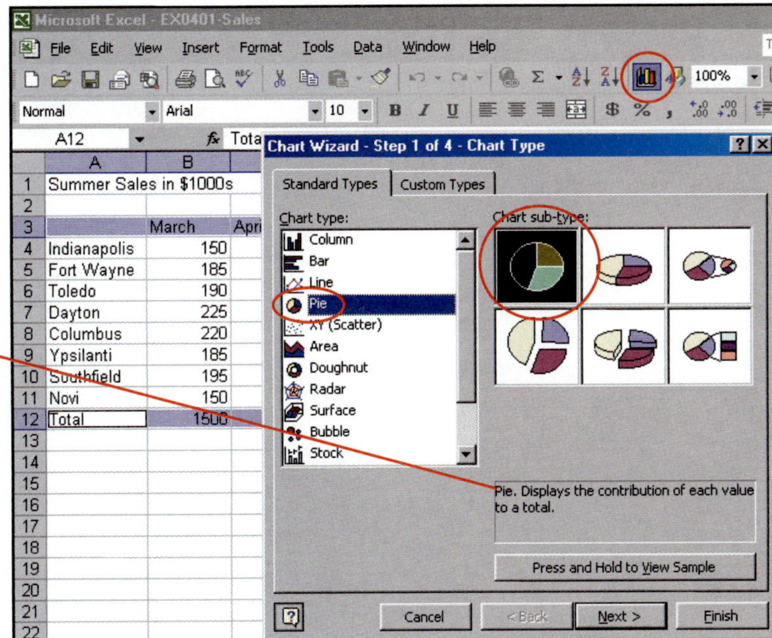

**3** Click **Next**.

*The second Chart Wizard dialog box is displayed.*

Make sure **Rows** is selected from the **Series in** area.

*The data you are charting is in rows.*

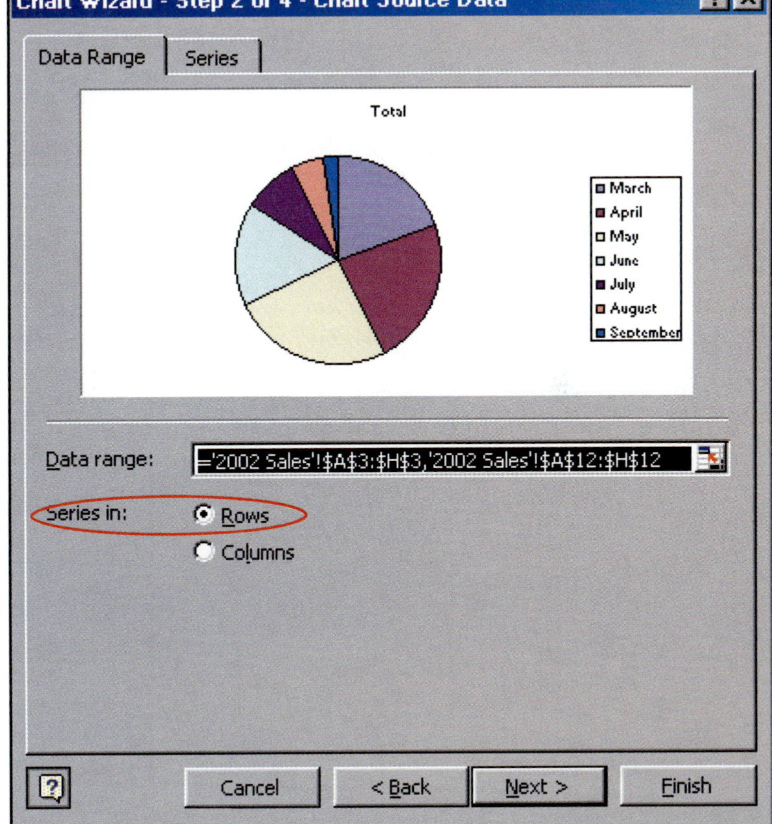

**4** Click **Next**.

*The third Chart Wizard dialog box is displayed.*

> Click the **Titles** tab, if necessary. Replace the default text in the **Chart title** box with **2002 Sales by Month**.

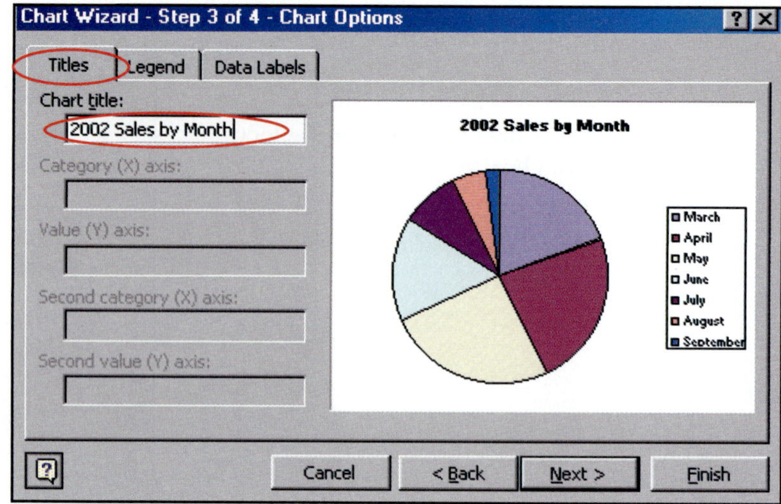

**5** Click **Next**.

*The fourth Chart Wizard dialog box is displayed.*

> Select **As new sheet** and type **2002 Sales by Month** in the adjacent box.

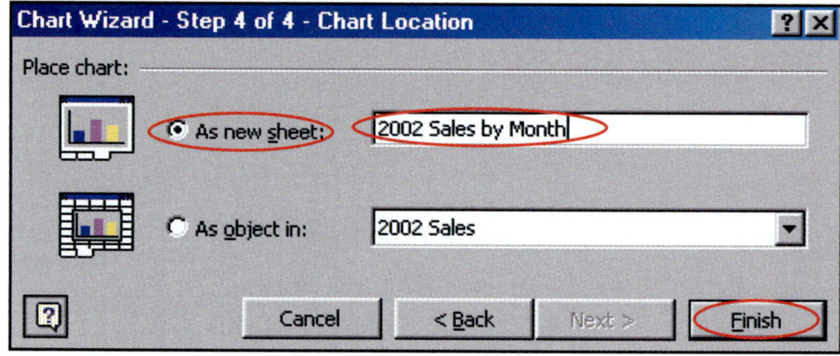

**6** Click **Finish**.

*The chart is placed on its own sheet. (You learn how to change the size of the title and legend in a later task.)*

> Save your work.

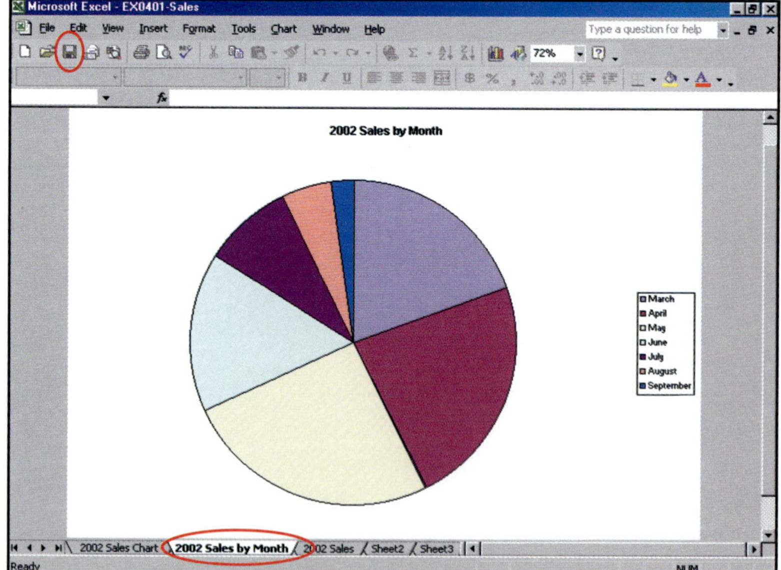

## *Why would I do this?*

Perhaps the most common use for a chart is to make comparisons. For example, you might want to compare oil production by country over a series of years. To illustrate this type of comparison, a *column chart* (with vertical bars) or *bar chart* (with horizontal bars) is most often used.

In this task, you learn how to create a column chart that compares sales by city.

**1** Click the **2002 Sales** sheet tab. Select cells **A3** through **H11**.

**IN DEPTH**

It is important that you do not include the total rows or columns when doing a comparison chart. If you included these figures, it would distort the chart, since the totals would be compared to regional and monthly sales amounts.

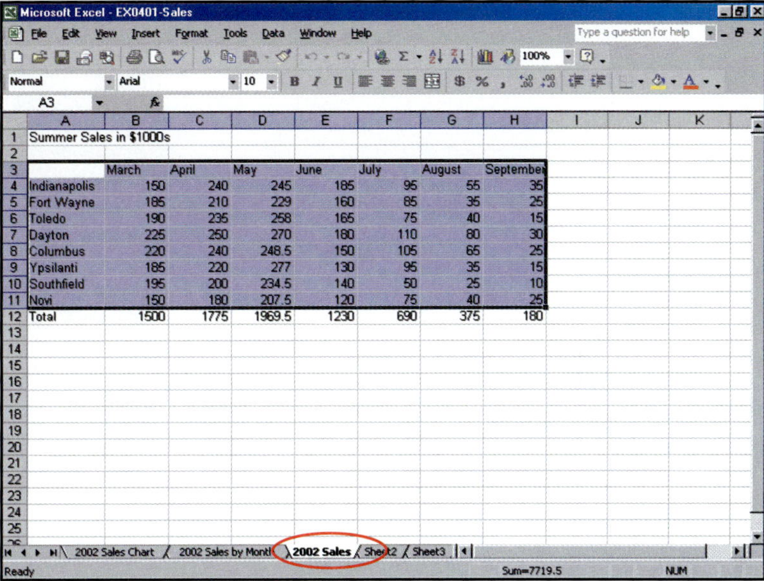

**2** Click the **Chart Wizard** button.

*The first Chart Wizard dialog box is displayed.*

Click **Column** in the **Chart type** area and accept the **Clustered Column** option in the **Chart sub-type** area.

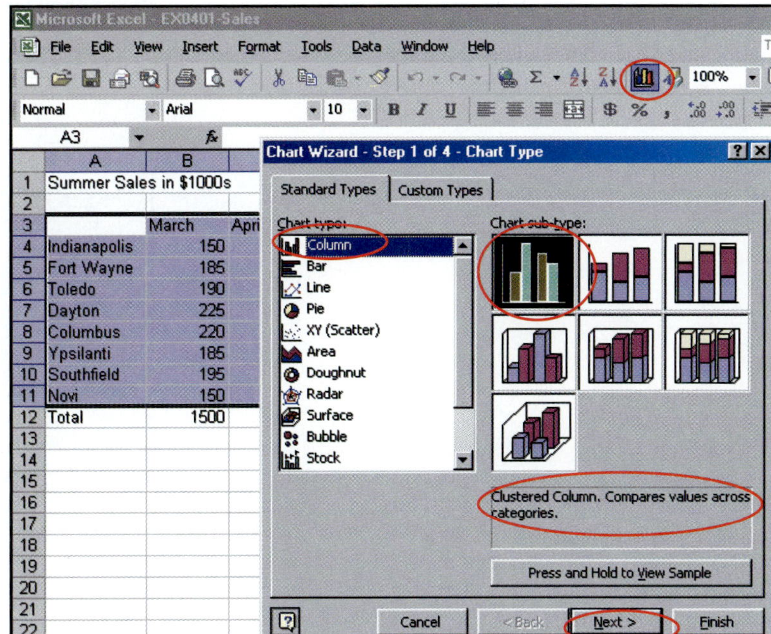

**3** Click **Next**.

*The second Chart Wizard dialog box is displayed.*

Select **Rows** in the **Series in** area.

*This keeps all of the sales figures from each month together.*

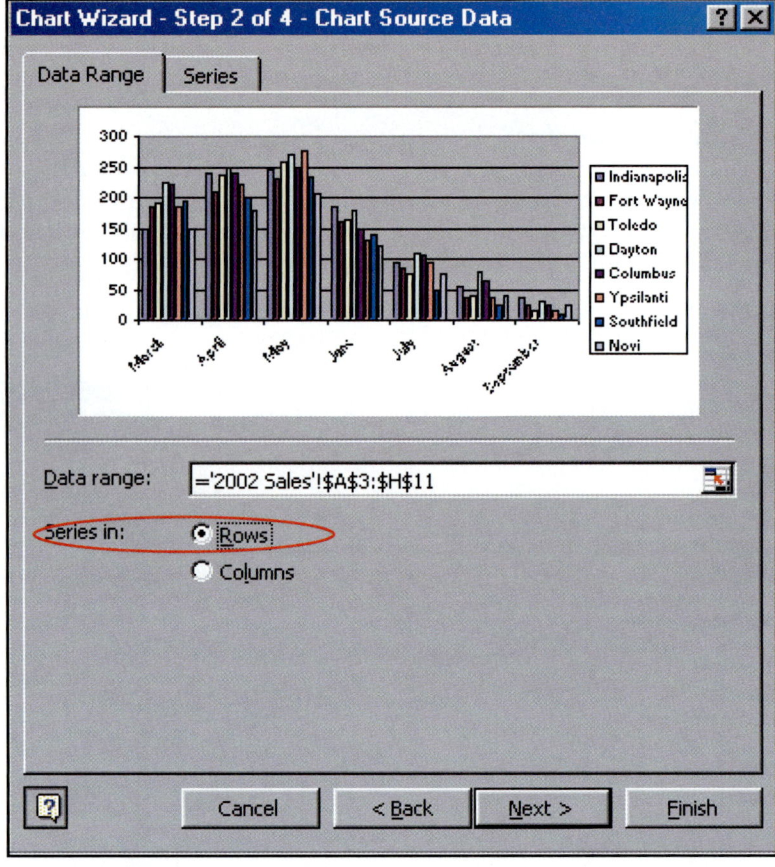


**4** Click **Next**.

*The third Chart Wizard dialog box is displayed.*

Click the **Titles** tab, if necessary, and type **Sales by Store** in the **Chart title** box. Type **($ thousands)** in the **Value (Y) axis** box.

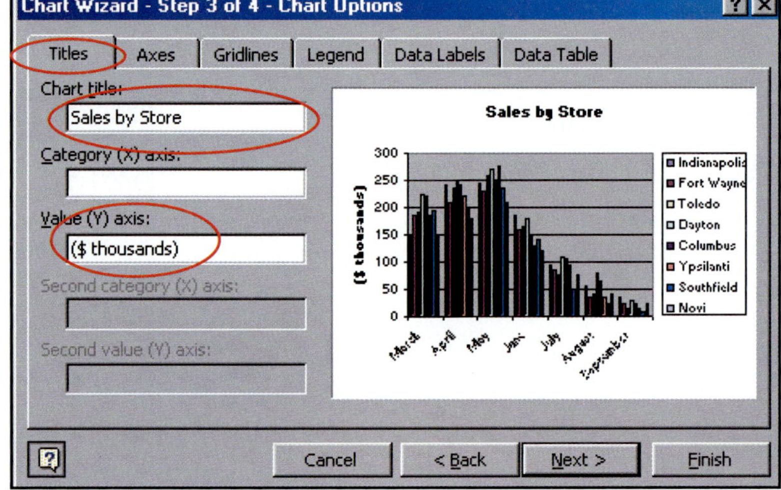

**5** Click **Next**. Select **As new sheet** and type
**2002 Sales by Store** in the adjacent box.

**6** Click **Finish**.

*The chart is on its own sheet.*

Click the **Save** button to save your work.

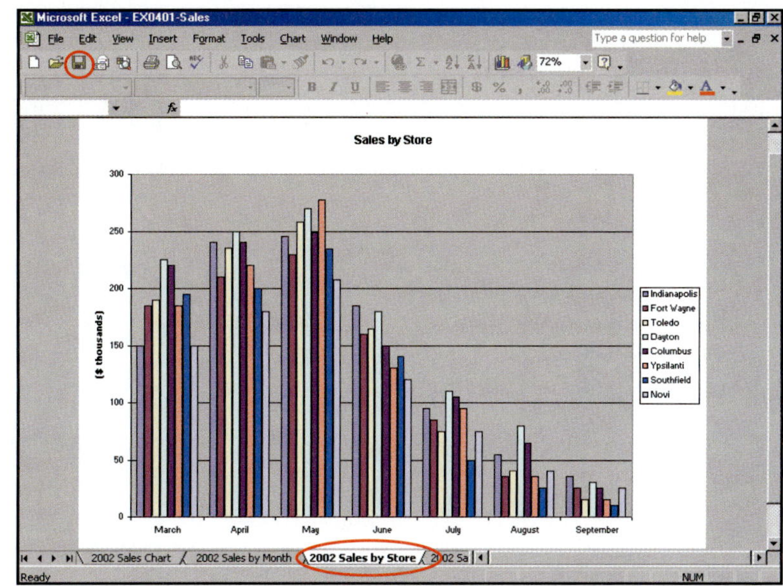


# Task 4

## EDITING THE ELEMENTS OF A CHART AND ADDING A CALLOUT

### Why would I do this?

When you create a chart in Excel, the proportions of the various elements often
need to be adjusted. For example, the text on the axes, titles, and legends on the
charts may be too small. There are many options for customizing your charts in
Excel, and they are easy to use.

In this task, you make changes to the 2002 Sales Chart to make it easier to read
and to emphasize the variation from one month to the next.

**1** Click the **2002 Sales Chart** sheet tab. Right-click on the title, **2002 Sales**.

*A shortcut menu appears.*

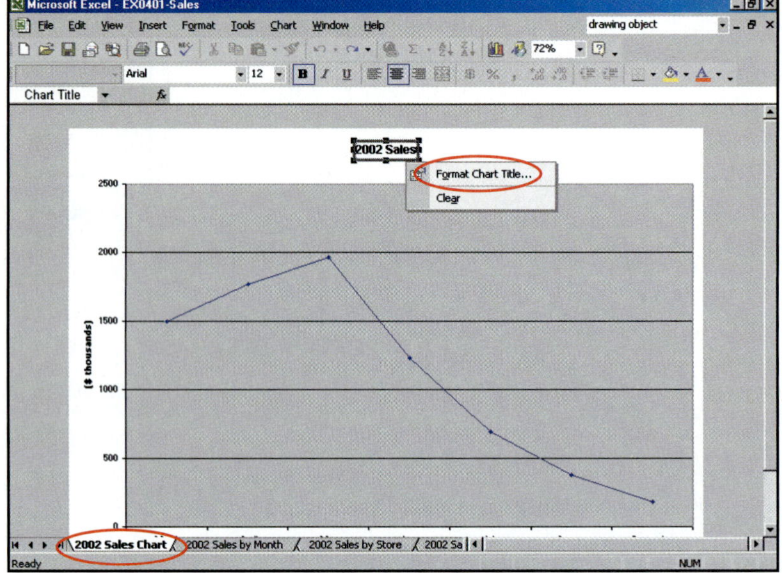

**2** Select **Format Chart Title** from the shortcut menu and click the **Font** tab in the Format Chart Title dialog box. Scroll down the list of available font sizes and select **18**.

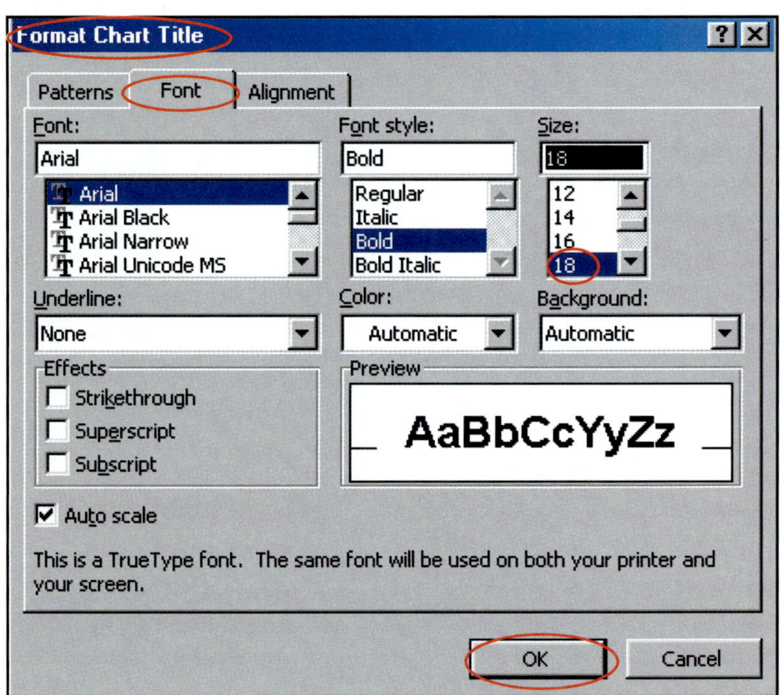

**3** Click **OK**.

*The title is now much easier to read.*

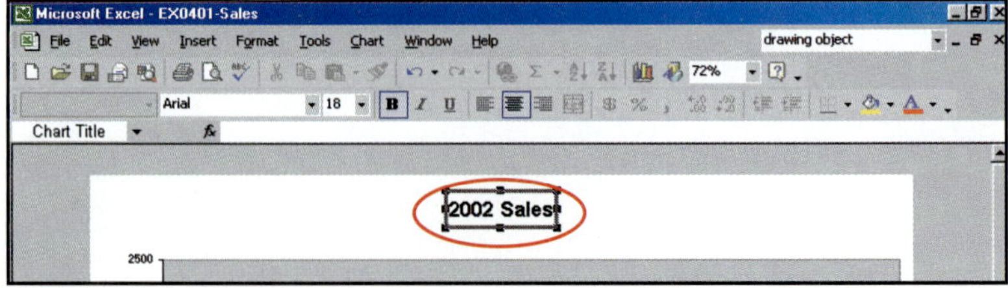

**4** Right-click on the **Value Axis Title ($ thou-sands)** and choose **Format Axis Title** from the shortcut menu. Change the size of the font to **14** points.



You can also open the Format dialog box quickly by double-clicking on any of the components of the chart. The dialog box that appears will contain all of the options available for the selected chart component.

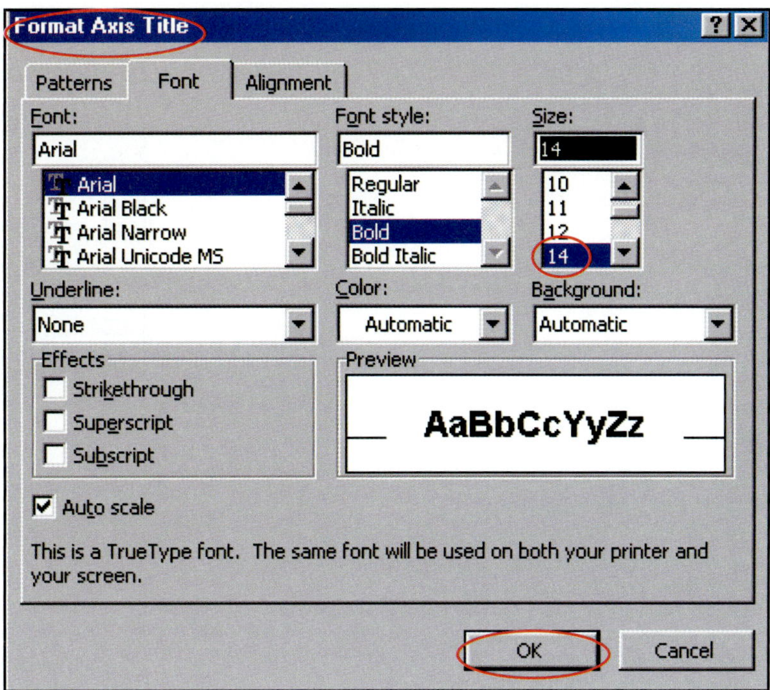

**5** Click **OK**. Use the same procedure to change the size of the category axis labels to **14** points.

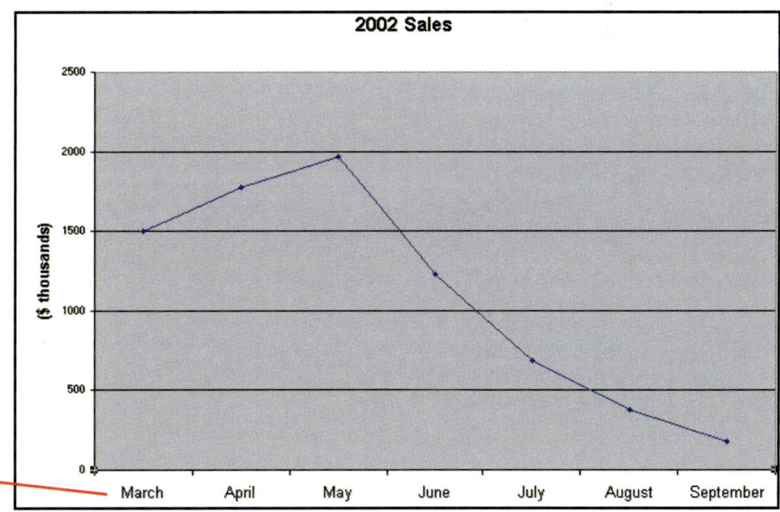

Category axis labels displayed using 14-point font

**6** Move the pointer onto the numbers on the value axis.

*The ScreenTip **Value Axis** is displayed.*

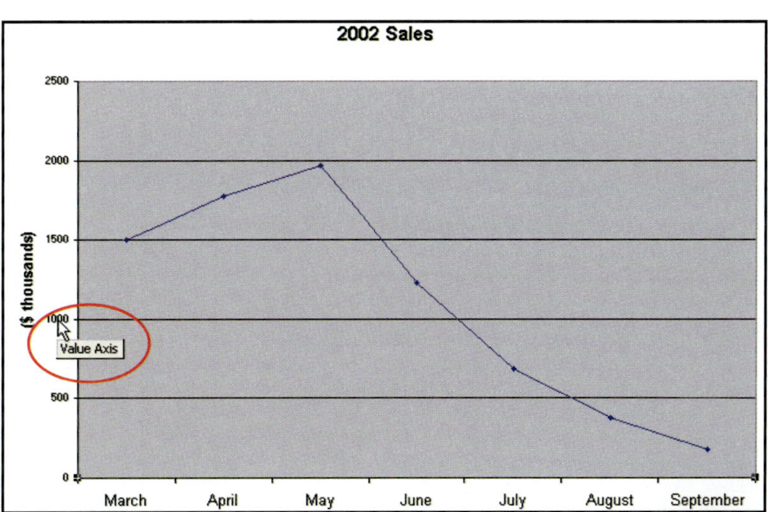

**7** Right-click and select **Format Axis** from the shortcut menu. Click the **Scale** tab. Change the **Maximum** value to **2000**.

*The highest point on the chart is below 2000.*

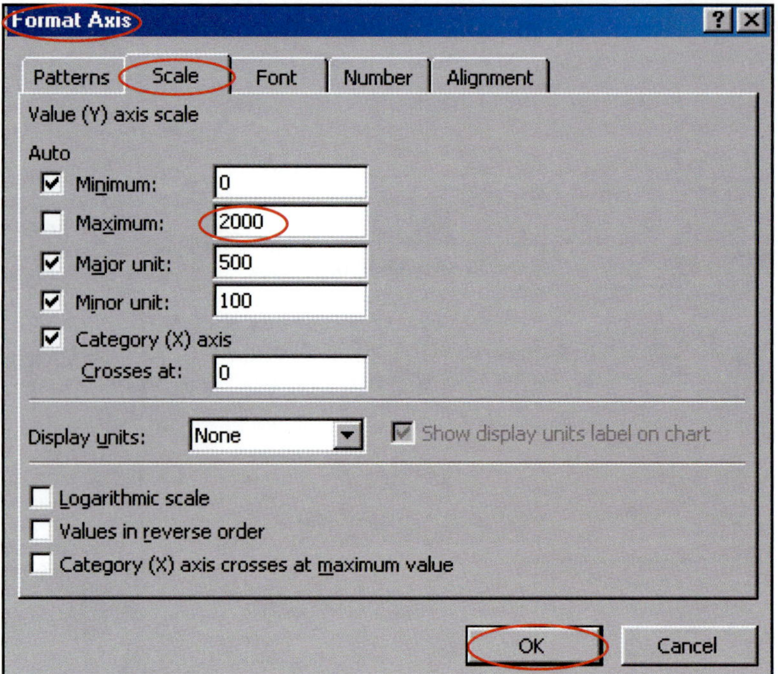

**8** Click **OK**.

*Notice the new scale emphasizes the difference in the values.*

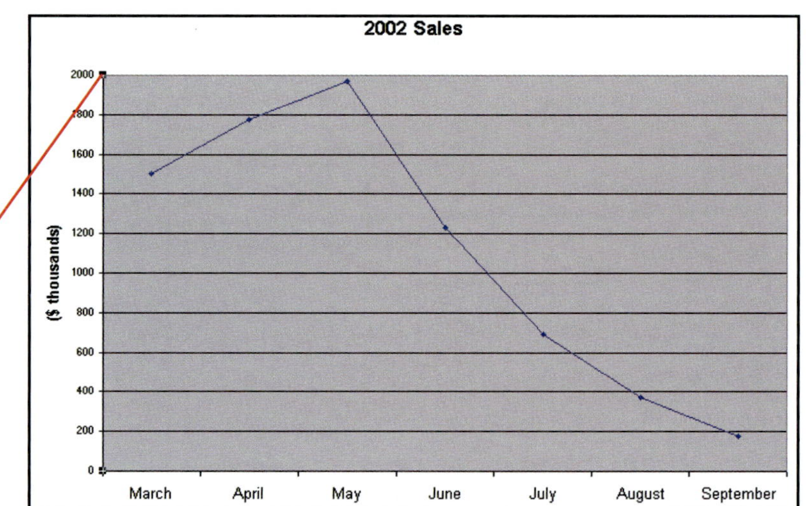



**9** Choose **Insert**, **Picture**, **AutoShapes**.

*The AutoShapes toolbar is displayed.*

Click the **Callouts** button on the **AutoShapes** toolbar.

*A menu of callout shapes is displayed.*

Point at the second callout in the first row and wait for the ScreenTip to display its name, **Rounded Rectangular Callout**.

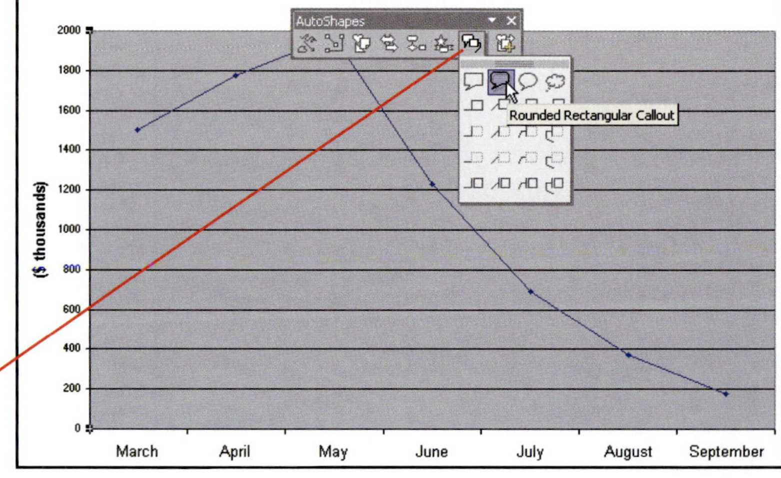

**10** Click the **Rounded Rectangular Callout**.

*The mouse pointer turns into cross hairs.*

Click and drag a rectangular area that defines the size of the callout and release the mouse button.

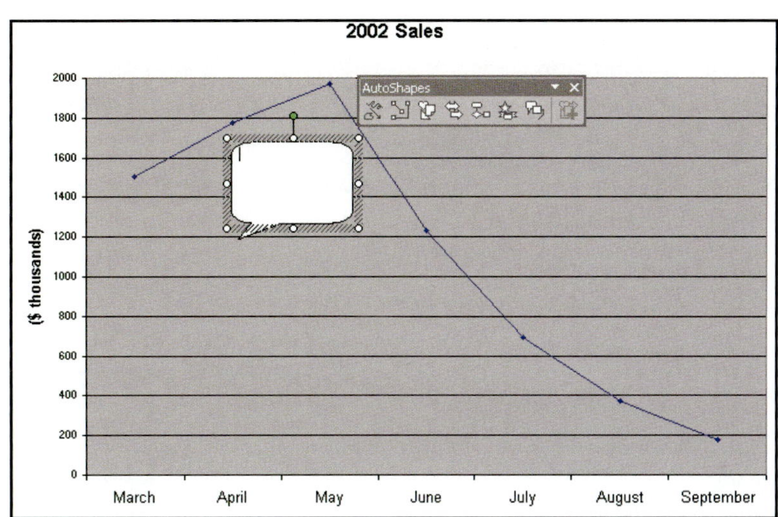

**11** Change the font size to **16**. Type **Hot spring weather increases sales**.

*The text wraps within the callout.*

Click and  drag the sizing handles so that the text fits on two lines.

*Notice the tip of the callout is a yellow diamond.*

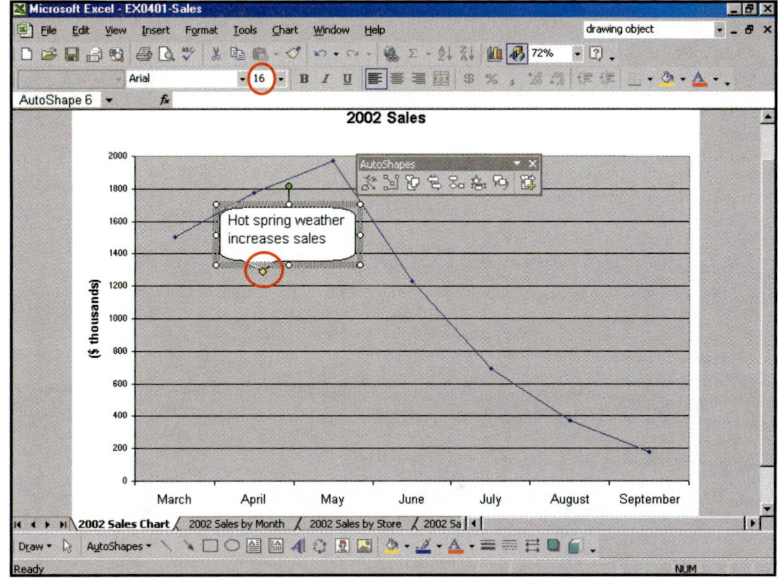


**12** Click-and-drag the yellow diamond so the callout points at the peak of the chart. Press Esc to deselect the callout.

Close the **AutoShapes** toolbar. Save the changes you have made and leave the workbook open for use in the next task.

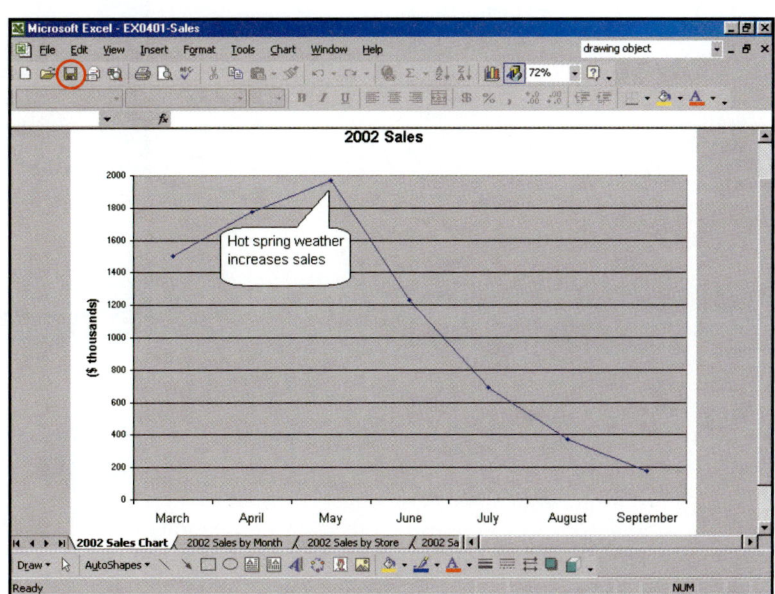

### Why would I do this?

Many spreadsheets are created for the sole purpose of generating one or more charts. These charts might be printed on paper to be included in a report or on overhead transparencies to be used as part of a presentation.

In this task, you learn how to print a chart.

**1** Click the **2002 Sales by Store** sheet tab.

*This sheet contains a column chart comparing sales by store.*

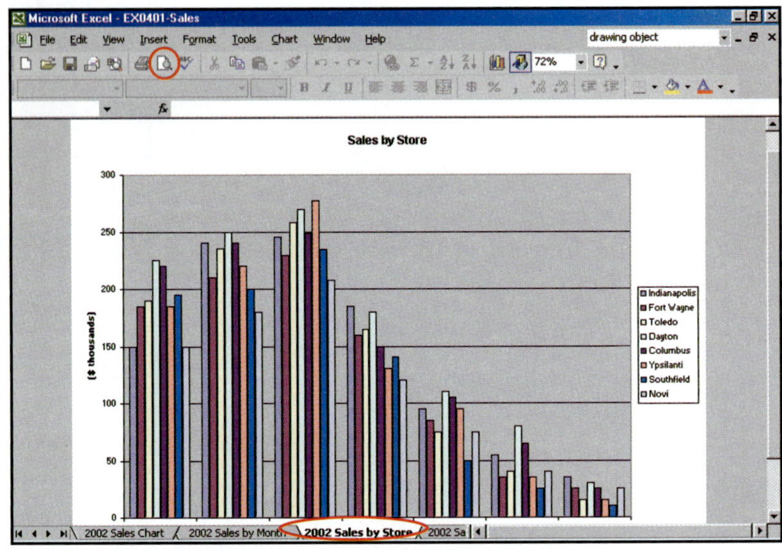

**2** Click the **Print Preview** button.

*The preview is displayed in grayscale in the figure. It may be in color if your default printer is a color printer.*

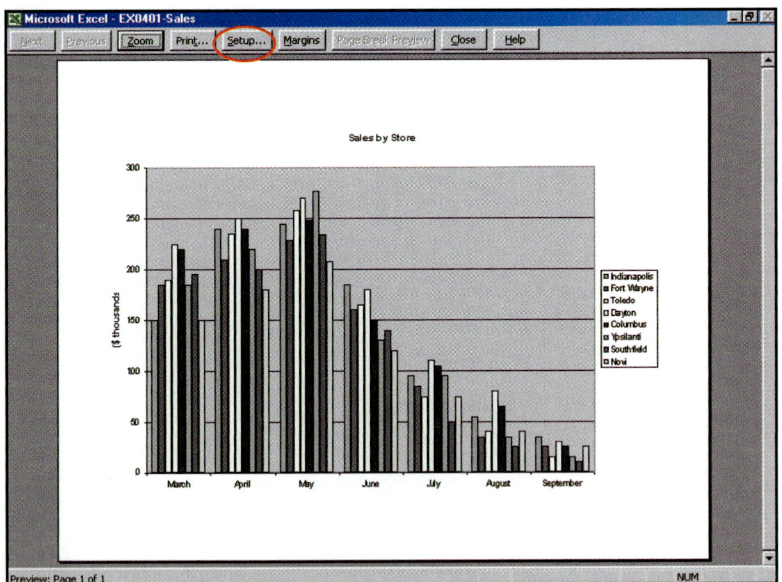

If your computer is connected to a color printer, the preview is displayed in color and the chart will print in color. Otherwise, the preview will not be shown in color.

**3** Click **Setup**. Click the **Header/Footer** tab.
Click **Custom Header** and type your name
in the **Left Section** of the header.

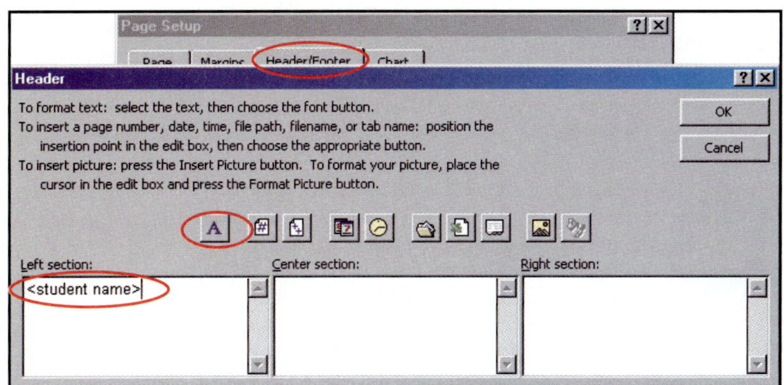


**4** Select your name. Click the button with the
large **A** on it and change the size of the font
to **14** points and the **Font style** to **Bold Italic**.

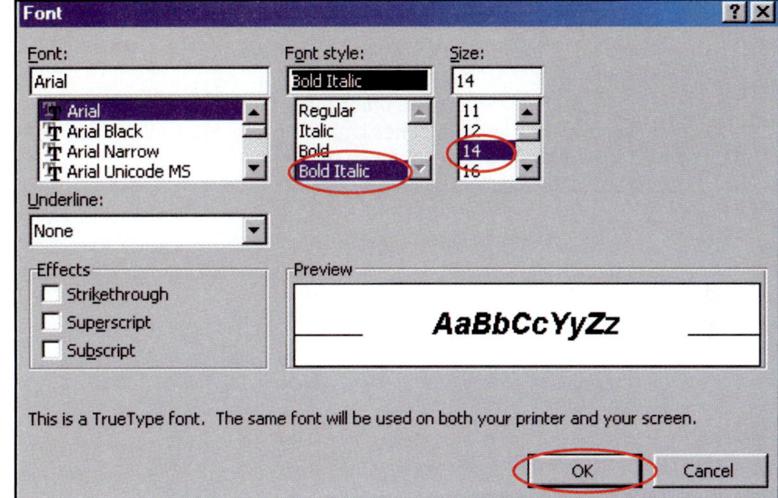


**5** Click **OK** to return to the Header dialog
box.

Click **OK** to return to the Page Setup dialog
box.

Click **OK** to return to the Print Preview.

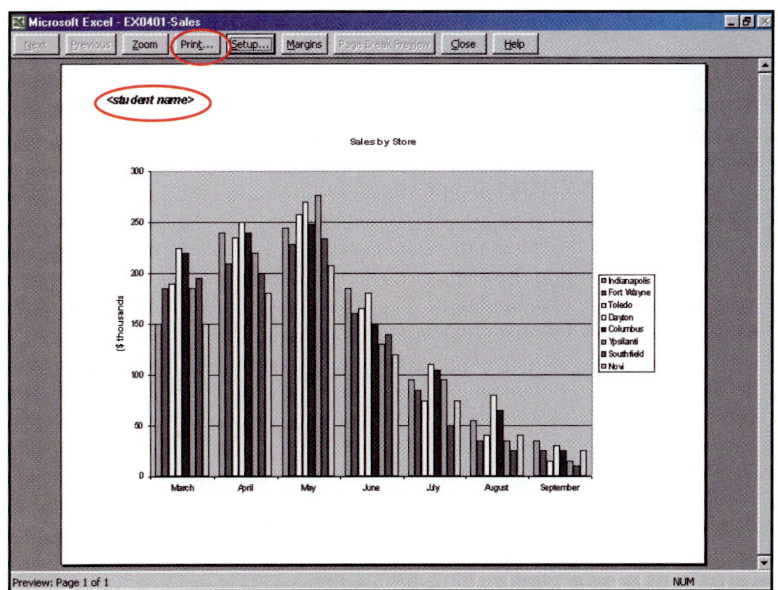

**6** Click the **Print** button to print the chart. Click **OK** in the Print dialog box. Close the workbook and save the changes.



If you plan to create transparencies from your charts, keep several issues in mind. If you plan to print the transparency directly from your printer, you must use a transparency that is designed for your type of printer. Colors on transparencies seldom look as dark or saturated as those onscreen or on paper. If your office has transparencies that work with your copier, you would be wise to print the charts on regular paper and then use the copier to transfer them to transparencies. Transparency material is expensive, and you usually have to buy an entire box. Preview your work and print samples on paper to avoid costly reprints. Also, be aware that transparencies sometimes jam when you try to feed several through the printer or copier.

The exercises that follow are designed for you to review and use what you have learned in this lesson. You also have the opportunity to practice your skills and then expand on them by applying them to new situations.

## COMPREHENSION

Comprehension exercises are designed to check your memory and understanding of the basic concepts in this lesson. You distinguish between true and false statements, identify new screen elements, and match terms with related statements. If you are uncertain of the correct answer, refer to the task number following each item (for example, T4 refers to Task 4), and review that task until you are confident you can provide a correct response.

## TRUE-FALSE

Circle either T or F.

T   F   **1.** The Chart Wizard walks you through the creation of a chart. **(T1)**

T   F   **2.** Pie charts are used to show trends. **(T2)**

T   F   **3.** If the printer you use is a color printer, the print preview will be in color. **(T5)**

T   F   **4.** When selecting data to chart, always include the row and column totals. **(T3)**

T   F   **5.** When you right-click on a chart title, it automatically sizes the font to produce a title that spans three-fourths of the printed page. **(T4)**

T   F   **6.** Column charts and bar charts are both used to illustrate data that shows comparisons. **(T3)**

## MATCHING QUESTIONS

**A.** Column chart  **D. Print Preview** button

**B.** Category (X) axis  **E.** Line chart

**C.** Value (Y) axis  **F.** Pie chart

Match the following statements to the word or phrase that is the best match from the list. Write the letter of the matching word or phrase in the space provided next to the number.

**1.** ____ A chart type used to make comparisons **(T3)**

**2.** ____ Displays chart as it will look when printed **(T5)**

**3.** ____ A chart type used to show trends over time **(T1)**

**4.** ____ The chart axis at the bottom of the chart **(T4)**

**5.** ____ The chart axis at the left side of the chart **(T4)**

**6.** ____ A chart type used to show contributions to a whole **(T2)**

# IDENTIFYING PARTS OF THE EXCEL SCREEN

Refer to the figure and identify the numbered parts of the screen. Write the letter of the correct label in the space next to the number.

1. _______________

2. _______________

3. _______________

4. _______________

5. _______________

6. _______________

7. _______________

8. _______________

9. _______________

10. _______________

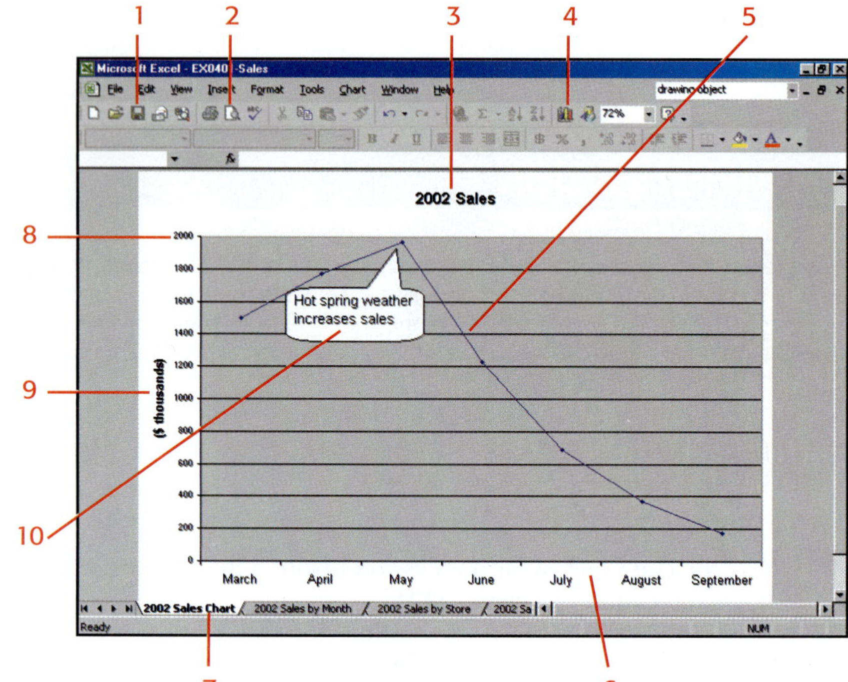


A. **Save** button  **(T1)**

B. Category axis  **(T4)**

C. **Print Preview** button  **(T6)**

D. Callout  **(T4)**

E. Value axis title  **(T4)**

F. **Chart Wizard** button  **(T1)**

G. Sheet tab  **(T2)**

H. Chart title  **(T1)**

I. Maximum scale value  **(T4)**

J. Line connecting data points  **(T1)**

Reinforcement exercises are designed to reinforce the skills you have learned by applying them to new situations. Detailed instructions are provided along with a figure, where appropriate, to illustrate the result. The reinforcement exercises that follow should be completed sequentially. Leave the file open at the end of each exercise for use in the next exercise until you are specifically directed to close it.

Open **EX0402** and save it as **EX0402-Reinforcement** on your floppy disk for use in the following exercises.

In these exercises, you examine a table of statistics showing the fatalities and injuries due to tornadoes in Michigan over a forty-year period. Charts are very useful when displaying trends, comparisons, or contributions to the whole.

## R1—Creating and Printing a Pie Chart

A pie chart may be used to show how each decade has contributed to the total number of casualties. See the following steps for more detail.

1. Select cells **A2** through **A6**. Hold down Ctrl and select cells **E2** through **E6** on the **Casualties** sheet.

2. Click the **Chart Wizard** button. In the first dialog box, choose the **Pie** chart type, and then choose the **Pie with a 3-D visual effect** chart sub-type (the middle choice on the top row).

3. In the second dialog box, choose **Columns**, if necessary.

4. In the third dialog box, change the title to **Michigan Tornado Casualties by Decade**.

5. In the fourth dialog box, choose to save the chart as a new sheet named **Pie Chart**.

6. Change the size of the font in the title and the legend to **18** points.

7. Choose **File**, **Page Setup** and add your name to the custom header on the left side using **Bold Italic**, **12**-point font. Preview and print the chart if your instructor requires it. Save your work.

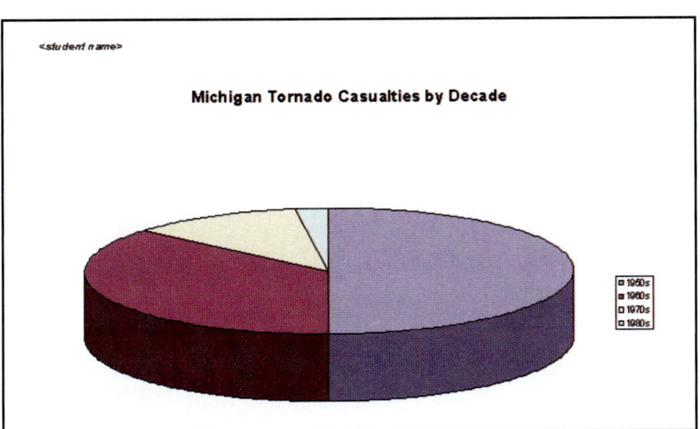


## R2—Creating and Printing a Column Chart

Column charts are useful for showing comparisons. In this exercise, you compare the number of tornadoes in each decade. See the following steps for more detail.

1. Select the **Casualties** sheet. Select cells **A2** through **B6**.

2. Click the **Chart Wizard** button. Choose the **Column** chart type, and then choose the **Clustered column with a 3-D visual effect** chart sub-type (the first choice in the second row).

3. Proceed to step 3 of the Chart Wizard and change the title to **Michigan Tornadoes by Decade**.

4. In the fourth dialog box, place the chart on a new sheet named **Column Chart**.

5. Change the size of the title font to **18** points. Select and delete the legend. Change the size of the X and Y axis labels to **12** points.

6. Choose **File**, **Page Setup** and add your name to a custom footer in the lower left. Print the chart if your instructor requires it. Save your work.

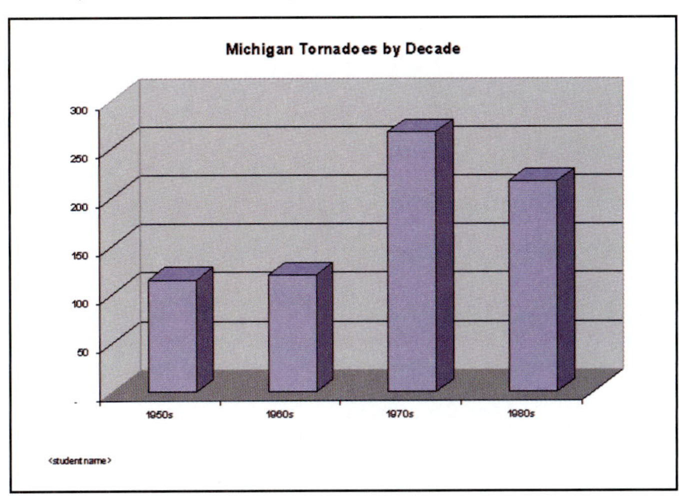

# R3—Showing a Trend with a Line Chart

Create a chart to show the trend in total casualties. See the steps below for more detail.

1. Select the **Casualties** sheet. Select cells **A2** through **A6** and cells **E2** through **E6**.

2. Click the **Chart Wizard** button and select the **Line** chart type and **3-D Line** as the sub-type.

3. Proceed with the Chart Wizard and change the chart title to **Tornado Casualties in Michigan**.

4. Save as a new sheet with the name **Line Chart**.

5. Delete the legend. Change the size of the font in the title to **18** points.

6. Add your name to the custom header in the upper left. Preview and print the chart if your instructor requires it. Save the workbook and close it.

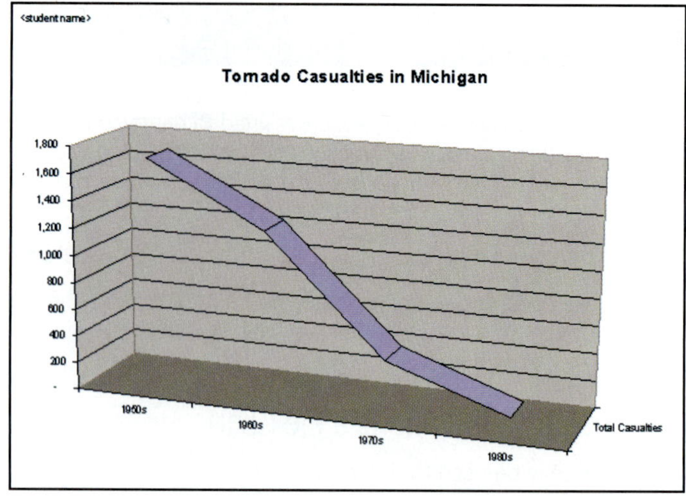

Challenge exercises are designed to test your ability to apply your skills to new situations with less-detailed instructions. These exercises also challenge you to expand your repertoire of skills by using commands that are similar to those you have already learned. The desired outcome is clearly defined, but you have more freedom to choose the steps needed to achieve the required result.

Challenge exercises C1 through C4 use the workbook **EX0403-Challenge**. The exercises are related but may be done individually. Open **EX0403** from the **Student** folder and save it as **EX0403-Challenge**.

In these Challenge exercises, you work with data concerning the consumption of energy compared to gross national product (GNP) for sixteen countries around the world. You will use Excel's charting capability to determine if the amount of energy that a person uses is proportional to the amount of goods they produce. In other words, if a person in an affluent country consumes ten times as much energy as a person in a poor country, do they produce ten times as much? If the amount of goods produced is directly proportional to the energy consumed, a line chart of the data should be a fairly straight line.

In these exercises, you examine this data to see if such a relationship exists, using some of the advanced Excel charting tools.

## C1—Placing a Chart on the Same Sheet as the Data

If a chart is small, it may be placed on the same sheet as the rest of the data. In this example, you chart the energy used per person by country, and then save it on the same sheet as the data. This makes it easier to compare the chart with the data.

*Goal:* Create a column chart that displays the country and the energy used per capita and place it on Sheet1 with the data. Adjust the font size of the category labels so they all display.

Use the following guidelines:

1. Select **Sheet1**. Select the data (and headings) in the **Country** and **Energy** columns.

2. Create a column chart and save it as an object in **Sheet1**. Accept all defaults, including the chart title.

3. Delete the legend.

4. Deselect the chart and change the **Zoom** to **50%** so you can see more of the page. Click-and-drag the chart to a place below the data and drag one of its handles to stretch the chart so that it spans columns **A** through **H**.

5. Change the font of the Category (X) axis labels to **8** point. Change the **Zoom** back to **100%**. All the country names should display. If they do not, widen the chart further.

6. Change **Page Setup** to **Landscape** orientation. Work with the **Print Preview** option to make sure the chart will fit on one page and all the country names will print (see the figure).

7. Add your name to the custom header. Print the page with the chart.

8. Save the workbook. Leave the workbook open for use in the next exercise.

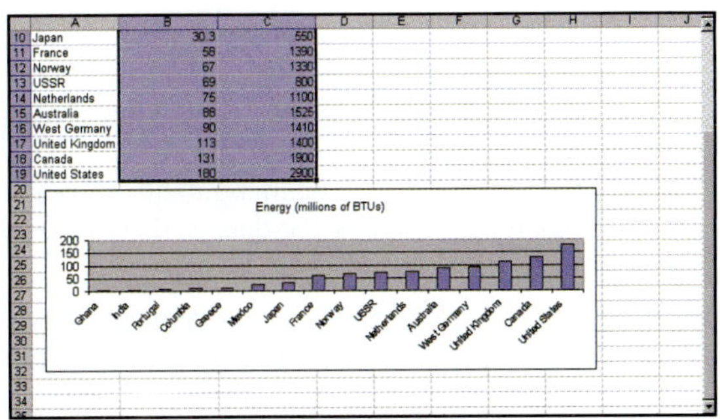

## C2—Charting Related Data Using the X-Y Chart

If you are charting two columns of numbers where the second column is dependent on (or related to) the first column, you should use an X-Y chart, sometimes called a scatter chart. The data points are scattered on the chart to indicate each intersection of the X and Y coordinates, and the intervals on the category (X) axis are forced to be equal.

When plotting real-life data, you seldom get an exact relationship. You look to see if the points represent a general trend, such as a straight line or a curve. In our example, the energy used per person is displayed on the category (X) axis and the GNP per person is displayed on the value (Y) axis.

*Goal:* Represent the per capita Gross National Product as it relates to the amount of energy used per person.

Use the following guidelines:

1. Select **Sheet1**. Select the **Energy** and **GNP** columns (cells **B3** through **C19**). Use the Chart Wizard and create an X-Y scatter chart.

2. Enter **GNP per Energy Used** as the chart title, **Millions of BTUs** for the X axis title, and **Dollars** for the Y axis title.

3. Delete the legend.

4. Save the chart on its own sheet named **My X-Y chart.**

5. Add your name to the custom header and print the chart if your instructor requires it.

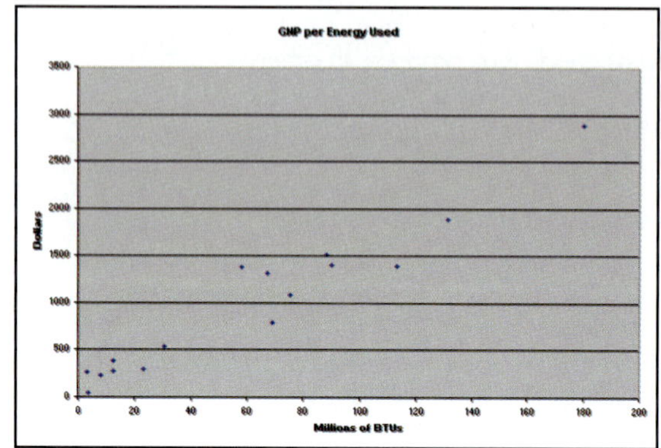

## C3—Adding Data Labels to an X-Y Chart

Excel makes it easier to determine the exact values of a point on a data chart by displaying the data value next to the data point.

You can add data labels to a chart using the shortcut menu that displays when you right-click on a data point on the chart.

*Goal:* Use the shortcut menu to display the Y-axis value next to each data point on an X-Y chart.

1. Select the **XY Chart** sheet. It is similar to the chart that you may have created if you did the previous Challenge exercise. Right-click on one of the chart's data points.

2. Choose **Format Data Series** from the shortcut menu. Choose **Data Labels** and select labels for both the **X Value** and the **Y Value**.

3. Add your name to the custom header and print the chart. Leave the workbook open.

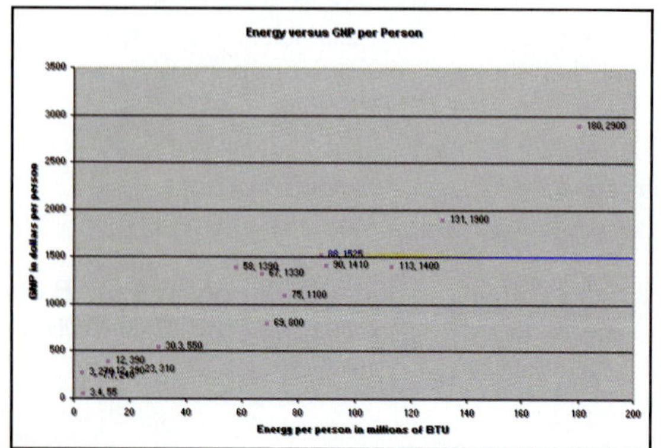

## C4—Adding a Trend Line to an X-Y Chart

If there is a linear relationship between the values displayed on the category (X) axis and those on the Y-axis of an X-Y chart, the data points will be close to a straight line. Excel can calculate the straight line that is the best fit to the data points and add it to the chart.

The method of determining the formula for the best fitting straight line is called a linear regression analysis. The degree of fit is represented by the $R^2$ value. A perfect fit would have an $R^2$ value equal to 1. If the $R^2$ value is close to 1, you may use the equation of the straight line to estimate new values of GNP if you know the energy used per person.

*Goal:* Add the trend line to the XY chart that is the best fit to the data. Use the $R^2$ value to evaluate the relationship between the X values and the Y values. Display an equation of the relationship.

1. Select the **XY chart** sheet. Right-click on one of the data points and choose **Add Trendline**.

2. Choose the **Linear** trend line. Click the **Options** tab and choose to display the R-squared value and the equation on the chart.

3. Locate the R-squared value and the equation. Drag them to the upper-left portion of the chart. Change the font to **14** points.

4. Add your name to the custom header and print the chart. Save and close the workbook.

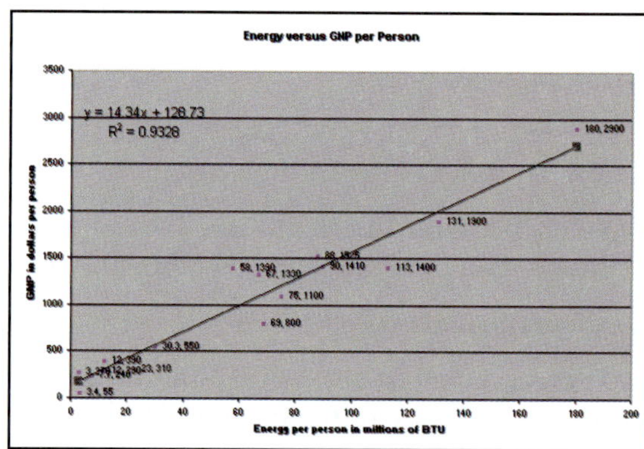

## C5—Charting Problem Data

The Chart Wizard makes assumptions that are often helpful when setting up charts. If a table of data has an unexpected value in it, the wizard can produce unusable results unless you know how to change some of the settings.

The data in this exercise represents the number of passengers that rode on commercial airlines from 1981 to 1998. The data for one of the years is missing, and the text, **Not Available**, occupies that cell. The wizard does not handle this well.

*Goal:* Manually adjust the settings used in the Chart Wizard to display a chart where one of the pieces of data is missing.

1. Open **EX0404** from the **Student** folder and save it as **EX0404-Challenge**.

2. Select cells **A3** through **B21**. Click the **Chart Wizard** button. Choose the **Column** chart type and the **Clustered Column** sub-type, if necessary, and then go to the next step.

The sample chart in this step indicates that there is a problem. **Columns** is selected, as it should be; the problem is that the wizard guessed incorrectly when it assigned the cells to their respective roles in the chart.

3. Click the **Series** tab. The years should be used as Category (X) labels, but they are shown in the **Series** box as data to be charted. Select the series that starts with **Year** and click **Remove**.

4. Click the **Collapse Dialog Box** button next to the **Category (X) axis labels** box. Select cells **A4** through **A21**. Click the **Expand Dialog Box** button. This helps but there is still a problem. The label and legend are wrong and there should be eighteen years of data displayed, but there are only eleven.

5. Click the **Collapse Dialog Box** button next to the **Name** box. Select cell **B3**. Click the **Expand Dialog Box** button. This fixes the title and legend.

6. Click the **Collapse Dialog Box** button next to the **Values** box. Select cells **B4** through **B21**. Click the **Expand Dialog Box** button. All of the years display properly with a gap for 1987, when there was no data (see figure).

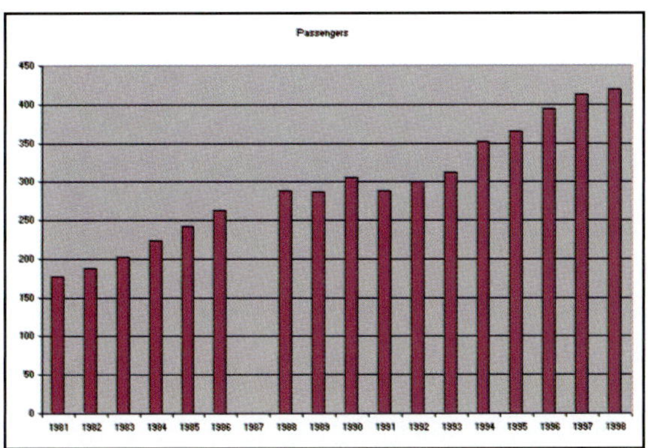

7. Go to step 3 of the wizard. Click the **Legend** tab and deselect **Show legend**.

8. Go to step 4 of the wizard. Choose **As new sheet** and enter **Passengers** as the sheet name.

9. Add your name to a custom header. Save the workbook and close it.

## C6—Exploding, Rotating, and Annotating a Chart

Sometimes you want to make a point dramatically. An attractive chart that isolates and identifies the key elements is very helpful.

Excel has several advanced charting options to help create more dramatic charts. In this exercise, you learn to use a pie chart that separates the individual slices. You will rotate the chart to bring the element of most interest to the front, and then add a callout to explain its significance.

*Goal*: Make an exploded pie chart of the sources of electric energy and identify the amount of new capacity we would need from sources that do not emit carbon dioxide if we are to reduce our carbon dioxide output to 1990 levels from electricity generation.

1. Open **EX0405** from the Student folder and save it as **EX0405-Challenge**.

2. Select cells **A1** to **E2**. Click the **Chart Wizard** button. Click the **Custom Types** tab, scroll down, and choose the **Pie Explosion**.

3. Change the chart title to **Electric Energy in the United States**.

4. Place the chart on a new sheet named **Electricity**.

5. Choose **Chart**, **3-D View**. Choose a rotation of **180** to bring the **New** slice to the front.

6. Choose **Insert**, **Picture**, **AutoShapes** from the menu bar. Click the **Callouts** button and choose the **Rounded Rectangular Callout**. Drag the outline of the callout below and to the right of the **New** slice.

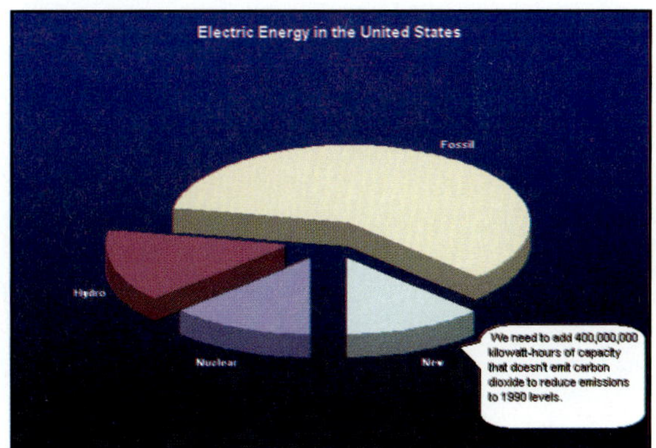


7. Change the font size to **12** and type **We need to add 400,000,000 kilowatt-hours of capacity that doesn't emit carbon dioxide.**

8. Adjust the size of the callout if necessary and move the yellow diamond to point at the **New** slice.

9. Change the font color of the title to **white** and its font size to **16**. Close the **AutoShapes** toolbar.

10. Add your name to the custom header. Save your work and print the chart. Close the workbook.

When you are trying to determine where the household money is going or when you are discussing this topic with other members of the household, it is useful to be able to display the situation with a chart.

Set up a worksheet that shows how much of the household's income is spent by category. Create a pie chart that displays how each expenditure compares to the other. The following criteria will be used for grading:

1. Demonstration of the use of the charting skills taught in this lesson.

2. Demonstration of a pie chart to display the household expenses.

Some examples of features that students have learned to use in previous classes to enhance their personal household expenses chart are listed below:

- Use of a legend or labels to identify slices of the pie chart

- Labels of adequate size for easy reading

- Use of data labels to place dollar amounts or percentages next to each slice

- 3-D effects when appropriate

- Identification of amounts as weekly, monthly, or yearly

- Saved as its own sheet

- Name in the header or footer

3. Identify yourself. Place your name in the footer so that it is visible in **Print Preview**.

4. To complete the project:

- Save your file on your own disk. Name it **EX0405-Expenses**.

- Check with your instructor to determine if the project should be submitted in electronic or printed form. If necessary, print out a copy of the worksheet to hand in.

# Lesson 5

## Integrating Excel with Word and the Internet

Task 1    Deleting, Inserting, Renaming, and Moving Sheets
Task 2    Designing a Summary Sheet
Task 3    Linking the Results of Several Sheets to a Summary Sheet
Task 4    Pasting a Worksheet into a Word Document
Task 5    Saving a Worksheet as a Web Page
Task 6    Previewing the Web Page

### INTRODUCTION

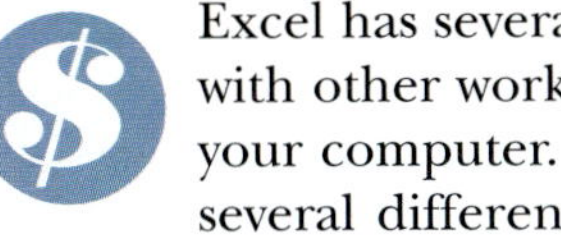

Excel has several powerful tools that you can use to connect a worksheet with other worksheets or to connect a worksheet to other documents on your computer. You can create summary sheets to compare the totals of several different sheets and paste the results into a Word document to illustrate the message in that document.

You can share the worksheet with a wider audience by saving it as a Web page that can be loaded on a Web server.

In this lesson, you learn how to link the totals from individual product sheets to a summary sheet. You also learn how to paste this worksheet into a letter and save it as a Web page.

Jack Armstrong, president of Armstrong Pool, Spa, and Sauna Company, decided to share the sales results from the previous year with his employees. He plans to send out a letter that shows a summary of quarterly sales figures and to provide these figures on an interactive web page.

# VISUAL SUMMARY

By the time you have completed this lesson, you will have created a year-end summary worksheet and pasted it into a document. You will also have a web page that could be uploaded to a server and shared on the Internet. The worksheet, Word document, and web page will look like this:

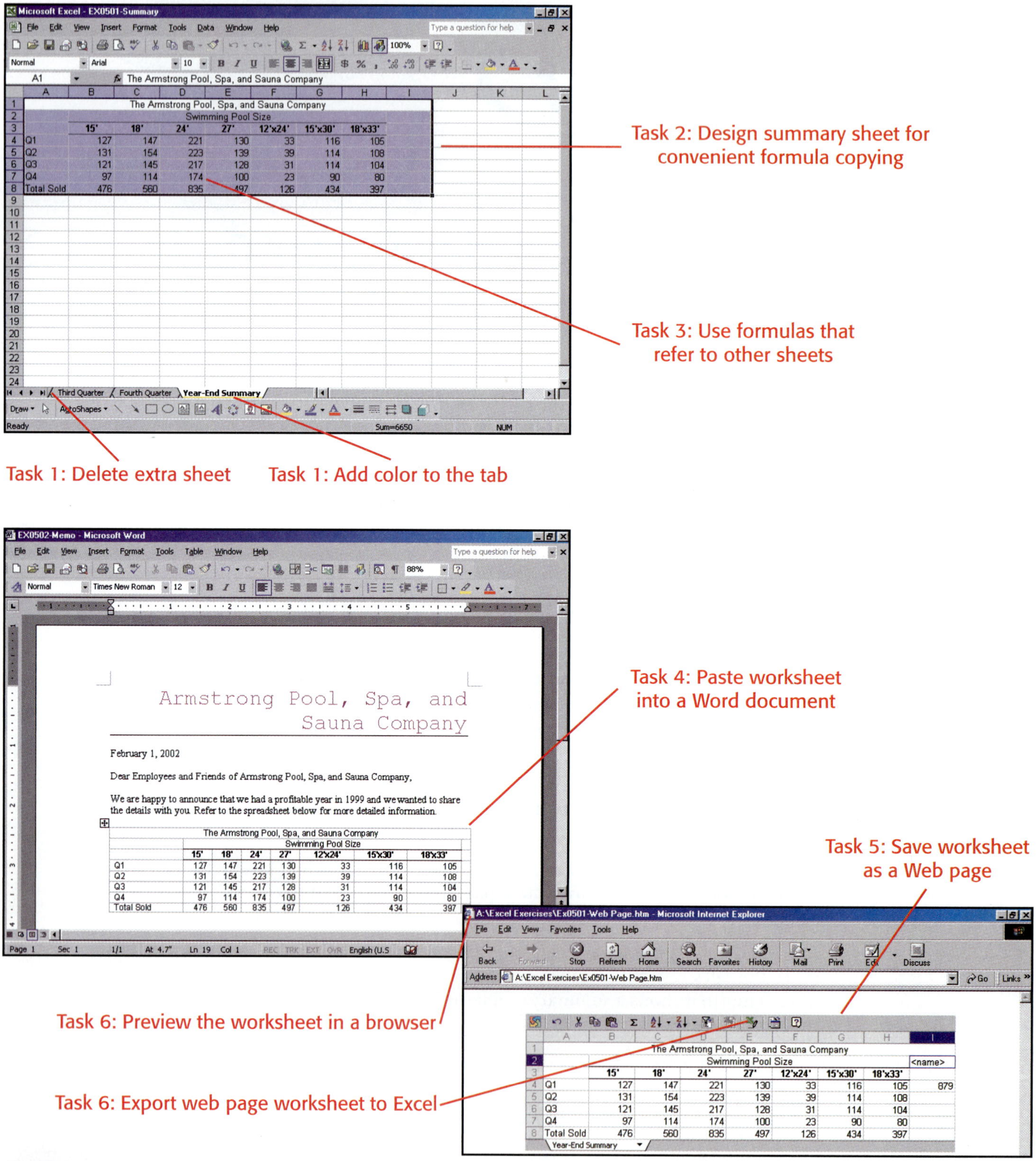

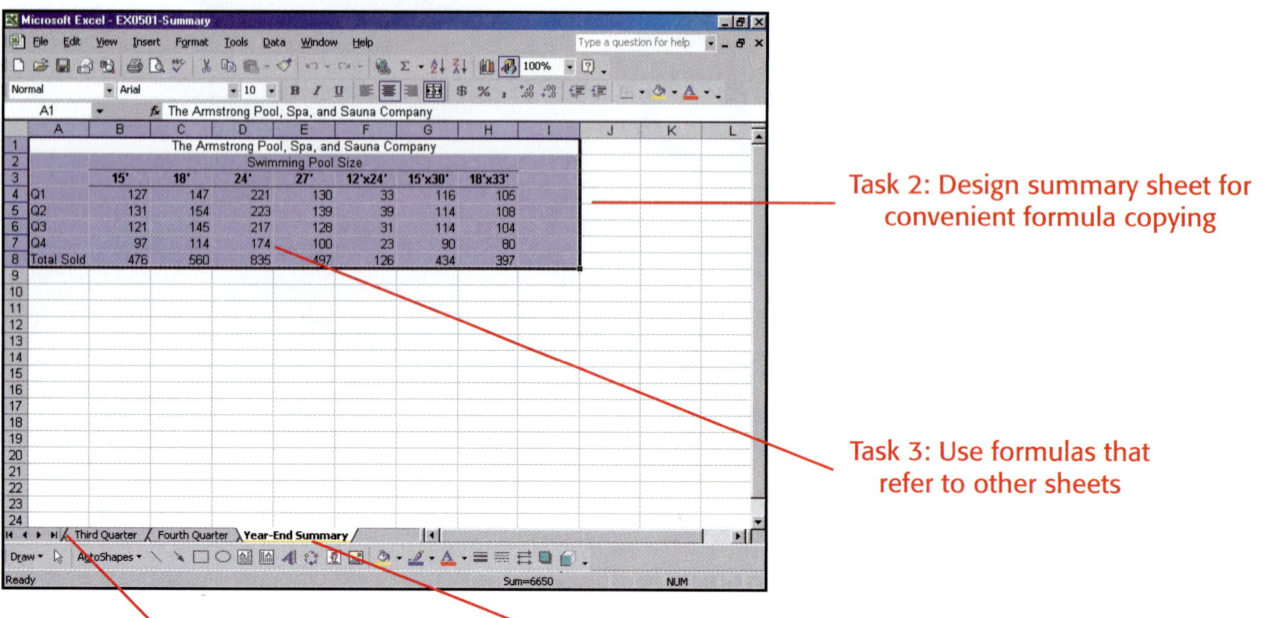

# Task 1
## DELETING, INSERTING, RENAMING, AND MOVING SHEETS

### Why would I do this?

It may make sense to divide your data into several separate sheets when you are working with it. This makes the data easier to manage and to chart. However, you often need to bring the results of these sheets together in one place so that they can be compared and summarized. When you are ready to summarize your work, you may need to add a worksheet and place it into your workbook in a particular location.

In this task, you delete a sheet, add a new sheet to use as a year-end summary sheet, give it a name, and move the sheet to a new position in the sequence of worksheets.

**1** Open **EX0501** from the **Student** folder. Save it as **EX0501-Summary** on your disk.

*The new title appears in the title bar.*

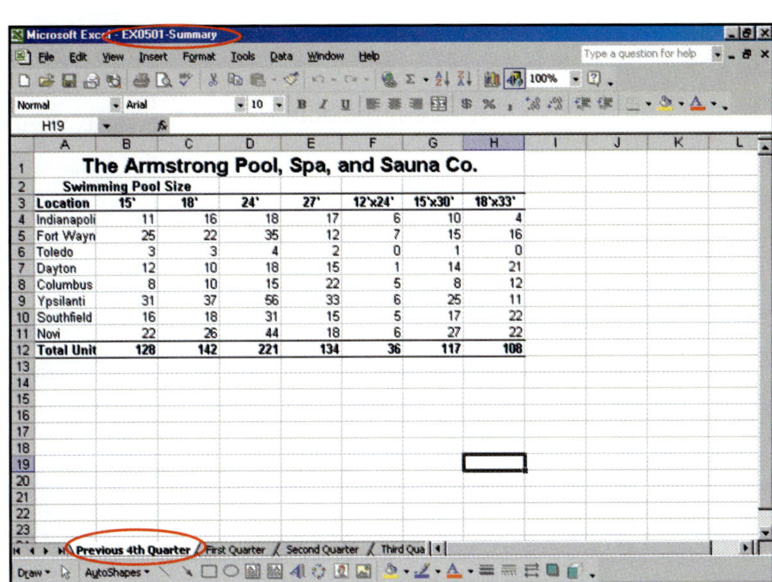

**2** Right-click on the **Previous 4th Quarter** sheet tab and choose **Delete** from the short-cut menu. Click the **Delete** button to confirm the deletion.

*The sheet is deleted from the workbook.*

Choose **Insert**, **Worksheet**.

*A blank worksheet is added. It is called Sheet1.*

Double-click the **Sheet1** tab to select it and type **Year-End Summary**. Press ⏎Enter.

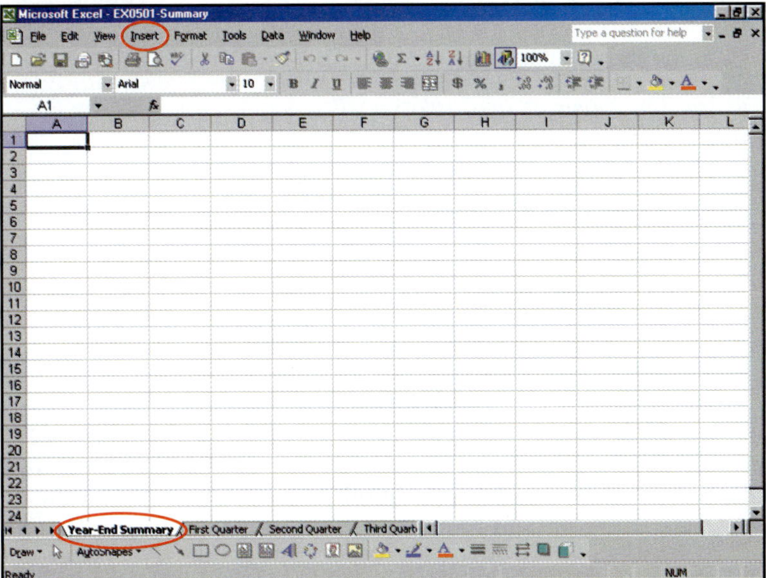

**3** Move the pointer onto the new tab. Click-and-drag the tab to the right to make this sheet the last one.

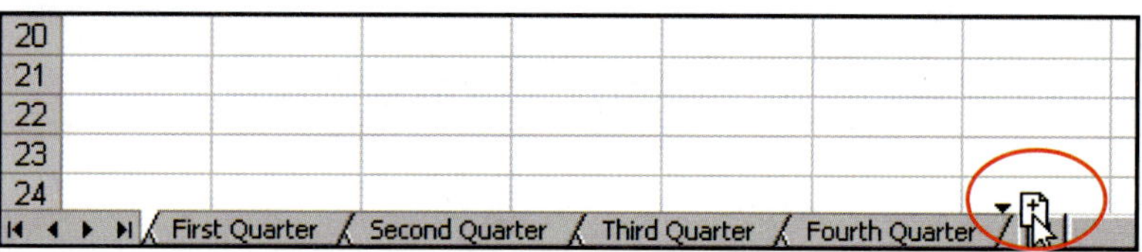

*Notice that there is a small arrow indicating where the sheet will be placed.*

**4** Release the mouse button.

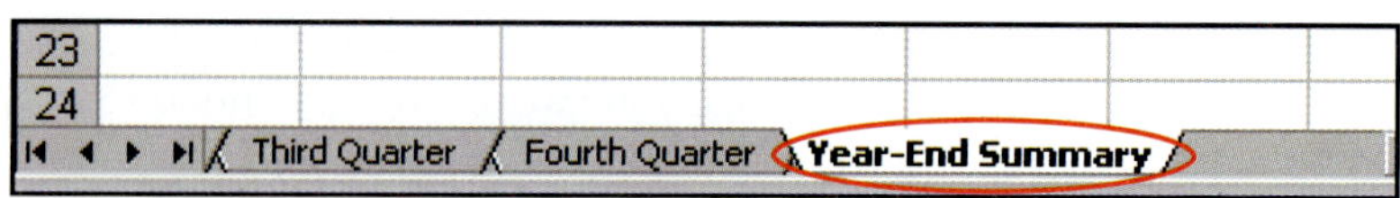

*The sheet is placed last.*

**5** Right-click on the **Year-End Summary** tab and choose **Tab Color** from the shortcut menu

*The Format Tab Color dialog box is displayed.*

Click the **Yellow** color box in the bottom row.

**6** Click **OK**.

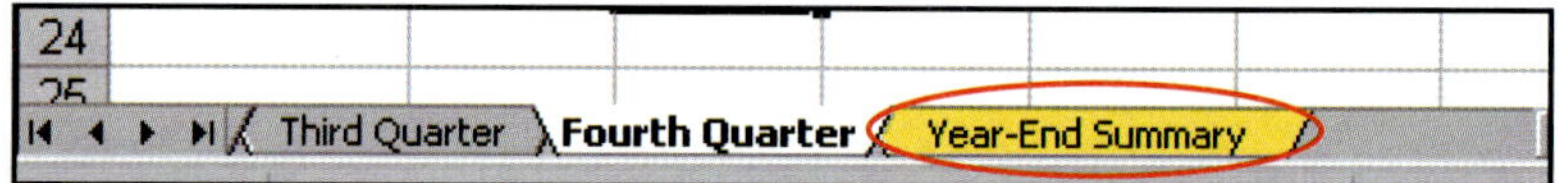

*A thin yellow line is displayed beneath the text.*

Click the **Fourth Quarter** tab.

*The Year-End Summary tab displays a yellow background color.*

# Task 2

## DESIGNING A SUMMARY SHEET

### Why would I do this?

The summary sheet consolidates the data from several other sheets. Because this is summary information that may be communicated to others, you want to organize it so that it is easy to chart. To create charts the data must be arranged into adjacent cells in rows or columns. Therefore it is important that the design of the worksheet allows for easy comparison charting.

In this task, you set up labels for a sheet that summarizes the sales from each of the quarters represented by the other four sheets.

**1** Click the **Year-End Summary** tab. Select cell **A1** and type **The Armstrong Pool, Spa, and Sauna Company**. Press ↵Enter.

Select cells **A1** through **I1.** Click the **Merge and Center** button.

**2** Select cell **B2.** Type **Swimming Pool Size**. Press ↵Enter.

Select cells **B2** through **H2.** Click the **Merge and Center** button.

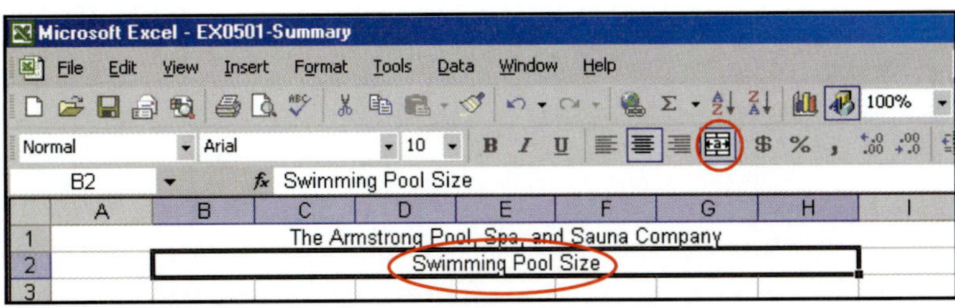

**3** Click the **Fourth Quarter** sheet tab and select cells **B3** through **H3.**

Click the **Copy** button.

*Cells B3 through H3 have a marquee around them to show that they have been copied.*

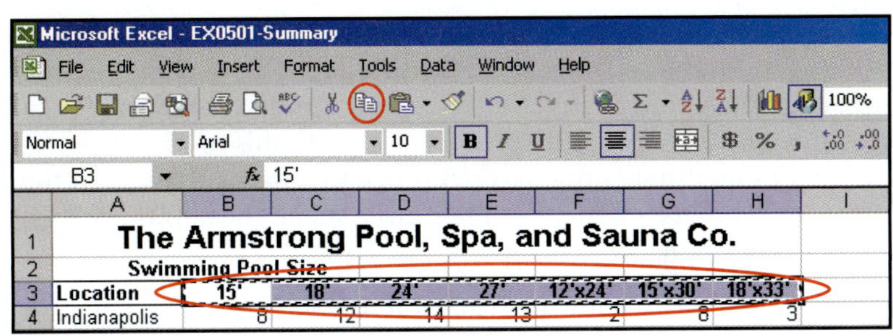

**4** Click the **Year-End Summary** sheet tab and select cell **B3.**

Click the **Paste** button.

*The column headings from the Fourth Quarter sheet are pasted into these cells.*

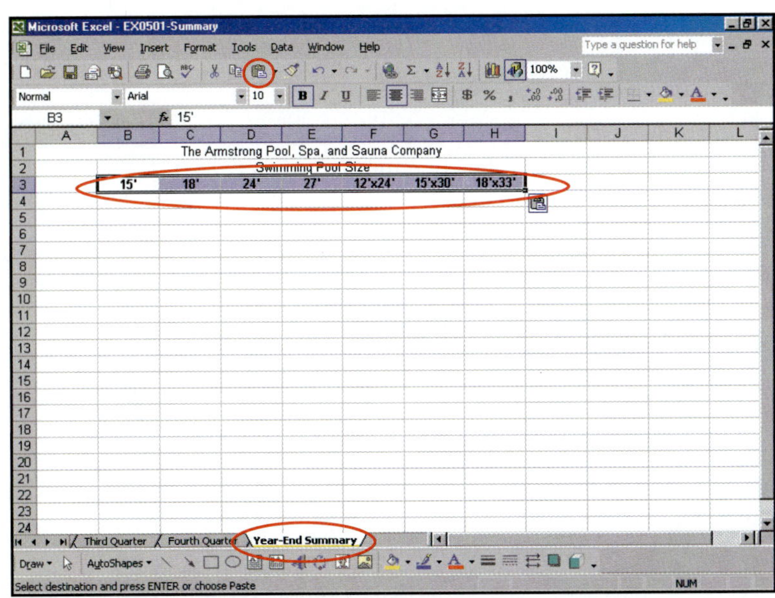

**5** Select cell **A4**, type **Q1**, and press ↵Enter.

IN DEPTH

When labeling columns or rows that will be charted at a later time, use brief labels that will not take up too much space on the chart, such as the Q1 label.

**6** Select cell **A4**. Drag the fill handle down from cell **A4** to **A7** and release the mouse button.

*The cells fill with a series from Q1 through Q4.*

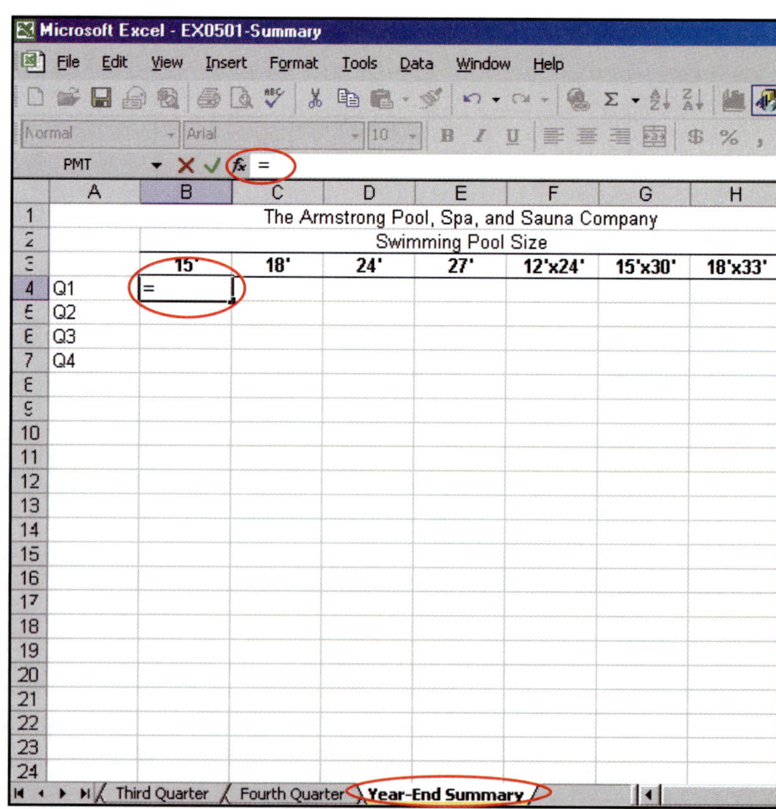


# Task 3

## LINKING THE RESULTS OF SEVERAL SHEETS TO A SUMMARY SHEET

### Why would I do this?

When you copy and paste information from one sheet to another, no link is established between the data in the two worksheets. To be able to change data in one sheet and have that change reflected in a summary worksheet, you need to create a connection between the worksheets. You do this by entering a formula in the summary sheet that contains a reference to a particular cell in the source worksheet. If you make changes in the source sheet, the summary sheet will reflect the change automatically.

For example, if you copy the data from the First through Fourth Quarter sheets and paste it into your Year-End Summary sheet, the values do not change in the Year-End Summary whenever you update the data in the quarterly report sheets. However, if you place a formula in a cell in the Year-End Summary sheet, you can make it refer to specific cells in the quarterly worksheet and it will update itself automatically.

In this task, you place formulas in the summary sheet that refer to the totals by category in each of the quarterly sales sheets.

**1** Make sure that the **Year-End Summary** sheet is selected and select cell **B4**.

Type **=** to indicate that the following entry is a formula.

**IN DEPTH**

After the = sign, you could type the complete formula in cell B4 if you knew the cell references you wanted to select. In this case, as you will see, it is easier to use your mouse to locate the cell references because the cells to which you refer are on another sheet.

**2** Click the leftmost **Tab Scrolling** button to find the **First Quarter** sheet tab.

Click the **First Quarter** tab.

*Notice that the name of the sheet is written in the Formula bar between single quotation marks, followed by an exclamation mark.*

Tab scrolling buttons

**3** Click cell **B12**.

*Notice that the formula in the Formula bar now refers to this sheet and cell.*

QUICK TIP

You could have typed the formula shown in B12 into cell B4 in step 2 if you knew the cell reference was B12 and how to state the formula.

**4** Click the **Enter** button on the Formula bar.

*The screen automatically returns to the Year-End Summary sheet, and the value from cell B12 on the First Quarter sheet is displayed in cell B4 where you placed the formula.*

**5** Drag the fill handle from cell **B4** to **H4** and release the mouse button.

*The cells from C4 through H4 are filled with relative formulas that refer to cells C12 through H12 on the First Quarter sheet.*

**6** Select cell **B5** and type **=**. (Do not type the period shown at the end of the previous sentence, just the equals sign.) Switch to the **Second Quarter** sheet, select cell **B12**, and click the **Enter** button.

Drag the fill handle from cell **B5** to **H5** and release the mouse button.

*The values from the second quarter are filled in.*

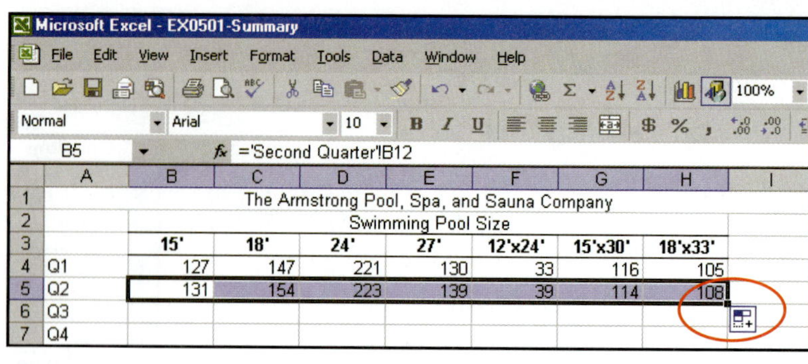

**7** Repeat this process in rows **6** and **7** to display the values from the **Third Quarter** and **Fourth Quarter** sheets.

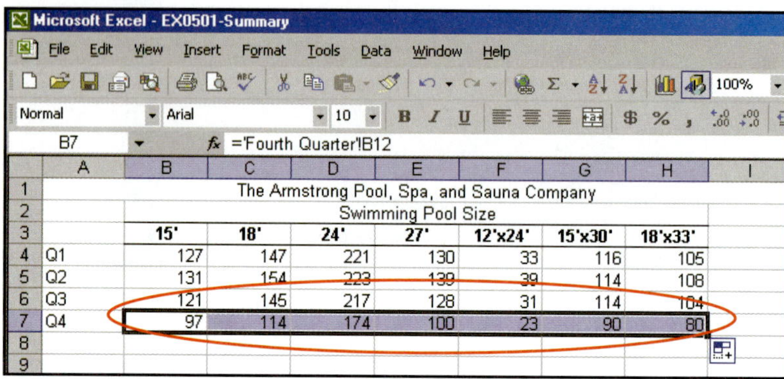

**8** Select cell **A8.** Type **Total Sold** and press Tab.

Select cells **B4** through **H8**.

*The selected area includes the columns to be totaled and the empty cells at the bottom of each column.*

Include the empty cells in row 8 →

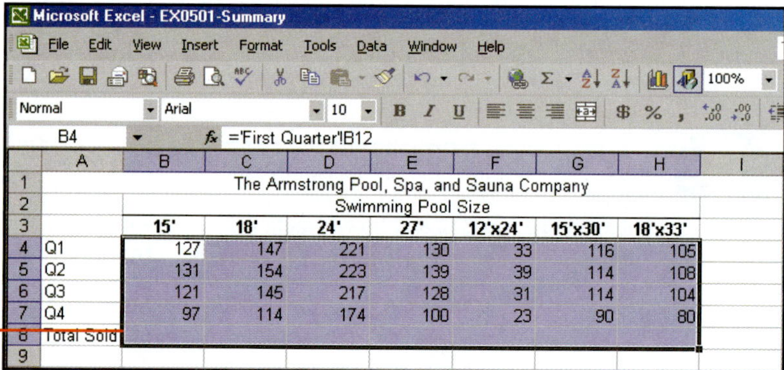

**9** Click the **AutoSum** button.

*Each column is totaled.*

Click the **Save** button.

*You may leave the workbook open for use in the next task.*

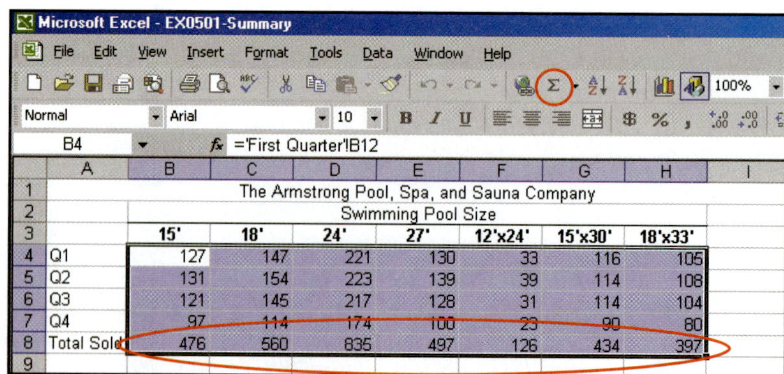

# Task 4
## PASTING A WORKSHEET INTO A WORD DOCUMENT

### Why would I do this?

A worksheet can be used to calculate summary information, but it usually needs further explanation. If you paste the worksheet into a Word document, you can use the document to explain the accompanying numbers.

In this task, you paste the Year-End Summary worksheet into a memo document.

**1** Launch Word and open the document **EX0502** from the **Student** folder. Save the file on your disk as **EX0502-Memo**.

*The letter has a space for the table.*

Choose **View**, **Print Layout**, if necessary, to select this view of the document.

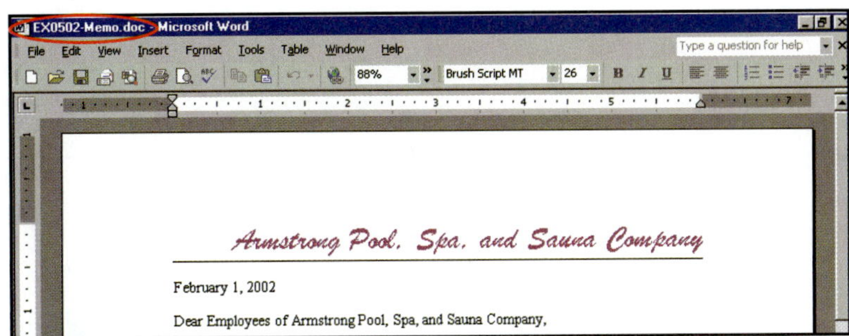

IN DEPTH

It is usually a good idea to view a document in the Print Layout view to see how inserted objects will really look when the document is printed.

**2** Use the taskbar to switch to the **EX0501-Summary** workbook in Excel.

Select the **Year-End Summary** worksheet if necessary.

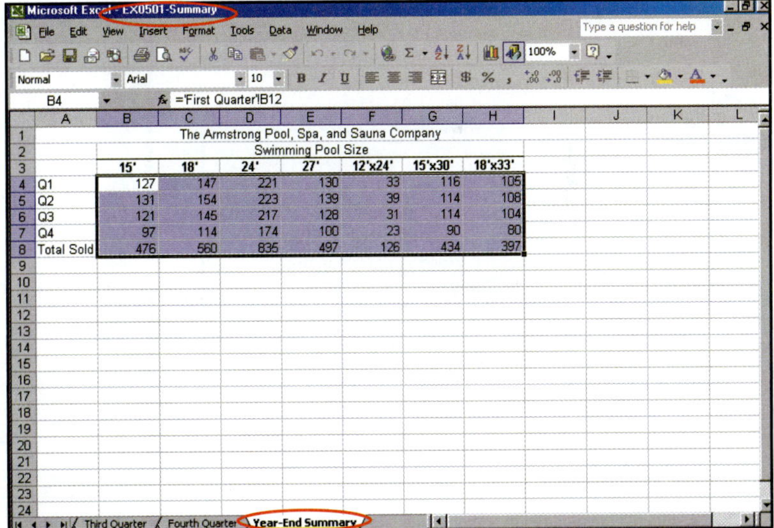

**3** Select cells **A1** through **I8**.

Click the **Copy** button.

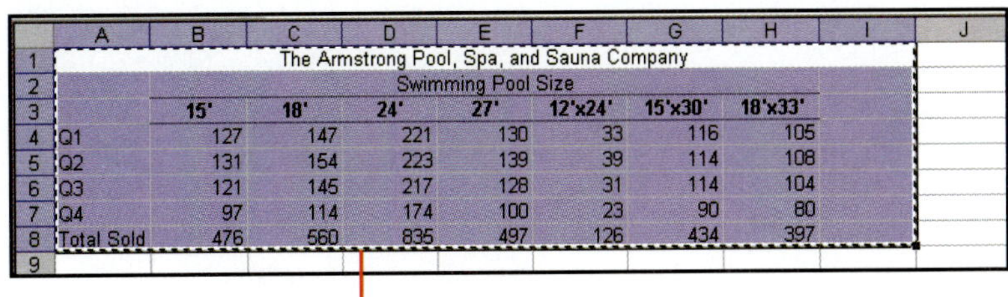

CAUTION

The range of cells in the previous step ends at cell I8. Be careful not to confuse the letter I with the number 1.

**4**  Use the taskbar to switch to the **EX0502-Memo** document.

Click on one of the blank lines between the body text paragraphs.

*The worksheet will be inserted at the insertion point.*

**QUICK TIP**

You can switch between applications and open worksheets and documents quickly by holding Alt and pressing Tab to display icons for each open document or application. The application used most recently prior to the current one is selected. If you release the Alt key, the selection will jump to it. If you press Tab, the selection moves to the next icon and will select this item if you release the Alt key.

**5**  Click the **Paste** button on the toolbar.

*The selected cells of the worksheet are pasted into the document as a Word table.*

**IN DEPTH**

If you change the values in the worksheet, the values in the new table in Word will not automatically update. If you would like to connect the worksheet and the document so that the table in the Word document updates when changes are made to the worksheet, choose Edit, Paste Special. A dialog box is displayed in which you can choose to Paste link the worksheet.

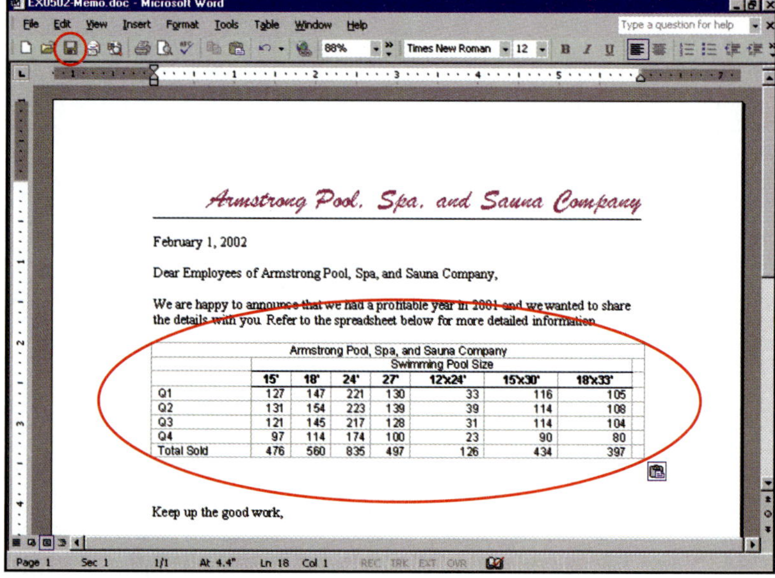



| | Armstrong Pool, Spa, and Sauna Company | | | | | | |
| | Swimming Pool Size | | | | | | |
| | 15' | 18' | 24' | 27' | 12x24' | 15x30' | 18x33' |
| Q1 | 127 | 147 | 221 | 130 | 33 | 116 | 105 |
| Q2 | 131 | 154 | 223 | 139 | 39 | 114 | 108 |
| Q3 | 121 | 145 | 217 | 128 | 31 | 114 | 104 |
| Q4 | 97 | 114 | 174 | 100 | 23 | 90 | 80 |
| Total Sold | 476 | 560 | 835 | 497 | 126 | 434 | 397 |

**6** Click the **Save** button, then close Word.

Switch back to the **EX0501-Summary** workbook if necessary.

Click the **Save** button to save the workbook.

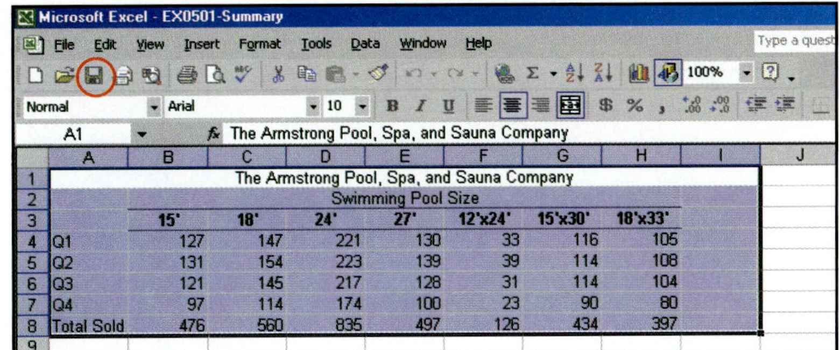


| | A | B | C | D | E | F | G | H | I | J |
|---|---|---|---|---|---|---|---|---|---|---|
| 1 | The Armstrong Pool, Spa, and Sauna Company | | | | | | | | | |
| 2 | Swimming Pool Size | | | | | | | | | |
| 3 | | 15' | 18' | 24' | 27' | 12'x24' | 15'x30' | 18'x33' | | |
| 4 | Q1 | 127 | 147 | 221 | 130 | 33 | 116 | 105 | | |
| 5 | Q2 | 131 | 154 | 223 | 139 | 39 | 114 | 108 | | |
| 6 | Q3 | 121 | 145 | 217 | 128 | 31 | 114 | 104 | | |
| 7 | Q4 | 97 | 114 | 174 | 100 | 23 | 90 | 80 | | |
| 8 | Total Sold | 476 | 560 | 835 | 497 | 126 | 434 | 397 | | |
| 9 | | | | | | | | | | |

# Task 5

## SAVING A WORKSHEET AS A WEB PAGE

### Why would I do this?

Excel 2002 uses a Web language called Extensible Markup Language, or **XML**, that was introduced with Office 2000. It allows you to interact with a worksheet using a browser. You can save your worksheet as an interactive Web page that can be used by anyone on the Web who has permission to view your site.

In this task, you learn how save the Year-End Summary worksheet as an XML Web page.

**1** Confirm that cells **A1** through **I8** are still selected.

*The empty cells in column I will be used in the next task.*

| | A | B | C | D | E | F | G | H | I | J |
|---|---|---|---|---|---|---|---|---|---|---|
| 1 | The Armstrong Pool, Spa, and Sauna Company | | | | | | | | | |
| 2 | Swimming Pool Size | | | | | | | | | |
| 3 | | 15' | 18' | 24' | 27' | 12'x24' | 15'x30' | 18'x33' | | |
| 4 | Q1 | 127 | 147 | 221 | 130 | 33 | 116 | 105 | | |
| 5 | Q2 | 131 | 154 | 223 | 139 | 39 | 114 | 108 | | |
| 6 | Q3 | 121 | 145 | 217 | 128 | 31 | 114 | 104 | | |
| 7 | Q4 | 97 | 114 | 174 | 100 | 23 | 90 | 80 | | |
| 8 | Total Sold | 476 | 560 | 835 | 497 | 126 | 434 | 397 | | |
| 9 | | | | | | | | | | |

Include the empty cells

**2** Choose **File**, **Save as Web Page**.

*The Save As dialog box opens.*

Select the **Excel Exercises** folder in the **Save in** box, if necessary.

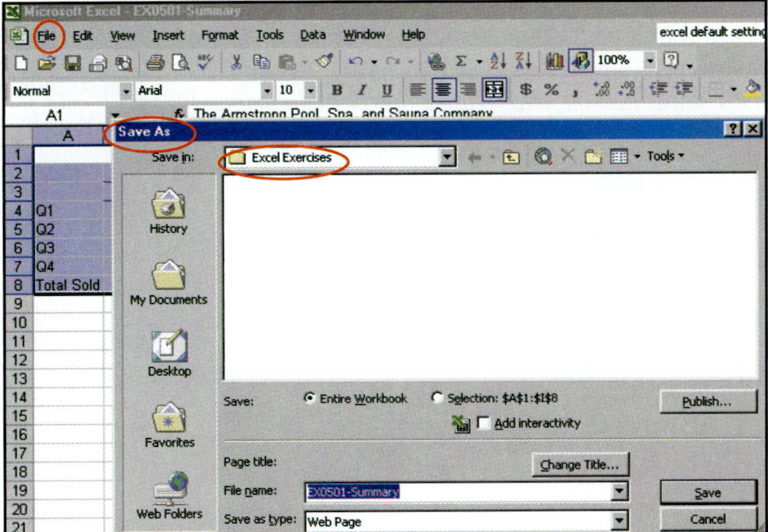

**3** Enter the name **EX0501-Web Page** in the **File name** box.

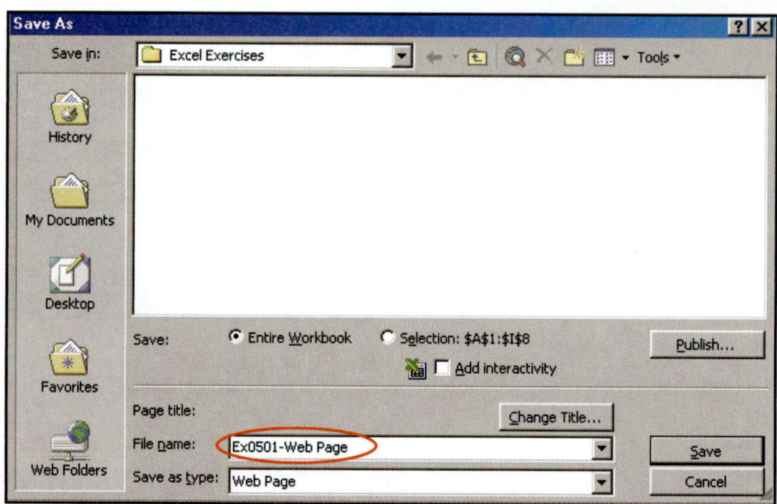

**4** Click the **Selection: $A$1:$I$8** option and the **Add interactivity** check box.

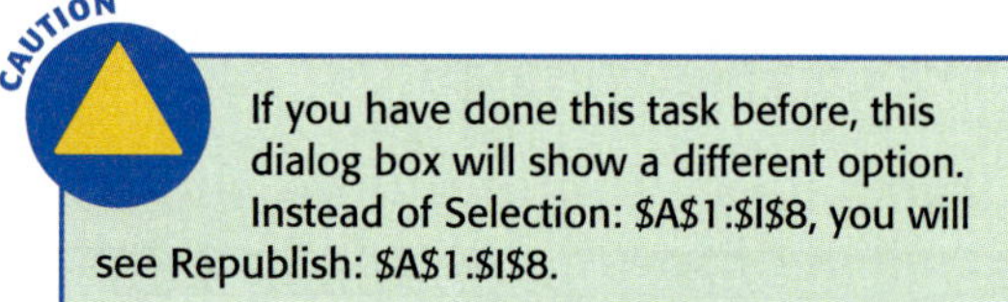

If you have done this task before, this dialog box will show a different option. Instead of Selection: $A$1:$I$8, you will see Republish: $A$1:$I$8.

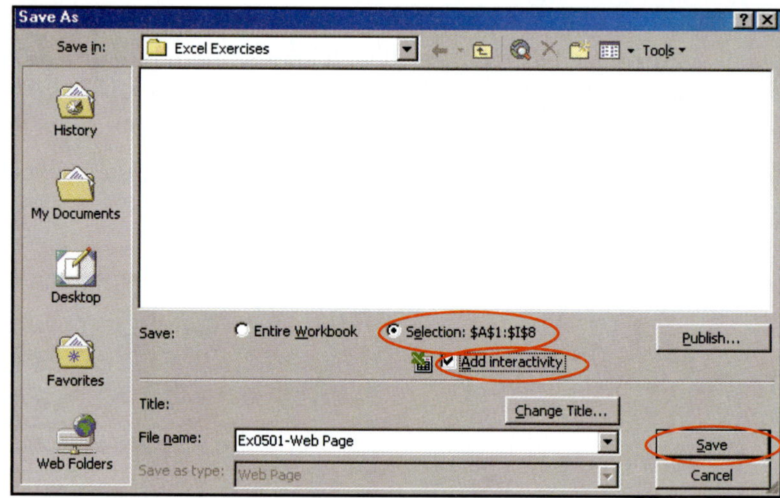

**5** Click **Save**.

*A warning box tells you that the formulas that refer to the other worksheets will not work on the Web page. This means that the Web page will not be linked to the quarterly sales worksheets.*

Click **OK**.

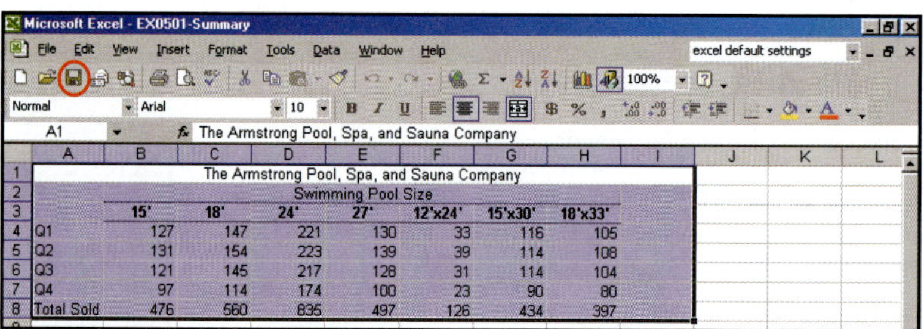

**6** Click the **Save** button on the toolbar to save your changes, then close Excel.

### Why would I do this?

Recent versions of Web browsers, such as Microsoft's Internet Explorer 5.0 or later versions, can read files that have XML features. Older browsers display a static page. Using the XML feature, you can interact with a worksheet on the Web in new ways.

In this task, you launch Internet Explorer 5.0 or 5.5 and browse the **EX0501-Web Page** file on your disk as if it were posted to a Web server.

**1** Launch Microsoft Internet Explorer or another browser that supports XML.

*The browser opens and displays the default home page. Yours will differ from the figure.*

Choose **File**, **Open**. Click the **Browse** button. Locate the folder in which you saved the web page in the previous task and select it.

*The Open dialog box displays options for opening existing web pages. You can browse your disks to locate the web pages. Notice the file name uses .htm to identify it as a web page.*

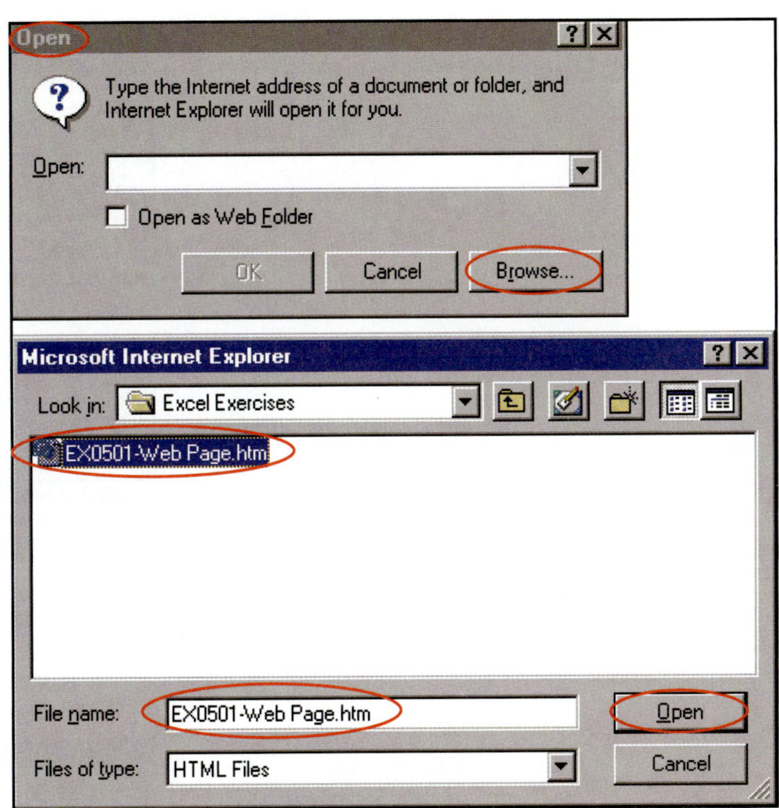


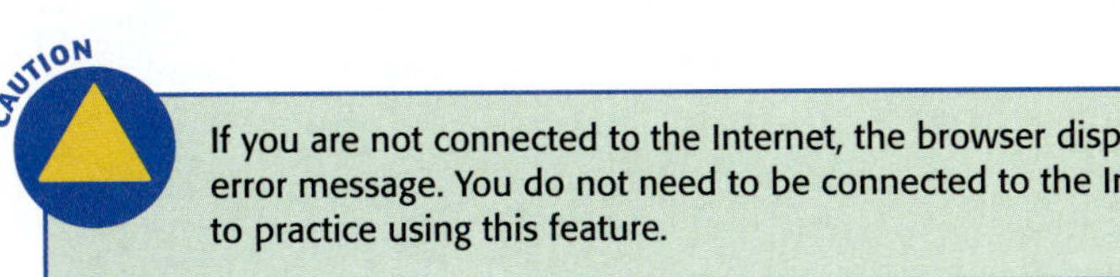


**2** Click **Open**.

*The Open dialog box displays the location of the web page.*

Click **OK**.

*The worksheet displays in the browser as an interactive web page.*

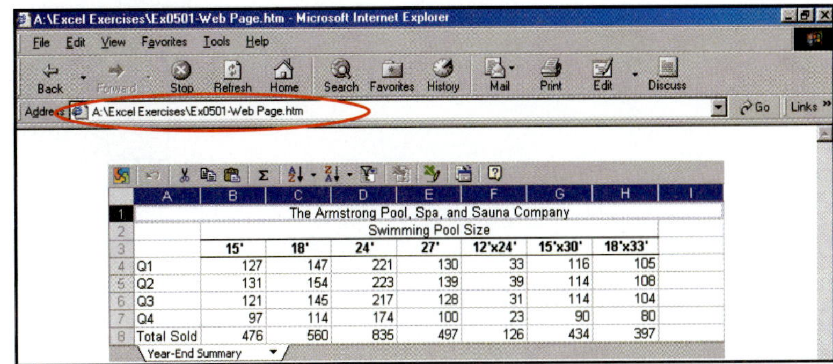

**3** Select cell **I4**.

*Notice that this worksheet summarized the total number of pools sold by size of pool at the bottom of each column but did not summarize the total number of pools sold each quarter at the end of each row. Notice that some of the worksheet tools from Excel are available on a toolbar at the top of the page.*

Double-click the **AutoSum** button.

*The Q1 row total is displayed.*

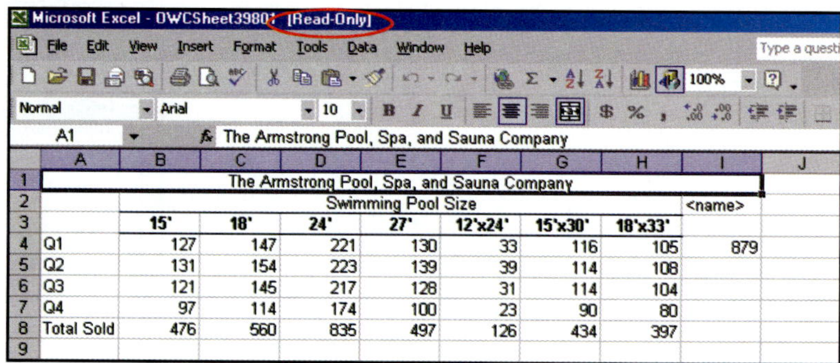


**4** Select cell **I2** and enter your last name.

**5** Click the **Export to Excel** button.

*The Excel program launches and the worksheet displays in **Read Only** mode.*

**6** Choose **File**, **Save As**. Type the name **EX0501-Web Sheet**, in the **File name** box. Set the **Save as type** box to **Microsoft Excel Workbook**. Change the folder displayed in the **Save in** box to the disk and folder where you keep your files.

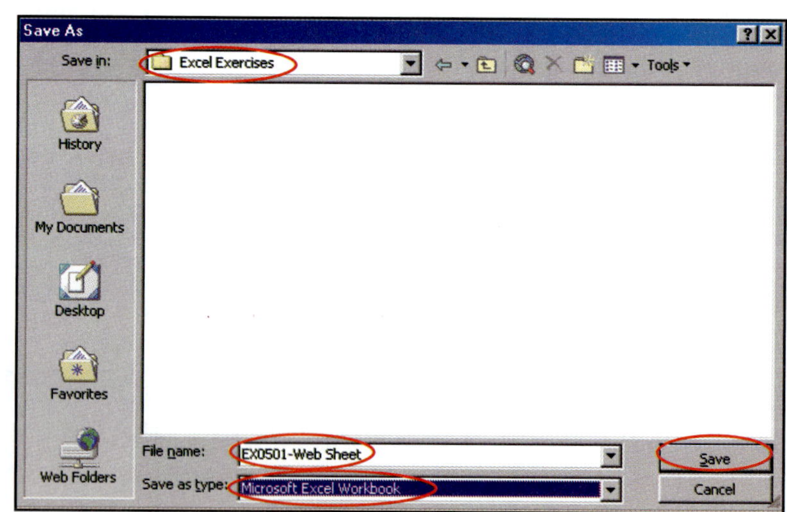

**7** Click **Save**.

Close the workbook and Excel. Close the browser.

The exercises that follow are designed for you to review and use what you have learned in this lesson. You also have the opportunity to practice your skills and then expand on them by applying them to new situations.

# COMPREHENSION

Comprehension exercises are designed to check your memory and understanding of the basic concepts in this lesson. You distinguish between true and false statements, identify new screen elements, and match terms with related statements. If you are uncertain of the correct answer, refer to the task number following each item (for example, T4 refers to Task 4), and review that task until you are confident you can provide a correct response.

## TRUE-FALSE

Circle either T or F.

T   F   **1.** To move a worksheet in Excel, you click-and-drag the sheet tab to a new position. **(T1)**

T   F   **2.** If you want cells in one worksheet to reflect changes that are made in another worksheet, you start with an equal sign in the destination cell. **(T3)**

T   F   **3.** In a formula, a reference to another worksheet is indicated by an exclamation point at the beginning and the end of the worksheet name. **(T3)**

T   F   **4.** If a cell contains a formula that refers to a cell in another sheet, you cannot use the Fill function with that cell. **(T3)**

T   F   **5.** To save the sheet as an interactive page suitable for publishing on the Internet, choose **File**, **Save as HTML**. **(T5)**

T   F   **6.** The Extensible Markup Language that makes interactive worksheets possible is known by the acronym, EML. **(T5)**

## MATCHING QUESTIONS

**A.** table     **D.** XML

**B.** insertion point     **E.** Export to Excel

**C.** ='Sheet1!A2'     **F.** Tab scrolling buttons

Match the following statements to the word or phrase that is the best match from the list. Write the letter of the matching word or phrase in the space provided next to the number.

**1.** ____ Used to move a sheet tab into view so it can be selected **(T1)**

**2.** ____ A range of cells turns into this when pasted into a document using the **Paste** button **(T4)**

**3.** ____ A button on an interactive Web page that sends a worksheet to Excel **(T6)**

**4.** ____ A formula showing a reference to a cell on another worksheet **(T3)**

**5.** ____ A language used to make worksheets interactive on the Internet **(T5)**

**6.** ____ Place where the cells will go if pasted into a document **(T4)**

# IDENTIFYING PARTS OF
# THE EXCEL SCREEN

Refer to the figure and identify the numbered parts of
the screen. Write the letter of the correct label in the
space next to the number.

1. _______________

2. _______________

3. _______________

4. _______________

5. _______________

6. _______________

7. _______________

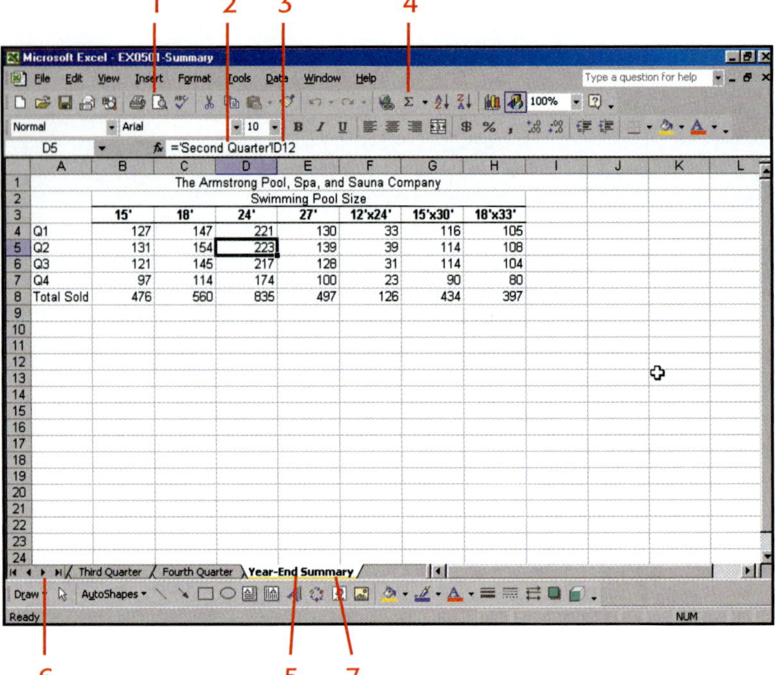

**A.** Reference to a cell in the Second
Quarter sheet  **(T3)**

**B.** Name of a sheet as it is used in a
formula  **(T3)**

**C.** **Print Preview** button  **(T4)**

**D.** Name of currently displayed sheet  **(T2)**

**E.** **AutoSum** button  **(T4)**

**F.** Tab scroll buttons  **(T1)**

**G.** Color added to sheet tab  **(T1)**

Reinforcement exercises are designed to reinforce the skills you have learned by applying them to new situations. Detailed instructions are provided along with a figure, where appropriate, to illustrate the result. The reinforcement exercises that follow should be completed sequentially. Leave the file open at the end of each exercise for use in the next exercise until you are specifically directed to close it.

Open **EX0503** and save it as **EX0503-Reinforcement** on your floppy disk for use in the following exercises. Replace source file with new file that uses year 2001 instead of 2000.

## R1—Summarizing Income and Expenses by Quarter

Many companies provide quarterly reports to stockholders. The data provided in the first sheet displays the income and expenses by month. You summarize this data on Sheet2 into three-month periods or quarters.

1. Select **Sheet2**. Select cell **B4**, where the sum of the incomes for the months of January, February, and March should be displayed.

2. Click the **AutoSum** button once to place the SUM function in cell **B4**.

3. Click the **2001** sheet tab and drag across cells **B9** though **D9** to identify the total income for the first three months of the year.

4. Press **⏎Enter** or click the **Enter** button on the formula bar. The total income for those three months, **66699**, displays in cell **B4** of **Sheet2**.

5. Repeat this process to represent the total income for April, May, and June in cell **C4**. The number **74549** displays in cell **C4**. (Do not use the fill handle for this exercise.)

6. Repeat this process to find the remaining two quarterly summations of income and the four quarterly expenses.

7. Select cell **F4** and use the **AutoSum** function to add the four quarters of income. (The total should be **321668**.) Repeat this process for the total expenses in cell **F5**. (The total expenses should be **312352**.)

8. Rename **Sheet2** as **Quarterly Report**.

9. Right-click on the Quarterly Report tab and change the tab color to light blue. Save the workbook and leave it open for use in the next exercise.

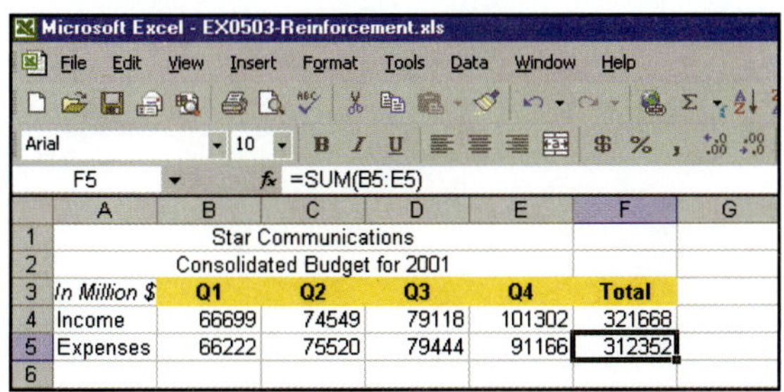

## R2—Pasting the Quarterly Report into a Word Document

The Quarterly Report worksheet may be copied and pasted into a Word document for convenient reporting.

1. Select the **Quarterly Report** sheet, if necessary. Select cells **A1** through **F5**.

2. Click the **Copy** button.

3. Start Word and open a blank document, if necessary.

4. Click the **Paste** button on the toolbar. The worksheet cells are pasted into the document as a table.

5. Save the document on your disk as **EX0503-Report**.

6. Close the document and close Word.

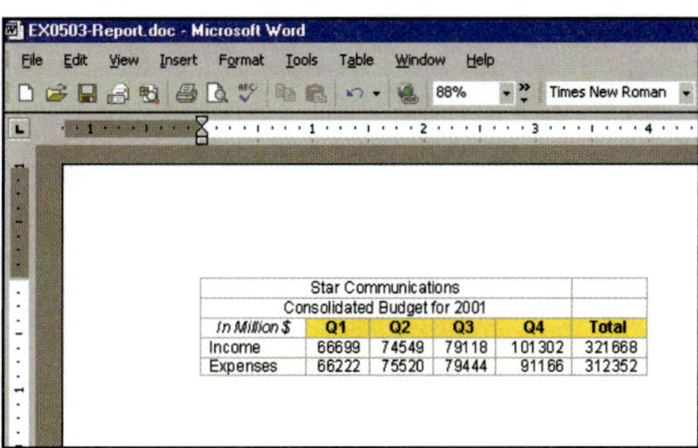

## R3—Saving a Summary Sheet as an Interactive Web Page

You can share this data with others by saving it as a Web page that can be placed on a Web server or in a folder that is available to others on a local area network.

1. Select the **Quarterly Report** sheet, if necessary. Select cells **A1** through **F6**. (Be sure to include row **6**.)

2. Save the selected area as a Web page on your disk. Choose the **Add interactivity** option and name it **EX0503-Web Page**.

3. Start your browser and enter the file's location in the browser's **Address** box or browse for its location using **File**, **Open**, and the **Browse** button.

4. In cell **B6**, type **=B4-B5** and press ⏎Enter to determine the difference between income and expenses for the first quarter.

5. Select cell **B6**, if necessary, and click the **Copy** button. Select cells **C6** through **F6** and click the **Paste** button.

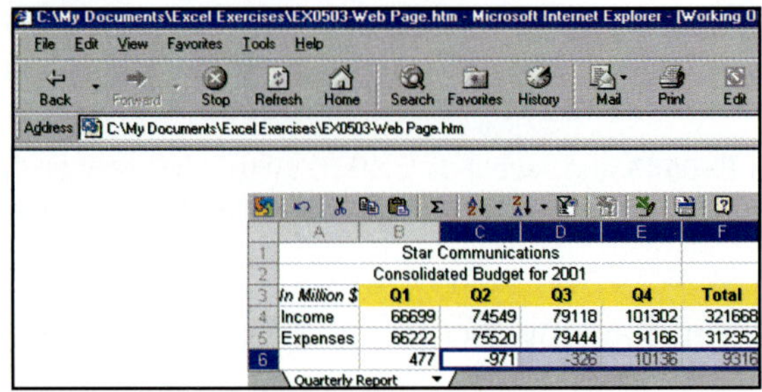

6. Click the **Export to Excel** button. Save the file as an Excel workbook named **EX0503-Web Sheet**.

7. Close the workbook.

Challenge exercises are designed to test your ability to apply your skills to new situations with less detailed instruction. These exercises also challenge you to expand your repertoire of skills by using commands that are similar to those you have already learned. The desired outcome is clearly defined, but you have more freedom to choose the steps needed to achieve the required result.

The following Challenge exercises use the file **EX0504,** which is similar to the file you edited in the lesson. They also use a Word document file, **EX0502**, that is opened in Word. Challenge exercises C1 to C3 use the same files, but they may be done independently.

Start Microsoft Word. Open **EX0502** from the **Student** folder and save it on your disk as **EX0502-Challenge**.

Start Excel, if necessary. Open **EX0504** from the **Student** folder and save it on your floppy disk as **EX0504-Challenge**.

### C1—Pasting a Worksheet into a Document as a Workbook

It is possible to paste a worksheet into a Word document in several ways depending on the application. A worksheet can be copied and pasted in such a way that it is converted into a Word table. It is also possible to paste it as an actual worksheet that you can activate and edit. If you paste the worksheet into a Word document as a working worksheet, you also can choose to maintain a link between the document and the parent worksheet so that changes in one are reflected in the other.

*Goal:* Paste the Armstrong Pool, Spa, and Sauna Co. worksheet into a letter to the employees, then activate the worksheet and look at various sheets within the workbook.

Use the following guidelines:

1. Select cells **A1** through **I8** on the **Year-End Summary** sheet and copy it.

2. Switch to the **EX0502-Challenge** document in Word and place the insertion point in one of the blank lines between the paragraphs.

3. Choose **Edit**, **Paste Special**. Paste the object as a **Microsoft Excel Worksheet Object** (do not link it).

4. Delete extra blank lines in the document as needed. Double-click on the table to activate the worksheet.

5. Save the document. Close the Word document and close Word. Close the workbook.

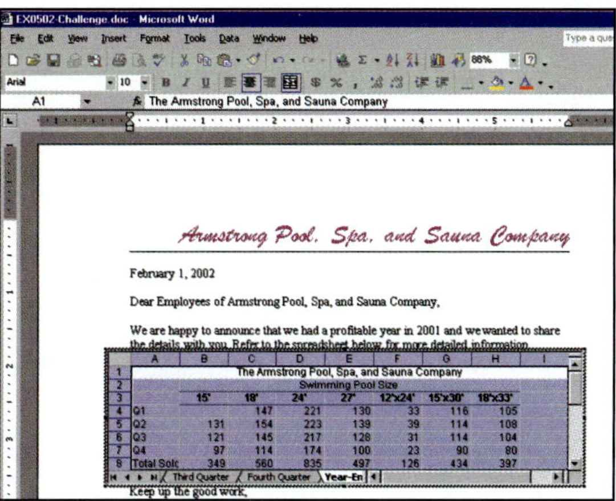

### C2—Saving a Workbook as a Web Page

If a workbook has several sheets, you can save the entire workbook as a Web page.

*Goal:* Save the workbook as a series of Web pages that can be selected using navigation buttons.

Use the following guidelines:

1. Open **EX0504-Challenge**, if necessary. See the instructions preceding the first Challenge exercise if you do not have this file.

2. Choose **File, Save as Web page** from the menu. Choose **Entire Workbook**. Change the name of the file to **EX0504-Web Pages** in the **File name** box. Save it to your disk.

3. Launch your Web browser (Internet Explorer 5.0 or later, or another browser capable of reading XML). Choose **File**, **Open**, **Browse** to locate the file on your disk and open it. (If your file is on the floppy disk, the address is probably A:\Excel Exercises\EX0504-Web Pages.htm).

4. Open the Web page. The workbook has sheet tabs as shown in the figure.

5. Navigate the different sheets of the workbook using the sheet tabs at the bottom of the page.

6. Close the browser. Close the workbook.

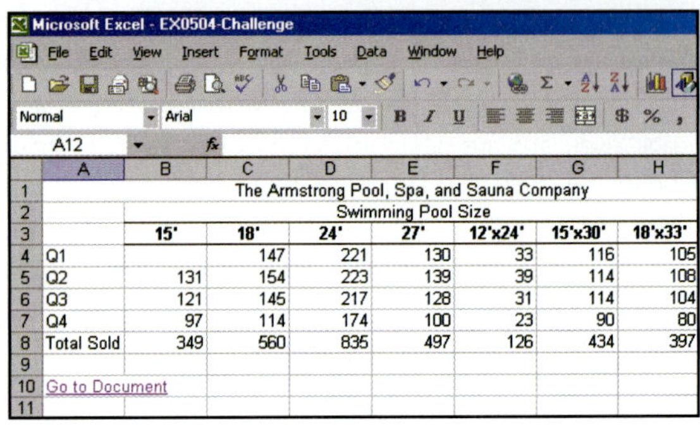

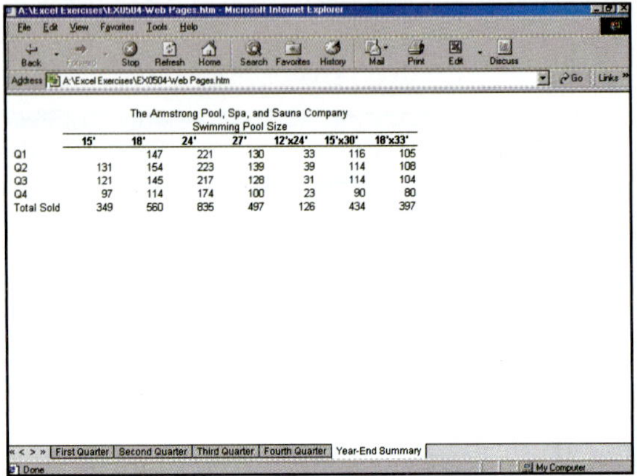

## C3—Inserting a Hyperlink to a Document

If you are using a Word document with a worksheet, it is useful to jump directly to the document, even if it isn't open. A convenient way to do this is to insert a *hyperlink*. A hyperlink is a connection between a word or label in one location to a file in another location. When you click on a hyperlink, it connects you directly to information in another file.

*Goal:* Place a hyperlink in a worksheet that links to a Word document.

1. Open **EX0504-Challenge**, select the **Year-End Summary** sheet if necessary, and select cell **A10**. Type **Go to Document** and enter it. Select the cell again if necessary.

2. Click the **Insert Hyperlink** button.

3. Click the down arrow next to the **Look in** box. Locate the Word document **EX0502-Memo**, select it, and click **OK**. The text will change color to indicate that it is a hyperlink.

4. Click the new hyperlink. The document opens in Word. Notice the Web navigation toolbar above the document.

5. Click the **Back** button to return to the worksheet.

6. Save the changes you have made and close the workbook.

## C4—Using Named Cells and Adding Comments

If a cell or range of cells is often copied, used in formulas, or returned to frequently, it is useful to give it a name of its own. The name of the cell may be used when selecting, copying, or writing formulas.

You may also add comments that provide additional information to a worksheet. Cells with small red triangles in the corners indicate the presence of a comment. The comment appears when the pointer is placed on the cell.

*Goal:* Assign names to cells and ranges of cells and then use those names in place of the cell address. Add a comment to the summary sheet to explain the new section.

1. Open **EX0504-Challenge** and select the **First Quarter** sheet. Select cell **I12** and double-click the **AutoSum** button to add up the total number of pools sold of all sizes.

2. Click on the name of the cell **I12** in the **Name** box at the left end of the formula bar to select it and type **Q1_Total**. Press Enter. (Names of cells cannot have spaces in them. The underscore character may be used to simulate a space between words.)

3. Repeat this process for the other three quarters, naming the cells **Q2_Total**, **Q3_Total**, and **Q4_Total** respectively.

4. Go to the **Year-End Summary** sheet and select cell **A1**. Click the cell name in the **Name** box and type **Title**. Press Enter.

5. Click the new name, **Title**, in the **Name** box to select it and click the **Copy** button.

6. Select cell **A13** and click the **Paste** button. The title is pasted into cells A13 through I13.

7. Select cells **A4** through **A8**. Click the name of the cell in the **Name** box and type **Row_Labels**. Press Enter.

8. Click the new name, **Row_Labels**, in the **Name** box and click the **Copy** button. Select cell **A14** and click the **Paste** button.

9. Select cell **B14**. Enter **=Q1_Total**. The value of the named cell from the First Quarter sheet is displayed. Select cell **B15** and enter **=Q2_Total**. Repeat this process for cells **B16** and **B17** to enter formulas that refer to the totals in the third and fourth quarters respectively.

10. Select cell **B18**. Enter **=Q1_Total + Q2_Total + Q3_Total + Q4_Total**. Cell names can be used in formulas.

11. Choose **Edit**, **Go To** from the menu. Choose **Q1_Total** from the list in the **Go to** dialog box and click **OK.** You can use this method to go directly to a named cell in a worksheet.

12. Return to the **Year-End Summary** sheet. Select cell **B18** and choose **Insert**, **Comment** from the menu. Select the default user name and type your name followed by **This cell uses named cells in a formula**. Click in an unused cell to finish. Move the mouse pointer onto cell **B18** to view your comment.

13. Save the workbook and close it.

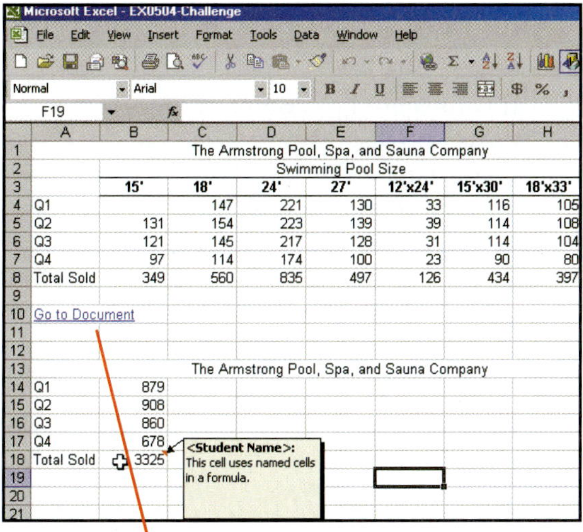

Not present if you did not do exercise C3

 C5—Pasting a Table from Word into a Worksheet

You may find a table of data in a Word document and desire to analyze it in more detail using Excel. You may copy a table and paste it directly into Excel.

*Goal:* Copy a table of fatality statistics from a Word document into a blank worksheet.

1. Launch Word and open **EX0505** from the **Student** folder.

2. Scroll to the second page of the document and click anywhere in the table. Choose **Table**, **Select**, **Table** from the menu.

3. Click the **Copy** button. Close the document and close Word.

4. Switch to Excel. Click the **New** button at the left end of the **Standard** toolbar or select it from the **Toolbar Options** list if it is not displayed on your combined toolbar.

5. Click the **Paste** button. The table is inserted but is not formatted properly. Widen column **A** to display **North Carolina** on a single line.

6. Choose **Format**, **AutoFormat** from the menu. Choose **Classic 2** and click **OK**.

7. Save the file on your disk as **EX0505-Word Table**. Close the workbook.

Create a set of worksheets to help itemize your deductions for tax purposes. Create a set of individual worksheets that are used to list and summarize your tax-deductible expenses. Create a summary sheet that displays the total from each of the other sheets next to a label. Write a brief letter in Word to an accountant and paste the summary table into the letter.

Criteria for grading will be:

1. Demonstration of the use of formulas that refer to cells on other worksheets.

2. Demonstration of the ability to paste a worksheet into a Word document.

Some examples of features that students have learned to use in previous classes to enhance their personal tax worksheets are as follows:

- Set up a worksheet for one expense with attractive formatting and copy that sheet for use with the other types of expenses

- Round all dollar amounts displayed to the nearest dollar

- Refer to an itemized tax return to see what categories a person would use to itemize expenses

- Rename each sheet tab to identify the type of deduction

- Include at least three of the four most common categories: Medical, Taxes, Gifts, Job Expenses, and Miscellaneous

- Set up a summary sheet that would be easy to chart with the labels and totals for each expense in a simple row-and-column format.

1. Identify yourself and the year. Place your name in a cell that is clearly visible on the summary worksheet and use your name in the letter at the bottom.

2. To complete the project:

- Save the workbook and the letter on your own disk. Name the workbook **EX0506-Tax** and the letter **EX0507-Tax**.

- Check with your instructor to determine if the project should be submitted in electronic or printed form. If necessary, print out a copy of the workbook and the letter to hand in.

- If your school or company has a server that supports web discussions, place the workbook on the discussion server. Post comments from two different computers that simulate a discussion between yourself and your accountant. Use Tools, Online Collaboration, Web Discussions to post comments.

# Lesson 6

## Becoming Proficient with Editing Cells

Task 1    Changing Numbers and Editing Text

Task 2    Creating Sequential Text Headings

Task 3    Creating a Series of Numbers

Task 4    Copying Cell Contents

Task 5    Using Find and Replace

Task 6    Creating Hyperlinks

## INTRODUCTION

When Dan Bricklin and Bob Frankston created *VisiCalc*, the first spreadsheet program for the personal computer, they announced it with an advertisement that asked the question "How did you ever do without it?" At the time, accountants and bookkeepers had to spend a great deal of time recalculating worksheets by hand or on a calculator if they found an error or if they wanted to compare scenarios. VisiCalc was so useful and saved so much time for anyone who worked with numbers that it was sufficient reason to go out and buy a computer just to run it.

Excel is a direct descendant of VisiCalc and offers several new features that are also convenient time-savers. If you find that you are entering the same text repeatedly, or if the text you want to enter is a simple sequence like the days of the week, there is probably a feature in Excel that makes entering it faster and easier.

In this lesson, you learn how to change numbers and text, create sequential headings and series of numbers, copy cells, find and replace cell contents, and create hyperlinks to related cells or content in other documents. You will be working with data from the Armstrong Pool, Spa, and Sauna Co.

# VISUAL SUMMARY

When you have completed this entire lesson, you will have a worksheet that looks like this:

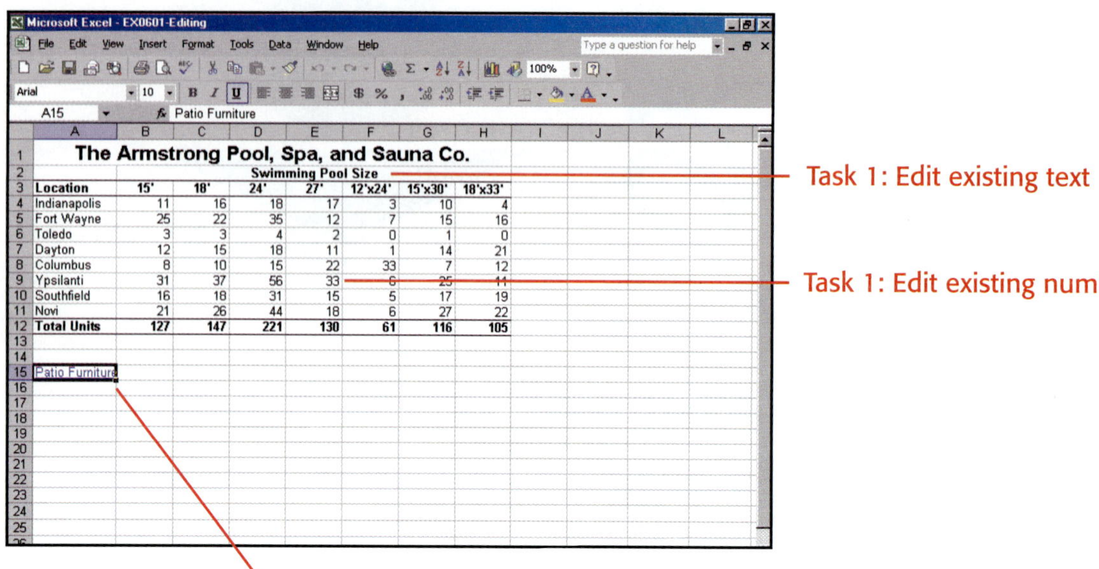

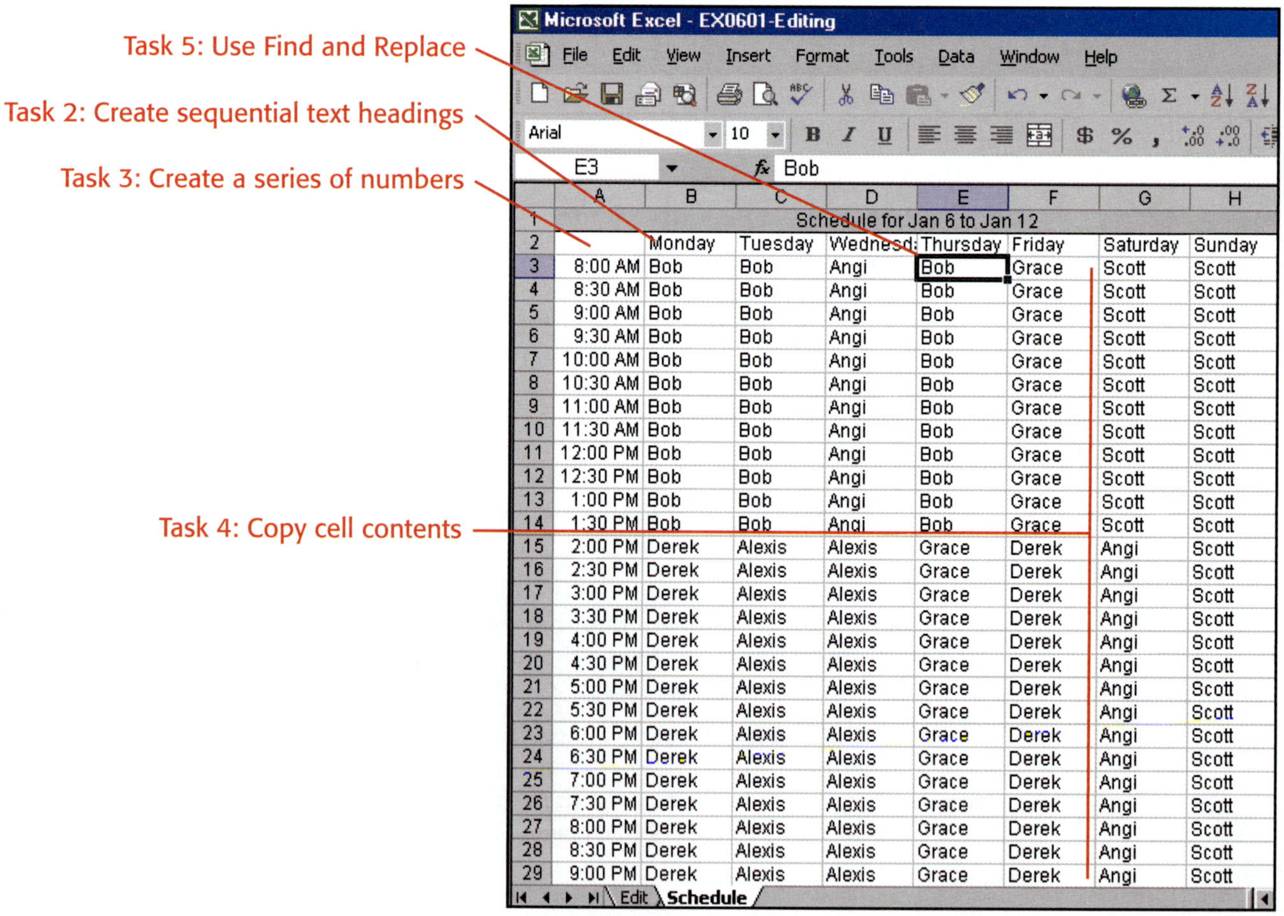

# Task 1
## CHANGING NUMBERS AND EDITING TEXT

### Why would I do this?

When you enter a lot of data into a worksheet, you will sometimes make errors. There will also be times when you enter data or labels correctly, but decide to change them later. In either case, you will need to edit the contents of a cell.

In this task, you change data in one cell and edit text in another.

**1** Launch Excel and click the **Open** button. Find **EX0601** in the **Student** folder and open it. Save the file as **EX0601-Editing**.

*The new file name appears in the title bar.*

Select the **Edit** sheet, if necessary.

*This worksheet summarizes pool sales by city.*

| | A | B | C | D | E | F | G | H |
|---|---|---|---|---|---|---|---|---|
| 1 | The Armstrong Pool, Spa, and Sauna Co. | | | | | | | |
| 2 | | | | | Pool Size | | | |
| 3 | Location | 15' | 18' | 24' | 27' | 12'x24' | 15'x30' | 18'x33' |
| 4 | Indianapolis | 11 | 16 | 18 | 17 | 3 | 10 | 4 |
| 5 | Fort Wayne | 25 | 22 | 35 | 12 | 7 | 15 | 16 |
| 6 | Toledo | 3 | 3 | 4 | 2 | 0 | 1 | 0 |
| 7 | Dayton | 12 | 15 | 18 | 11 | 1 | 14 | 21 |
| 8 | Columbus | 8 | 10 | 15 | 22 | 5 | 7 | 12 |
| 9 | Ypsilanti | 31 | 37 | 56 | 33 | 6 | 25 | 11 |
| 10 | Southfield | 16 | 18 | 31 | 15 | 5 | 17 | 19 |
| 11 | Novi | 21 | 26 | 44 | 18 | 6 | 27 | 22 |
| 12 | Total Units | 127 | 147 | 221 | 130 | 33 | 116 | 105 |

**2** Select cell **F8**, type **33,** and press ⏎Enter.

*The new number replaces the old one, and the sum at the bottom of the column is recalculated.*

| | A | B | C | D | E | F | G | H |
|---|---|---|---|---|---|---|---|---|
| 1 | The Armstrong Pool, Spa, and Sauna Co. | | | | | | | |
| 2 | | | | | Pool Size | | | |
| 3 | Location | 15' | 18' | 24' | 27' | 12'x24' | 15'x30' | 18'x33' |
| 4 | Indianapolis | 11 | 16 | 18 | 17 | 3 | 10 | 4 |
| 5 | Fort Wayne | 25 | 22 | 35 | 12 | 7 | 15 | 16 |
| 6 | Toledo | 3 | 3 | 4 | 2 | 0 | 1 | 0 |
| 7 | Dayton | 12 | 15 | 18 | 11 | 1 | 14 | 21 |
| 8 | Columbus | 8 | 10 | 15 | 22 | 33 | 7 | 12 |
| 9 | Ypsilanti | 31 | 37 | 56 | 33 | 6 | 25 | 11 |
| 10 | Southfield | 16 | 18 | 31 | 15 | 5 | 17 | 19 |
| 11 | Novi | 21 | 26 | 44 | 18 | 6 | 27 | 22 |
| 12 | Total Units | 127 | 147 | 221 | 130 | 61 | 116 | 105 |

**3** Select cell **B2.**

*This heading has been merged and centered over seven columns. Notice that the contents of the cell are shown both in the cell and in the Formula bar. The cell location is also shown in the Name box.*

**QUICK TIP**

To edit the contents of the cell in the cell itself, double-click on the cell to place the insertion point into the cell.

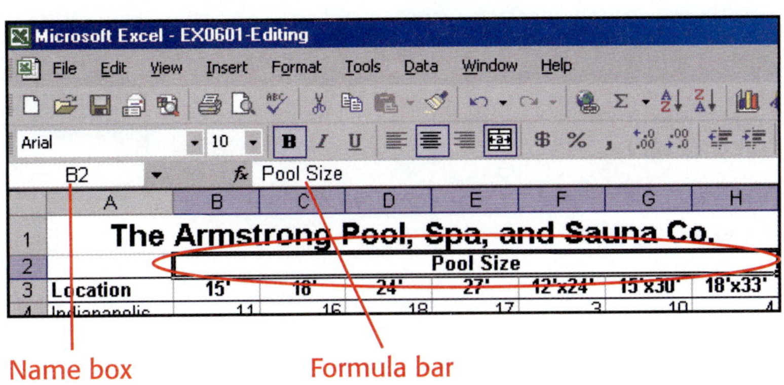

**4** Move the pointer to the left of the word **Pool** in the Formula bar and click once to position the insertion point in front of the word **Pool**.

*The insertion point indicates where new text will go when you start typing.*

Type **Swimming**, then press Spacebar, and then press ↵Enter.

*The contents of cell B2 reflect the change you made.*

# Task 2

## CREATING SEQUENTIAL TEXT HEADINGS

### Why would I do this?

Many worksheets use days of the week, months of the year, fiscal quarters, or other sequences of labels as column or row headings. Excel recognizes text that begins such sequences and assists you in entering them. This feature of Excel increases your efficiency in creating your worksheet.

In this task, you learn how to create sequential labels.

**1** Click the **Schedule** tab.

*This worksheet will display a schedule of workers. Each cell will represent a half-hour of time worked.*

Select cell **B2**, type **Monday**, and press ↵Enter.

*Excel can recognize text that is typically used in a sequence.*

**2** Select cell **B2** again. Move the pointer to the small black square at the lower-right corner of the cell.

*This small square is called a **fill handle**. The pointer changes to a black plus sign.*

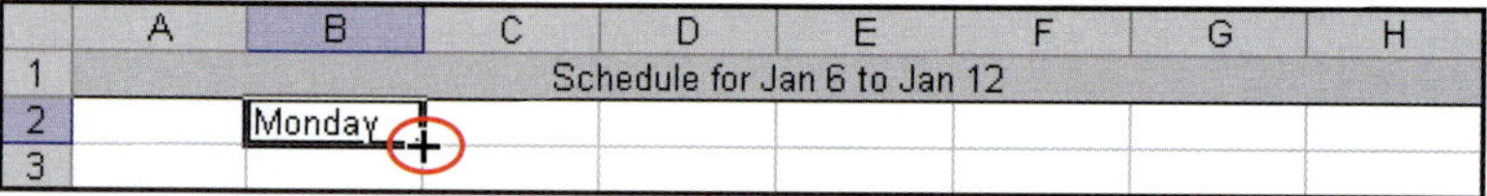

**3** Click-and-drag the fill handle to the right, to cell **H2**.

*Notice that the name of the next day in the sequence is displayed in a ScreenTip as you drag.*

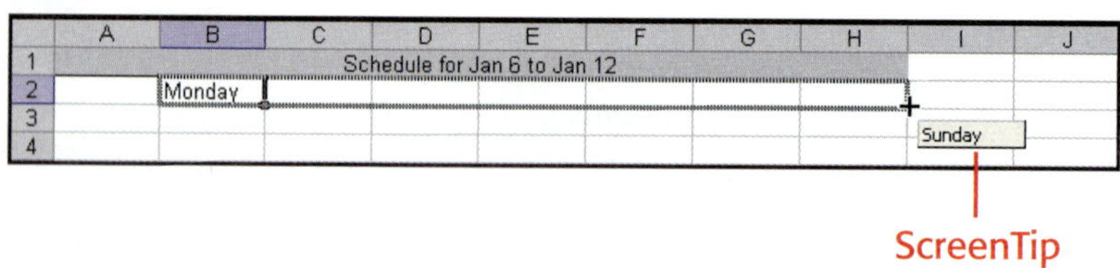

**4** Release the mouse button.

*The sequence of days is filled in.*

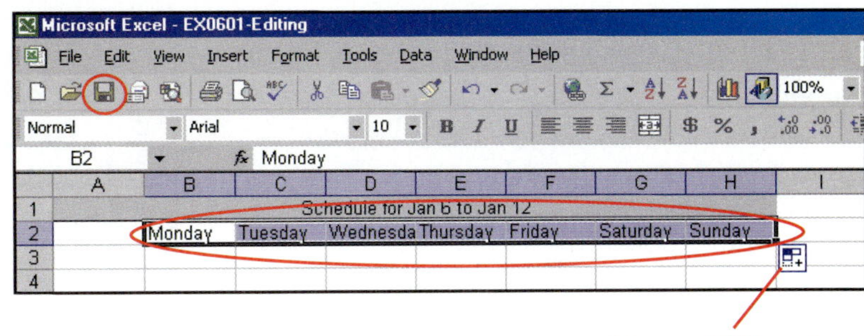


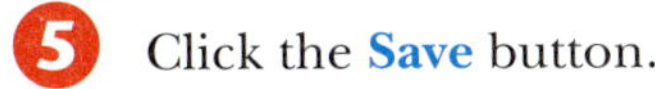



Several interesting options are available when you fill cells with dates or numbers. When the days are filled, a drop-down menu is attached to the fill handle's ScreenTip. One option on this menu is to fill weekdays, excluding weekend days. Other choices are explored in the end-of-lesson exercises.

**5** Click the **Save** button.

*The workbook is saved on your disk.*

# Task 3
## CREATING A SERIES OF NUMBERS

### Why would I do this?

Normally, numbers in a worksheet are entered in order to make calculations, which is why they are entered in separate cells. Sometimes you use numbers to represent dates or times as the labels for rows or columns. Excel is able to recognize when date formats such as 9/5 or 9-5-01 are entered in a cell. It can also recognize typical time formats such as 8:00. Numbers representing dates or times can be filled into a series of cells to be used as row or column headings.

In this task, you learn how to create a series of times as row labels. You also learn how to set both common and custom intervals.

**1** Select cell **A3**, type **8:00**, and press ⏎Enter.

*We would like the first time interval to be the half hour between 8:00 and 8:30 in the morning.*

| | A | B | C | D | E | F | G | H |
|---|---|---|---|---|---|---|---|---|
| 1 | | | | Schedule for Jan 6 to Jan 12 | | | | |
| 2 | | Monday | Tuesday | Wednesda | Thursday | Friday | Saturday | Sunday |
| 3 | 8:00 | | | | | | | |
| 4 | | | | | | | | |

**2** Select cell **A3** again. Click-and-drag the fill handle down to cell **A10**.

Release the mouse button.

*The program assumes that times will increase in one-hour intervals. If we want to use a different time interval, we need to provide an example. The default format is 24-hour, which can be changed using the Format options.*

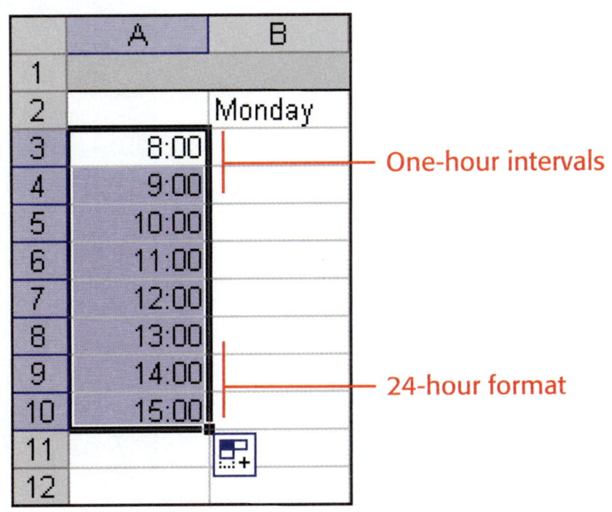

**3** Click the **Undo** button.

*The fill is undone. This company schedules its part-time workers on the half hour. In order to establish this half-hour pattern, you need to enter data in at least two cells before applying the fill.*

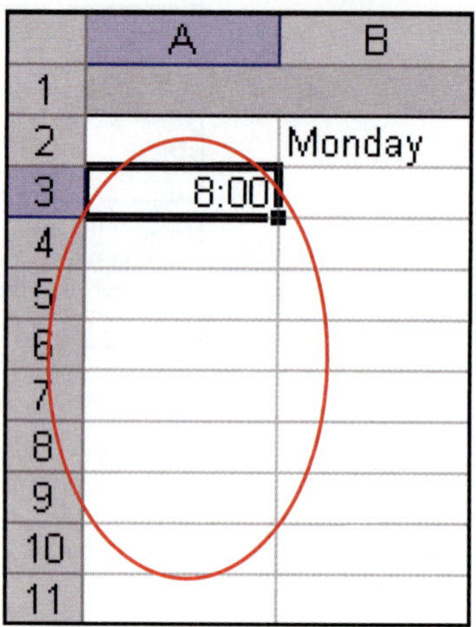

**4** Select cell **A4**, type **8:30**, and press ⏎Enter.

Select cells **A3** and **A4**.

*When you select a pair of cells, the difference between them is used to determine the difference between cells in a series if you use the fill handle.*

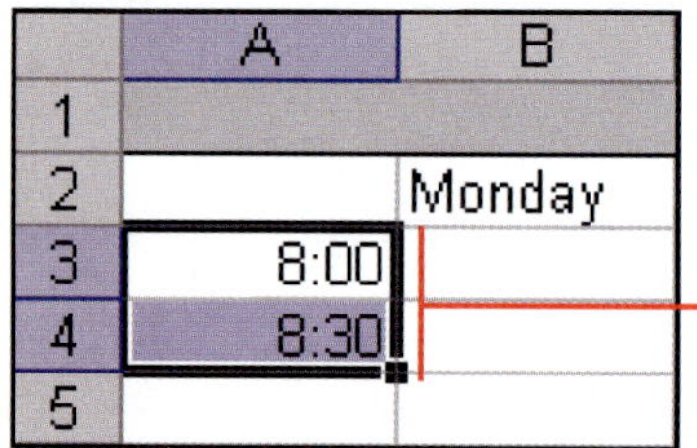




Remember, since the first cell of a selected group does not change background color, cell A3 may not appear to be selected. The thick line border encloses both cells if they are both selected. It is important that both cells are selected to indicate what interval to use to create the rest of the series.

**5** Click-and-drag the fill handle down to cell **A18**.

Release the mouse button.

*The sequence is filled in half-hour increments.*

**6** Use the vertical scroll bar, if necessary, to scroll down to show rows **18** through **29**.

*Sometimes it is useful to extend an existing series.*

Click-and-drag the fill handle down to cell **A29**. Release the mouse button.

*The sequence is extended to 21:00 (9 PM).*

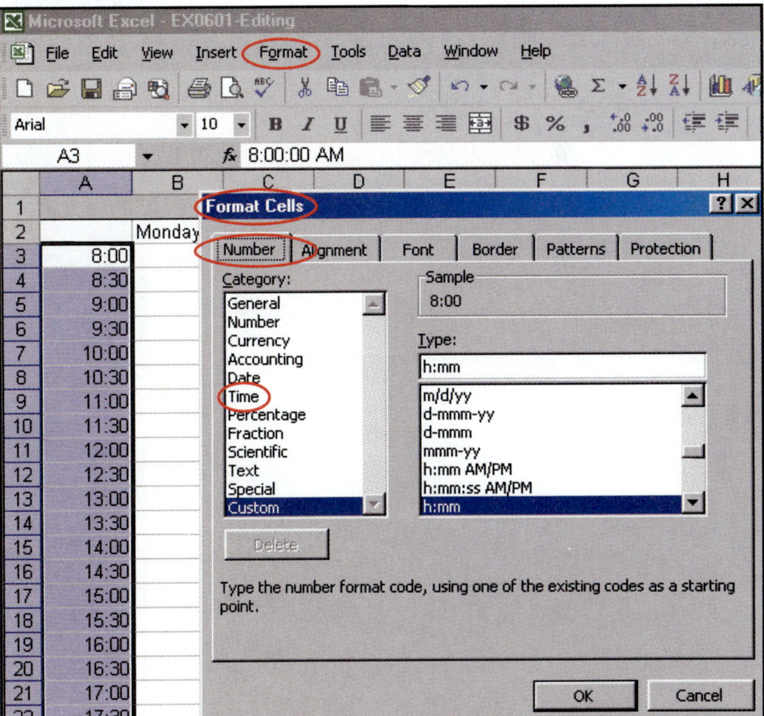

**7** With cells **A3** through **A29** still selected, choose **Format**, **Cells** to open the Format Cells dialog box. Click the **Number** tab, if necessary.

QUICK TIP

Many formatting options are also available from a shortcut menu that opens when you right-click on the selected cells.

**8** Click the **Time** option in the **Category** box.

*A series of examples is displayed in the **Type** box.*

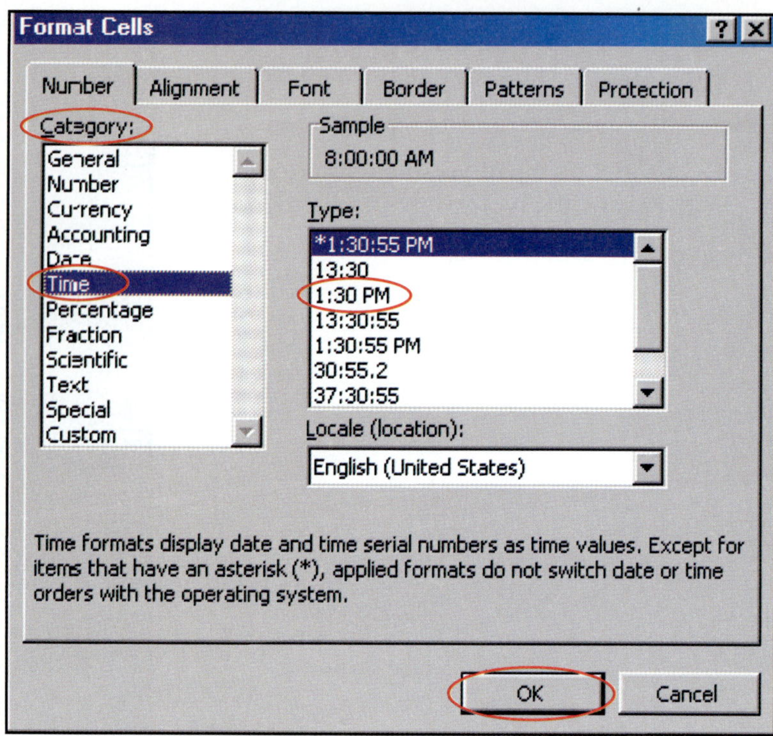

**9** Click the **1:30 PM** sample format and click **OK**.

*The series of times are displayed using the selected format.*

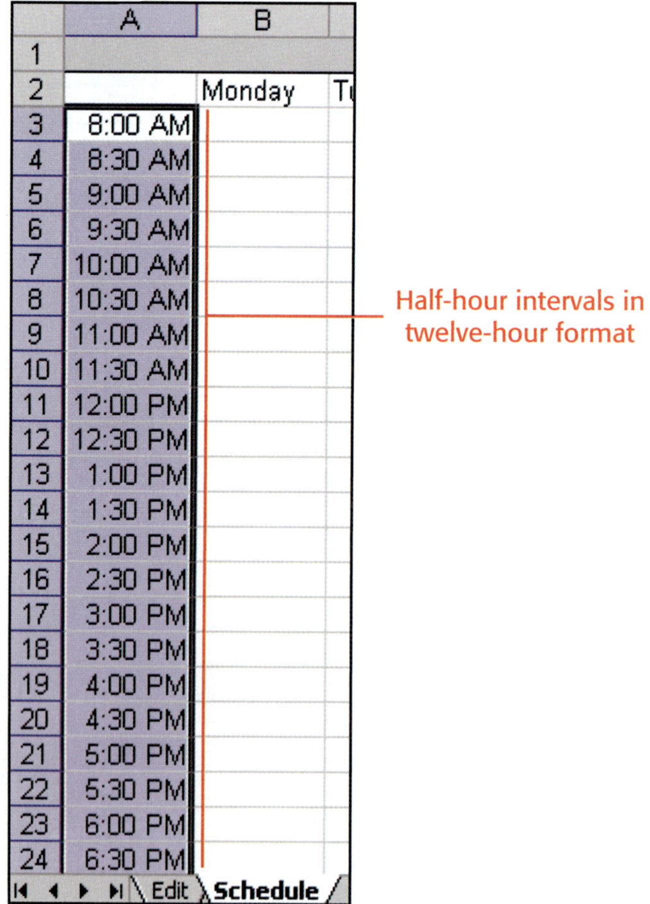

# Task 4
## COPYING CELL CONTENTS

### Why would I do this?

Some worksheets require the display of the same data in many cells. For example, a business that is open from 8 AM to 9 PM, Monday through Sunday, uses six different part-time employees. If you wanted to post a work schedule for these employees, you would have to fill out a table with more than 200 cells.

In this task, you learn how to use the fill, copy, and paste techniques to fill out a form with repetitive data.

**1** Select cell **B3**, type **Bill**, and press ↵Enter.

Select cell **B3** again. Click-and-drag the fill handle down through cell **B14**. Release the mouse button.

*Bill's name is filled into the cells from B4 through B14.*

| | A | B | C |
|---|---|---|---|
| 1 | | | Sc |
| 2 | | Monday | Tuesday |
| 3 | 8:00 AM | Bill | |
| 4 | 8:30 AM | Bill | |
| 5 | 9:00 AM | Bill | |
| 6 | 9:30 AM | Bill | |
| 7 | 10:00 AM | Bill | |
| 8 | 10:30 AM | Bill | |
| 9 | 11:00 AM | Bill | |
| 10 | 11:30 AM | Bill | |
| 11 | 12:00 PM | Bill | |
| 12 | 12:30 PM | Bill | |
| 13 | 1:00 PM | Bill | |
| 14 | 1:30 PM | Bill | |
| 15 | 2:00 PM | | |
| 16 | 2:30 PM | | |

**2** Click-and-drag the fill handle to the right to cell **C14**. Release the mouse button.

*The cells to the right are filled with Bill's name.*

**CAUTION**

If someone else has used this computer to create a custom list that starts with Bill, you may see the custom list rather than Bill's name. If this occurs, you can either use the copy-and-paste method or delete the custom list. To delete the custom list, choose <u>T</u>ools, <u>O</u>ptions, click the Custom Lists tab, select the list you want to delete, and click <u>D</u>elete.

| | A | B | C | D |
|---|---|---|---|---|
| 1 | | | | Schedule for J |
| 2 | | Monday | Tuesday | Wednesda |
| 3 | 8:00 AM | Bill | Bill | |
| 4 | 8:30 AM | Bill | Bill | |
| 5 | 9:00 AM | Bill | Bill | |
| 6 | 9:30 AM | Bill | Bill | |
| 7 | 10:00 AM | Bill | Bill | |
| 8 | 10:30 AM | Bill | Bill | |
| 9 | 11:00 AM | Bill | Bill | |
| 10 | 11:30 AM | Bill | Bill | |
| 11 | 12:00 PM | Bill | Bill | |
| 12 | 12:30 PM | Bill | Bill | |
| 13 | 1:00 PM | Bill | Bill | |
| 14 | 1:30 PM | Bill | Bill | |
| 15 | 2:00 PM | | | |
| 16 | 2:30 PM | | | |

**3** Click cell **B3**.

*If the cells to which you want to copy Bill's name are not adjacent to those already containing his name, the fill handle is not the best choice. In this case, you want to show that Bill works on Thursday but not Wednesday.*

Click the **Copy** button on the Standard toolbar.

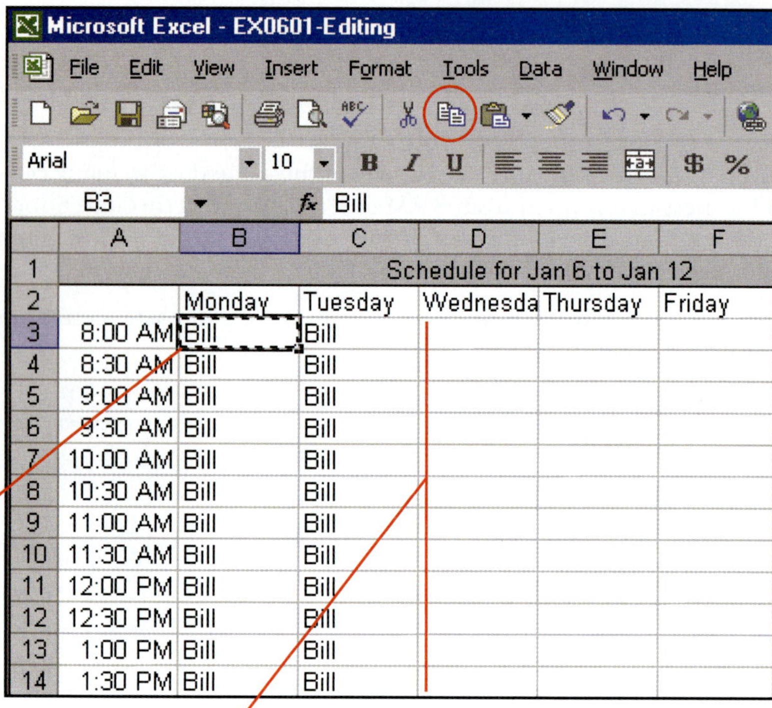




**4** Select cells **E3** through **E14**.

*Bill is scheduled to work from 8 AM to 2 PM on Thursday.*

Click the **Paste** button on the Standard toolbar.

*Bill's name is pasted into the entire cell range.*

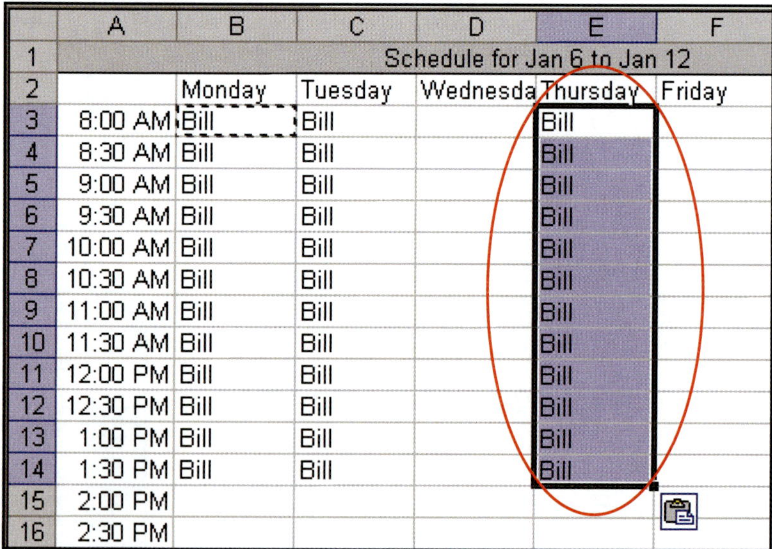

The marquee displays around cell B3 to indicate that it is still selected for further pasting if necessary. You may press Esc to deselect it, or it will automatically be deselected when you start entering data in another cell.

**5** Use the fill and copy techniques to fill out the rest of the schedule for the following employees:

**Angi**: Wednesday 8 AM to 2 PM and Saturday 2 PM to 9:30 PM

**Grace**: Thursday 2 PM to 9:30 PM and Friday 8 AM to 2 PM

**Scott**: Saturday 8 AM to 2 PM and Sunday 8 AM to 9:30 PM

**Alexis**: Tuesday 2 PM to 9:30 PM and Wednesday 2 PM to 9:30 PM

**Derek**: Monday 2 PM to 9:30 PM and Friday 2 PM to 9:30 PM

*The business closes at 9:00 PM, but it takes the employees an extra half hour to clean up. Each cell represents a half hour of work and is represented by the time at the beginning of the half hour. Someone who works until 9:30 PM has his name in the 9:00 cell.*

Click the **Save** button to save your work.

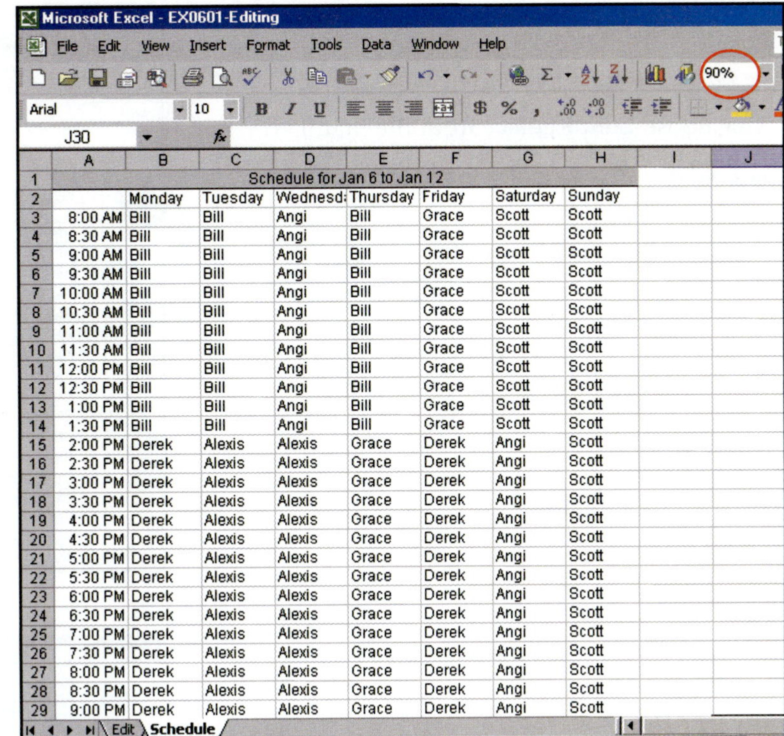



| | A | B | C | D | E | F | G | H | I | J |
|---|---|---|---|---|---|---|---|---|---|---|
| 1 | | | | Schedule for Jan 6 to Jan 12 | | | | | | |
| 2 | | Monday | Tuesday | Wednesd: | Thursday | Friday | Saturday | Sunday | | |
| 3 | 8:00 AM | Bill | Bill | Angi | Bill | Grace | Scott | Scott | | |
| 4 | 8:30 AM | Bill | Bill | Angi | Bill | Grace | Scott | Scott | | |
| 5 | 9:00 AM | Bill | Bill | Angi | Bill | Grace | Scott | Scott | | |
| 6 | 9:30 AM | Bill | Bill | Angi | Bill | Grace | Scott | Scott | | |
| 7 | 10:00 AM | Bill | Bill | Angi | Bill | Grace | Scott | Scott | | |
| 8 | 10:30 AM | Bill | Bill | Angi | Bill | Grace | Scott | Scott | | |
| 9 | 11:00 AM | Bill | Bill | Angi | Bill | Grace | Scott | Scott | | |
| 10 | 11:30 AM | Bill | Bill | Angi | Bill | Grace | Scott | Scott | | |
| 11 | 12:00 PM | Bill | Bill | Angi | Bill | Grace | Scott | Scott | | |
| 12 | 12:30 PM | Bill | Bill | Angi | Bill | Grace | Scott | Scott | | |
| 13 | 1:00 PM | Bill | Bill | Angi | Bill | Grace | Scott | Scott | | |
| 14 | 1:30 PM | Bill | Bill | Angi | Bill | Grace | Scott | Scott | | |
| 15 | 2:00 PM | Derek | Alexis | Alexis | Grace | Derek | Angi | Scott | | |
| 16 | 2:30 PM | Derek | Alexis | Alexis | Grace | Derek | Angi | Scott | | |
| 17 | 3:00 PM | Derek | Alexis | Alexis | Grace | Derek | Angi | Scott | | |
| 18 | 3:30 PM | Derek | Alexis | Alexis | Grace | Derek | Angi | Scott | | |
| 19 | 4:00 PM | Derek | Alexis | Alexis | Grace | Derek | Angi | Scott | | |
| 20 | 4:30 PM | Derek | Alexis | Alexis | Grace | Derek | Angi | Scott | | |
| 21 | 5:00 PM | Derek | Alexis | Alexis | Grace | Derek | Angi | Scott | | |
| 22 | 5:30 PM | Derek | Alexis | Alexis | Grace | Derek | Angi | Scott | | |
| 23 | 6:00 PM | Derek | Alexis | Alexis | Grace | Derek | Angi | Scott | | |
| 24 | 6:30 PM | Derek | Alexis | Alexis | Grace | Derek | Angi | Scott | | |
| 25 | 7:00 PM | Derek | Alexis | Alexis | Grace | Derek | Angi | Scott | | |
| 26 | 7:30 PM | Derek | Alexis | Alexis | Grace | Derek | Angi | Scott | | |
| 27 | 8:00 PM | Derek | Alexis | Alexis | Grace | Derek | Angi | Scott | | |
| 28 | 8:30 PM | Derek | Alexis | Alexis | Grace | Derek | Angi | Scott | | |
| 29 | 9:00 PM | Derek | Alexis | Alexis | Grace | Derek | Angi | Scott | | |

The figure is shown at 90% percent Zoom to show the whole work schedule. You do not have to make this change to your worksheet.

# Task 5

## USING FIND AND REPLACE

### Why would I do this?

The Find and Replace features can be time-savers in Excel just as they are in Word. If Bill quits and is replaced by Bob, you need to replace Bill's name with Bob's in numerous cells, and you need to be sure you find all of them.

In this task, you use the Replace feature to find each occurrence of Bill and replace it with Bob.

**1** Click cell **A2.**

*The search will begin from this location.*

Choose **Edit**, **Replace** from the menu.

*The Find and Replace dialog box is displayed.*

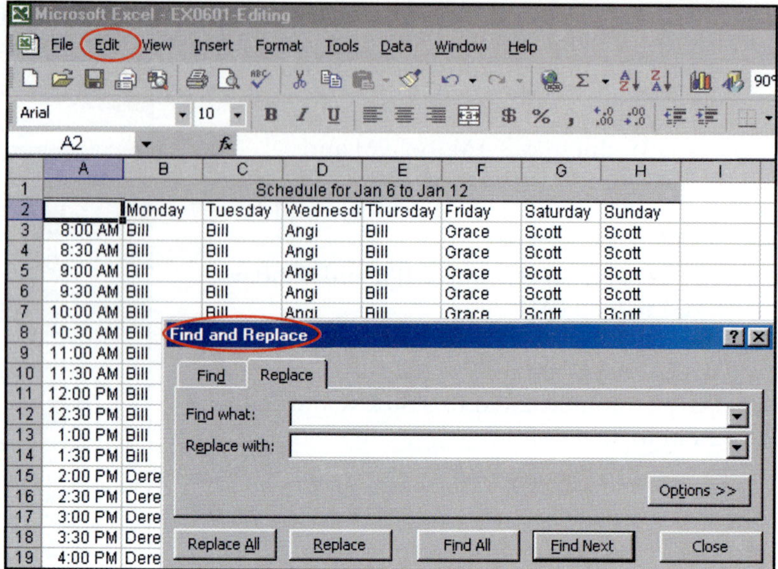

**2** Type **Bill** in the **Find what** box and press Tab.

Type **Bob** in the **Replace with** box.

*Excel has some replacement options that are different than those found in Word. These options are displayed if you use the Options button.*

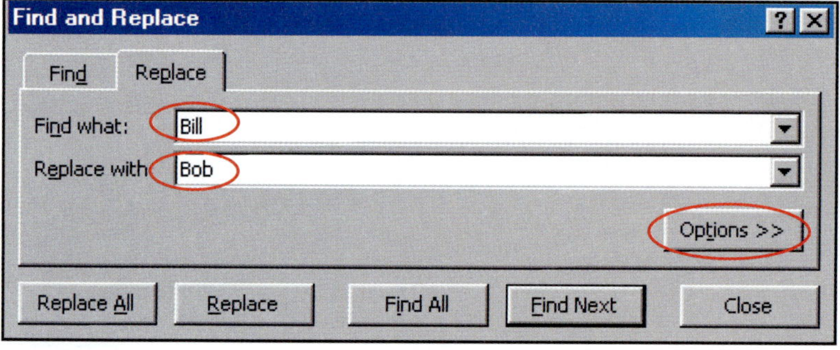

**3** Click the **Options** button.

*You may search within the current sheet or the whole workbook, and you can search by column or row.*

Click the down arrow next to the **Search** box and select **By Rows**, if necessary.

*The search will move across the sheet a row at a time.*

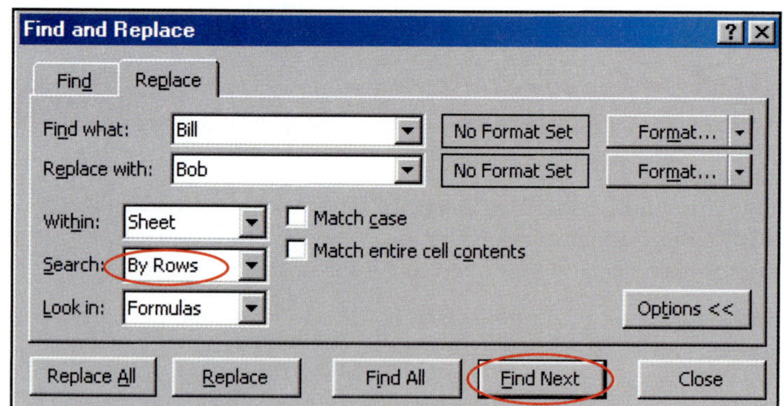

**4** Click the **Find Next** button.

*The selection moves to cell B3.*

Click the **Replace** button.

*Bill is replaced by Bob in cell B3, and the search moves on to the next occurrence in row 3.*

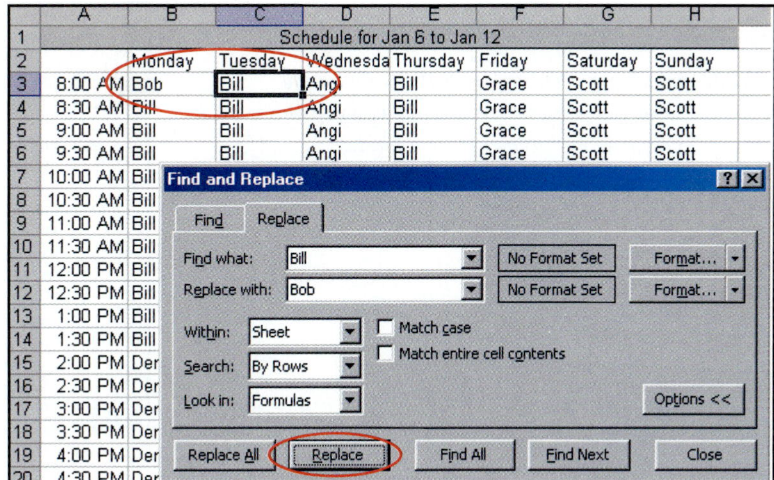

**5** Click **Find All**.

*A list displays the location of each remaining occurrence of Bill's name.*

Click **Replace**.

*The replacement is made in cell C3, and the search finds the next occurrence in cell E3.*

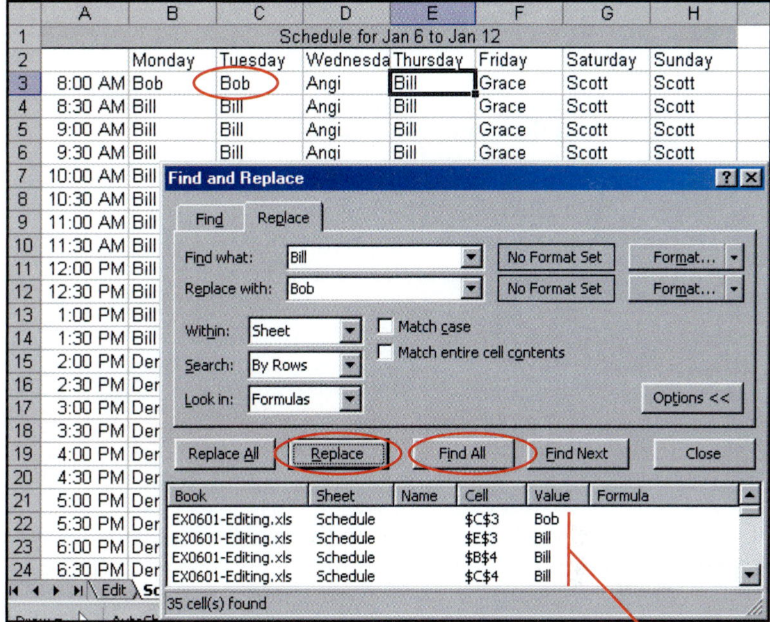

List of cells found
with Bill's name

IN DEPTH

The Find All option produces a list of all the cells in which Bill's name occurs. It also keeps track of new values that are placed in those cells, which is why the first item in the list shows Bob's name.

**6** Click the **Replace All** button.

*All the remaining occurrences of Bill's name are replaced with Bob's name. A message box informs you of how many replacements were made.*

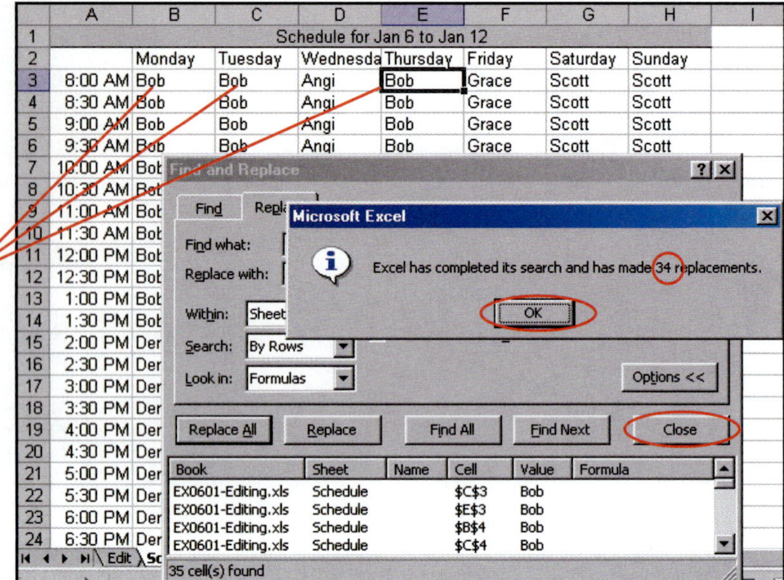


**7** Click **OK** and then close the dialog box.

Type your name in the Left Section area of the Custom Header, and then print the worksheet. Save your work and leave the workbook open for use in the next task.

# Task 6
## CREATING HYPERLINKS

### Why would I do this?

If worksheets get too large to view on the screen, it may be useful to put in some hyperlinks to jump to specific locations. Hyperlinks can also be used to jump to other related documents or to Web sites on the Internet.

In this task, you learn how to add a hyperlink that will take you to a worksheet in another workbook.

**1** Click the **Open** button. Find **EX0602** in the **Student** folder and open it.

*This file is similar to one you worked on in a previous lesson but some changes have been made. Notice that one of the worksheets is named Patio Furniture.*

Save the file as **EX0602-Hyperlink** on your disk and then close it.

In the **EX0601-Editing** file, click the **Edit** tab. Select cell **A15**, type **Patio Furniture** and press Enter.

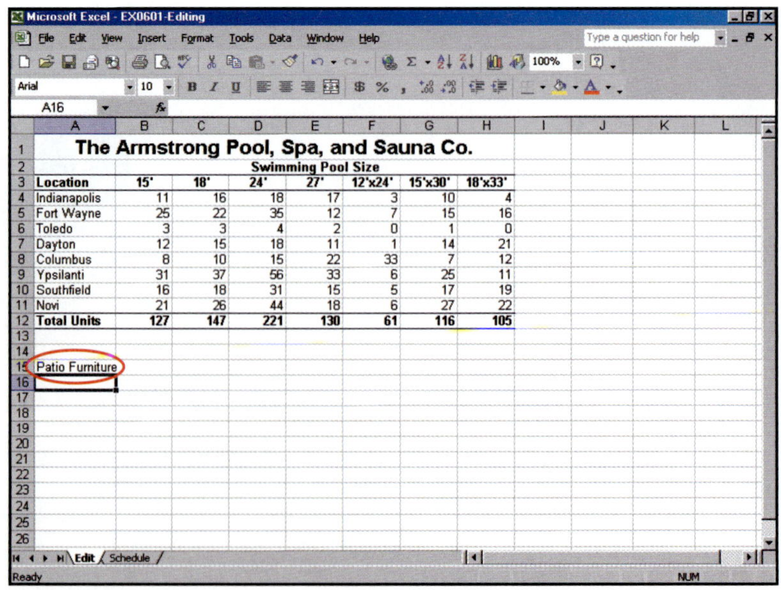

**2** Select cell **A15** again. Click the **Insert Hyperlink** button on the toolbar.

*The Insert Hyperlink dialog box is displayed.*

Use the **Look in** box to locate **EX0602-Hyperlink** on your disk and select it.

*The name of the folder in which you stored the file may differ from the example in the figure.*

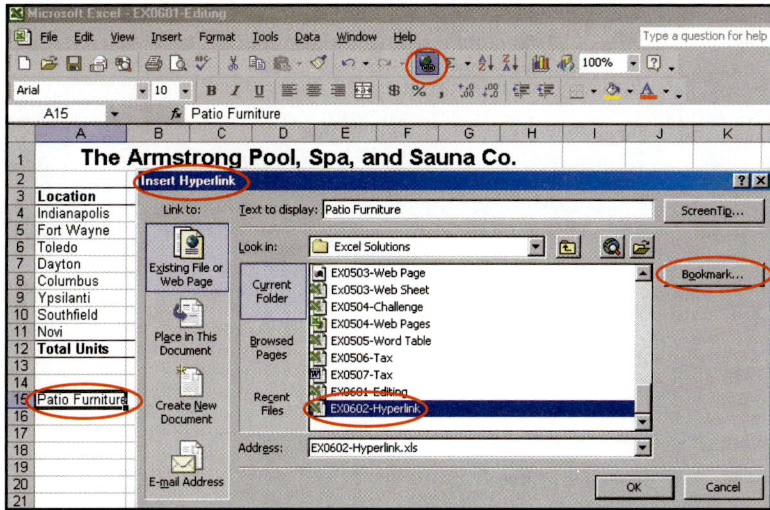

**3** Click the **Bookmark** button.

*Hyperlinks can connect directly to individual worksheets in a workbook.*

Select **Patio Furniture**. This is the name of the worksheet in the EX0602-Hyperlink workbook.

Names of worksheets in the target workbook

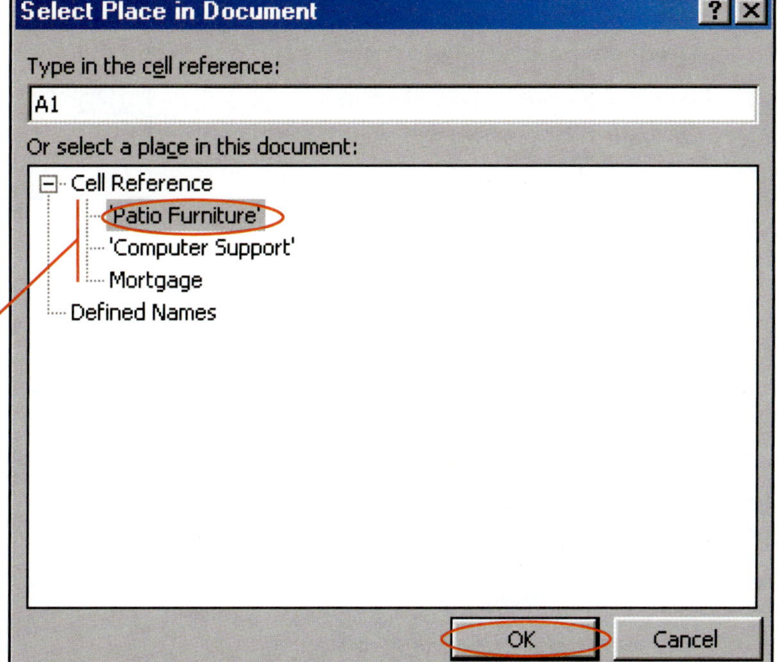




Bookmarks are used in Word to mark a specific location in a document. In Excel, you can use bookmarks that refer to worksheets or *named ranges*. A named range is one or more cells that have been assigned a name.

**4** Click **OK**.

*Notice that the worksheet name is included in the Address box.*

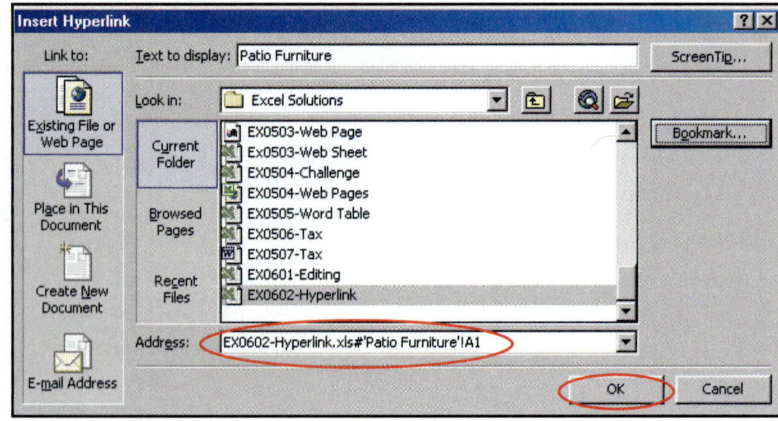

**5** Click **OK**.

*The text in cell A15 changes color to indicate that it is a hyperlink.*

Move the pointer onto the hyperlink.

*The pointer changes into a small hand, and a ScreenTip displays the address. Your ScreenTip address will be different from the one in the figure.*

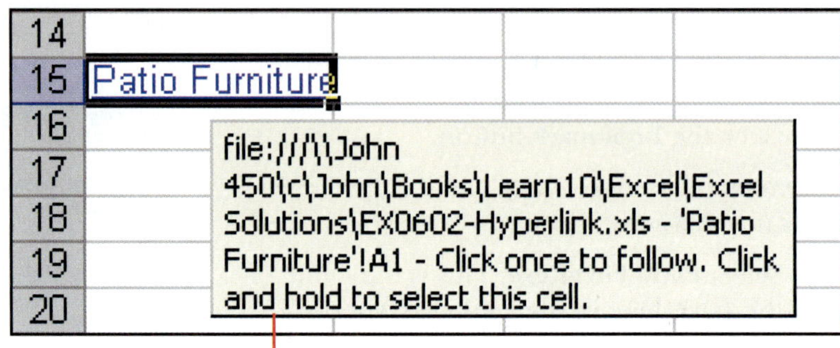


ScreenTip displays hyperlink
address and editing directions

When you hover the mouse pointer over the hyperlink, it also tells you how to select the cell using click-and-hold if you do not want to activate the hyperlink.

**6** Click the hyperlink.

*Excel opens the EX0602-Hyperlink workbook and selects the Patio Furniture worksheet. The Web toolbar opens, and the Back button is active.*

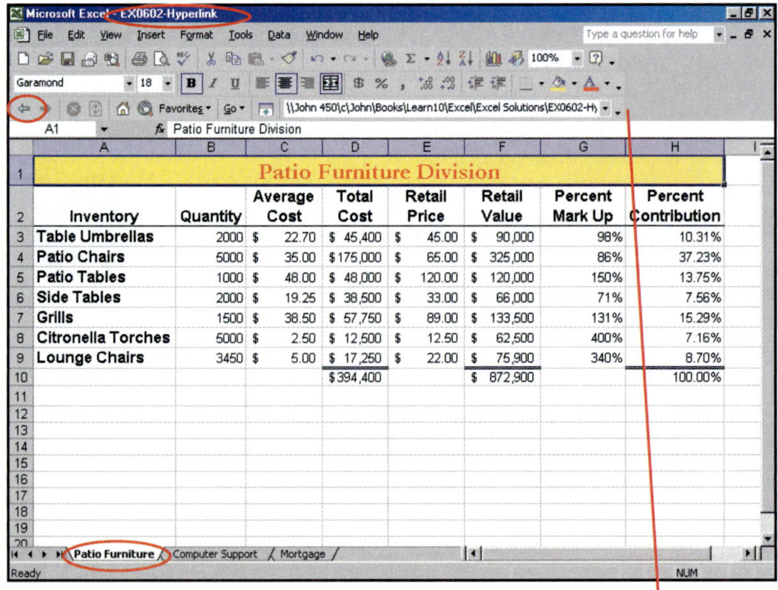

Web toolbar

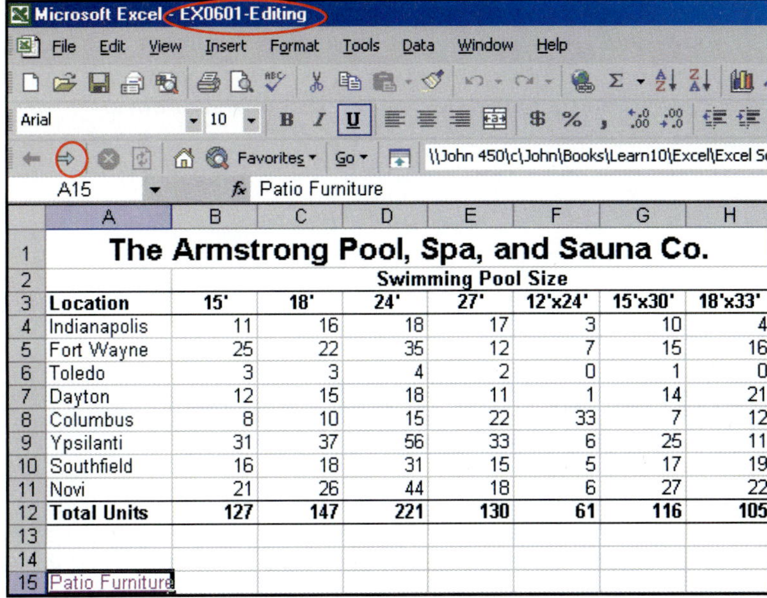

**7** Click the **Back** button.

*The previous worksheet with its hyperlink is displayed. Notice that the Web toolbar is still displayed and the Forward button is active. The color of the hyperlink text has changed to indicate this link has been used.*

**8** Click the **Forward** button. Close the **EX0602-Hyperlink** workbook.

*The EX0602-Hyperlink workbook is displayed.*

Type your name in the <u>L</u>eft Section area of the Custom Header, and then print the worksheet. Close the **EX0601-Editing** workbook. Save your changes when prompted.

The exercises that follow are designed for you to review and use what you have learned in this lesson. You also have the opportunity to practice your skills and then expand on them by applying them to new situations.

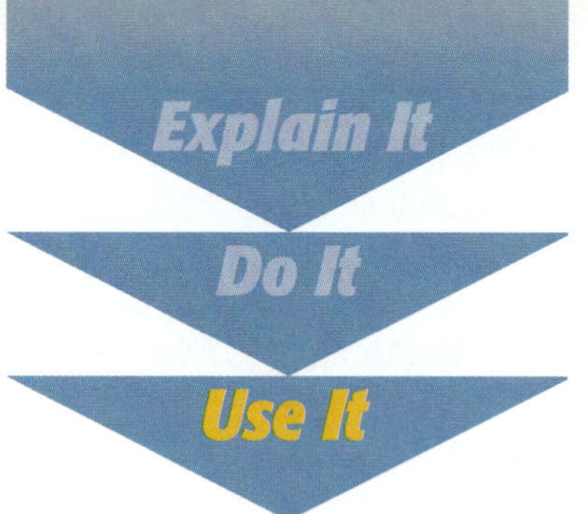


## COMPREHENSION

Comprehension exercises are designed to check your memory and understanding of the basic concepts in this lesson. You distinguish between true and false statements, identify new screen elements, and match terms with related statements. If you are uncertain of the correct answer, refer to the task number following each item (for example, T4 refers to Task 4), and review that task until you are confident you can provide a correct response.

### TRUE-FALSE

Circle either T or F.

T   F   **1.** One way to change a number in a cell is to select the cell and type the new number. **(T1)**

T   F   **2.** When you select a cell, the contents are shown both in the cell and in a box on the Formula bar near the top of the screen. **(T1)**

T   F   **3.** The fill handle is located in the lower-left corner of the selected cell. **(T2)**

T   F   **4.** Once a series of values has been created using the fill handle, you can extend the series further using the fill handle. **(T3)**

T   F   **5.** The Copy button on the Standard toolbar looks like a small clipboard with a page in front of it. **(T4)**

T   F   **6.** If you want to copy the contents of a single cell into a contiguous column of cells, you must do it one at a time. **(T4)**

### MATCHING QUESTIONS

**A.** Double-click     **D.** Fill handle

**B.** January     **E.** Name box

**C.** Replace     **F.** 9:00, 9:15

Match the following statements to the word or phrase that is the best match from the list. Write the letter of the matching word or phrase in the space provided next to the number.

**1.** _____ Shows the cell that is selected **(T1)**

**2.** _____ Action that may be used to begin editing the contents of a cell **(T1)**

**3.** _____ An example of a first label in a sequence **(T2)**

**4.** _____ Values that can be used to fill a column or row with times that are separated by fifteen-minute increments **(T3)**

**5.** _____ Method used to change numerous entries from one value to another **(T5)**

**6.** _____ Small box at the lower-right corner of a selected cell **(T2)**

Refer to the figure and identify the numbered parts of
the screen. Write the letter of the correct label in the
space next to the number.

1. ______________

2. ______________

3. ______________

4. ______________

5. ______________

6. ______________

7. ______________

8. ______________

9. ______________

10. ______________

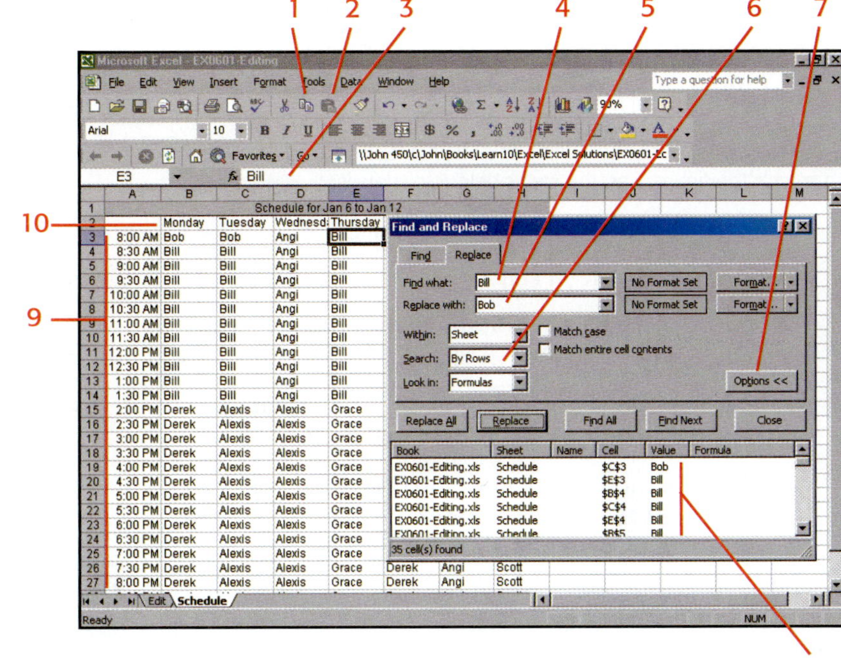

A. Formula bar  **(T1)**

B. List of cells found with "Bill"  **(T5)**

C. Copy button  **(T4)**

D. Paste button  **(T4)**

E. Repeating series at half-hour intervals  **(T3)**

F. Sequential text headings  **(T3)**

G. Text used for replacement  **(T5)**

H. Text or number to be found  **(T5)**

I. Direction of search  **(T5)**

J. Displays search options  **(T5)**

# REINFORCEMENT

Reinforcement exercises are designed to reinforce the skills you have learned by applying them to new situations. Detailed instructions are provided along with a figure, where appropriate, to illustrate the result. The reinforcement exercises that follow should be completed sequentially. Leave the workbook open at the end of each exercise for use in the next exercise until you are specifically directed to close it.

Open **EX0603** and save it as **EX0603-Reinforcement** on your disk for use in the following exercises.

## R1—Changing Numbers and Editing Text

Edit the Budget sheet by editing the titles, headings, and numbers to match the figure. See the steps below for details.

1. Select the **Budget** sheet, if necessary.

2. Enter your name in cell **A22**.

3. Double-click cell **A2**. Edit the year in this cell and change it from **2000** to **2002**.

4. Select cell **G8** (Other Income for June). Change the value in this cell from **2500** to **25000**.

5. Adjust the width of column **N** to display the full contents of cell **N20**. Save and print the worksheet. Leave the workbook open for use in the next exercise.

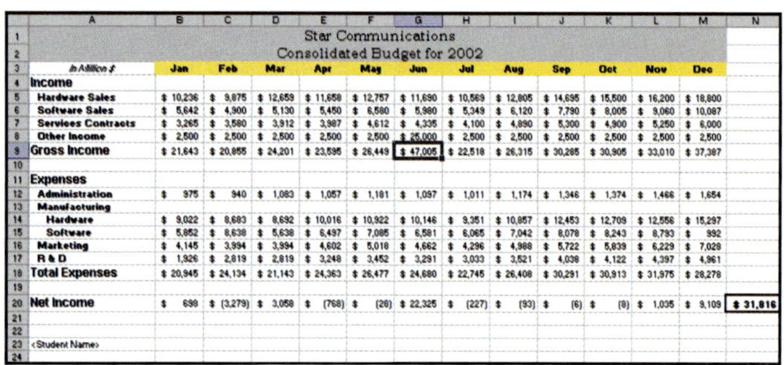

| | A | Jan | Feb | Mar | Apr | May | Jun | Jul | Aug | Sep | Oct | Nov | Dec | N |
|---|---|---|---|---|---|---|---|---|---|---|---|---|---|---|
| 1 | | | | | Star Communications | | | | | | | | | |
| 2 | | | | | Consolidated Budget for 2002 | | | | | | | | | |
| 3 | In Millions $ | Jan | Feb | Mar | Apr | May | Jun | Jul | Aug | Sep | Oct | Nov | Dec | |
| 4 | **Income** | | | | | | | | | | | | | |
| 5 | Hardware Sales | $ 10,236 | $ 9,875 | $ 12,659 | $ 11,658 | $ 12,757 | $ 11,690 | $ 10,569 | $ 12,805 | $ 14,695 | $ 15,500 | $ 16,200 | $ 18,800 | |
| 6 | Software Sales | $ 5,642 | $ 4,900 | $ 5,130 | $ 5,450 | $ 6,580 | $ 5,980 | $ 5,349 | $ 6,120 | $ 7,790 | $ 8,005 | $ 9,060 | $ 10,087 | |
| 7 | Services Contracts | $ 3,265 | $ 3,580 | $ 3,912 | $ 3,987 | $ 4,612 | $ 4,335 | $ 4,100 | $ 4,890 | $ 5,300 | $ 4,900 | $ 5,250 | $ 6,000 | |
| 8 | Other Income | $ 2,500 | $ 2,500 | $ 2,500 | $ 2,500 | $ 2,500 | $ 25,000 | $ 2,500 | $ 2,500 | $ 2,500 | $ 2,500 | $ 2,500 | $ 2,500 | |
| 9 | **Gross Income** | $ 21,643 | $ 20,855 | $ 24,201 | $ 23,595 | $ 26,449 | $ 47,005 | $ 22,518 | $ 26,315 | $ 30,285 | $ 30,905 | $ 33,010 | $ 37,387 | |
| 10 | | | | | | | | | | | | | | |
| 11 | **Expenses** | | | | | | | | | | | | | |
| 12 | Administration | $ 975 | $ 940 | $ 1,083 | $ 1,057 | $ 1,181 | $ 1,097 | $ 1,011 | $ 1,174 | $ 1,346 | $ 1,374 | $ 1,466 | $ 1,654 | |
| 13 | Manufacturing | | | | | | | | | | | | | |
| 14 | Hardware | $ 9,022 | $ 8,683 | $ 8,692 | $ 10,016 | $ 10,922 | $ 10,146 | $ 9,351 | $ 10,857 | $ 12,453 | $ 12,709 | $ 12,556 | $ 15,297 | |
| 15 | Software | $ 5,852 | $ 8,638 | $ 5,638 | $ 6,497 | $ 7,085 | $ 6,581 | $ 6,065 | $ 7,042 | $ 8,078 | $ 8,243 | $ 8,793 | $ 992 | |
| 16 | Marketing | $ 4,145 | $ 3,994 | $ 3,994 | $ 4,602 | $ 5,018 | $ 4,662 | $ 4,296 | $ 4,988 | $ 5,722 | $ 5,839 | $ 6,229 | $ 7,028 | |
| 17 | R & D | $ 1,326 | $ 2,819 | $ 2,819 | $ 3,248 | $ 3,452 | $ 3,291 | $ 3,033 | $ 3,521 | $ 4,038 | $ 4,122 | $ 4,397 | $ 4,961 | |
| 18 | **Total Expenses** | $ 20,945 | $ 24,134 | $ 21,143 | $ 24,363 | $ 26,477 | $ 24,680 | $ 22,745 | $ 26,408 | $ 30,291 | $ 30,913 | $ 31,975 | $ 28,278 | |
| 19 | | | | | | | | | | | | | | |
| 20 | **Net Income** | $ 698 | $ (3,279) | $ 3,058 | $ (768) | $ (28) | $ 22,325 | $ (227) | $ (93) | $ (6) | $ (8) | $ 1,035 | $ 9,109 | $ 31,816 |
| 21 | | | | | | | | | | | | | | |
| 22 | | | | | | | | | | | | | | |
| 23 | ‹Student Name› | | | | | | | | | | | | | |
| 24 | | | | | | | | | | | | | | |

5. Use Fill and/or Copy to put **Tax** (a tax accounting firm) in office 104 from July to December and in offices 108 through 118. Place **Arch** (an architectural firm) in 106 and **Admin** (administrative staff) in 120.

6. Adjust column widths of each column to fit the contents as shown.

7. Center the column headings in row **3**.

8. Use **File**, **Page Setup** and put your name in a custom footer.

9. Save and print the worksheet. Leave the workbook open for use in the next exercise.

| | A | 100 | 102 | 104 | 106 | 108 | 110 | 112 | 114 | 116 | 118 | 120 |
|---|---|---|---|---|---|---|---|---|---|---|---|---|
| 1 | | | | Office Leases | | | | | | | | |
| 2 | | | | Office Number | | | | | | | | |
| 3 | Month | 100 | 102 | 104 | 106 | 108 | 110 | 112 | 114 | 116 | 118 | 120 |
| 4 | January | Armstrong | Armstrong | Armstrong | Arch | Tax | Tax | Tax | Tax | Tax | Tax | Admin |
| 5 | February | Armstrong | Armstrong | Armstrong | Arch | Tax | Tax | Tax | Tax | Tax | Tax | Admin |
| 6 | March | Armstrong | Armstrong | Armstrong | Arch | Tax | Tax | Tax | Tax | Tax | Tax | Admin |
| 7 | April | Armstrong | Armstrong | Armstrong | Arch | Tax | Tax | Tax | Tax | Tax | Tax | Admin |
| 8 | May | Armstrong | Armstrong | Armstrong | Arch | Tax | Tax | Tax | Tax | Tax | Tax | Admin |
| 9 | June | Armstrong | Armstrong | Armstrong | Arch | Tax | Tax | Tax | Tax | Tax | Tax | Admin |
| 10 | July | Armstrong | Armstrong | Tax | Arch | Tax | Tax | Tax | Tax | Tax | Tax | Admin |
| 11 | August | Armstrong | Armstrong | Tax | Arch | Tax | Tax | Tax | Tax | Tax | Tax | Admin |
| 12 | September | Armstrong | Armstrong | Tax | Arch | Tax | Tax | Tax | Tax | Tax | Tax | Admin |
| 13 | October | Armstrong | Armstrong | Tax | Arch | Tax | Tax | Tax | Tax | Tax | Tax | Admin |
| 14 | November | Armstrong | Armstrong | Tax | Arch | Tax | Tax | Tax | Tax | Tax | Tax | Admin |
| 15 | December | Armstrong | Armstrong | Tax | Arch | Tax | Tax | Tax | Tax | Tax | Tax | Admin |

## R2—Creating a Sheet to Track Leases

In this exercise, you create a lease report worksheet for a small office building. Refer to the figure and fill in the sheet. Use the following steps to make sure that you completed all of the required steps.

1. Click the **Leases** tab to select the Leases sheet.

2. Fill in the months in column **A**.

3. Select the first two office numbers in cells **B3** and **C3**; then fill in the column labels up to **120** in column **L**.

4. Type **Armstrong** in cell **B4**. Fill the name into all the cells for offices 100 and 102. Copy the name into the cells for January through June for office 104.

## R3—Replacing One Name with Another

In this exercise, you modify the Leases worksheet when you find out that the tax accounting firm is moving out in September to be replaced by a hair salon.

1. Select cell **D12**.

2. Choose **Edit**, **Replace** from the menu.

3. Type **Tax** in the **Find what** box and **Hair** in the **Replace with** box.

4. Click the **Options** button. Choose to search by rows.

5. Drag the Find and Replace dialog up and to the left so that you can see rows **12** through **15**.

6. Click the **Replace** button.

7. Click **Replace** repeatedly until all the occurrences of **Tax** have been changed to **Hair** for September through December as shown.

8. Close the dialog box and save your changes. Print the worksheet. Leave the workbook open for use in the next exercise.

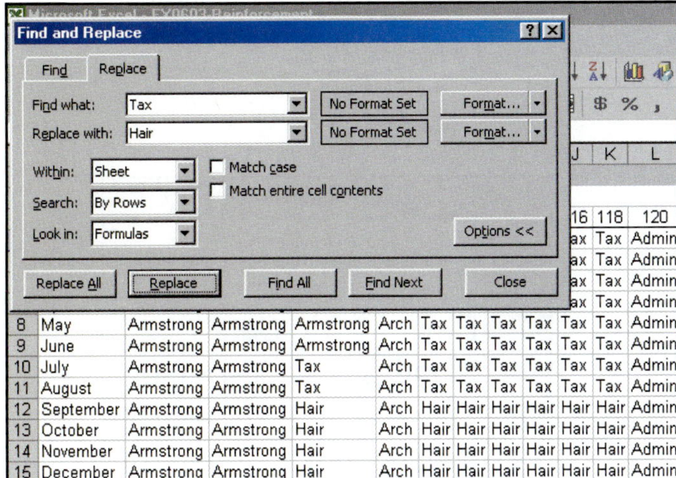

## R4—Replacing Data and Formats

In this exercise, search for and replace numbers and formatting.

1. Click the **Budget** sheet tab and select cell **A1**.

2. Choose **Edit**, **Replace**. Type **2500** in the **Find what** box and **3000** in the **Replace with** box.

3. Click the check box next to **Match entire cell contents** to avoid partial matches. (This is very important when replacing numbers.) Confirm that **By Rows** is selected in the **Search** box.

4. Click the **Find Next** button. The selection will jump to cell **B8**. Click the **Replace** button.

5. Click the **Replace** button repeatedly to change the values in row **8**. Notice that it skips cell **G8**, where you changed the value in exercise R1.

6. Delete the values in the **Find what** box and the **Replace with** box.

7. Click the down arrow next to the **Format** button in line with the **Find what** box and choose **Format**. Choose the **Font** tab if necessary and select **Italic** in the **Font style** list. Click **OK**.

8. Click the down arrow next to the **Format** button in line with the **Replace with** box and choose **Format**. Choose the **Font** tab if necessary and select **Regular** in the **Font style** list. Click **OK**.

9. Click the **Find Next** button. It will find the only cell that is formatted in italics. Click the **Replace** button.

10. Close the dialog box. Save your changes and print the worksheet.

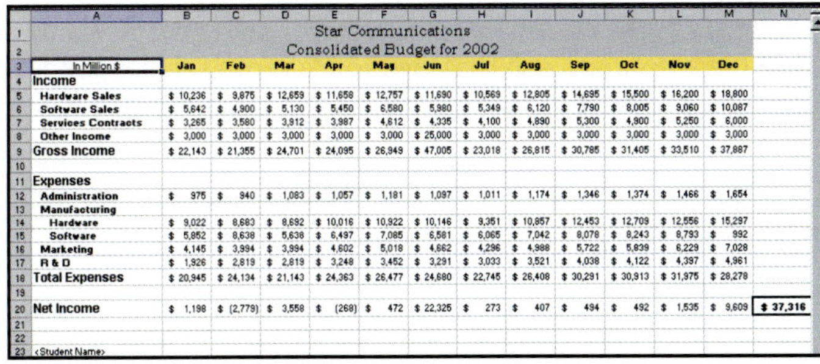

## R5—Hyperlink to a Worksheet in Another Workbook

In this exercise, you place a hyperlink in the **Budget** sheet to the Mortgage sheet in the **EX0602-Hyperlink** workbook.

This exercise uses the same file, **EX0602-Hyperlink**, that you created in Task 6. If you did not do Task 6, open **EX0602** in the **Student** folder and save it as **EX0602-Hyperlink**. Close the workbook.

1. Click the **Budget** sheet tab, if necessary, and select cell **A25**.

2. Type **Loan Calculation** and press ↵Enter.

3. Select cell **A25** again and click the **Insert Hyperlink** button on the toolbar.

4. Find and select the **EX0602-Hyperlink** workbook. Click the **Bookmark** button.

5. Choose **Mortgage** and click **OK** in both dialog boxes to close them.

6. Click the **Loan Calculation** hyperlink to jump to the **Mortgage** worksheet in the **EX0602-Hyperlink** workbook.

7. Click the **Back** button on the Web toolbar to return to the **EX0602-Reinforcement** workbook.

8. Save your changes to the **EX0603-Reinforcement** workbook. Print the worksheet and close both workbooks.

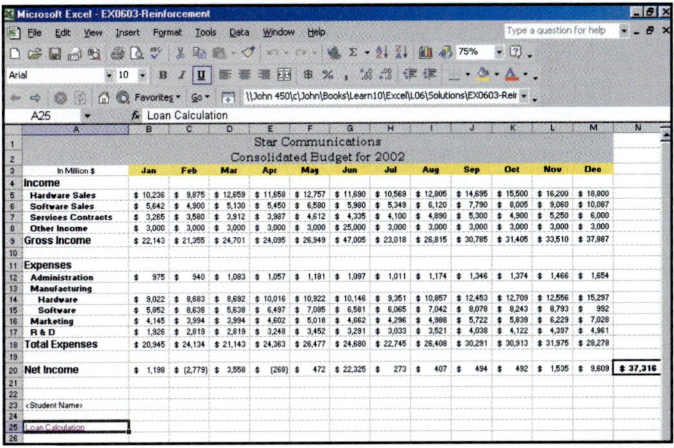

Challenge exercises are designed to test your ability to apply your skills to new situations with less-detailed instructions. These exercises also challenge you to expand your repertoire of skills by using commands that are similar to those you have already learned. The desired outcome is clearly defined, but you have more freedom to choose the steps needed to achieve the required result.

The Challenge exercises use separate sheets in the workbook, EX0604-Challenge. The exercises are not sequential and do not depend on each other.

Open **EX0604** and save it on your disk as **EX0604-Challenge**.

### C1—Filling Workdays Only and Checking Spelling

Several different series are commonly used in business. Excel can fill in weekdays only, as well as each day of the week.

*Goal:* Set up a worksheet to track time worked during the Monday through Friday work week.

1. Select the **Schedule** worksheet.

2. Select cell **A4**. Use the fill handle to fill down through cell **A23**.

3. Click the down arrow on the **AutoFill Options** button that is attached to the fill handle and select **Fill Weekdays**.

4. Use the same method to fill the corresponding dates in column **B**.

5. Click in an unused cell to deselect the cells in column **B**. Choose **Tools**, **Spelling**. Choose **Yes** if asked to continue at the beginning of the sheet. A misspelled word, **Workd**, is located in the title.

6. Confirm that **Worked** is selected from the list of **Suggestions** and click the **Change** button.

7. The next word found, **Ferrett**, is a proper name in the heading of column **E**. Click the **Ignore Once** button. Click **OK** to finish the spelling check.

8. Save the workbook. Type your name in cell **A25**, and then print the worksheet. Leave this file open for use in the next Challenge exercise.

| | A | B |
|---|---|---|
| 1 | | |
| 2 | | |
| 3 | Day | Date |
| 4 | Monday | 30-Dec-02 |
| 5 | Tuesday | 31-Dec-02 |
| 6 | Wednesday | 1-Jan-03 |
| 7 | Thursday | 2-Jan-03 |
| 8 | Friday | 3-Jan-03 |
| 9 | Monday | 6-Jan-03 |
| 10 | Tuesday | 7-Jan-03 |
| 11 | Wednesday | 8-Jan-03 |
| 12 | Thursday | 9-Jan-03 |
| 13 | Friday | 10-Jan-03 |
| 14 | Monday | 13-Jan-03 |
| 15 | Tuesday | 14-Jan-03 |
| 16 | Wednesday | 15-Jan-03 |
| 17 | Thursday | 16-Jan-03 |
| 18 | Friday | 17-Jan-03 |
| 19 | Monday | 20-Jan-03 |
| 20 | Tuesday | 21-Jan-03 |
| 21 | Wednesday | 22-Jan-03 |
| 22 | Thursday | 23-Jan-03 |
| 23 | Friday | 24-Jan-03 |
| 24 | | |

Schedule / Cruise

## C2—Filling Dates with a Weekly Interval

The menu of options for filling dates includes workdays, monthly, and yearly, but not weekly. In this exercise, you fill out a schedule of dates for a cruise ship line whose ships depart every Sunday and return every Friday.

*Goal:* Establish an interval of seven days and then fill in the dates that are one week apart.

1. Select the **Cruise Dates** worksheet. Select cell **A5**.

2. Enter the date for the next Sunday in the series.

3. Select the first two dates in the series (cells **A4** and **A5**).

4. Use the fill handle to fill in the dates to March 30, 2003.

5. Use the same method to fill in the second column of dates for the Fridays in the schedule.

6. Save the workbook. Type your name in cell **A23** and print the worksheet. Leave the workbook open for the next exercise.

|    | A | B | C | D |
|----|---|---|---|---|
| 1  | Cruise Ships leave on Sunday and Return on Friday | | | |
| 2  | | | | |
| 3  | Departure | Return | | |
| 4  | 1-Dec-02 | 6-Dec-02 | | |
| 5  | 8-Dec-02 | 13-Dec-02 | | |
| 6  | 15-Dec-02 | 20-Dec-02 | | |
| 7  | 22-Dec-02 | 27-Dec-02 | | |
| 8  | 29-Dec-02 | 3-Jan-03 | | |
| 9  | 5-Jan-03 | 10-Jan-03 | | |
| 10 | 12-Jan-03 | 17-Jan-03 | | |
| 11 | 19-Jan-03 | 24-Jan-03 | | |
| 12 | 26-Jan-03 | 31-Jan-03 | | |
| 13 | 2-Feb-03 | 7-Feb-03 | | |
| 14 | 9-Feb-03 | 14-Feb-03 | | |
| 15 | 16-Feb-03 | 21-Feb-03 | | |
| 16 | 23-Feb-03 | 28-Feb-03 | | |
| 17 | 2-Mar-03 | 7-Mar-03 | | |
| 18 | 9-Mar-03 | 14-Mar-03 | | |
| 19 | 16-Mar-03 | 21-Mar-03 | | |
| 20 | 23-Mar-03 | 28-Mar-03 | | |
| 21 | 30-Mar-03 | 4-Apr-03 | | |
| 22 | | | | |
| 23 | | | | |
| 24 | | | | |

Schedule \ **Cruise Dates** / Population / Car Payn

## C3—Projecting Population Growth

Increases in population require social services to provide for more people each year, and it is important to project that growth when planning for the future. If the population is growing at a steady rate, the actual number of additional people is not the same each year but increases because it is a percentage of the previous year. You can use Excel to fill in a series of numbers which grows by a given percentage increase over the previous year.

*Goal:* Use the Fill Series options to fill in a range of years and a series of population figures that increase by 1% each year.

1. Click the **Population** worksheet tab.

2. Select cell **A3**. Click-and-drag the fill handle down to cell **A31**. (Excel cannot be certain that 2002 is a date, so it does not automatically increment the number.)

3. Click the down arrow on the **Auto Fill Options** button attached to the fill handle and choose **Fill Series**.

4. Select cell **B3**. This time, use the right mouse button to click-and-drag the fill handle down to cell **B31**.

5. Select **Series** from the shortcut menu.

6. Choose **Growth** as the **Type**. Enter a **Step value** of **1.01** (this is how you get a 1% increase each year) and click **OK**.

7. Format the numbers in column **B** to display one decimal place.

8. Save the workbook. Type your name in cell **A25** and print the worksheet. Leave the workbook open for the next exercise.

|    | A | B | C | D |
|----|---|---|---|---|
| 1  | Population Growth at 1% per year | | | |
| 2  | Year | Population in Millions | | |
| 3  | 2002 | 265.0 | | |
| 4  | 2003 | 267.7 | | |
| 5  | 2004 | 270.3 | | |
| 6  | 2005 | 273.0 | | |
| 7  | 2006 | 275.8 | | |
| 8  | 2007 | 278.5 | | |
| 9  | 2008 | 281.3 | | |
| 10 | 2009 | 284.1 | | |
| 11 | 2010 | 287.0 | | |
| 12 | 2011 | 289.8 | | |
| 13 | 2012 | 292.7 | | |
| 14 | 2013 | 295.7 | | |
| 15 | 2014 | 298.6 | | |
| 16 | 2015 | 301.6 | | |
| 17 | 2016 | 304.6 | | |
| 18 | 2017 | 307.7 | | |
| 19 | 2018 | 310.7 | | |
| 20 | 2019 | 313.8 | | |
| 21 | 2020 | 317.0 | | |
| 22 | 2021 | 320.1 | | |
| 23 | 2022 | 323.4 | | |

Schedule / Cruise Dates \ **Population**

## C4—Customizing a Fill List

Excel recognizes several common sequences of names. You may want to create your own. For example, if your company works six days a week (closed Sunday), you may want to fill in a sequence of days that does not include Sundays. In this example, three friends decide to buy a car together and take turns making the car payment. Their names will appear many times, in the same sequence. If you create a custom list, you can fill in a column of names using the fill handle.

*Goal:* Create a custom list of three names that can be used to fill in the column that shows whose turn it is to pay the loan.

1. Select the **Car Payment** sheet. Select cell **E4**.

2. Enter the names **Jack**, **Bill**, and **Mary** in cells **E4**, **E5**, and **E6**, respectively. Select these three cells.

3. Choose **Tools**, **Options**, click the **Custom Lists** tab, and click the **Import** button. Your list of entries is displayed. Click **OK**.

4. Confirm that the three names are selected and use the fill handle to fill in the rest of the names in column **E**. The three names should repeat so that each person is responsible for a payment every third month.

5. Save the workbook. Type your name in cell **A9** and print the worksheet. Leave the workbook open for the next exercise.

| | A | B | C | D | E | F | G |
|---|---|---|---|---|---|---|---|
| 1 | Payment Schedule for Car Owned by Jack, Bill, and Mary | | | | | | |
| 2 | | | | | | | |
| | | | | Date | Person who will pay | Payment | Balance |
| 3 | Loan | 5000 | | | | | |
| 4 | Months | 48 | | 9/1/99 | Jack | ($122.06) | $4,911.27 |
| 5 | Annual Interest Rate | 8% | | 10/1/99 | Bill | ($122.06) | $4,821.95 |
| 6 | Interest rate per month | 0.667% | | 11/1/99 | Mary | ($122.06) | $4,732.03 |
| 7 | Payment | ($122.06) | | 12/1/99 | Jack | ($122.06) | $4,641.51 |
| 8 | | | | 1/1/00 | Bill | ($122.06) | $4,550.39 |
| 9 | | | | 2/1/00 | Mary | ($122.06) | $4,458.66 |
| 10 | | | | 3/1/00 | Jack | ($122.06) | $4,366.32 |
| 11 | | | | 4/1/00 | Bill | ($122.06) | $4,273.36 |
| 12 | | | | 5/1/00 | Mary | ($122.06) | $4,179.79 |
| 13 | | | | 6/1/00 | Jack | ($122.06) | $4,085.59 |
| 14 | | | | 7/1/00 | Bill | ($122.06) | $3,990.76 |
| 15 | | | | 8/1/00 | Mary | ($122.06) | $3,895.30 |
| 16 | | | | 9/1/00 | Jack | ($122.06) | $3,799.21 |
| 17 | | | | 10/1/00 | Bill | ($122.06) | $3,702.47 |
| 18 | | | | 11/1/00 | Mary | ($122.06) | $3,605.09 |
| 19 | | | | 12/1/00 | Jack | ($122.06) | $3,507.06 |

Schedule / Cruise Dates / Population / **Car Payment** / Keyboard / Fill

## C5—Using Keyboard Shortcuts to Fill and Format Cells

People who have to perform the same operation over and over find that it takes too long to take their hands off the keyboard to use the mouse. If your goal is higher productivity, you need to know how to use keyboard shortcuts.

If you have to do a lot of cutting, copying, and pasting, it is time consuming to take your hand off the keyboard and use a mouse to click a button on a toolbar or select an option from a menu. You may also need to cut, copy, or paste when a dialog box is open and the toolbars and menus are not available. At times like these, you can use the Ctrl key plus a keyboard letter to perform the task.

Some tasks require that you use menu options, but it will still be faster to use the keyboard to make the selection. In these cases, you can hold the Alt key and press the key that is underlined (the hot key) in the menu option to choose that option.

When you are done specifying your selections in a dialog box or window, you may need to choose a button such as **OK**, **Next**, or **Finish**. If a button has a bold outline, it can be selected by pressing ↵Enter.

*Goal:* Learn how to use the Ctrl key with another key to perform functions, the Alt key to select menu options, the ⬆Shift key with arrow keys to select cells, and ↵Enter to push buttons.

1. In the **EX0604-Challenge** workbook, select the **Keyboard** sheet.

2. Use the arrow keys to move the selection to cell **A1**. Press ⬆Shift and use the down arrow to select cells **A1** through **A12**.

3. Press Ctrl+C to copy the contents of the cells.

4. Use the arrow key to move the selection to cell **C1**. Press Ctrl+V to paste the selection.

5. Use the arrow keys to select cell **C3**. Use Ctrl+X to mark **Wednesday** to be cut out of cell **C3**. Use the arrow keys to move to cell **E3** and use Ctrl+V to paste **Wednesday** into cell **E3**.

6. Use keyboard shortcuts to copy **Wednesday**, select cells **E4** through **E12**, and paste it into them.

7. Use keyboard shortcuts to select cells **A1** through **E12**.

8. Notice that the **Format** menu option has an underlined letter **o**. (This is called a hot key.) Hold the Alt key and press the O key. Type the letter **e** (the underlined letter in **Cells**) to open the Format Cells dialog box.

9. Use `Ctrl`+`Tab`, if necessary to select the **Font** tab.
Use `Alt`+`O` to choose **Font style;** then use the arrow
keys to select **Bold Italic**.

10. Notice that the **OK** button has a darker border.
Press `Enter` to produce the same result as clicking
the **OK** button.

11. Save the workbook. Type your name in cell **A14** and
print the worksheet. Leave the workbook open for
the next exercise.

| | A | B | C | D | E | F |
|---|---|---|---|---|---|---|
| 1 | Monday | | Monday | | | |
| 2 | Tuesday | | Tuesday | | | |
| 3 | Wednesday | | | | Wednesday | |
| 4 | Thursday | | Thursday | | Wednesday | |
| 5 | Friday | | Friday | | Wednesday | |
| 6 | Saturday | | Saturday | | Wednesday | |
| 7 | Monday | | Monday | | Wednesday | |
| 8 | Tuesday | | Tuesday | | Wednesday | |
| 9 | Wednesday | | Wednesday | | Wednesday | |
| 10 | Thursday | | Thursday | | Wednesday | |
| 11 | Friday | | Friday | | Wednesday | |
| 12 | Saturday | | Saturday | | Wednesday | |

## C6—Using Advanced Fill Options

The right mouse button can be used with the fill handle
to provide several useful options.

*Goal:* Use the fill handle with the right mouse button to fill in the
columns as shown in the figure.

1. In the **EX0604-Challenge** workbook, select the **Fill**
sheet.

2. Select cell **A2**. Click-and-drag the fill handle down
through **A14** to copy the name into the cells.

3. Select cell **B2**. Click-and-drag the fill handle down
to **B14**. Click the down arrow on the **Auto Fill
Options** button and choose **Fill Series**.

4. Repeat this process for the values in columns **C**
through **H**. Refer to the heading of the column to
determine which option to use. Refer to the figure
to confirm each operation.

5. Select cell **I2**. Use the right mouse button to click-
and-drag the fill handle down to **I14**. Choose **Series**
from the shortcut menu. Select a **Linear** type with a
**Step value** of **1.1**.

6. Select cell **J2**. Use the right mouse button to click-
and-drag the fill handle down to **J14**. Choose **Series**
from the shortcut menu. Select a **Growth** type with
a **Step value** of **1.1**.

7. Save the workbook. Type your name in cell **A16** and
print the worksheet. Leave the workbook open for
the next exercise.

| | A | B | C | D | E | F | G | H | I | J |
|---|---|---|---|---|---|---|---|---|---|---|
| 1 | Copy Cells | Fill Series | Fill Formats | Fill Values | Fill Days | Fill Weekdays | Fill Months | Fill Years | Linear Trend | Growth Trend |
| 2 | Ralph | 100 | 100 | 100 | 9/15/99 | 9/15/99 | 9/15/99 | 9/15/99 | 100 | 100 |
| 3 | Ralph | 100 | 100 | 100 | 9/16/99 | 9/16/99 | 10/15/99 | 9/15/00 | 101.1 | 110 |
| 4 | Ralph | 100 | 100 | 100 | 9/17/99 | 9/17/99 | 11/15/99 | 9/15/01 | 102.2 | 121 |
| 5 | Ralph | 100 | 100 | 100 | 9/18/99 | 9/20/99 | 12/15/99 | 9/15/02 | 103.3 | 133.1 |
| 6 | Ralph | 100 | 100 | 100 | 9/19/99 | 9/21/99 | 1/15/00 | 9/15/03 | 104.4 | 146.41 |
| 7 | Ralph | 100 | 100 | 100 | 9/20/99 | 9/22/99 | 2/15/00 | 9/15/04 | 105.5 | 161.051 |
| 8 | Ralph | 100 | 100 | 100 | 9/21/99 | 9/23/99 | 3/15/00 | 9/15/05 | 106.6 | 177.1561 |
| 9 | Ralph | 100 | 100 | 100 | 9/22/99 | 9/24/99 | 4/15/00 | 9/15/06 | 107.7 | 194.8717 |
| 10 | Ralph | 100 | 100 | 100 | 9/23/99 | 9/27/99 | 5/15/00 | 9/15/07 | 108.8 | 214.3589 |
| 11 | Ralph | 100 | 100 | 100 | 9/24/99 | 9/28/99 | 6/15/00 | 9/15/08 | 109.9 | |
| 12 | Ralph | 100 | 100 | 100 | 9/25/99 | 9/29/99 | 7/15/00 | 9/15/09 | 111 | |
| 13 | Ralph | 100 | 100 | 100 | 9/26/99 | 9/30/99 | 8/15/00 | 9/15/10 | 112.1 | |
| 14 | Ralph | 100 | 100 | 100 | 9/27/99 | 10/1/99 | 9/15/00 | 9/15/11 | 113.2 | |

Values required but not shown

Create a worksheet to determine the income you would need in the future that would have as much buying power as a given income today. If we save a certain amount each year during our working years, we may have a large sum of money available to us to live on when we retire. Many people are misled by such figures because they do not consider that an income that looks adequate by today's standards may be too small after twenty or thirty years of inflation. We need to determine what it would take to live on at tomorrow's cost of living. We can estimate the effect of inflation on income by taking an amount that would seem sufficient today and creating a series of values, each of which is increased by a percentage that represents the rate of inflation.

Set up a worksheet that will contain a growth series that calculates how much your future retirement income would have to be each year in the future to have today's buying power.

Criteria for grading will be:

1. Demonstration of the ability to fill a series of years

2. Demonstration of the use of a growth series

Some examples of features that students have learned to use in previous classes to enhance their personal retirement income worksheet are listed below:

- Use of a growth series to show how an amount that would be sufficient to live on today must be adjusted upward by the inflation rate to determine what would be necessary in the future

- The rate of inflation and years to retirement are stated in separate cells.

- Since the income column is to be filled using the fill growth series feature, it will not be interactive with the cells that show the assumptions.

- The year column starts with this year and extends to the year when the student expects to retire.

- All dollar amounts are formatted with zero decimal places to reduce the clutter on the screen.

- Assume that inflation is usually about 3% less than the interest rate on very conservative investments like bank savings accounts.

3. Identify yourself. Place your name in a cell that is clearly visible.

4. To complete the project:

- Save your file on your own disk. Name it **EX0605-Income**.

- Check with your instructor to determine if the project should be submitted in electronic or printed form. If necessary, print out a copy of the worksheet to hand in.

# Lesson 7

## Becoming Proficient with Formatting Cells and Worksheets

**Task 1**  Copying, Deleting, Inserting, and Hiding Sheets
**Task 2**  Inserting, Deleting, Hiding, and Unhiding Rows and Columns
**Task 3**  Using the Format Painter and Applying AutoFormats
**Task 4**  Defining, Applying, and Removing a Style
**Task 5**  Changing the Zoom and Freezing Panes

## INTRODUCTION

Excel has many features that proficient users take advantage of to improve their efficiency. You can copy entire worksheets and paste them into other workbooks. You can hide worksheets, rows, or columns, change the magnification, and freeze parts of the window to make it easier to work with large sheets. For those who work in an organization that desires a uniform look to their documents, there are ways to quickly apply styles and formats that provide professional-looking results that are consistent from one worker to the next.

In this lesson, you will take a summary of four quarters of the previous year's sales and revise it for use in the next year. You will copy sheets from the original workbook into a new workbook and learn how to hide sheets and parts of worksheets. You will also learn how to change formatting more efficiently.

# VISUAL SUMMARY

When you have completed this entire lesson, you will have a worksheet that looks like this:

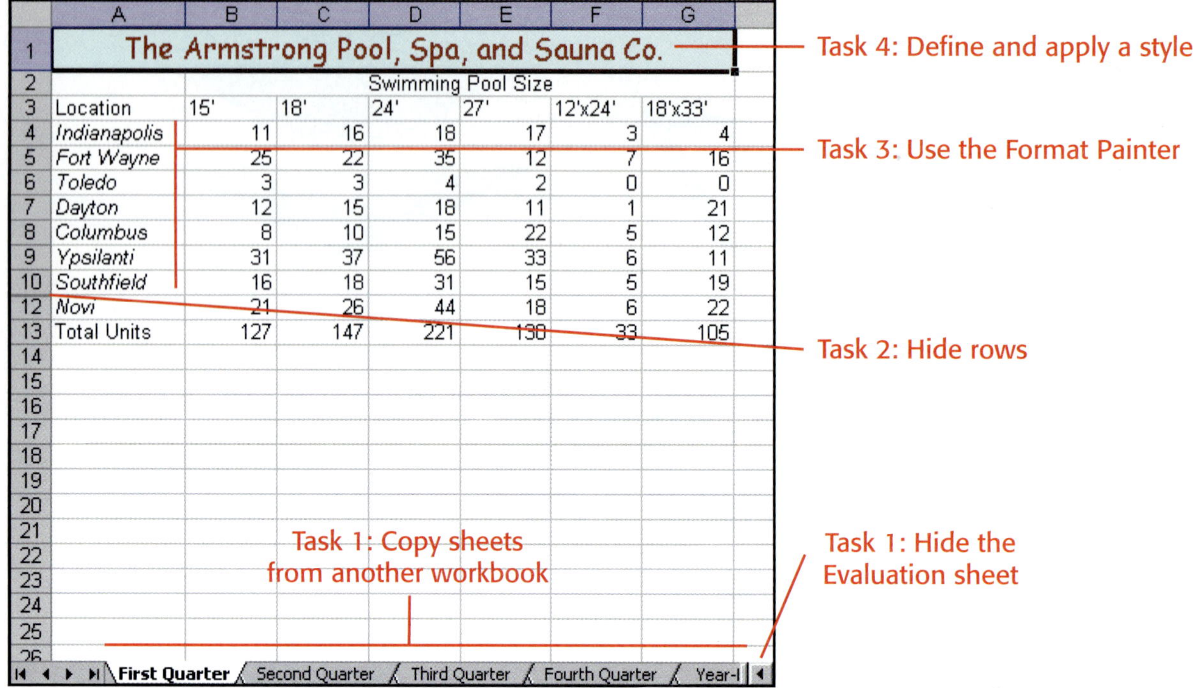



| | A | B | C | D | E | F | G |
|---|---|---|---|---|---|---|---|
| 1 | The Armstrong Pool, Spa, and Sauna Co. | | | | | | |
| 2 | | Swimming Pool Size | | | | | |
| 3 | Location | 15' | 18' | 24' | 27' | 12'x24' | 18'x33' |
| 4 | Indianapolis | 11 | 16 | 18 | 17 | 3 | 4 |
| 5 | Fort Wayne | 25 | 22 | 35 | 12 | 7 | 16 |
| 6 | Toledo | 3 | 3 | 4 | 2 | 0 | 0 |
| 7 | Dayton | 12 | 15 | 18 | 11 | 1 | 21 |
| 8 | Columbus | 8 | 10 | 15 | 22 | 5 | 12 |
| 9 | Ypsilanti | 31 | 37 | 56 | 33 | 6 | 11 |
| 10 | Southfield | 16 | 18 | 31 | 15 | 5 | 19 |
| 12 | Novi | 21 | 26 | 44 | 18 | 6 | 22 |
| 13 | Total Units | 127 | 147 | 221 | 130 | 33 | 105 |

First Quarter / Second Quarter / Third Quarter / Fourth Quarter / Year-l

| | A | B | C | D | E | F | G |
|---|---|---|---|---|---|---|---|
| 1 | The Armstrong Pool, Spa, and Sauna Co. | | | | | | |
| 2 | | Swimming Pool Size | | | | | |
| 3 | Location | 15' | 18' | 24' | 27' | 12'x24' | 18'x33' |
| 4 | Indianapolis | 15 | 16 | 18 | 17 | 3 | 4 |
| 5 | Fort Wayne | 25 | 29 | 35 | 12 | 7 | 16 |
| 6 | Toledo | 3 | 3 | 6 | 2 | 0 | 0 |
| 7 | Dayton | 12 | 15 | 18 | 20 | 1 | 21 |
| 8 | Columbus | 8 | 10 | 15 | 22 | 7 | 12 |
| 9 | Ypsilanti | 31 | 37 | 56 | 33 | 10 | 11 |
| 10 | Southfield | 16 | 18 | 31 | 15 | 5 | 19 |
| 12 | Novi | 21 | 26 | 44 | 18 | 6 | 25 |
| 13 | Total Units | 131 | 154 | 223 | 139 | 39 | 108 |

Task 5: Change the zoom

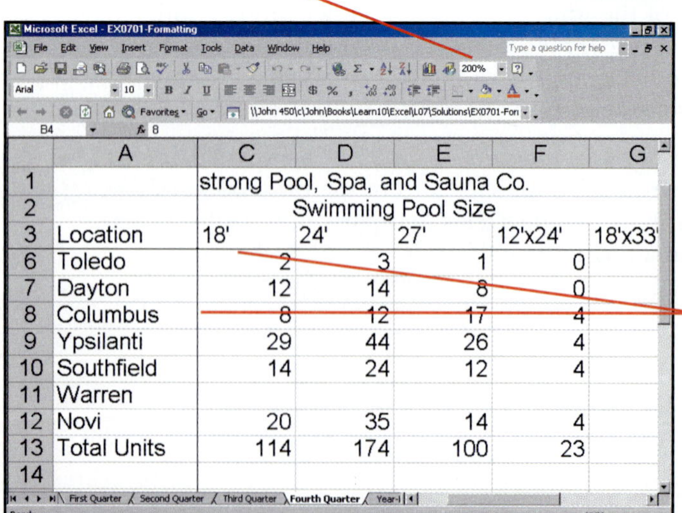



| | A | C | D | E | F | G |
|---|---|---|---|---|---|---|
| 1 | | strong Pool, Spa, and Sauna Co. | | | | |
| 2 | | Swimming Pool Size | | | | |
| 3 | Location | 18' | 24' | 27' | 12'x24' | 18'x33' |
| 6 | Toledo | 2 | 3 | 1 | 0 | |
| 7 | Dayton | 12 | 14 | 8 | 0 | |
| 8 | Columbus | 8 | 12 | 17 | 4 | |
| 9 | Ypsilanti | 29 | 44 | 26 | 4 | |
| 10 | Southfield | 14 | 24 | 12 | 4 | |
| 11 | Warren | | | | | |
| 12 | Novi | 20 | 35 | 14 | 4 | |
| 13 | Total Units | 114 | 174 | 100 | 23 | |
| 14 | | | | | | |

First Quarter / Second Quarter / Third Quarter / Fourth Quarter / Year-l

Task 5: Freeze panes

# Task 1
## COPYING, DELETING, INSERTING, AND HIDING SHEETS

### Why would I do this?

It is usually much easier to modify an existing worksheet than it is to reenter all the column and row headings.

In this task, you copy one of the sheets from an existing workbook into a new workbook. You will also make copies of the sheet within the new workbook, delete unneeded sheets, and hide a sheet used to evaluate store managers.

**1** Start Excel and click the **Open** button. Find **EX0701** in the **Student** folder and open it.

*This worksheet summarizes pool sales by city.*

Click the **New** button on the toolbar.

*This button is used to open a new workbook. The EX0701 workbook is still open, but it is not displayed.*

Save the new file as **EX0701-Formatting** on your disk.

*The new file name appears in the title bar.*

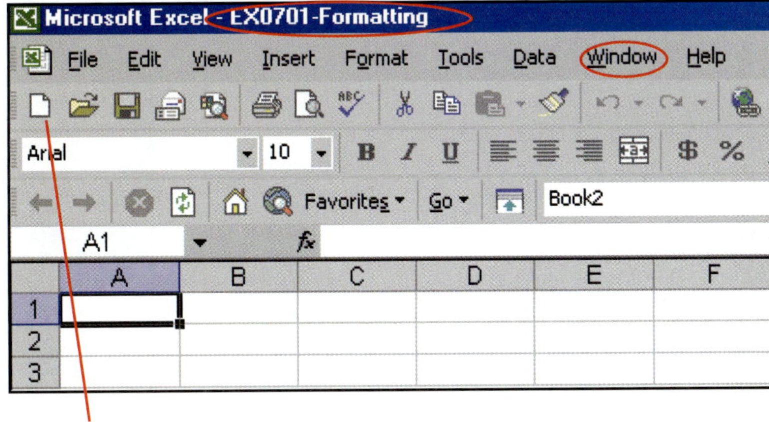

New button

**2** Choose **Window**, **EX0701** from the menu.

*The Window menu may be used to switch between open workbooks.*

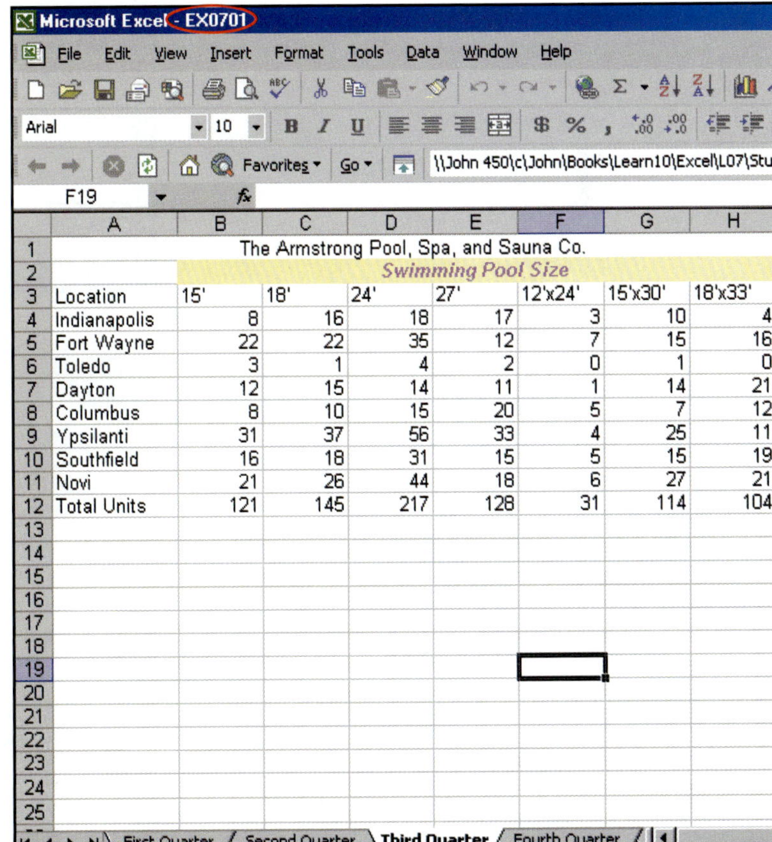

The Armstrong Pool, Spa, and Sauna Co.

Swimming Pool Size

| Location | 15' | 18' | 24' | 27' | 12'x24' | 15'x30' | 18'x33' |
|---|---|---|---|---|---|---|---|
| Indianapolis | 8 | 16 | 18 | 17 | 3 | 10 | 4 |
| Fort Wayne | 22 | 22 | 35 | 12 | 7 | 15 | 16 |
| Toledo | 3 | 1 | 4 | 2 | 0 | 1 | 0 |
| Dayton | 12 | 15 | 14 | 11 | 1 | 14 | 21 |
| Columbus | 8 | 10 | 15 | 20 | 5 | 7 | 12 |
| Ypsilanti | 31 | 37 | 56 | 33 | 4 | 25 | 11 |
| Southfield | 16 | 18 | 31 | 15 | 5 | 15 | 19 |
| Novi | 21 | 26 | 44 | 18 | 6 | 27 | 21 |
| Total Units | 121 | 145 | 217 | 128 | 31 | 114 | 104 |

First Quarter / Second Quarter / **Third Quarter** / Fourth Quarter

 Right-click the **First Quarter** sheet tab and choose **Move or Copy** from the shortcut menu.

*The Move or Copy dialog box is displayed. This dialog box may be used to move the sheet, or a copy of it, within the current workbook or move it to another open workbook.*

Click the down arrow next to the **To book** box and select **EX0701-Formatting**. Click the **Create a copy** option to select it. Confirm that **Sheet1** is selected in the **Before sheet** box.

*These settings will create a copy of the First Quarter sheet and place it in the EX0701-Formatting workbook to the left of Sheet1.*

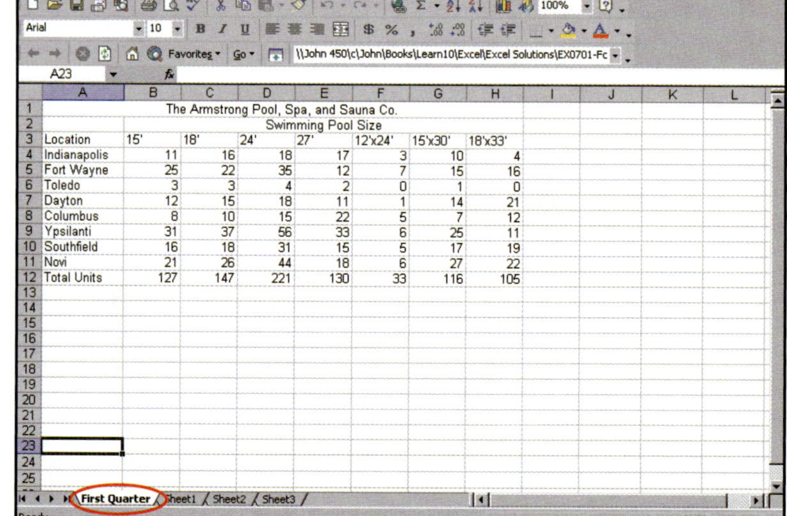

**4** Click **OK**.

*The display switches to EX0701-Formatting. A copy of the First Quarter sheet is placed before Sheet1.*

**5** Use the taskbar or **Window** menu option to switch back to the **EX0701** workbook.

Right click the **Second Quarter** tab and choose **Move or Copy** from the shortcut menu. Select **EX0701-Formatting** in the **To book** box, select **Sheet1** in the **Before sheet** box, and click the **Create a copy** box.

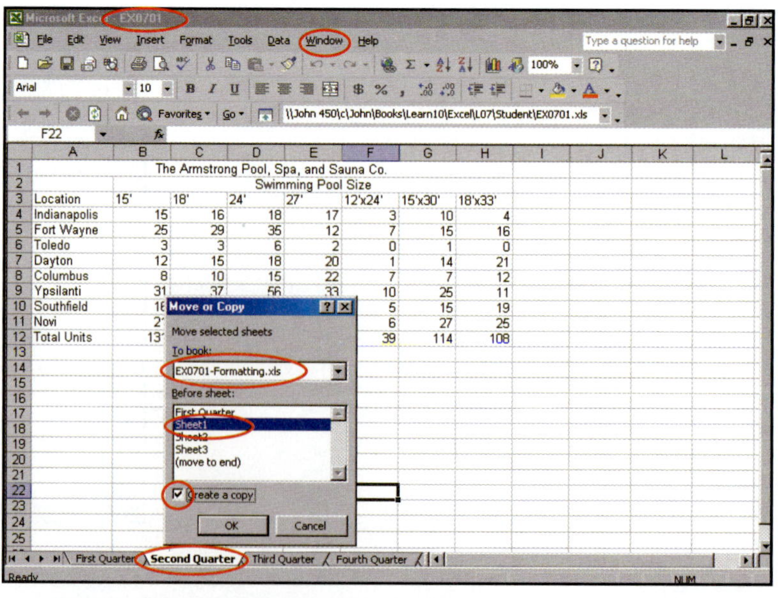

**6** Click **OK**.

*The Second Quarter sheet is also copied and moved.*

Repeat this process to move the Third and Fourth Quarter sheets and the Year-End Summary sheet.

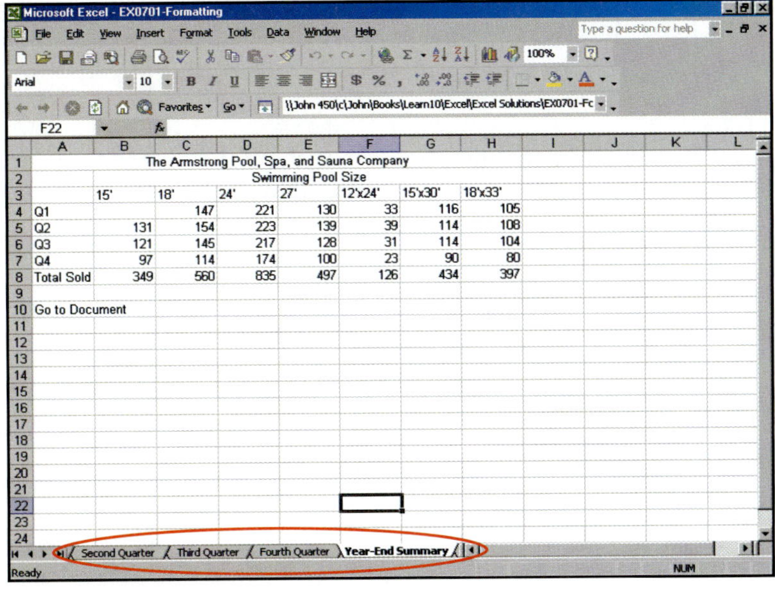

**7** In the **EX0701-Formatting** workbook, use the right **Tab Scrolling** button to display the tab for **Sheet1**. Right-click on the **Sheet1** tab and choose **Delete** from the shortcut menu.

Delete **Sheet2** and **Sheet3**.

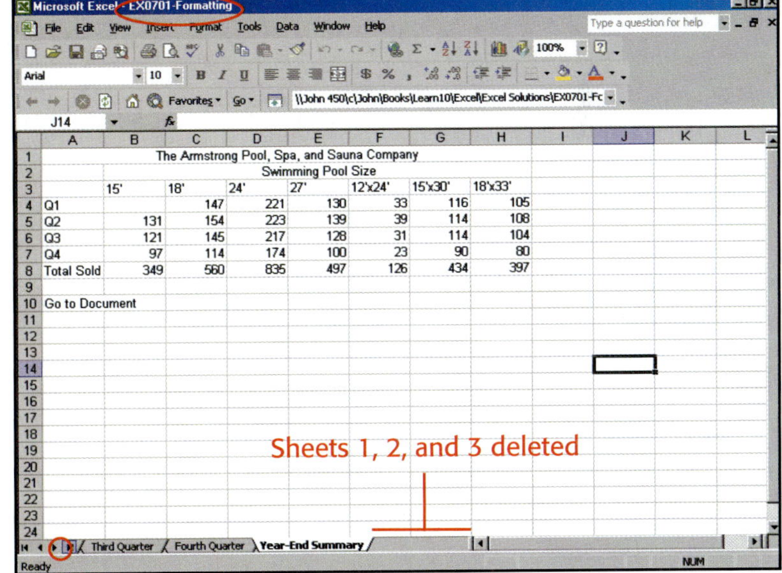


**QUICK TIP**

If you wanted only to create a new version of an existing workbook, it would have been quicker to open it and save it with a new name. This exercise is designed to demonstrate more than one way to copy sheets.

**8** Choose **Insert, Worksheet** from the menu.

*A new worksheet is placed before the Year-End Summary sheet.*

Click-and-drag the new sheet tab to the right and drop it to the right of the **Year-End Summary** sheet.

Double-click the new sheet name and type **Evaluation**. Press ↵Enter.

*The new workbook now has six worksheets.*

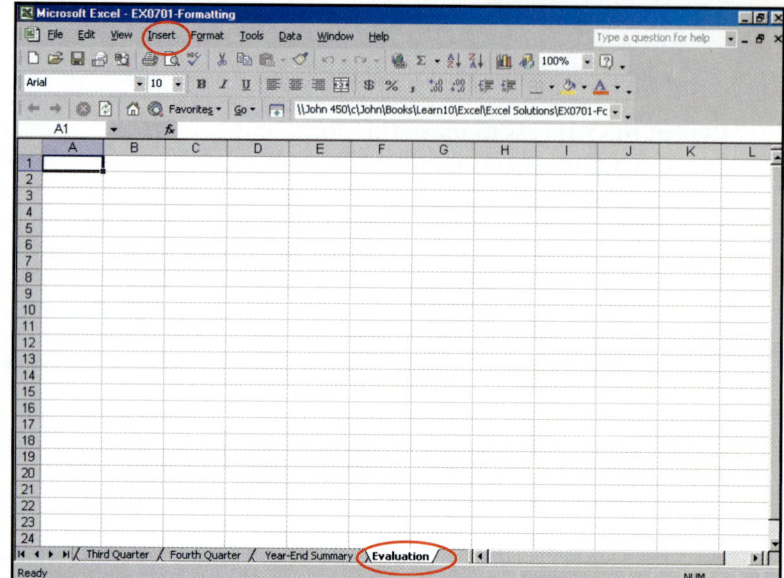

**9** Choose **Format, Sheet,** and **Hide** from the menu.

*The Evaluation sheet is not displayed with the other sheets. You will learn how to unhide sheets in the Reinforcement exercises.*

Switch to EX0701 and close the workbook. Do not save any changes if asked.

Hidden sheet tab not displayed

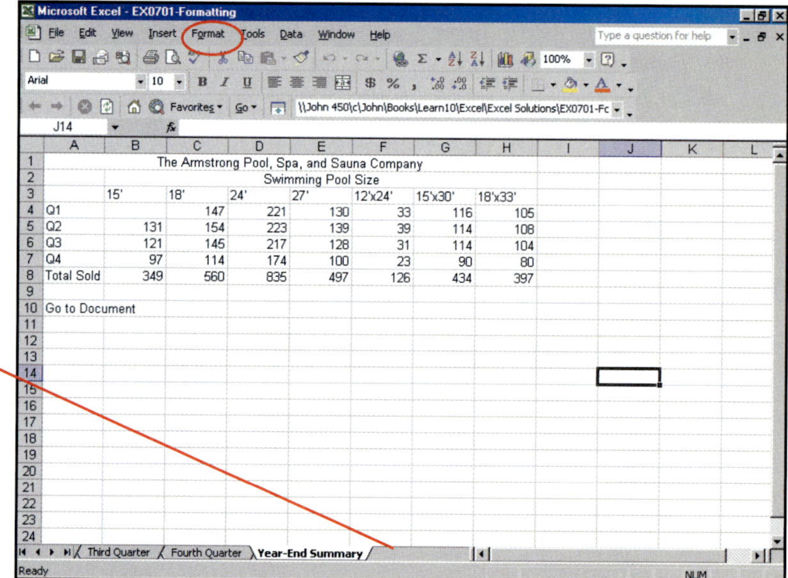

# Task 2



## INSERTING, DELETING, HIDING, AND UNHIDING ROWS AND COLUMNS

### *Why would I do this?*

Modifying worksheets often involves inserting or deleting rows or columns of data. Excel will automatically revise formulas that are affected by these changes, but there are some circumstances where the formulas are not revised. It is also convenient to be able to hide rows or columns that are not often used or are not intended for others to see.

In this task, you learn how to insert and delete rows and columns as well as how to hide and reveal them. You will insert a row for a store that is expected to open in the near future and then hide it. You will delete a column that represents a pool size that is no longer available.

**1** Click the **Tab Scroll** button to display the **First Quarter** tab and click it.

Click cell **B12**.

*Notice that the formula includes cells B4 through B11.*

| | B12 | | $f_x$ =SUM(B4:B11) | | | | | |
|---|---|---|---|---|---|---|---|---|
| | A | B | C | D | E | F | G | H |
| 1 | | The Armstrong Pool, Spa, and Sauna Co. | | | | | | |
| 2 | | Swimming Pool Size | | | | | | |
| 3 | Location | 15' | 18' | 24' | 27' | 12'x24' | 15'x30' | 18'x33' |
| 4 | Indianapolis | 11 | 16 | 18 | 17 | 3 | 10 | 4 |
| 5 | Fort Wayne | 25 | 22 | 35 | 12 | 7 | 15 | 16 |
| 6 | Toledo | 3 | 3 | 4 | 2 | 0 | 1 | 0 |
| 7 | Dayton | 12 | 15 | 18 | 11 | 1 | 14 | 21 |
| 8 | Columbus | 8 | 10 | 15 | 22 | 5 | 7 | 12 |
| 9 | Ypsilanti | 31 | 37 | 56 | 33 | 6 | 25 | 11 |
| 10 | Southfield | 16 | 18 | 31 | 15 | 5 | 17 | 19 |
| 11 | Novi | 21 | 26 | 44 | 18 | 6 | 27 | 22 |
| 12 | Total Units | 127 | 147 | 221 | 130 | 33 | 116 | 105 |
| 13 | | | | | | | | |

**2** Click row heading **12**. Choose **Insert**, **Rows**.

*A new row is inserted above the selected row.*

Click cell **B13**.

*Notice that the formula was not revised to include the new row.*

Formula does not include new row.

New row

| | B13 | | $f_x$ =SUM(B4:B11) | | | | | |
|---|---|---|---|---|---|---|---|---|
| | A | B | C | D | E | F | G | H |
| 1 | | The Armstrong Pool, Spa, and Sauna Co. | | | | | | |
| 2 | | Swimming Pool Size | | | | | | |
| 3 | Location | 15' | 18' | 24' | 27' | 12'x24' | 15'x30' | 18'x33' |
| 4 | Indianapolis | 11 | 16 | 18 | 17 | 3 | 10 | 4 |
| 5 | Fort Wayne | 25 | 22 | 35 | 12 | 7 | 15 | 16 |
| 6 | Toledo | 3 | 3 | 4 | 2 | 0 | 1 | 0 |
| 7 | Dayton | 12 | 15 | 18 | 11 | 1 | 14 | 21 |
| 8 | Columbus | 8 | 10 | 15 | 22 | 5 | 7 | 12 |
| 9 | Ypsilanti | 31 | 37 | 56 | 33 | 6 | 25 | 11 |
| 10 | Southfield | 16 | 18 | 31 | 15 | 5 | 17 | 19 |
| 11 | Novi | 21 | 26 | 44 | 18 | 6 | 27 | 22 |
| 12 | | | | | | | | |
| 13 | Total Units | 127 | 147 | 221 | 130 | 33 | 116 | 105 |
| 14 | | | | | | | | |

**3** Click the **Undo** button.

*The new row is deleted.*

Click row heading **11**. Choose **Insert**, **Rows**. Select cell **B13**.

*The formula has been revised to include values in the new row.*

| | B13 | | $f_x$ =SUM(B4:B12) | | | | | |
|---|---|---|---|---|---|---|---|---|
| | A | B | C | D | E | F | G | H |
| 1 | | The Armstrong Pool, Spa, and Sauna Co. | | | | | | |
| 2 | | Swimming Pool Size | | | | | | |
| 3 | Location | 15' | 18' | 24' | 27' | 12'x24' | 15'x30' | 18'x33' |
| 4 | Indianapolis | 11 | 16 | 18 | 17 | 3 | 10 | 4 |
| 5 | Fort Wayne | 25 | 22 | 35 | 12 | 7 | 15 | 16 |
| 6 | Toledo | 3 | 3 | 4 | 2 | 0 | 1 | 0 |
| 7 | Dayton | 12 | 15 | 18 | 11 | 1 | 14 | 21 |
| 8 | Columbus | 8 | 10 | 15 | 22 | 5 | 7 | 12 |
| 9 | Ypsilanti | 31 | 37 | 56 | 33 | 6 | 25 | 11 |
| 10 | Southfield | 16 | 18 | 31 | 15 | 5 | 17 | 19 |
| 11 | | | | | | | | |
| 12 | Novi | 21 | 26 | 44 | 18 | 6 | 27 | 22 |
| 13 | Total Units | 127 | 147 | 221 | 130 | 33 | 116 | 105 |
| 14 | | | | | | | | |

**IN DEPTH**

In general, a formula that uses a range of cells will be revised if you insert a new row or column between the outermost rows or columns in its range. In this case, a new row inserted below row 12 or above row 4 would not be included in the summation formulas in the row labeled Total Units.

**4** Select cell **A11** and type **Warren**. Press ↵Enter.

*This is the name of the city in which a new store is opening later in the quarter.*

|   | A | B | C | D | E | F | G | H |
|---|---|---|---|---|---|---|---|---|
| 1 | The Armstrong Pool, Spa, and Sauna Co. | | | | | | | |
| 2 | Swimming Pool Size | | | | | | | |
| 3 | Location | 15' | 18' | 24' | 27' | 12'x24' | 15'x30' | 18'x33' |
| 4 | Indianapolis | 11 | 16 | 18 | 17 | 3 | 10 | 4 |
| 5 | Fort Wayne | 25 | 22 | 35 | 12 | 7 | 15 | 16 |
| 6 | Toledo | 3 | 3 | 4 | 2 | 0 | 1 | 0 |
| 7 | Dayton | 12 | 15 | 18 | 11 | 1 | 14 | 21 |
| 8 | Columbus | 8 | 10 | 15 | 22 | 5 | 7 | 12 |
| 9 | Ypsilanti | 31 | 37 | 56 | 33 | 6 | 25 | 11 |
| 10 | Southfield | 16 | 18 | 31 | 15 | 5 | 17 | 19 |
| 11 | Warren | | | | | | | |
| 12 | Novi | 21 | 26 | 44 | 18 | 6 | 27 | 22 |
| 13 | Total Units | 127 | 147 | 221 | 130 | 33 | 116 | 105 |

**5** Click row heading **11**.

*This action selects the entire row.*

Choose **Format**, **Row**, **Hide**.

*Row 11 is not displayed.*

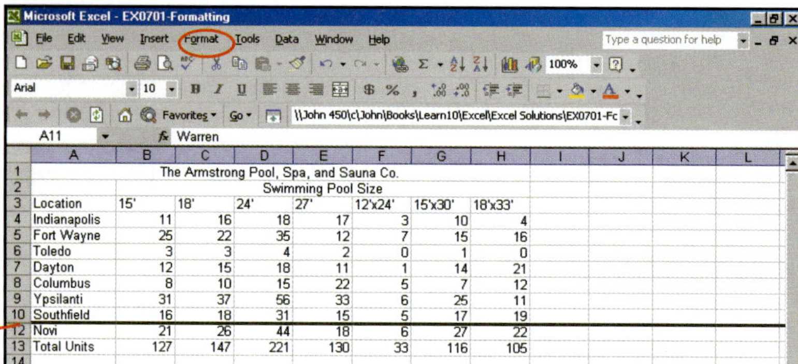



Row 11 is hidden.

**6** Click column heading **G**.

*Column G is selected. The 15' × 30' pools are no longer made.*

Choose **Edit**, **Delete**.

*The contents of the column are deleted, and the columns to the right are moved to the left to replace it.*

|   | A | B | C | D | E | F | G | H |
|---|---|---|---|---|---|---|---|---|
| 1 | The Armstrong Pool, Spa, and Sauna Co. | | | | | | | |
| 2 | Swimming Pool Size | | | | | | | |
| 3 | Location | 15' | 18' | 24' | 27' | 12'x24' | 18'x33' | |
| 4 | Indianapolis | 11 | 16 | 18 | 17 | 3 | 4 | |
| 5 | Fort Wayne | 25 | 22 | 35 | 12 | 7 | 16 | |
| 6 | Toledo | 3 | 3 | 4 | 2 | 0 | 0 | |
| 7 | Dayton | 12 | 15 | 18 | 11 | 1 | 21 | |
| 8 | Columbus | 8 | 10 | 15 | 22 | 5 | 12 | |
| 9 | Ypsilanti | 31 | 37 | 56 | 33 | 6 | 11 | |
| 10 | Southfield | 16 | 18 | 31 | 15 | 5 | 19 | |
| 12 | Novi | 21 | 26 | 44 | 18 | 6 | 22 | |
| 13 | Total Units | 127 | 147 | 221 | 130 | 33 | 105 | |

15' × 30' pool size deleted

**7** Click the **Second Quarter** sheet tab. Hold the ↑Shift key and click the **Third Quarter**, **Fourth Quarter**, and **Year-End Summary** sheet tabs.

*All four sheets are selected.*

Click the heading in column **G**. Choose **Edit**, **Delete**.

*The same column is deleted in all four selected sheets.*

|   | A | B | C | D | E | F | G |
|---|---|---|---|---|---|---|---|
| 1 | The Armstrong Pool, Spa, and Sauna Co. | | | | | | |
| 2 | Swimming Pool Size | | | | | | |
| 3 | Location | 15' | 18' | 24' | 27' | 12'x24' | 18'x33' |
| 4 | Indianapolis | 15 | 16 | 18 | 17 | 3 | 4 |
| 5 | Fort Wayne | 25 | 29 | 35 | 12 | 7 | 16 |
| 6 | Toledo | 3 | 3 | 6 | 2 | 0 | 0 |
| 7 | Dayton | 12 | 15 | 18 | 20 | 1 | 21 |
| 8 | Columbus | 8 | 10 | 15 | 22 | 7 | 12 |
| 9 | Ypsilanti | 31 | 37 | 56 | 33 | 10 | 11 |
| 10 | Southfield | 16 | 18 | 31 | 15 | 5 | 19 |
| 11 | Novi | 21 | 26 | 44 | 18 | 6 | 25 |
| 12 | Total Units | 131 | 154 | 223 | 139 | 39 | 108 |
| 13 | | | | | | | |
| 14 | | | | | | | |
| 15 | | | | | | | |
| 16 | | | | | | | |
| 17 | | | | | | | |
| 18 | | | | | | | |
| 19 | | | | | | | |
| 20 | | | | | | | |
| 21 | | | | | | | |
| 22 | | | | | | | |
| 23 | | | | | | | |
| 24 | | | | | | | |
| 25 | | | | | | | |

Second Quarter / Third Quarter / Fourth Quarter / Year-End Summary

15' × 30' pool column deleted in selected sheets

**QUICK TIP**

If you need to make changes to several sheets at once, use the ↑Shift key while clicking the sheet tabs. You can add text and numbers as well as insert and delete rows and columns, and all the sheets will be affected the same way. If the sheets are not next to each other, use Ctrl instead of ↑Shift when you click on the sheet tabs.

**8** Right-click the **Second Quarter** tab and choose <u>Ungroup Sheets</u> from the shortcut menu. Select the **Second Quarter**, **Third Quarter**, and **Fourth Quarter** sheets.

Click the heading for row **11** in one of the sheets. Choose <u>Insert</u>, <u>Rows</u>. Type **Warren** in cell **A11** and press ↵Enter.

*This row is added to all the selected sheets.*

New row added to selected sheets

| | A | B | C | D | E | F | G |
|---|---|---|---|---|---|---|---|
| 1 | The Armstrong Pool, Spa, and Sauna Co. | | | | | | |
| 2 | Swimming Pool Size | | | | | | |
| 3 | Location | 15' | 18' | 24' | 27' | 12'x24' | 18'x33' |
| 4 | Indianapolis | 15 | 16 | 18 | 17 | 3 | 4 |
| 5 | Fort Wayne | 25 | 29 | 35 | 12 | 7 | 16 |
| 6 | Toledo | 3 | 3 | 6 | 2 | 0 | 0 |
| 7 | Dayton | 12 | 15 | 18 | 20 | 1 | 21 |
| 8 | Columbus | 8 | 10 | 15 | 22 | 7 | 12 |
| 9 | Ypsilanti | 31 | 37 | 56 | 33 | 10 | 11 |
| 10 | Southfield | 16 | 18 | 31 | 15 | 5 | 19 |
| 11 | Warren | | | | | | |
| 12 | Novi | 21 | 26 | 44 | 18 | 6 | 25 |
| 13 | Total Units | 131 | 154 | 223 | 139 | 39 | 108 |

First Quarter / Second Quarter / Third Quarter / Fourth Quarter / Year-

**9** Click the heading for row **11**. Choose <u>Format</u>, <u>Row</u>, <u>Hide</u>.

*The row is hidden in all the selected sheets.*

Right-click the **Fourth Quarter** sheet tab. Choose <u>Ungroup Sheets</u>.

Hidden row

Only one sheet selected

| | A | B | C | D | E | F | G |
|---|---|---|---|---|---|---|---|
| 1 | The Armstrong Pool, Spa, and Sauna Co. | | | | | | |
| 2 | Swimming Pool Size | | | | | | |
| 3 | Location | 15' | 18' | 24' | 27' | 12'x24' | 18'x33' |
| 4 | Indianapolis | 8 | 12 | 14 | 13 | 2 | 3 |
| 5 | Fort Wayne | 20 | 17 | 28 | 9 | 5 | 12 |
| 6 | Toledo | 2 | 2 | 3 | 1 | 0 | 0 |
| 7 | Dayton | 9 | 12 | 14 | 8 | 0 | 16 |
| 8 | Columbus | 6 | 8 | 12 | 17 | 4 | 9 |
| 9 | Ypsilanti | 24 | 29 | 44 | 26 | 4 | 8 |
| 10 | Southfield | 12 | 14 | 24 | 12 | 4 | 15 |
| 12 | Novi | 16 | 20 | 35 | 14 | 4 | 17 |
| 13 | Total Units | 97 | 114 | 174 | 100 | 23 | 80 |

First Quarter / Second Quarter / Third Quarter / Fourth Quarter / Year-

 Click-and-drag to select row headings **10** and **12**.

*Since you cannot select the hidden row, you select the two rows that are on either side of it.*

Choose **Format**, **Row**, **Unhide**.

*The row for the new Warren store is displayed.*

Previously hidden row

| | A | B | C | D | E | F | G |
|---|---|---|---|---|---|---|---|
| 1 | The Armstrong Pool, Spa, and Sauna Co. | | | | | | |
| 2 | Swimming Pool Size | | | | | | |
| 3 | Location | 15' | 18' | 24' | 27' | 12'x24' | 18'x33' |
| 4 | Indianapolis | 8 | 12 | 14 | 13 | 2 | 3 |
| 5 | Fort Wayne | 20 | 17 | 28 | 9 | 5 | 12 |
| 6 | Toledo | 2 | 2 | 3 | 1 | 0 | 0 |
| 7 | Dayton | 9 | 12 | 14 | 8 | 0 | 16 |
| 8 | Columbus | 6 | 8 | 12 | 17 | 4 | 9 |
| 9 | Ypsilanti | 24 | 29 | 44 | 26 | 4 | 8 |
| 10 | Southfield | 12 | 14 | 24 | 12 | 4 | 15 |
| 11 | Warren | | | | | | |
| 12 | Novi | 16 | 20 | 35 | 14 | 4 | 17 |
| 13 | Total Units | 97 | 114 | 174 | 100 | 23 | 80 |

# Task 3

## USING THE FORMAT PAINTER AND APPLYING AUTOFORMATS

### Why would I do this?

Formatting a worksheet can be time consuming. Fortunately, there are several features that speed up the process.

In this task, you learn two valuable time-saving techniques that make it much faster to format documents. You will use the *Format Painter* to copy a format, and you will use the *autoformat* option to format a table of data.

**1** Select the **First Quarter** sheet. Select cell **A4**.

*You will format the store names.*

Click the **Italic** button on the Formatting toolbar.

Click the **Format Painter** button on the Formatting toolbar and move the pointer onto cell **A5**.

*The format of the currently selected cell is stored. Notice the Format Painter button seems to be depressed, indicating that it is active and has a format stored and ready to apply. The pointer includes a small paintbrush.*

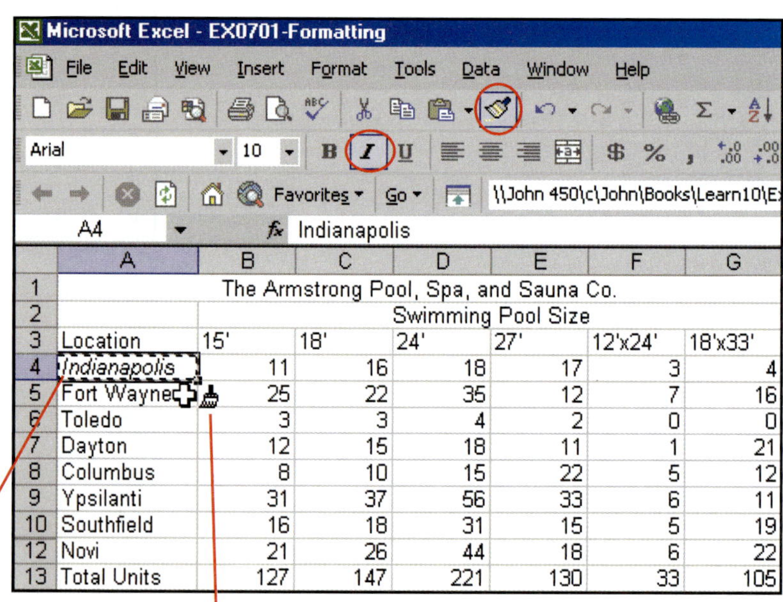

| | A | B | C | D | E | F | G |
|---|---|---|---|---|---|---|---|
| 1 | The Armstrong Pool, Spa, and Sauna Co. | | | | | | |
| 2 | Swimming Pool Size | | | | | | |
| 3 | Location | 15' | 18' | 24' | 27' | 12'x24' | 18'x33' |
| 4 | Indianapolis | 11 | 16 | 18 | 17 | 3 | 4 |
| 5 | Fort Wayne | 25 | 22 | 35 | 12 | 7 | 16 |
| 6 | Toledo | 3 | 3 | 4 | 2 | 0 | 0 |
| 7 | Dayton | 12 | 15 | 18 | 11 | 1 | 21 |
| 8 | Columbus | 8 | 10 | 15 | 22 | 5 | 12 |
| 9 | Ypsilanti | 31 | 37 | 56 | 33 | 6 | 11 |
| 10 | Southfield | 16 | 18 | 31 | 15 | 5 | 19 |
| 12 | Novi | 21 | 26 | 44 | 18 | 6 | 22 |
| 13 | Total Units | 127 | 147 | 221 | 130 | 33 | 105 |

Cell whose format will be copied

Format Painter pointer

**2** Click cell **A5**.

*The next city name is also formatted as italic. The Format Painter button returns to its normal appearance to indicate that it is not active.*

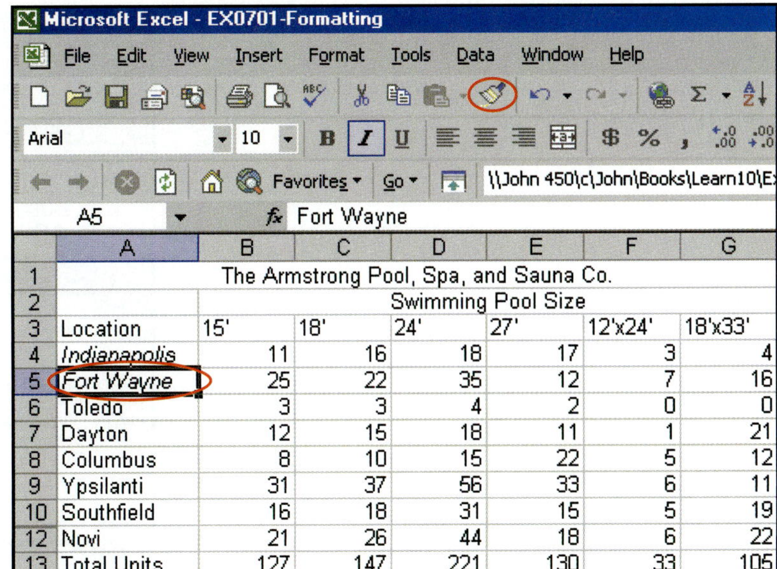

**3** Double-click the **Format Painter** button.

*The format of the current cell is stored. The button will remain active for use on multiple occasions until it is clicked to deactivate it.*

Click cell **A6**. Click cell **A7**. Click-and-drag cells **A8** through **A12**.

*All the store names are italicized.*

**CAUTION**

If you have trouble double-clicking the Format Painter button, you can copy the cell that has the format you desire and paste only the format. Choose <u>E</u>dit, Paste <u>S</u>pecial. Click the Format<u>s</u> option, then click OK.

**IN DEPTH**

The name of the Warren store is also formatted. Even though it was hidden, it was included when you selected the cells on either side of it.

**4**  Click the **Format Painter** button.

*The Format Painter is turned off, and the button resumes its normal appearance.*

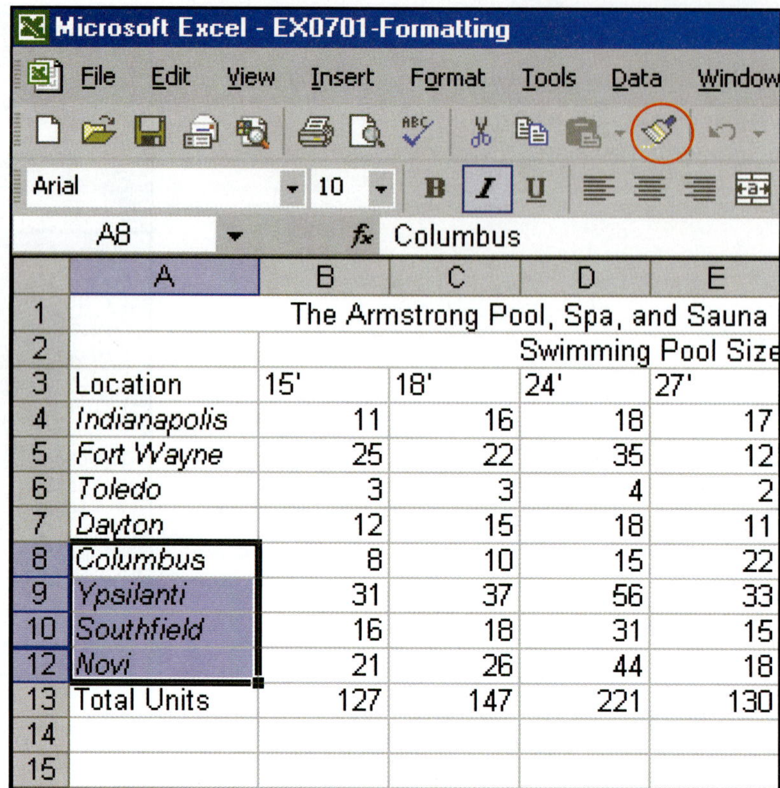

**5**  Click the **Second Quarter** sheet tab. Select cells **A3** through **G13**.

Choose **Format**, **AutoFormat**. Click the **Options** button.

*The AutoFormat dialog box is displayed. Its options range from simple enhancements and borders to 3D effects with color.*

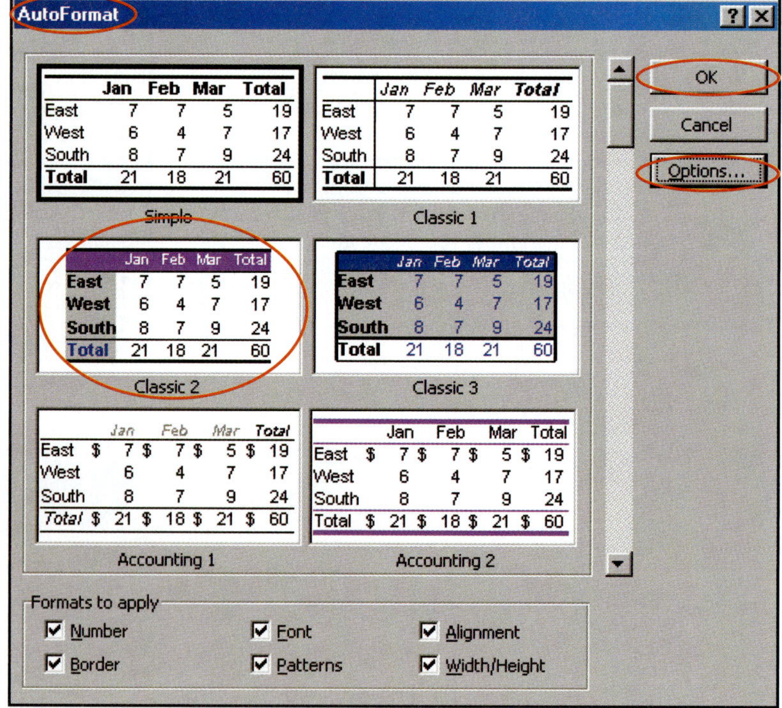

**6** Click the **Classic 2** option.

*The column and row headings will be formatted and a Top and Bottom border applied to the cells in the bottom row.*

Click **OK**. Click in an empty cell to deselect the data and view the formatting.

*The selected cells are formatted.*

The Armstrong Pool, Spa, and Sauna Co.

Swimming Pool Size

| | Location | 15' | 18' | 24' | 27' | 12'x24' | 18'x33' |
|---|---|---|---|---|---|---|---|
| 4 | Indianapolis | 15 | 16 | 18 | 17 | 3 | 4 |
| 5 | Fort Wayne | 25 | 29 | 35 | 12 | 7 | 16 |
| 6 | Toledo | 3 | 3 | 6 | 2 | 0 | 0 |
| 7 | Dayton | 12 | 15 | 18 | 20 | 1 | 21 |
| 8 | Columbus | 8 | 10 | 15 | 22 | 7 | 12 |
| 9 | Ypsilanti | 31 | 37 | 56 | 33 | 10 | 11 |
| 10 | Southfield | 16 | 18 | 31 | 15 | 5 | 19 |
| 12 | Novi | 21 | 26 | 44 | 18 | 6 | 25 |
| 13 | Total Units | 131 | 154 | 223 | 139 | 39 | 108 |

**7** Save the changes you have made. Leave the workbook open for use in the next task.

# Task 4
## DEFINING, APPLYING, AND REMOVING A STYLE

### Why would I do this?

Companies spend a lot of advertising money to create customer awareness of their name. It is often important that the company name is always displayed using the same font and colors for the text and background. In situations such as this, it is useful to create a *style* that can be applied whenever it is needed. A style may be a combination of font, color, and emphasis.

In this task, you learn how to define a style and apply it. You will also learn how to delete a style if it is no longer needed.

**1** Click the **First Quarter** sheet tab and select cell **A1**.

*The company name is selected.*

Change the font to **Comic Sans MS** and make it **14** point.

Click the down arrow next to the **Font Color** button and choose **Dark Red**. Click the down arrow next to the **Fill Color** button and choose **Light Turquoise**.

*This format will be used for all occurrences of the company name in this workbook.*

**2** Confirm that the title is still selected and choose **Format**, **Style** from the menu.

*The Style dialog box is displayed, and the style name is selected.*

Type **Company Name** in the **Style name** box.

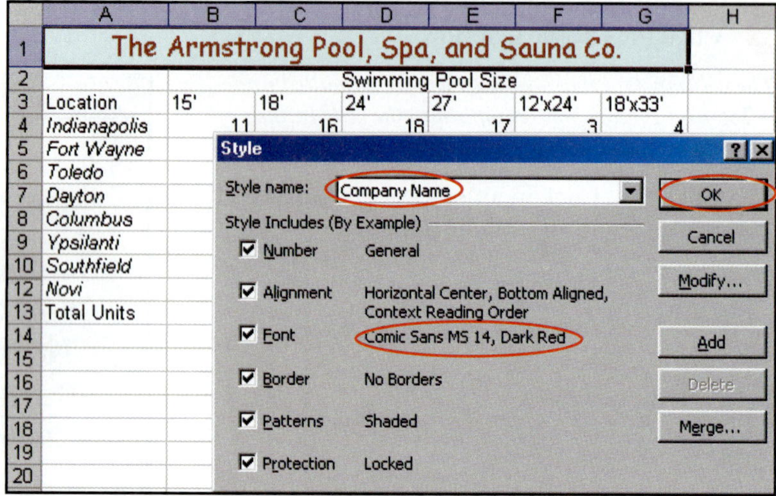

**3** Click **OK**.

*This format is stored as Company Name and may be applied when needed.*

Click the **Second Quarter** sheet tab and select cell **A1**.

*The title on the next sheet is selected.*

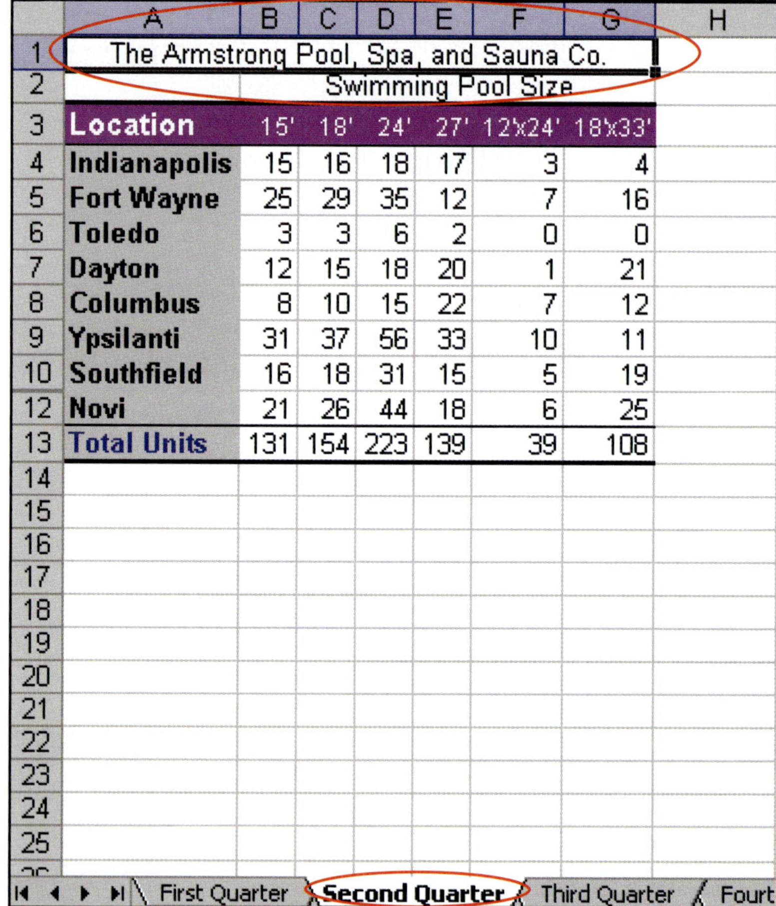

**4** Choose **Format**, **Style**.

*The Style dialog box is displayed.*

Click the down arrow next to the **Style name** box and select **Company Name** from the list.

*The style you created is selected.*



**5** Click **OK**.

*The style is applied to the title. Notice that it doesn't automatically adjust the width of the columns to display the text.*

Click-and-drag across column headings **B** through **G** to select them. Move the pointer onto the boundary between any two of the selected columns. Click-and-drag the boundary to the right slightly and release the mouse button.

*The selected columns are resized and equalized. If the title is still not completely displayed, adjust the column widths until it is.*

Click on an empty cell to deselect the columns.

Adjust all the selected columns at once

| | A | B | C | D | E | F | G |
|---|---|---|---|---|---|---|---|
| 1 | The Armstrong Pool, Spa, and Sauna Co. | | | | | | |
| 2 | | | | Swimming Pool Size | | | |
| 3 | Location | 15' | 18' | 24' | 27' | 12'x24' | 18'x33' |
| 4 | Indianapolis | 15 | 16 | 18 | 17 | 3 | 4 |
| 5 | Fort Wayne | 25 | 29 | 35 | 12 | 7 | 16 |
| 6 | Toledo | 3 | 3 | 6 | 2 | 0 | 0 |
| 7 | Dayton | 12 | 15 | 18 | 20 | 1 | 21 |
| 8 | Columbus | 8 | 10 | 15 | 22 | 7 | 12 |
| 9 | Ypsilanti | 31 | 37 | 56 | 33 | 10 | 11 |
| 10 | Southfield | 16 | 18 | 31 | 15 | 5 | 19 |
| 12 | Novi | 21 | 26 | 44 | 18 | 6 | 25 |
| 13 | Total Units | 131 | 154 | 223 | 139 | 39 | 108 |

Title formatted using a style

**6** Click the **Third Quarter** sheet and select the title in cell **B2**.

*This sheet has a column heading style for Swimming Pool Size that is not acceptable.*

Choose **Format**, **Style**. Confirm that **Normal** is selected in the **Style name** box and click **OK**.

*The style is deleted and replaced by the style that is defined as Normal for this workbook. Notice that it is no longer centered across the columns, but the cells are still merged. Formatting does not affect the merging of cells.*

| | A | B | C | D | E | F | G |
|---|---|---|---|---|---|---|---|
| 1 | | The Armstrong Pool, Spa, and Sauna Co. | | | | | |
| 2 | | Swimming Pool Size | | | | | |
| 3 | Location | 15' | 18' | 24' | 27' | 12'x24' | 18'x33' |

Style deleted by replacing with Normal style

# Task 5
## CHANGING THE ZOOM AND FREEZING PANES

### Why would I do this?

Worksheets can often become too large to view easily. The *zoom* feature allows you to change the magnification of the onscreen display. If you adjust the zoom to display all of the columns or rows, the data may be too small to read. If you increase the zoom to make the numbers easy to read, the column and row headings may be off the screen. If this problem arises, you can use a feature called *freeze panes*. This feature freezes the rows and columns above and to the left of a selected cell so that they stay on the screen when you scroll through the worksheet.

In this task, you learn how to use zoom along with the freeze panes feature to view the Fourth Quarter worksheet.

**❶** Click the **Fourth Quarter** sheet tab. Select cell **B4**.

*The rows above the selected cell will be frozen as will the columns to the left.*

Choose **Window**, **Freeze Panes**.

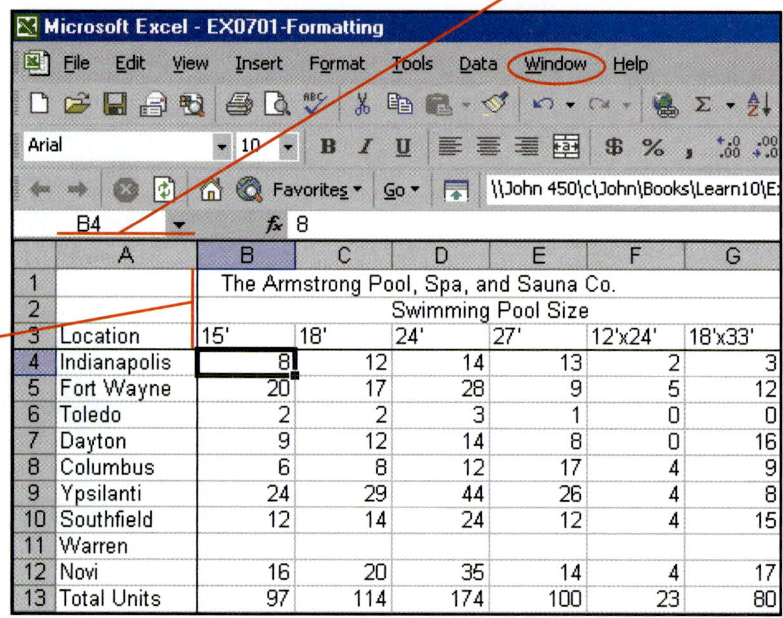


**❷** Click the down arrow next to the **Zoom** button. Choose **200%**.

*The worksheet is displayed at twice the normal size.*

**3** Use the vertical scrollbar to scroll down to display rows **1** through **3** and **6** through **13**.

*Notice that the first three rows do not move.*

Use the horizontal scrollbar to scroll to the right to display columns **A** and **D** through **G**.

*Notice that column A does not move.*

Rows above this line are frozen.

Columns to the left of this line are frozen.

| | A | D | E | F | G | H |
|---|---|---|---|---|---|---|
| 1 | | ol, Spa, and Sauna Co. | | | | |
| 2 | | Swimming Pool Size | | | | |
| 3 | Location | 24' | 27' | 12'x24' | 18'x33' | |
| 6 | Toledo | 3 | 1 | 0 | 0 | |
| 7 | Dayton | 14 | 8 | 0 | 16 | |
| 8 | Columbus | 12 | 17 | 4 | 9 | |
| 9 | Ypsilanti | 44 | 26 | 4 | 8 | |
| 10 | Southfield | 24 | 12 | 4 | 15 | |
| 11 | Warren | | | | | |
| 12 | Novi | 35 | 14 | 4 | 17 | |
| 13 | Total Units | 174 | 100 | 23 | 80 | |
| 14 | | | | | | |

**IN DEPTH**

The zoom setting does not affect the size of the worksheet when it is printed. Notice the font size did not change. The zoom feature is useful for workers whose eyesight is not as acute as others. There is another feature that is similar to zoom that is part of the Windows 98 and later operating systems. It is installed as one of the accessibility options. The feature is called ***magnifier***. It displays a panel at the top of the screen that zooms in on the portion of the screen under the mouse pointer. To find out more about magnifier, click the Start button on the taskbar; then click <u>H</u>elp on the Startup menu and look for magnifier in the Index.

**4** Save the workbook. Close the workbook. Leave Excel open if you plan to do the exercises at this time.

The exercises that follow are designed for you to review and use what you have learned in this lesson. You also have the opportunity to practice your skills and then expand on them by applying them to new situations.

## COMPREHENSION

Comprehension exercises are designed to check your memory and understanding of the basic concepts in this lesson. You distinguish between true and false statements, identify new screen elements, and match terms with related statements. If you are uncertain of the correct answer, refer to the task number following each item (for example, T4 refers to Task 4), and review that task until you are confident you can provide a correct response.

## TRUE-FALSE

Circle either T or F.

T   F   1. A workbook always has three sheets. If you need more sheets, you hyperlink two workbooks together. **(T1)**

T   F   2. All of the sheets in a workbook do not have to be visible. Some of them may be hidden. **(T1)**

T   F   3. If a summation formula adds the values in rows 3 through 10 in a column, the formula will be automatically updated if you add a new row between rows 5 and 6. **(T2)**

T   F   4. If you want to copy the format of a given cell into several other cells that are scattered around the worksheet, you can right-click the Format Painter button so it will stay active until you turn it off. **(T3)**

T   F   5. If you apply a style to a cell, it will not affect the number of cells across which the text is merged. **(T4)**

T   F   6. Changing the zoom to 50% will allow you to get more columns and rows on a printed page. **(T5)**

## MATCHING QUESTIONS

**A.** Right-click on the sheet tab

**B.** Row 2

**C.** Click the Format option on the menu

**D.** Row 4

**E.** Row 3

**F.** Click on the Format Painter button

Match the following statements to the word or phrase that is the best match from the list. Write the letter of the matching word or phrase in the space provided next to the number. The same answer may match more than one statement. All of the answers are not necessarily used.

1. ____ To begin the process of hiding a sheet, you select it, and then do this **(T1)**

2. ____ To copy a sheet, you do this to start the process **(T1)**

3. ____ To insert a new row between rows 2 and 3, you start by selecting **(T2)**

4. ____ Once you double-click on the Format Painter button to turn it on, you then do this to disable it **(T3)**

5. ____ To begin the process of creating a style, you format a cell the way you want it, then **(T4)**

6. ____ To freeze the first two rows of the worksheet, start by clicking any cell in **(T5)**

# IDENTIFYING PARTS OF
# THE EXCEL SCREEN

Refer to the figure and identify the numbered parts of
the screen. Write the letter of the correct label in the
space next to the number.

1. ____________

2. ____________

3. ____________

4. ____________

5. ____________

6. ____________

7. ____________

8. ____________

9. ____________

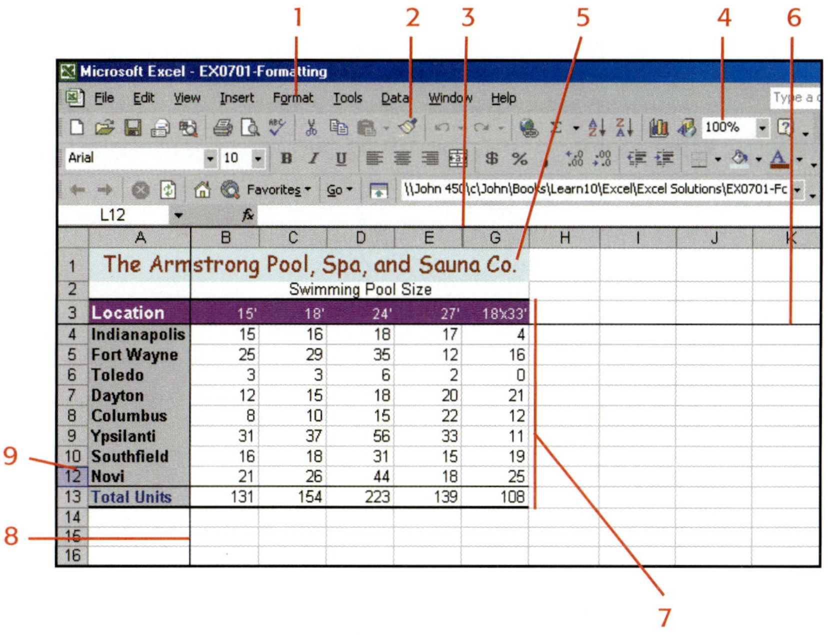

**A.** Format menu option  **(T3,T4)**

**B.** Zoom button  **(T5)**

**C.** Format Painter button  **(T4)**

**D.** Freeze rows above this line  **(T5)**

**E.** Freeze columns to the left of this line  **(T5)**

**F.** An example of an AutoFormat  **(T3)**

**G.** A hidden row  **(T2)**

**H.** A hidden column  **(T2)**

**I.** Example of the Company Name style  **(T4)**

# REINFORCEMENT

Reinforcement exercises are designed to reinforce the skills you have learned by applying them to new situations. Detailed instructions are provided along with a figure, where appropriate, to illustrate the result. The reinforcement exercises that follow should be completed sequentially. Leave the file open at the end of each exercise for use in the next exercise until you are specifically directed to close it.

Open **EX0702** and save it as **EX0702-Reinforcement** on your disk for use in the following exercises.

We will use the table of swimming pool sales to practice and reinforce the skills learned in this lesson.

## R1—Copying, Deleting, Inserting, and Hiding Sheets

1. Right-click the **First Quarter** sheet tab and use the **Move or Copy** option to create a copy. Place it after the **First Quarter** sheet.

2. Double-click the sheet name of the copy and type **Second Quarter**. Press ⏎Enter.

3. Repeat this process to create copies and name them **Third Quarter**, **Fourth Quarter**, and **Summary**.

4. Right-click the new **Summary** sheet and choose **Delete**. Confirm that you want to delete it.

5. Choose **Insert**, **Worksheet**. Click-and-drag the new sheet tab to a position to the right of the **Fourth Quarter** sheet. Double-click its tab and type **Summary**. Press ⏎Enter.

6. Choose **Format**, **Sheet**, **Hide**.

7. Save the workbook. Leave the workbook open for use in the next exercise.

| | A | B | C | D | E | F | G |
|---|---|---|---|---|---|---|---|
| 1 | The Armstrong Pool, Spa, and Sauna Co. | | | | | | |
| 2 | | | | Swimming Pool Size | | | |
| 3 | Location | 15' | 18' | 24' | 27' | 12'x24' | 15'x30' |
| 4 | Indianapolis | 11 | 16 | 18 | 17 | 3 | 10 |
| 5 | Fort Wayne | 25 | 22 | 35 | 12 | 7 | 15 |
| 6 | Toledo | 3 | 3 | 4 | 2 | 0 | 1 |
| 7 | Dayton | 12 | 15 | 18 | 11 | 1 | 14 |
| 8 | Columbus | 8 | 10 | 15 | 22 | 5 | 7 |
| 9 | Ypsilanti | 31 | 37 | 56 | 33 | 6 | 25 |
| 10 | Southfield | 16 | 18 | 31 | 15 | 5 | 17 |
| 11 | Novi | 21 | 26 | 44 | 18 | 6 | 27 |
| 12 | Total Units | 127 | 147 | 221 | 130 | 33 | 116 |

First Quarter / Second Quarter / Third Quarter / Fourth Quarter

## R2—Inserting, Deleting, Hiding, and Unhiding Rows and Columns

1. Select the **First Quarter** sheet. Insert a row between **Dayton** and **Columbus**. Insert a new column between **24'** and **27'** pools.

2. Select column **C** and choose **Edit**, **Delete** to delete the column for **18'** pools.

3. Hide the column for **27'** pools.

4. Select columns **D** and **F**. Choose **Format**, **Column**, **Unhide** to unhide column **E**.

5. Save the workbook. Leave the workbook open for use in the next exercise.

| | A | B | C | D | E | F | G |
|---|---|---|---|---|---|---|---|
| 1 | The Armstrong Pool, Spa, and Sauna Co. | | | | | | |
| 2 | | | | Swimming Pool Size | | | |
| 3 | Location | 15' | 24' | | 27' | 12'x24' | 15'x30' |
| 4 | Indianapolis | 11 | 18 | | 17 | 3 | 10 |
| 5 | Fort Wayne | 25 | 35 | | 12 | 7 | 15 |
| 6 | Toledo | 3 | 4 | | 2 | 0 | 1 |
| 7 | Dayton | 12 | 18 | | 11 | 1 | 14 |
| 8 | | | | | | | |
| 9 | Columbus | 8 | 15 | | 22 | 5 | 7 |
| 10 | Ypsilanti | 31 | 56 | | 33 | 6 | 25 |
| 11 | Southfield | 16 | 31 | | 15 | 5 | 17 |
| 12 | Novi | 21 | 44 | | 18 | 6 | 27 |
| 13 | Total Units | 127 | 221 | | 130 | 33 | 116 |

## R3—Unhiding a Sheet, Using the Format Painter, and Applying an AutoFormat

Unhide the Executive Salaries sheet and use the Format Painter. Use the AutoFormat feature to format the Second Quarter sheet.

1. Choose **Format**, **Sheet**, **Unhide**. Select **Executive Salaries** in the **Unhide sheet** box. Click **OK**.

2. Select cell **A3**. Double-click the **Format Painter** button. Click cells **B3** and **C3**. Click the **Format Painter** button to turn it off.

3. Select the **Second Quarter** sheet. Select cells **A3** through **G12**.

4. Choose **Format, AutoFormat**. Choose **3D Effects 2** from the list of options.

5. Click the **Options** button and deselect the **Width/ Height** option. Click **OK**. Click an empty cell to deselect the table and view the new format.

6. Save the workbook and leave it open for use in the next exercise.

|   | A | B | C | D | E | F | G |
|---|---|---|---|---|---|---|---|
| 1 | **The Armstrong Pool, Spa, and Sauna Co.** | | | | | | |
| 2 | | | | Swimming Pool Size | | | |
| 3 | **Location** | 15' | 18' | 24' | 27' | 12'x24' | 15'x30' |
| 4 | Indianapolis | 11 | 16 | 18 | 17 | 3 | 10 |
| 5 | Fort Wayne | 25 | 22 | 35 | 12 | 7 | 15 |
| 6 | Toledo | 3 | 3 | 4 | 2 | 0 | 1 |
| 7 | Dayton | 12 | 15 | 18 | 11 | 1 | 14 |
| 8 | Columbus | 8 | 10 | 15 | 22 | 5 | 7 |
| 9 | Ypsilanti | 31 | 37 | 56 | 33 | 6 | 25 |
| 10 | Southfield | 16 | 18 | 31 | 15 | 5 | 17 |
| 11 | Novi | 21 | 26 | 44 | 18 | 6 | 27 |
| 12 | **Total Units** | 127 | 147 | 221 | 130 | 33 | 116 |

## R4—Defining and Applying a Style

1. Select the **Third Quarter** sheet. Select cell **A4**.

2. Change the font to **Courier New** and make it **Bold**. Change the font color to **Pink** and the fill color to **Black**.

3. Choose **Format, Style**. Type **Store Name** in the **Style name** box and click **OK**.

4. Select cells **A5** through **A11**. Choose **Format, Style**. Select **Store Name** from the list of styles and click **OK**.

5. Save the workbook. Leave the workbook open for use in the next exercise.

|   | A | B | C | D |
|---|---|---|---|---|
| 1 | **The Armstrong Pool, Spa** | | | |
| 2 | | | | Swimming |
| 3 | **Location** | 15' | 18' | 24' |
| 4 | Indianapol: | 11 | 16 | 18 |
| 5 | Fort Wayne | 25 | 22 | 35 |
| 6 | Toledo | 3 | 3 | 4 |
| 7 | Dayton | 12 | 15 | 18 |
| 8 | Columbus | 8 | 10 | 15 |
| 9 | Ypsilanti | 31 | 37 | 56 |
| 10 | Southfield | 16 | 18 | 31 |
| 11 | Novi | 21 | 26 | 44 |
| 12 | **Total Units** | 127 | 147 | 221 |

## R5—Changing the Zoom and Freezing Panes

1. Select the **Fourth Quarter** sheet.

2. Click the **Zoom** box and type **150**. Press **⏎Enter**.

3. Select cell **A4**. Choose **Window, Freeze Panes**.

4. Use the vertical scroll bar to scroll the worksheet so that row **12**, the **Total Units** row, is directly below row **3**.

5. Save the workbook and close it.

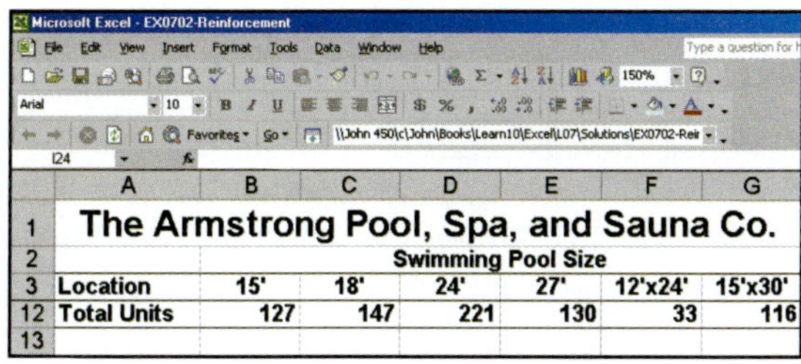

|   | A | B | C | D | E | F | G |
|---|---|---|---|---|---|---|---|
| 1 | **The Armstrong Pool, Spa, and Sauna Co.** | | | | | | |
| 2 | | | | Swimming Pool Size | | | |
| 3 | Location | 15' | 18' | 24' | 27' | 12'x24' | 15'x30' |
| 12 | Total Units | 127 | 147 | 221 | 130 | 33 | 116 |
| 13 | | | | | | | |

Challenge exercises are designed to test your ability to apply your skills to new situations with less-detailed instructions. These exercises also challenge you to expand your repertoire of skills by using commands that are similar to those you have already learned. The desired outcome is clearly defined, but you have more freedom to choose the steps needed to achieve the required result.

The following exercises use separate sheets in the same workbook. The exercises are not sequential and do not depend on each other. Open **EX0703** and save it on your disk as **EX0703-Challenge**.

## C1—Selecting Custom Zoom Settings

The down arrow next to the Zoom box lists several fixed zoom options. There are two other options that are useful. You can select a range of cells and zoom the display to maximize the selected cells or you can enter your own zoom factor. The percentage of zoom used to fill the screen with the selected text depends upon the **Screen Area** setting used by the Windows operating system. The screen area setting controls how many picture elements, or **pixels**, are displayed on the screen. This book is written using a screen setting of 800 pixels by 600 pixels. If a screen is set to display more pixels, the individual cells of the worksheet appear smaller, but more of them fit on the screen at one time.

*Goal:* Change the zoom so that the table is maximized on the screen.

1. Click the **C1** sheet tab, if necessary. Select cells **A1** through **I12**. Click the down arrow next to the **Zoom** box and click **Selection**.

2. Notice the customized zoom setting that fits the selection to the display window. Select cell **B18** and type this percentage into that cell. This value depends upon the Screen Area setting used in Windows.

3. Save the workbook. Leave this file open for use in the next Challenge exercise.

## C2—Sorting Rows of Data

Excel can sort tables by column. Include the column headings in the range of cells to be sorted but do not include merged headings or totals.

*Goal:* Sort the table alphabetically by location.

1. Click the **C2** sheet tab. Select cells **A3** through **H11**.

2. Choose **Data, Sort**. The Sort dialog box opens.

3. Confirm that the **Header row** option is selected.

4. Click the down arrow next to the **Sort by** box to see a list of columns by which you can sort. Choose **Location**.

5. Confirm that the **Ascending** option is selected and click **OK**. Notice that the totals at the right recalculated to reflect the new row totals.

6. Save the workbook and keep it open for the next exercise.

| | A | B | C | D | E | F | G | H | I |
|---|---|---|---|---|---|---|---|---|---|
| 1 | The Armstrong Pool, Spa, and Sauna Co. | | | | | | | | |
| 2 | | | Swimming Pool Size | | | | | | |
| 3 | Location | 15' | 18' | 24' | 27' | 12'x24' | 15'x30' | 18'x33' | Total Units |
| 4 | Columbus | 8 | 10 | 15 | 22 | 5 | 7 | 12 | 79 |
| 5 | Dayton | 12 | 15 | 18 | 11 | 1 | 14 | 21 | 92 |
| 6 | Fort Wayne | 25 | 22 | 35 | 12 | 7 | 15 | 16 | 132 |
| 7 | Indianapolis | 11 | 16 | 18 | 17 | 3 | 10 | 4 | 79 |
| 8 | Novi | 21 | 26 | 44 | 18 | 6 | 27 | 22 | 164 |
| 9 | Southfield | 16 | 18 | 31 | 15 | 5 | 17 | 19 | 121 |
| 10 | Toledo | 3 | 3 | 4 | 2 | 0 | 1 | 0 | 13 |
| 11 | Ypsilanti | 31 | 37 | 56 | 33 | 6 | 25 | 11 | 199 |
| 12 | Total Units | 127 | 147 | 221 | 130 | 33 | 116 | 105 | 879 |

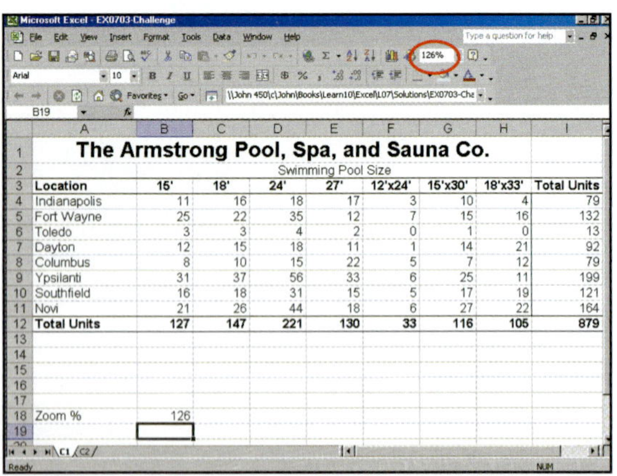

## C3—Deleting a Style

If a style has been created but is no longer in use, it is prudent to delete it.

*Goal:* Apply a style and then delete the style.

1. Click the **C2** sheet tab. Select cells **A4** through **A11**. Choose **Format**, **Style**.

2. Click the down arrow next to the **Style name** box and select **Cities**. Click **OK**. The city names are displayed in Comic Sans MS with Bold and Italic emphasis.

3. Click the **Undo** button to remove the style from the selected cells.

4. Choose **Format**, **Style**. Click the down arrow next to the **Style name** box and select **Cities**.

5. Click the **Delete** button. Notice that the Normal style is displayed in the **Style name** box but the Delete button is inactive. The Normal style may not be deleted.

6. Click the down arrow next to the **Style** box and confirm that the **Cities** style is no longer listed. Click **OK**.

7. Click the **C1** sheet tab. Choose **Format**, **Style** to display the **Style** dialog box. Click the down arrow next to the **Style name** box to display the available styles and confirm that the **Cities** style is no longer listed. Close the **Style** dialog box. Deleting the style removes it from the whole workbook.

8. Save the workbook and leave it open for use in the next exercise.

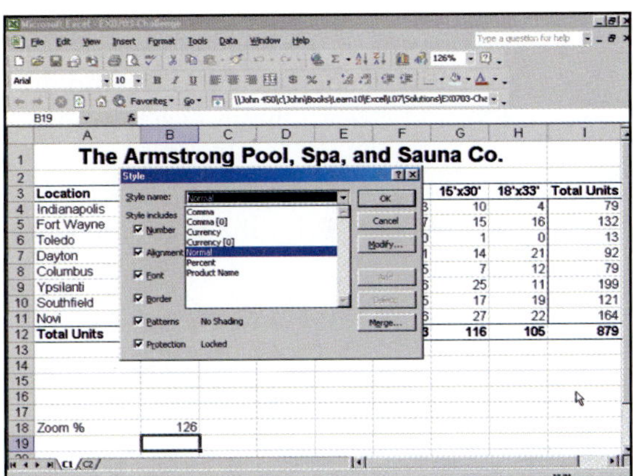

## C4—Customizing the Toolbar to Add the Styles Button

If you use styles very much, it is time consuming to apply them using the menu options. You can customize the Formatting toolbar to include a box that shows the current style and also has a down arrow that will display the available styles. It works just like the Font box. Customizations of the toolbar do not attach themselves to the workbook, so you will document this exercise by capturing a screen image that shows the toolbar with the style box and then pasting the image into a Word document.

*Goal:* Customize the Formatting toolbar to display the Style box.

1. Choose **View**, **Toolbars**, **Customize**. Click the **Commands** tab, if necessary.

2. Click **Format** in the **Categories** box. Select the **Style** option in the **Commands** box that includes a box with a down arrow.

3. Click-and-drag the selected style box from the Customize dialog box onto the Formatting toolbar and drop it at the left end, next to the Font name box.

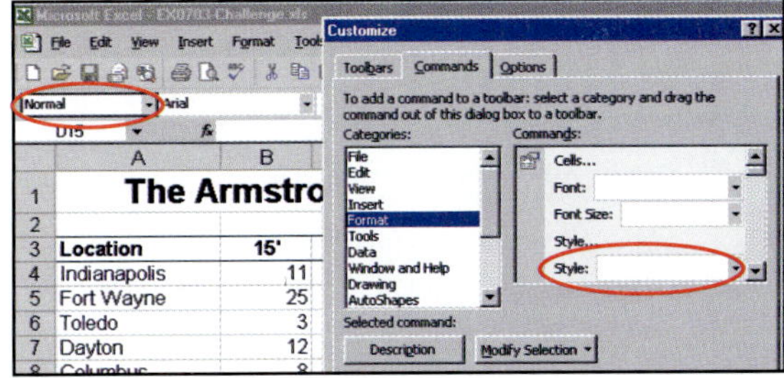

4. Click the **Close** button.

5. Select cell **B2**. Click the down arrow on the new Style box and select **Product Name**.

6. Press the PrtSc button on your keyboard. (It may be abbreviated as PrtScr or PrtSc on some keyboards.) An image of the screen is captured and placed in the clipboard.

7. Start Microsoft Word and open a new document if necessary. Click the **Paste** button on the toolbar.

8. Save the document as **EX0704-Style**. Close the document and close Word. Switch back to the workbook.

9. Choose **View**, **Toolbars**, **Customize**. Click and drag the new **Styles** box downward, off of the toolbar. Release the mouse button once the mouse pointer is no longer above any of the toolbars. This action removes the Styles box from the toolbar. Click the **Close** button on the Customize dialog box.

10. Save the changes you have made. Close the workbook.

## C5–Creating a New Workbook from a Template

Excel has some worksheets that are already completely designed and ready for use. You can open one of these **templates** and fill in the information. Formulas are already included, so you simply insert the data and save the workbook by a new name.

*Goal:* Use a template to create a timecard that shows how much time a person spent working on three different projects.

1. Choose **View**, **Task Pane**. Choose **General Templates** in the **New from template** section.

2. Click the **Spreadsheet Solutions** tab. Click the **Timecard** option and click **OK**. Change the **zoom** to **75%** if necessary to see the entire width of the worksheet.

3. Enter your name in the Name box. Enter the following information in the indicated cells:

| | |
|---|---|
| **Emp #:** | 111 |
| **Position:** | Designer |
| **SSN** | 111-11-1111 |
| **Department:** | Design |
| **Manager:** | Smith |
| **From:** | 2/4/02 |
| **To:** | 2/8/02 |

| ACCOUNT DESCRIPTION | ACCOUNT CODE | M | T | W | TH | F | SA | SU |
|---|---|---|---|---|---|---|---|---|
| Miller Building | 555 | 2 | 1 | 5 | 4 | 3 | 0 | 0 |
| Dexter Plaza | 345 | 3 | 6 | 2 | 4 | 1 | 0 | 0 |
| French Landing | 876 | 3 | 2 | 1 | 0 | 3 | 0 | 0 |

4. Save the workbook on your disk as **EX0705-Time Card** and close it.

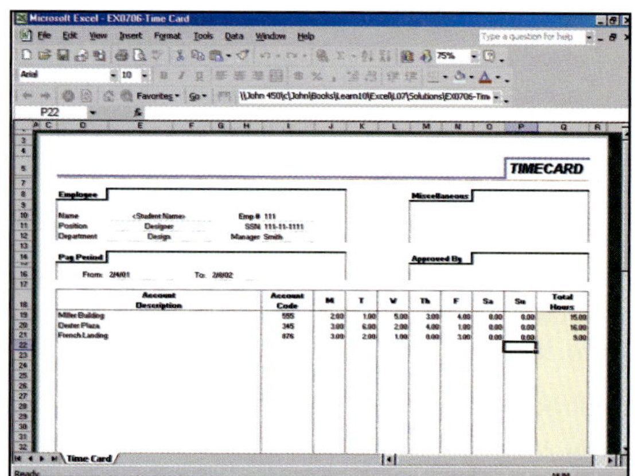

## C6–Inserting and Deleting Cells

When you enter columns of names and numbers, it is easy to lose track and enter values twice or skip one. To repair this type of mistake, you need to insert or delete a single cell and move the rest of the data in the column up or down without moving the data in the other columns.

In this exercise, the employees at several branch banks are in a contest to see who sells the most bank services. When you review this worksheet, you realize that someone entered the values by column and made two mistakes that result in misalignment of most of the branch names. You need to delete one entry and insert another to correct this mistake.

*Goal:* Delete and insert cells and move the other values in the column to adjust for the deletion and insertion.

1. Open the file **EX0706** from the **Student** folder and save it on your disk as **EX0706-Insert Cells**.

2. Pam works at the Jackson branch and you recognize that Dexter has been entered a third time incorrectly. Right-click on the third **Dexter** entry in cell **E6** and choose **Delete**.

3. Chose **Shift cells up**.

4. Scroll down the list and examine the name of the sales representatives and the names and the Branches. Select cell **E32**. An entry is missing.

5. Choose **Insert**, **Cells**.

6. Confirm that **Shift cells down** is selected and click **OK**.

7. Scroll the window so you can see rows **32** through **50**.

8. Click on cell **E47** which contains an extra entry for **Jackson**.

9. Move the pointer to the edge of the cell where it becomes a four-headed arrow. Click-and-drag this cell to **E32** and release the mouse button.

10. Add your name to cell **A49**.

11. Save the workbook. Print the sheet then close the workbook.

12. Save your changes and close the workbook.

| | A | B | C | D | E | F |
|---|---|---|---|---|---|---|
| 1 | | Sales Record for January 2000 for First National Bank | | | | |
| 2 | Date | Product | Amount | Sales Rep | Branch | Points |
| 3 | 2-Jan | Checking | $ 2,000 | Diane | Plymouth | 6 |
| 4 | 5-Jan | Savings | $ 10,000 | Sharon | Dexter | 20 |
| 5 | 6-Jan | Auto Loan | $ 17,700 | Sharon | Dexter | 35.4 |
| 6 | 6-Jan | Certificate | $ 30,000 | Pam | Jackson | 60 |
| 7 | 6-Jan | Credit Card | $ 5,000 | Paula | Main | 15 |
| 8 | 6-Jan | Certificate | $ 12,500 | Jonell | Ypsilanti | 25 |
| 9 | 7-Jan | Mortgage | $ 150,000 | Richard | Dexter | 300 |

## C7—Filtering a Table of Data

Many people use Excel in place of a database if all the information can be saved in a single table. Excel can sort, filter, and subtotal  the data to provide simple summary reports.

In this exercise, the employees at several branch banks are in a contest to see who sells the most bank services. You want to look at how each branch is doing.

*Goal:* Filter the table based on branch name or product name.

1. Open the file **EX0707** from the **Student** folder and save it on your disk as **EX0707-Filter**.

2. Click anywhere in the table and choose **Data**, **Filter**, **AutoFilter**. Down arrows appear at the top of each column in the table.

3. Click the down arrow at the top of the **Branch** column and select **Jackson** from the list. (↵Enter).

4. Click cell **F48** and click the **AutoSum** button on the toolbar. The SUBTOTAL function is inserted but it does not have the correct range.

5. Click and drag the cells that are showing in column **F** from **F6** to **F43** and press (↵Enter).

6. Add your name to cell **F51** and save the workbook.

7. Print the sheet. Close the workbook.

| | A | B | C | D | E | F |
|---|---|---|---|---|---|---|
| 1 | | Sales Record for January 2000 for First National Bank | | | | |
| 2 | Date | Product | Amount | Sales Rep | Branch | Points |
| 6 | 6-Jan | Certificate | $ 30,000 | Pam | Jackson | 60 |
| 11 | 8-Jan | Auto Loan | $ 30,000 | Pam | Jackson | 60 |
| 13 | 9-Jan | Mortgage | $ 125,000 | Rhonda | Jackson | 250 |
| 23 | 16-Jan | Savings | $ 4,000 | Pam | Jackson | 12 |
| 31 | 21-Jan | Savings | $ 2,500 | Pam | Jackson | 7.5 |
| 32 | 22-Jan | Certificate | $ 25,000 | Pam | Jackson | 50 |
| 34 | 23-Jan | Auto Loan | $ 17,750 | Rhonda | Jackson | 35.5 |
| 36 | 27-Jan | Mortgage | $ 165,000 | Pam | Jackson | 330 |
| 39 | 28-Jan | Certificate | $ 15,000 | Rhonda | Jackson | 30 |
| 42 | 30-Jan | Auto Loan | $ 25,000 | Pam | Jackson | 50 |
| 43 | 30-Jan | Certificate | $ 15,600 | Pam | Jackson | 31.2 |
| 48 | | | | | | 916.2 |

You may have a way of formatting worksheets that you want to use consistently. Set up a workbook with a set of your own styles.

Criteria for grading will be:

**1.** Demonstration of the use of the styles feature.

Some examples of features that students have learned to use in previous classes to enhance their personal style workbook are as follows:

- The example workbook had several different opportunities for using a style such as a workbook of tax deductions like the one done in the On Your Own section of Lesson 5.

- The style names were easy to recognize and associated with their function.

- The styles worked together to form a consistent look.

- The styles are applied in more than one place.

**2.** Identify yourself. Place your name in a cell that is clearly visible.

**3.** To complete the project:

- Save your file on your own disk. Name it **EX0706-MyStyles**.

- Check with your instructor to determine if the project should be submitted in electronic or printed form. If necessary, print out a copy of the worksheet to hand in.

# Lesson 8

## Becoming Proficient with Printing Workbooks and Getting Help

Task 1  Selecting a Range of Cells to Print and Previewing the Worksheet
Task 2  Inserting, Moving, and Removing a Page Break
Task 3  Clearing the Print Area, Setting Page Orientation and Scaling
Task 4  Setting Headings and Margins
Task 5  Using Headers and Footers
Task 6  Using the Office Assistant and Help

## INTRODUCTION

Printing a worksheet is as easy as clicking the Print button, but the resulting output is often more than you need or is less useful than it could be. You may also need to send the workbook to someone at another location. In that case, you can attach the workbook to an email message.

Excel has many features that have not been addressed in this book. To learn more, you can use the Office Assistant to look up instruction from the built-in help manual.

In this lesson you use a worksheet that calculates and displays the monthly payments for a home mortgage. You learn how to control the appearance of the worksheet printout, send a worksheet as an email attachment, and use the Office Assistant to get additional help.

# VISUAL SUMMARY

When you have completed this entire lesson, you will have a worksheet printout that looks like this:

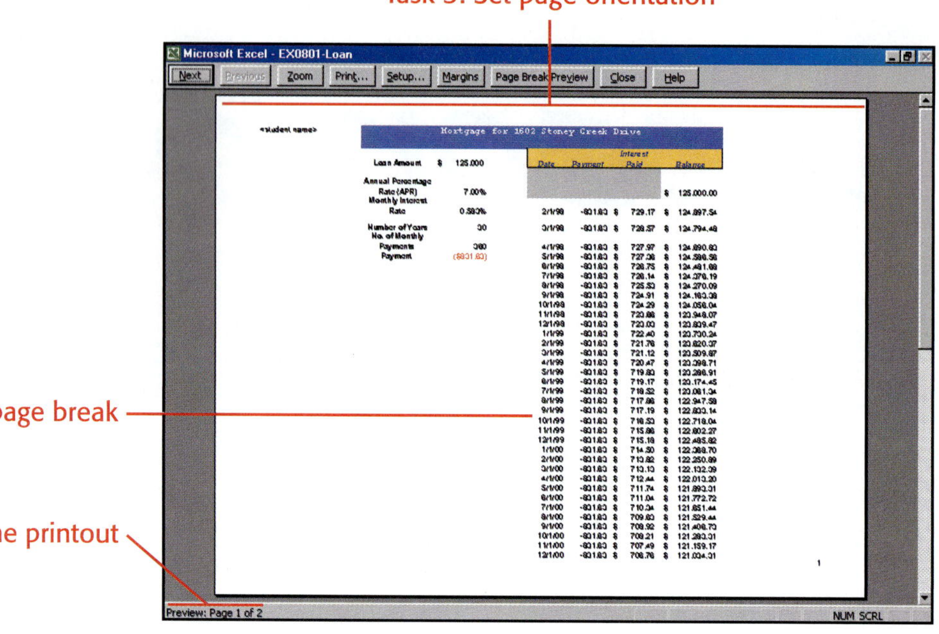



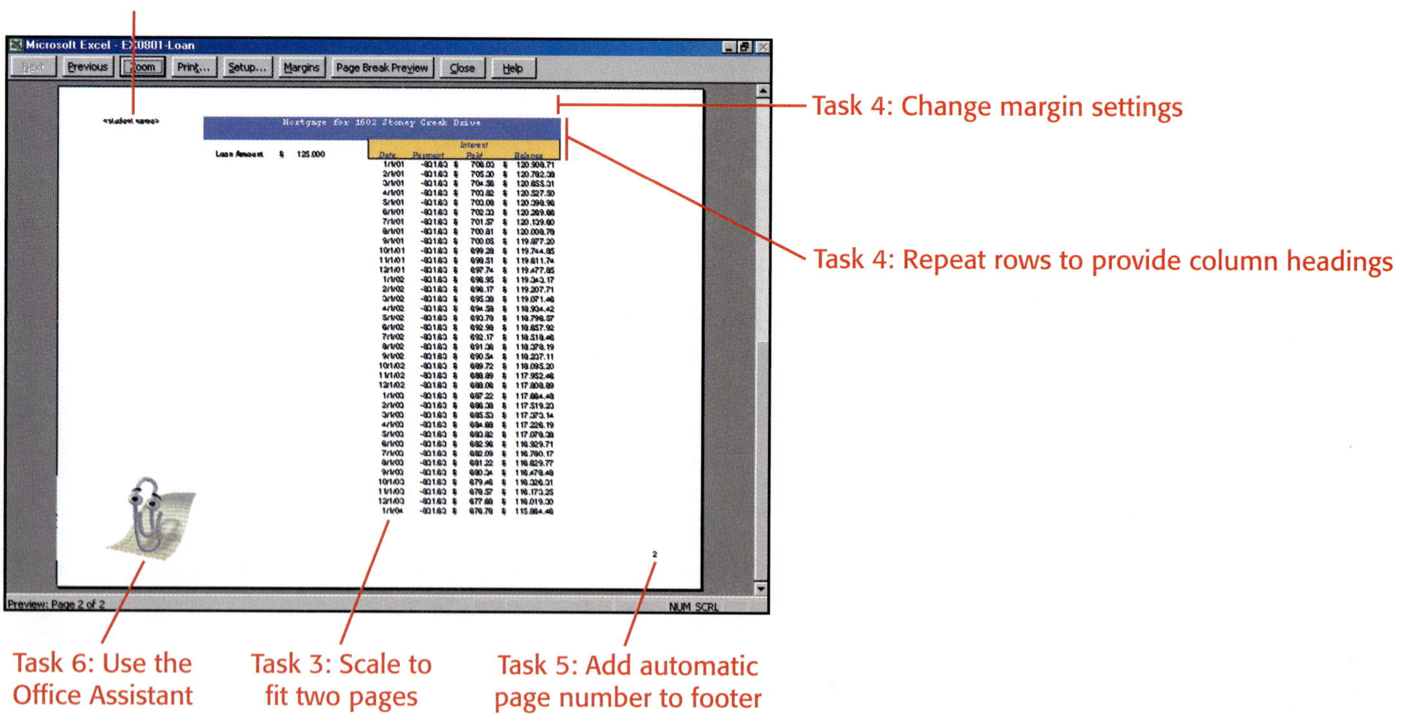

# Task 1

## SELECTING A RANGE OF CELLS TO PRINT AND PREVIEWING THE WORKSHEET

*Explain It*

*Do It*

*Use It*

### Why would I do this?

If a worksheet is too large to fit on one page or for some other reason you do not want to print an entire worksheet, you may select a portion of the sheet to print. It is useful to first preview the printout on the screen to catch errors in layout and formatting, such as one column printing on a page by itself. You can make the needed adjustments and save time and paper by not printing mistakes.

In this task, you learn how to print a portion of the loan repayment schedule and to preview it before printing.

**1** Launch Excel and click the **Open** button. Find **EX0801** in the **Student** folder and open it.

*This worksheet displays monthly payments for a loan amortized over 30 years.*

Save the file as **EX0801-Loan** on your disk.

*The new file name appears in the title bar.*

Select the **Loan 1** sheet, if necessary, and click cell **D3**. Scroll down to display row **364**. Press ⬆Shift) and click cell **G364**.

*The column headings and payments for the 30 years are selected.*

| | A | B | C | D | E | F | G |
|---|---|---|---|---|---|---|---|
| 347 | | | | 8/1/26 | -895.52 | $ 97.94 | $ 14,368.04 |
| 348 | | | | 9/1/26 | -895.52 | $ 92.79 | $ 13,565.31 |
| 349 | | | | 10/1/26 | -895.52 | $ 87.61 | $ 12,757.40 |
| 350 | | | | 11/1/26 | -895.52 | $ 82.39 | $ 11,944.27 |
| 351 | | | | 12/1/26 | -895.52 | $ 77.14 | $ 11,125.89 |
| 352 | | | | 1/1/27 | -895.52 | $ 71.85 | $ 10,302.22 |
| 353 | | | | 2/1/27 | -895.52 | $ 66.54 | $ 9,473.24 |
| 354 | | | | 3/1/27 | -895.52 | $ 61.18 | $ 8,638.90 |
| 355 | | | | 4/1/27 | -895.52 | $ 55.79 | $ 7,799.17 |
| 356 | | | | 5/1/27 | -895.52 | $ 50.37 | $ 6,954.02 |
| 357 | | | | 6/1/27 | -895.52 | $ 44.91 | $ 6,103.41 |
| 358 | | | | 7/1/27 | -895.52 | $ 39.42 | $ 5,247.31 |
| 359 | | | | 8/1/27 | -895.52 | $ 33.89 | $ 4,385.68 |
| 360 | | | | 9/1/27 | -895.52 | $ 28.32 | $ 3,518.48 |
| 361 | | | | 10/1/27 | -895.52 | $ 22.72 | $ 2,645.68 |
| 362 | | | | 11/1/27 | -895.52 | $ 17.09 | $ 1,767.25 |
| 363 | | | | 12/1/27 | -895.52 | $ 11.41 | $ 883.14 |
| 364 | | | | 1/1/28 | -895.52 | $ 5.70 | $ (6.68) |

Not always zero

**IN DEPTH**

The final balance (as shown in cell G364) should be zero but is often slightly higher or lower. This is due to the practice of rounding the interest and payment to the nearest penny. If you select cell B8 or one of the calculated interest payments in column F, you will see that the formula used to calculate the value is nested inside the **ROUND()** function. This function is used to round the result of the payment or interest calculation to two decimal places, the way it is done at banks.

**2** Choose **File**, **Print Area**, **Set Print Area**.

*This range of cells may be printed by itself.*

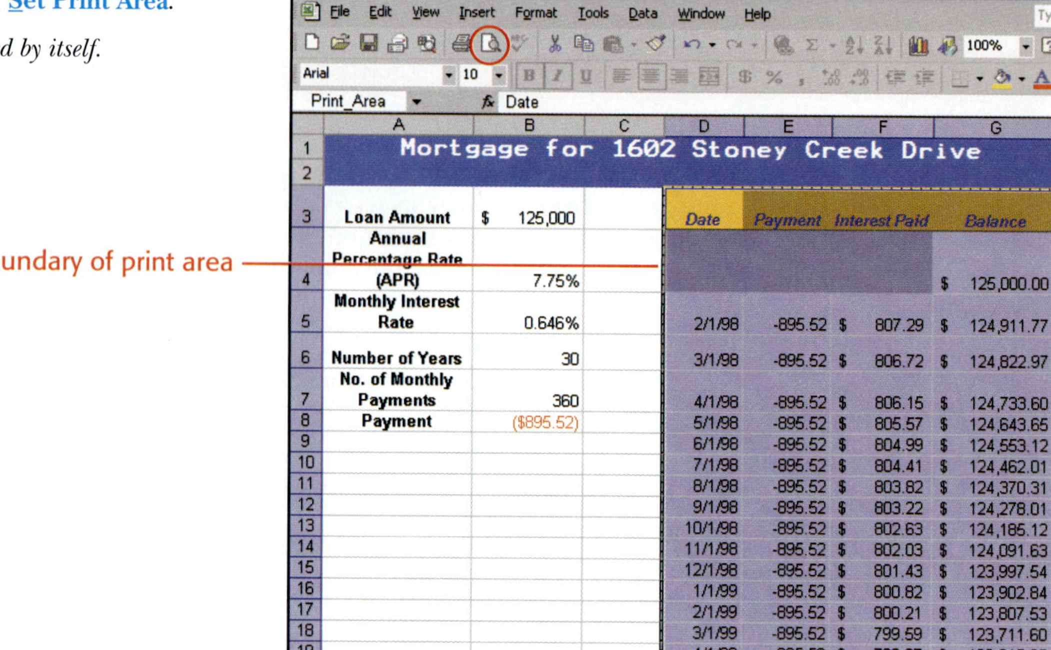



**3** Click the **Print Preview** button.

*A preview of the first of eight pages is displayed.*

**CAUTION**

Your computer may be set up to operate with different top and bottom margins. This will affect the number of pages used and where the automatic page breaks are placed. This example assumes the top and bottom margins are both set to one inch. You will learn more about setting margins in Task 4.

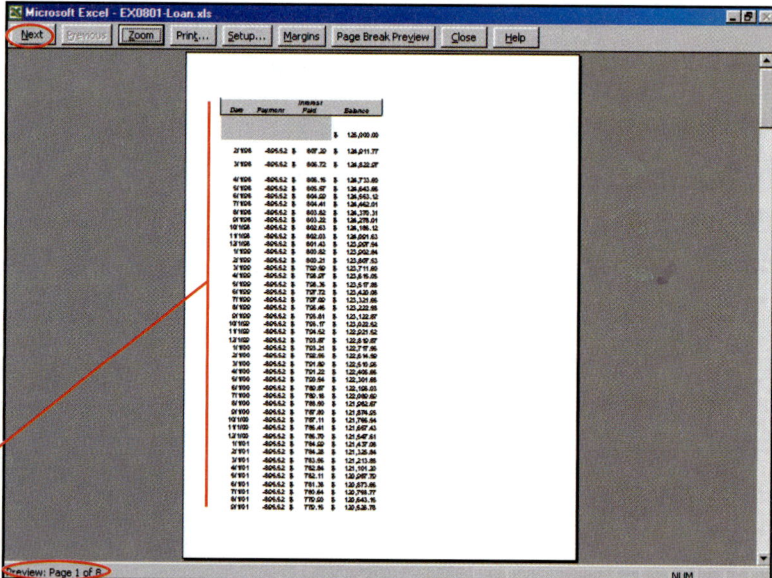



**4** Click the **Next** button.

*The second page displays the payments through 12/01/2002. Notice that the Previous button becomes active.*

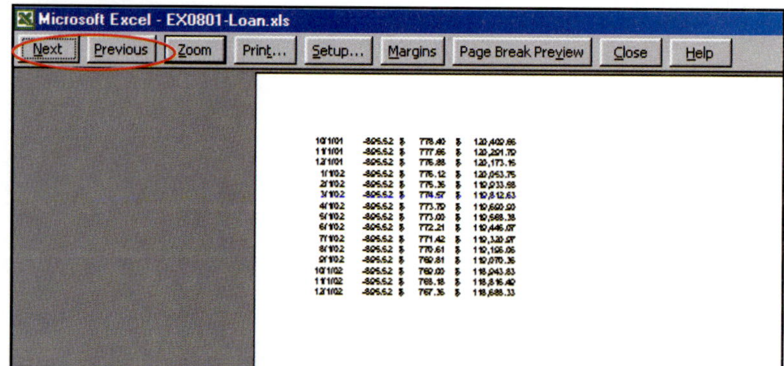

**5** Click the **Next** button again.

*Unlike the second page, the third page is filled with data.*

Click the **Previous** button to return to page **2**.

*This short page is the result of a page break inserted by the authors that you will work with in the next task.*

Result of a page break ——

**6** Move the pointer to the last row of the data.

*The pointer becomes a magnifying glass.*

Click on the last row.

*The display zooms in on the spot where you clicked.*

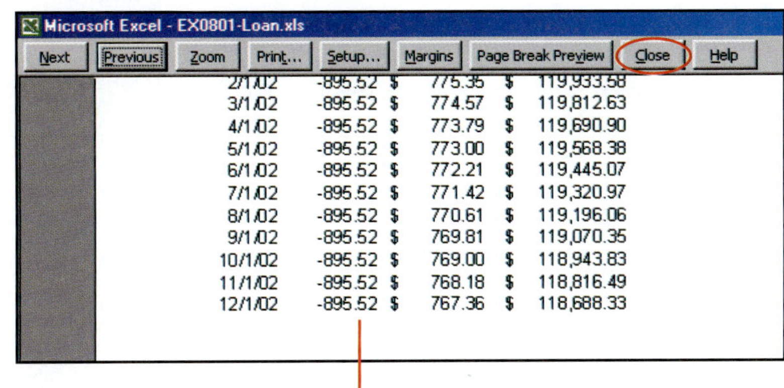


Zooms to last row

**7** Click anywhere on the sheet.

*The full page is displayed.*

Click the **Close** button on the toolbar.

*The **Normal view** of the worksheet is displayed.*

Leave the workbook open for use in the next task.

Normal view ——

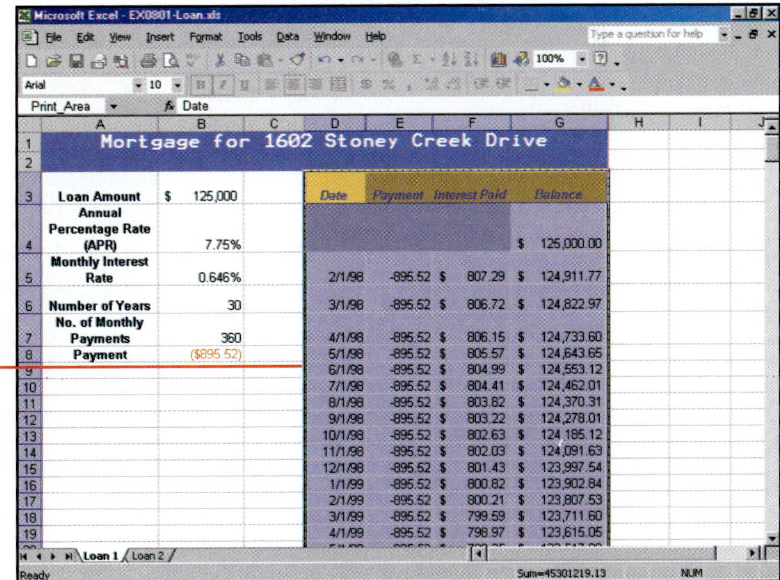

### Why would I do this?

Worksheets that consist of long columns or rows of numbers that extend beyond a single sheet will automatically be divided into sections that fit the current setting for the paper size. You may prefer to break the columns at different locations.

In this task, you learn how to insert, move, and delete page breaks.

**1** Choose **View**, **Page Break Preview**. The Welcome to Page Break Preview dialog box may appear. If so, click **OK**.

*The **Page Break Preview** view displays the selected cells with a color border around the perimeter.*

Scroll down to display rows **35** through **65**. Select cell **D39**.

*This range of cells contains the first calculated page break and a page break that has been inserted. The selected cell contains the date, 12/1/00. It is our intention to place a page break after this row.*

**IN DEPTH**

The dotted line indicates a break at the bottom of the available space on a page. The position of this line is determined by font size, paper size, margin settings, and the positions of inserted page breaks. The solid line represents a page break that has been previously inserted in this worksheet and will not move unless you specifically move it yourself.

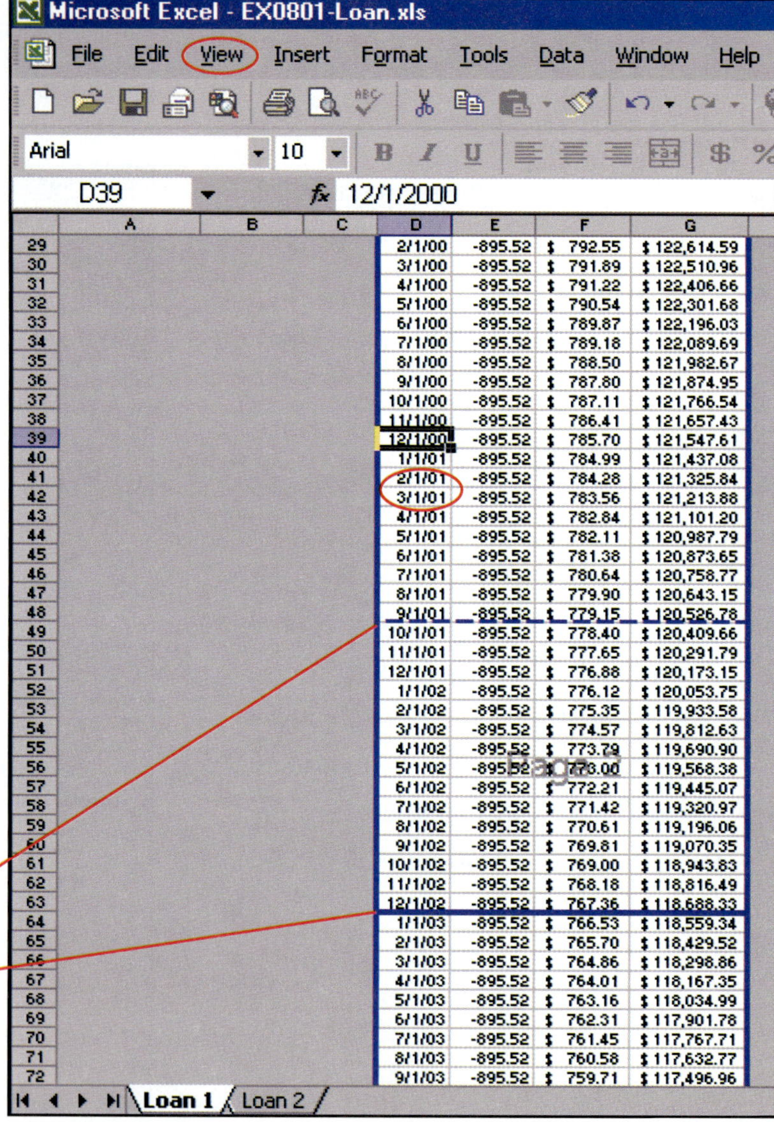



Calculated page break

Previously inserted page break

**2** Choose **Insert**, **Page Break**. Click an empty cell in the worksheet to view the location of the new page break.

*A page break is inserted above the selected cell rather than below it so the break is not in the correct position. You will move it in the next step. Notice that the calculated page break has been moved but the previously inserted page break has not.*

Page break inserted above the selected cell

Calculated page break removed

Previously inserted page break

| | A | B | C | D | E | F | G |
|---|---|---|---|---|---|---|---|
| 29 | | | | 2/1/00 | -895.52 | $ 792.55 | $ 122,614.59 |
| 30 | | | | 3/1/00 | -895.52 | $ 791.89 | $ 122,510.96 |
| 31 | | | | 4/1/00 | -895.52 | $ 791.22 | $ 122,406.66 |
| 32 | | | | 5/1/00 | -895.52 | $ 790.54 | $ 122,301.68 |
| 33 | | | | 6/1/00 | -895.52 | $ 789.87 | $ 122,196.03 |
| 34 | | | | 7/1/00 | -895.52 | $ 789.18 | $ 122,089.69 |
| 35 | | | | 8/1/00 | -895.52 | $ 788.50 | $ 121,982.67 |
| 36 | | | | 9/1/00 | -895.52 | $ 787.80 | $ 121,874.95 |
| 37 | | | | 10/1/00 | -895.52 | $ 787.11 | $ 121,766.54 |
| 38 | | | | 11/1/00 | -895.52 | $ 786.41 | $ 121,657.43 |
| 39 | | | | 12/1/00 | -895.52 | $ 785.70 | $ 121,547.61 |
| 40 | | | | 1/1/01 | -895.52 | $ 784.99 | $ 121,437.08 |
| 41 | | | | 2/1/01 | -895.52 | $ 784.28 | $ 121,325.84 |
| 42 | | | | 3/1/01 | -895.52 | $ 783.56 | $ 121,213.88 |
| 43 | | | | 4/1/01 | -895.52 | $ 782.84 | $ 121,101.20 |
| 44 | | | | 5/1/01 | -895.52 | $ 782.11 | $ 120,987.79 |
| 45 | | | | 6/1/01 | -895.52 | $ 781.38 | $ 120,873.65 |
| 46 | | | | 7/1/01 | -895.52 | $ 780.64 | $ 120,758.77 |
| 47 | | | | 8/1/01 | -895.52 | $ 779.90 | $ 120,643.15 |
| 48 | | | | 9/1/01 | -895.52 | $ 779.15 | $ 120,526.78 |
| 49 | | | | 10/1/01 | -895.52 | $ 778.40 | $ 120,409.66 |
| 50 | | | | 11/1/01 | -895.52 | $ 777.65 | $ 120,291.79 |
| 51 | | | | 12/1/01 | -895.52 | $ 776.88 | $ 120,173.15 |
| 52 | | | | 1/1/02 | -895.52 | $ 776.12 | $ 120,053.75 |
| 53 | | | | 2/1/02 | -895.52 | $ 775.35 | $ 119,933.58 |
| 54 | | | | 3/1/02 | -895.52 | $ 774.57 | $ 119,812.63 |
| 55 | | | | 4/1/02 | -895.52 | $ 773.79 | $ 119,690.90 |
| 56 | | | | 5/1/02 | -895.52 | $ 773.00 | $ 119,568.38 |
| 57 | | | | 6/1/02 | -895.52 | $ 772.21 | $ 119,445.07 |
| 58 | | | | 7/1/02 | -895.52 | $ 771.42 | $ 119,320.97 |
| 59 | | | | 8/1/02 | -895.52 | $ 770.61 | $ 119,196.06 |
| 60 | | | | 9/1/02 | -895.52 | $ 769.81 | $ 119,070.35 |
| 61 | | | | 10/1/02 | -895.52 | $ 769.00 | $ 118,943.83 |
| 62 | | | | 11/1/02 | -895.52 | $ 768.18 | $ 118,816.49 |
| 63 | | | | 12/1/02 | -895.52 | $ 767.36 | $ 118,688.33 |
| 64 | | | | 1/1/03 | -895.52 | $ 766.53 | $ 118,559.34 |
| 65 | | | | 2/1/03 | -895.52 | $ 765.70 | $ 118,429.52 |
| 66 | | | | 3/1/03 | -895.52 | $ 764.86 | $ 118,298.86 |
| 67 | | | | 4/1/03 | -895.52 | $ 764.01 | $ 118,167.35 |
| 68 | | | | 5/1/03 | -895.52 | $ 763.16 | $ 118,034.99 |
| 69 | | | | 6/1/03 | -895.52 | $ 762.31 | $ 117,901.78 |
| 70 | | | | 7/1/03 | -895.52 | $ 761.45 | $ 117,767.71 |
| 71 | | | | 8/1/03 | -895.52 | $ 760.58 | $ 117,632.77 |
| 72 | | | | 9/1/03 | -895.52 | $ 759.71 | $ 117,496.96 |

|◄ ◄ ► ►|\ **Loan 1** / Loan 2 /

**3** Move the pointer onto the line between rows **38** and **39**. When the pointer changes to a two-headed arrow, click-and-drag the line down one row. Release the mouse button.

*The page break is now between the last payment of 2000 and the first payment of 2001.*

| | D | E | F | G |
|---|---|---|---|---|
| 30 | 3/1/00 | -895.52 | $ 791.89 | $ 122,510.96 |
| 31 | 4/1/00 | -895.52 | $ 791.22 | $ 122,406.66 |
| 32 | 5/1/00 | -895.52 | $ 790.54 | $ 122,301.68 |
| 33 | 6/1/00 | -895.52 | $ 789.87 | $ 122,196.03 |
| 34 | 7/1/00 | -895.52 | $ 789.18 | $ 122,089.69 |
| 35 | 8/1/00 | -895.52 | $ 788.50 | $ 121,982.67 |
| 36 | 9/1/00 | -895.52 | $ 787.80 | $ 121,874.95 |
| 37 | 10/1/00 | -895.52 | $ 787.11 | $ 121,766.54 |
| 38 | 11/1/00 | -895.52 | $ 786.41 | $ 121,657.43 |
| 39 | 12/1/00 | -895.52 | $ 785.70 | $ 121,547.61 |
| 40 | 1/1/01 | -895.52 | $ 784.99 | $ 121,437.08 |
| 41 | 2/1/01 | -895.52 | $ 784.28 | $ 121,325.84 |
| 42 | 3/1/01 | -895.52 | $ 783.56 | $ 121,213.88 |
| 43 | 4/1/01 | -895.52 | $ 782.84 | $ 121,101.20 |
| 44 | 5/1/01 | -895.52 | $ 782.11 | $ 120,987.79 |
| 45 | 6/1/01 | -895.52 | $ 781.38 | $ 120,873.65 |

Two-headed arrow pointer used to click-and-drag page break

 Select cell **D64**. Choose **Insert**, **Remove Page Break**.

*The page break is removed. The Remove Page Break option is displayed in the Insert menu if a cell is selected below a page break.*

Click the **Save** button and leave the workbook open for use in the next task.

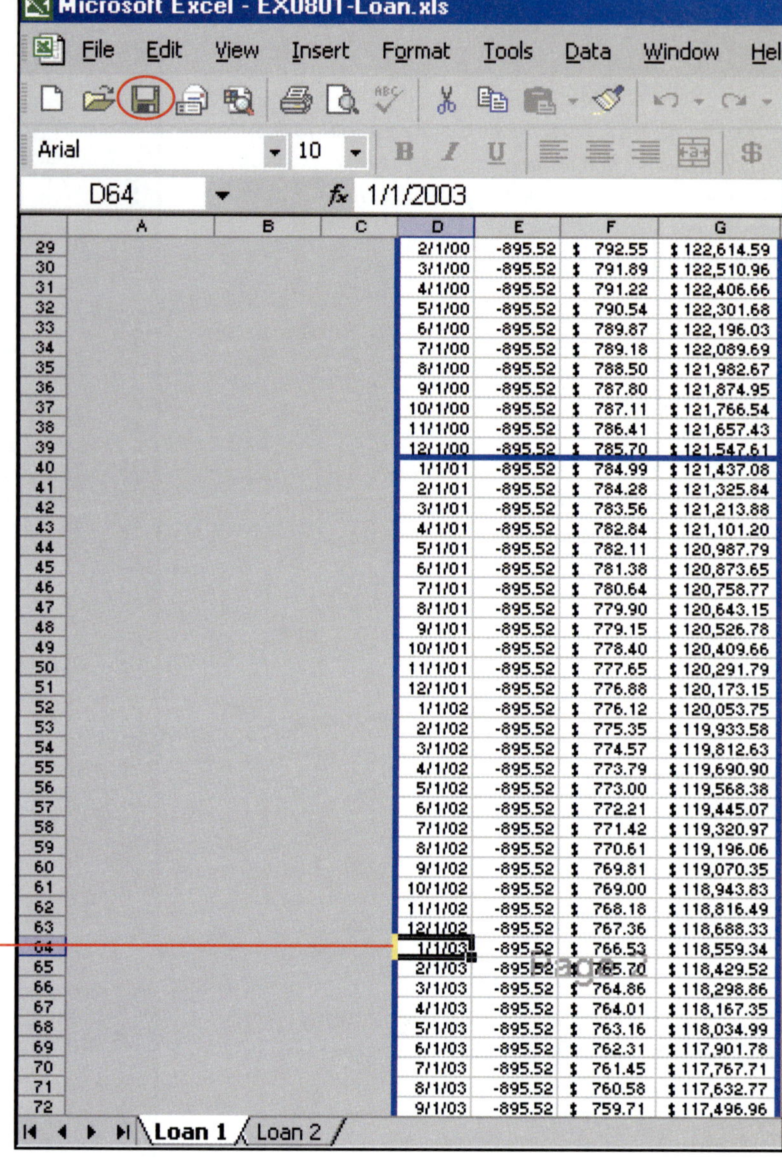

Page break removed

# Task 3

## CLEARING THE PRINT AREA, SETTING PAGE ORIENTATION, AND SCALING

### Why would I do this?

Once the print area is set, you need to know how to change it so you can print other areas of the worksheet. Some tables of data are long with few columns whereas others have many columns with few rows. If the area you wish to print has more columns than rows, it may fit the page better if you use Landscape orientation, which uses the width of the paper. If the selected area is slightly too large to fit on a page, you can adjust the columns or rows manually or you can use the scaling option to adjust the size automatically, which can be much faster.

In this task, you learn how to change the print area and the orientation of the printed page. You will also adjust the size automatically using the scaling feature.

**1** Click the **Loan 2** tab.

*In this worksheet, you will set up to print the first five years of payments on two pages in Landscape orientation.*

Choose **File**, **Print Area**, **Clear Print Area**.

*This returns the print area to the default setting, which is all of the worksheet that contains data.*

Dotted line indicates edge of print area.

|  | A | B | C | D | E | F | G |
|---|---|---|---|---|---|---|---|
| 1 | Mortgage for 1602 Stoney Creek Drive | | | | | | |
| 2 | | | | | | | |
| 3 | Loan Amount | $ 125,000 | | Date | Payment | Interest Paid | Balance |
| 4 | Annual Percentage Rate (APR) | 7.75% | | | | | $ 125,000.00 |
| 5 | Monthly Interest Rate | 0.646% | | 2/1/98 | -895.52 | $ 807.29 | $ 124,911.77 |
| 6 | Number of Years | 30 | | 3/1/98 | -895.52 | $ 806.72 | $ 124,822.97 |
| 7 | No. of Monthly Payments | 360 | | 4/1/98 | -895.52 | $ 806.15 | $ 124,733.60 |
| 8 | Payment | ($895.52) | | 5/1/98 | -895.52 | $ 805.57 | $ 124,643.65 |
| 9 | | | | 6/1/98 | -895.52 | $ 804.99 | $ 124,553.12 |
| 10 | | | | 7/1/98 | -895.52 | $ 804.41 | $ 124,462.01 |
| 11 | | | | 8/1/98 | -895.52 | $ 803.82 | $ 124,370.31 |
| 12 | | | | 9/1/98 | -895.52 | $ 803.22 | $ 124,278.01 |
| 13 | | | | 10/1/98 | -895.52 | $ 802.63 | $ 124,185.12 |
| 14 | | | | 11/1/98 | -895.52 | $ 802.03 | $ 124,091.63 |
| 15 | | | | 12/1/98 | -895.52 | $ 801.43 | $ 123,997.54 |
| 16 | | | | 1/1/99 | -895.52 | $ 800.82 | $ 123,902.84 |
| 17 | | | | 2/1/99 | -895.52 | $ 800.21 | $ 123,807.53 |
| 18 | | | | 3/1/99 | -895.52 | $ 799.59 | $ 123,711.60 |

Loan 1 \ Loan 2

**QUICK TIP**

It is not necessary to clear the current print area setting before you set a new one.

**2** Click cell **A1**. Scroll to row **76**, then press **Shift** and click cell **G76**.

*This will select the loan information, headings, and first five years of payments.*

Choose **File**, **Print Area**, **Set Print Area**.

|  | A | B | C | D | E | F | G |
|---|---|---|---|---|---|---|---|
| 1 | Mortgage for 1602 Stoney Creek Drive | | | | | | |
| 2 | | | | | | | |
| 3 | Loan Amount | $ 125,000 | | Date | Payment | Interest Paid | Balance |
| 4 | Annual Percentage Rate (APR) | 7.75% | | | | | $ 125,000.00 |
| 5 | Monthly Interest Rate | 0.646% | | 2/1/98 | -895.52 | $ 807.29 | $ 124,911.77 |
| 6 | Number of Years | 30 | | 3/1/98 | -895.52 | $ 806.72 | $ 124,822.97 |
| 7 | No. of Monthly Payments | 360 | | 4/1/98 | -895.52 | $ 806.15 | $ 124,733.60 |
| 8 | Payment | ($895.52) | | 5/1/98 | -895.52 | $ 805.57 | $ 124,643.65 |
| 9 | | | | 6/1/98 | -895.52 | $ 804.99 | $ 124,553.12 |
| 10 | | | | 7/1/98 | -895.52 | $ 804.41 | $ 124,462.01 |
| 11 | | | | 8/1/98 | -895.52 | $ 803.82 | $ 124,370.31 |
| 12 | | | | 9/1/98 | -895.52 | $ 803.22 | $ 124,278.01 |
| 13 | | | | 10/1/98 | -895.52 | $ 802.63 | $ 124,185.12 |
| 14 | | | | 11/1/98 | -895.52 | $ 802.03 | $ 124,091.63 |
| 15 | | | | 12/1/98 | -895.52 | $ 801.43 | $ 123,997.54 |
| 16 | | | | 1/1/99 | -895.52 | $ 800.82 | $ 123,902.84 |
| 17 | | | | 2/1/99 | -895.52 | $ 800.21 | $ 123,807.53 |
| 18 | | | | 3/1/99 | -895.52 | $ 799.59 | $ 123,711.60 |

Loan 1 \ Loan 2

**IN DEPTH**

Some loans are calculated as if they were going to be paid off over a long period of time, such as 30 years, but the outstanding balance must be paid off or refinanced at the end of a much shorter period, such as five years. This type of loan that has a large final payment is called a balloon mortgage.

**3** Choose **File**, **Page Setup**.

*The Page Setup dialog box opens.*

Click the **Page** tab. Click the **Landscape** option button.

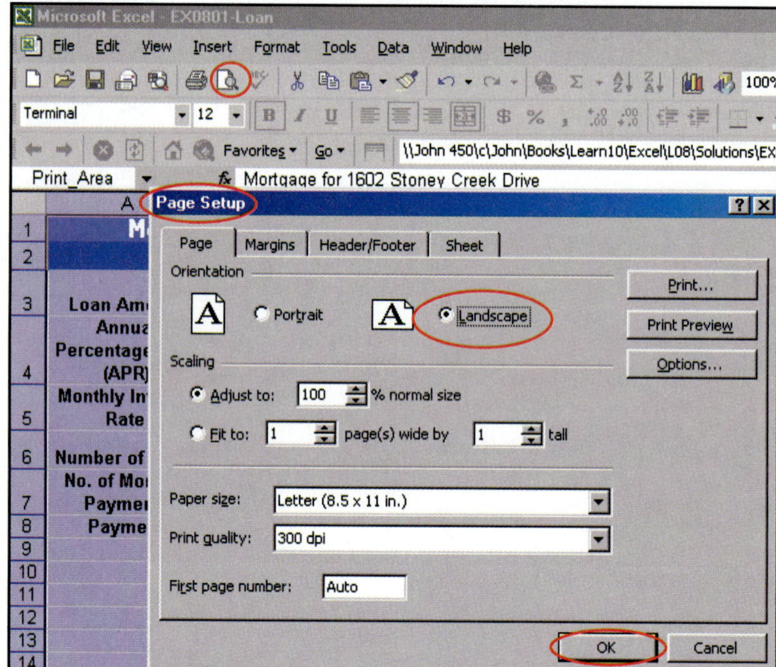

**4** Click **OK**. Click the **Print Preview** button.

*The table could be printed on three pages.*

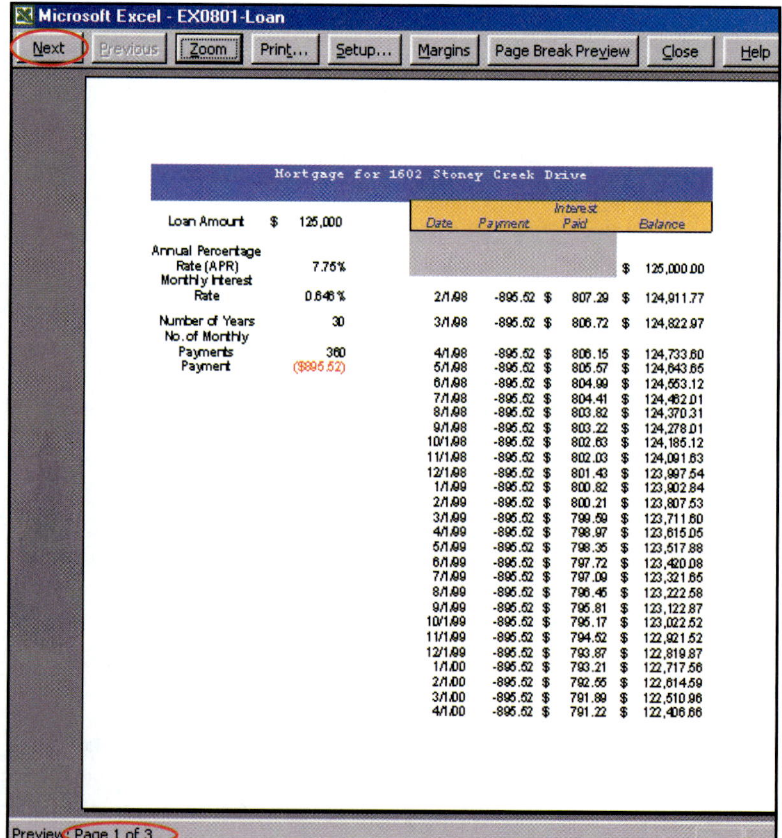

**5** Click the **Next** button twice to move to the third page.

*Notice that the last page does not have a full page of data.*

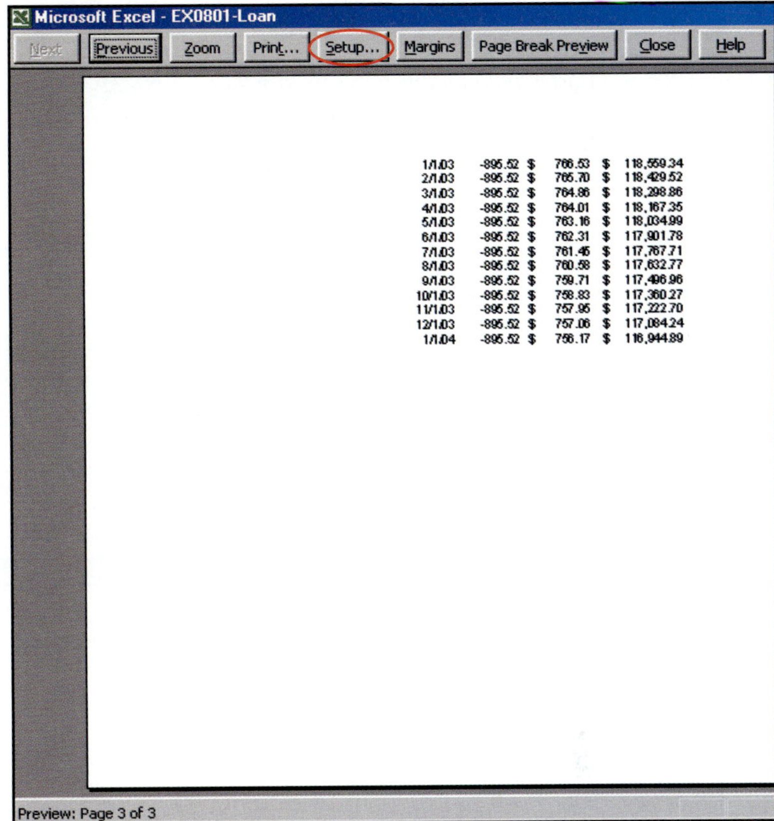

**6** Click the **Setup** button.

*The Page Setup dialog box is displayed.*

Click the **Fit to** option button and change the printout to **1** page wide by **2** tall.

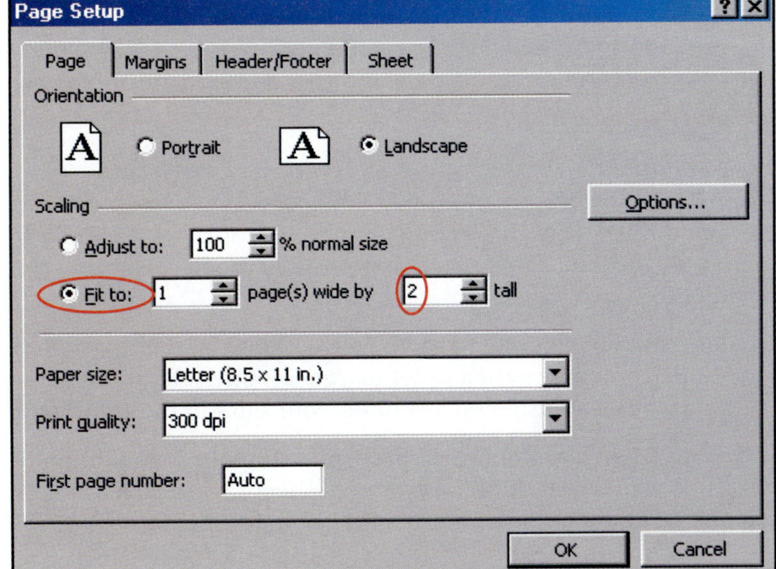

 **7** Click **OK**.

*The printout is adjusted to fit on two pages. Notice that the columns do not have headings on the second page. You will fix this problem in the next task.*

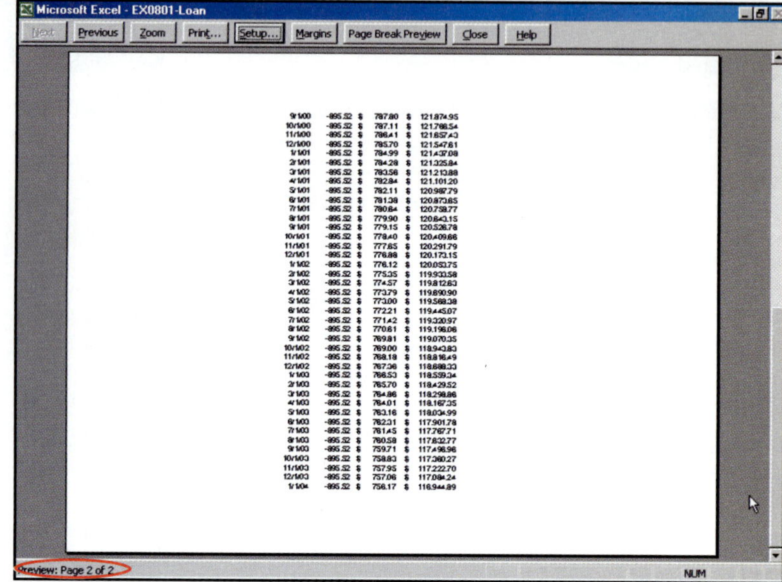

**8** Click the **Previous** button.

*The type size is smaller, but the entire printout fits on two pages instead of three.*

Click the **Close** button. Leave the workbook open for use in the next task.

# Task 4
## SETTING HEADINGS AND MARGINS

### Why would I do this?

When a table extends to more than one page, the column or row headings that identified the data in those columns are not displayed. This may make it difficult to identify the data. Fortunately, it is possible to select rows or columns to serve as headings on each page.

In some cases, a table will fit on the page if the margins are slightly narrower. In other cases, you may want a wider margin on one side to allow for binding. The margins may be adjusted on any of the four sides of the printout.

In this task, you learn how to choose the first three rows of the worksheet to act as headings that repeat on the subsequent sheets. You also learn how to reduce the top and bottom margin to make more room for the data.

**1** Choose **File, Page Setup**. Select the **Sheet** tab.

*The Sheet tab of the Page Setup dialog box allows the user to select rows or columns to repeat on each page.*

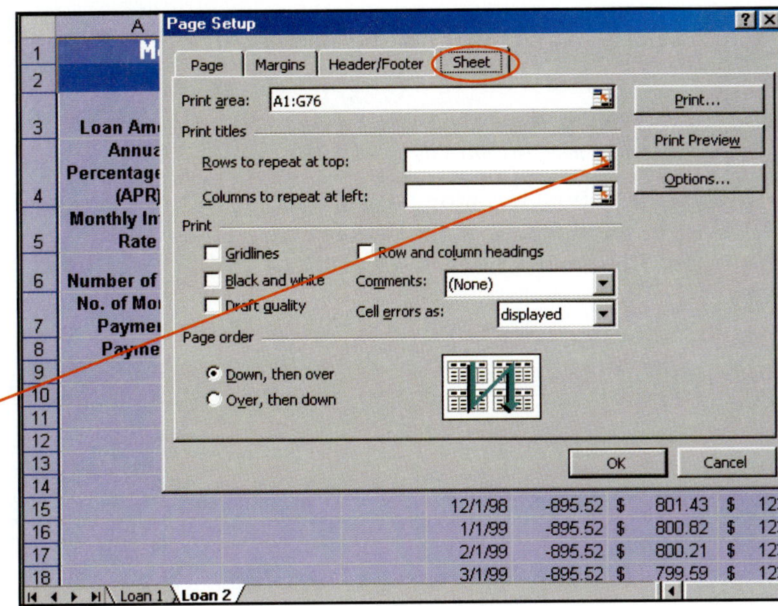

Collapse dialog box button

**2** Click the **Collapse dialog box** button at the right end of the **Rows to repeat at top** box.

*The dialog box collapses to display a single box with an expand dialog box button.*

Click-and-drag row headings **1** through **3**.

*The rows are selected and the range is added to the dialog box.*

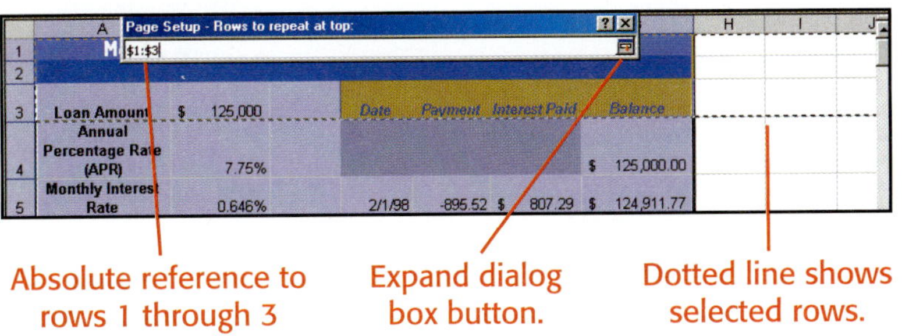

Absolute reference to rows 1 through 3

Expand dialog box button.

Dotted line shows selected rows.

**3** Click the **Expand dialog box** button.

*The dialog box expands.*

Click the **Print Preview** button in the Page Setup dialog box. Click the **Next** button.

*The first three rows are also displayed at the top of the second sheet. The extra rows are fit into the second sheet by making the data even smaller.*

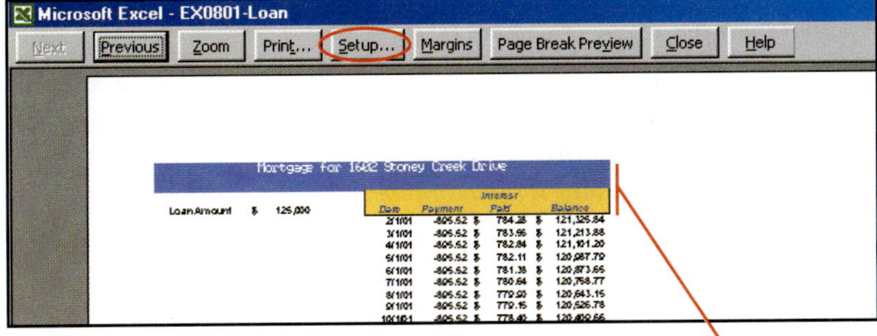

First three rows repeated

**4**  Click the **Setup** button. Click the **Margins** tab.

*It is possible to enlarge the size of the data if we make the top and bottom margins narrower.*

Click the bottom arrow on the **Top** box twice to select **0.5**. Click the bottom arrow on the **Bottom** box twice to select **0.5**.

*The bottom and top margins are reduced to 0.5 inches. This gives the data an extra inch on the page and allows for use of a larger font.*

Click the check box next to **Horizontally**.

*This action centers the data from left to right.*

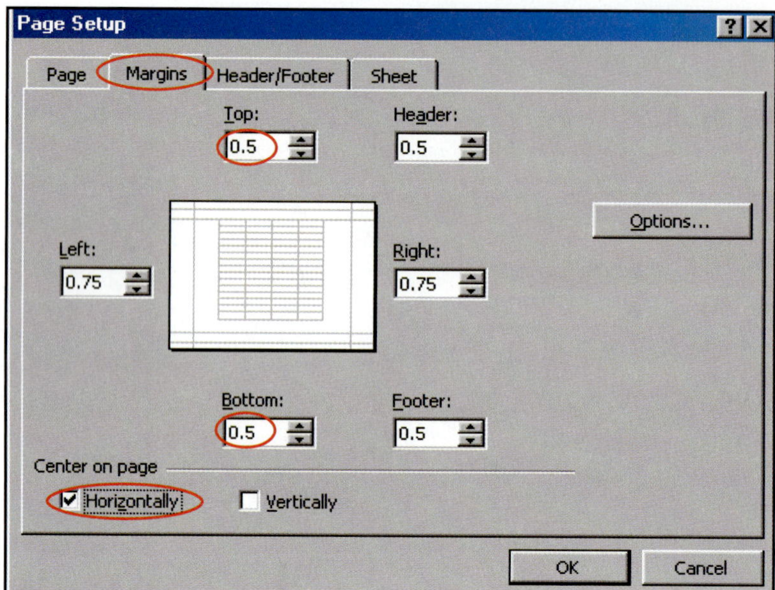

CAUTION

Some printers will print closer to the edge of the paper than others. If you notice that the bottom or top of the table is clipped off when you use a margin of 0.5 inches, increase it to 0.75 inches.

QUICK TIP

If you click the **Margins** button on the toolbar, you can drag the margins to the preferred position.

**5**  Click **OK**. Click the **Previous** button.

*The top and bottom margins are smaller, the font is slightly larger, and the data is centered from left to right.*

Leave the workbook open for use in the next task.

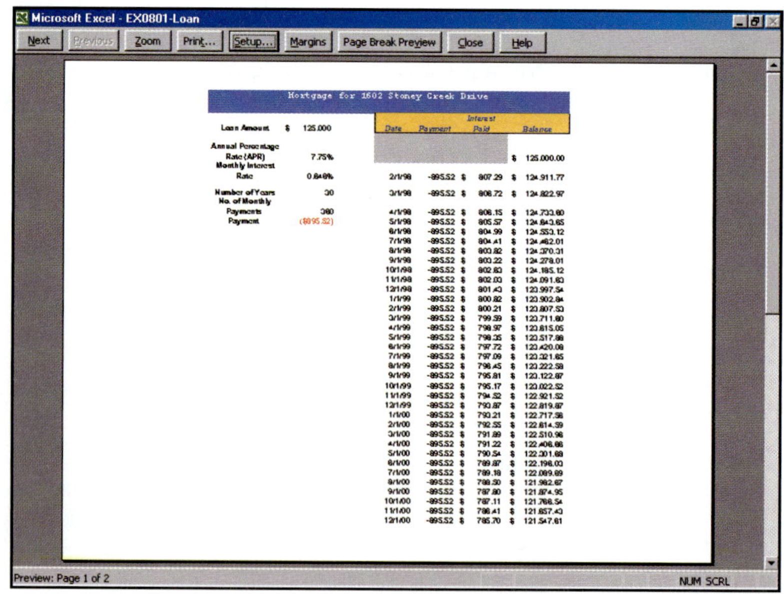

# Task 5
## USING HEADERS AND FOOTERS

### Why would I do this?

Identifying a printout is always important. You can add your name, page numbers, date, time, and other information to a printout.

In this task, you learn how to place your name and page numbers in a header and footer.

**1** Click the **Setup** button. Click the Header/Footer tab.

*The top of the dialog box is a preview of the header, and the bottom is a preview of the footer. A standard header may be selected using the down arrow next to the Header box, or a custom header may be created using the Custom Header button. The same is true for the footer.*

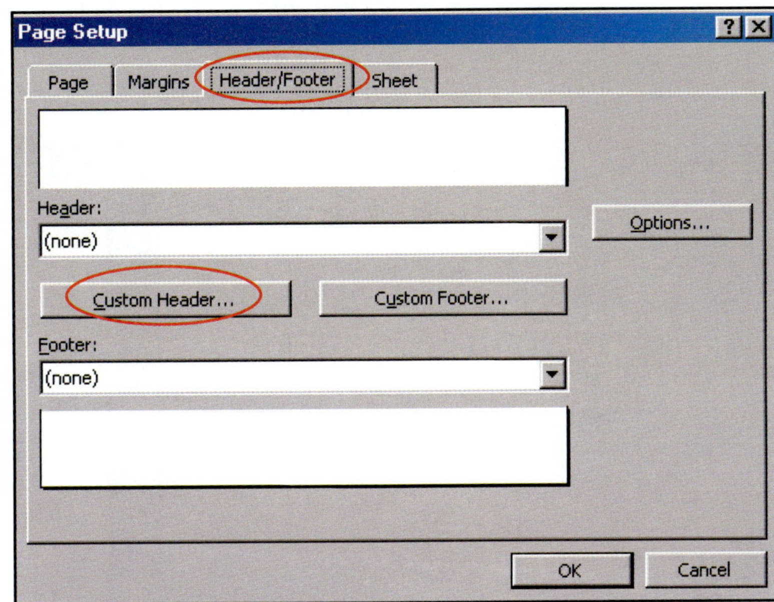

**2** Click the **Custom Header** button.

*The Header dialog box is displayed. The left section is left aligned, the center section is centered, and the right section is right aligned. The insertion point is placed in the left section by default.*

Type your name in the **Left section** box and click **OK**.

*Your name is displayed in the header preview section.*

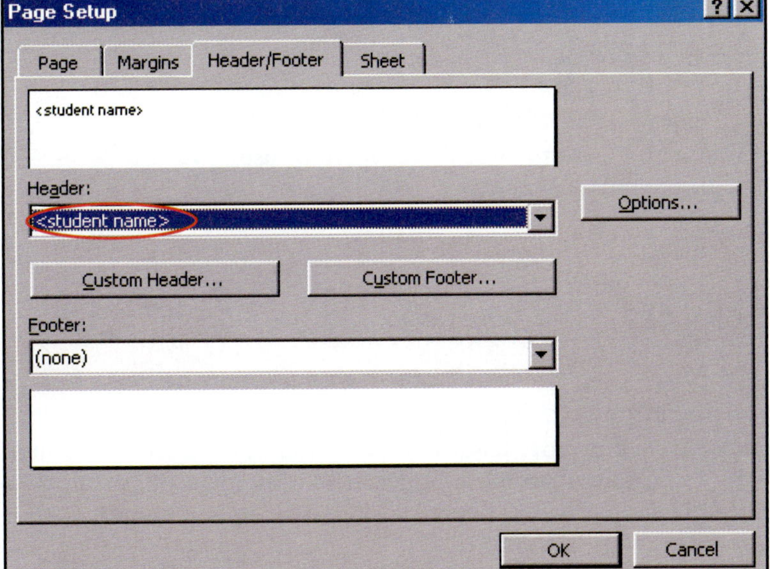

**3** Click the **Custom Footer** button. Click inside the **Right section** box. Click the **Page Number** button.

*The automatic page number function is placed in the right section of the footer.*

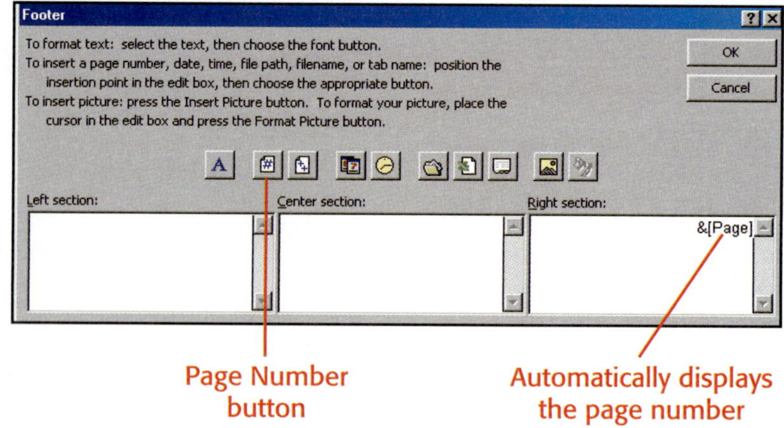



Page Number
button

Automatically displays
the page number

**4** Click **OK**.

*The page number is displayed in the footer preview.*

Click **OK**. Click the **Next** button.

*Your name is displayed in the upper-left corner of the page, and the page number is displayed in the lower-right corner.*

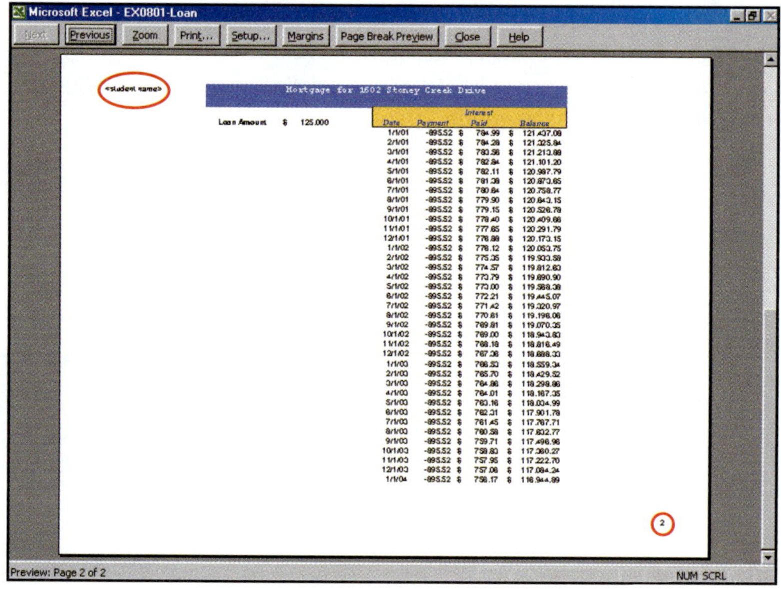

**5** Click the **Close** button. Click the **Save** button and leave the workbook open for use in the next task.

# Task 6

## USING THE OFFICE ASSISTANT AND HELP

### Why would I do this?

There are many more features and capabilities of Excel that you may find useful. It is very valuable to learn how to teach yourself new skills using the built-in help in Excel. Help may be obtained by using the Help menu options or by using the Office Assistant.

In this task, you learn how to use the Office Assistant and the Help menu to unprotect the worksheet.

**1** If the Office Assistant is not currently displayed, choose **Help**, **Show the Office Assistant**.

*The Office Assistant is displayed.*

Select **B4**, type **7** and press ↵Enter.

*The new annual interest rate is accepted, and the formulas that depend on it are recalculated.*

Select **B5** and attempt to type **.5%**.

*A caution message appears along with the Office Assistant that explains the problem and gives a suggested course of action. You will learn more about protecting worksheets in the following steps, so you will not act on these instructions at this time.*

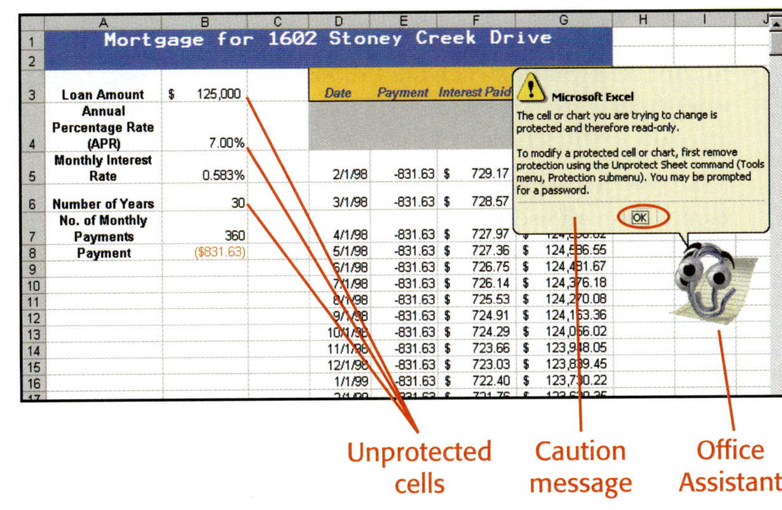


Unprotected cells    Caution message    Office Assistant

**2** Click OK. Choose **Help**, **Microsoft Excel Help**.

*A dialog box opens above or beside the Office Assistant that has option buttons and a box into which you can type questions using natural language.*

Type **How do I make changes to a protected sheet?**.

*The program will extract key words from your question and try to match them with topics. It will display its best matches as options in the assistant's dialog box. You do not have to type a complete sentence.*

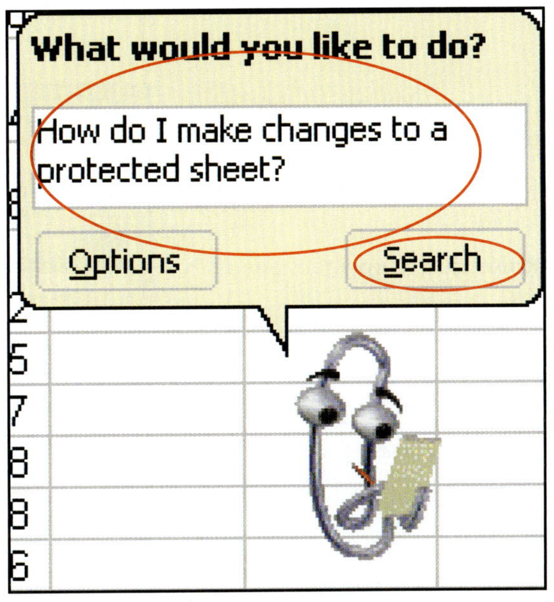


**3** Click the **Search** button.

*A list of topics is displayed.*

Click the **About worksheet protection** topic.

*The Microsoft Excel Help window opens and shares the screen with the Excel window.*

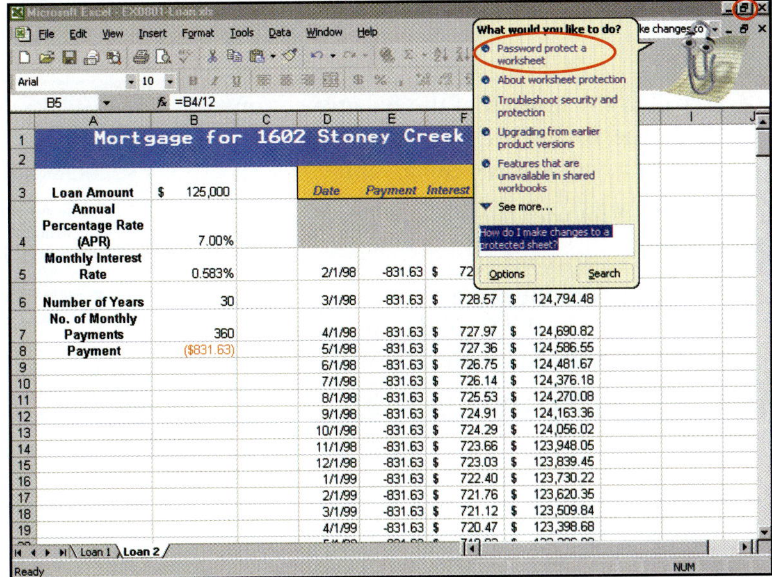

**4** Maximize the **Microsoft Excel Help** window. In the Help window, click the **Protecting worksheet elements** hyperlink. Drag the assistant to the left side of the screen.

Read the first section on **Protecting elements from all users**. It explains how to unlock the cells that you want users to be able to modify.

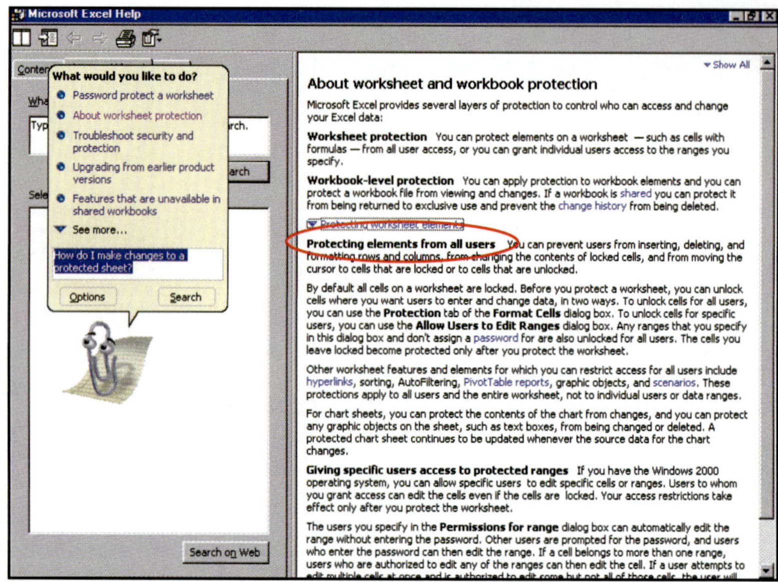

**5** Click the **Close** button on the **Microsoft Excel Help** window.

*The Microsoft Excel Help window closes and the Office Assistant icon remains on the screen.*

Choose **Tools**, **Protection**, **Unprotect Sheet**.

*The sheet is unprotected and all the cells may be edited.*

**IN DEPTH**

Protecting a sheet while leaving some cells unprotected is a two-step process. While the sheet is unprotected, you select the cells you wish to leave unprotected then choose Format, Cells, click the Protection tab, and remove the check from the Locked option. The second step is to protect the rest of the sheet by choosing Tools, Protection, Protect Sheet.

**6** Scroll to the bottom of the **Balance** column and observe that the final balance is not zero but is almost two dollars off.

*The payment is rounded to the nearest penny, which causes this error.*

Scroll back to the top and select cell **B8**. Edit the formula in the formula bar to remove the **ROUND()** function.

*The formula should be =PMT(B5,B7,B3).*

**7** Click the **Enter** button on the formula bar.

*The amount displayed in cell B8 does not appear to change but the formulas that use this number are using a number that is not rounded and is more accurate.*

Scroll to the bottom of the **Balance** column and observe that the final balance is still not zero but is much closer. Scroll back to the top and select cell **F5**.

*The formulas in the Interest Paid column are also rounded to the nearest penny, which also causes a small error. If you removed the Round function from all the formulas in the Interest Paid column, the final balance in cell G364 would be zero.*

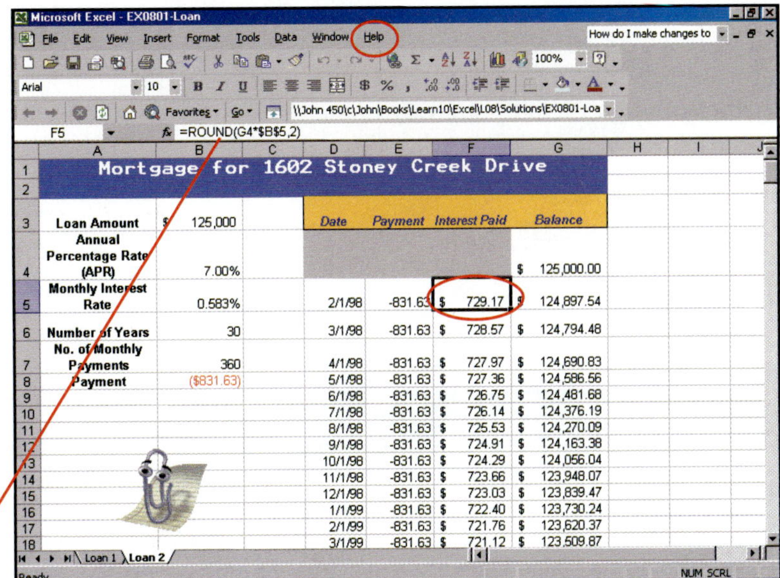


**8** Choose **Help**, **Hide the Office Assistant**.

*The Office Assistant is turned off.*

Save the workbook and close it.

The exercises that follow are designed for you to review and use what you have learned in this lesson. You also have the opportunity to practice your skills and then expand on them by applying them to new situations.

## COMPREHENSION

Comprehension exercises are designed to check your memory and understanding of the basic concepts in this lesson. You distinguish between true and false statements, identify new screen elements, and match terms with related statements. If you are uncertain of the correct answer, refer to the task number following each item (for example, T4 refers to Task 4), and review that task until you are confident you can provide a correct response.

### TRUE-FALSE

Circle either T or F.

T   F   **1.** When you select a range of cells to be printed, they will be automatically re-sized to fit on a single page. **(T1)**

T   F   **2.** A page break must be deleted and then inserted in a different location to move it. **(T2)**

T   F   **3.** Scaling allows you to force the table into a selected number of pages. **(T3)**

T   F   **4.** If a table spans several sheets, rows may be selected that will repeat at the top of each sheet. **(T4)**

T   F   **5.** There is an automatic page numbering feature that may be placed in a footer. **(T5)**

T   F   **6.** The Office Assistant is able to accept questions written in normal language. **(T6)**

### MATCHING QUESTIONS

**A.** Page Preview     **D.** Help

**B.** Right     **E.** Collapse dialog box

**C.** Page Break Preview     **F.** Landscape

Match the following statements to the word or phrase that is the best match from the list. Write the letter of the matching word or phrase in the space provided next to the number.

**1.** ____ The view used to move page breaks **(T2)**

**2.** ____ The view that displays the table on each printed page including the header and footer **(T1)**

**3.** ____ The "sideways" orientation **(T3)**

**4.** ____ The alignment automatically set in the right section of the footer **(T5)**

**5.** ____ The button that shrinks the dialog box when you are selecting the range of rows to repeat at the top of each page **(T4)**

**6.** ____ If the Office Assistant is not displayed, use this menu option to locate the choice that turns it on **(T6)**

# REINFORCEMENT

Reinforcement exercises are designed to reinforce the skills you have learned by applying them to new situations. Detailed instructions are provided along with a figure, where appropriate, to illustrate the result. The reinforcement exercises that follow should be completed sequentially. Leave the file open at the end of each exercise for use in the next exercise until you are specifically directed to close it.

Open **EX0802** and save it as **EX0802-Reinforcement** on your disk for use in the following exercises.

Due to the unique geography of the United States, it has over 95% of the world's tornadoes. The United States Government has put a lot of effort into warning people about oncoming tornadoes. In this set of reinforcement exercises, you set up the printout of a table of statistics about tornadoes that have killed more than five people. It is sorted by year so the reader can determine if the number of people killed by tornadoes has been reduced. You will determine how the pages are divided and place headings, headers, and footers on the pages.

## R1—Selecting a Range of Cells to Print, and Setting the Page Orientation and Scaling

1. Click the Sheet 1 tab, if necessary. Select cells **A2** through **L162**. Choose **File**, **Print Area**, **Set Print Area**.

2. Choose **View**, **Page Break Preview.** The dotted lines indicate where the calculated page breaks are. Notice that the last four columns do not fit the width of the paper.

3. Choose **File**, **Page Setup**. Click the **Page** tab if necessary.

4. Select the **Landscape** option. Click **OK**. All the columns fit except the last one.

5. Choose **File**, **Page Setup**. Click the **Margins** tab.

6. Change the **Right** and **Left** margins to **0.5**. Click **OK**. All the columns fit on the page in landscape orientation if smaller margins are used.

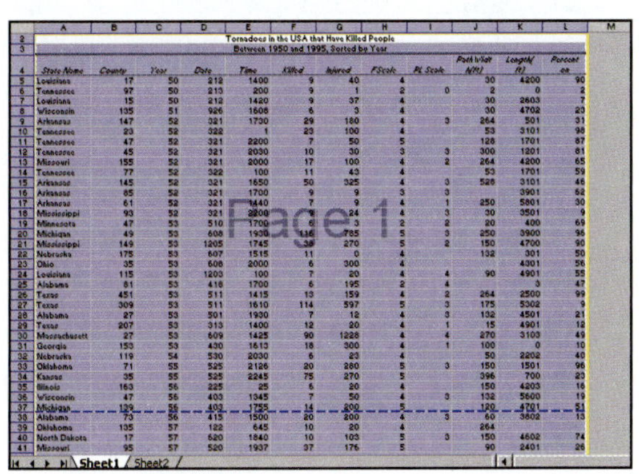


## R2—Setting and Moving Page Breaks

1. Select cell **A33** and choose **Insert**, **Page Break**. This will force a page break after the first five years (50–54) of records.

2. Select cell **A55** and insert another page break. Notice the values in the **Year** column. The first page has all the tornadoes from the first five years, 50–54, and the next page has the tornadoes from the next five-year period, 55–59. Repeat this process to insert page breaks that group the tornado records into five-year periods on each page.

3. Check to make sure you have placed a page break between the row representing the last tornado of the five-year group and the row representing the first tornado of the next group. Move the page breaks if necessary. You should have nine pages.

4. Click the **Print Preview** button.

5. Click the **Next** button repeatedly to review the data to make sure that each page represents a five-year group.

6. Click the **Close** button. If you found any errors, move or delete the incorrect page breaks.

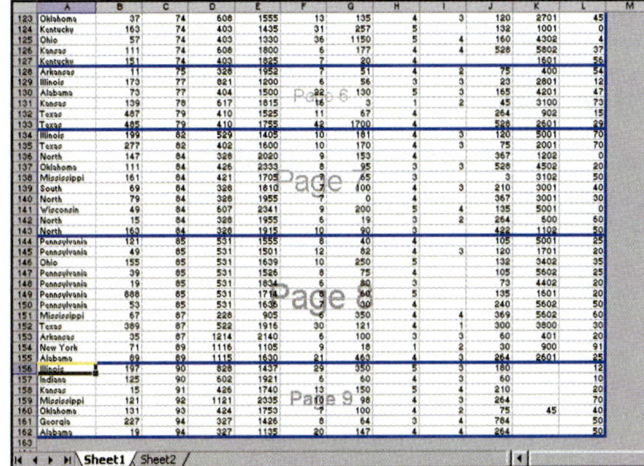

# IDENTIFYING PARTS OF THE EXCEL SCREEN

Refer to the figures and identify the numbered parts of
the screen. Write the letter of the correct label in the
space next to the number.

1. _______________

2. _______________

3. _______________

4. _______________

5. _______________

6. _______________

7. _______________

8. _______________

9. _______________

10. _______________

**A.** Cells selected for printing  **(T1)**

**B.** Inserted page break  **(T2)**

**C.** Calculated page break  **(T2)**

**D.** Selected cell-new page break would
go above it  **(T2)**

**E.** Name in header  **(T5)**

**F.** Rows repeated on each page  **(T4)**

**G.** Automatic page number  **(T5)**

**H.** Top margin  **(T4)**

**I.** Office Assistant  **(T6)**

**J.** Displays current page and total
number of pages  **(T3)**

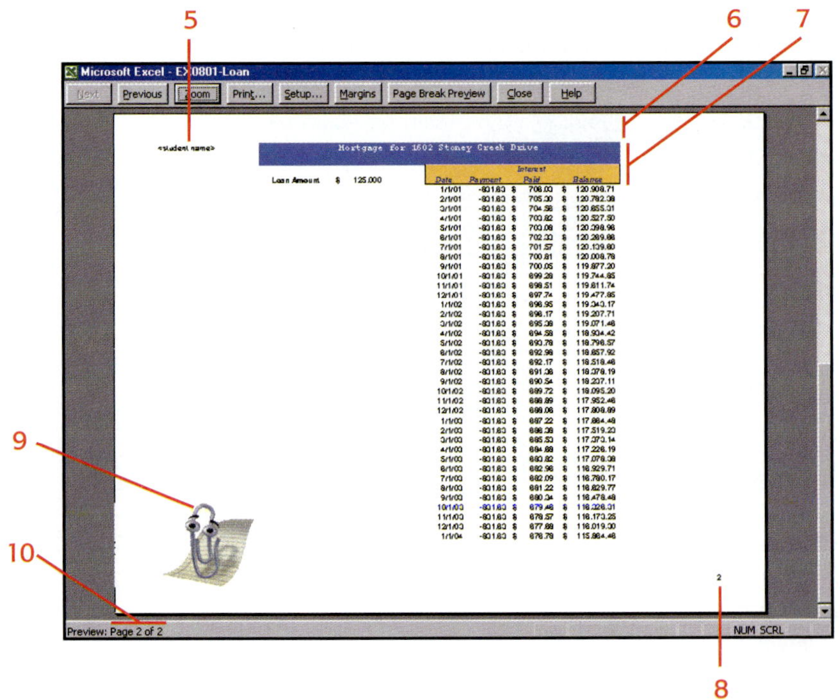

## R3—Setting a Row to Repeat on Each Page

In this sheet, the column headings are in row 4. Set this row to repeat at the top of each page after the first one to identify the data in the columns. See the following steps for detailed instructions.

1. Choose **File**, **Page Setup**. Click the **Sheet** tab.

2. Click the **Collapse dialog** box button next to the **Rows to repeat at top** box and click row heading number **4**.

3. Click the **Expand dialog box** button and click **OK**.

4. Click the **Print Preview** button. Click the **Next** button a few times to confirm that the headings in row 4 repeat at the top of each page after page 1.

5. Click the **Close** button. Click the **Save** button to save your work.

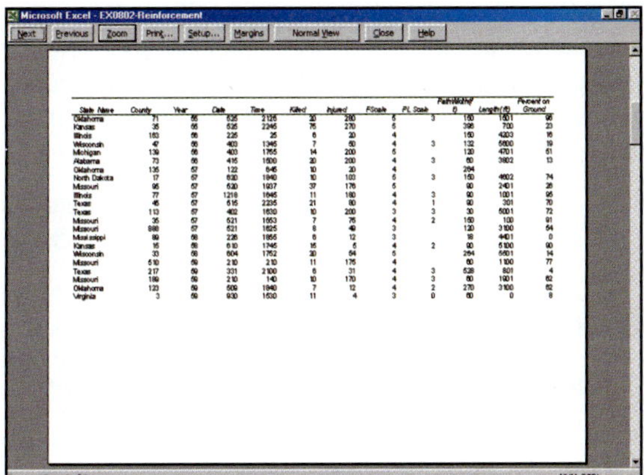

## R4—Placing Your Name in the Header and the Page Number in the Footer

Place your name in the upper right corner of each page using the header. Use the date option to place today's date in the footer.

1. Choose **File**, **Page Setup**. Click the **Header/Footer** tab.

2. Click **Custom Header** and click the **Right section**. Type your name. Click **OK**.

3. Click **Custom Footer** and click the **Center section**.

4. Click the **Date** button. (It looks like a small calendar.) The automatic date function is placed in the center section.

5. Click **OK**. Check the preview sections, then click **OK**.

6. Click the **Print Preview** button. Confirm that your name is in the header and today's date is in the footer. Click **Close**.

7. Save the workbook.

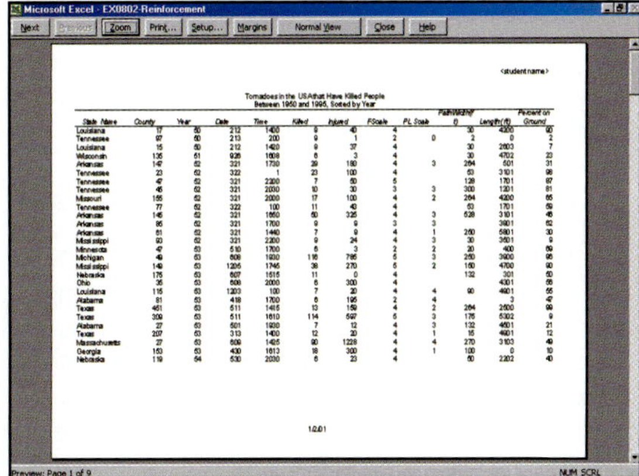

## R5—Automatically Scaling a Worksheet

If it is not necessary to insert page breaks at fixed places, you may automatically scale the worksheet. Scale the table in Sheet2 to automatically fit to one page wide and let the program determine the number of pages in length.

1. Click the **Sheet2** tab. Choose **File**, **Page Setup**. Click the **Page** tab.

2. Change the orientation to **Landscape**.

3. Click the **Fit to** option button and confirm that it is set to one page wide. Change the **tall** setting to **20**. Click **OK**.

4. Click the **Print Preview** button. Notice that the width was adjusted to one page but the length stops at five pages.

5. Click the **Close** button. Click the **Save** button to save your work, and then close the workbook.

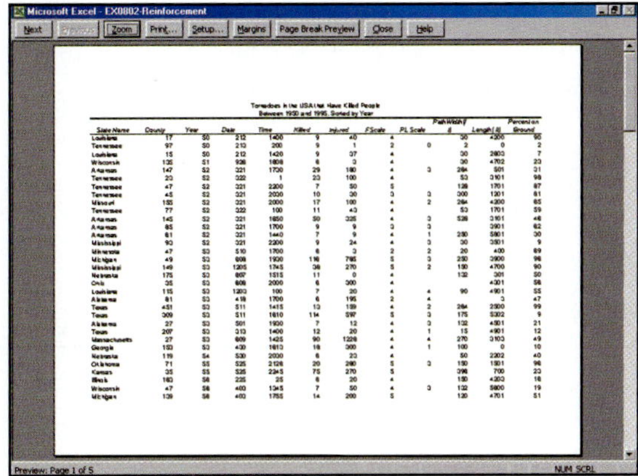

Challenge exercises are designed to test your ability to apply your skills to new situations with less-detailed instructions. These exercises also challenge you to expand your repertoire of skills by using commands that are similar to those you have already learned. The desired outcome is clearly defined, but you have more freedom to choose the steps needed to achieve the required result.

The following exercises use separate sheets in the same workbook. The exercises are not sequential and do not depend on each other. Open **EX0803** and save it on your floppy disk as **EX0803-Challenge**.

## C1—Printing Row Headings

Some tables are much wider than they are long. If the table will not fit on the paper in landscape orientation, the table will be repeated on subsequent pages. In that case, it is useful to repeat a column of headings at the left side of each page. The table of data used in this exercise displays a summary of the number of tornadoes that killed more than five people. It is organized vertically by state and horizontally by year. The rows used to represent the states can fit on one page, but the columns used for the years from 1950 to 1995 extend much beyond one page to the right.

*Goal:* Set the column that displays the state names to repeat on each page.

1. Select sheet **C1**. Select the table from cell **A2** to cell **AN31** and set this range to be the print area.

2. Choose **File, Page Setup**.

3. Set the page orientation to **Landscape** on the **Page** sheet.

4. Use the **Columns to repeat at left** option on the **Sheet** tab to display column **A** on each sheet. Click **OK**.

5. Use the **Print Preview** to confirm that the first column repeats on each page.

6. Save the workbook. Leave it open if you plan to continue with the Challenge exercises.

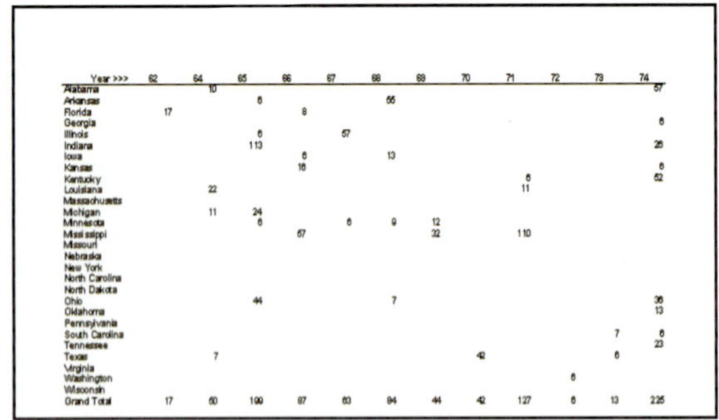

| | Year >>> | 62 | 64 | 65 | 66 | 67 | 68 | 69 | 70 | 71 | 72 | 73 | 74 |
|---|---|---|---|---|---|---|---|---|---|---|---|---|---|
| Alabama | | | 10 | | | | | | | | | | 57 |
| Arkansas | | | | 6 | | | 66 | | | | | | |
| Florida | | 17 | | | 8 | | | | | | | | |
| Georgia | | | | | | | | | | | | | 6 |
| Illinois | | | | 6 | | 57 | | | | | | | |
| Indiana | | | | 113 | | | | | | | | | 26 |
| Iowa | | | | | 6 | | 13 | | | | | | |
| Kansas | | | | | 16 | | | | | | | | 6 |
| Kentucky | | | | | | | | | | 6 | | | 62 |
| Louisiana | | | 22 | | | | | | | 11 | | | |
| Massachusetts | | | | | | | | | | | | | |
| Michigan | | | 11 | 24 | | | | | | | | | |
| Minnesota | | | | 6 | | 6 | 9 | 12 | | | | | |
| Mississippi | | | | | 67 | | | 32 | | 110 | | | |
| Missouri | | | | | | | | | | | | | |
| Nebraska | | | | | | | | | | | | | |
| New York | | | | | | | | | | | | | |
| North Carolina | | | | | | | | | | | | | |
| North Dakota | | | | | | | | | | | | | |
| Ohio | | | | 44 | | | | 7 | | | | | 36 |
| Oklahoma | | | | | | | | | | | | | 13 |
| Pennsylvania | | | | | | | | | | | | | |
| South Carolina | | | | | | | | | | | | 7 | 6 |
| Tennessee | | | | | | | | | | | | | 23 |
| Texas | | | 7 | | | | | | 42 | | | 6 | |
| Virginia | | | | | | | | | | | | | |
| Washington | | | | | | | | | | | 6 | | |
| Wisconsin | | | | | | | | | | | | | |
| Grand Total | | 17 | 60 | 100 | 87 | 63 | 94 | 44 | 42 | 127 | 6 | 13 | 225 |

## C2—Changing the Print Quality

Printers represent images, text, and numbers by placing small dots of ink or toner on the paper. Finer detail is obtained by using more dots per inch but it takes more ink or toner and it often takes longer to print. Some printers allow you to choose how many dots per inch are used to print a page. If you are just printing draft copies of a multi-page table, you may want to speed things up by changing the print quality to fewer dots per inch. This setting varies from one printer to the next. In some printers, you can change this setting from the Page Setup dialog box. In other printers, it is a property that is controlled by the printer itself and may be selected from the Print dialog box.

*Goal:* Determine if your printer can be set to print at a different quality; then change the quality setting to see if it affects printing speed.

1. Select sheet **C2**. Place your name in cell **A1**.

2. Choose **File, Page Setup**. Select the **Page** tab.

3. Click the down arrow next to the **Print quality** box. Make note of the highest and lowest setting available. Also make note of the make and model of the printer. (Dpi stands for dots per inch.) If there is only one quality, proceed to step 9.

4. Select the highest print quality. Enter the quality setting in cell **A33**. Enter the make and model of the printer in cell **D33**.

5. Print the first page of this worksheet. Use a watch or clock with a second hand to time the printout.

6. Enter the time it took to print the page in cell **B33**.

7. Repeat this process with the lowest print quality. Enter the quality setting in cell **A34** and the time it took in cell **B34**.

8. Save the workbook. Set the quality back to the original setting. Skip the following steps. Leave the workbook open if you intend to continue with the Challenge exercises.

9. Some printers control the quality with their own internal settings. If your printer displayed only one quality setting in step 3 above, choose **File**, **Print**. Click the **Properties** button. If your printer supports different print quality settings and they can be changed using this dialog box, proceed with steps four through eight above.

10. If your printer cannot be set to different quality settings, enter the make and model in cell **D33** and write a brief note in cell **A34** that explains this fact.

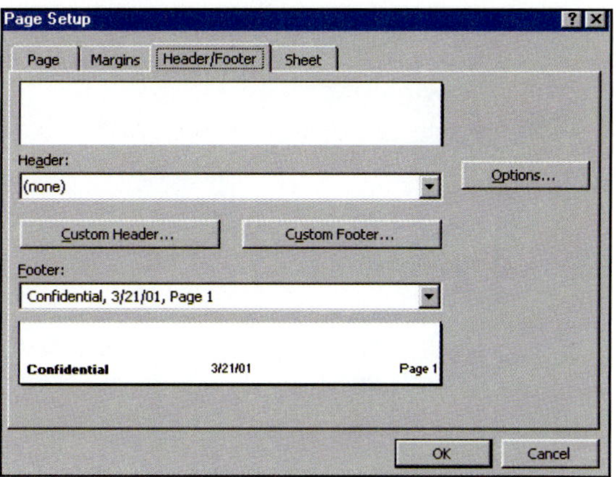

 ## C3—Using Preselected Header and Footer Options

If your printout will be sent to a customer, you may want to identify it with a date and time or use a more formal style. In this exercise, you use a worksheet that is designed to prepare a bid document for a company that prints custom logos on shirts. They handle a variety of T-shirts, sweatshirts, and polo shirts and they buy them in case lots of 144 (a gross). The price per shirt depends upon the type of shirt and whether or not the company buys more than 144 shirts. The employee enters the shirt code in the first column and the quantity in the second column. Formulas in columns C and D calculate the prices. You just want to print the range of cells from A1 to D17 to send to the customer.

*Goal:* Choose a footer for a bid document from the list of preselected footers.

1. Select sheet **C3**. Edit cell **A1** and enter your name to the right of **Customer Name**.

2. Set the print area to cells **A1** through **D17**.

3. Choose **File**, **Page Setup**. Select the **Header/Footer** tab.

4. Click the down arrow next to the **Footer** box. Select the option that prints **Confidential** in the left section, today's date in the middle section, and the word **Page** followed by the page number in the right section. Use the preview area to check your choice.

5. Close the dialog box. Use **Print Preview** to confirm that the cells that make up the bid document will be printed with the selected footer. Zoom in on the footer if necessary.

6. Close the preview and save the workbook. Leave it open if you plan to continue with the Challenge exercises.

## C4—Transposing Tables

Some worksheets are oriented the wrong way for convenient printing. In this exercise, you have a table of data showing deaths from tornadoes by year for each state that is only three rows long but is composed of 159 columns and takes fifteen pages to print.

You can transpose the data in this table into a table that is three columns wide by 159 rows long that will print on only four pages.

*Goal:* Copy the table on sheet **C4a** and transpose it onto sheet **C4b**.

1. Select sheet **C4a**. Select cells **A1** through **FC3**.

2. Click the **Copy** button. Select sheet **C4b**.

3. Select cell **A1**, if necessary. Choose **Edit**, **Paste Special**.

4. Click the **Transpose** check box and then click **OK**. The table is pasted into the first three columns with the formatting from the first table.

5. Choose **Edit**, **Clear**, **Formats** to remove the borders and formatting that was part of the previous table but is not appropriate here. Refer to the figure on the next page.

6. Add your name to the header in the upper left corner. Use **Print Preview** to confirm that this sheet would print on four pages.

7. Save the changes you have made. Print the first page of the worksheet.

| | A | B | C |
|---|---|---|---|
| 1 | State Name | Year | Killed |
| 2 | Louisiana | 50 | 9 |
| 3 | Tennessee | 50 | 9 |
| 4 | Louisiana | 50 | 9 |
| 5 | Wisconsin | 51 | 6 |
| 6 | Arkansas | 52 | 29 |
| 7 | Tennessee | 52 | 23 |
| 8 | Tennessee | 52 | 7 |
| 9 | Tennessee | 52 | 10 |
| 10 | Missouri | 52 | 17 |
| 11 | Tennessee | 52 | 11 |
| 12 | Arkansas | 52 | 50 |
| 13 | Arkansas | 52 | 9 |
| 14 | Arkansas | 52 | 7 |
| 15 | Mississippi | 52 | 9 |
| 16 | Minnesota | 53 | 6 |
| 17 | Michigan | 53 | 116 |
| 18 | Mississippi | 53 | 38 |
| 19 | Nebraska | 53 | 11 |
| 20 | Ohio | 53 | 6 |
| 21 | Louisiana | 53 | 7 |
| 22 | Alabama | 53 | 6 |
| 23 | Texas | 53 | 13 |
| 24 | Texas | 53 | 114 |
| 25 | Alabama | 53 | 7 |
| 26 | Texas | 53 | 12 |
| 27 | Massachusetts | 53 | 90 |
| 28 | Georgia | 53 | 18 |
| 29 | Nebraska | 54 | 6 |
| 30 | Oklahoma | 55 | 20 |
| 31 | Kansas | 55 | 75 |
| 32 | Illinois | 56 | 6 |
| 33 | Wisconsin | 56 | 7 |
| 34 | Michigan | 56 | 14 |

C1 / C2 / C3 / C4a \ **C4b**

## C5—Sending a Workbook by Email

If you have Microsoft Outlook set up on your computer, you can send a worksheet to someone by email. If Outlook is not set up on your computer, set it up and add yourself as a contact with your email address. If your instructor wants this exercise submitted by email, include the instructor as a contact with the appropriate email address. Set up Outlook's email functions and test them by sending an email to yourself before you start this exercise.

Excel works with Outlook to make it easy to send a worksheet to someone else as part of a message or as an attachment. If the person is on the same local area network and has permission to read files from the disk where your workbook is stored, you can send them a review request with the path to your workbook.

*Goal:* Send the bid portion of the worksheet to yourself as part of an email message.

1. Select sheet **C5**. Edit cell **A1** and add your name as the customer.

2. Select cells **A1** through **D17**. Choose **File, Send to, Mail Recipient**.

3. Click the **To** button, scroll the list of names in the **Name** box, and locate your name in the list. Click your name to select it. Click the **To** button to select your name from the list of contacts. If your instructor wants a copy, select his or her name in the list and click the **Cc** button.

4. Click **OK**. Click the **Introduction** box and type your name. After your name, type **Lesson 8, C5**.

5. Click the **Send this Selection** button.

6. Open Outlook or the email client that you use to view your email and display the email message.

7. Close Outlook. Save your changes and close the workbook.

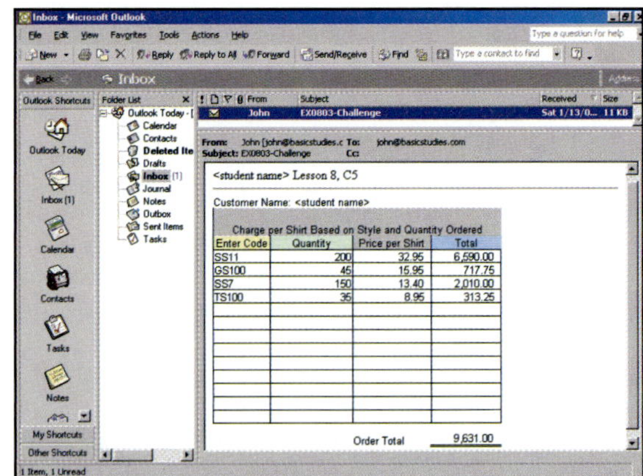

Choose or create a worksheet that spans several pages and place page breaks to divide the pages in a logical way.

**1.** Demonstrate the ability to insert page breaks and to set rows or columns to repeat on each page when appropriate.

Some examples of features that students have learned to use in previous classes to enhance their multipage printouts are listed below:

- The page breaks were used to divide the rows or columns into equal groups.

- If the data displayed was vertically oriented, the column headings were repeated on each page; if the table was horizontally oriented, the row headings repeated on each page.

- The margins were adjusted or scaling was used to prevent a few rows or columns from ending up on the last page by themselves.

- The print area selected was appropriate for displaying the results for someone else.

- The table was centered on the page if appropriate.

- The orientation matched the dimensions of the table.

- Automatic page numbering was used in the footer.

**2.** Identify yourself. Place your name in the header.

**3.** To complete the project, perform the following:

- Save your file on your own disk. Name it **EX0804-Breaks**.

- Check with your instructor to determine if the project should be submitted in electronic or printed form. If necessary, print out a copy of the worksheet to hand in.

# Lesson 9

## Importing and Exporting Tables and Creating a Workspace

Task 1    Copying a Worksheet from Another Workbook
Task 2    Importing Data from a Web Page
Task 3    Importing Data from an Access Table
Task 4    Copying a Table from a Word Document
Task 5    Creating a Summary Sheet
Task 6    Saving a Sheet in CSV Format
Task 7    Publishing Interactive Web Pages
Task 8    Saving Related Files in a Workspace

## INTRODUCTION

Excel is a good place to analyze and summarize data obtained from several different sources. Its charting and statistical capabilities make it ideal for this purpose. To make use of Excel as a summary tool, you import data into a workbook from several different sources.

Once you summarize the data and chart it, you may export the data to other programs using common data formats or you can create an interactive Web page that you can transfer to a Web server.

If you are working with a group of related workbooks, you can create a *workspace* which is a single name for a group of workbooks. Opening a workspace automatically opens all the workbooks.

In this lesson, you gather data about the budget of the United States from another workbook, a Web page, an Access Table, and a Word table. You create a summary sheet to compare the data from these sources and chart it for analysis. Once you have the summary sheet, you export it in a common format that many other programs can read and save it as an interactive Web page. Finally, you create a workspace that makes it convenient to open all the workbooks at once.

# VISUAL SUMMARY

When you complete this entire lesson, you will have worksheets that look like these:

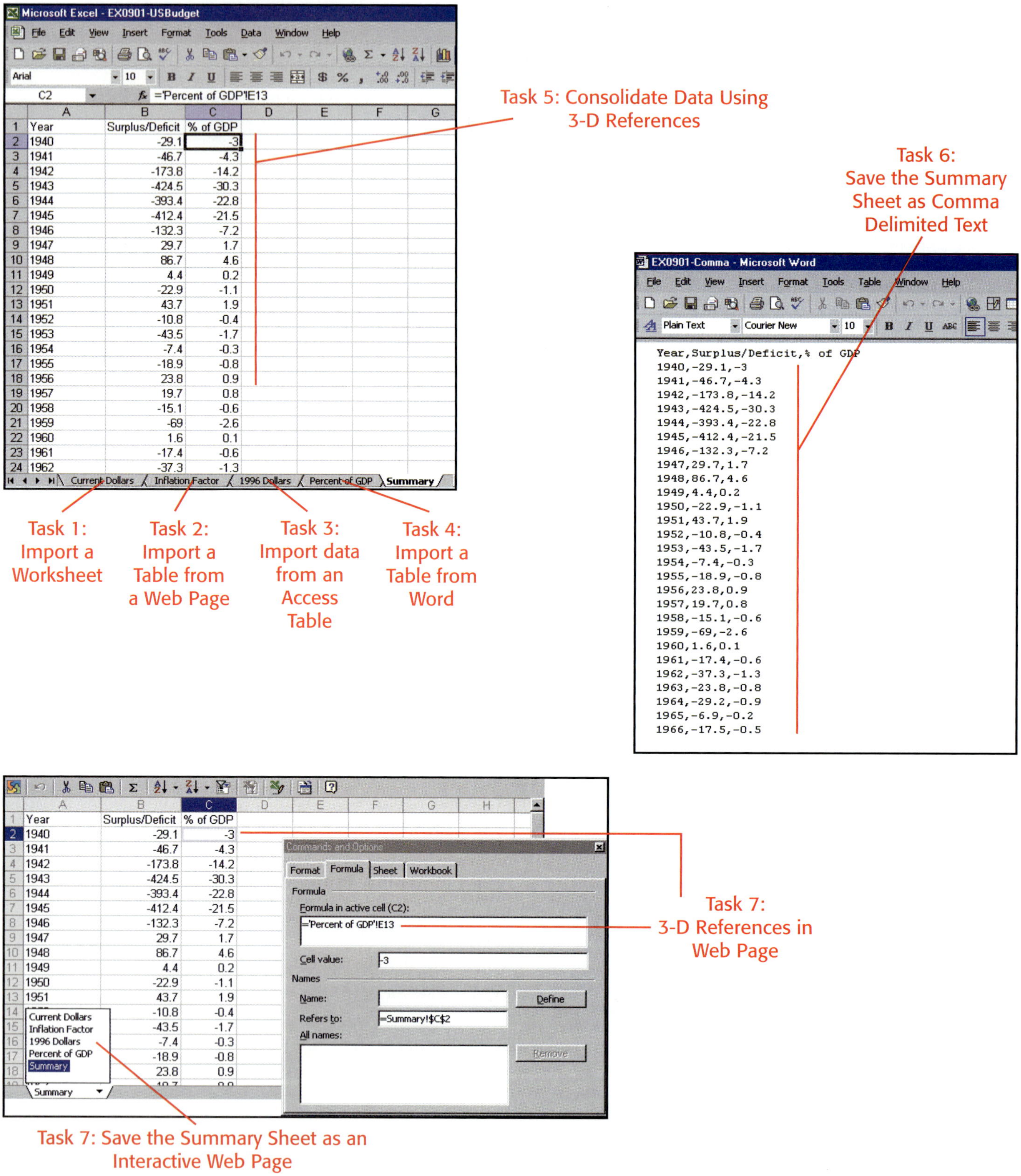

Task 5: Consolidate Data Using 3-D References

Task 6: Save the Summary Sheet as Comma Delimited Text

Task 1: Import a Worksheet

Task 2: Import a Table from a Web Page

Task 3: Import data from an Access Table

Task 4: Import a Table from Word

The Excel worksheet (Current Dollars, Inflation Factor, 1996 Dollars, Percent of GDP, Summary) shows:

| Year | Surplus/Deficit | % of GDP |
|------|-----------------|----------|
| 1940 | -29.1 | -3 |
| 1941 | -46.7 | -4.3 |
| 1942 | -173.8 | -14.2 |
| 1943 | -424.5 | -30.3 |
| 1944 | -393.4 | -22.8 |
| 1945 | -412.4 | -21.5 |
| 1946 | -132.3 | -7.2 |
| 1947 | 29.7 | 1.7 |
| 1948 | 86.7 | 4.6 |
| 1949 | 4.4 | 0.2 |
| 1950 | -22.9 | -1.1 |
| 1951 | 43.7 | 1.9 |
| 1952 | -10.8 | -0.4 |
| 1953 | -43.5 | -1.7 |
| 1954 | -7.4 | -0.3 |
| 1955 | -18.9 | -0.8 |
| 1956 | 23.8 | 0.9 |
| 1957 | 19.7 | 0.8 |
| 1958 | -15.1 | -0.6 |
| 1959 | -69 | -2.6 |
| 1960 | 1.6 | 0.1 |
| 1961 | -17.4 | -0.6 |
| 1962 | -37.3 | -1.3 |

The Word document (EX0901-Comma - Microsoft Word) shows:

```
Year,Surplus/Deficit,% of GDP
1940,-29.1,-3
1941,-46.7,-4.3
1942,-173.8,-14.2
1943,-424.5,-30.3
1944,-393.4,-22.8
1945,-412.4,-21.5
1946,-132.3,-7.2
1947,29.7,1.7
1948,86.7,4.6
1949,4.4,0.2
1950,-22.9,-1.1
1951,43.7,1.9
1952,-10.8,-0.4
1953,-43.5,-1.7
1954,-7.4,-0.3
1955,-18.9,-0.8
1956,23.8,0.9
1957,19.7,0.8
1958,-15.1,-0.6
1959,-69,-2.6
1960,1.6,0.1
1961,-17.4,-0.6
1962,-37.3,-1.3
1963,-23.8,-0.8
1964,-29.2,-0.9
1965,-6.9,-0.2
1966,-17.5,-0.5
```

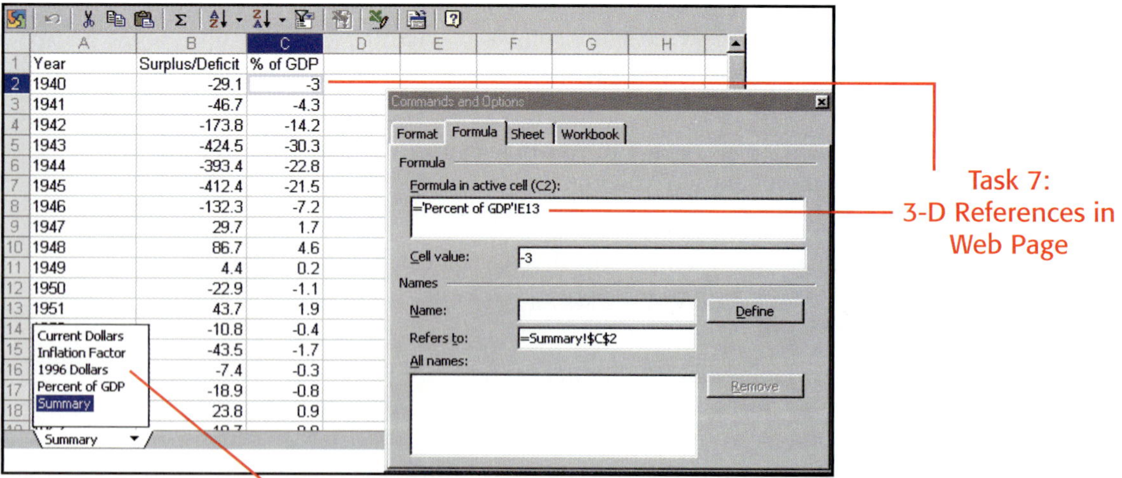


Task 7: 3-D References in Web Page

Task 7: Save the Summary Sheet as an Interactive Web Page

# Task 1
## COPYING A WORKSHEET FROM ANOTHER WORKBOOK

### Why would I do this?

You can copy and paste worksheets within a workbook or between open workbooks. If you have a worksheet that is already set up the way you like it, it is faster to copy it and paste it into your current workbook than it is to create it again.

In this task, you learn how to copy a worksheet that shows information about the income and expenses of the United States government. This sheet displays the receipts, outlays, and the surplus or deficit for each year from 1901 to estimated values for 2001 through 2006.

**1** Start Excel. Confirm that an empty workbook is displayed and choose **File**, **Save As**. Select the folder on your disk in which you are saving your files in the **Save in** box.

*The workbook will be saved on your disk.*

Change the name in the **File name** box to **EX0901-USBudget**. Click the **Save** button.

*The empty workbook is saved on your disk with a new file name that appears in the title bar.*

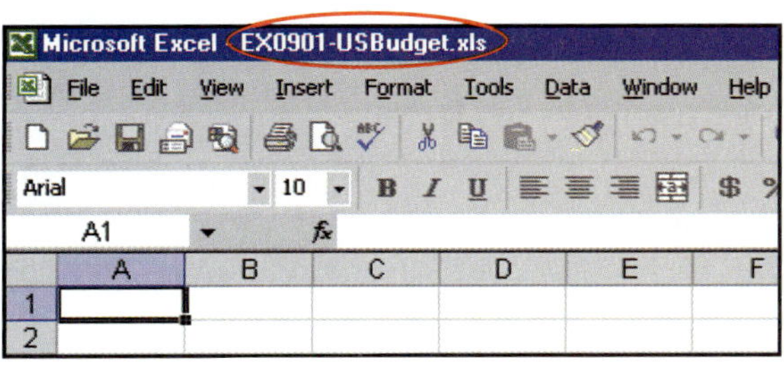

**2** Open the Task Pane, if necessary, by choosing **View**, **Task Pane**. Click **More workbooks** from the **Open a workbook** area of the task pane. Change the **Look in** box to display the student files for this lesson. Select **EX0901** and click the **Open** button.

*The workbook opens and displays a table that lists the receipts, outlays, and the surplus or deficit for each year from 1901 to estimated values through 2006.*

The values in the Year column have small green triangles in the upper left corner to indicate that the Error Checking feature is turned on and there is something unusual about these cells. The cells in this column are formatted as text rather than number to accommodate the values at the end of the column which contains both dates and text.

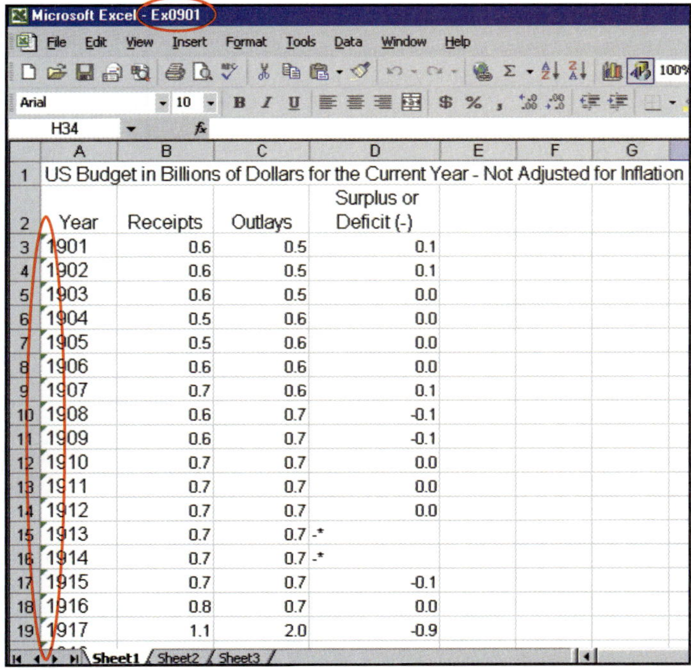

| Year | Receipts | Outlays | Surplus or Deficit (-) |
|------|----------|---------|-------|
| US Budget in Billions of Dollars for the Current Year - Not Adjusted for Inflation | | | |
| 1901 | 0.6 | 0.5 | 0.1 |
| 1902 | 0.6 | 0.5 | 0.1 |
| 1903 | 0.6 | 0.5 | 0.0 |
| 1904 | 0.5 | 0.6 | 0.0 |
| 1905 | 0.5 | 0.6 | 0.0 |
| 1906 | 0.6 | 0.6 | 0.0 |
| 1907 | 0.7 | 0.6 | 0.1 |
| 1908 | 0.6 | 0.7 | -0.1 |
| 1909 | 0.6 | 0.7 | -0.1 |
| 1910 | 0.7 | 0.7 | 0.0 |
| 1911 | 0.7 | 0.7 | 0.0 |
| 1912 | 0.7 | 0.7 | 0.0 |
| 1913 | 0.7 | 0.7 -* | |
| 1914 | 0.7 | 0.7 -* | |
| 1915 | 0.7 | 0.7 | -0.1 |
| 1916 | 0.8 | 0.7 | 0.0 |
| 1917 | 1.1 | 2.0 | -0.9 |

**3** Choose **Edit**, **Move or Copy Sheet**.

*The Move or Copy dialog box opens.*

Click the arrow at the right side of the **To book** box and select **EX0901-USBudget**. Click the **Create a copy** check box.

*A copy of the current sheet will be placed before Sheet1 in the EX0901-Budget workbook.*

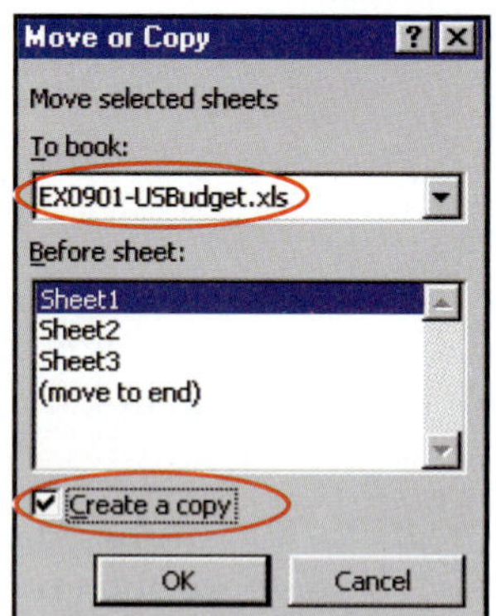

**4** Click the **OK** button.

*A copy of the sheet is placed before Sheet1 in the EX0901-USBudget workbook and the display automatically switches to the EX0901-USBudget workbook.*

Double-click the sheet tab to select it and type **Current Dollars**. Press ⏎Enter.

*The sheet tab is renamed.*

Print this sheet if your instructor requires it.

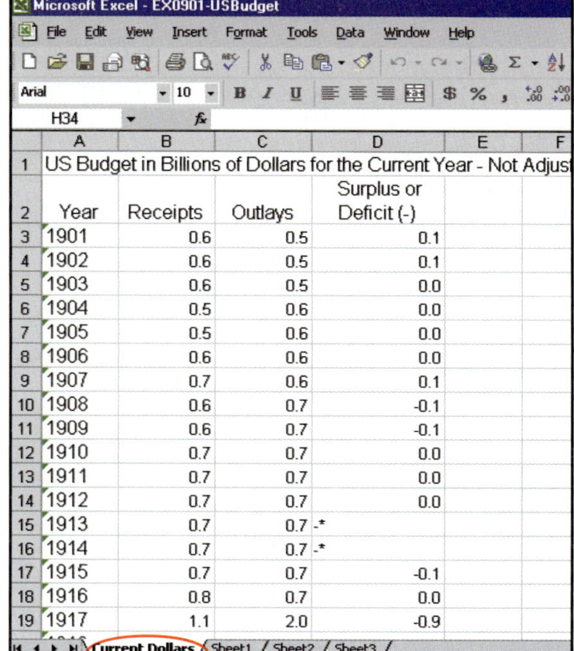

**5** Switch back to **EX0901** and close it.

# Task 2



### *Why would I do this?*

Many Web pages contain useful tables that you can import into Excel. Web pages change often on the Internet so we have saved a simple table as a Web page as part of the student files to be used for this task. See the challenge or supplementary exercises to practice importing tables from Web pages on the Internet.

In this task, you learn how to import a table from a Web page.

**1** Launch Internet Explorer. Choose **File**, **Open**. Click the **Browse** button.

*You can locate Web pages stored on your disk or network using this method.*

Locate the folder that contains the student files for this lesson and select **EX0902**. Click the **Open** button. Click **OK**.

*The table on this Web page is displayed.*

**IN DEPTH**

When you start the wizard that imports the table from a Web page, it has an address box into which you may type the Web address. Unfortunately, this dialog box does not have a browse option so you must have the address before you begin the process. To do this, you can use a Web browser like Internet Explorer to locate the desired page and copy its address to the clipboard for use in the Excel dialog box.

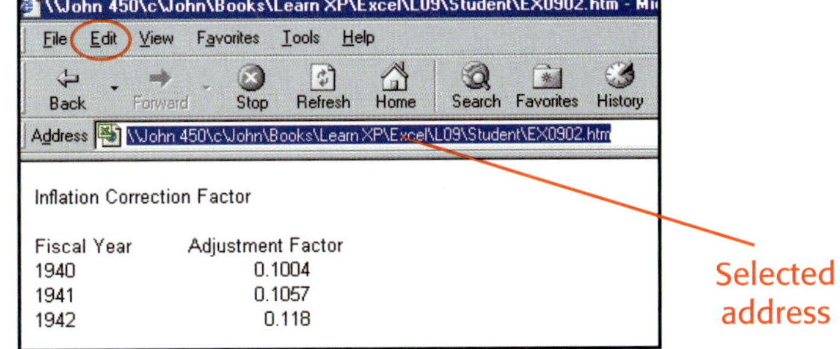

Table of data on the Web page

**2** Select the address in the **Address** box. Choose **Edit**, **Copy**.

*The address is copied to the Office Clipboard. Your address will differ from the one shown in the figure since your student files are stored in your folder.*

Selected address

**3** Click the **Close** button on the title bar of the Internet Explorer window. Double-click the **Sheet1** tab to select it and type **Inflation Factor**. Press **↵Enter**.

*The sheet tab is renamed. This sheet will display the factor used to convert current dollars into constant 1996 dollars so budgets from different years may be compared using the same dollar value.*

**4** Choose **Data**, **Import External Data**, **New Web Query**.

*The New Web Query dialog box opens and displays the default Web page.*

> Confirm that the address is selected. Hold the [Ctrl] key and press **V**.

*The address of the Web page is pasted into the box.*

> Click the **Go** button.

*Tables in the Web page are identified with a small black arrow on a yellow background.*

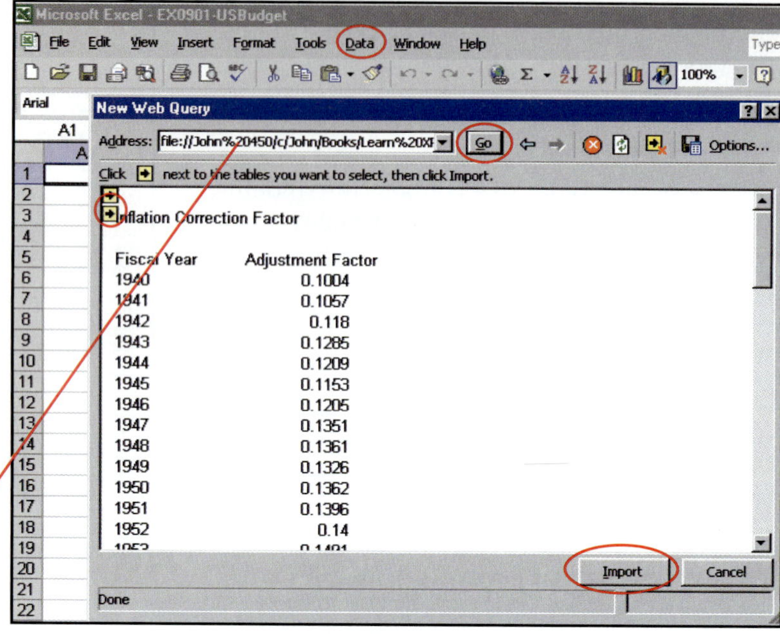


Address pasted from Office Clipboard

**5** Click the arrow next to the title, **Inflation Correction Factor**.

*The arrow changes to a check mark and the background changes to blue.*

> Click the **Import** button.

*The Import Data dialog box opens.*

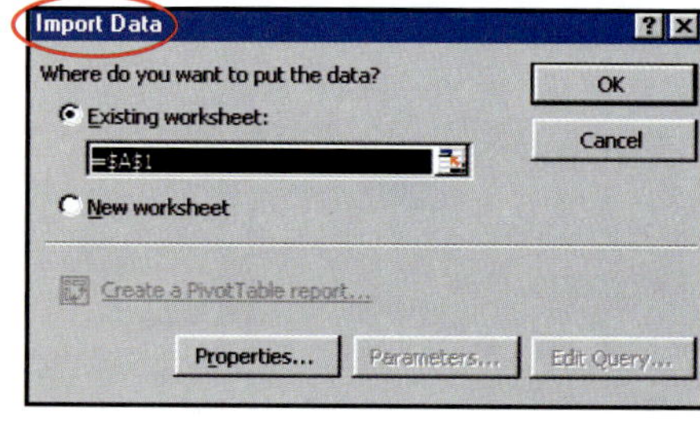


**6** Type **=$A$2**.

*The upper left corner of the table will be placed in the cell you choose and the rest of the table will be placed in the cells to the right and below the chosen cell.*

> Click **OK**. Close the Data toolbar if it appears.

*The data is imported into the worksheet.*

> Print this sheet if your instructor requires it.

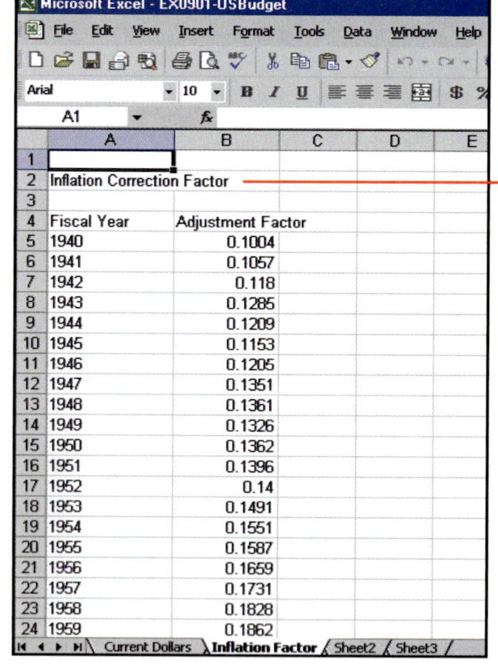


First cell of the imported table placed in cell A2

# Task 3

## IMPORTING DATA FROM AN ACCESS TABLE

### *Why would I do this?*

Access is database management software that can store large tables of data. You import data from an Access table and filter the records to import only those records you need.

In this task, you learn how to import annual budget records from a table in Access that has been adjusted for inflation based on constant 1996 dollars. One of the records in the table is for an interim report and the value in the year field is TQ. You will import all the records except that one.

**1** Double-click the **Sheet2** tab and type **1996 Dollars**. Press ↵Enter.

*The sheet tab is renamed.*

Choose **Data**, **Import External Data**, **New Database Query**.

*The Choose Data Source dialog box opens.*

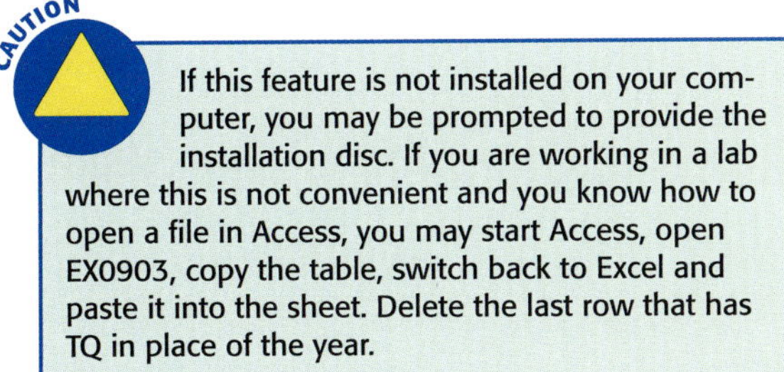

**CAUTION**

If this feature is not installed on your computer, you may be prompted to provide the installation disc. If you are working in a lab where this is not convenient and you know how to open a file in Access, you may start Access, open EX0903, copy the table, switch back to Excel and paste it into the sheet. Delete the last row that has TQ in place of the year.

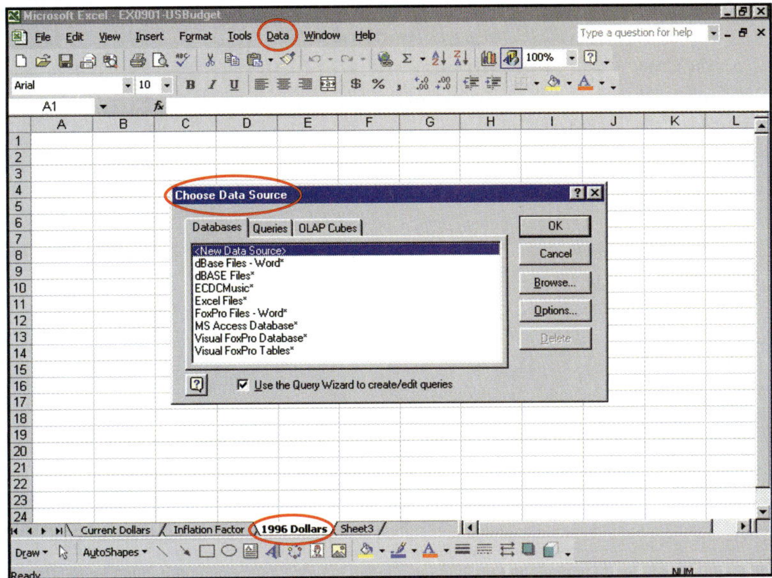

**2** Click the **Databases** tab, if necessary and click **MS Access Database***.

*You can import data from a variety of database files.*

Confirm that the checkbox next to **Use the Query Wizard to create/edit queries** displays a check mark.

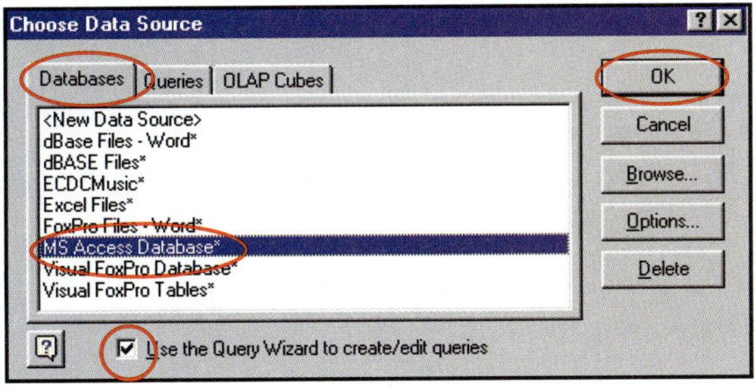

**3** Click the **OK** button.

*The Select Database dialog box opens.*

Select the drive where the student files are located in the **Drives** box. Select the folder where the student files are located in the **Directories** box. Select **EX0903** in the **Database Name** box.

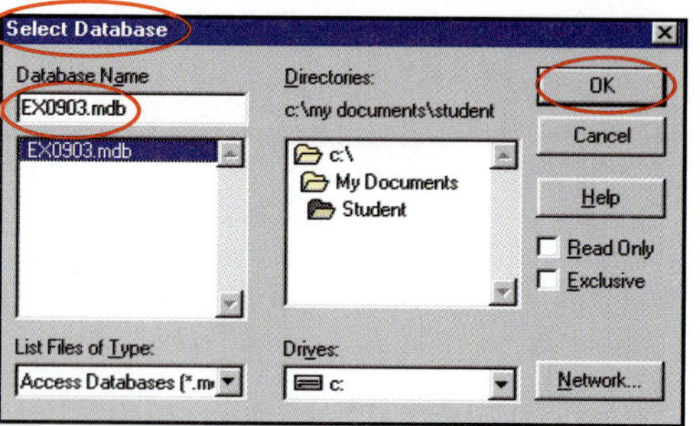

**4** Click **OK**.

*The Query Wizard starts.*

Confirm that **Budget in Billions of 1996 Dollars** is selected and click the add button to add all of the table's columns to the query.

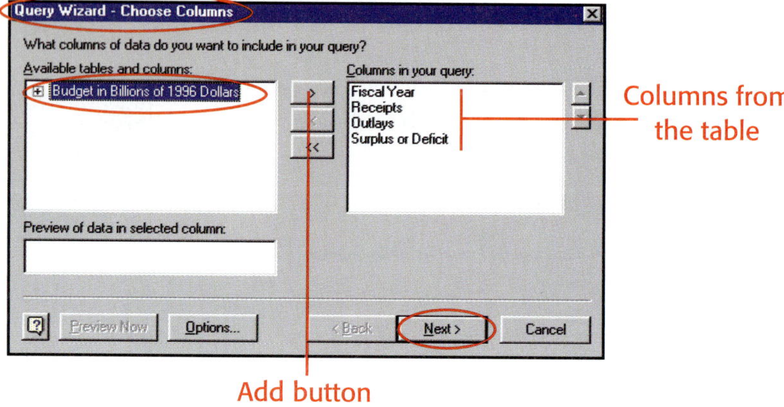


> **IN DEPTH**
>
> You do not have to import all the columns. You may click the plus sign next to the name of the table then select and add the columns individually. If you are familiar with Access, these columns are the fields in the table.

**5** Click the **Next** button to move to the **Filter Data** dialog box of the wizard. Click **Fiscal Year**.

*This column contains the name of the year. One of the rows in this table has TQ in this column to indicate a special case which you do not want to import.*

Click the arrow on the first box in the **Only include rows where** area and choose **does not equal**.

*You want all the rows that do not have TQ in this column.*

Type **TQ** in the second box.

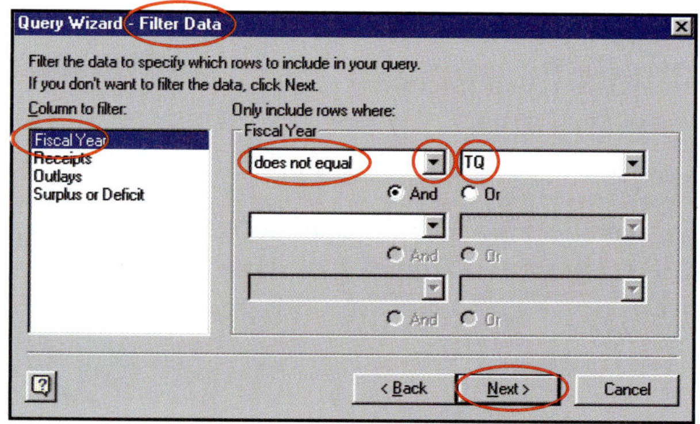

**6** Click the **Next** button.

*The Sort Order page of the wizard is displayed. The rows are already sorted by year, so no change is needed on this page.*

Click the **Next** button.

*The Finish dialog box of the wizard is displayed and provides three options for dealing with this data.*

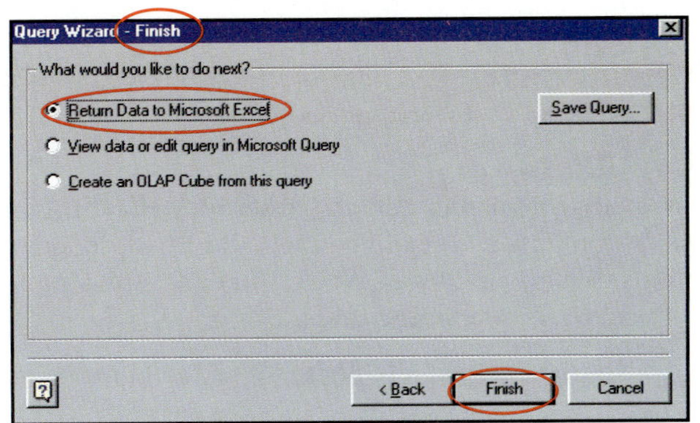


**7** Confirm that **Return Data to Microsoft Excel** is selected. Click **Finish**.

*The Import Data dialog box is displayed.*

Confirm that **Existing worksheet** is selected and type **=$A$2**.

*The upper left corner of the table will be placed in cell A2 to provide room for adding a label in the first row.*

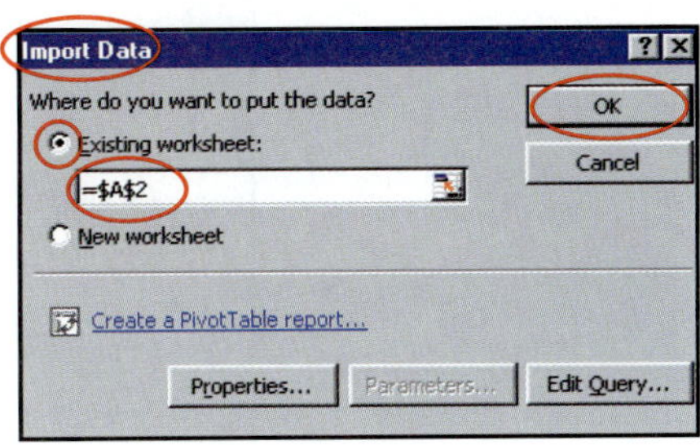


**8** Click the **OK** button.

*The table is imported to the worksheet without the row with TQ in the year cell.*

Print this sheet if your instructor requires it.

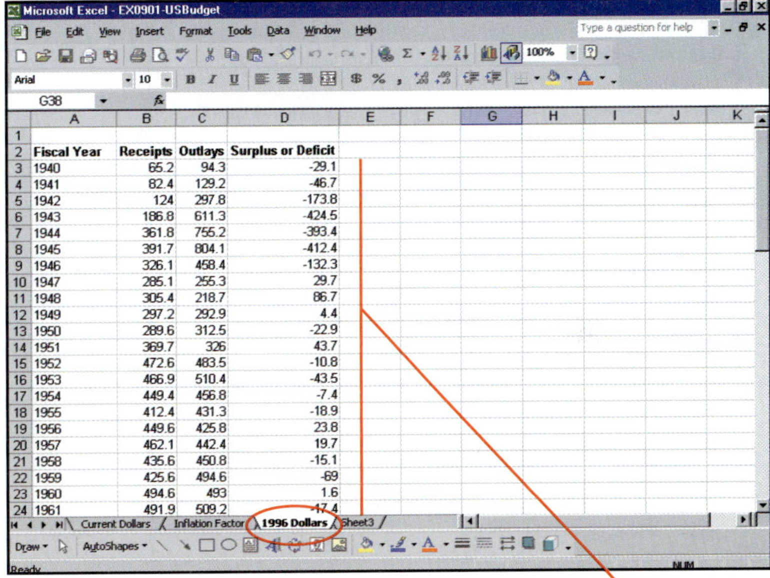

Data imported from Access table

# Task 4
## COPYING A TABLE FROM A WORD DOCUMENT

### Why would I do this?

Some people make tables of names and addresses in Microsoft Word that they use to create merged documents and mailing labels. Tables of data may also exist in research documents that are written in Word. You can import tables like these from Word into Excel without retyping them.

In this task, you learn how to select a table in a Word document, copy it, and paste it into a worksheet.

**1** Double click the **Sheet3** tab and type **Percent of GDP**. Press ↵Enter.

*The name of the sheet is changed.*

**IN DEPTH**

*GDP* stands for Gross Domestic Product and is used in the field of economics to measure the economic productivity of a country. Comparing the surplus or deficit in the budget to the GDP provides some insight into how significant the deficit or surplus may be. For example, if a person with an annual income of $100,000 overspends his budget by $2,000 it isn't as significant as a person who overspends by the same amount but who only makes $20,000 per year.

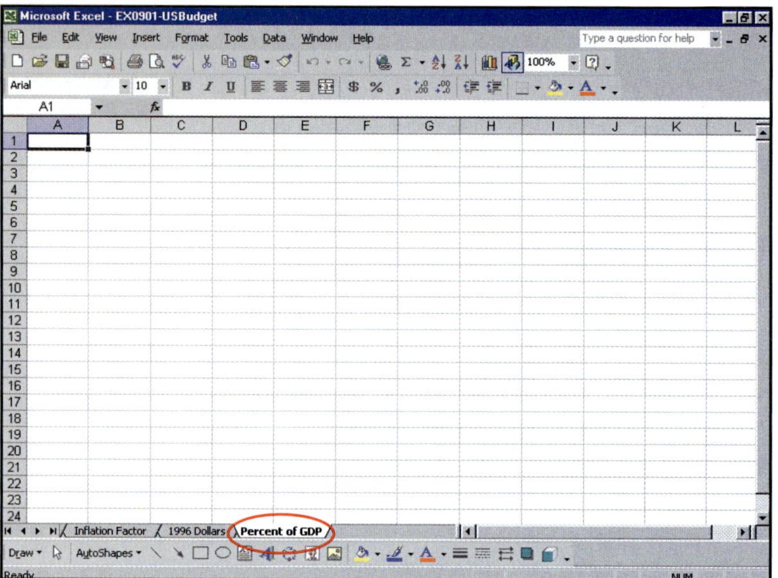

**2** Start Word and click the **Open** button on the toolbar. Locate the folder where the student files for this lesson are stored. Select **EX0904** and click the **Open** button.

*The Word file EX0904 opens and displays a table of data.*

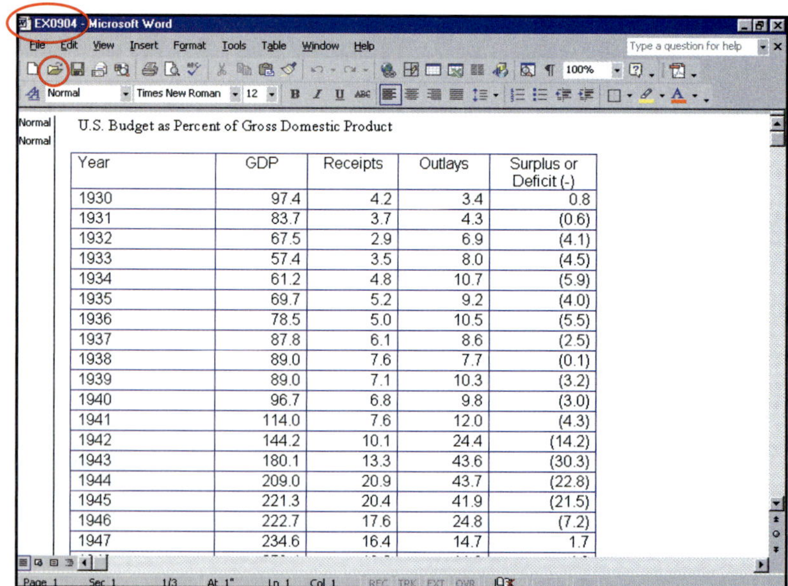

U.S. Budget as Percent of Gross Domestic Product

| Year | GDP | Receipts | Outlays | Surplus or Deficit (-) |
|------|------|----------|---------|------------------------|
| 1930 | 97.4 | 4.2 | 3.4 | 0.8 |
| 1931 | 83.7 | 3.7 | 4.3 | (0.6) |
| 1932 | 67.5 | 2.9 | 6.9 | (4.1) |
| 1933 | 57.4 | 3.5 | 8.0 | (4.5) |
| 1934 | 61.2 | 4.8 | 10.7 | (5.9) |
| 1935 | 69.7 | 5.2 | 9.2 | (4.0) |
| 1936 | 78.5 | 5.0 | 10.5 | (5.5) |
| 1937 | 87.8 | 6.1 | 8.6 | (2.5) |
| 1938 | 89.0 | 7.6 | 7.7 | (0.1) |
| 1939 | 89.0 | 7.1 | 10.3 | (3.2) |
| 1940 | 96.7 | 6.8 | 9.8 | (3.0) |
| 1941 | 114.0 | 7.6 | 12.0 | (4.3) |
| 1942 | 144.2 | 10.1 | 24.4 | (14.2) |
| 1943 | 180.1 | 13.3 | 43.6 | (30.3) |
| 1944 | 209.0 | 20.9 | 43.7 | (22.8) |
| 1945 | 221.3 | 20.4 | 41.9 | (21.5) |
| 1946 | 222.7 | 17.6 | 24.8 | (7.2) |
| 1947 | 234.6 | 16.4 | 14.7 | 1.7 |

**3** Click anywhere in the table to place the insertion point in one of its cells. Choose **Table**, **Select**, **Table**.

*The table is selected but not the row of text above it.*

Click the **Copy** button.

*The table is copied to the Office Clipboard.*

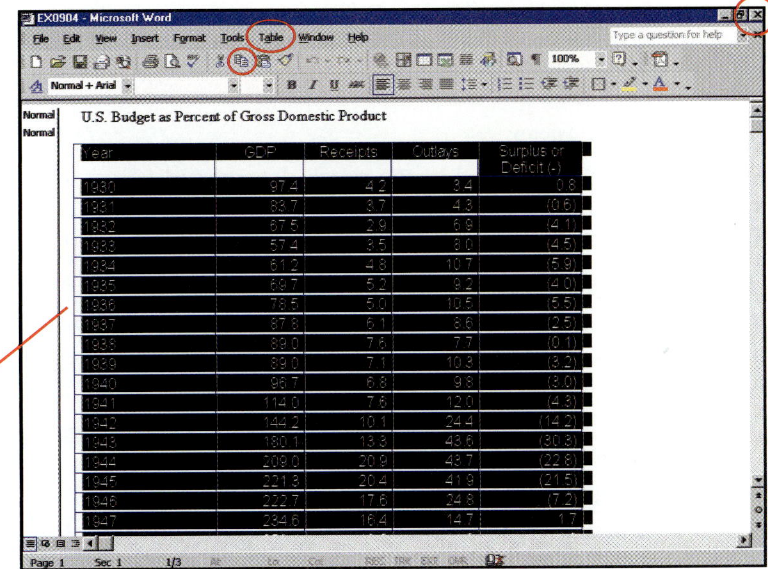

Selected table copied to the Office Clipboard

**4** Close Word. Do not save any changes.

*The table is still in the Office Clipboard.*

Click cell **A2** in the **Percent of GDP** sheet to select it. Click the **Paste** button.

*The table is imported with some of its formatting.*

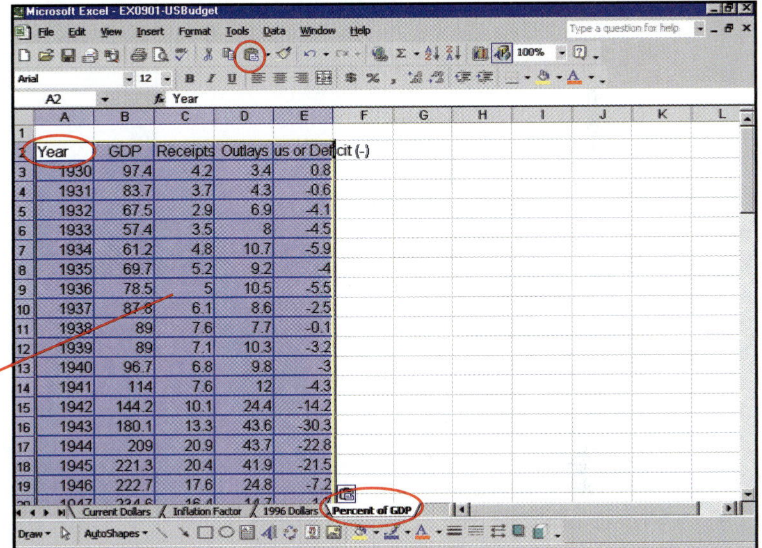

Table imported with borders around cells

**5** Confirm that the table is still selected. Choose **Edit**, **Clear**, **Formats**.

*The formatting is removed from the table.*

Print this sheet if your instructor requires it.

Save the workbook. Overwrite the original copy of the workbook, if necessary.

Leave the workbook open for use in the next task.

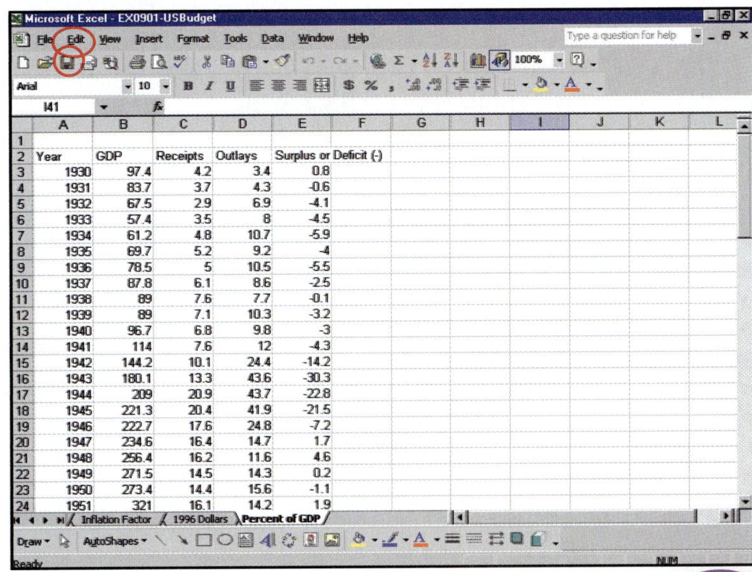

# Task 5
## CREATING A SUMMARY SHEET

### *Why would I do this?*

It is easy to get overwhelmed by too much data spread across several worksheets. If you want to extract meaningful information from the data, it is a good idea to bring the important data together on a single worksheet and then chart it.

In this task, you learn how to create a summary sheet and use formulas to transfer data into it. The custom chart type allows you to chart two different sets of related data on the same chart using two different value axes.

**1** Choose Insert, Worksheet.

*A new worksheet is inserted.*

Double-click the tab on the new sheet and type **Summary**. Press ⏎Enter.

*The sheet is renamed.*

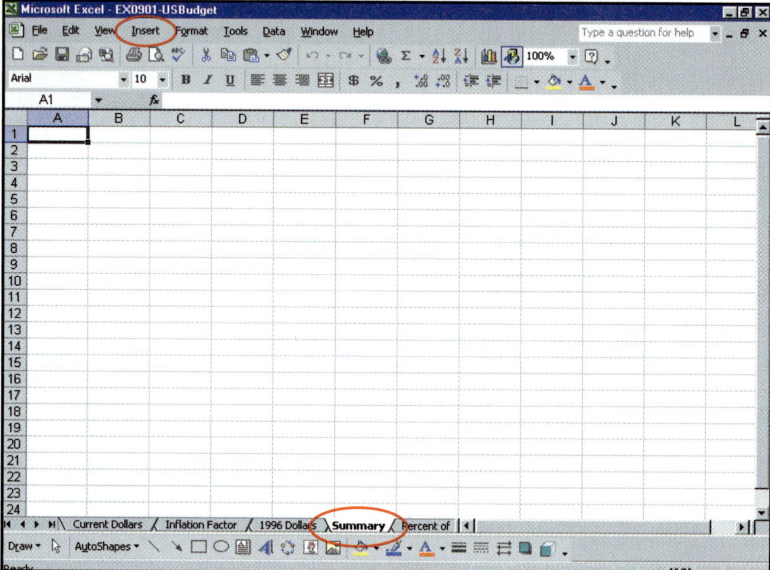

**2** Move the mouse pointer onto the **Summary** sheet tab. Drag the sheet tab to the right of the **Percent of GDP** sheet tab and release the mouse.

*The Summary sheet is moved to the last position in the list of sheets.*

Select cell **A1** and type **Year**. Select cell **B1**. Type **Surplus/Deficit**. Select cell **C1**. Type **% of GDP**. Press ⏎Enter. Widen column **B** to display the full title.

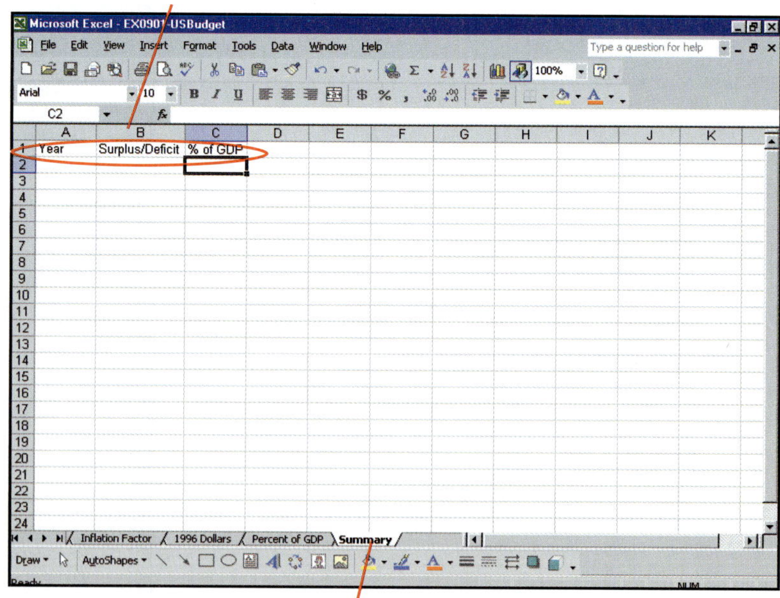

**3** Click cell **A2**. Type **=** to start an equation.

*Equations can refer to other worksheets. This type of reference is called a* **three-dimensional reference**. *If you consider the sheets to be stacked on top of each other, the third dimension is the depth of the stack of worksheets.*

> Click the **1996 Dollars** tab. Click cell **A3** on the 1996 Dollars sheet which contains the year **1940**. Press ⏎Enter.

*The formula on the Summary sheet refers to the first cell in the list of years on the 1996 Dollars sheet.*

> Select **A2** on the **Summary** sheet.

*Notice the 3-D reference on the formula toolbar.*

**IN DEPTH**

You can type a formula with a 3-D reference if you use the correct syntax. Like all formulas in Excel, it starts with an equal sign. The sheet name is enclosed in single quotation marks and followed by an exclamation mark. The cell name follows the sheet name. This combination of sheet name and cell name can be used with other cell names and mathematical functions.

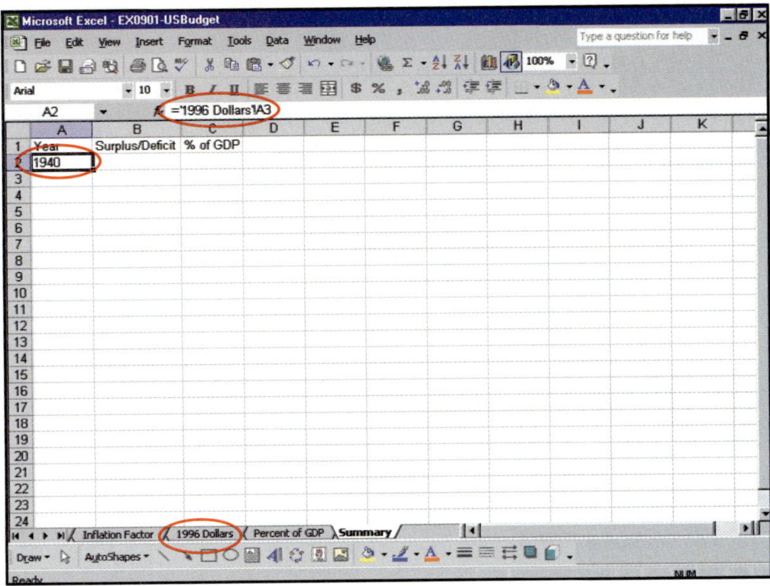

**4** Click the fill handle on cell **A2** and drag it to cell **A68**. Release the fill handle.

*The Summary sheet displays the values from the corresponding cells in the 1996 Dollars sheet. If actual values are used to replace the estimates in the last six cells in the 1996 Dollars sheet, the changes will be reflected in the Summary sheet.*

> Widen column **A** to accommodate the last six values.

Column widened

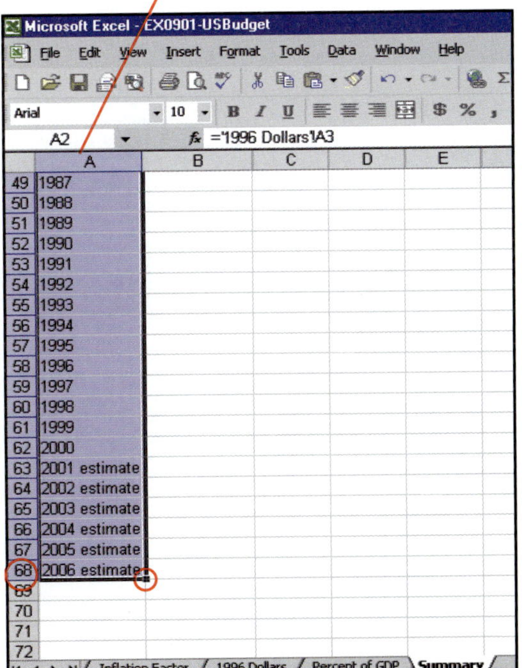

**5** Select cell **B2**. Type **=**, click the **1996 Dollars** sheet tab, click cell **D3**, and press ↵Enter.

*The Summary sheet displays the budget deficit for 1940.*

Select cell **B2**. Drag the fill handle down to cell **B68**.

*The formula in B2 is filled into the cells below it through cell B68.*



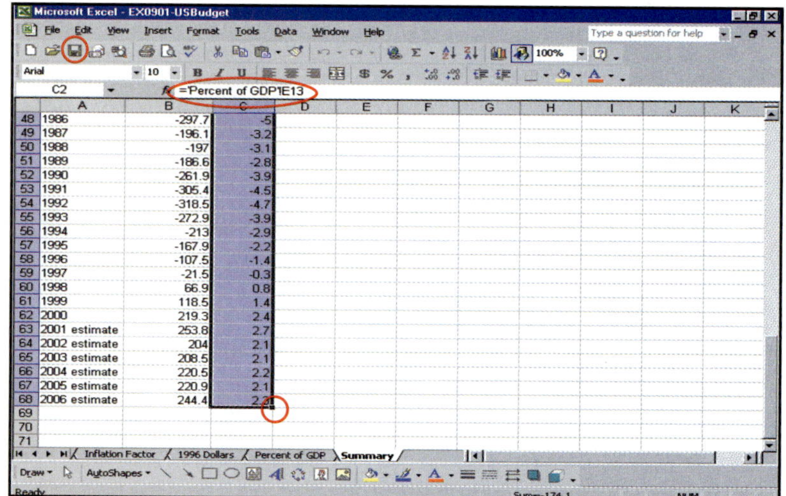

**6** Select cell **C2**. Type **=**, click the **Percent of GDP** sheet tab, click cell **E13**, and press ↵Enter.

*The Summary sheet displays the budget deficit as a percent of GDP for 1940 .*

Select cell **C2**. Drag the fill handle down to cell **C68**.

*The summary sheet has the surplus or deficit value in 1996 dollars and the percent of GDP for each year. You can now compare and evaluate this data.*

Print this sheet if your instructor requires it.

Save the workbook and leave it open for use in the next task.

# Task 6
## SAVING A SHEET IN CSV FORMAT

### Why would I do this?

Programs that handle data use proprietary formats to display the data. Codes that control the format are saved as part of the data and can confuse a program made by a different vendor.

Data can be transferred between different programs if the proprietary formatting codes are removed. The result is a series of text or numbers separated by a character such as a comma, tab, or semicolon that is used to separate the values that were formerly in different columns in the sheet. If commas are used, the file format is called *CSV*, which stands for *Comma Separated Values*. When a character such as a comma is used to separate values, the characters are called *delimiters*. This type of file is also called a comma delimited file. A CSV file can be imported into almost any other program that manages data.

In this task, you learn how to save a worksheet as a CSV file and open it in a word processor to view the file structure.

**1** Confirm that the **Summary** sheet is selected. Choose **File**, **Save As**. Click the arrow next to the **Save as type** box and select **CSV (Comma delimited)**.

*The worksheet will be saved with a file extension of .csv.*

Select the file name and type **EX0901-Comma**.

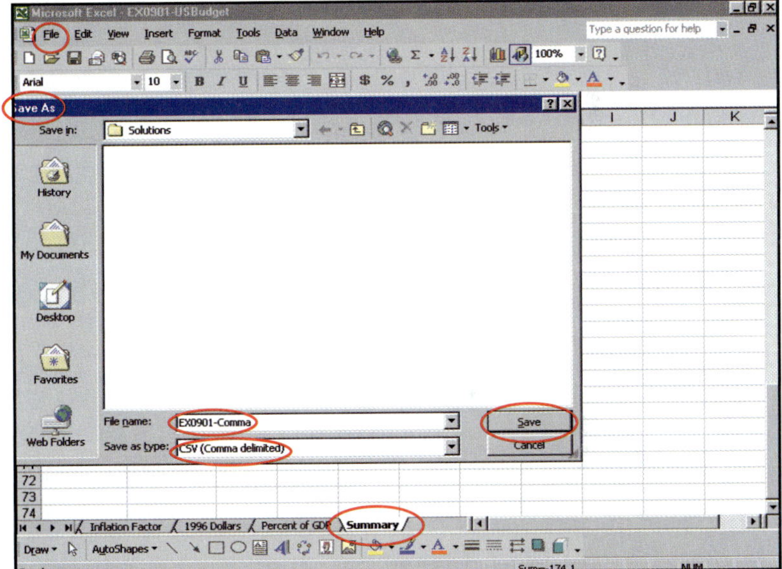

**IN DEPTH**

You can display the file extension as part of the file name or you can hide the file extensions for known file types. If you want to see the file extensions for the known file types, start Windows Explorer and choose Tools, Folder Options. Click the View tab and deselect the option, Hide file extensions for known file types.

**2** Confirm that the folder in which you store your solutions is selected in the **Save in** box. Click **Save**.

*A dialog box opens and explains that this format does not work with multiple worksheets and that only the currently selected sheet will be saved.*

Click **OK**.

*Another dialog box opens to warn you that your worksheet contains features that will be lost. This worksheet uses formulas. Only the values will be saved, not the formulas*

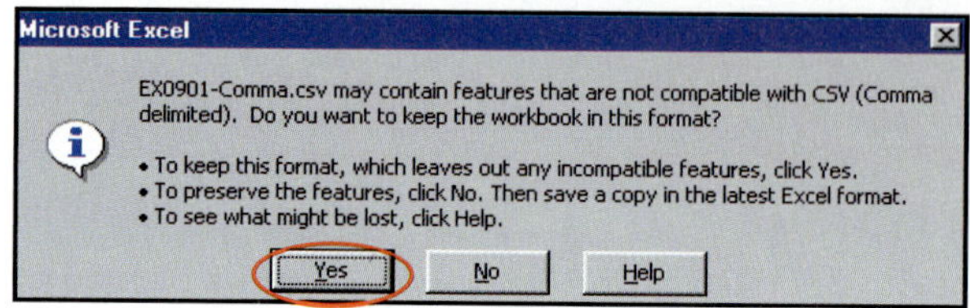


**3** Click **Yes**.

*The Summary worksheet is saved as a comma separated values file named EX0901-Comma. The name on the sheet tab is changed to the new name. If you close this file and open it again, the other sheets will not be there.*

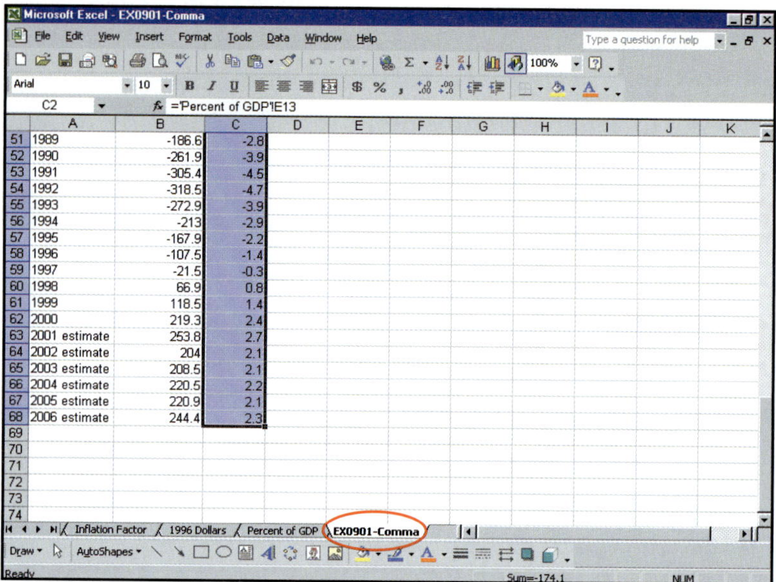

**4** Close Excel and the workbook. When asked if you want to save your changes, click **No**.

Start Microsoft Word. Choose **File**, **Open**. Locate the folder in which you store your files. Change the **Files of type** box to **All Files**. Select **EX0901-Comma** and click **Open**.

*The File Conversion dialog box opens. The default settings will work to open this file.*

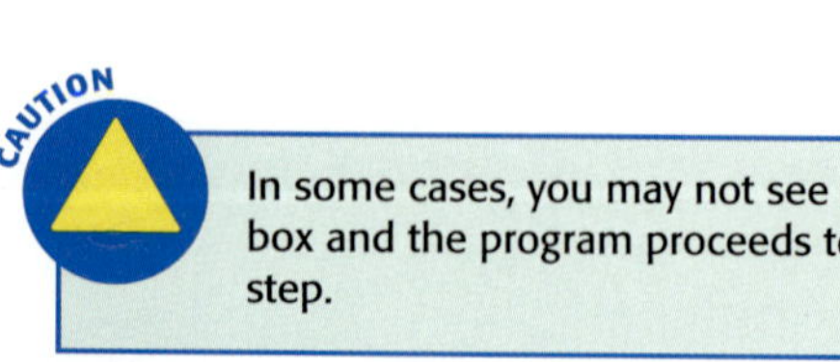


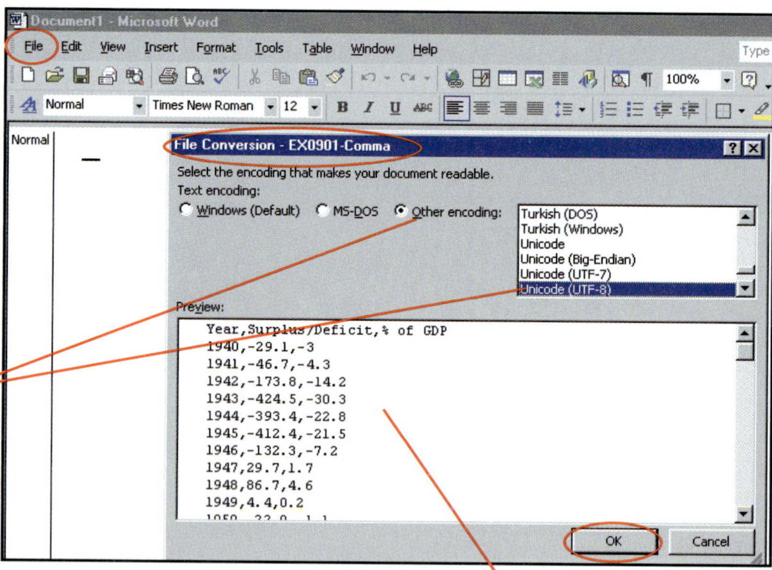

Default settings

Preview of data before it is imported

**5** Click **OK**.

*The file opens and displays the data from the summary sheet separated by commas.*

> Print this sheet if your instructor requires it.

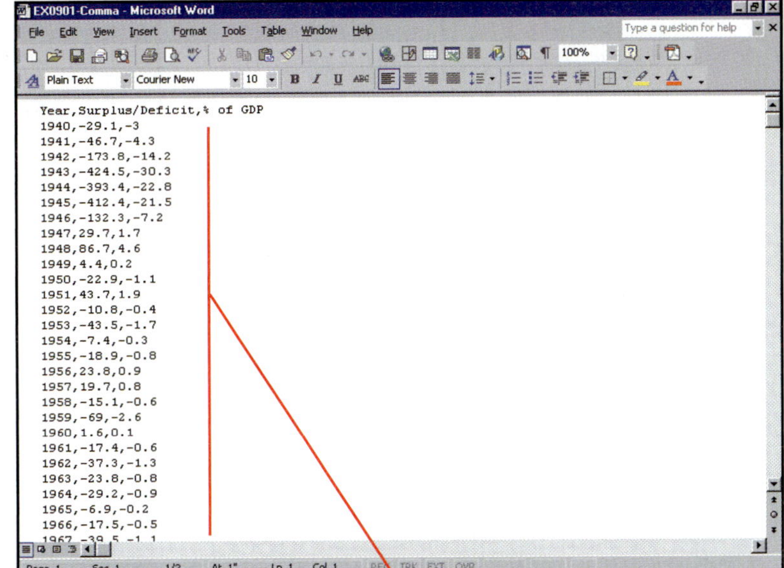


Comma Separated Values

**6** Close the file and close Word.

# Task 7
## PUBLISHING INTERACTIVE WEB PAGES

### Why would I do this?

Interactive Web pages allow you to interact with the worksheet using a Web browser. You can provide the data to the entire company or a small workgroup where people can sort, filter, and calculate values for themselves. The people who view the Web page cannot alter the data permanently so you do not have to worry about them corrupting the data. They can download a working copy of the worksheet if they want to use it off-line as a normal Excel worksheet.

In this task, you learn how to save the budget pages as a Web page that you can view with a browser.

**1** Start Excel. Open **EX0901-USBudget** from the folder where you store your work.

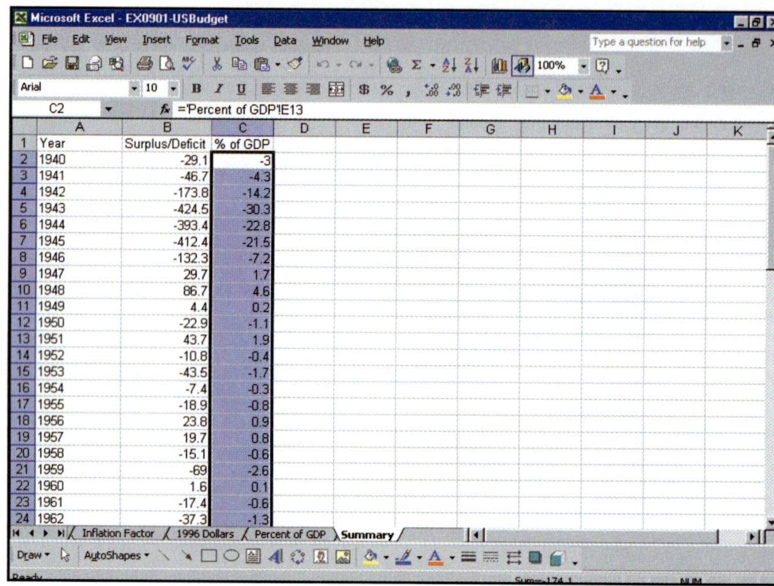

**CAUTION**

This workbook should have all the worksheets. If you did not save the workbook at the end of Task 5, you may have lost most of your work when you saved the file as CSV in Task 6. If the workbook only has one worksheet, you need to start this lesson over. Be sure to save the work as directed in Task 5.

**QUICK TIP**

Excel keeps a short list of recently opened workbooks that you can use to open a workbook again without taking the time to look for it. One of these lists is part of the File menu and the other is found in the task pane under Open a workbook. You can use either one to open the recently used workbook.

**2** Choose **File**, **Save as Web Page**.

*The Save As dialog box opens.*

Click the **Add interactivity** box. Select the current name in the **File name** box and type **EX0901-Web**. Confirm that the folder in the **Save in** box is the one where you save your work.

*When you choose the Add interactivity option, the page is saved using the* **XML** *language which provides more interactivity with Web pages. XML stands for eXtensible Mark-up Language.*

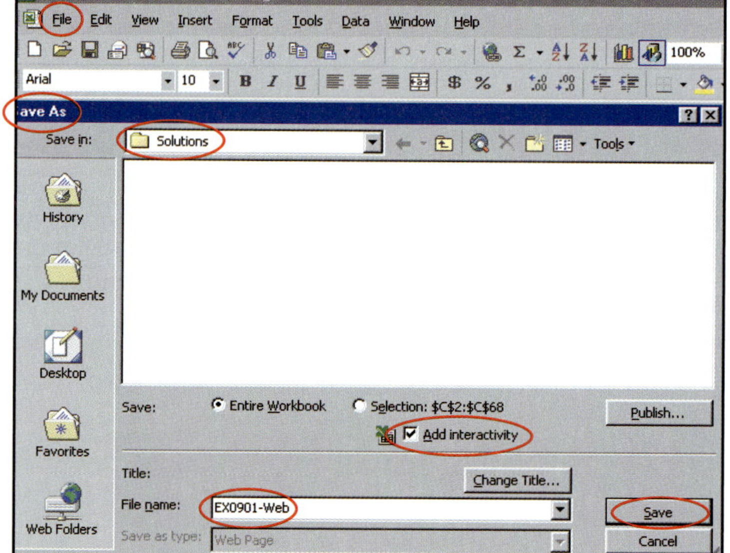

**3** Click the **Save** button. Close Excel. Do not save any changes if asked.

*The workbook is saved as a Web page.*

Start Internet Explorer. Choose **File**, **Open**, and click the **Browse** button. Locate the folder where you saved the Web page, select **EX0901-Web**, and then click the **Open** button.

*The Open dialog box displays the location of the file in your folder.*

Click **OK**.

*The browser opens the Web page.*

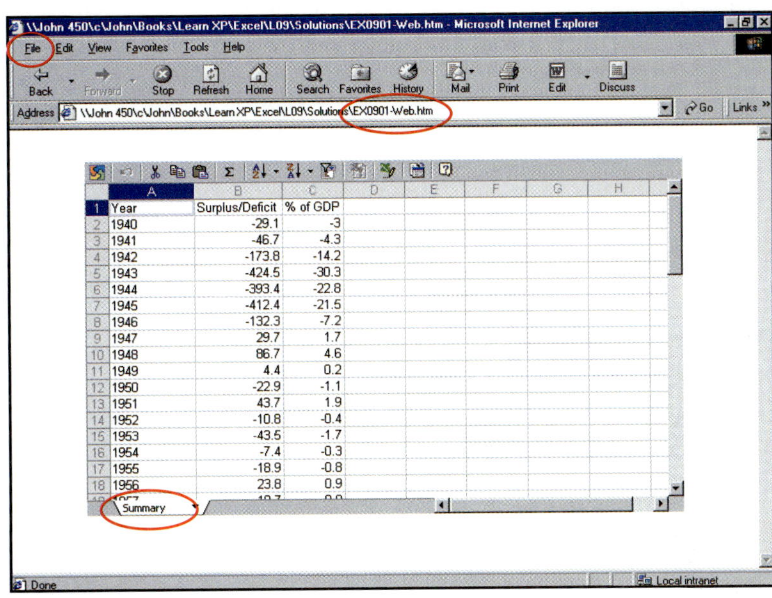

**4** Click the **Summary** tab.

*A list of the other worksheets in the workbook is displayed.*

Click **Percent of GDP** on the list.

*The Percent of GDP sheet is displayed and its name is displayed on the sheet tab.*

**5** Click the **Percent of GDP** sheet tab and choose **Summary** from the list. Click cell **C2** to select it.

*This cell had a formula with a 3-D reference in it in the Excel workbook.*

Click the **Commands and Options** button on the toolbar.

*The Commands and Options dialog box opens.*

Click the **Formula** tab.

*The formula is still there.*

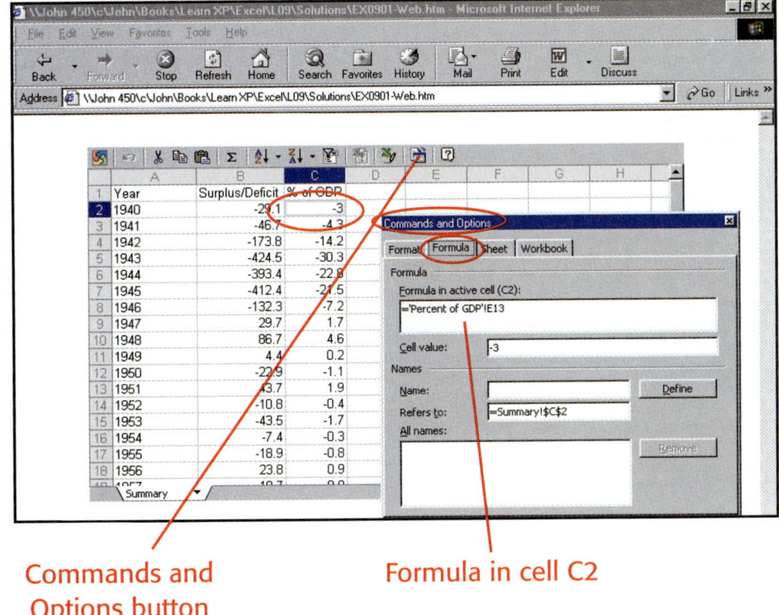

**6** Print this page if your instructor requires it.
Close the browser.

# Task 8
## SAVING RELATED FILES IN A WORKSPACE

### *Why would I do this?*

When you regularly work with several related Excel files, it is convenient to create a workspace. This is a file that automatically opens several workbooks at once.

In this task, you learn how to create a workspace that opens the budget files you have been using.

**1** Start Excel. Choose **File**, **Open**. Locate the folder you use to store your work in the **Look in** box. Click the arrow at the right of the **Files of type** box and select **All Files**.

*All the files in this folder are displayed. You may have more files than those shown in the figure. Confirm that there are three different files that begin with EX0901.*

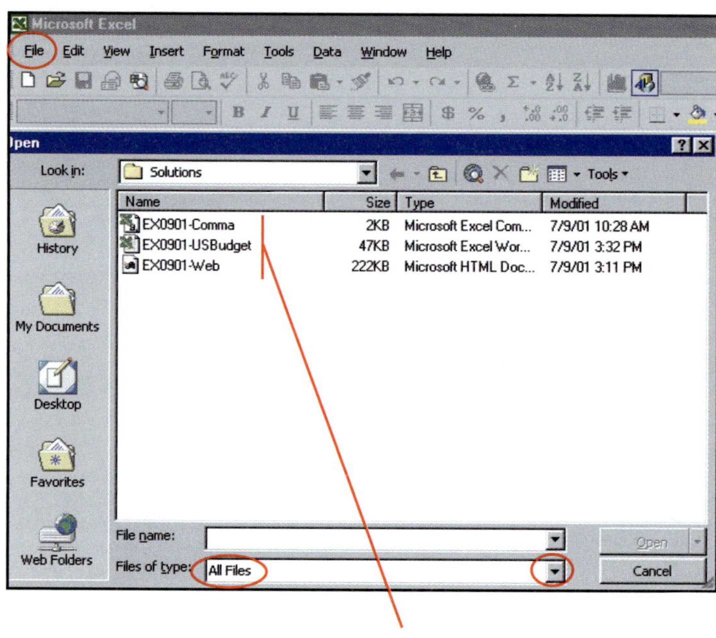

**2** Select **EX0901-USBudget** and click the **Open** button. Repeat this process to open **EX0901-Comma** and **EX0901-Web**.

*You have a workbook, a CSV file, and a Web page open at the same time.*

Choose **Window**.

*A list of the open files is displayed at the bottom of this menu.*

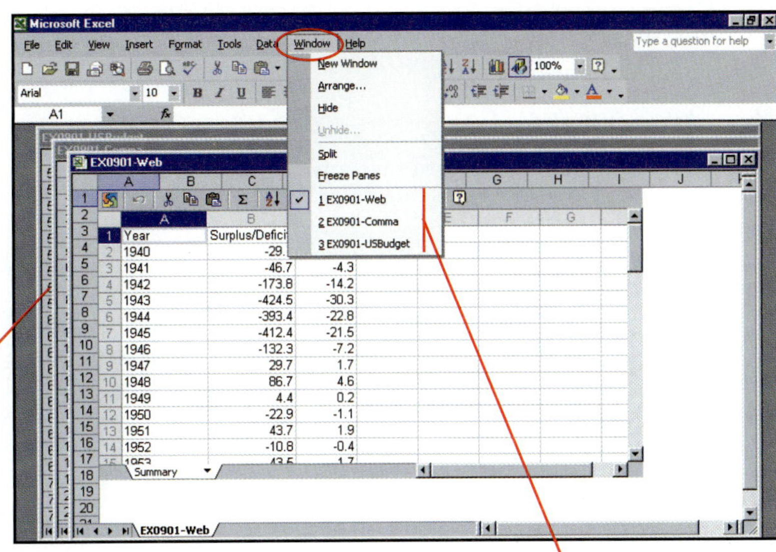


**IN DEPTH**

The three windows are arranged using the Cascade option. If your windows do not display this way by default, choose Window, Arrange, Cascade, and click OK.

**QUICK TIP**

You can open several files at once by selecting them in the Open dialog box. Hold the Ctrl key and click on each workbook you want to select and then click the Open button.

**3** Choose **File**, **Save Workspace**.

*The Save Workspace dialog box opens.*

Confirm that the folder where you store your work is selected in the **Save in** box. Select the default name in the **File name** box and type **EX0901-Workspace**.

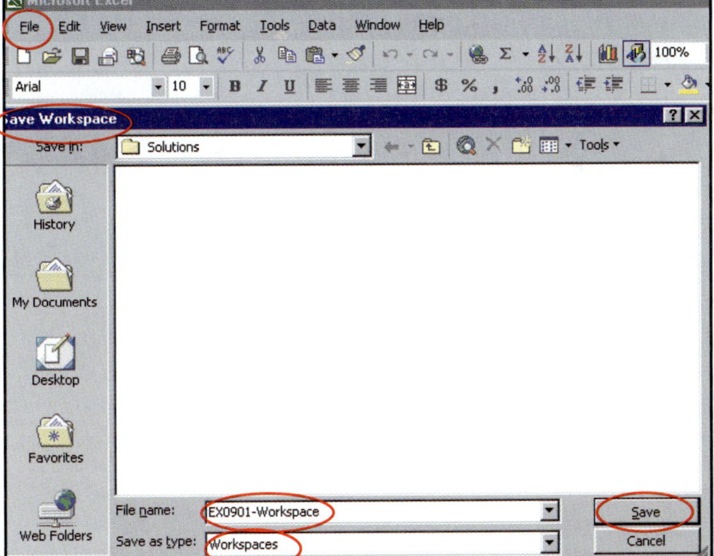

**4** Click **Save**. Choose **No** if you are asked if you want to save changes.

*The workspace is created.*

Close all three files. Do not save any changes.

*This time, you can open all three files at once by opening the workspace file. It will open the other files for you automatically.*

**5** Choose **File**, **Open**. Select your folder in the **Look in** box. Change the **Files of type** box to **All Files**, if necessary.

*The file names are listed.*

Click the arrow on the **Views** button and choose **Details** if this view is not already in use.

*This view displays the file size. Notice that the workspace file is very small. It only contains instructions on how to open the other files.*

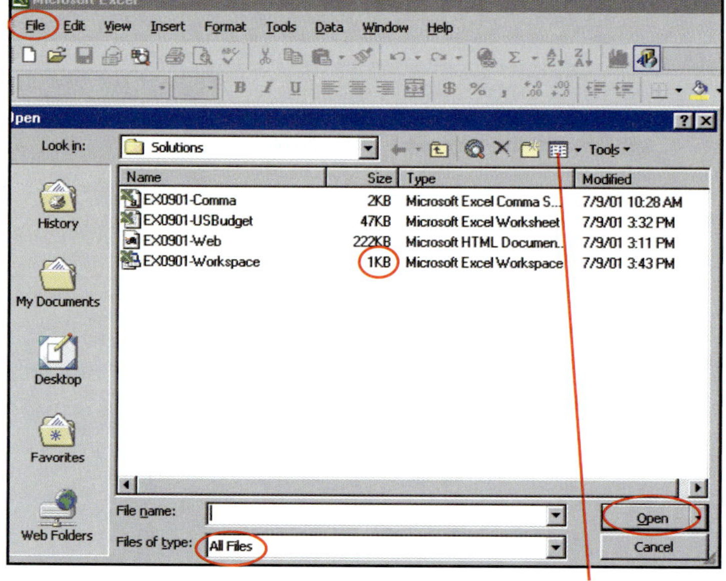

**6** Select **EX0901-Workspace** and click **Open**.

*The three files in the workspace open automatically.*

Choose **Window** to display the list of open files.

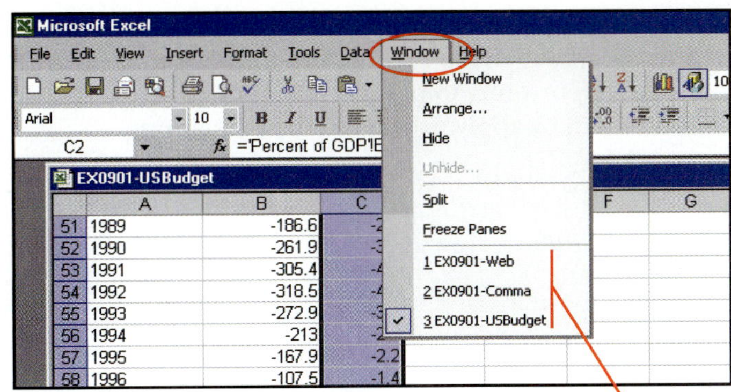



List of files opened automatically

**7** Close Excel. Do not save any changes.

The exercises that follow are designed for you to review and use what you have learned in this lesson. You also have the opportunity to practice your skills and then expand on them by applying them to new situations.

## COMPREHENSION

Comprehension exercises are designed to check your memory and understanding of the basic concepts in this lesson. You distinguish between true and false statements, identify new screen elements, and match terms with related statements. If you are uncertain of the correct answer, refer to the task number following each item (for example, T4 refers to Task 4) and review that task until you are confident that you can provide a correct response.

### TRUE-FALSE

Circle either T or F.

T  F  **1.** To import a table from Access, you must first convert it to a CSV file. **(T3)**

T  F  **2.** When you copy a table from a Word document and paste it in an Excel worksheet, the existing formatting is automatically removed. **(T4)**

T  F  **3.** A 3-D reference can include cells from other worksheets. **(T5)**

T  F  **4.** When you save an Excel worksheet as a CSV file, formulas will be saved. **(T6)**

T  F  **5.** Only one worksheet can be selected at a time when viewing your Excel workbook as a Web page in a Web browser. **(T7)**

T  F  **6.** A workspace is a file that automatically opens several workbooks at once. **(T8)**

### MATCHING QUESTIONS

**A.** CSV

**B.** Workspace

**C.** 3-D reference

**D.** Add Interactivity box

**E.** Import External <u>Data</u>

**F.** Move or Copy dialog box

Match the following statements to the word or phrase that is the best match from the list. Write the letter of the matching word or phrase in the space provided next to the number.

**1.** _____ An option when saving the file as a Web page to use the XML language to provide more interaction with Web pages **(T7)**

**2.** _____ A file format that uses commas to separates values **(T6)**

**3.** _____ A menu item that allows you to create a new Web or database query **(T2 & T3)**

**4.** _____ An equation that can use references to other worksheets **(T5)**

**5.** _____ A place where you indicate where you want to copy a worksheet **(T1)**

**6.** _____ A file that automatically opens several workbooks at once **(T8)**

# IDENTIFYING PARTS OF THE EXCEL SCREEN

Refer to the figure and identify the numbered parts of the screen. Write the letter of the correct label in the space next to the number.

1. _______________

2. _______________

3. _______________

4. _______________

5. _______________

6. _______________

7. _______________

8. _______________

9. _______________

10. _______________

A. Database query dialog box  (T3)

B. 3-D reference  (T5)

C. Name of Access database table  (T3)

D. Button to add database columns to your query  (T3)

E. Web query dialog box  (T2)

F. Address of Web page that contains table to import  (T2)

G. Identified Web table to import  (T2)

H. Formatting marks to indicate number  (T6)

I. Formatting marks to indicate separation of data  (T6)

J. CSV file  (T6)

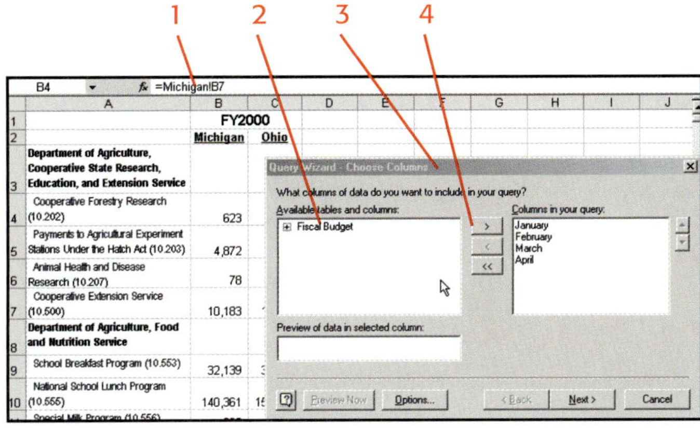

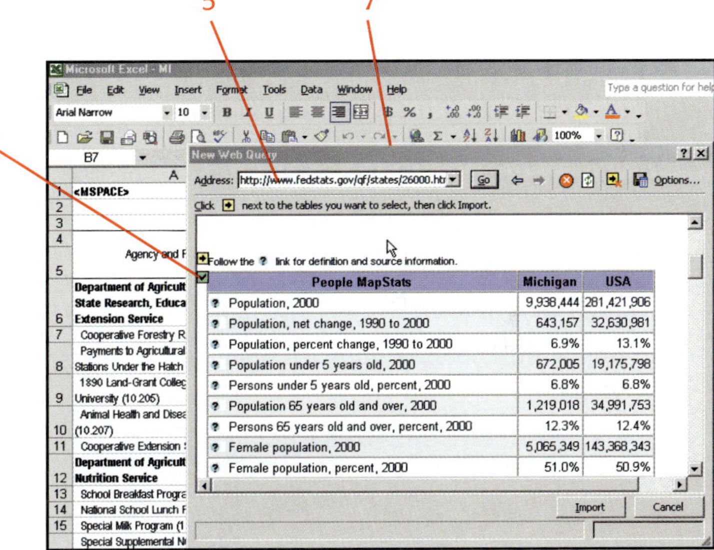

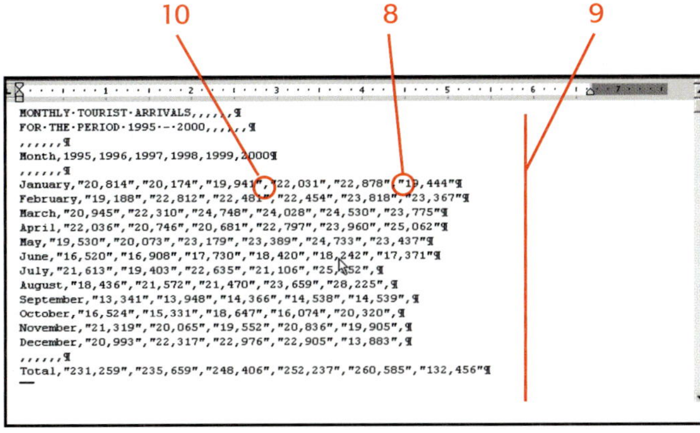

Reinforcement exercises are designed to reinforce the skills you have learned by applying them to a new situation. Detailed instructions are provided along with a figure, where appropriate, to illustrate the result. Complete the reinforcement exercises sequentially. Leave the workbook open at the end of each exercise for use in the next exercise until you are specifically directed to close it.

## R1—Copying a Worksheet from another Workbook

In this exercise, you create a new workbook and then copy information from another workbook into it. The information you will be copying is a list of how many employees the executive branch of the U.S. government employed between 1962 and 2000.

1. Start Excel. Confirm that an empty workbook is displayed and save it in your folder as **EX0905-USEmployees**.

2. Open the Task Pane, if necessary, by choosing **View**, **Task Pane**. Click **More workbooks** from the **Open a workbook** area. Change the **Look in** box to display the student files for this lesson. Select **EX0905** and click the **Open** button.

3. Choose **Edit**, **Move or Copy Sheet**.

4. Click the down arrow at the right side of the **To book** box and select **EX0905-USEmployees**.

5. Click the **Create a copy** check box, and then click the **OK** button.

6. Double-click the sheet tab to select it and type **Executive**. Press **⏎Enter**.

7. Switch back to EX0905 and close it.

8. Save the workbook, and leave it open for the next exercise.

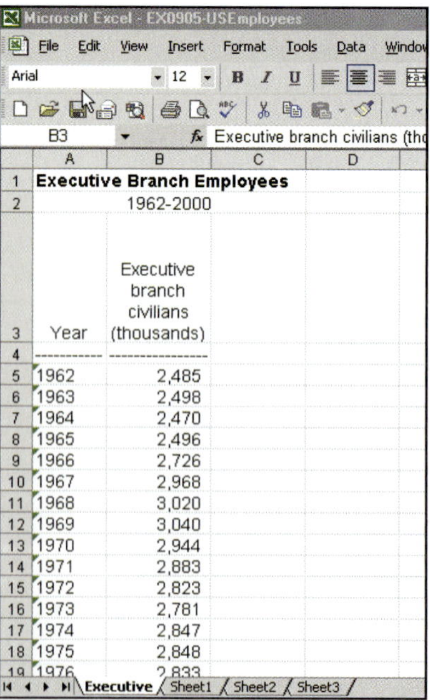


## R2—Importing Data from a Web Page

The information that lists how many employees the legislative and judicial branches employ is located on a Web page. You will import this information into your workbook using a New Web Query.

1. Launch Internet Explorer. Choose **File**, **Open**. Click the **Browse** button.

2. Locate the folder that contains the student files for this lesson and select **EX0906**. Click the **Open** button. Click **OK**.

3. Select the address in the **Address** box. Choose **Edit**, **Copy**.

4. Click the **Close** button on the title bar of the Internet Explorer window. Double-click the **Sheet1** tab and type **Legislative & Judicial**. Press **⏎Enter**.

5. Choose **Data**, **Import External Data**, **New Web Query**.

6. Confirm that the address is selected. Hold the **Ctrl** key and press **V**, then click the **Go** button.

7. Click the **Import** button; then click the **OK** button. Widen column **B** to accommodate the heading.

8. Save the workbook, and leave it open for the next exercise.

|  | A | B |
|---|---|---|
| 1 | Year | Legislative and judicial branch personnel (thousands) |
| 2 | - | - |
| 3 | 1962 | 30 |
| 4 | 1963 | 30 |
| 5 | 1964 | 31 |
| 6 | 1965 | 32 |
| 7 | 1966 | 33 |
| 8 | 1967 | 34 |
| 9 | 1968 | 35 |
| 10 | 1969 | 36 |
| 11 | 1970 | 38 |
| 12 | 1971 | 40 |
| 13 | 1972 | 42 |
| 14 | 1973 | 44 |
| 15 | 1974 | 46 |
| 16 | 1975 | 49 |
| 17 | 1976 | 50 |
| 18 | 1977 | 53 |
| 19 | 1978 | 55 |
| 20 | 1979 | 53 |
| 21 | 1980 | 55 |
| 22 | 1981 | 54 |
| 23 | 1982 | 55 |
| 24 | 1983 | 56 |

Executive \ **Legislative & Judicial** \ Sheet2 \ Sheet3

## R3–Importing Data from an Access Table

Information on how many people the U.S. military employs is located in an Access database. You will use a new database query to import this information into your workbook.

1. Double click the **Sheet2** tab and type **Military**. Press ↵Enter.

2. Choose **Data**, **Import External Data**, **New Database Query**.

3. Click the **Databases** tab, if necessary, and click **MS Access Database***. Confirm that the checkbox next to **Use the Query Wizard to create/edit queries** displays a check mark.

4. Click the **OK** button. Select the drive where the student files are located in the **Drives** box. Select the folder where the student files are located in the **Directories** box. Select **EX0907** in the **Database Name** box.

5. Click **OK**. Confirm that **Military Table** is selected and click the add button to add all of the table's columns to the query.

6. Click the **Next** button twice to move to the **Sort Order** box. Click the down arrow to the right of the **Sort by** box, and select **Year**.

7. Click **Next**. Confirm that **Return Data to Microsoft Excel** is selected. Click **Finish**.

8. Confirm that **Existing worksheet** is selected and click **OK**.

9. Save the workbook, and leave it open for the next task.

| | A | B | C | D | E | F |
|---|---|---|---|---|---|---|
| 1 | Year | Military | | | | |
| 2 | 1962 | 2840 | | | | |
| 3 | 1963 | 2732 | | | | |
| 4 | 1964 | 2719 | | | | |
| 5 | 1965 | 2687 | | | | |
| 6 | 1966 | 3129 | | | | |
| 7 | 1967 | 3413 | | | | |
| 8 | 1968 | 3584 | | | | |
| 9 | 1969 | 3499 | | | | |
| 10 | 1970 | 3104 | | | | |
| 11 | 1971 | 2752 | | | | |
| 12 | 1972 | 2360 | | | | |
| 13 | 1973 | 2289 | | | | |
| 14 | 1974 | 2198 | | | | |
| 15 | 1975 | 2164 | | | | |
| 16 | 1976 | 2119 | | | | |
| 17 | 1977 | 2112 | | | | |
| 18 | 1978 | 2099 | | | | |
| 19 | 1979 | 2063 | | | | |
| 20 | 1980 | 2090 | | | | |
| 21 | 1981 | 2122 | | | | |
| 22 | 1982 | 2147 | | | | |
| 23 | 1983 | 2163 | | | | |
| 24 | 1984 | 2178 | | | | |

Executive / Legislative & Judicial / **Military** / Sheet3 /

## R4–Getting a Table from a Word Document

In this exercise, you retrieve state and local employment numbers from a Word document and paste them in your workbook.

1. Double click the **Sheet3** tab and type **State & Local**. Press ↵Enter.

2. Start Word and click the **Open** button on the toolbar. Locate the folder where the student files for this lesson are stored. Select **EX0908** and click the **Open** button.

3. Click anywhere in the table to place the insertion point in one of its cells. Choose **Table**, **Select**, **Table**. Click the **Copy** button. Close Word.

4. Click cell **A1** in the **State & Local** sheet to select it. Click the **Paste** button.

5. Choose **Edit**, **Clear**, **Formats**. Widen column **B** to accommodate heading.

6. Save the workbook, and leave it open for the next task.

| | A | B | C |
|---|---|---|---|
| 1 | Year | State and local governments  (thousands) | |
| 2 | 1962 | 6549 | |
| 3 | 1963 | 6868 | |
| 4 | 1964 | 7248 | |
| 5 | 1965 | 7696 | |
| 6 | 1966 | 8221 | |
| 7 | 1967 | 8673 | |
| 8 | 1968 | 9102 | |
| 9 | 1969 | 9437 | |
| 10 | 1970 | 9822 | |
| 11 | 1971 | 10184 | |
| 12 | 1972 | 10649 | |
| 13 | 1973 | 11069 | |
| 14 | 1974 | 11446 | |
| 15 | 1975 | 11937 | |
| 16 | 1976 | 12138 | |
| 17 | 1977 | 12400 | |
| 18 | 1978 | 12920 | |
| 19 | 1979 | 13174 | |
| 20 | 1980 | 13375 | |
| 21 | 1981 | 13259 | |
| 22 | 1982 | 13098 | |
| 23 | 1983 | 13096 | |
| 24 | 1984 | 13216 | |

Executive / Legislative & Judicial / Military / **State & Local**

## R5–Creating a Summary Sheet

In this exercise, you create a summary worksheet that uses formulas with 3-D references to the Executive and State & Local worksheets.

1. Choose **Insert**, **Worksheet**. Double click the tab on the new sheet and type **Summary**. Press ↵Enter.

2. Move the mouse pointer onto the **Summary** sheet tab. Click and drag the sheet tab to the right of the **State & Local** sheet tab and release the mouse.

3. Select cell **A1** and type **Year**. Press Tab↹ to move the selection to cell **B1**. Type **Executive**. Press Tab↹. Type **State & Local**. Press ↵Enter. Widen column **C** to display the full title.

4. Click cell **A2**. Type **=** to start an equation. Click the **Executive** sheet tab. Click cell **A5**, and then press ⏎**Enter**. Select **A2** on the **Summary** sheet. Click the fill handle on cell **A2** and drag it to cell **A40**. Release the fill handle.

5. Select cell **B2**. Type **=**, click the **Executive** sheet tab, click cell **B5**, and then press ⏎**Enter**. Select cell **B2**. Click and drag the fill handle down to cell **B40**.

6. Select cell **C2**. Type **=**, click the **State & Local** sheet tab, click cell **B2**, and then press ⏎**Enter**. Select cell **C2**. Click and drag the fill handle down to cell **C40**.

7. Select column **C**. Click the **Comma Style** button to format the numbers. Click the **Decrease Decimal** button twice to remove zeros.

8. Print each sheet of the workbook if your instructor requires it.

9. Save the workbook, and leave it open for the next task.

| | A | B | C | D | E | F |
|---|---|---|---|---|---|---|
| 1 | Year | Executive | State & Local | | | |
| 2 | 1962 | 2,485 | 6,549 | | | |
| 3 | 1963 | 2,498 | 6,868 | | | |
| 4 | 1964 | 2,470 | 7,248 | | | |
| 5 | 1965 | 2,496 | 7,696 | | | |
| 6 | 1966 | 2,726 | 8,221 | | | |
| 7 | 1967 | 2,968 | 8,673 | | | |
| 8 | 1968 | 3,020 | 9,102 | | | |
| 9 | 1969 | 3,040 | 9,437 | | | |
| 10 | 1970 | 2,944 | 9,822 | | | |
| 11 | 1971 | 2,883 | 10,184 | | | |
| 12 | 1972 | 2,823 | 10,649 | | | |
| 13 | 1973 | 2,781 | 11,069 | | | |
| 14 | 1974 | 2,847 | 11,446 | | | |
| 15 | 1975 | 2,848 | 11,937 | | | |
| 16 | 1976 | 2,833 | 12,138 | | | |
| 17 | 1977 | 2,840 | 12,400 | | | |
| 18 | 1978 | 2,875 | 12,920 | | | |
| 19 | 1979 | 2,823 | 13,174 | | | |
| 20 | 1980 | 2,821 | 13,375 | | | |
| 21 | 1981 | 2,806 | 13,259 | | | |
| 22 | 1982 | 2,770 | 13,098 | | | |
| 23 | 1983 | 2,820 | 13,096 | | | |
| 24 | 1984 | 2,854 | 13,216 | | | |

`|◄ ◄ ► ►|\ Executive / Legislative & Judicial / Military / State & Local \ Summar`

## R6—Saving a Sheet in CSV Format

1. Confirm that the **Summary** sheet is selected. Choose **File**, **Save As**. Click the down arrow next to the **Save as type** box and select **CSV (Comma delimited)**. Select the file name and type **EX0905-Comma**.

2. Confirm that the folder in which you store your solutions is selected in the **Save in** box. Click **Save**. Click **OK**.

3. Click **Yes**. Close Excel and the workbook. When asked if you want to save your changes, click **No**.

4. Start Microsoft Word. Choose **File**, **Open**. Locate the folder in which you store your files. Change the **Files of type** box to **All Files**. Select **EX0905-Comma** and click **Open**. Click **OK**.

5. Print this sheet if your instructor requires it. Close the file and close Word.

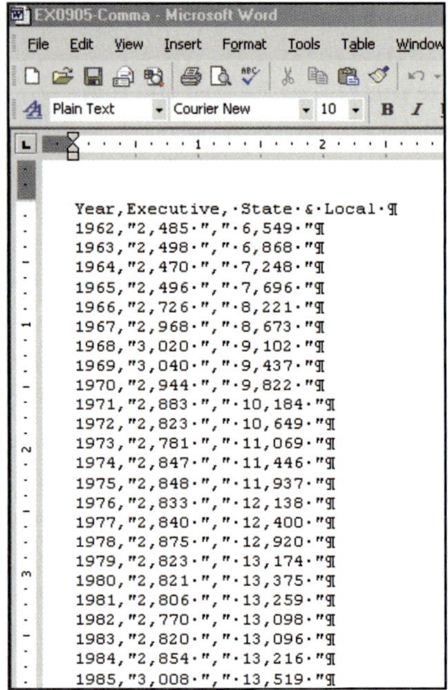


## R7—Publishing Interactive Web Pages

1. Start Excel. Open **EX0905-USEmployees** from the folder where you store your work.

2. Choose **File**, **Save as Web Page**. Click the **Add interactivity** box. Select the current name in the **File name** box and type **EX0905-Web**. Confirm that the folder in the **Save in** box is the one where you save your work.

3. Click the **Save** button. Close Excel. Do not save any changes if asked.

4. Start Internet Explorer. Choose **File**, **Open**, and click the **Browse** button. Locate the folder where you saved the Web page, select **EX0905-Web**, and then click the **Open** button. Click **OK**.

5. Click the arrow on the sheet tab and choose **Military**.

6. Click the arrow on the sheet tab and choose **Summary**. Click cell **C2** to select it.

7. Print this page if your instructor requires it. Close the browser.

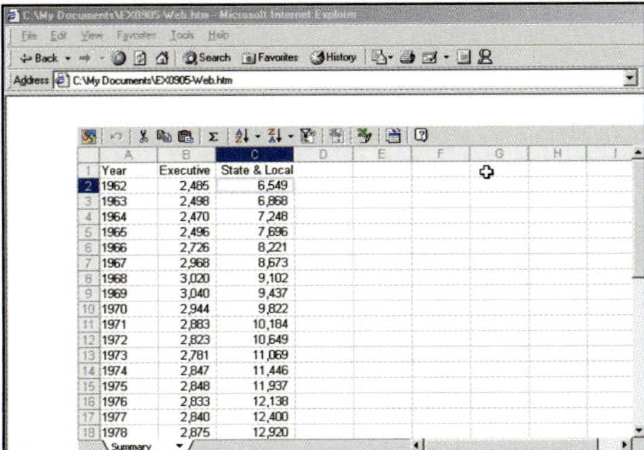

## R8—Saving Related Files in a Workspace

1. Start Excel. Choose **File**, **Open**. Locate the folder you use to store your work in the **Look in** box. Click the arrow at the right of the **Files of type** box and select **All Files.** Confirm that there are three different files that begin with EX0905. Select **EX0905-USEmployees** and click the **Open** button. Repeat this process to open **EX0905-Comma** and **EX0905-Web.**

2. Choose **File**, **Save Workspace**. Confirm that the folder where you store your work is selected in the **Save in** box. Select the default name in the **File name** box and type **EX0905-Workspace**.

3. Click **Save**. Choose **No** if you are asked if you want to save changes. Close all three files. Do not save any changes.

4. Choose **File**, **Open**. Select your folder in the **Look in** box. Change the **Files of type** box to **All Files**, if necessary. Click the arrow on the **Views** button and choose **Details** if this view is not already in use.

5. Select **EX0905-Workspace** and click **Open**. All three Excel files in the workspace open.

6. Close Excel. Do not save any changes.

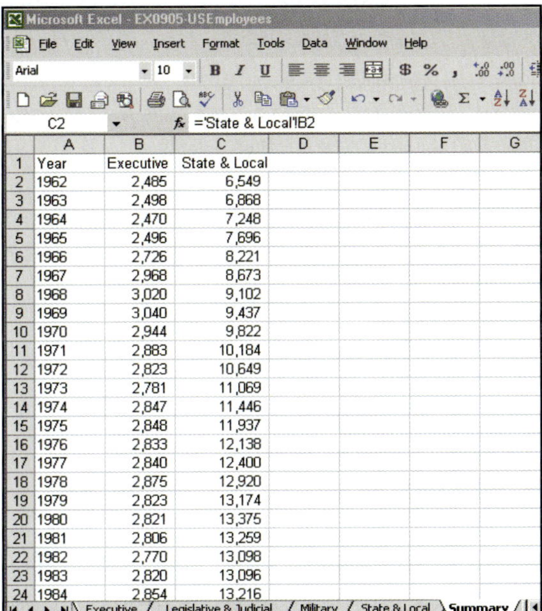

Challenge exercises are designed to test your ability to apply your skills to new situations with less detailed instruction. These exercises also challenge you to expand your repertoire of skills by using commands that are similar to those you have already learned. The desired outcome is clearly defined, but you have more freedom to choose the steps needed to achieve the required result.

The following exercises use separate sheets in the same workbook. The exercises are not sequential and do not depend on each other.

## C1—Copying and Importing Information into the Same Worksheet

When you copy or import information into an Excel workbook from another file, you do not need to place it in its own worksheet. You can place it in your active worksheet beside existing information and then reformat it if necessary.

In this exercise, you obtain information from three different weather service agencies that are responsible for tracking temperature data. All three services use a different software application, and you will create a single worksheet from the separate files. You will also deal with some of the formatting issues that arise when you create a single worksheet from several different files.

*Goal:* Retrieve information from other files and place in an existing worksheet.

1. Open **EX0909** and save it in your folder as **EX0909-Challenge1**.

2. Start Word and open **EX0910.** Place your mouse pointer at the top of the second column (above **May**) so it becomes a down button. Click and drag to the right to highlight all columns containing names of months. Click the **Copy** button, and close Word.

3. Select cell F4 in the Temperatures worksheet and click the **Paste** button. Clear the formats.

4. Select cell J4. Choose **Data, Import External Data, New Database Query**. On **Databases** tab, click **MS Access Database***, and click **OK**. Locate the student files, select **EX0911** and click **OK**.

5. Click the add button. In the **Columns in your query** box, select **Year**. Click the remove button that has a single arrow to remove Year from your query.

6. Click **Next** three times to advance to the **Finish** dialog box. Confirm that **Return Data to Microsoft Excel** is selected, and click **Finish**.

7. In the **Import Data** dialog box, click **OK**. Place your name in **A3**.

8. Remove bold formatting from the month headings. Adjust the column widths and size of the font to fit the data on one printed sheet. (Hint: Use the **Fit to** option in Page Setup.) Change the titles in rows 1 and 2 to merge across all the columns of data.

9. Save the changes, print the **Temperatures** worksheet, and then close the file.

## C2—Consolidating Data in a Summary Sheet

When you create a summary worksheet, is it useful to obtain numbers from different worksheets and have them automatically totaled when placed in the summary sheet. Excel allows you to do this with the Consolidate feature. You create references to the desired cells in various worksheets, and Excel then adds them together.

The U.S. Census Bureau tracks total monthly income by region and income bracket. In this exercise you use a workbook that contains two worksheets: one for households whose total monthly income is $0–$24,999 and one for households whose total monthly income is $25,000–$49,999. The summary sheet you create will take the totals in each worksheet and automatically sum them.

*Goal:* Use the Consolidate feature in a summary worksheet.

1. Open **EX0912** and save it in your folder as **EX0912-Challenge2**.

2. Double-click **Sheet3** and rename it **Summary**.

3. Select the **Under25k** worksheet. Select cells **A6** through **A19**. Click the **Copy** button. Select cell **A2** in the Summary worksheet, and click the **Paste** button. Widen column **A** to accommodate the information.

4. Select cell B2 and type **Total**.

5. Select cell **B3**. Choose **Data, Consolidate**. Confirm that **SUM** is selected in the **Function** box and the insertion point is in the **Reference** box.

6. Click the **Under25k** worksheet, and select cells L7 to L19. You may need to move the open dialog box to view the worksheet. Click **Add** in the **Consolidate** dialog box.

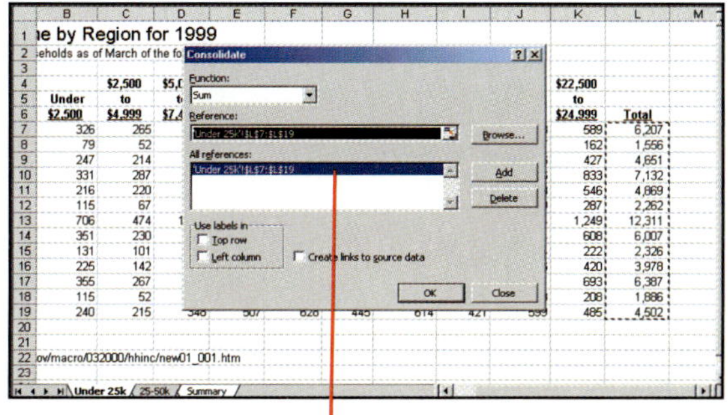

Stores the formulas to be used again

7. Click the **25-50k** tab, and select cells **L7** to **L19**. Click **Add**.

8. Click **OK**. The numbers added to your worksheet are summed by region.

9. Type your name in **A1**. Save the changes, print the **Summary** worksheet and close the workbook.

## C3—Saving Excel Workbook in Different File Formats

*Goal:* Save an Excel workbook in different file formats and compare them in Word.

1. Open **EX0913**. Choose **File, Save As**. Click the arrow next to the **Save as type** box and select **CSV (Comma delimited)**. Select the file name and type **EX0913-CSV**.

2. Click **OK**. Click **Yes** when prompted about certain features not being compatible with CSV format. Notice that you were not prompted about the selected file not being compatible with multiple worksheets (as you were in Task 6) since the file only contains a single worksheet.

3. Close **EX0913-CSV**, and do not save changes.

4. Reopen **EX0913**. Choose **File, Save As**. Click the arrow next to the **Save as type** box and select **Text (Tab delimited)**. Select the file name and type **EX0913-Text**.

5. Click **Save**. Click **Yes** when prompted, and do not save changes. Close Excel.

6. Start Word. Click **File, Open**. Confirm that **All Files** is selected in the **Files of type** box. Open **EX0913-CSV**. Click **OK** when prompted. Click the **Show/Hide** button if formatting is not displayed.

7. Click **File, Open**. Confirm that **All Files** is selected in the **Files of type** box. Open **EX0913-Text**. Click **OK** when prompted. Click the **Show/Hide** button if formatting is not displayed.

8. Create a new Word document and save it as **EX0913-Questions**. Enter your name and section number then type and answer the following questions regarding **EX0913-CSV** and **EX0913-Text**. Keep the two files open for reference and toggle between them using the **Windows** menu or clicking on them in the Task bar.

   1) **What font do the files use and why do you think the fonts are different from the original worksheet?**

   2) **How are the files similar?**

   3) **What differences do you notice between the files?**

   4) **The CSV file uses commas to separate the numbers. How does the file treat the column headings that contain commas versus the column heading that contains no commas? What could be done so that all headings are treated equally?**

9. Save **EX0913-Questions** and print the file. Close all files.

## C4—Using Multiple Worksheets in 3-D References

You previously learned how to create a 3-D reference that used a cell located on another worksheet. A 3-D reference can also contain functions using cells from multiple worksheets, providing that the desired information is located in the same cell on each worksheet.

This exercise uses an Excel workbook that contains multiple worksheets. Each worksheet contains information on a single department of the U.S. Executive branch. In the Summary worksheet you create a 3-D reference that uses cells in each worksheet.

*Goal:* Using Microsoft Help to create a 3-D reference that refers to the same cell on multiple worksheets.

1. Open **EX0914** and save it on your disk as **EX0914-Challenge4**.

**2.** View the various worksheets to become familiar with them.

**3.** Select the **Summary** worksheet, which is the first worksheet in the workbook.

**4.** Select **Help, Microsoft Excel Help**. Search for information on 3-D reference and locate the item that explains how to refer to the same cell on multiple sheets. Print the help screen titled **Refer to the same cell or range on multiple sheets**. Close the Help window.

**5.** Create a 3-D reference in cell **D7** of the **Summary** worksheet to sum all the values that occur in cell **B4** in each of the other worksheets. The function you will use in the 3-D reference is **SUM**.

**6.** Click the fill handle of cell D7 and drag it down to cell D26. Format the numbers to include a decimal and no zeros and the comma separator. Place your name in **A1** or in a location your instructor prefers.

**7.** Print the Summary worksheet.

**8.** Save the changes and close the workbook.

## C5—Importing Data from a Text File

In addition to importing data from the Internet and Access, Excel contains a wizard to import data from other file types. In this exercise, you import a text file.

*Goal:* Use Paste Special to copy formula values to another worksheet.

**1.** Start Excel, and save the blank workbook on your floppy disk as **EX0915-Challenge5**.

**2.** Choose **Data, Import External Data, Import Data**.

**3.** Confirm that **All Data Sources** is displayed in the **Files of type** box. In the **Look in box**, select **EX0915**. Click **Open**.

**4.** In **Step 1** of the **Text Import Wizard** box, click the arrow of the scroll bar to view the data that will be imported.

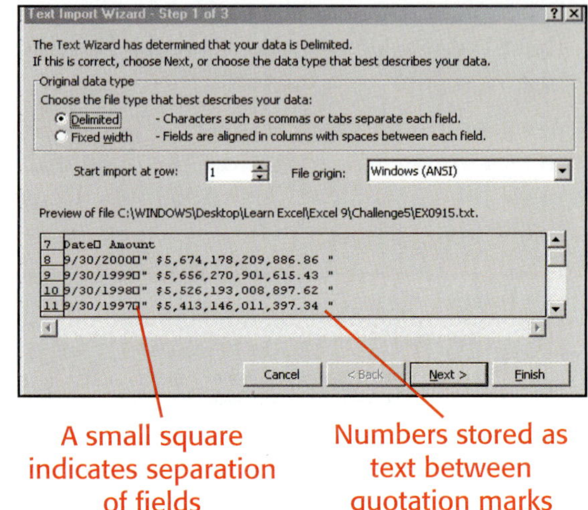



A small square indicates separation of fields

Numbers stored as text between quotation marks

**5.** Click **Next**. **Step 2** previews how the data will look when imported into your worksheet. Notice that Excel has removed the quotation marks from the numbers and correctly guessed that tabs were used as delimiters.

**6.** Click **Next**. **Step 3** allows you to set the data format. In the **Data preview** box, **General** appears above each column and the first column is highlighted. This dialog box allows you to format each column separately. The General format recognizes the date and currency formats automatically so you do not need to specify them in this box.

**7.** Click **Finish**. Confirm that **Existing worksheet** is selected, and click **OK**.

**8.** Save the file, print the worksheet, and close the workbook.

## C6—Copying Values Produced by Formulas

Creating and using formulas in Excel is an easy and accurate way to manipulate numbers. Once you create them, these formulas can even be copied to adjacent cells using the click and drag method. However, if you want to use the resulting values in another worksheet or application, using copy/paste will not work since it is the formula that gets copied and not the number. This results in a reference error message. Excel provides an option called Paste Special to copy values produced by formulas. Paste Special also allows you to copy formulas, formats, and comments.

In this exercise you use a workbook that contains two worksheets. One worksheet contains Michigan travel information that is broken down by regional areas. The SUM function is used in cells to total each region. The second worksheet contains headings but no numbers. You will copy information from the first worksheet and paste it into the second worksheet using Paste Special.

1. Start Excel and open **EX0916** from the folder of student files. Save the new workbook on your floppy disk as **EX0916-Challenge6**.

2. Select the **Regional Breakdown** worksheet, and click cell **D9**. Notice that the cell contains a SUM function. In fact, all cells located beneath **Total** headings contain SUM functions.

3. Select the **Region Totals** worksheet. Notice that the headings in the first column match the **Regional Breakdown** worksheet. The other four columns contain only region names.

4. Select the **Regional Breakdown** worksheet. Highlight cells **D9** through **D51**. Click the **Copy** button.

5. Select the **Region Totals** worksheet. Click cell **B5**.

6. Choose **Edit**, **Paste Special**. Under **Paste**, click **Values**. Click **OK**.

7. Repeat steps 4 through 6 to finish filling in the Region Totals worksheet. The following cell ranges need to be selected for each region: Midwest, **G9** through **G51**; South, **K9** through **K51**; and West, **N9** through **N51**.

8. Select cells **E5** through **E47** and add a right border.

9. Add your name to **A2** or a location your instructor prefers. Make any formatting changes your instructor requires. Save the file, and print the **Region Totals** worksheet.

10. Close the file and close Excel.

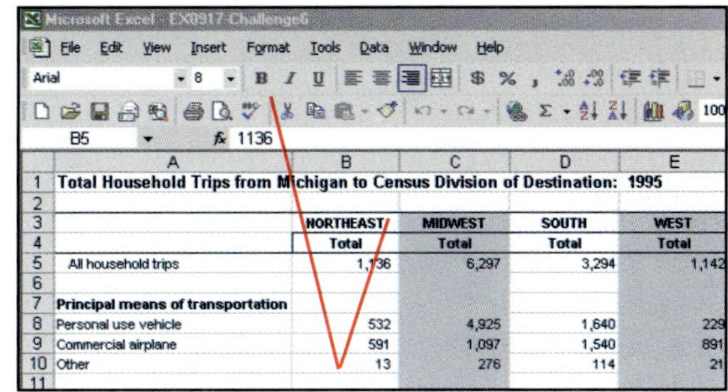

Value pasted, not the formula

Pick a topic that draws information from at least two different types of tables which are stored as text: a database table, or a table on a web page. Tables should come from at least two different types of files, not including Excel worksheets.

Criteria for grading will be:

1. Demonstrate the ability to import the tables into separate sheets in the same workbook.

2. In a separate sheet in the same workbook, create a summary sheet using 3-D references or the Consolidate option.

To complete the project:

- Submit the source files and/or the Web address for the tables you imported.

- Save your file on your own disk. Name it **EX0918-Importing**.

- Check with your instructor to determine if you should submit the project in electronic or printed form. If necessary, print out a copy of the worksheet to hand in.

# Lesson 10

## Templates and Macros

Task 1    Creating and Running Macros
Task 2    Editing Macros Using VBA Editor
Task 3    Creating a Custom Toolbar
Task 4    Adding and Removing Buttons from Toolbars
Task 5    Assigning a Macro to a Toolbar Button
Task 6    Customizing Menus
Task 7    Creating Templates
Task 8    Applying Templates

## INTRODUCTION

If you use Excel in the workplace, you may find yourself doing the same task repeatedly. It could be formatting the title of a worksheet to conform to company standards or performing a series of moves and operations on a range of cells. If you or your employees are spending time doing the same tasks over and over, you can automate these steps to make the operation faster and to assure that it is done the same way each time. One way to accomplish this objective is to record the steps in a *macro*. A macro in Excel is a program that is created automatically by recording a sequence of commands. It can be assigned to menus, buttons, or keys on the keyboard. You can edit the macro using the *Visual Basic Editor,* which is a text editor that allows you to see and edit the programming code that was created automatically when you recorded the macro.

If your work uses a collection of toolbar commands that are not usually available or are found on several different toolbars, you can create your own toolbar to make it easier to use these commands. You can *customize* the new toolbar by adding existing buttons to it. You can also create your own buttons and assign macros to them. Your toolbar can even have menus with a selection of options just like the standard menu toolbar.

Once you create a worksheet with its own macros and customized toolbars, you can use it as a *template*. Templates are workbooks that are already formatted with formulas in place. They only lack the specific information the user provides in certain cells.

In this lesson, you record a macro to format a title with a given font, color, alignment, and background. You edit the macro using the Visual Basic Editor to change the selected font. You also create a new toolbar to which you add a button that runs your macro. Then you add other buttons and a menu to the new toolbar. Finally, you save this worksheet as a template and apply it to a new worksheet.

## VISUAL SUMMARY

When you complete this entire lesson, you will have a worksheet that looks like this:

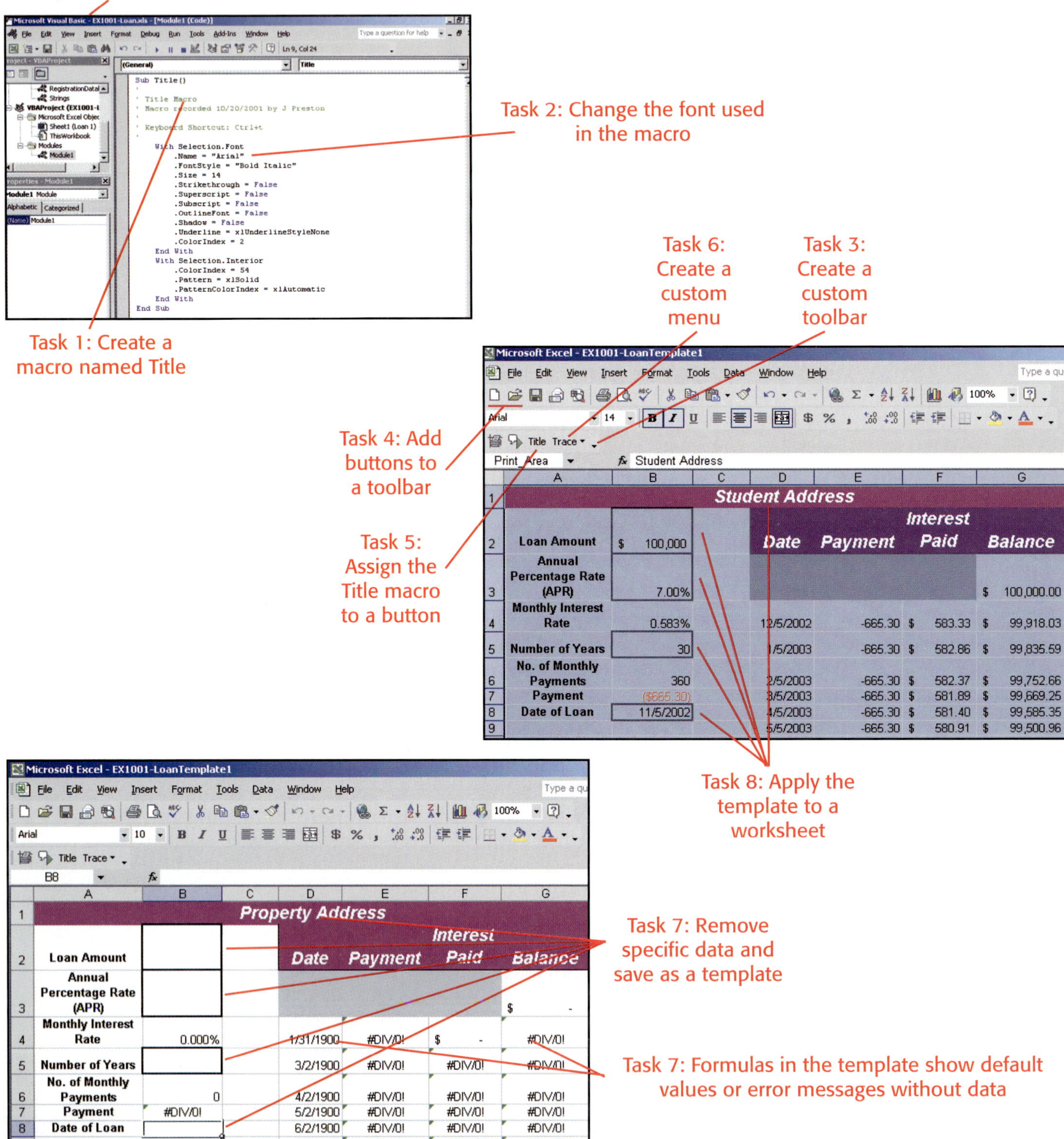

# Task 1
## CREATING AND RUNNING MACROS

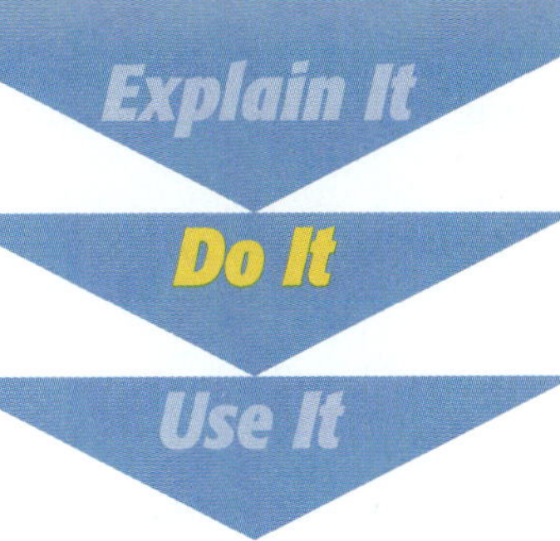


### Why would I do this?

Companies spend a lot of advertising money on creating a company name that customers recognize. The company name is represented by the same font and colors wherever it appears to take advantage of this investment. If you have to go through numerous steps to format the company name every time you type it into a worksheet, you can automate this process by using a macro.

If you know Visual Basic programming code, you can write sophisticated macros. Fortunately, Excel has a feature that writes this code for you. If you know how to do what you want in Excel, the program can create a macro for you by recording your actions. It is a good idea to practice the process you want to record so you can do it without errors while you are recording the macro.

In this task, you set the security level to allow the creation of macros and then record a macro to format the company name.

**1** Launch Excel and click the **Open** button. Find **EX1001** in the **Student** folder and open it.

*This worksheet calculates the repayment schedule for an amortized loan.*

Save the new file as **EX1001-Loan** on your disk.

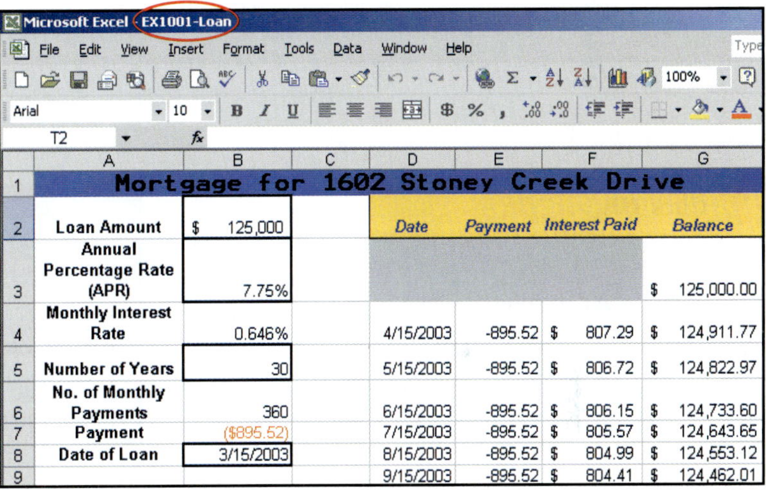

**2** Choose **Tools**, **Macro**, **Security** from the menu.

*The Security dialog box displays security options for the workbook.*

Click the **Security Level** tab, if necessary. Click the **Medium** option to select it.

*This allows you to create a macro and run it without allowing unknown macros to run without your approval.*

**CAUTION**

Macros are designed to help you with repetitive tasks, but be aware that malicious people can use macros to destroy your work. Macros that are written for these purposes are called *macro viruses*. If you receive a worksheet or other file from someone else and it has a macro in it, do not run the macro unless you know what it is supposed to do and you trust the creator of the file. If you are in doubt, scan the file with a security program to check for known macro viruses.

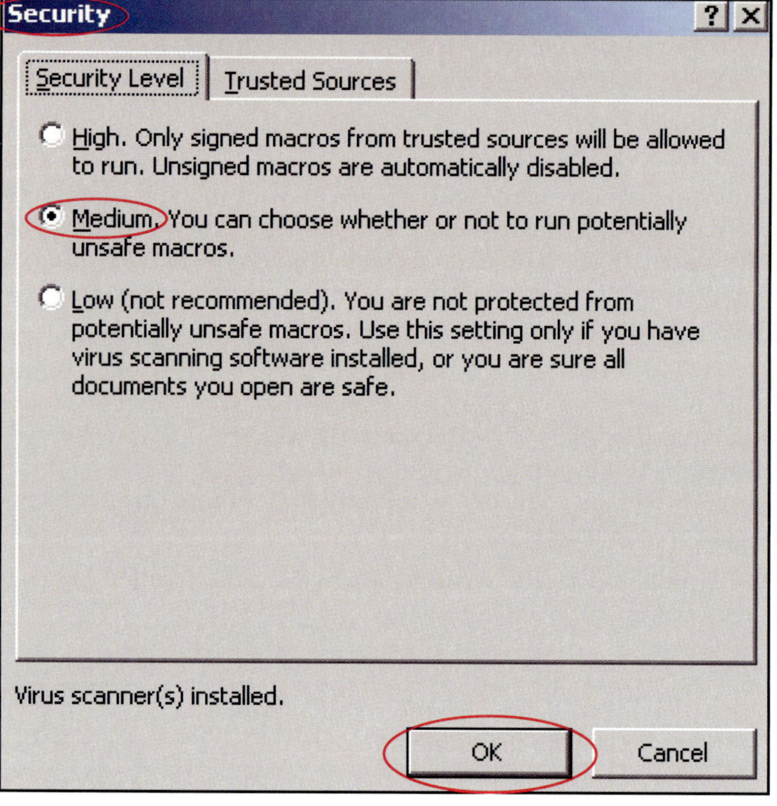

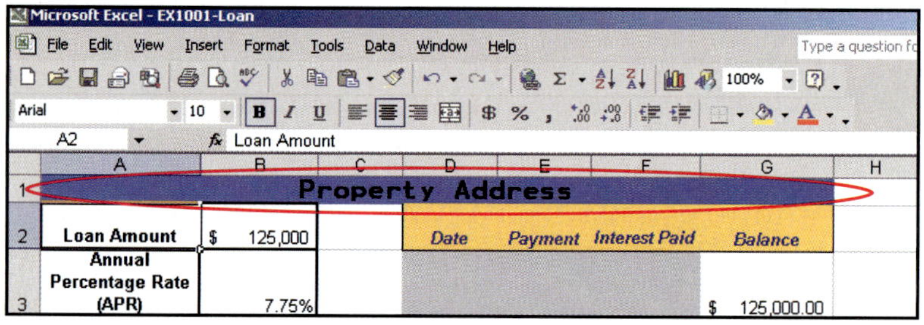

**3** Click **OK**.

*The Security dialog box closes.*

Click in **A1** to select cells **A1** through **G1,** type **Property Address**, and press ↵Enter.

*The marketing department wants document and worksheet titles to appear as white letters on a plum colored background using bold, italic, Bookman Old Style font.*

**4** Select the title in cells **A1** through **G1.** Choose **Tools**, **Macro**, **Record New Macro** from the menu.

*The Record Macro dialog box opens.*

Confirm that the default name is selected in the **Macro name** box and type **Title**. Confirm that **This Workbook** is selected in the **Store macro in** box. Select the **Shortcut key** box and type **t**.

*The macro is stored in the workbook with the name you typed. You can run it using the* Ctrl *key plus the letter t.*

Confirm that your name is used in the **Description** box or replace the default name with your name, if necessary.

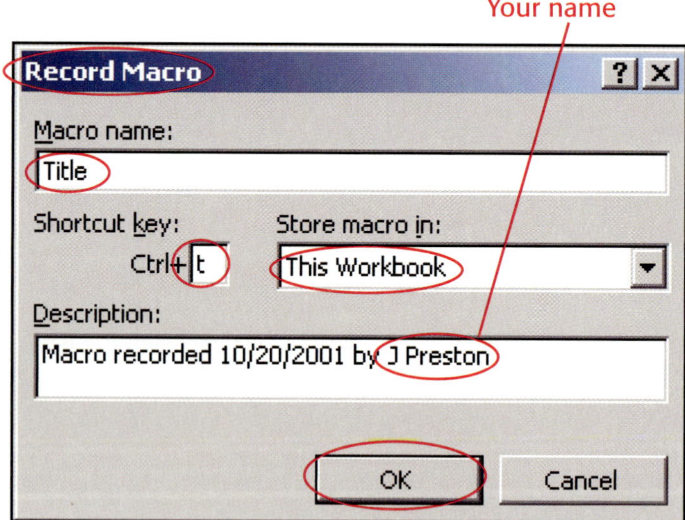

**5** Click **OK**.

*The Record Macro toolbar is displayed. The program is ready to record each step you take and write a program to reproduce them.*

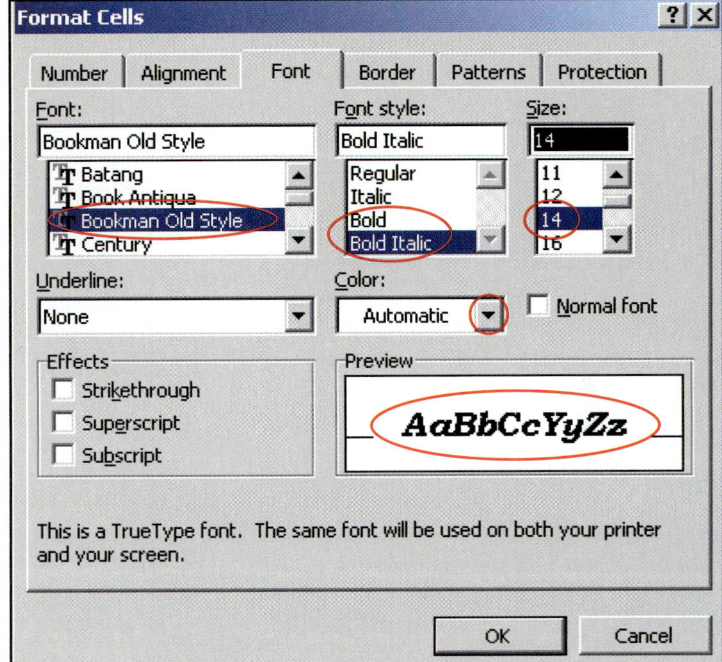

**6** Choose **Format**, **Cells** and click the **Font** tab.

*You can make all the formatting changes from this dialog box.*

    Change the **Font** to **Bookman Old Style**. Change the **Font style** to **Bold Italic**. Change the **Size** to **14**.

*An example is displayed in the Preview box.*

**7** Click the **Color** arrow to display the options for font colors. Click the White box.

*The font will be white. While the background is still white, the font cannot be seen in the preview box.*

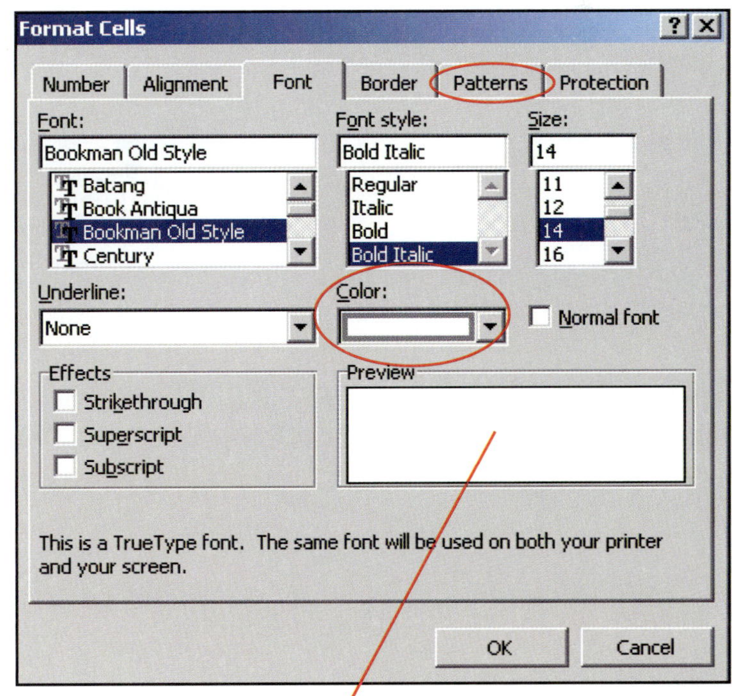

**8**  Click the **Patterns** tab. Click the plum color in the fourth row.

*This color contrasts with the white font.*

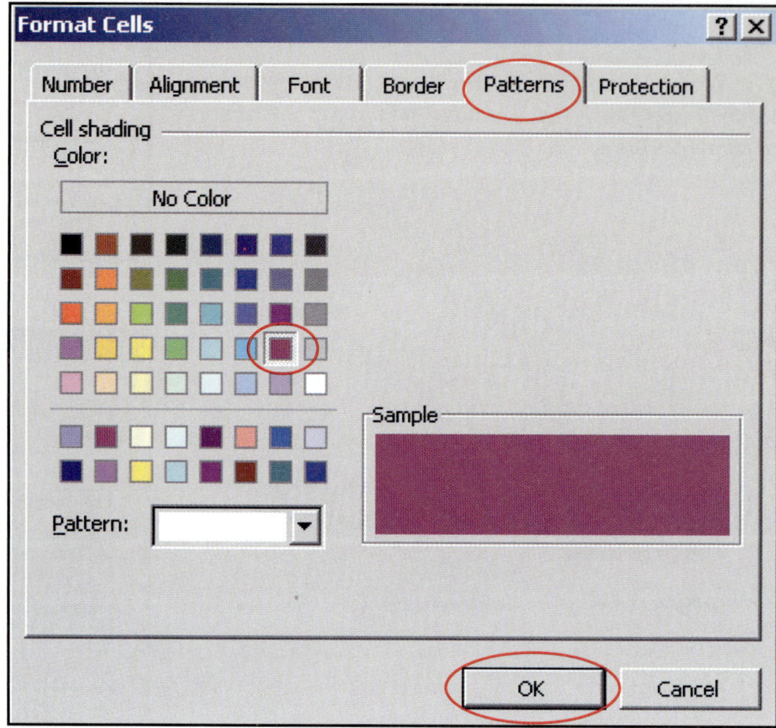

**9**  Click **OK**.

*The title is formatted and the Record Macro toolbar is displayed to indicate that you are recording these steps.*

Click the **Stop Recording** button on the Record Macro toolbar.

*The macro is recorded and named Title.*

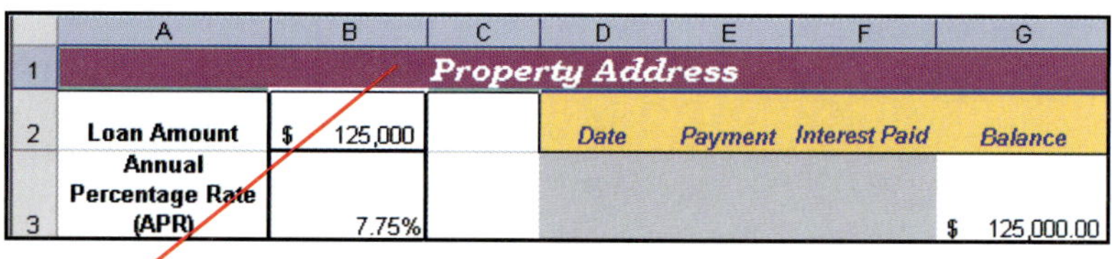



> **CAUTION**
>
> If you do not see the Stop Recording button on the Record Macro toolbar, the toolbar may be hidden behind another window. You can stop recording by selecting Tools, Macro, Stop Recording option.

**10** Scroll down and select cell **A365**. Type your name and press ↵Enter. Select the cell again.

*You can duplicate all the formatting steps required to format a title by running the macro.*

Confirm that your name is selected. Hold the Ctrl and press the letter **t**. If your name is wider than a single cell, select cell **A365** and as many cells to the right as necessary and click the **Merge and Center** button.

*Your name is formatted just like the title.*

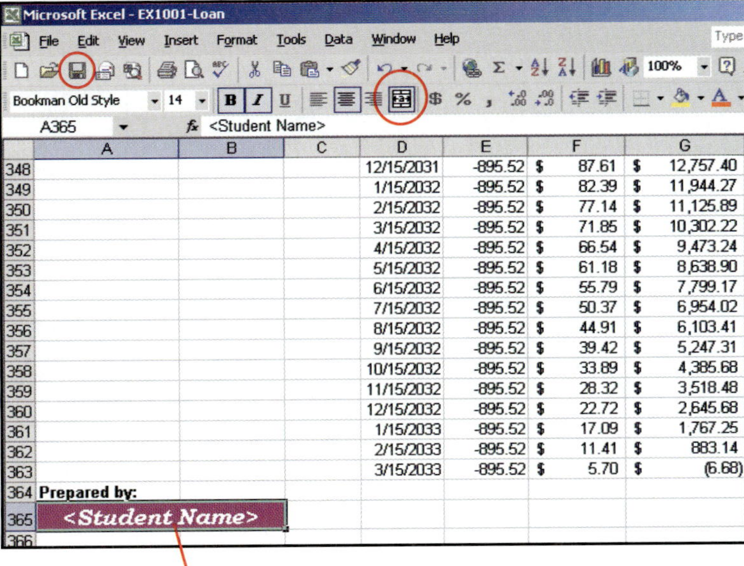

Formatted using the macro

QUICK TIP

If want to move to a particular cell in a large worksheet, you can enter the cell address in the Name box. If you want to go to the end of a long column, use Ctrl + End.

**11** Click the **Save** button to save your work.

*The macro is saved as part of the workbook and is available for use any time the workbook is open.*

# Task 2

## EDITING MACROS USING VBA EDITOR

### *Why would I do this?*

The macro you created in the previous task is a program written in **VBA** that you can edit. ***Visual Basic for Applications*** or VBA is a programming language and the VBA Editor is a program that allows you to edit the programs.

Learning how to write programs in Visual Basic could be a separate course and is beyond the scope of this text. You can use the VBA editor to make some simple changes to an existing program without knowing how to write the program yourself. Using the VBA editor also provides insight as to how macros work.

In this task, you learn how to open the Title macro in the VBA editor and change the font used for the title.

**1** Choose **Tools**, **Macro**, **Macros**. Select the **Title** macro and click the **Edit** button.

*The Microsoft Visual Basic editor starts and the EX1001-Loan.xls-Module1(code) window opens.*

> Maximize the **EX1001-Loan.xls-[Module1(code)]** window.

*This is the VBA program that runs when you run the Title macro. Notice the name of the font.*

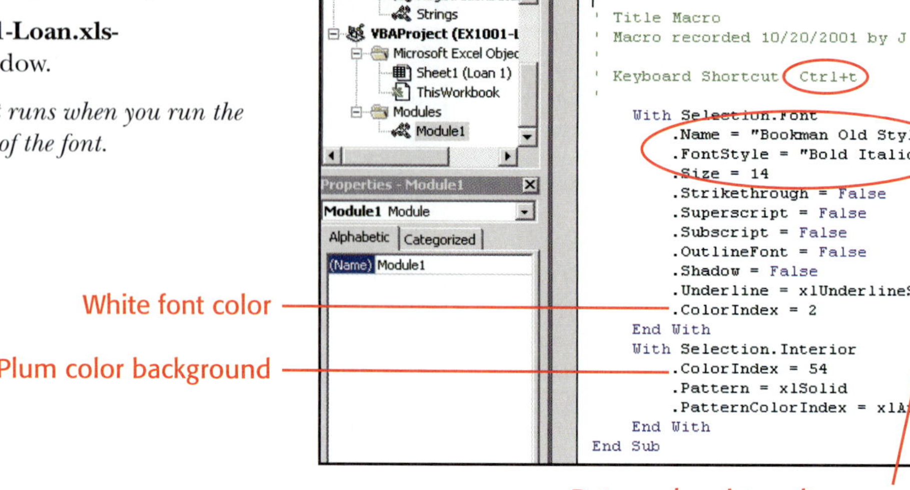


**2** Drag to select **"Bookman Old Style"**. Type **"Arial"**.

*Arial is the name of one of the fonts available in Excel.*

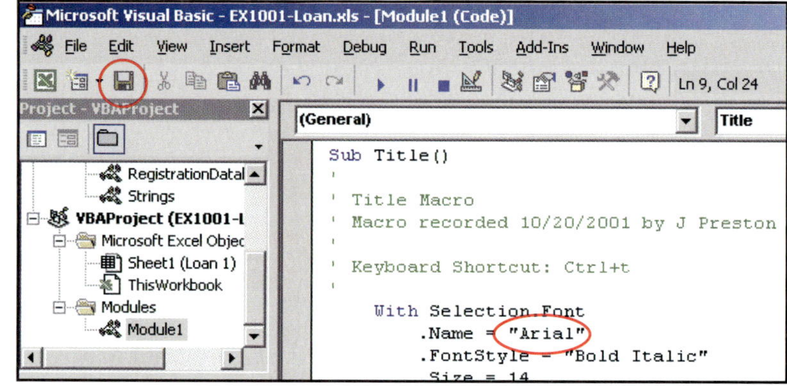

**3** Click the **Save** button. Close the VBA editor program.

*You can use the macro to apply the new formatting to selected cells.*

> Select the title in cells **A1** through **G1**. Hold the Ctrl key and press **t**.

*The same colors and font size are used but the font is now Arial. This does not affect the formatting of your name, which is still in Bookman Old Style.*

> Save the workbook.

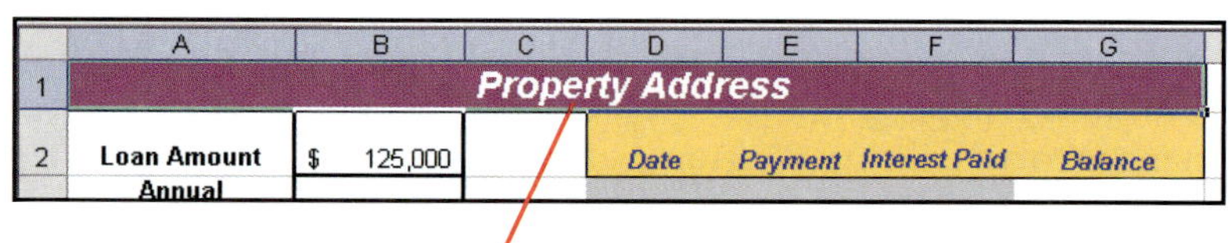


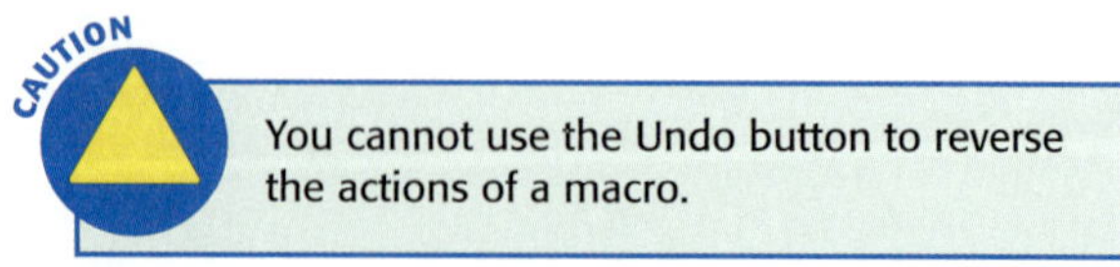

# Task 3

## CREATING A CUSTOM TOOLBAR

### *Why would I do this?*

There are many buttons available for use on toolbars that are not normally displayed on the Standard or Formatting toolbar. You can add or remove buttons from existing toolbars or create your own toolbar and add buttons to it. You can add buttons that run macros and you can also add menus.

In this task, you create a new toolbar that can display buttons that do not normally appear on the other toolbars.

**1** Choose **View**, **Toolbars**, **Customize**.

*The Customize dialog box is displayed.*

    Click the **Toolbars** tab.

*A list of toolbars is displayed. Checkmarks indicate toolbars that are currently displayed on the worksheet.*

Displayed toolbars

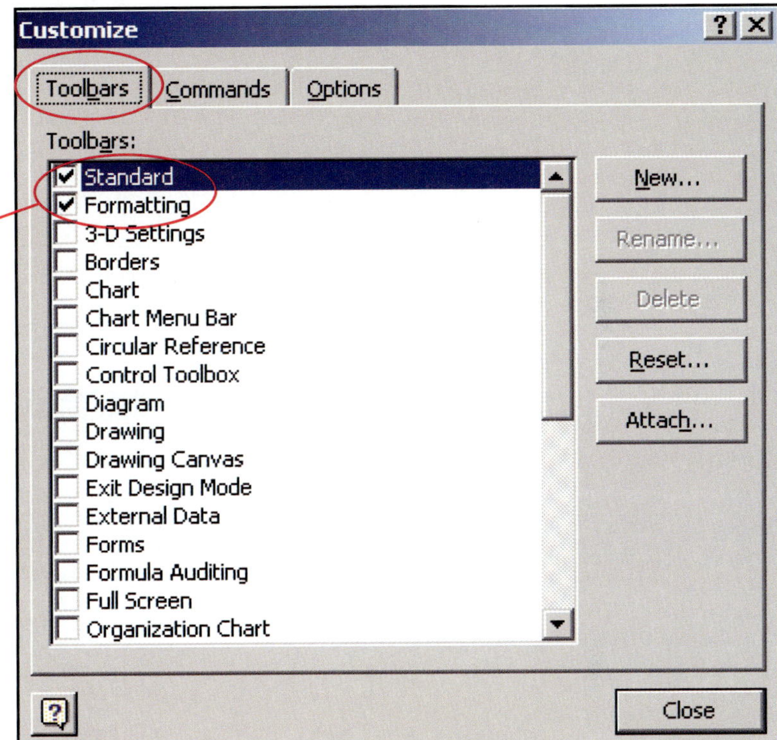

Your screen may show other toolbars that are open. For example, it is common for the Drawing toolbar to be open in Excel.

**2** Click the **New** button.

*The New Toolbar dialog box is displayed.*

Select the default name in the **Toolbar name** box and type your last name.

*The toolbar will be referred to by your last name.*

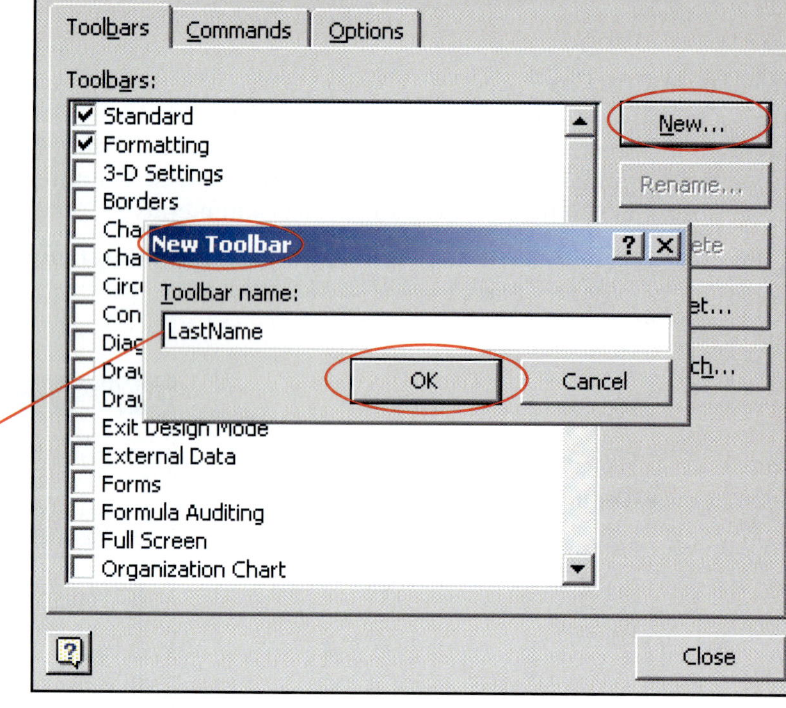


**3** Click the **OK** button.

*A short toolbar with no buttons is displayed on the worksheet and the toolbar name is added to the list. A check indicates the toolbar is displayed. The toolbar appears on the worksheet. This is called a floating toolbar.*

Leave this dialog box open for use in the next task.

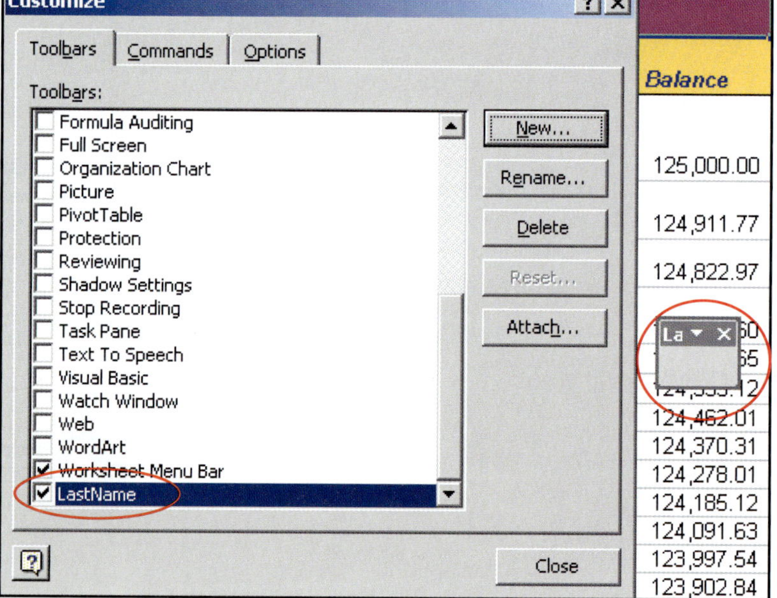

# Task 4
## ADDING AND REMOVING BUTTONS FROM TOOLBARS

### Why would I do this?

You can add many special buttons to your toolbar. If there is a function that you use often but have to go through several layers of menus to get to it, you can probably find a button for it to add to your toolbar.

In this task, you add the Set Print Area button and the Speak Cells button to your toolbar.

**1** Click the **Commands** tab in the **Customize** dialog box.

*The Categories pane on the left of the dialog box displays the categories of buttons. Buttons within the category are displayed on the right in the Commands pane.*

Choose the **File** category on the left and scroll down the commands to the button labeled **Set Print Area**.

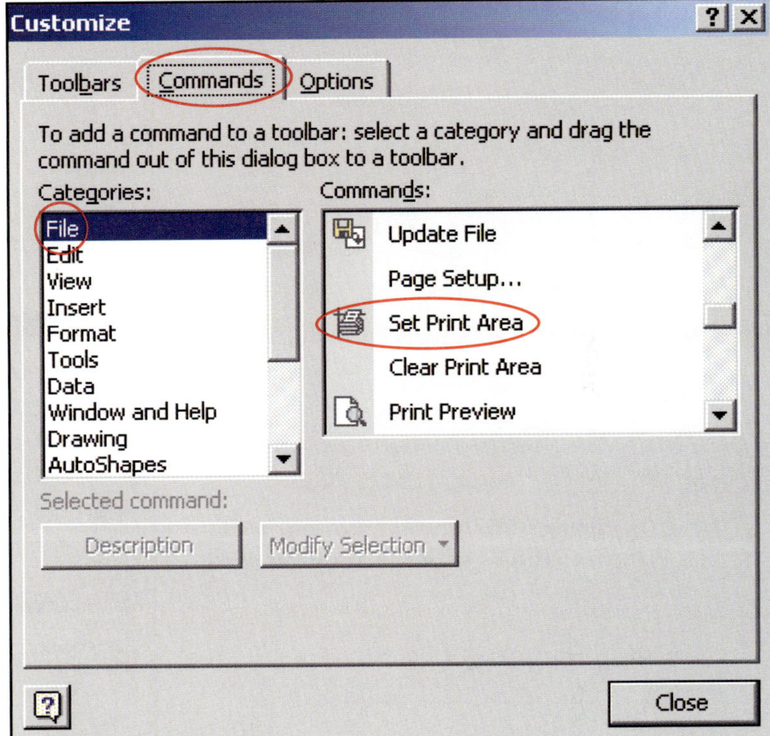



**CAUTION**

Your screen may show the Standard and Formatting toolbars on one row. You can move the formatting toolbar to a position under the standard toolbar by dragging the move handle of the formatting toolbar below the standard toolbar.

**2** Drag the **Set Print Area** button from the Commands pane to your toolbar.

*A vertical line on the toolbar indicates where the button will be placed.*

Release the mouse button and a copy of the Set Print Area button is added to the toolbar.

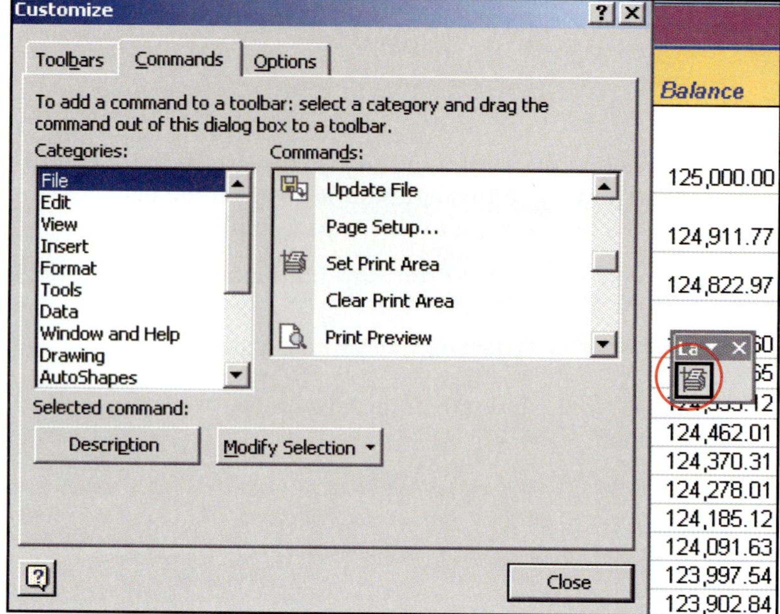

**3** Choose **Tools** in the **Categories** pane. Scroll down the list of commands to the **Speak Cells** button.

*If your computer has speakers and they are turned on, Office XP will speak the contents of selected cells.*

Drag the **Speak Cells** button onto your toolbar. Place it to the right of the **Set Print Area** button.

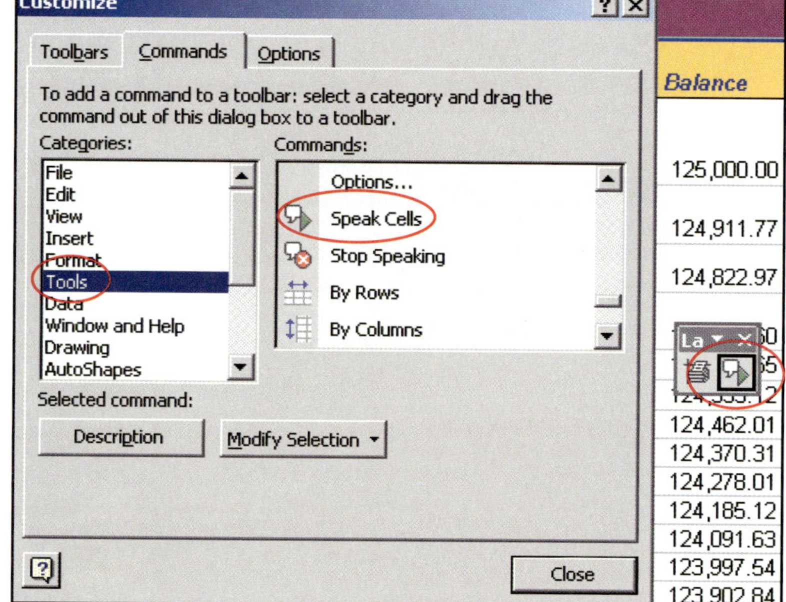

**CAUTION**

The new toolbar is small and may be in a different location on your screen.

**4** Drag the **Stop Speaking** button onto your toolbar.

*The stop speaking command cancels the Speak Cells command. The stop speaking command can be used if you select a large range of cells and do not wish to wait until they are all spoken. Pressing the* Esc *key accomplishes the same thing. This button is not as useful as the Speak Cells button, so it would be a good one to remove.*

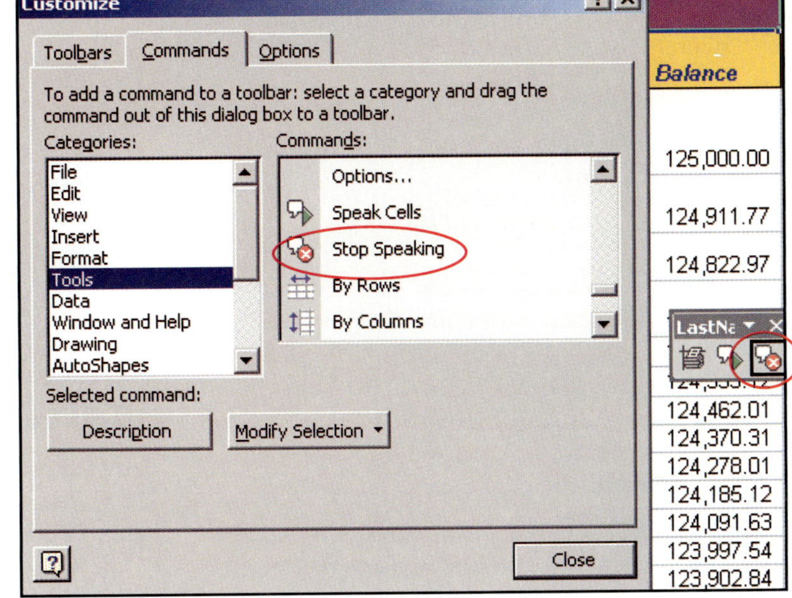

**5** Move the mouse pointer onto the **Stop Speaking** button. Drag the button off of the toolbar onto any other part of the screen except another toolbar. Release the mouse button.

*The Stop Speaking button is removed from the toolbar. You can use this method to add or remove command buttons from existing toolbars as well as toolbars you create.*

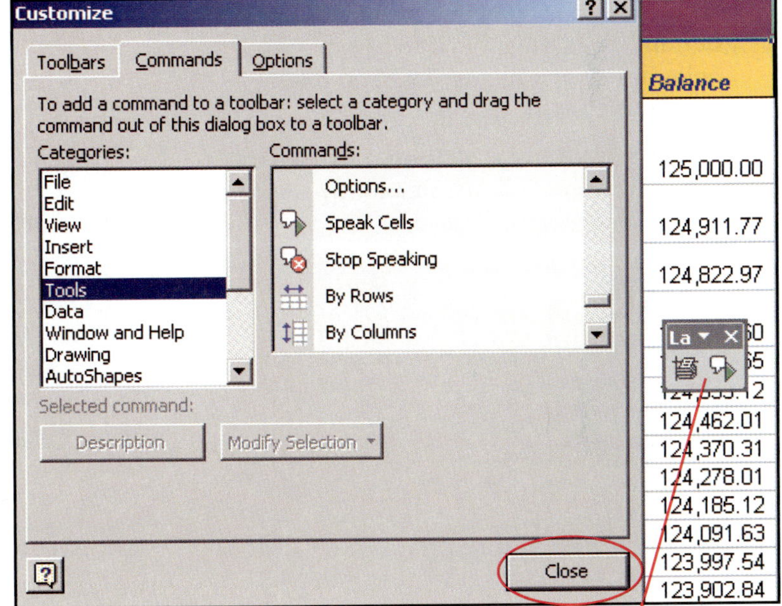

**6** Click the **Close** button on the Customize dialog box.

*The new toolbar is active.*

Select cells **A2** through **B8**. Click the **Set Print Area** button.

*A dotted line is displayed around the selected area.*

Click the **Print Preview** button.

*The range of cells you selected is now the print area.*

**7** Click the **Close** button on the toolbar. Confirm that cells **A2** through **B8** are still selected and click the **Speak Cells** button.

*If you have speakers attached to your computer and they are turned on, you hear a computer-generated voice speak the content of the cells.*

Move the mouse pointer onto the title bar of the new toolbar but not onto one of the buttons. Drag the toolbar to a point just below the formatting toolbar and release the mouse.

*The toolbar becomes a **docked toolbar** below the formatting toolbar. Docked toolbars are located at the top, bottom, or either side of the window.*

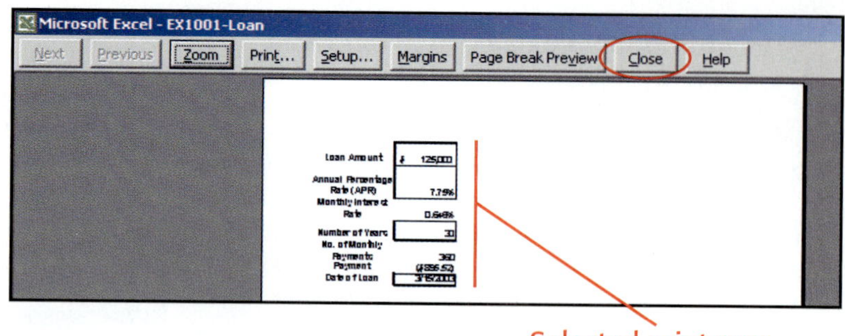


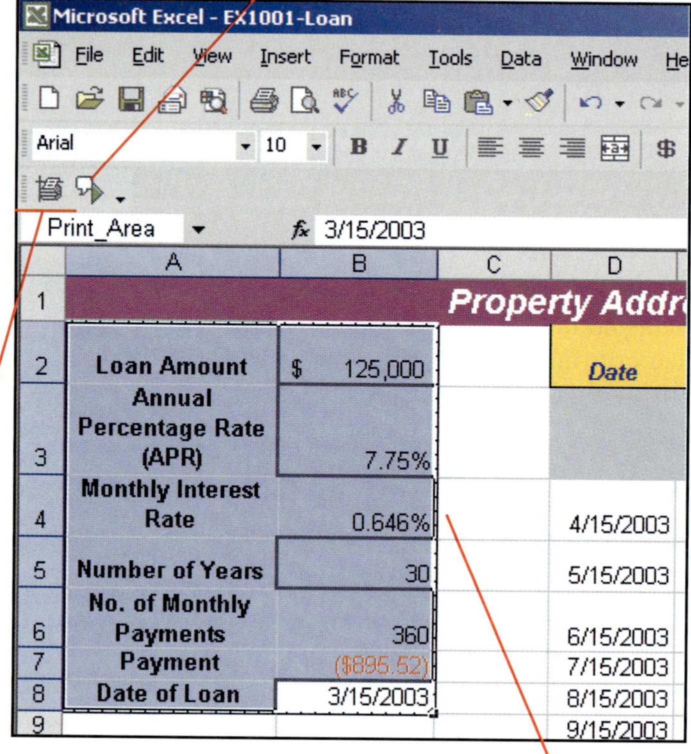


**CAUTION**

The Speak Cells feature will try to pronounce abbreviations like APR and No. as if they were words. This could be confusing if someone was relying on this feature to determine the content of cells.

# Task 5
## ASSIGNING A MACRO TO A TOOLBAR BUTTON

### Why would I do this?

A toolbar button can run a macro. This is faster than using the menus and doesn't require that you remember a keyboard shortcut.

In this task, you learn how to add a custom button to the toolbar and use it to run the Title macro.

**1** Choose **View**, **Toolbars**, **Customize**. Click the **Commands** tab if necessary. Scroll down the list of **Categories** and select **Macros**.

*Two commands are listed in the Commands pane.*

Drag the **Custom Button** from the **Commands** pane to a position just to the right of the **Speak Cells** button on your new toolbar. Release the mouse button.

*The Custom button is placed on your toolbar and it is still selected.*

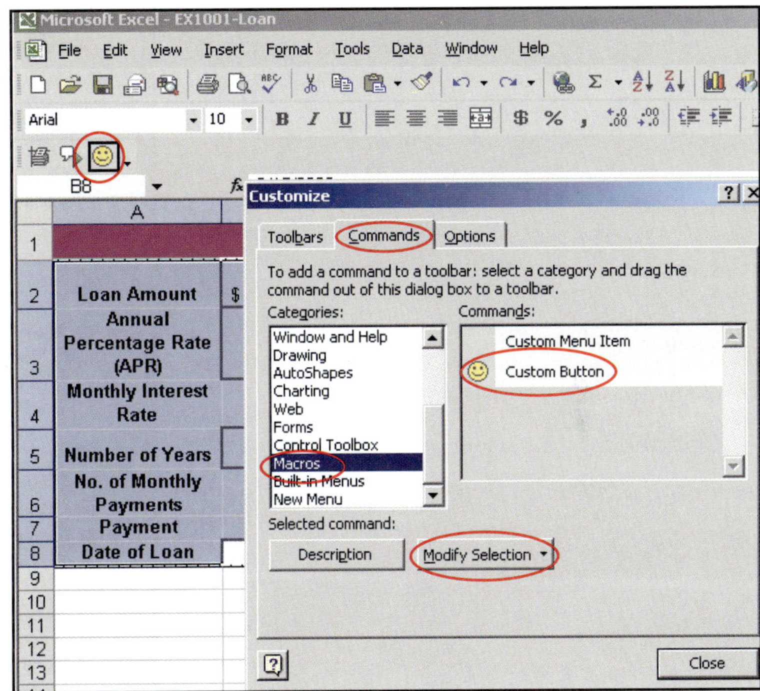

**2** Click the **Modify Selection** button.

*A menu of options is displayed.*

Select the default name in the **Name** box and type **Title**.

*The new name of the button is Title.*

> **IN DEPTH**
>
> A *hotkey* is a letter in a menu or button name that can be used in place of clicking on the menu or button item. To turn one of the letters in your button name into a hotkey, place an ampersand, &, to the left of the letter when you type the name of the button in the Name box. Check the other menus displayed on the screen to be sure that the letter you want to use is not a hotkey in another menu. To use a hotkey, hold the Alt key and press the hotkey letter on the keyboard.

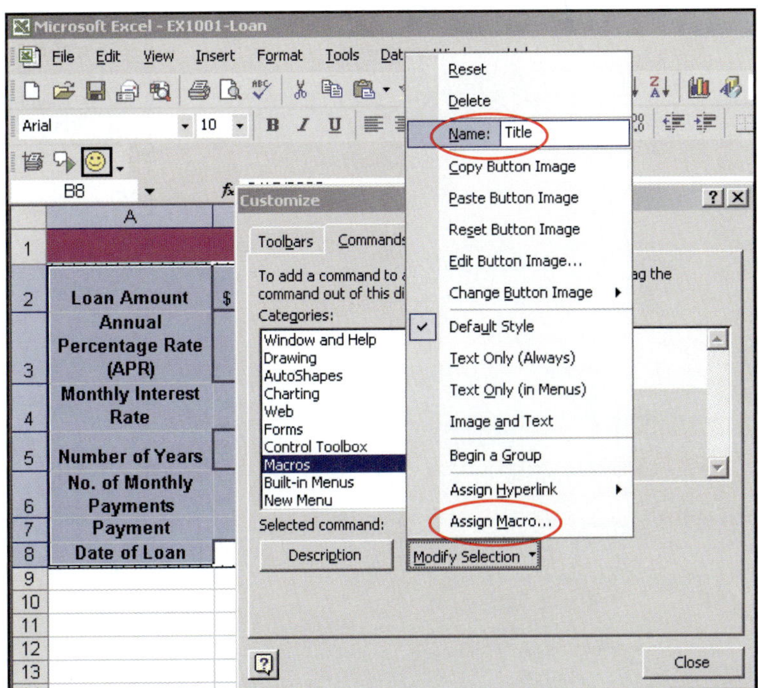

**3** Choose **Assign Macro**.

*The Assign Macro dialog box is displayed and existing macros are listed on the Macro Name pane.*

    Click **Title** to select it.

*The Title macro is assigned to the custom button.*

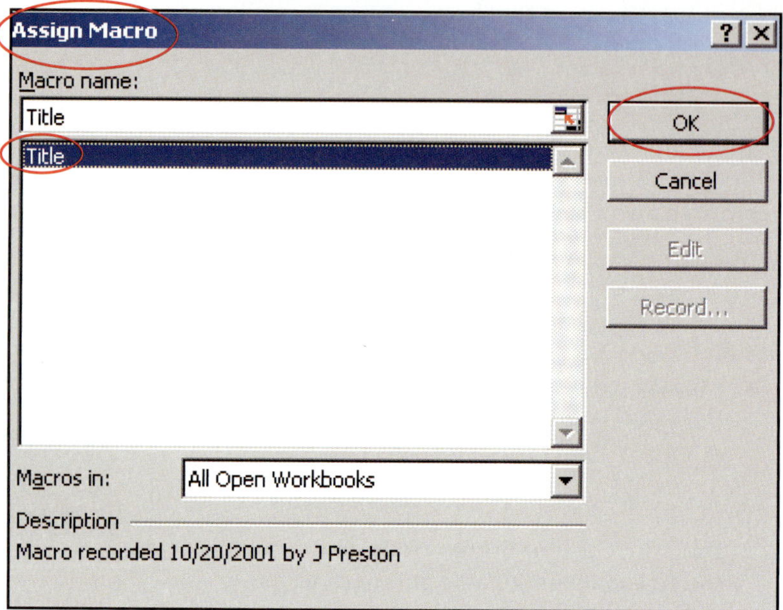


**4** Click **OK**.

*The Assign Macro dialog box closes.*

    Click the **Modify Selection** button.

*The menu of modifications is displayed.*

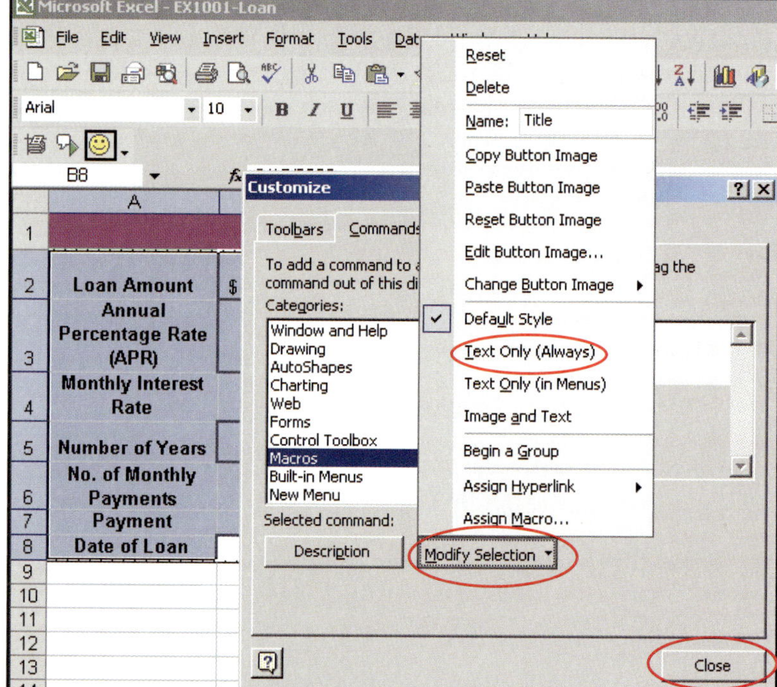

**5** Click **Text Only (Always)**.

*The button displays the name instead of the icon.*

Click the **Close** button on the Customize dialog box.

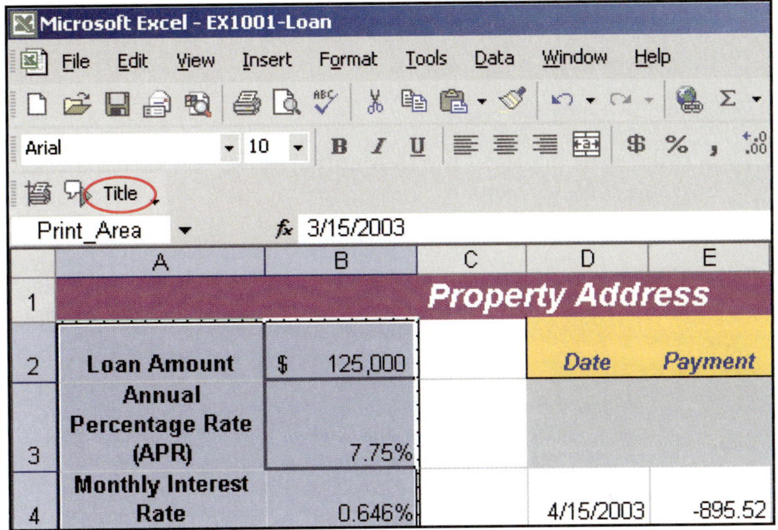

**6** Select cells **D2** through **G2** and click the new **Title** button on your toolbar.

*The column headings are reformatted to match the title.*

Adjust the width of column **E** to display the larger heading. Save the workbook and leave it open for the next task.

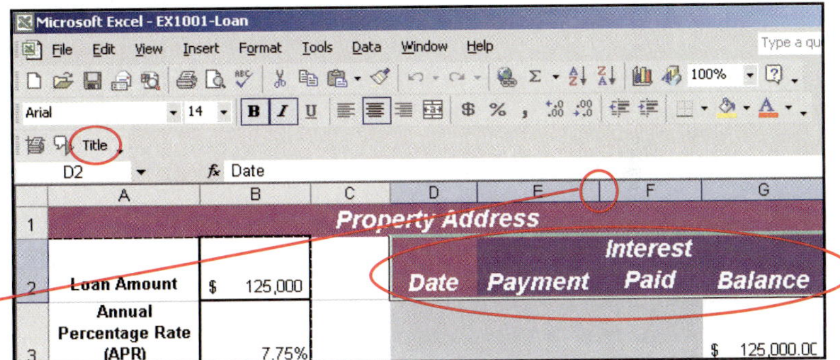


# Task 6
## CUSTOMIZING MENUS

### Why would I do this?

You can add your own menus to toolbars or customize existing menus. First you add the menu item to the toolbar and then you populate it with command buttons. Generally, you use menus when you have a group of related commands. Just like adding buttons, you may want to customize a menu for frequently used tasks that do not otherwise appear on buttons.

In this task, you add a menu to your toolbar that has command buttons designed to help you troubleshoot formulas.

**1** Choose <u>**View**</u>, <u>**Toolbars**</u>, <u>**Customize**</u>. Click the <u>**Commands**</u> tab, if necessary.

*The Customize dialog box opens.*

Scroll down the list in the **Categories** pane and select **New Menu**.

*The New Menu command is displayed in the Commands pane.*

**QUICK TIP**

To view the Customize dialog box in fewer steps, right-click on one of the toolbars and choose Customize from the shortcut menu.

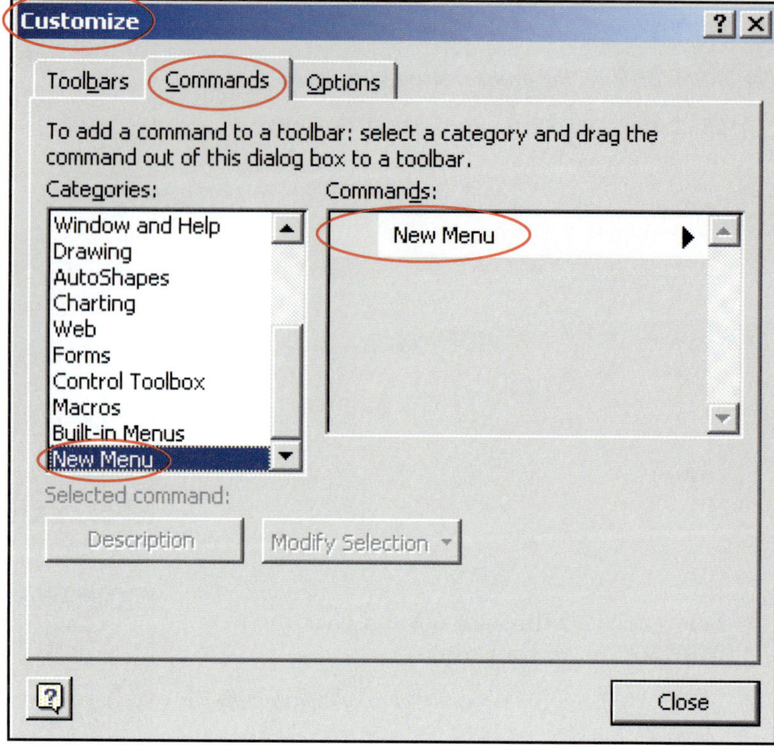

**2** Drag the **New Menu** command from the **Commands** pane onto your toolbar. Place it at the right end of the toolbar.

*The New Menu is part of the toolbar.*

Click the arrow on the **New Menu** button on your toolbar.

*A blank menu item is displayed below the New Menu button. The first command button will be placed in this area.*

First menu item

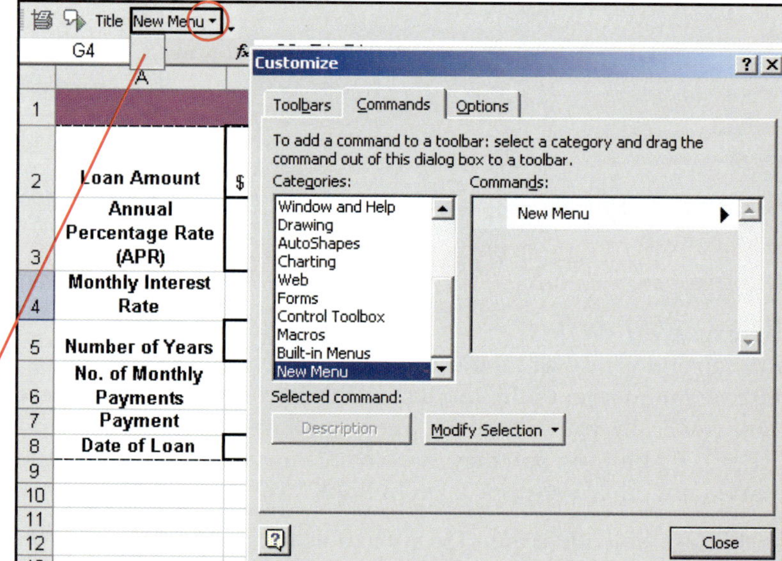

**3** Select **Tools** in the **Categories** pane. Scroll down the list of commands in the **Commands** pane and locate **Trace Precedents**.

*You can add a menu item by dragging a command button onto the blank area.*

Drag the **Trace Precedents** command to the blank area below the **New Menu** button.

*The first menu item is Trace Precedents. You can add more command buttons by dragging them from the Commands pane to the menu.*

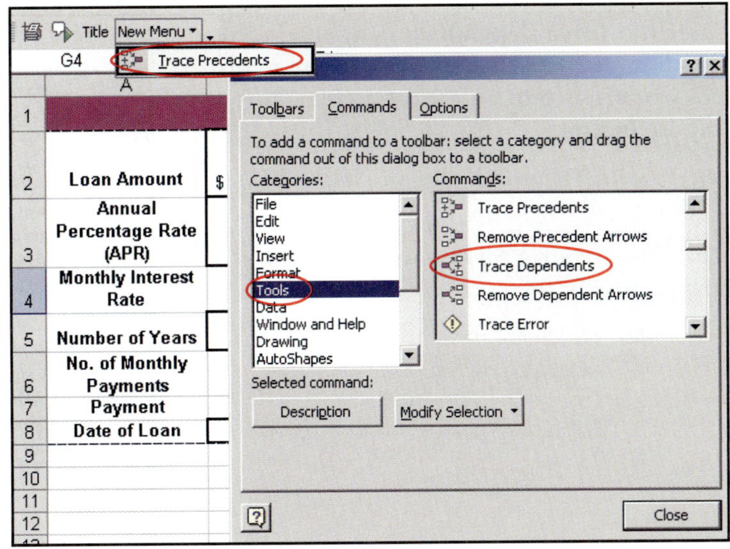

**4** Drag **Remove Precedent Arrows** from the command list to the new menu. Position the pointer to drop the **Remove Precedent Arrows** below the **Trace Precedents** menu item.

*A horizontal line indicates where the new menu item will appear in the list.*

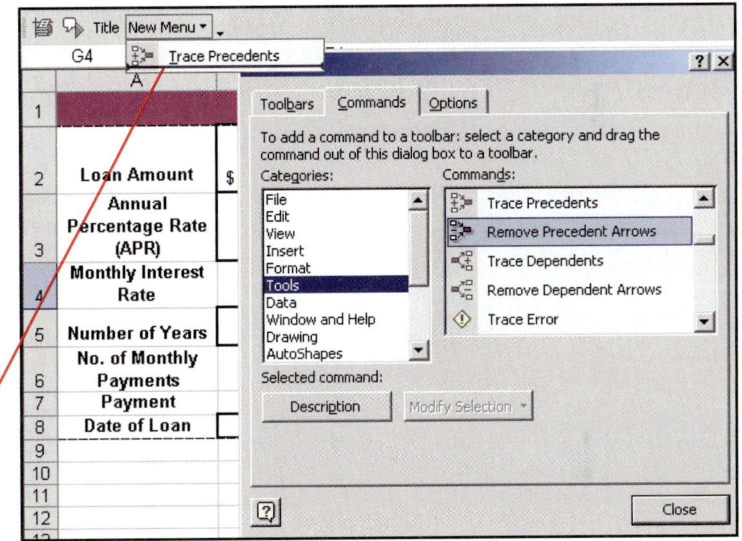


**5** Release the mouse button. The **Remove Precedent Arrows** command is the second menu option.

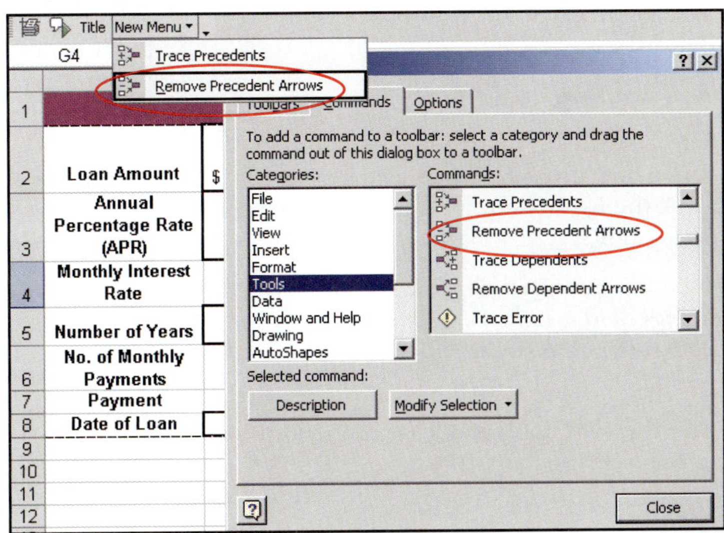

**6** Drag the **Trace Dependents** command to a position between the other two menu items so that it is second on the list. Release the mouse button.

*You can place new commands anywhere in the list of menu items.*

Drag the **Remove All Arrows** command to the bottom of the list of menu options.

*In this example, you do not need the Remove Precedent Arrows option. You will remove it in the next step.*

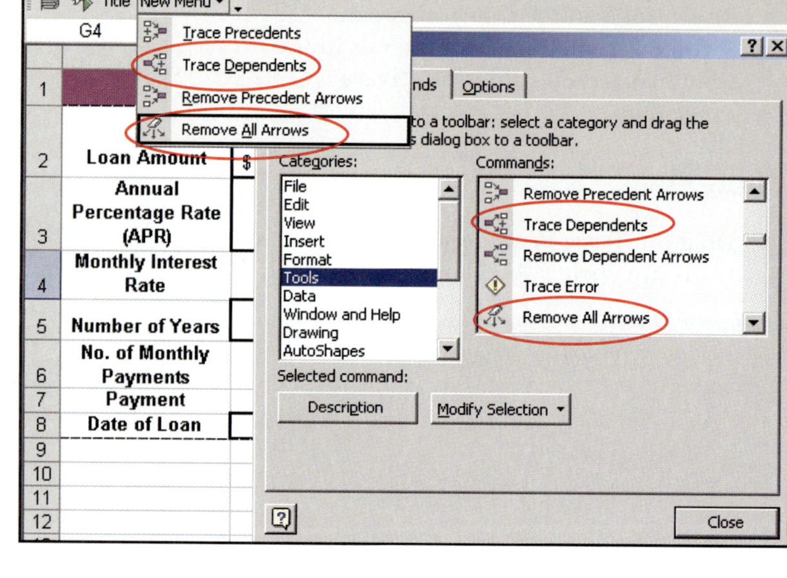

**7** Move the pointer onto the **Remove Precedent Arrows** item in the new menu. Drag the menu item off the menu.

*You can remove an item from the menu by dragging it off the menu. It does not matter where you drag it as long as it is off the menu and not on another toolbar.*

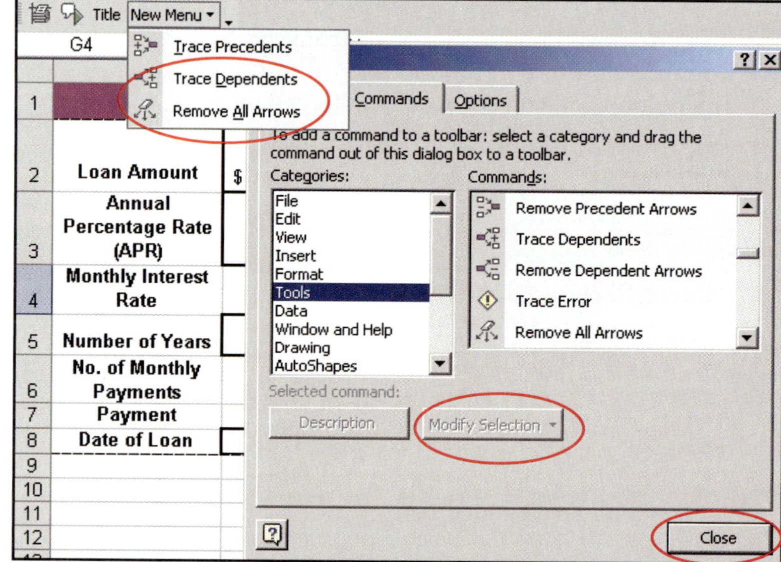

**8** Click the **New Menu** button on your toolbar to select it. Click the **Modify Selection** button.

*A shortcut menu appears.*

Select the default name for the menu in the **Name** box and type **Trace**. Press ⏎Enter. Click the **Close** button on the Customize dialog box.

*The new name appears on the menu bar. Keep the menu names short to conserve space on the menu bar. You will learn to use these commands to audit formulas in Lesson 11.*

Save the workbook and leave it open for use in the next task.

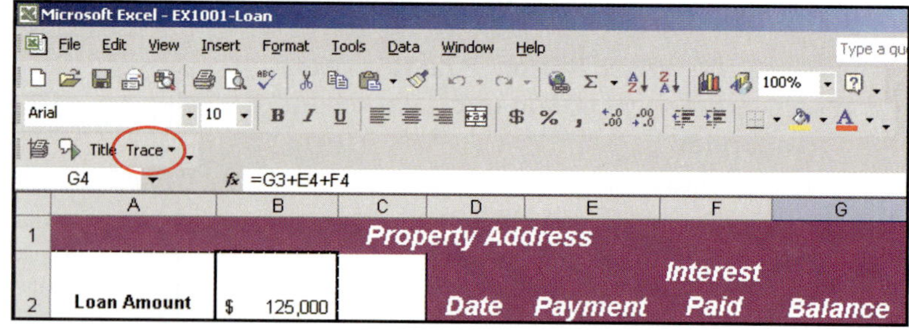

# Task 7
## CREATING TEMPLATES

### Why would I do this?

If you invest a lot of time designing a workbook and creating toolbars and macros to do a particular task, you can use it again and share it with others who do similar work. You can remove the data but leave the formulas and formatting. You can also attach custom toolbars. The resulting workbook can be used as a template. Templates are workbooks that contain formulas, formatting, and other special features that allow you to simply enter specific data to achieve a sophisticated result.

There are two common ways to use a workbook as a template. The first is to save the workbook normally. Whenever you want to use it, you locate the file, open it, add the data, and save it with a different name. The problem with this method is that you may accidentally save the file without changing the name and overwrite the original file with new data. The second method is to save the file as a template file type in a special folder that the Windows operating system uses for templates. Your file will display with the other template files and is not easily overwritten when you save the file.

In this task, you learn how to attach a toolbar and save a workbook as an Excel template. You also learn how to save the file as a normal workbook that you can use as a template.

**1** Delete the values in cells **B2**, **B3**, **B5**, and **B8**.

*The values that determine the specifics of a particular loan are removed. The formulas that depend upon these values show errors, zeros, or dates that start at the beginning of the century.*

Loan values deleted



| | A | B | C | D | E | F | G |
|---|---|---|---|---|---|---|---|
| 1 | | | | Property Address | | | |
| 2 | Loan Amount | | | Date | Payment | Interest Paid | Balance |
| 3 | Annual Percentage Rate (APR) | | | | | | $   - |
| 4 | Monthly Interest Rate | 0.000% | | 1/31/1900 | #DIV/0! | $   - | #DIV/0! |
| 5 | Number of Years | | | 3/2/1900 | #DIV/0! | #DIV/0! | #DIV/0! |
| 6 | No. of Monthly Payments | 0 | | 4/2/1900 | #DIV/0! | #DIV/0! | #DIV/0! |
| 7 | Payment | #DIV/0! | | 5/2/1900 | #DIV/0! | #DIV/0! | #DIV/0! |
| 8 | Date of Loan | | | 6/2/1900 | #DIV/0! | #DIV/0! | #DIV/0! |
| 9 | | | | 7/2/1900 | #DIV/0! | #DIV/0! | #DIV/0! |

**CAUTION**

If you are working in a laboratory that restores the computers to original settings on a regular basis, the security setting may have been changed since you set it to Medium in Task 1. If you cannot run your macro because the security setting is High, return to Task 1 and follow the directions to set it to Medium for this task.

**2** Choose **View**, **Toolbars**, **Customize**. Click the **Toolbars** tab, if necessary. Scroll down and select your new toolbar.

*You can attach a toolbar to a workbook so that it will be available to someone else.*

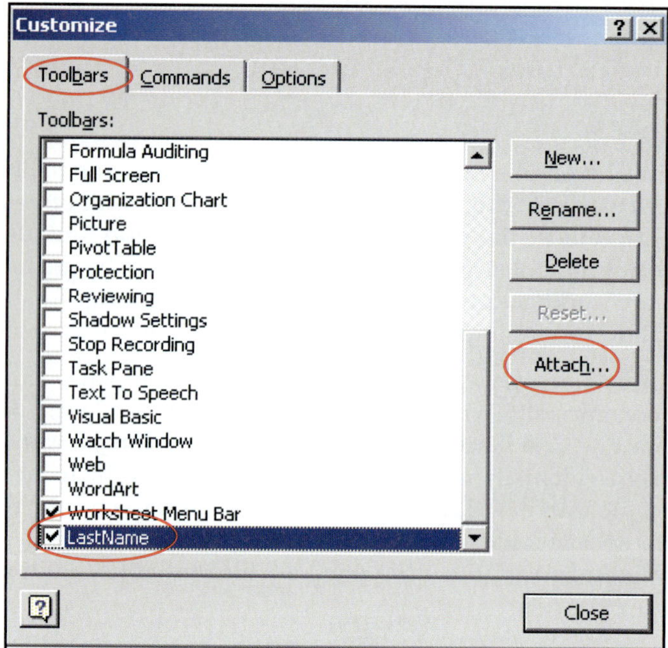

**IN DEPTH**

Toolbars are normally saved on a computer rather than in a workbook. If you send the workbook to another person who will use it on a different computer, you must attach the toolbar to the workbook to make it available to them. The same is true of templates that are shared by people who work on other computers.

**3** Click the **Attach** button.

*A list of custom toolbars is displayed on the left.*

Select your toolbar and click the **Copy** button.

*Your toolbar will be attached to the workbook.*

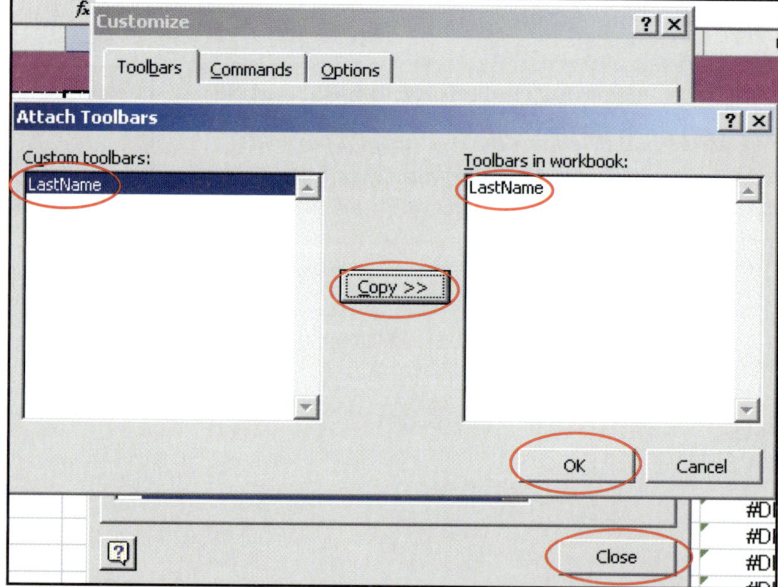

**4** Click **OK**.

*Your toolbar is attached.*

Click the **Close** button.

*You can save this workbook as a template that you can use whenever you need to calculate a loan repayment schedule.*

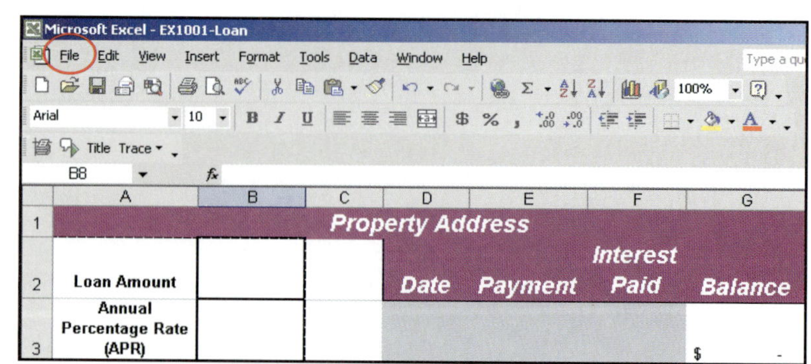

**5** Choose **File**, **Save As**. Click the arrow next to the **Save as type** box and choose **Template**. Change the name of the file to **EX1001-LoanTemplate**.

*The Templates folder is automatically displayed in the Save in box.*

Click the drop-down arrow next to the **Save in** box.

*The location of the Templates folder for your computer is displayed. The location of this folder depends on the operating system so your screen may not match the figure. Leave this folder selected.*

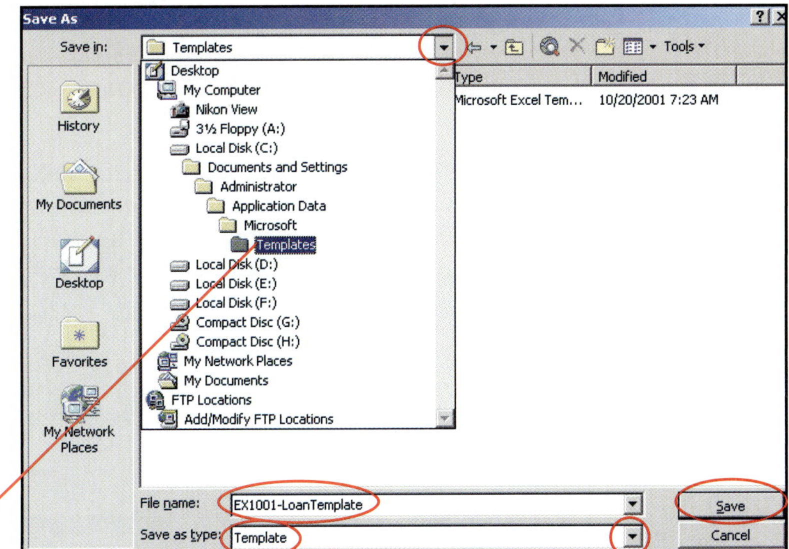




**6** Click the **Save** button.

*The workbook is saved as a template. If you do not have permission to save files to this folder, you may get an error message. Proceed to the next step.*

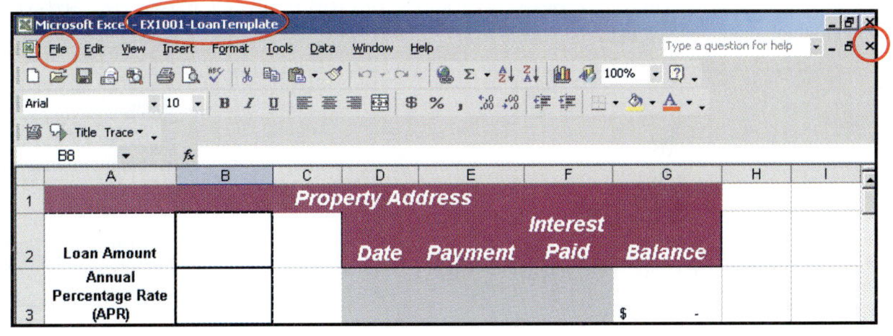

**7** Choose **File**, **Save As**. Choose the folder where you keep the other solution files for this book. Change the file type to **Microsoft Excel Workbook** and click the **Save** button.

*Your workbook is stored with your other files as a normal workbook. If you are not allowed to save files in the template folder, you can open this file from your folder as you would a normal file.*

Close the workbook but leave Excel open.

# Task 8
## APPLYING TEMPLATES

### Why would I do this?

Templates are designed to be used repeatedly without accidentally overwriting them. When you create a new workbook using a template, the Save command does not save the new workbook over the template but opens the Save As dialog box and automatically chooses the workbook file type. If you were not able to save your template to the Templates folder on a shared computer, you may use a normal workbook as a template but you must remember to save it with a different name to avoid overwriting the original file.

In this task, you learn how to apply a template and save the resulting workbook without changing the template.

**1** Start Excel. Choose **File**, **New**.

*The New Workbook task pane opens.*

**CAUTION**

If you were able to save your template to the Templates folder on your computer, the EX1001-LoanTemplate file will be available from General Templates. The EX1001-LoanTemplate file may be listed by name under the New from template heading in the task pane. However, it may not be listed if you have changed computers since you did Task 7. If you cannot find the EX1001-LoanTemplate file in General Templates, open the file from your folder and go to step 3.

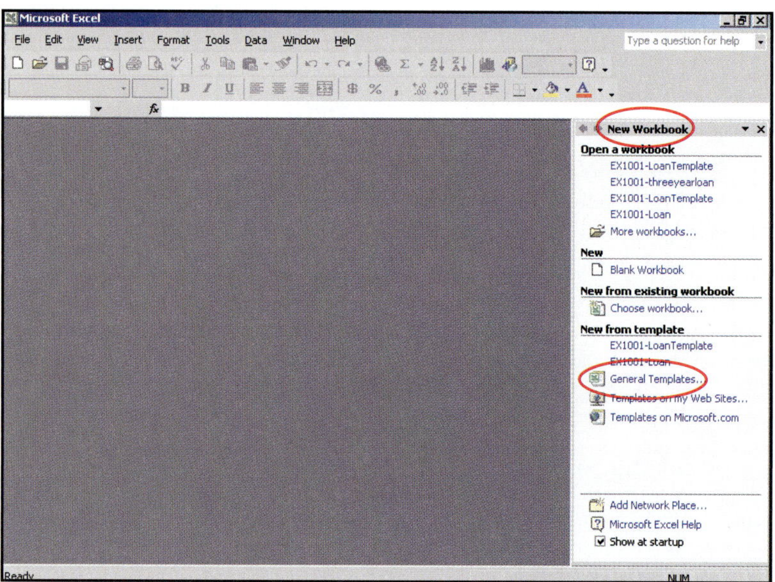

**2** Click **General Templates**. Click the **General** tab, if necessary.

*If you were able to save your template to the Templates folder on your computer, it will be listed in this window.*

Click the icon that represents **EX1001-LoanTemplate**.

*The selected template is applied to a new workbook.*

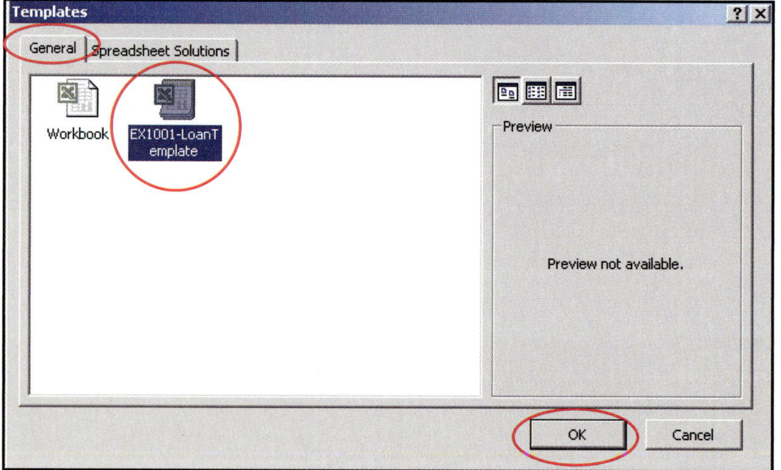

**3** Click **OK**.

*If your security setting is still Medium, a dialog box opens that allows you to enable macros.*

Click the **Enable Macros** button.

*A new workbook opens with the formatting and formulas from the template.*

If your custom toolbar is not displayed, choose **View**, **Toolbars**. Select your toolbar from the list.

**4** Select **B2** and type **100000**. Select **B3** and type **7**. Select **B5** and type **30**. Select **B8** and enter today's date.

*The formulas calculate the loan.*

Select the title in cells **A1** through **G1** and enter your personal home address.

*A loan repayment schedule is ready to print.*

**5** Select **A1** through **G39**.

*The loan information and three years of payments are selected.*

Click the **Set Print Area** button on your custom toolbar.

*The print area is set.*

Click the **Print** button.

*A copy of the first three years of the loan repayment schedule is printed.*

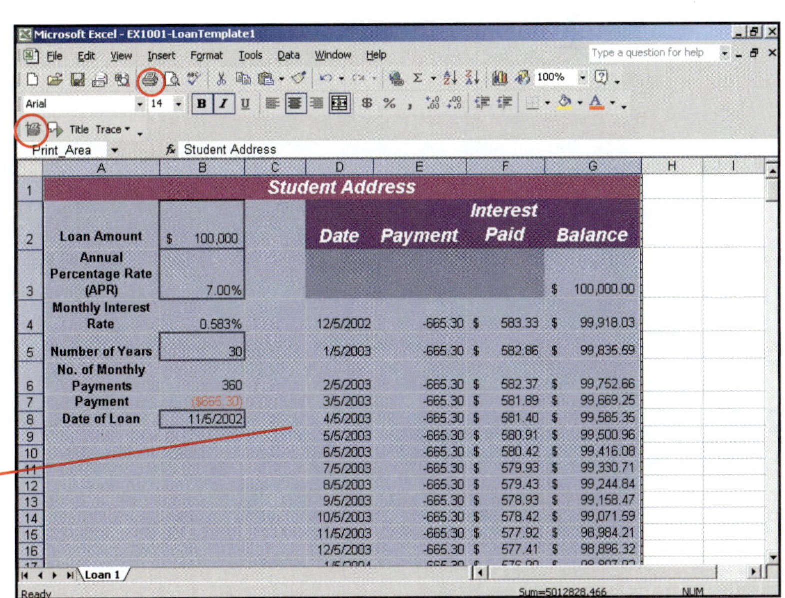

 **6** Choose **File**, **Save As**.

*The Save As dialog box opens and the Save as type box is automatically set to Microsoft Excel Workbook.*

Select the folder where you save your files in the **Save in** box. Change the name of the file in the **File name** box to **EX1001-threeyearloan**. Confirm that the type of file is **Microsoft Excel Workbook**.

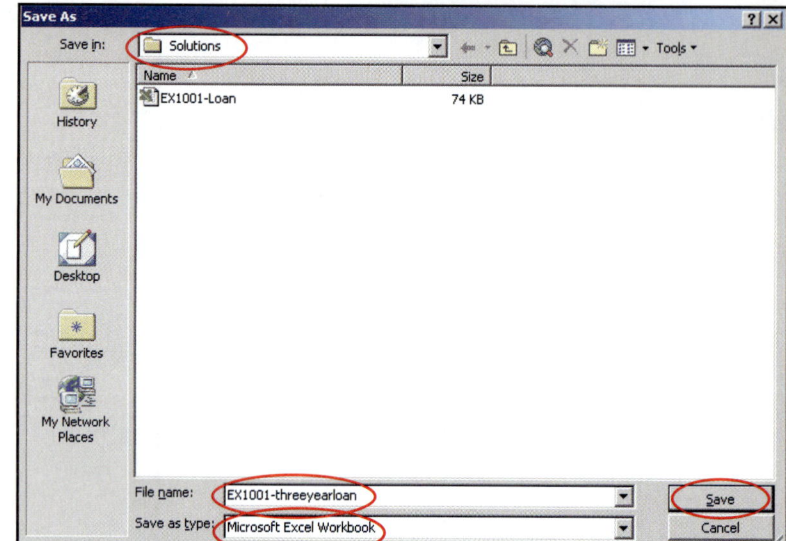

IN DEPTH

If you applied the template to the workbook from the General Templates option, it will open the Save As dialog box if you choose the Save or the Save As options.

**7** Click the **Save** button. Close the workbook. Leave Excel open.

The exercises that follow are designed for you to review and use what you have learned in this lesson. You also have the opportunity to practice your skills and then expand on them by applying them to new situations.

## COMPREHENSION

Comprehension exercises are designed to check your memory and understanding of the basic concepts in this lesson. You distinguish between true and false statements, identify new screen elements, and match terms with related statements. If you are uncertain of the correct answer, refer to the task number following each item (for example, T4 refers to Task 4) and review that task until you are confident that you can provide a correct response.

### TRUE-FALSE

Circle either T or F.

T  F  **1.** The Security level must be set to High when you create a macro. **(T1)**

T  F  **2.** You can assign macros to a key on the keyboard and run them by holding the Ctrl key and pressing the assigned key. **(T1)**

T  F  **3.** To edit a macro, you use the Visual Basic editor. **(T2)**

T  F  **4.** You can create custom toolbars, but you have to choose a name for the toolbar from a list of names provided in the Customize dialog box. **(T3)**

T  F  **5.** To remove a button from a toolbar while the Customize dialog box is open, you double-click on the button. **(T4)**

T  F  **6.** You can assign a macro to a button on a toolbar. **(T5)**

T  F  **7.** You can add menu buttons to a toolbar that display a list of commands that you can customize. **(T6)**

T  F  **8.** Templates are stored in a special folder named Templates by default where the Excel program can find them automatically. **(T7)**

### MATCHING QUESTIONS

**A.** VBA editor      **D.** Template

**B.** New Menu      **E.** Tools

**C.** Attach      **F.** Macro

Match the following statements to the word or phrase that is the best match from the list. Write the letter of the matching word or phrase in the space provided next to the number.

**1.** _____ The command used to link a custom menu to a workbook **(T7)**

**2.** _____ The type of program you create by recording a series of actions in Excel **(T1)**

**3.** _____ A workbook that has all the formulas and formatting but no specific data **(T7)**

**4.** _____ Allows you to edit a macro **(T2)**

**5.** _____ Name of the category of customized commands used to add a menu to a toolbar **(T3)**

**6.** _____ Name of the category of customized commands used to add the Speak Cells command to a toolbar **(T3)**

# IDENTIFYING PARTS OF
# THE EXCEL SCREEN

Refer to the figure and identify the numbered parts of
the screen. Write the letter of the correct label in the
space next to the number.

1. _______________

2. _______________

3. _______________

4. _______________

5. _______________

6. _______________

7. _______________

8. _______________

9. _______________

10. _______________

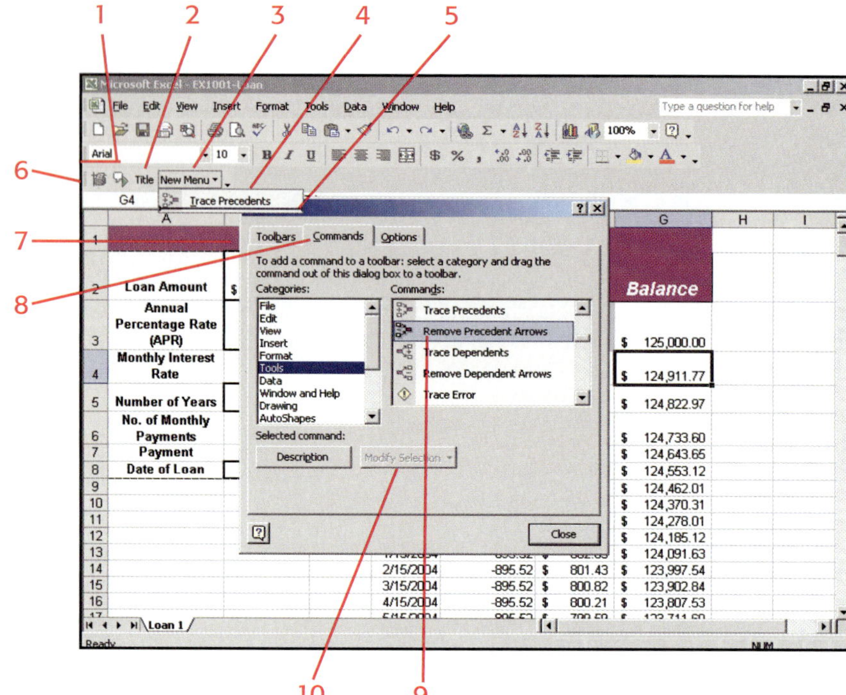

A. Command that can be added to a toolbar  (T4)

B. Indicates where a new menu item will be placed  (T6)

C. Buttons on a custom toolbar  (T2)

D. Custom toolbar  (T3)

E. Used to change names of buttons  (T6)

F. Button used to run a macro  (T5)

G. Custom menu  (T6)

H. Command in a custom menu  (T6)

I. Used to create a new custom toolbar  (T3)

J. Displays available commands  (T4)

Reinforcement exercises are designed to reinforce the skills you have learned by applying them to a new situation. Detailed instructions are provided along with a figure, where appropriate, to illustrate the result. Complete the reinforcement exercises sequentially. Leave the workbook open at the end of each exercise for use in the next exercise until you are specifically directed to close it.

Excel is commonly used to report quarterly sales of products. You can create a template to help with this task that provides consistent input. In the following exercises, you record macros to print each of the quarterly statements and the summary sheet. You assign these macros to buttons that you place on a custom menu in a custom tool-bar. You attach the toolbar to the workbook, remove the data but not the formatting or formulas, and save it to use as a template.

## R1—Create Macros to Print Each Sheet of a Workbook

When you create the macros in this exercise, be sure to select the worksheet or menu option, even if they are already selected. The current default choice may not be the same the next time you run the macro.

1. Open **EX1002** and save it as **EX1002-Reinforcement** on your disk for use in the following exercises.

2. Choose **Tools**, **Macros**, **Record New Macro**. Type **PrintQ1** in the **Macro name** box (do not use a space between Print and Q1). Confirm that your name is displayed in the **Description** box and click **OK**.

3. Click the **First Quarter** sheet tab. Choose **File**, **Print**, **Active sheet(s)**, **OK**.

4. Choose **Tools**, **Macros**, **Stop Recording**.

5. Choose **Tools**, **Macros**, **Record New Macro**. Type **PrintQ2** in the **Macro name** box (do not use a space between Print and Q2) and click **OK**.

6. Click the **Second Quarter** sheet tab. Choose **File**, **Print**, **Active sheet(s)**, **OK**.

7. Choose **Tools**, **Macros**, **Stop Recording**.

8. Repeat this process for the third- and fourth-quarter sheets.

9. Choose **Tools**, **Macros**, **Record New Macro**. Type **PrintSum** in the **Macro name** box (do not use a space between Print and Sum) and click **OK**.

10. Click the **Year-End Summary** sheet tab. Choose **File**, **Print**, **Active sheet(s)**, **OK**.

11. Choose **Tools**, **Macros**, **Stop Recording**.

12. Choose **Tools**, **Macro**, **Macros**. A list of the five macros is displayed.

13. Capture a screen shot of the Macro Dialogue box by pressing and holding Alt and then pressing the PrtSc key. Launch Word and type your name and section number at the top of a blank page. Paste your screen shot. Save the file as **EX1002-R1** and print it if required by your instructor.

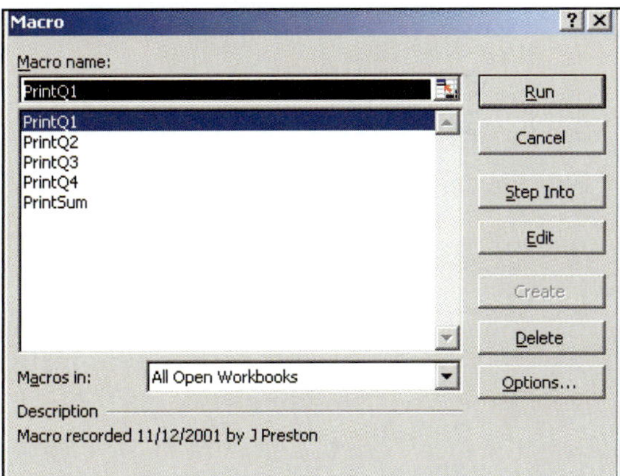

## R2—Change the Name of the Macro in VBA Editor

The name for the macro that prints the summary may be misleading. Edit the macro to change the name.

1. Select **PrintSum** and click **Edit**.

2. Change **PrintSum** to **PrintSummary** in the first two lines of the macro.

3. Capture a screen shot of the VBA Editor window by pressing and holding Alt and then pressing the PrtSc key. Launch Word and type your name and section number at the top of a blank page. Paste your screen shot. Save the file as **EX1002-R2** and print it if required by your instructor. Close Word.

**4.** Save the changes and close the VBA editor.

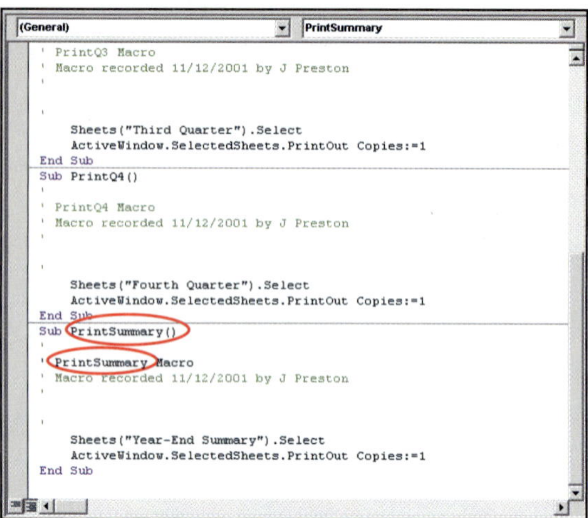

## R3—Create a Custom Toolbar with a Custom Menu

You can add these print options to a custom toolbar.
Create a custom toolbar and attach it to this workbook.

**1.** Choose **View**, **Toolbars**, **Customize**. Click the **Toolbars** tab and click the **New** button.

**2.** Type your initials in the **Toolbar name** box and click **OK**.

**3.** Double-click the title bar of the new toolbar to dock it.

**4.** Click the **Commands** tab. Scroll down the list of categories and click **New Menu**.

**5.** Drag the **New Menu** command to the custom toolbar.

**6.** Click **Modify Selection**. Select the default value in the **Name** box and type **Print Sheets**.

**7.** Click **Macros** in the Categories pane. Drag the **Custom Menu Item** onto the new menu on your toolbar, just below the name of the menu.

**8.** Click the **Modify Selection** button and choose **Assign Macro**. Select **PrintQ1** from the list of macros and click **OK**.

**9.** Click the **Custom Menu Item** that you just placed on your custom toolbar. Click the **Modify Selection** button and change the name of the button to **Q1**.

**10.** Repeat Steps 4-6 to create a total of five menu items on your toolbar to print the four quarterly sheets and the summary sheet.

**11.** Select the name of your toolbar in the **Toolbars** box and click the **Attach** button.

**12.** Select the custom toolbar named with your initials and click the **Copy** button. Click **OK**.

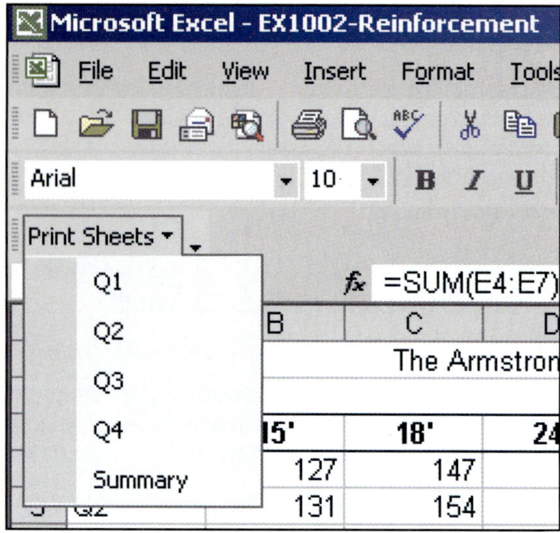

## R4—Remove data and save as a template

You can use this workbook as a template without saving it to the Templates folder. Remove the data from the first four sheets but do not disturb the formulas in the Year-End Summary sheet.

**1.** Choose the **First Quarter** sheet. Select **B4** through **H11** and delete the data.

**2.** Repeat this process for the other three quarters.

**3.** Choose the **Year-End Summary** sheet. Do not delete the formulas.

**4.** Click the **Save** button to save your work, and then close the workbook.

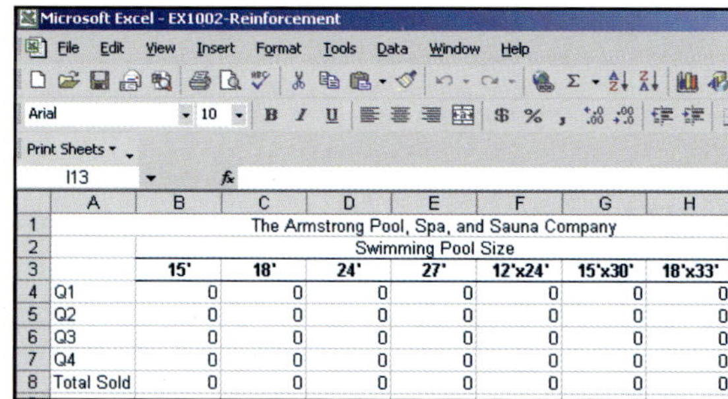

# R5—Apply the template

You can use this workbook as a template if you open it,
save it with a new name, and fill in the data.

1. Open **EX1002-Reinforcement**.

2. Choose the **First Quarter** sheet. Enter the following
   numbers in row 4 for sales at the Indianapolis store:
   11, 16, 18, 17, 3, 10, 4.

3. Choose the **Year-End Summary** sheet and confirm
   that the numbers you entered were added to the
   fourth row to show first-quarter sales.

4. Save the workbook as **EX1002-Applied Template**.
   Close the workbook.

|  | 15' | 18' | 24' | 27' | 12'x24' | 15'x30' | 18'x33' |
|---|---|---|---|---|---|---|---|
| Q1 | 11 | 16 | 18 | 17 | 3 | 10 | 4 |
| Q2 | 0 | 0 | 0 | 0 | 0 | 0 | 0 |
| Q3 | 0 | 0 | 0 | 0 | 0 | 0 | 0 |
| Q4 | 0 | 0 | 0 | 0 | 0 | 0 | 0 |
| Total Sold | 11 | 16 | 18 | 17 | 3 | 10 | 4 |

Challenge exercises are designed to test your ability to apply your skills to new situations with less detailed instruction. These exercises also challenge you to expand your repertoire of skills by using commands that are similar to those you have already learned. The desired outcome is clearly defined, but you have more freedom to choose the steps needed to achieve the required result.

## C1—Use Templates Installed with Microsoft Office XP

A few templates are provided with Microsoft Office. Most of them use protection features to hide the formulas and prevent the user from making changes. You will learn how to add these features to your templates in a later lesson. The templates provided with Excel have little flexibility but are very fast and useful for specific needs.

Partial installations of Microsoft Office XP may not include these templates. If you have none listed when you do Step two of this exercise, you need to install them from the Microsoft Office XP CD-ROM. If you do not have that privilege on the computer you are using, contact the administrator or make arrangements with your instructor to do a different assignment.

*Goal:* Use the Loan Amortization template to determine two loans and comment on the benefits and limitations of the template.

1. Choose **File**, **New**. Select **General Templates** from the task pane under **New from template**.

2. Click the **Spreadsheet Solutions** tab to see the templates installed with Office.

3. Select **Loan Amortization** and click **OK**.

4. Select the cell to the right of **Loan Amount**, type **100000**, and press **⏎Enter**.

5. Enter the following values in the next three cells: **7.25%**, **30**, **12**. Enter today's date for the start date of the loan. Leave the **Optional Extra Payments** cell empty and enter your name as the lender.

6. Notice that the total interest you would pay on this loan is $145,583.46. Scroll to the bottom of the sheet and confirm that there are 360 payments on this 30-year loan.

7. Click the **Save** button. Notice that the **Save As** dialog box opens. This is a characteristic of templates that prevents you from saving your changes over the original template. Name the file **EX1003-CH1a**.

8. Select the cell to the right of **Optional Extra Payments** and enter **50**. Notice the actual number of combined payments is reduced to 290 if an extra $50 is added to each payment.

9. Start Word and open the file, **EX1003**. Save the file as **EX1003-CH1b**. Print this sheet and fill it out if required by your instructor. If your instructor prefers the file in electronic form, switch back and forth between this document and the worksheet and answer the questions in this document. Save it and close it when you are finished.

10. Close the workbook and do not save it again. Leave Excel open if you plan to continue with the Challenge exercises.

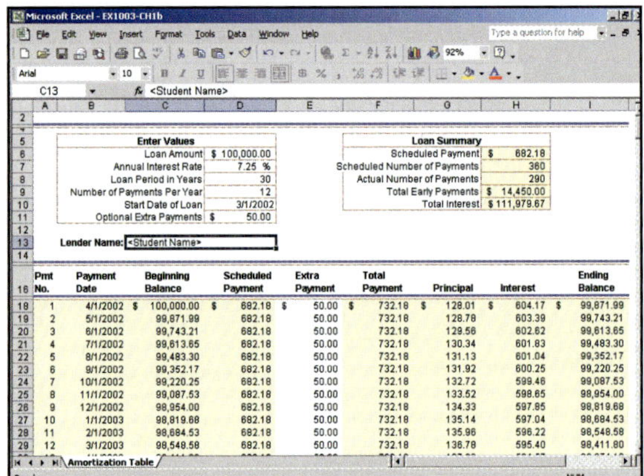

## C2—Use a Finance and Accounting Template from the Microsoft Web Site

Microsoft maintains a library of templates that you can use if you have Internet access. The templates are organized by category and within each category are templates in Word, Excel, PowerPoint, and Access. Excel is primarily a financial tool and the greatest number of templates is in the Finance and Accounting section.

*Goal:* Use a finance or accounting template from the library of templates on Microsoft's Web site.

1. Choose **File**, **New**. Click **Templates on Microsoft.com** under **New from Template** in the task pane.

2. Choose the **Finance and Accounting** topic. Browse through the options and choose an Excel template that you may find useful in your major area of study or an area of personal interest. Do not choose the loan amortization with optional payments template if you did the first challenge exercise in this lesson.

**3.** Fill out the template with some sample data and save it as **EX1004-CH2**.

## C3—Use Templates of Your Choice from the Microsoft Web Site

Explore Microsoft's library of templates. The templates are organized by category and within each category are templates in Word, Excel, PowerPoint, and Access. Excel is primarily a financial tool but it can be used for other purposes

*Goal:* Use a template of your choice that is not from the Finance and Accounting area of the library of templates on Microsoft's Web site.

**1.** Choose **File**, **New**. Click **Templates on Microsoft.com** under **New from Template** in the task pane.

**2.** Browse through the Template Gallery and choose an Excel template that you may find useful in your major area of study or an area of personal interest.

**3.** Fill out the template with some sample data and save it as **EX1004-CH3**.

## C4—Manage Toolbar Attachments

A toolbar is stored in a special folder on the computer you are using and continues to reside there after the workbook is closed. You can attach it to another workbook. If you delete it from your list of toolbars, it will be restored when you open the workbook.

If you are working in a laboratory environment, the toolbars stored on your computer in the special folder may be erased periodically and replaced with the default toolbars. This is another good reason to attach them to specific workbooks.

*Goal:* Attach an existing toolbar to a new workbook.

**1.** Click the **New** button on the toolbar to automatically open a new workbook without opening the task pane.

**2.** Choose **View**, **Toolbars**, **Customize**. Click the **Toolbars** tab, if necessary. Click the **Attach** button.

**3.** Click the custom toolbar with your last name and click the **Copy** button. (This step assumes you have done the tasks in this lesson.) Click **OK**.

**4.** Type your name in cell **A1**. Save the workbook as **EX1004-CH4** and close the workbook.

**5.** Choose **View**, **Toolbars**, **Customize**. Click the **Toolbars** tab, if necessary. Scroll to find the custom toolbar named with your last name and click it to select it.

**6.** Click the **Delete** button. Click **OK** to confirm the deletion. Click the **Close** button to close the dialog box.

**7.** Confirm that the toolbar is no longer on your list of toolbars. Open **EX1004-CH4** and confirm that the toolbar is available.

**8.** If your instructor requires a printout for grading purposes, capture a screen shot that displays the toolbar by pressing and holding Alt and then pressing the PrtSc key. Launch Word and type your name and section number at the top of a blank page. Paste your screen shot. Print the page to hand in. Close Word and do not save the file (you have EX1004-CH4 to confirm you have done the work).

**9.** Close the workbook. If you are working on a computer that others share, delete the toolbar from the list of available toolbars on the computer.

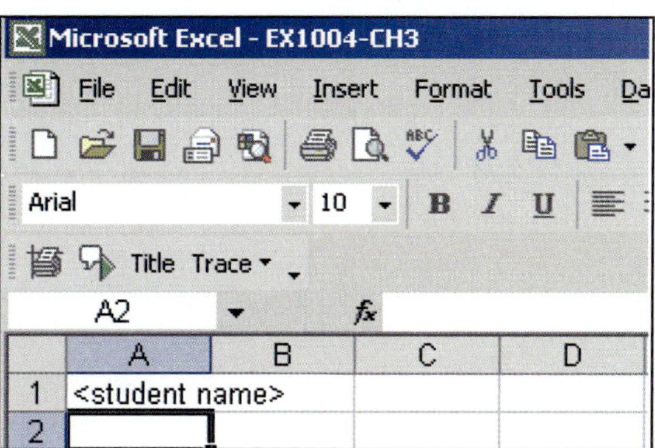

Create your own macro to do something you find repetitive and place it on a custom toolbar that is attached to a workbook.

Grading criteria will be:

1. Demonstrate the ability to record a macro.

2. Demonstrate the ability to create a custom toolbar.

3. Demonstrate the ability to attach a macro to a button on a toolbar.

4. Demonstrate the ability to attach a toolbar to a workbook.

Some examples of features that students have learned to use in previous classes to enhance their multipage printouts are listed below:

- Two or more ranges of cells on a single worksheet have buttons on a toolbar that are set to print each range.

- Several different text formats are attached to buttons that can be used for appropriate sections of the worksheet.

- Several different number formats, including specific number of decimal places displayed, are attached to buttons on a toolbar.

To complete the project, perform the following:

- Place your name in the header.

- Save your file on your own disk. Name it **EX1005-Macros**.

- Check with your instructor to determine if the project should be submitted in electronic or printed form. If necessary, capture an image of the screen using the PrtSc button on your keyboard and paste the image into a Word document that you can print to display your toolbar in a workbook.

# Lesson 11

## Managing Formulas



## INTRODUCTION

The strength of Excel is its ability to perform sophisticated calculations and display the results in useful ways. As your workbooks grow in size and complexity, you need to learn how to simplify formulas, make them easy to change, and analyze them for errors.

In this lesson, you use a template to produce invoices for a small company that sells customized shirts. The company buys shirts in several styles and prints designs or logos on them in one, two, or three colors. The price of the shirt depends on the style, quantity, and number of colors used. The owner of the company would like to simply enter the code for the shirt, the number ordered, and the number of colors used to produce an invoice. The owner would also like to prevent errors that may occur while entering the data.

In this lesson, you learn how to use *named ranges* to validate input and look up prices from lists on other worksheets. A named range is a cell or range of cells that has a name of your choice. You use *conditional functions* to determine the price range based on quantity ordered and *conditional formatting* to draw attention to important issues. Conditional functions evaluate a conditional statement and then perform one of two other functions depending on whether the statement is true or false. Conditional formatting evaluates a statement and applies a format of your choice if the statement is true. You also trace the *precedents* and *dependents* of formulas to analyze them and resolve an error that results from modifying the original template. Precedents are cells that are used by a formula in the selected cell and dependents are cells that use the contents of the current cell to calculate their own values.

# VISUAL SUMMARY

By the time you complete this lesson, you will have created an invoice worksheet that looks like this:

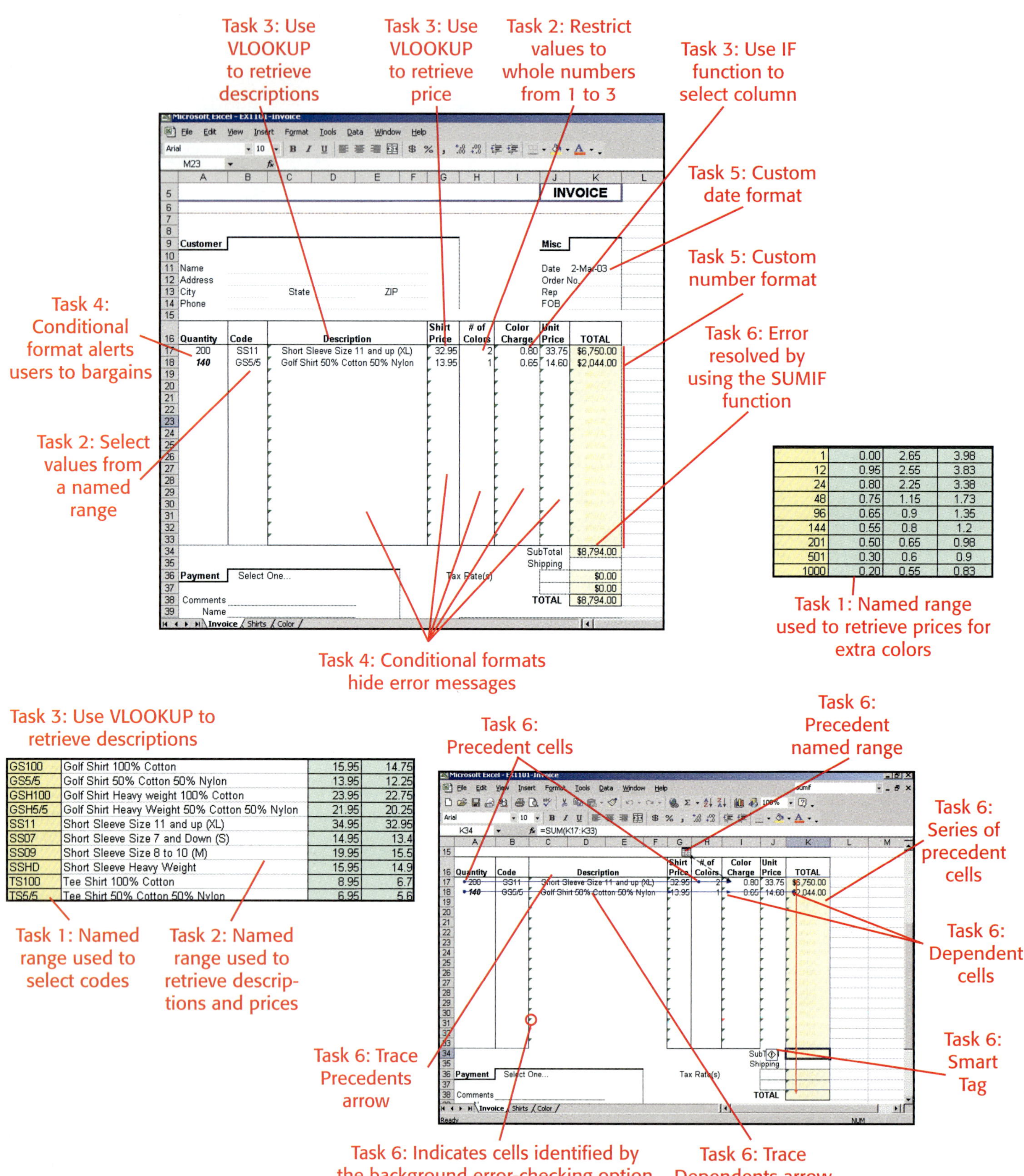

# Task 1
## NAMING A RANGE



### Why would I do this?

Some formulas refer to a range of cells. If the range of cells is a table of data, you must rewrite the formula whenever you modify the table or change the number of rows or columns. If you name the range of cells in the table and use that name in the formulas, you only have to rename the range if you change the size of the table. It is also easier to understand the formulas when the ranges have names.

Excel 2002 has a new feature that places a small colored triangle in the corner of cells that may have problems or could be improved. You turn this feature off in this task and turn it back on when you are finished revising the worksheet to check for errors.

In this task, you name ranges in two tables of data.

**1** Open **EX1101** from the **Student** folder. Save it as **EX1101-Invoice** on your disk.

*The new title appears in the title bar. The cells in the Unit Price column have small markers in the corners. These markers warn the user that the cells are not protected from accidental change. This issue is dealt with in a later lesson.*

    Choose **Tools**, **Options**. Click the **Error Checking** tab. Deselect **Enable background error checking**. Click **OK**.

*Many cells are marked with indicators while you are revising the worksheet. Removing these marks reduces the clutter on the screen. You will turn them back on in the last task.*

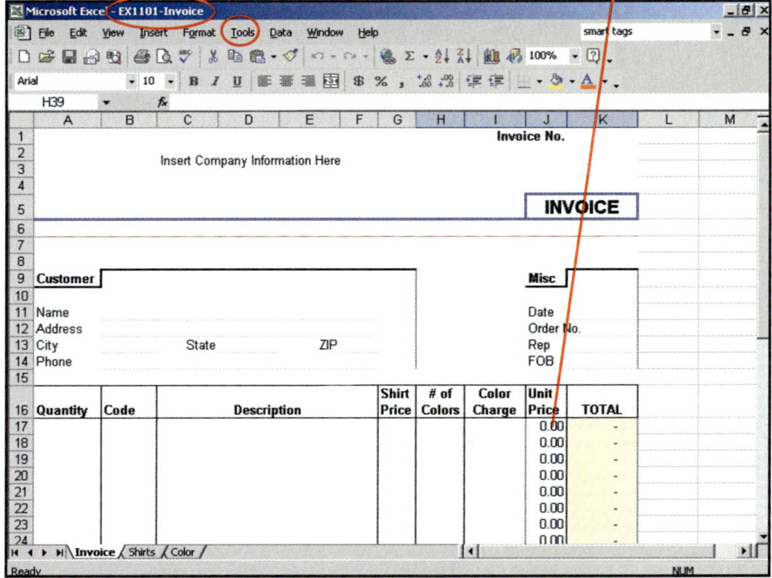


**2** Click the **Shirts** worksheet tab.

*This table of shirt products contains style codes, descriptions, and prices for quantities of less than, or more than, one case. In this example, a case holds 144 shirts.*

    Select cells **A3** through **A12**.

*This range of cells contains the shirt codes.*



| | Style Code | Description | Less than a case | More tha a case |
|---|---|---|---|---|
| 1 | Quantity Charge | | | |
| 2 | Style Code | Description | Less than a case | More tha a case |
| 3 | GS100 | Golf Shirt 100% Cotton | 15.95 | 14.7 |
| 4 | GS5/5 | Golf Shirt 50% Cotton 50% Nylon | 13.95 | 12.2 |
| 5 | GSH100 | Golf Shirt Heavy weight 100% Cotton | 23.95 | 22.7 |
| 6 | GSH5/5 | Golf Shirt Heavy Weight 50% Cotton 50% Nylon | 21.95 | 20.2 |
| 7 | SS11 | Short Sleeve Size 11 and up (XL) | 34.95 | 32.9 |
| 8 | SS07 | Short Sleeve Size 7 and Down (S) | 14.95 | 13 |
| 9 | SS09 | Short Sleeve Size 8 to 10 (M) | 19.95 | 15 |
| 10 | SSHD | Short Sleeve Heavy Weight | 15.95 | 14 |
| 11 | TS100 | Tee Shirt 100% Cotton | 8.95 | 6 |
| 12 | TS5/5 | Tee Shirt 50% Cotton 50% Nylon | 6.95 | 5 |

**3** Choose **Insert**, **Name**, **Define**.

*The Define Names dialog box opens.*

Type **Codes**. Click the **Add** button.

*The range of cells from A2 through A12 is named Codes. It will be used to validate the code entries.*

**IN DEPTH**

These tables are used in lookup functions in a later task. These functions do not use the column headings so they are not included in the selected range.

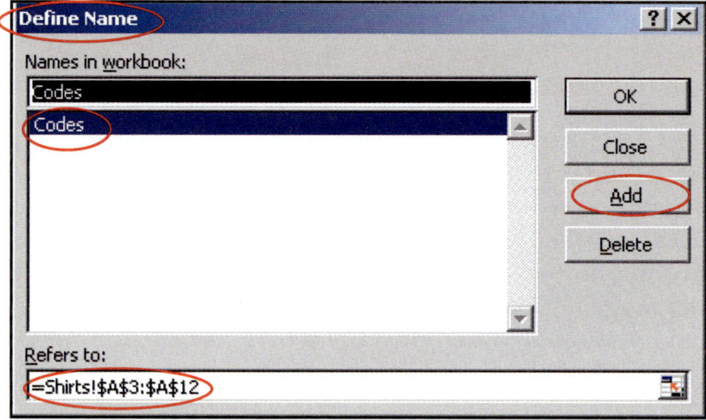

**QUICK TIP**

A faster way to name a range is to select the range of cells, click the Name box, and type the name of the range.

**4** Click **OK**. Select cells **A3** through **D12**.

*The table of shirt codes, descriptions, prices is selected.*

Choose **Insert**, **Name**, **Define**. Type **Shirts** and click the **Add** button.

*The table of shirt information is named.*

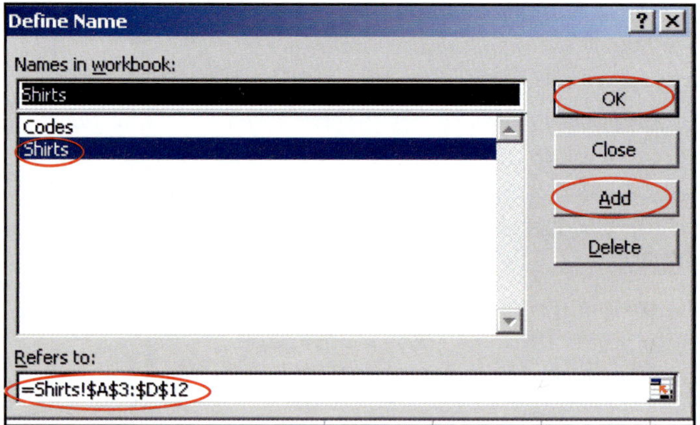

**5** Click **OK**. Click the **Color** sheet tab and select cells **A3** through **D11**.

*The table of prices for printing with color is selected.*

Choose **Insert**, **Name**, **Define**. Type **Colors** and click the **Add** button.

*The table of prices for printing in color is named.*

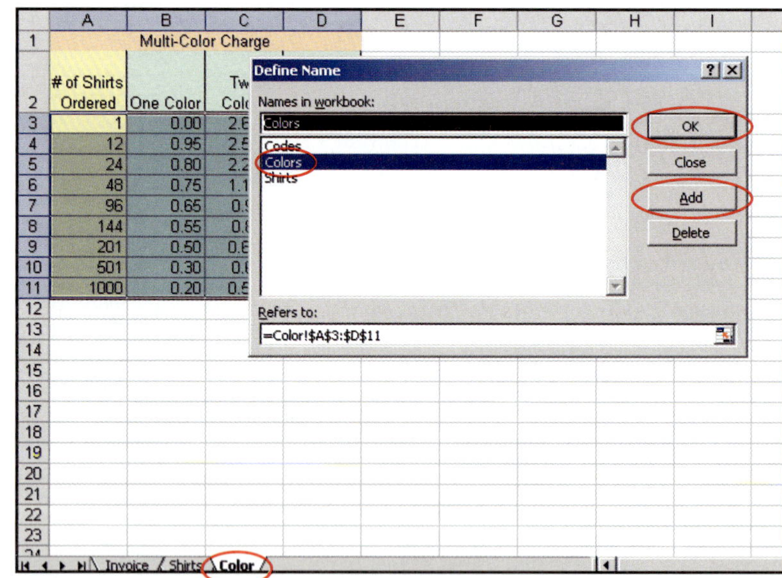

**6** Click **OK**. Click the **Invoice** sheet tab. Click the arrow on the **Name** box.

*Three ranges are named that you can use in formulas on this invoice.*

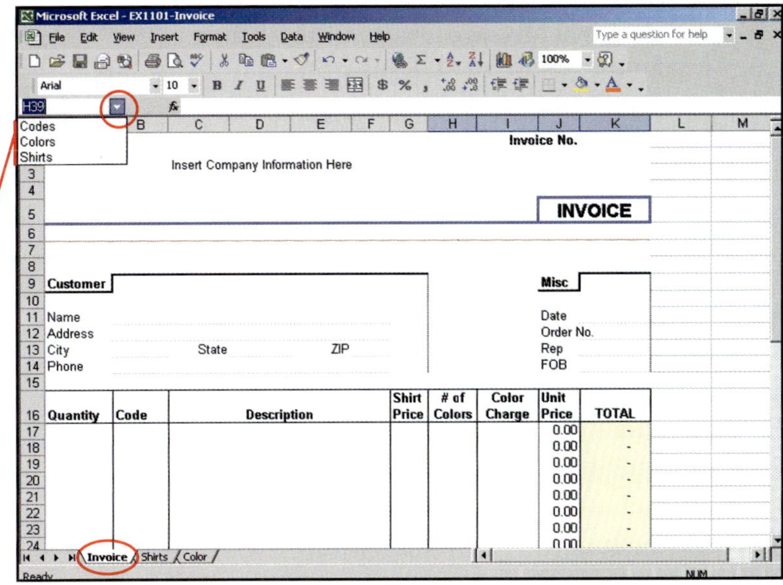


# Task 2
VALIDATING DATA INPUT

## Why would I do this?

You can use the validation option to restrict the input to a list of values or range of numbers. You can provide guidance to the user with a pop-up message that appears before the data is entered. You can also provide an error message that provides information on how the user can revise an incorrect entry. This makes data entry faster and more accurate.

In this task, you restrict the values entered in the Code column to those that exist in the table of shirts. You also restrict the values entered in the # of Colors column to integers from one to three.

**1** Select cells **B17** through **B33**. Choose **Data**, **Validation**.

*The Data Validation dialog box opens.*

Click the **Settings** tab, if necessary. Click the **Allow** arrow and choose **List**. In the **Source** box, type **=Codes**.

*Only values that exist in the named range are allowed.*

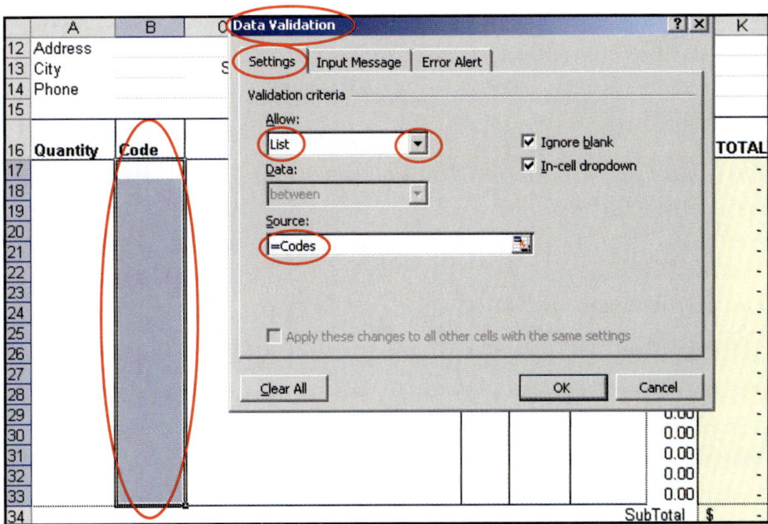

**2** Click the **Input Message** tab. Select the **Title** box and type **Code Validation**.

*The message is given a name for future reference.*

Select the **Input Message** box and type **Enter a shirt code from the list**.

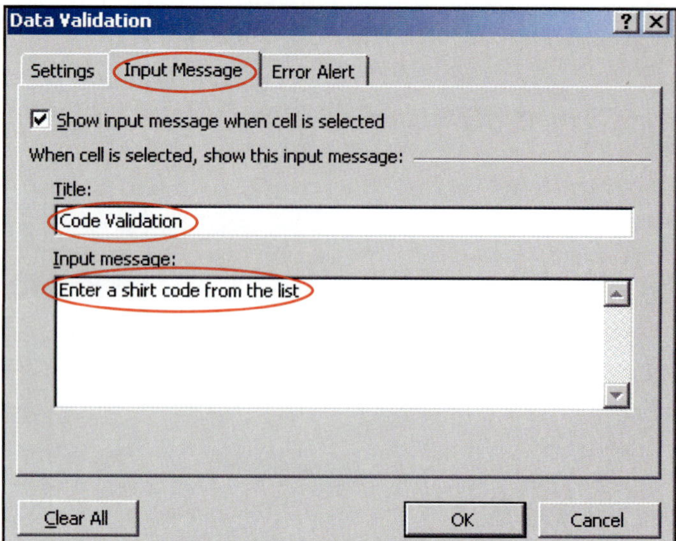

**3** Click the **Error Alert** tab. Click in the **Title** box and type **Code validation error**.

Click the **Error message** box and type **Refer to the list of codes on the Shirts worksheet**.

*The validation rule for this cell has been defined. It only allows values from the list and displays the messages you have entered.*

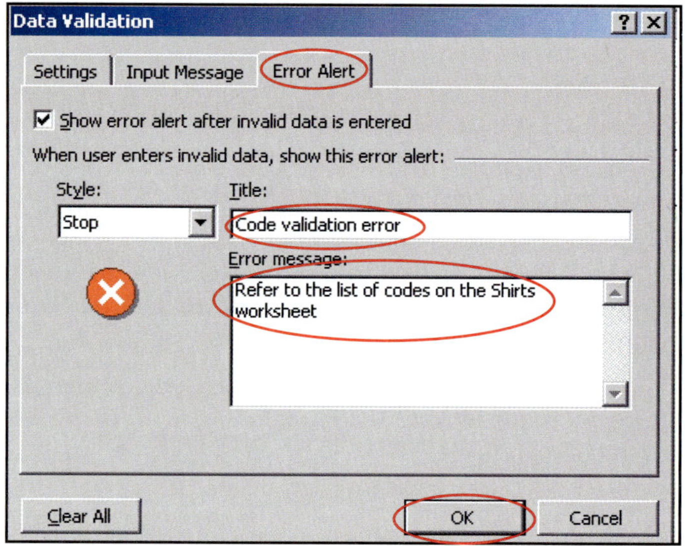

**4** Click **OK**.

*The input message is displayed next to the cell and an arrow is also displayed.*

Select **B17**, type **SS1**, and press ⏎Enter.

*The error message is displayed.*

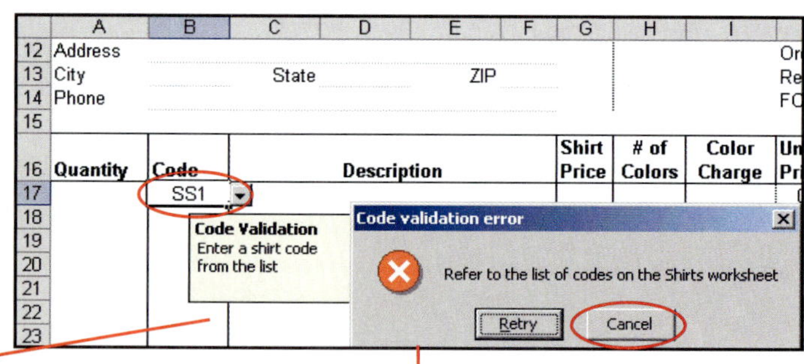

Input message

Error box with title and message

**5** Click **Cancel**. Click the arrow next to the box and select **SS11** from the list.

*This is a valid entry and no error message is displayed.*

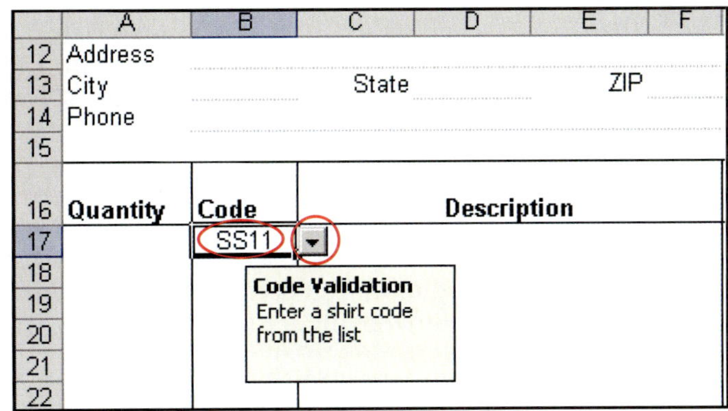

**6** Select cells **H17** through **H33**. Choose **Data**, **Validation**.

*The Data Validation dialog box opens.*

Click the **Settings** tab. Click the **Allow** arrow and choose **Whole Number**. Click the **Data** arrow and choose **between**, if necessary. Select the **Minimum** box and type **1**. Select the **Maximum** box and type **3**.

*The entry in this cell will be restricted to whole numbers from 1 to 3.*

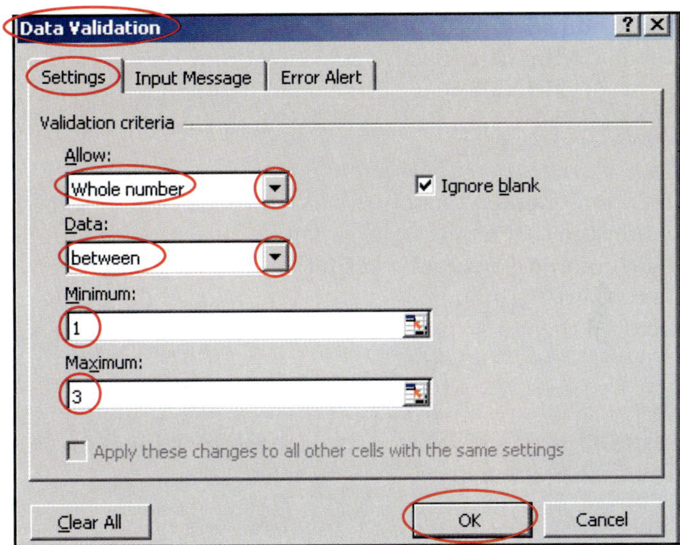

**7** Click **OK**. Select cell **H17**.

*No input message has been defined.*

Type **4** and press ↵Enter.

*If you do not define an error message, a default error message is displayed.*

Error warning with default title and message.

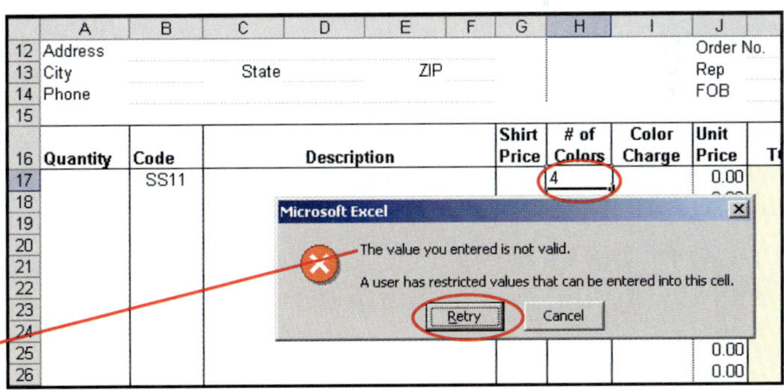

**8** Click **Retry**, type **2**, and then press ↵Enter.

*The entry is successful. The number entered in this cell is restricted to whole numbers from 1 to 3.*

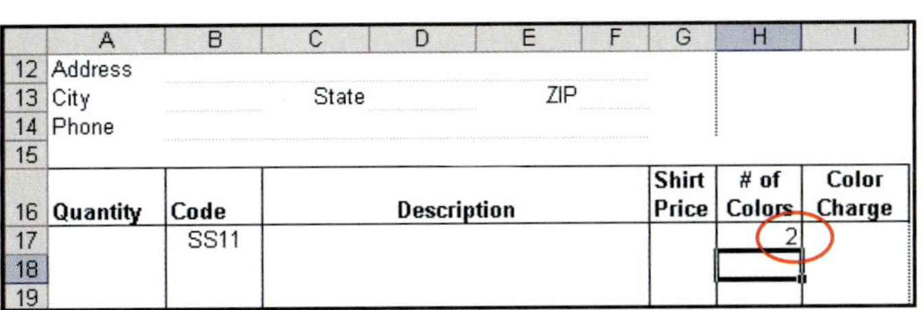

### *Why would I do this?*

If you need to retrieve data from tables for use in your formulas, lookup functions are powerful tools. The *VLOOKUP* function looks up values that are displayed vertically in a column. It is used most often because nearly all tables are arranged with a unique identifier in the first column. You use the *HLOOKUP* function to look up a value in a table by searching horizontally across a row of data. You will use the VLOOKUP function in this task.

The lookup functions can look up numbers or text. If you are searching for numbers, it is important to sort the column or row in ascending order.

If you name the table, you can use the name of the table in the lookup function. This has a major advantage. If you decide to add or remove rows or columns from the table, you simply redefine the table name to include the rows and columns of the revised table. You do not have to revise all the lookup formulas that refer to the table.

The *IF* function evaluates a statement and performs one of two options, depending on whether the statement is true or false. An IF function can be used to determine which column to look up by nesting it within the VLOOKUP function. The IF function has three arguments—a criterion, what to do if the criterion is true, and what to do if the criterion is false. The true and false results may be single values, blanks, or other functions.

In this task you use the VLOOKUP and IF functions to complete the body of the invoice. In steps 1 through 3, you use the VLOOKUP function to look up the description in the Shirts table.

In Steps 4 and 5, you fill this function into the other cells in the Description column and test it.

In Steps 6 through 8, you use the IF function to determine whether to use column 3 or 4 in the Shirts table to find the price. Column 3 has prices for quantities less than a case of 144 shirts and column 4 has prices for quantities of more than 144.

In Steps 9 and 10, you nest the IF function within a VLOOKUP function. This combination of functions lets you find the price per shirt based on the code and the quantity.

In Steps 11 and 12, you use a VLOOKUP function to find the additional charge for using colors by looking it up in the Color table.

**1** Select the **Invoice** sheet, if necessary. Select cell **C17**. Choose **Insert**, **Function**. If the Office Assistant opens, click **No, don't provide help now**, to close it.

*The Insert Function dialog box opens.*

Click the arrow on the **Or select a category** box and choose **Lookup & Reference**. Scroll to the bottom of the list in the **Select a function** box and click **VLOOKUP**.

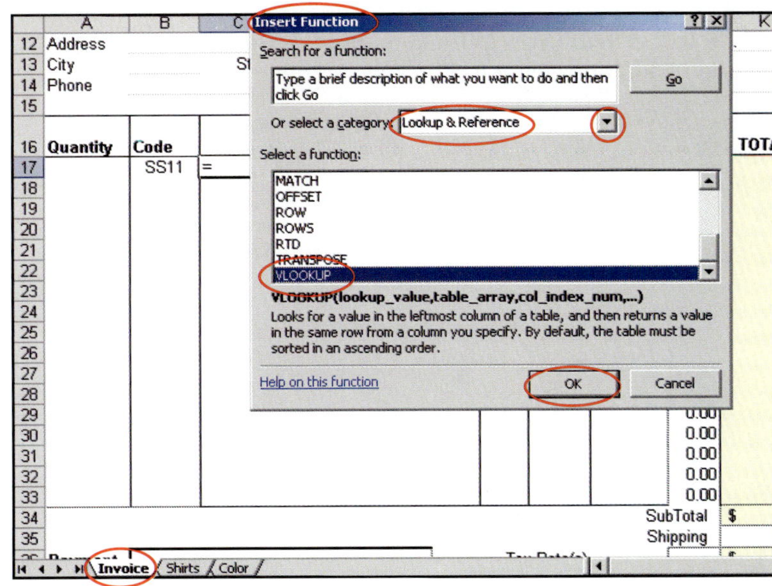

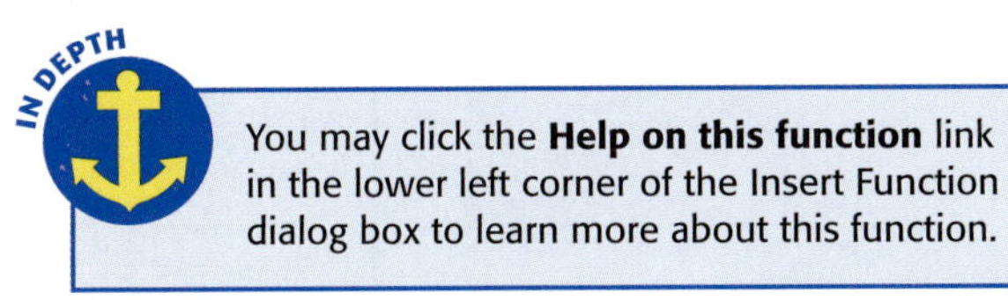

IN DEPTH

You may click the **Help on this function** link in the lower left corner of the Insert Function dialog box to learn more about this function.

CAUTION

The cells in the Description column are merged. If you try to click in D17, E17, or F17, you will still select C17. This isn't really a problem since you want to place the formula in cell C17 anyway.

**2** Click **OK**.

*The Function Arguments dialog box opens.*

Click the **Lookup_value** box then type **B17**.

*This is the code that will be looked up in the Shirts table.*

Click the **Table_array** box and type **Shirts**. Click the **Col_index_num** box and type **2**.

*You use the name of the range, defined in Task 1, in the Table_array box rather than the cell range for convenience. The column of the table that contains the descriptions is the second column in the table, which is why you entered the number 2 in the Col_index_num box.*

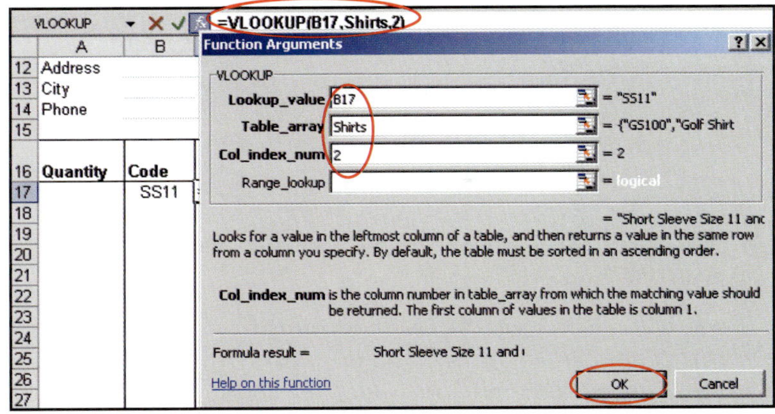

**3** Click **OK**.

*The description from the Shirts table is displayed for code SS11.*

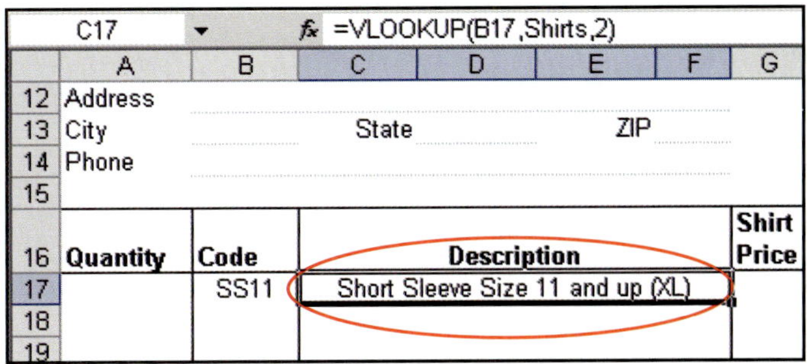

**4** Select cell **C17**. Drag the fill handle down to cell **F33** and release it.

*The VLOOKUP function is filled into the cells below. When there is no value in the cell to the left, #N/A is displayed to indicate that the function is not applicable yet. You learn how to hide this in a later task.*

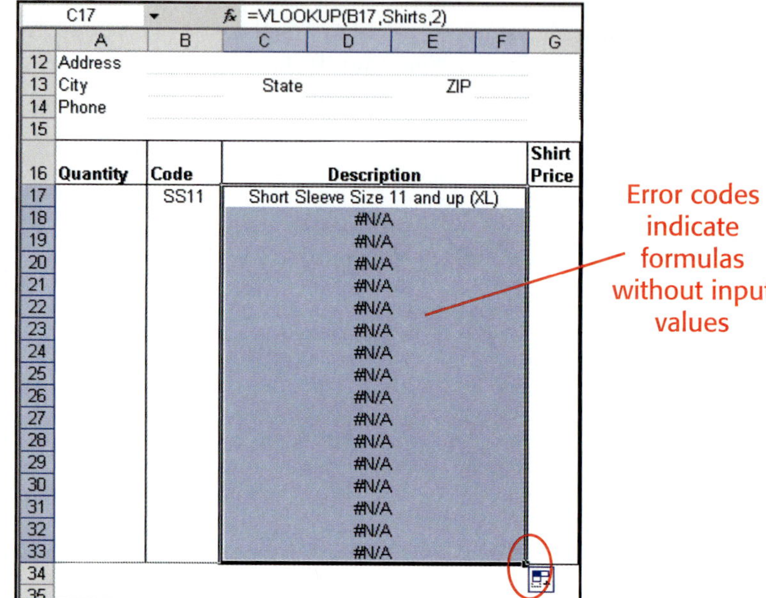


**5** Select cell **B18**. Click the arrow and select **GSH5/5**.

*The description is filled into cell C18.*

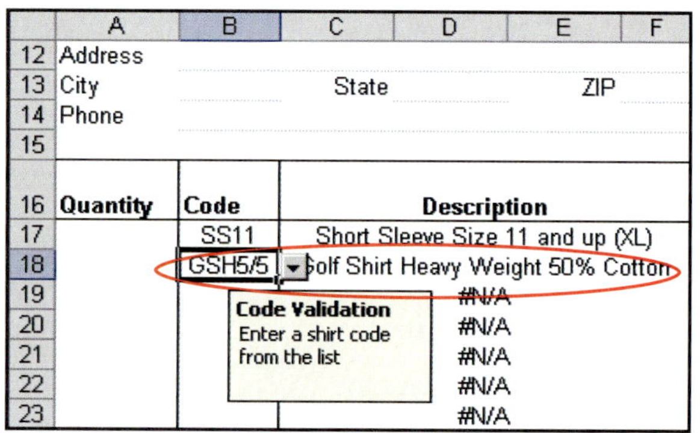

**6** Select cell **A17** and type **200**. Select cell **A18**, type **140**, and press ↵Enter.

*The price of the shirt depends on how many are purchased. To determine the price per shirt, you need to determine if the quantity purchased is less than a case. A case of shirts holds 144 shirts (a gross). The prices for quantities of less than a case are found in column 3 of the Shirts table and prices for a case or more are found in column 4. You will use an IF function to determine the column number.*

Select **G17**. Choose **Insert**, **Function**. Click the arrow on the **Or select a category** box and choose **Logical**. Select **IF** in the **Select a function** box.

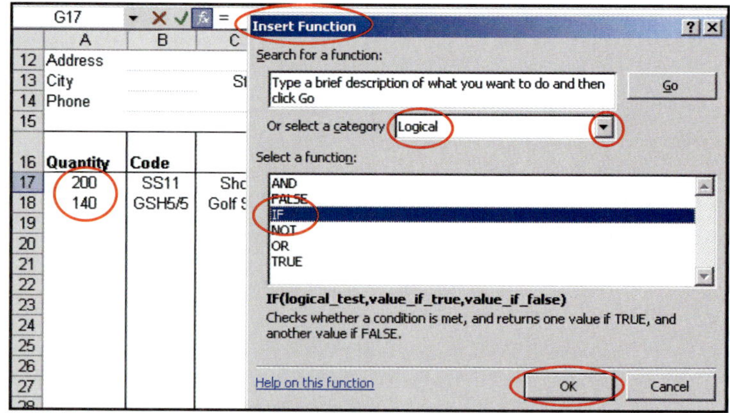

**7** Click **OK**. In the **Logical_test** box, type **A17<144**. In the **Value_if_true** box, type **3**. In the **Value_if_false** box, type **4**.

*If the quantity in cell A17 is less than 144, the result of the IF function will be 3, if the value is 144 or more, the result will be 4.*

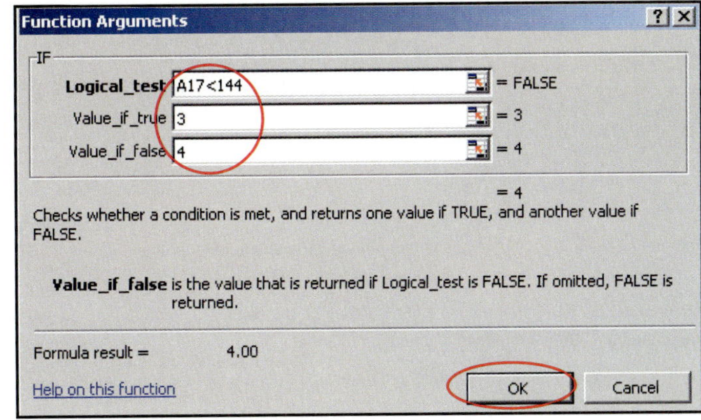

**8** Click **OK**.

*The correct value is column 4. The Shirt Price column is formatted with two decimal places to display the price. Do not be concerned about the display at this time. Next, this function will be nested within the VLOOKUP function to find the correct column number.*

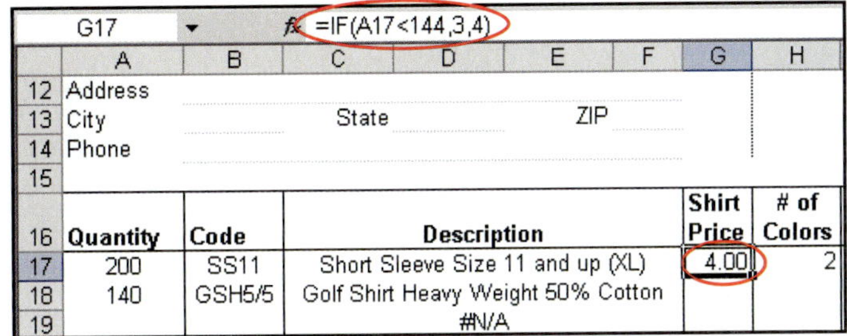

**9** Select **G17** and press Del.

*The IF function is deleted. You will start over and enter this function as the third argument of the VLOOKUP function to determine which column of the Shirts table to use when determining the price.*

> Choose **Insert**, **Function**. Click the **Or select a category** arrow and choose **Lookup & Reference**. Scroll to the bottom of the list in the **Select a function** box and click **VLOOKUP**. Click **OK**.

*The Function Arguments dialog box opens.*

> In the **Lookup_value** box, type **B17**. In the **Table_array** box, type **Shirts**. In the **Col_index_num** box, type **IF(A17<144,3,4)**.

*The function looks up the code from cell B17 in the Shirts range and uses the column determined by the IF function to return the correct price. The formula results are displayed in the dialog box.*

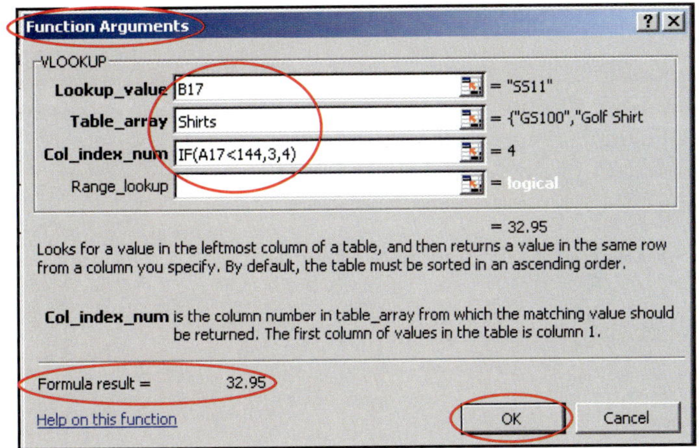

**10** Click **OK**.

*The formula looks up the price for this type of shirt in the fourth column of the Shirts table, which displays the lower cost for purchases that exceed 144 shirts.*

**11** Select **I17**. Choose <u>Insert</u>, <u>Function</u>. Click the **Or select a <u>c</u>ategory** arrow and choose **Lookup & Reference**. Scroll to the bottom of the list in the **Select a functio<u>n</u>** box and click **VLOOKUP**. Click **OK**.

*The Function Arguments dialog box opens. You will use the VLOOKUP function to find the price for extra colors in the color table. The color table has nine rows for different quantities ordered and three different columns for one, two, and three colors. The VLOOKUP function uses the value in the Quantity column and the value in the # of Colors column to find the additional price for extra colors. In this case the prices for one color are in column two of the table, the prices for two colors are in column three, and the prices for three colors are in column four. The correct column number in this case is the number of colors plus one.*

In the **Lookup_value** box, type **A17**. In the **Table_array** box, type **Colors**. In the **Col_index_num** box, type **H17+1**.

*The function looks up the number of shirts from cell A17 in the Colors range and uses the column determined by the value entered in H17 plus one. The formula result shows 0.80 as the cost per shirt for the number of colors used.*

**12** Click **OK**. Select **G17** and copy it. Select cells **G18** to **G33**. Choose **Edit**, **Paste Special**. Click **Formulas** then click **OK**. Repeat this process to copy the formula in **I17** to **I18** through **I33**.

*Both functions display #N/A in the rows that lack values in column A or H.*

Select **H18** and type **1** and then press ⏎**Enter**.

*The charge for one color is displayed in I18.*

Print the worksheet if your instructor requires it. Save your workbook and leave it open for the next task.

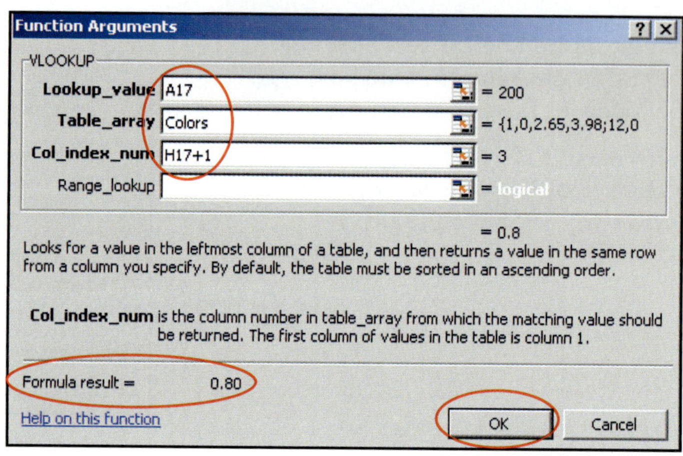


**CAUTION**

The first column of the table contains numbers to identify the minimum quantity for the prices in that row. The prices for one color start in column 2. In this example, you add 1 to the value the user enters in H17 to find the correct column in the table. This is specific to this particular example. You do not always add 1 to the cell used for the Col_index_num argument.

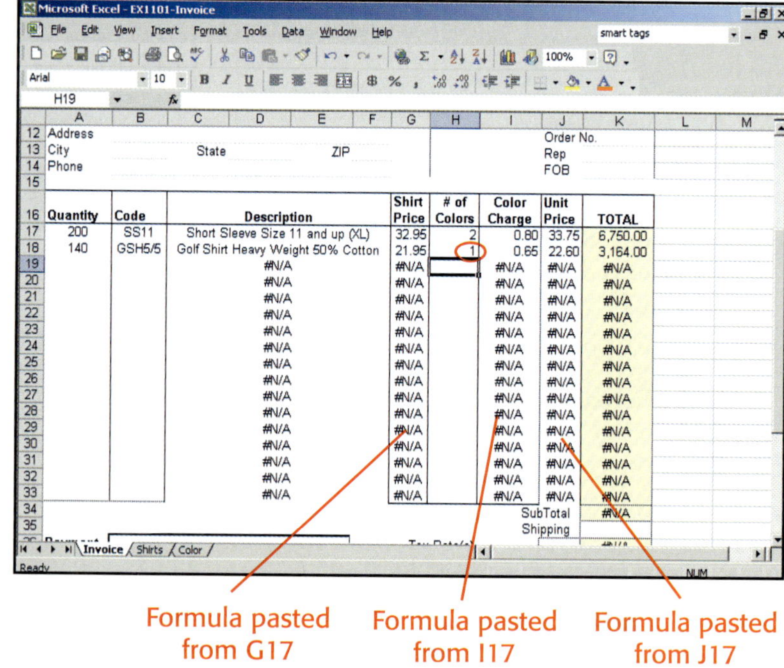

Formula pasted from G17

Formula pasted from I17

Formula pasted from J17

 **EXC** **Lesson 11** Managing Formulas

# Task 4
## USING CONDITIONAL FORMATS

### Why would I do this?

You can change the format of a cell based on the value in the cell. This is called conditional formatting. Conditional formatting is often used to warn the person who is entering data that they may have made a mistake. It can also be used to hide error messages that are displayed because cells referenced in formulas are empty. In this circumstance, you can hide the error messages, and when valid entries are supplied, the formulas calculate the results.

In this example, there is a significant price reduction if the order exceeds 144 shirts. If an order is just under 144, the buyer could increase the quantity ordered and actually pay less. It would be useful to flag this situation so the person taking the order can suggest to the buyer that it would be in their best interest to increase the quantity ordered to take advantage of the decreased price.

There are also numerous error codes in the rows that do not have values yet. The error code, #N/A, indicates that no value is available. It would improve the appearance of the invoice to hide these codes. A single function, *ISNA,* can be used to identify when a cell contains this error. You can hide error codes by using a conditional format to format the error code font to be the same color as the background, thereby hiding them from view.

In this task, you use conditional formatting to draw attention to quantities that are slightly less than 144 and to hide the error codes by making their font color the same as the background.

**1** Select A17 through A33. Choose **Format, Conditional Formatting.**

*The Conditional Formatting dialog box opens.*

Confirm that the first box displays **Cell Value is**. Click the arrow on the next box and choose **between**. In the third box, type **135**. In the fourth box, type **143**.

*This condition will identify values from 135 to 143 in the quantity cells.*

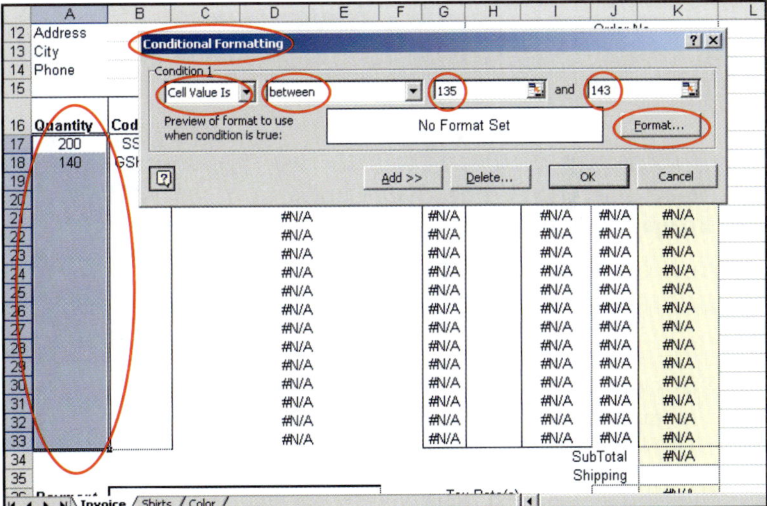

**2** Click the **Format** button.

*The Format Cells dialog box opens.*

Click **Bold Italic** in the **Font Style** box.

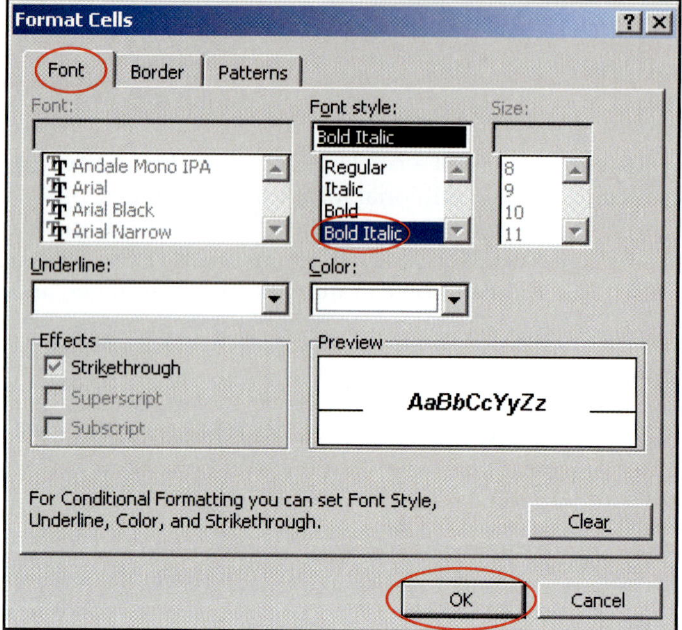

**3** Click **OK**.

*The Format Cells dialog box closes, and the selected format is displayed in the Conditional Formatting dialog box.*

Click **OK**.

*The value in cell A18 is displayed in bold italic font because it is between 135 and 143. The value in cell A17 does not change.*

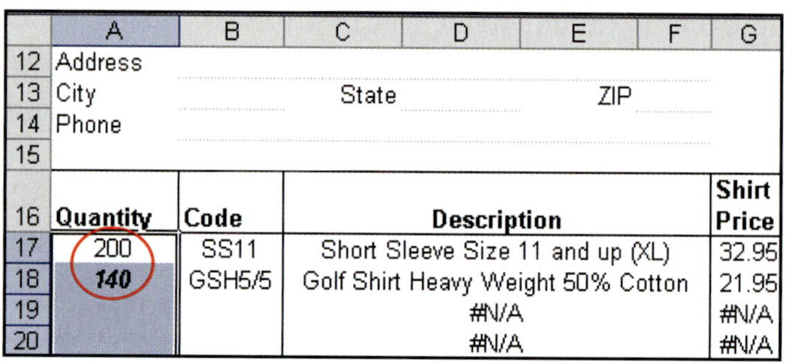

**4** Select cells **C18** through **F33**. Choose **Format, Conditional Formatting**.

*The Conditional Formatting dialog box opens. C17 is not selected because you would never have a blank invoice.*

Click the arrow on the first box and choose **Formula is**. Click the second box and type **=ISNA(C18)**.

*The argument for the ISNA function is the cell address that contains the error code.*

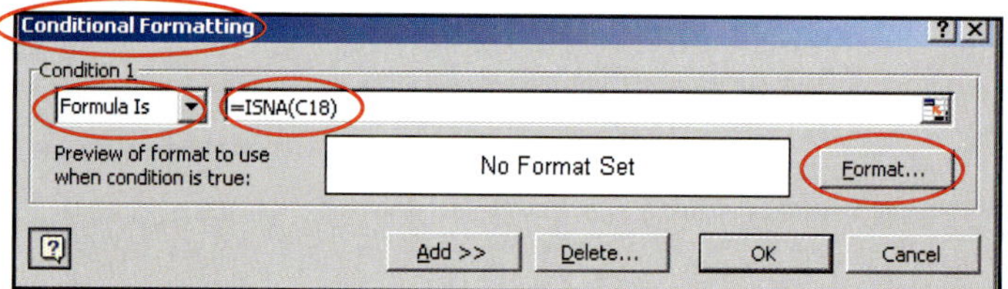

**5** Click the **Format** button. Click the **Color** arrow and choose **white**.

*To hide the code, format the font color to match the background in the cell, which in this case is white.*

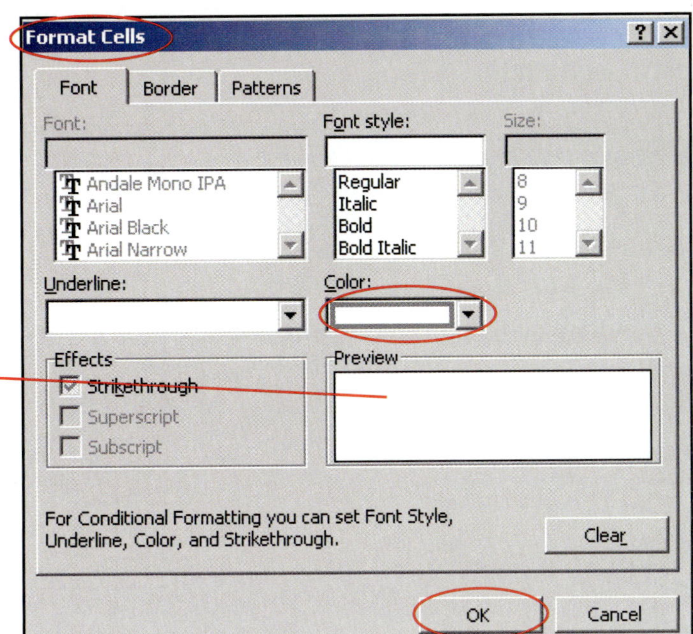



**CAUTION**

You must select the color white from the color palette, even though the color box appears to be white. The color box is actually empty—no color is selected.

**6** Click **OK**.

*Cells that contain an error message are formatted with a white font that does not appear against a white background.*

White font shows when the cell is selected

| 16 | Quantity | Code | Description | Shirt Price | # of Colors |
|---|---|---|---|---|---|
| 17 | 200 | SS11 | Short Sleeve Size 11 and up (XL) | 32.95 | 2 |
| 18 | 140 | GSH5/5 | Golf Shirt Heavy Weight 50% Cotton | 21.95 | 1 |
| 19 | | | #N/A | #N/A | |
| 20 | | | #N/A | #N/A | |
| 21 | | | #N/A | #N/A | |
| 22 | | | #N/A | #N/A | |
| 23 | | | #N/A | #N/A | |
| 24 | | | #N/A | #N/A | |
| 25 | | | #N/A | #N/A | |
| 26 | | | #N/A | #N/A | |
| 27 | | | #N/A | #N/A | |
| 28 | | | #N/A | #N/A | |
| 29 | | | #N/A | #N/A | |
| 30 | | | #N/A | #N/A | |
| 31 | | | #N/A | #N/A | |
| 32 | | | #N/A | #N/A | |
| 33 | | | #N/A | #N/A | |

**7** Select cells **G18** through **G33**. Choose **Format**, **Conditional Formatting**.

*The Conditional Formatting dialog box opens.*

Click the arrow on the first box and choose **Formula is**. Click the second box and type **=ISNA(G18)**. Set the format of the font color to white.

Repeat this process to hide the error messages in the **Color Charge** and **Unit Price** columns.

*The error messages are hidden in the columns with white backgrounds.*

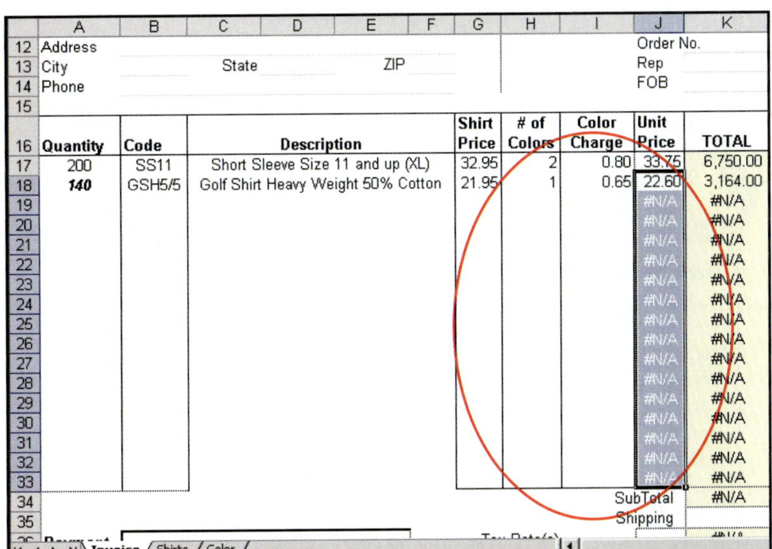

| | A | B | C | D | E | F | G | H | I | J | K |
|---|---|---|---|---|---|---|---|---|---|---|---|
| 12 | Address | | | | | | | | | Order No. | |
| 13 | City | | | State | | ZIP | | | | Rep | |
| 14 | Phone | | | | | | | | | FOB | |
| 15 | | | | | | | | | | | |
| 16 | Quantity | Code | | Description | | | Shirt Price | # of Colors | Color Charge | Unit Price | TOTAL |
| 17 | 200 | SS11 | | Short Sleeve Size 11 and up (XL) | | | 32.95 | 2 | 0.80 | 33.75 | 6,750.00 |
| 18 | 140 | GSH5/5 | | Golf Shirt Heavy Weight 50% Cotton | | | 21.95 | 1 | 0.65 | 22.60 | 3,164.00 |
| 19 | | | | | | | | | | #N/A | #N/A |
| 20 | | | | | | | | | | #N/A | #N/A |
| 21 | | | | | | | | | | #N/A | #N/A |
| 22 | | | | | | | | | | #N/A | #N/A |
| 23 | | | | | | | | | | #N/A | #N/A |
| 24 | | | | | | | | | | #N/A | #N/A |
| 25 | | | | | | | | | | #N/A | #N/A |
| 26 | | | | | | | | | | #N/A | #N/A |
| 27 | | | | | | | | | | #N/A | #N/A |
| 28 | | | | | | | | | | #N/A | #N/A |
| 29 | | | | | | | | | | #N/A | #N/A |
| 30 | | | | | | | | | | #N/A | #N/A |
| 31 | | | | | | | | | | #N/A | #N/A |
| 32 | | | | | | | | | | #N/A | #N/A |
| 33 | | | | | | | | | | #N/A | #N/A |
| 34 | | | | | | | | | | SubTotal | #N/A |
| 35 | | | | | | | | | | Shipping | |

**8** Select **K18** through **K38**. Use a conditional format to set the font color to light yellow when an error message is present.

*To hide the error messages in this column, the font must match the light yellow color of the background. If you are unsure which color is light yellow, point at the color and wait for a screen tip to appear with the name of the color.*

Click elsewhere on the worksheet to deselect the cells.

*The error messages are hidden.*

Save the workbook.

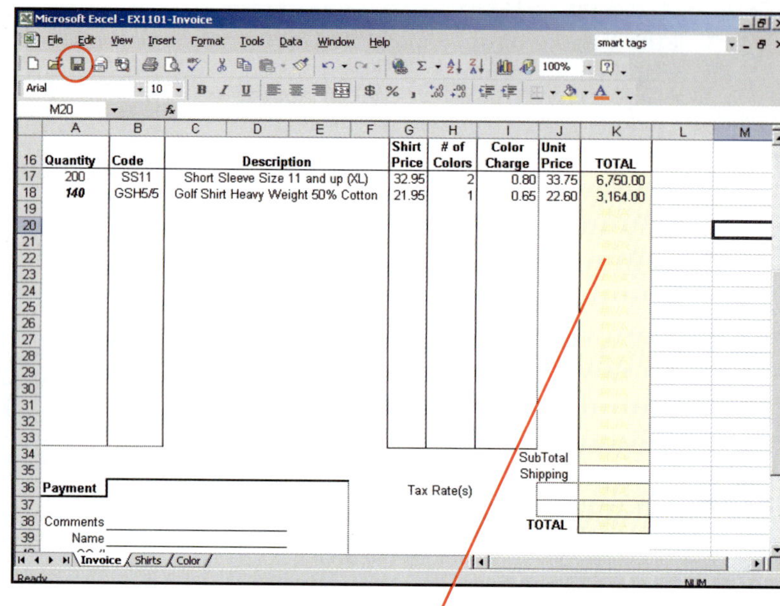

Yellow error code on yellow background

# Task 5



### Why would I do this?

Excel has many options for displaying numbers and dates. You can control the placement of commas in large numbers, as well as control how negative numbers are displayed. You can choose the type of currency settings used, including the symbols for different international currencies.

In this task, you learn how use a custom format for the date cell that displays the date in an unambiguous format, and to set the currency format for the Total column.

**1** Select **K11**. Type **3/2/03** and press Enter. Select **K11** again.

*The date is displayed using a four-digit format for the year.*

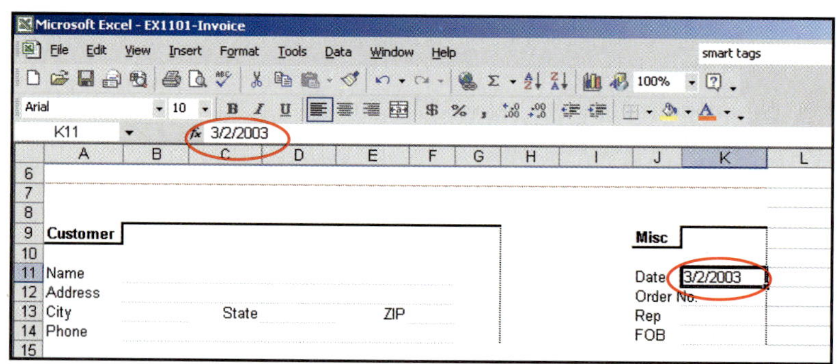

**CAUTION**

You can choose from a variety of displays for dates. If you work in an environment where people of different nationalities are using your worksheets, you need to be careful how you display dates. Most Europeans use a day-month-year format while most Americans use month-day-year. A date such as 3/2/03 is interpreted as February 3rd by Europeans and March 2nd by most Americans. The system your computer uses was determined when the Windows operating system was installed. The instructions in this task assume your operating system was set to United States English when it was installed. If your computer's operating system is set to a different date system, ask your instructor for options on how to do this task.

**IN DEPTH**

Notice the program converted 03 to 2003. To learn more about the assumptions Excel uses to convert two-digit years to four-digit years, use Help and search for: About Dates and Date Systems.

**2** Choose **Format**, **Cells**.

*The Format Cells dialog box opens.*

Click the **Number** tab, if necessary. Select **Date** in the **Category** pane. Select **14-Mar-01** in the **Type** pane. Confirm that the **Locale** is set to **English (United States)**.

*The month will be displayed using a three-character format.*

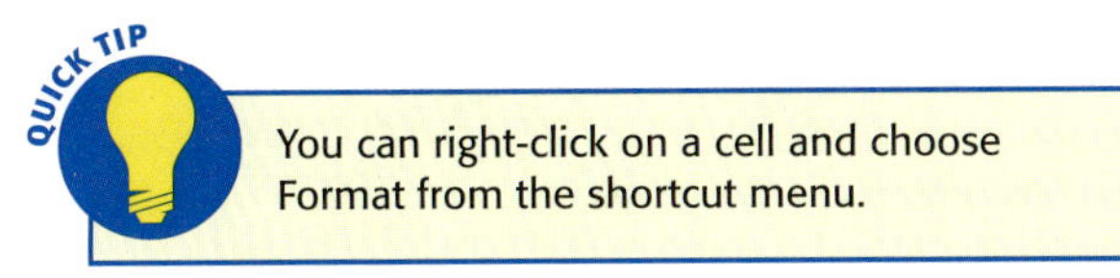

**QUICK TIP**

You can right-click on a cell and choose Format from the shortcut menu.

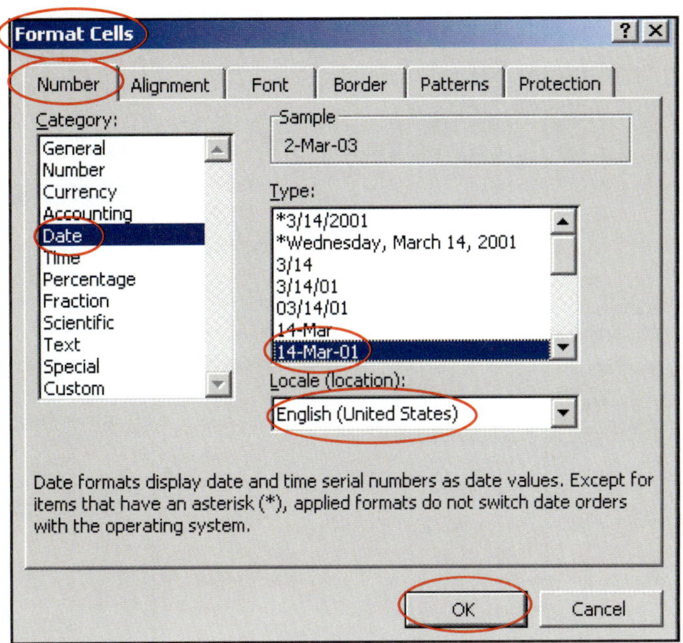


**3** Click **OK**. Select **K17** through **K38**. Choose **Format**, **Cells**.

*The Format Cells dialog box opens.*

Select **Currency** in the **Category** pane. Click the arrow on the **Symbol** box.

*A list of different currency styles is displayed.*

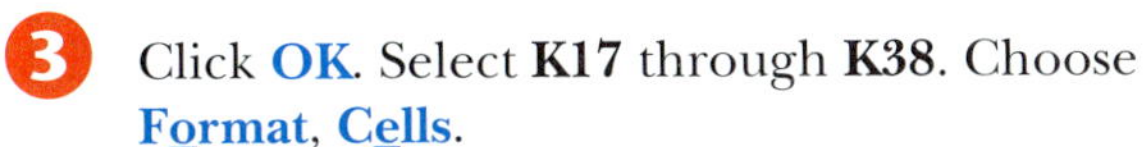
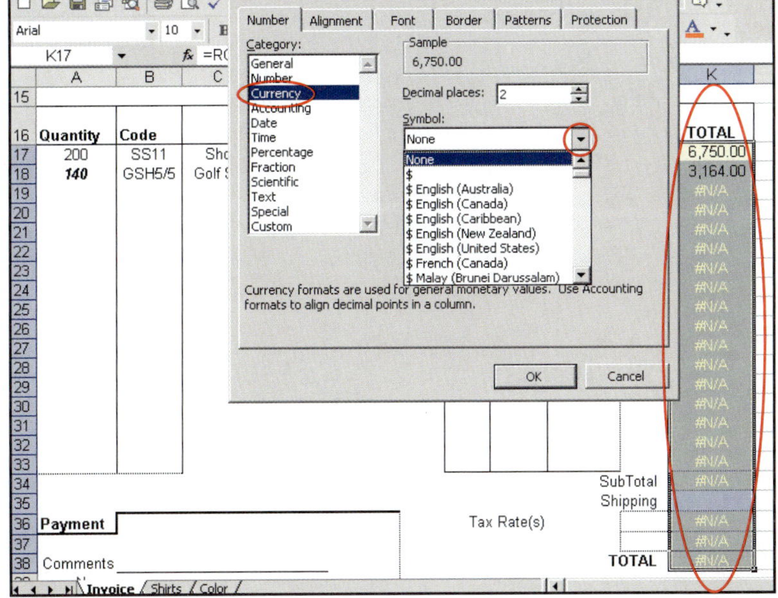

**4** Select **$ English (United States)**. Select **($1,234.10)** in the **<u>Negative numbers</u>** pane—the third option listed.

*Negative numbers, if they occur, are enclosed in parentheses.*

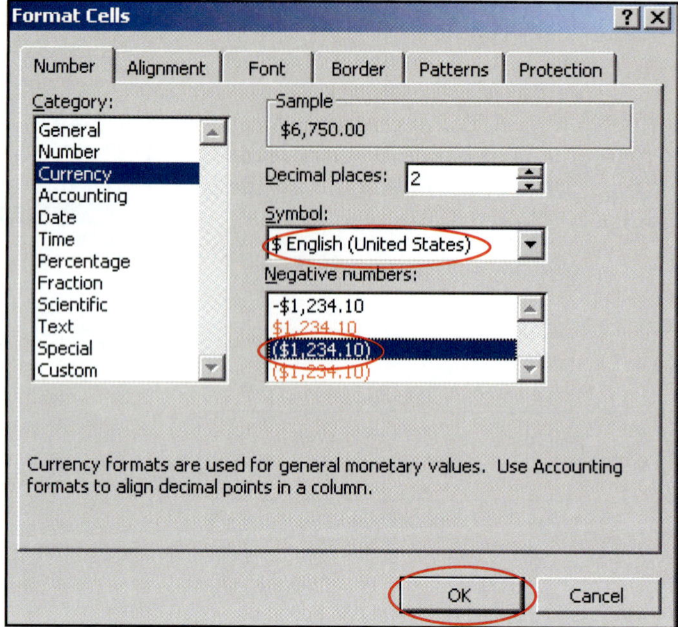

**5** Click **OK**.

*The numbers are formatted as currency in U.S. dollars. Negative numbers, if they occur, are enclosed in parentheses. The conditional format of the colors is not changed.*

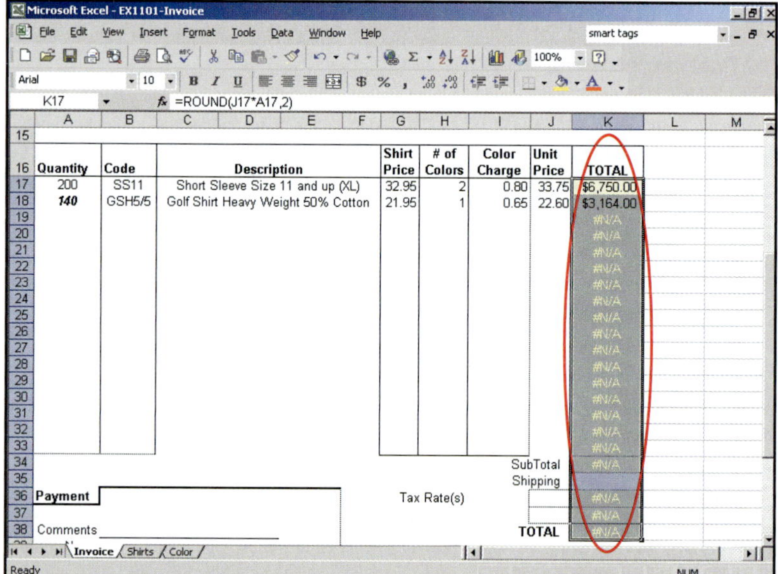

# Task 6
## AUDITING FORMULAS AND RESOLVING ERRORS

### Why would I do this?

The formulas used in this lesson are more complex than most and are more difficult to troubleshoot when there is an error. You may use a feature in Excel called *Formula Auditing,* which helps you identify the cells that affect or are affected by the current cell. The program draws arrows on the worksheet to show the cells used to calculate the formulas in the current cell when you use the *Trace Precedents* option. Arrows show which cells use the value in the current cell when you use the *Trace Dependents* option. The Undo button does not remove the arrows. You must use the *Remove All Arrows* option.

If a formula uses a range of cells and one of those cells contains an error message, such as #N/A, the formula also displays an error message. You turn the background error checking feature on to help identify the problem and then resolve this problem by using the *SUMIF* function that only sums cells in one range that meet certain criteria in another range.

In this task, you trace the precedents for a formula in the Color Charge column and you trace the dependents for a cell in the Quantity column. You resolve the problem in the SubTotal and Total cells by tracing the dependents and using the SUMIF function.

**1** Select **I17**. Choose **Tools, Formula Auditing, Trace Precedents**.

*The blue arrow indicates the precedent cells with a small circle in each precedent cell. The Shirts table is indicated with a small table and a dotted line to show that it is in another worksheet.*

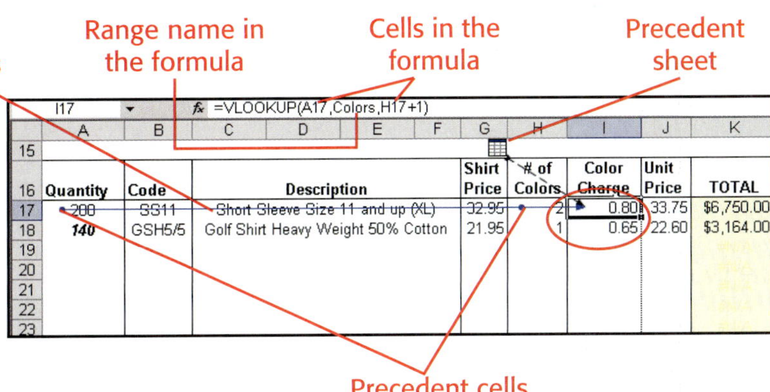


**2** Select **A18**. Choose **Tools, Formula Auditing, Trace Dependents**.

*A blue line indicates the dependent cells by placing an arrowhead at each dependent cell.*

The Undo button does not remove the arrows. You can remove the arrows by using the Remove All Arrows option that is also found on the Formula Auditing toolbar.

**3** Select **K34**. Choose **Tools, Formula Auditing, Trace Precedents**.

*The solid color line indicates that all the cells through which it passes are precedents of the selected cell.*

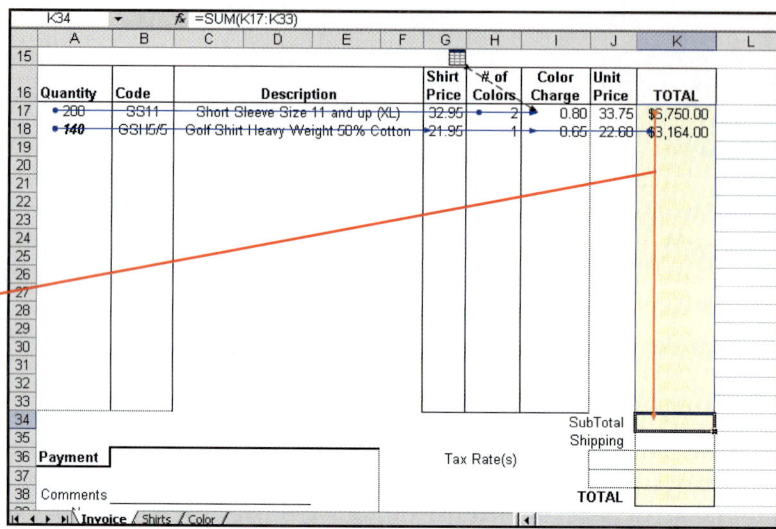


**4** Choose **Tools, Options**. Click the **Error Checking** tab. Click **Enable background error checking**. Click **OK**.

*Small green markers indicate the cells with error codes.*

Select **K38**. Move the pointer onto the *smart tag*.

*Smart tags detect situations in which you might need help. When you click on this one, it displays a message that tells you a value may not be available to this formula. The solid red trace precedent arrow tells you this formula uses values from the four cells above it and you can see that three of them have an error marker.*

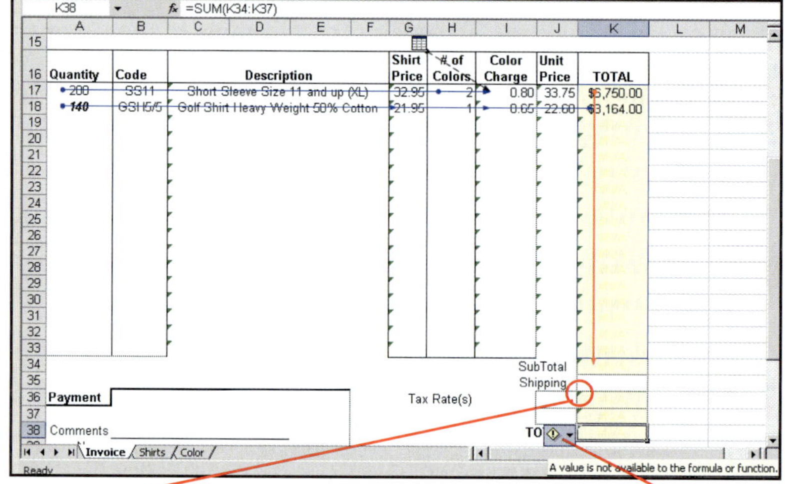


**5** Select **K34**.

*This cell has a formula that sums the cells above it, many of which have the #N/A error message. You will replace this formula with the SUMIF function.*

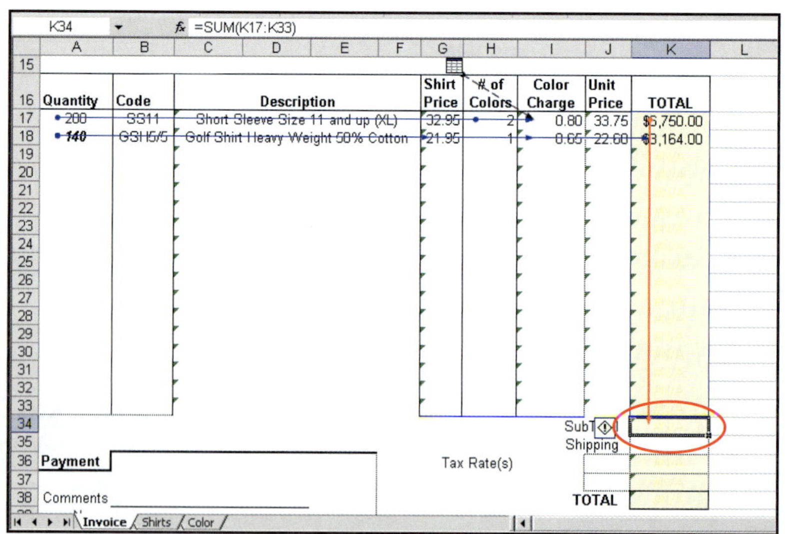

**6** Press `Del`. Choose **Insert, Function**. Click **Or select a category** arrow and choose **Math & Trig**. Scroll down and select **SUMIF**.

*This function examines one range of cells and sums the cells in a second range of cells if a criterion is met.*

Click **OK**. In the **Range** box, type **A17:A33**. In the **Criteria** box, type **>0**. In the **Sum_range** box, type **K17:K33**.

*The cells in the Total column that have a corresponding value greater than zero in the Quantity column will be summed. The cells with the #N/A error are not included and the SUMIF formula adds the cells that have values. The criteria is automatically enclosed in quotation marks that you do not have to type.*

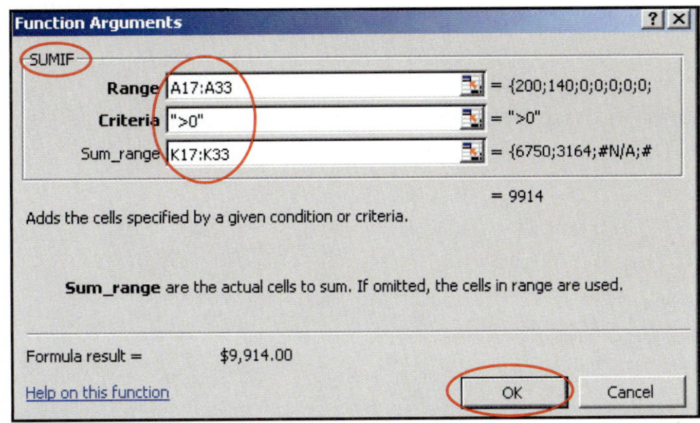

**IN DEPTH**

The two ranges in a SUMIF function must be the same size and consist of two columns that share the same rows. The criterion is applied to the cells in the range column one at a time. If the criterion is met, the corresponding cell in the sum_range is included in the summation.

**7** Click **OK**.

*The formula correctly sums the cells that have corresponding values in the Quantity column. This also removes the error markers in the three cells that are precedents of the Total formula in cell K38. The formula auditing lines are also removed.*

Cells no longer depend on a cell with an error

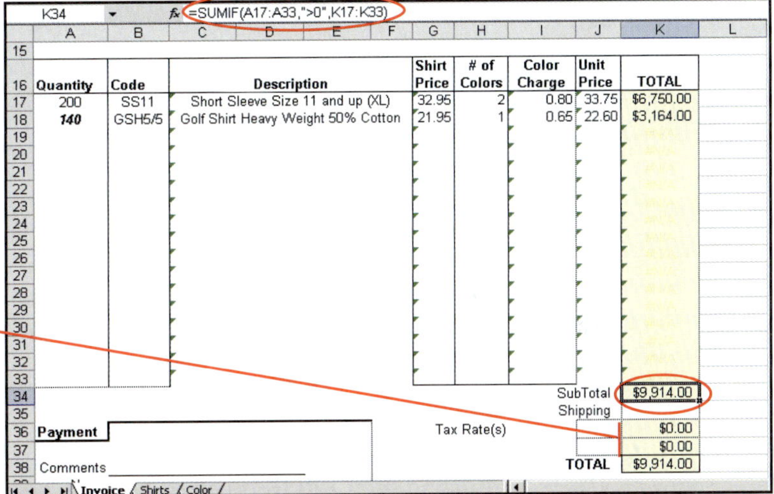

**8** Print the worksheet if your instructor requires it. Click **Save**. Close the workbook.

The exercises that follow are designed for you to review and use what you have learned in this lesson. You also have the opportunity to practice your skills and then expand on them by applying them to new situations.

## COMPREHENSION

Comprehension exercises are designed to check your memory and understanding of the basic concepts in this lesson. You distinguish between true and false statements, identify new screen elements, and match terms with related statements. If you are uncertain of the correct answer, refer to the task number following each item (for example, T4 refers to Task 4) and review that task until you are confident that you can provide a correct response.

### TRUE-FALSE

Circle either T or F.

T   F   **1.** If you use a named range in a formula, it must always be enclosed in double quotation marks. **(T1)**

T   F   **2.** You can validate the input of a cell by requiring that the value entered matches one of the values in a range of cells. **(T2)**

T   F   **3.** The VLOOKUP function finds a value in the first column of a range of data to determine the desired row. **(T3)**

T   F   **4.** You can use conditional formatting to hide errors by utilizing the ERROR function as the criterion. **(T4)**

T   F   **5.** The date, 3/2/2002, may be interpreted differently in the United States and Europe. You can use a custom date format to display the name of the month to reduce the likelihood of a misunderstanding. **(T5)**

T   F   **6.** To display the cells that depend on the currently selected cell graphically, you use the Trace Precedents tool. **(T6)**

### MATCHING QUESTIONS

**A.** Settings, Input message, Error Alert

**B.** Criteria, true, false

**C.** 2/3/2002

**D.** Define

**E.** Smart tags

**F.** Font color same as background color

Match the following statements to the word or phrase that is the best match from the list. Write the letter of the matching word or phrase in the space provided next to the number.

**1.** ____ Menu option used when naming a range for the first time **(T1)**

**2.** ____ Parts of defining validation **(T2)**

**3.** ____ Arguments of an IF statement **(T3)**

**4.** ____ Formatting method used to hide a message **(T4)**

**5.** ____ The way many Europeans would write March 2, 2002 **(T5)**

**6.** ____ Icons that display next to cells that may need attention **(T6)**

# IDENTIFYING PARTS OF THE EXCEL SCREEN

Refer to the figure and identify the numbered parts of the screen. Write the letter of the correct label in the space next to the number.

1. _______________

2. _______________

3. _______________

4. _______________

5. _______________

6. _______________

7. _______________

8. _______________

9. _______________

10. _______________

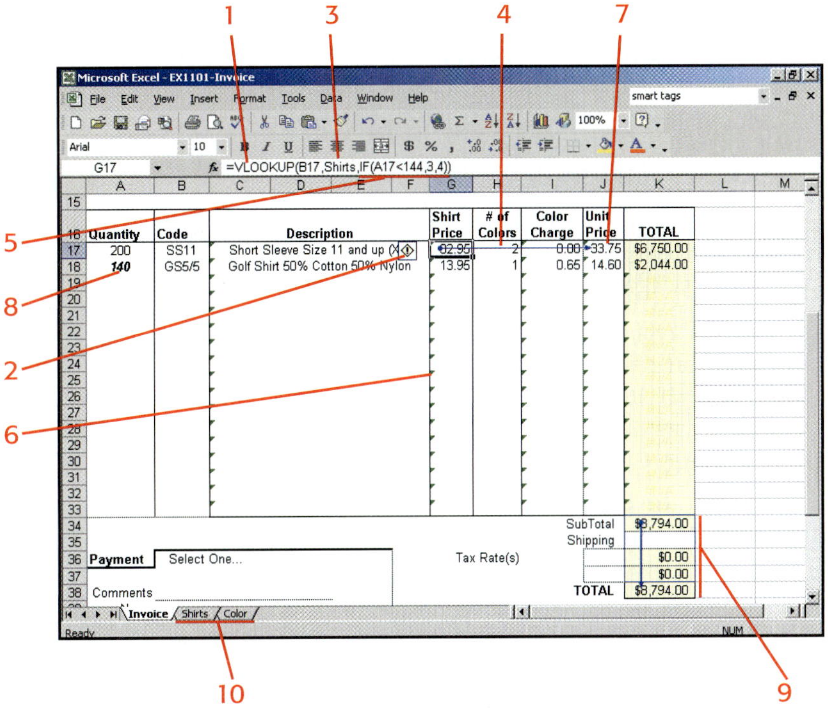

A. Precedents for K38  **(T6)**

B. Smart tag  **(T6)**

C. Conditional format  **(T4)**

D. A lookup function  **(T3)**

E. IF function  **(T3)**

F. Trace dependents line  **(T6)**

G. Error marker  **(T6)**

H. Dependent cell  **(T6)**

I. Named range  **(T1)**

J. Workheets where tables with named ranges are stored  **(T1)**

Reinforcement exercises are designed to reinforce the skills you have learned by applying them to a new situation. Detailed instructions are provided along with a figure, where appropriate, to illustrate the result. Complete the reinforcement exercises sequentially. Leave the workbook open at the end of each exercise for use in the next exercise until you are specifically directed to close it.

The workbook employed in the following reinforcement exercises is used to prepare an invoice for Armstrong Pool, Spa, and Sauna. It utilizes three tables that contain information about products, customers, and installation contractors.

## R1—Naming Ranges

You need two ranges for each of the four tables of data. One range will be used to validate the selection and the other will be used to look up specific information.

1. Open **EX1102** and save it as **EX1102-Armstrong** on your disk. Select the **Stores** worksheet. Select **A2** through **A9**. Define this range of cells as a named range with the name **StoreNumber**. Select **A2** through **G9** and name this range **StoreInfo**.

2. Select the **Products** worksheet. Select **A2** through **A20**. Define this range of cells as a named range with the name **ProductDescription**. Select **A2** through **D20** and name this range **ProductInfo**.

3. Select the **Customers** worksheet. Select **A2** through **A49**. Define this range of cells as a named range with the name **CustomerName**. Select **A2** through **I49** and name this range **CustomerInfo**.

4. Select the **Contractors** worksheet. Select **A2** through **A17**. Define this range of cells as a named range with the name **ContractorName**. Select **A2** through **I17** and name this range **ContractorInfo**.

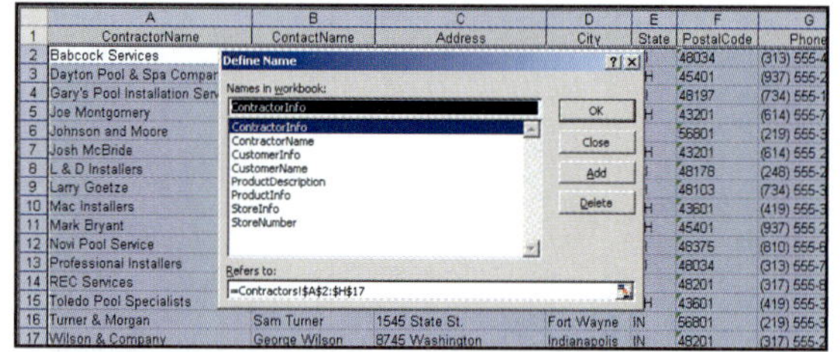

## R2—Validating Store, Customer, Contractor, and Product Information

To be sure that your invoice has the correct and current information, you validate the data from the other tables.

1. Select the **Invoice** sheet. Select cell **B1**. Validate the data in this cell by using a list. Use **=StoreNumber** as the source. Use the list to select **MI-100** for cell **B1**.

2. Select cells **B7** and **C7** (they are merged). Validate the data in this cell by using a list. Use **=CustomerName** as the source. Use the list to select **Shepard, Lucinda**.

3. Select cells **B13** through **D13** (they are merged). Validate the data in these cells by using a list. Use **=ContractorName** as the source. Use the list to select **Professional Installers**.

4. Select cells **B20** through **D20** (they are merged). Validate the data in these cells by using a list. Use **=ProductDescription** as the source. Use the list to select **Pool Oval 15'x24'**.

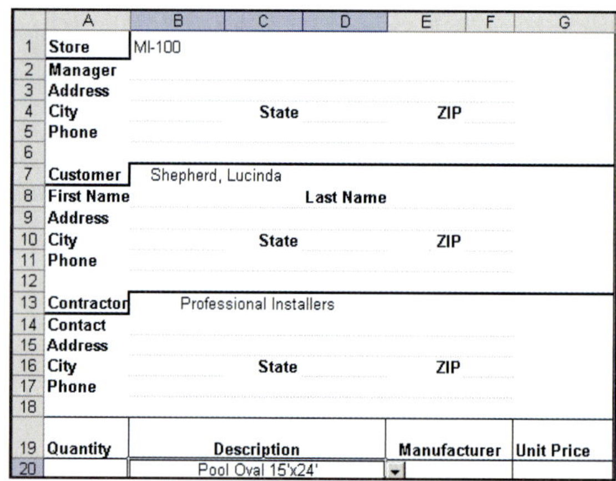

## R3—Using VLOOKUP functions to fill in the form

Once you have chosen the store, customer, contractor, and product, you can look up the related address and contact information.

1. Select the **Invoice** sheet, if necessary. The store manager's name is in column 2 of the StoreInfo range. Select the merged cells **B2** through **F2**. Type **=VLOOKUP(B1,StoreInfo,2)** and Press ⏎Enter. Use a VLOOKUP function in each of the following cells, **B3:F3**, **B4**, **D4**, **F4**, and **B5:C5**, to look up the value in cell B1 in the StoreInfo range. The address, city, state, postal code, and phone numbers are in columns 3 through 7. For example, in cells **B2:F3** you type **=VLOOKUP(B1,StoreInfo,3)**. In cell **B4**, you type **=VLOOKUP(B1,StoreInfo,4)** and so on.

2. The customer name is in column **1** of the
CustomerInfo range. The names in this column
are a combination of the last name, a comma,
and the first name. This is done to provide a
column of unique names that can be used with
a VLOOKUP function. Select the merged cells
**B8** through **C8** where the first name should go.
Type **=VLOOKUP(B7,CustomerInfo,3)**. Use a
VLOOKUP function in each of the following cells,
**E8:F8**, **B9:F9**, **B10**, **D10**, **F10**, and **B11:C11**, to look
up the value in cell **B7** in the CustomerInfo range.
The last name, address, city, state, postal code, and
phone numbers are in columns **4** through **9** of the
CustomerInfo range. For example, in cells **E8:F8**
you type **=VLOOKUP(B7,CustomerInfo,4)**. In cells
**B9:F9**, you type **=VLOOKUP(B7,CustomerInfo,5)**
and so on.

3. The contractor name is in column **1** of the
ContractorInfo range. Select the merged cells **B14**
through **C14** where the contact name should go.
Type **=VLOOKUP(B13,ContractorInfo,2)**. Use a
VLOOKUP function in each of the following cells,
**B15:F15**, **B16**, **D16**, **F16**, and **B16:C16**, to look up
the value in cell **B13** in the ContractorInfo range.
The address, city, state, postal code, and phone
numbers are in columns **3** through **7** of the
ContractorInfo range.

4. Place a VLOOKUP function in cell **E20** that can
look up the description in **B20** in the **ProductInfo**
range and return the manufacturer's name from
column **2**.

5. Place a VLOOKUP function in cell **G20** that can
look up the description in **B20** in the **ProductInfo**
range and return the unit price from column **3**.

6. Place a VLOOKUP function in cell **H20** that can
look up the description in **B20** in the **ProductInfo**
range and return the installation cost from
column **4**.

7. Select **A20** and type **1**. The unit price, installation
cost, and total are filled in.

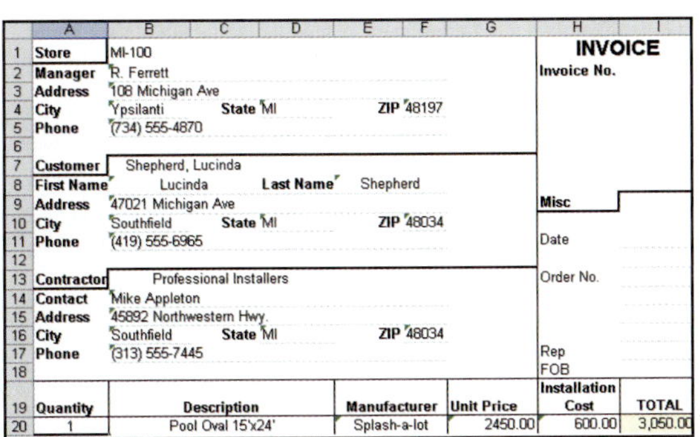

## R4—Using Conditional Formatting to Hide Error Messages

When you copy the validation and the formulas into the other cells
in the table, #REF error messages display due to the empty reference cells. You can hide them by formatting the font of the error
messages to match the background color.

1. Select the description in cells **B20** through **D20** and
click the **Copy** button. Select **B21** through **D36**.
Choose **Edit**, **Paste Special**. Choose **Validation** and
click **OK**.

2. Select the three formulas in cells **E20** through **H20**
and click the **Copy** button. Select **E21** through **H36**.
Choose **Edit**, **Paste Special**. Choose **Formulas** and
click **OK**.

3. Select **E21** through **H36**. Choose **Format**,
**Conditional Formatting**. Change the condition to
**Formula is** and type **=ISNA(E21)**. Click the **Format**
button and set the font to white, then click **OK**
twice to close the dialog boxes.

4. Select **I21** through **I41**. Choose **Format**,
**Conditional Formatting**. Change the condition to
**Formula is** and type **=ISNA(I21)**. Click the **Format**
button and set the font to light yellow, then click
**OK** twice to close the dialog boxes.

5. Format the numbers in columns **G**, **H**, and **I** to
**Currency** with two decimal places. Select cells **I20**
through **I41**. Click the **Borders** arrow and select
**Right Border**.

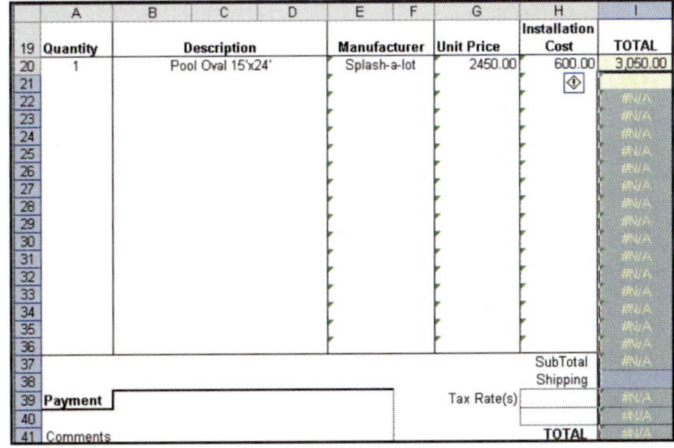

## R5—Using Formula Auditing to Resolve Errors

The subtotals and total figures do not display at the bottom of
TOTAL column.

1. Delete the formula in cell **I37**. Choose **Insert**,
**Function**. Click the **Or select a category** arrow and
choose **Math & Trig**. Scroll down and select **SUMIF**.
Click **OK**. In the **Range** box, type **A20:A36**. In the
**Criteria** box, type **>0**. In the **Sum_range** box, type
**I20:I36**. Click **OK**.

2. Select **I37** and choose **Tools**, **Formula Auditing**, **Trace Precedents**.

3. Print the **Invoice** sheet. Save the workbook and close it. The auditing arrows are not saved as part of the workbook.

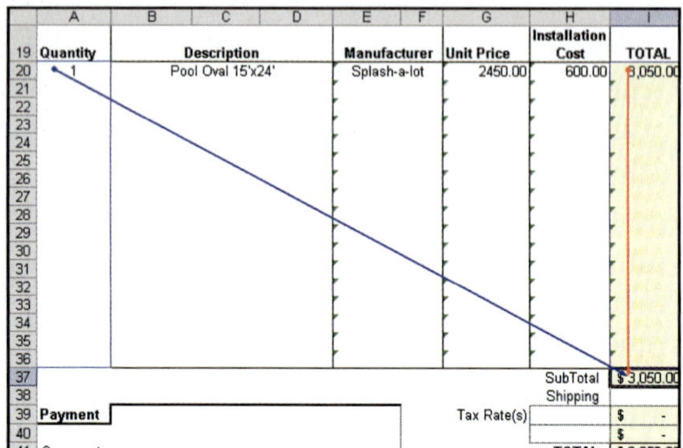

# CHALLENGE

Challenge exercises are designed to test your ability to apply your skills to new situations with less detailed instruction. These exercises also challenge you to expand your repertoire of skills by using commands that are similar to those you have already learned. The desired outcome is clearly defined, but you have more freedom to choose the steps needed to achieve the required result.

## C1—Using the INDEX function

If you know the row and column numbers of the cell you wish to look up from a table, you can use the INDEX function. The table used in this exercise is similar to the Colors table in EX1101-Invoice but it has been modified so that the number of shirts in the first column is in dozens and the number of colors ranges from 1 to 4 where 1 stands for black.

*Goal:* Use the INDEX function to find the cost of adding color to a printing job.

Use the following guidelines:

1. Locate **EX1103** in the student files and save it as **EX1103-C1-INDEX**.

2. Select **A22** and enter your name. Select **A12** and enter **Dozens of Shirts:**. Select **A13** and enter **Number of Colors:**. Select **A14** and enter **Cost per Shirt:**.

3. Enter a number between 1 and 8 in **B12** and a number between 1 and 4 in **B13**.

4. Select the data in cells **B3** through **E10**. Notice the row and column numbers are not included. Define a name for this range as **Colors**.

5. Select **B14**. Type **=INDEX(Colors,5,3)** and press **⏎Enter**. The answer should be **1.2**, which is the cost for five dozen shirts in three colors.

6. Select **B14** and type **=INDEX(Colors,B12,B13)**. Now the formula uses the values you selected in cells **B12** and **B13**.

7. Print the **Colors** sheet if your instructor requires it. Save the file. Close the workbook.

| B14 | ▼ | $f_x$ =INDEX(Colors,B12,B13) | | |
|---|---|---|---|---|
| | **A** | **B** | **C** | **D** | **E** |
| 1 | Dozens of Shirts | | Number of Colors | | |
| 2 | | 1 | 2 | 3 | 4 |
| 3 | 1 | 0.95 | 2.55 | 3.83 | 5.11 |
| 4 | 2 | 0.80 | 2.25 | 3.38 | 4.51 |
| 5 | 3 | 0.75 | 1.15 | 1.73 | 2.31 |
| 6 | 4 | 0.65 | 0.90 | 1.35 | 1.80 |
| 7 | 5 | 0.55 | 0.80 | 1.20 | 1.60 |
| 8 | 6 | 0.50 | 0.65 | 0.98 | 1.31 |
| 9 | 7 | 0.30 | 0.60 | 0.90 | 1.20 |
| 10 | 8 | 0.20 | 0.55 | 0.83 | 1.11 |
| 11 | | | | | |
| 12 | Dozens of Shirts: | 4.00 | | | |
| 13 | Number of Colors | 2.00 | | | |
| 14 | Cost per Shirt: | 0.9 | | | |
| 15 | | | | | |

## C2—Selecting Ranges using Column Headers or Whole Worksheets

If you want to add values to a table, you have to revise the named ranges if they are based on a specific range of cells. You can get around this limitation by naming the entire worksheet or a particular column as the range. The worksheet must be modified to remove column headings and other labels as well as any merged cells. You also use a combination of the Ctrl and ⃔ keys to display the formulas in each cell. The ***accent grave*** character, ⃔, is similar to a single quotation mark and is usually found at the left end of the row of numbers on your keyboard.

*Goal:* Revise the Colors sheet and create ranges that you can expand without revising the range names.

Use the following guidelines:

1. Locate **EX1103** in the student files and save it as **EX1103-C2-Range**.

2. Select row **1** and row **2**. Choose **Edit**, **Delete**.

3. Click the small box in upper-left corner of the sheet. It is above the first row header and to the left of the column **A** header. The entire sheet is selected. Name this range **Colors**.

4. Click the header for column **A** to select the entire column. Name this range **Dozens**.

5. Click the **Sheet1** tab. Enter your name in **A1**.

6. Select **A3** and type **Dozens:**. Select **B3** and type **5**.

7. Select **A4** and type **Colors:**. Select **B4** and type **3**.

8. Select **A5** and type **Cost:**. Select **B5** and type **=VLOOKUP(B3,Colors,B4+1)** and press **⏎Enter**. In this example, the number of the column is one more than the number of the colors because the first column is used for the number of dozens.

9. Click the **Colors** sheet tab. Add another row to the table. The new values in row 9 are: **9**, **0.18**, **0.50**, **0.78**, and **1.02**.

10. Click the **Sheet1** tab. Change the number of dozens to **9**. The correct cost per shirt for nine dozen with three colors should display.

11. Format **B5** to **Currency**.

12. Press Ctrl + ⃔ to display the formulas and print the Sheet1.

**13.** Save the workbook and close it.

| | A | B | C | D | E |
|---|---|---|---|---|---|
| 1 | 1 | 0.95 | 2.55 | 3.83 | 5.11 |
| 2 | 2 | 0.80 | 2.25 | 3.38 | 4.51 |
| 3 | 3 | 0.75 | 1.15 | 1.73 | 2.31 |
| 4 | 4 | 0.65 | 0.90 | 1.35 | 1.80 |
| 5 | 5 | 0.55 | 0.80 | 1.20 | 1.60 |
| 6 | 6 | 0.50 | 0.65 | 0.98 | 1.31 |
| 7 | 7 | 0.30 | 0.60 | 0.90 | 1.20 |
| 8 | 8 | 0.20 | 0.55 | 0.83 | 1.11 |
| 9 | 9 | 0.18 | 0.50 | 0.78 | 1.02 |

## C3—Using the True/False Option in a VLOOKUP Function

If you use a VLOOKUP function to look up a number, you need to know what will happen if the number for which you are searching does not match any of the values in the first column. You also need to know what happens if the value is outside the range of numbers in the first column. You can use a fourth argument, called *range_lookup*, in the function to force exact matches or allow approximate matches.

*Goal:* Create a small table that shows what happens with you exceed the range or use nonmatching numbers in a VLOOKUP function with and without the range_lookup option.

1. Locate **EX1103** in the student files and save it as **EX1103-C3-TRUE**.

2. Select **A3:E10** and name the range **Colors**.

3. Select **A13** and type **Dozens:**. Select **B13** and type **5**.

4. Select **A14** and type **Colors:**. Select **B14** and type **3**.

5. Select **A15** and type **Cost:**. Select **B15** and type **=VLOOKUP(B13,Colors,B14+1,TRUE)** and then press ⏎Enter. In this example, you use B14+1 as the third argument because the number of the column is one more than the number of the colors. This happens because the first column is used for the number of dozens. The fourth argument is used to determine if the match is approximate or exact.

6. Select **B12** through **D12**, click the **Merge and Center** button, and then type **TRUE**. Select **E12** through **G12**, click the **Merge and Center** button, and then type **FALSE**.

7. Select **B13** through **B15**. Drag the fill handle to column **G**.

8. Edit the three formulas in **E15** through **G15** and change the range_lookup options from TRUE to **FALSE**.

9. Replace the values in **B13:G13** to show three different options for both TRUE and FALSE: **0.50, 2.75, 9.00, 0.50, 2.75, 9.00**.

10. Select **A17** through **G23** and click the **Merge and Center** button. Choose **Format**, **Cells**, **Alignment**. Select **Left(Indent)** in the **Horizontal** box, **TOP**, in the **Vertical** box, and select **Wrap text**. Click **OK**.

11. Use this range of cells to write a short explanation of this function. Refer to the table of results in **A12** through **G15**. Describe how the range_error option deals with reference values that are less than the lowest value in the first column of the table (.5), how they each deal with a number that is between two values in the first column (2.75), and how they deal with numbers that are larger than the largest value in the first column (9).

12. Print the worksheet. Save your changes and close the workbook.

| | A | B | C | D | E | F | G |
|---|---|---|---|---|---|---|---|
| 3 | 1 | 0.95 | 2.55 | 3.83 | 5.11 | | |
| 4 | 2 | 0.80 | 2.25 | 3.38 | 4.51 | | |
| 5 | 3 | 0.75 | 1.15 | 1.73 | 2.31 | | |
| 6 | 4 | 0.65 | 0.90 | 1.35 | 1.80 | | |
| 7 | 5 | 0.55 | 0.80 | 1.20 | 1.60 | | |
| 8 | 6 | 0.50 | 0.65 | 0.98 | 1.31 | | |
| 9 | 7 | 0.30 | 0.60 | 0.90 | 1.20 | | |
| 10 | 8 | 0.20 | 0.55 | 0.83 | 1.11 | | |
| 11 | | | | | | | |
| 12 | | | TRUE | | | FALSE | |
| 13 | Dozens: | 0.50 | 2.75 | 9.00 | 0.50 | 2.75 | 9.00 |
| 14 | Colors: | 3.00 | 3.00 | 3.00 | 3.00 | 3.00 | 3.00 |
| 15 | Cost: | #N/A | 3.38 | 0.83 | #N/A | #N/A | #N/A |
| 16 | | | | | | | |
| 17 | Analyze the behaviour of the range_error option in the table above and write your | | | | | | |
| 18 | essay here. | | | | | | |
| 19 | | | | | | | |
| 20 | | | | | | | |
| 21 | | | | | | | |
| 22 | | | | | | | |
| 23 | | | | | | | |

## C4—Using the HLOOKUP Function and Transpose

You can orient a table of data horizontally rather than vertically. If the value you want to look up is arranged in a row across the top of the table, you can use the HLOOKUP function instead of the VLOOKUP function.

In some cases, you may wish to change the orientation of a table. To accomplish this, you copy the table and then paste it in another location using the *Transpose* option.

*Goal:* Transpose the Colors table and use the HLOOKUP function to find the price for color printing.

1. Locate **EX1103** in the student files and save it as **EX1103-C4-Horizontal**.

2. Select **A2** through **E10** and click the **Copy** button.

3. Click **A12**. Choose **Edit**, **Paste Special**. Click the **Transpose** option and click **OK**. The number of colors is now listed in column **A**, and the number of dozens is in row **12**.

4. Select **B12** through **I16** and name the range **Colors**. You do not include the row headings in the HLOOKUP argument in the same manner that you did not include the column headings in a VLOOKUP argument.

5. Select **A18** and type **Dozens:**. Select **B18** and type **5**.

6. Select **A19** and type **Colors:**. Select **B19** and type **3**.

7. Select **A20** and type **Cost:**. Select **B20** and type **=HLOOKUP(B18,Colors,B19+1)** and press **⏎Enter**. In this example, you use B19+1 as the third argument because the number of the rows is one more than the number of the colors. This happens because the first row is used for the number of dozens.

8. Select **A22** and enter your name. Print the sheet. Save the workbook and close it.

| | A | B | C | D | E | F | G | H | I |
|---|---|---|---|---|---|---|---|---|---|
| 1 | Dozens of Shirts | | Number of Colors | | | | | | |
| 2 | | 1 | 2 | 3 | 4 | | | | |
| 3 | 1 | 0.95 | 2.55 | 3.83 | 5.11 | | | | |
| 4 | 2 | 0.80 | 2.25 | 3.38 | 4.51 | | | | |
| 5 | 3 | 0.75 | 1.15 | 1.73 | 2.31 | | | | |
| 6 | 4 | 0.65 | 0.90 | 1.35 | 1.80 | | | | |
| 7 | 5 | 0.55 | 0.80 | 1.20 | 1.60 | | | | |
| 8 | 6 | 0.50 | 0.65 | 0.98 | 1.31 | | | | |
| 9 | 7 | 0.30 | 0.60 | 0.90 | 1.20 | | | | |
| 10 | 8 | 0.20 | 0.55 | 0.83 | 1.11 | | | | |
| 11 | | | | | | | | | |
| 12 | | 1 | 2 | 3 | 4 | 5 | 6 | 7 | 8 |
| 13 | 1 | 0.95 | 0.80 | 0.75 | 0.65 | 0.55 | 0.50 | 0.30 | 0.20 |
| 14 | 2 | 2.55 | 2.25 | 1.15 | 0.90 | 0.80 | 0.65 | 0.60 | 0.55 |
| 15 | 3 | 3.83 | 3.38 | 1.73 | 1.35 | 1.20 | 0.98 | 0.90 | 0.83 |
| 16 | 4 | 5.11 | 4.51 | 2.31 | 1.80 | 1.60 | 1.31 | 1.20 | 1.11 |
| 17 | | | | | | | | | |
| 18 | Dozens: | 5.00 | | | | | | | |
| 19 | Colors: | 3.00 | | | | | | | |
| 20 | Cost: | 1.2 | | | | | | | |
| 21 | | | | | | | | | |
| 22 | <student name> | | | | | | | | |

## C5—Using Custom Number Formats

Most formatting needs can be met using one of the pre-defined formatting options. If you want to control the number of digits displayed, how zero values are handled, or if you want to add different text labels to positive and negative numbers you can create your own rules for handling these options.

In this exercise, you learn about the options for formatting numbers and create your own formatting options to handle positive, negative, and zero values.

*Goal:* Create and describe your own custom number format.

1. Save a new, blank workbook as EX1104-C5.

2. Enter your name and section in A1.

3. Select the Ask a Question box in the upper right corner of the window and enter Create a custom number format. Choose the option Create or delete a custom number format. Read the instructions in this topic.

4. Select B3 and create a custom format that will display positive numbers as currency. Negative numbers display in blue followed by your last name.

5. Test your format by typing in positive and negative numbers. Print a copy to hand in if your instructor requires it. Save the workbook and close it.

| B3 | | ▾ | *fx* | -1 |
|---|---|---|---|---|
| | A | | B | C |
| 1 | <student name and section> | | | |
| 2 | | | | |
| 3 | | | ($1.00 lastname) | |
| 4 | | | | |
| 5 | | | | |

Create a workbook that consists of at least two worksheets. The first sheet prepares a statement of some kind that uses values from the second sheet.

Criteria for grading will be:

1. Demonstration of the use of reference formulas such as VLOOKUP, HLOOKUP, and IF formulas that refer to a named range of cells on the second worksheet.

2. Demonstration of the ability to use conditional formatting.

3. Demonstration of the ability to check for errors and hide #N/A error messages with conditional formatting.

Some examples of projects that students have created that meet these criteria are:

- A workbook that creates a Material Safety Data Sheet (MSDS) for substances that contain several chemicals. A list of chemicals and the required warnings resided in a table on the second worksheet while VLOOKUP functions retrieved the various attributes of the chemicals.

- A workbook that determines the safety and cost of flying freight to various destinations. This project had tables of airport information and airplane characteristics. The student used VLOOKUP and IF statements to determine if the runways were long enough at a given airport to accommodate a selected aircraft. Conditional formatting was used to warn of a safety problem. The student also looked up the longitude and latitude of the airports and calculated the distance between them. Another lookup formula determined the fuel consumption of the selected aircraft and calculated the fuel needed to fly between the two airports. The final product allowed the user to select an aircraft and enter the airports on its route. The distance, fuel consumption, and flight time were calculated and the user was warned if the airport did not have long enough runways for the aircraft selected.

1. Identify yourself and the year. Place your name in a cell that is clearly visible on the first worksheet.

2. To complete the project:

- Save the workbook on your own disk. Name the workbook **EX1104-OnYourOwn**.

- Check with your instructor to determine if you should submit the project in electronic or printed form. If necessary, print out a copy of the workbook.

# Lesson 12

## Analyzing Data



## INTRODUCTION

Many people who are not familiar with database management software, such as Microsoft Access, use Excel as a simple database manager to store records of invoices or other transactions. You can manage data in Excel if the data is stored in a simple table format where each row is a record of one transaction and the columns are types of data. The column headings should not be merged across columns and each column heading should be short and unique. If the data is stored in this form, you can sort, filter, group, and subtotal the columns of data. These features are especially useful for preparing reports that allow someone to focus on particular sections of the data. You can summarize the data by groups and categories by creating a *PivotTable* on another worksheet. You select the row and column headings and how the cells in the table will be calculated.

Excel can help you chart your data and find a line that is the best fit through your data points. This type of line is called a *trendline*. Excel can also provide the formula for that line and a statistical measurement called an *R-squared value* that gives you an idea of how well the trend line fits the data. You can use the formula to estimate other data points on the trend line.

If your calculations depend on several assumptions, you can calculate the best option for each variable using *Goal Seek* and save the result of each calculation as a separate *scenario*. Goal Seek is a tool that automatically tries different values to achieve a goal, and a scenario saves the values of the variable for use at a later time.

In this lesson, you learn how to sort the data by each of the columns and how to filter the data by selecting values within certain columns. You group the data and add subtotals. You create a PivotTable to compare sales by branch and product. Finally, you save different scenarios that result from changing the size limit and point values for large and small sales.

307

# VISUAL SUMMARY

By the time you complete this lesson; you will have sorted, grouped, subtotaled, and filtered the data. You will have charted the data and added a trend line. You will also have calculated and compared four different scenarios. The worksheets will look like these:

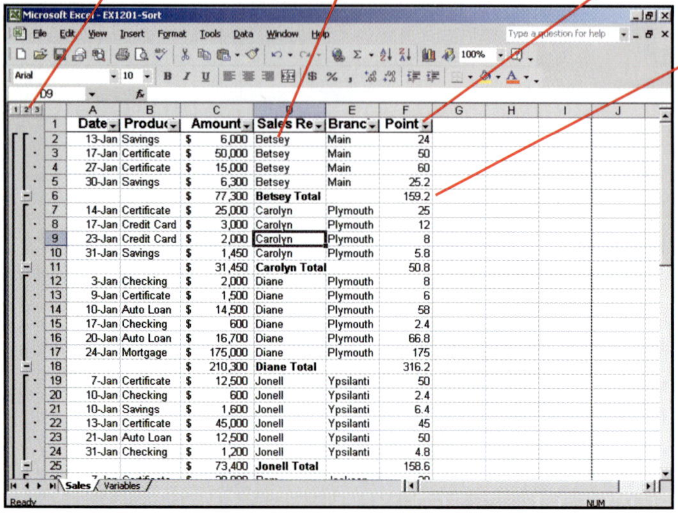

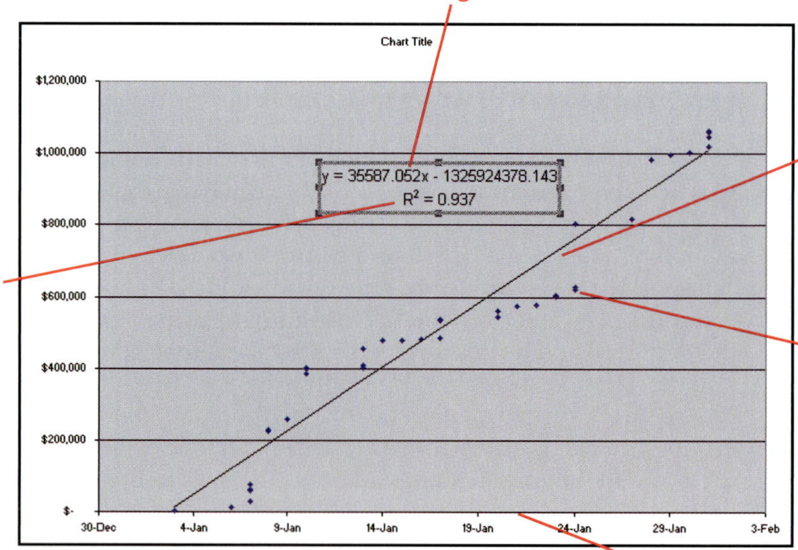

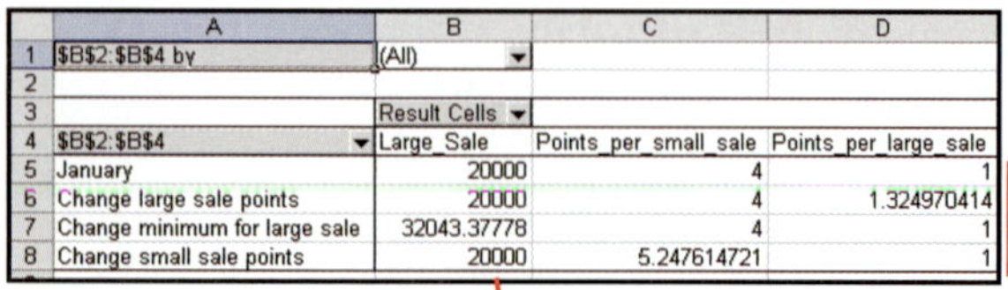

| | A | B | C | D | E | F |
|---|---|---|---|---|---|---|
| 1 | Date | Product | Amount | Sales Re | Branch | Point |
| 2 | 13-Jan | Savings | $ 6,000 | Betsey | Main | 24 |
| 3 | 17-Jan | Certificate | $ 50,000 | Betsey | Main | 50 |
| 4 | 27-Jan | Certificate | $ 15,000 | Betsey | Main | 60 |
| 5 | 30-Jan | Savings | $ 6,300 | Betsey | Main | 25.2 |
| 6 | | | $ 77,300 | **Betsey Total** | | 159.2 |
| 7 | 14-Jan | Certificate | $ 25,000 | Carolyn | Plymouth | 25 |
| 8 | 17-Jan | Credit Card | $ 3,000 | Carolyn | Plymouth | 12 |
| 9 | 23-Jan | Credit Card | $ 2,000 | Carolyn | Plymouth | 8 |
| 10 | 31-Jan | Savings | $ 1,450 | Carolyn | Plymouth | 5.8 |
| 11 | | | $ 31,450 | **Carolyn Total** | | 50.8 |
| 12 | 3-Jan | Checking | $ 2,000 | Diane | Plymouth | 8 |
| 13 | 9-Jan | Certificate | $ 1,500 | Diane | Plymouth | 6 |
| 14 | 10-Jan | Auto Loan | $ 14,500 | Diane | Plymouth | 58 |
| 15 | 17-Jan | Checking | $ 600 | Diane | Plymouth | 2.4 |
| 16 | 20-Jan | Auto Loan | $ 16,700 | Diane | Plymouth | 66.8 |
| 17 | 24-Jan | Mortgage | $ 175,000 | Diane | Plymouth | 175 |
| 18 | | | $ 210,300 | **Diane Total** | | 316.2 |
| 19 | 7-Jan | Certificate | $ 12,500 | Jonell | Ypsilanti | 50 |
| 20 | 10-Jan | Checking | $ 600 | Jonell | Ypsilanti | 2.4 |
| 21 | 10-Jan | Savings | $ 1,600 | Jonell | Ypsilanti | 6.4 |
| 22 | 13-Jan | Certificate | $ 45,000 | Jonell | Ypsilanti | 45 |
| 23 | 21-Jan | Auto Loan | $ 12,500 | Jonell | Ypsilanti | 50 |
| 24 | 31-Jan | Checking | $ 1,200 | Jonell | Ypsilanti | 4.8 |
| 25 | | | $ 73,400 | **Jonell Total** | | 158.6 |

Sales / Variables

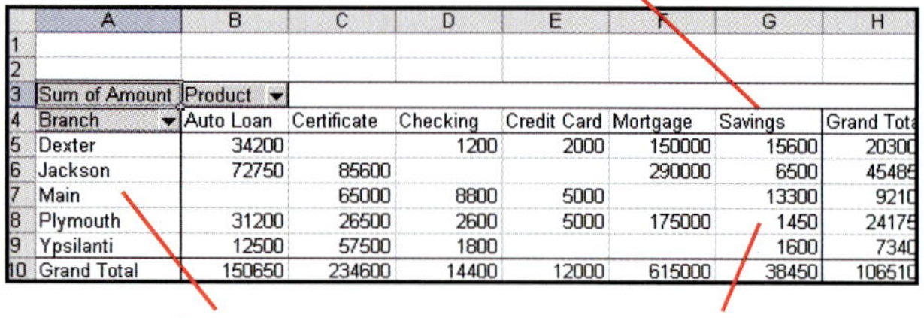

| | A | B | C | D | E | F | G | H |
|---|---|---|---|---|---|---|---|---|
| 3 | Sum of Amount | Product | | | | | | |
| 4 | Branch | Auto Loan | Certificate | Checking | Credit Card | Mortgage | Savings | Grand Total |
| 5 | Dexter | 34200 | | 1200 | 2000 | 150000 | 15600 | 20300 |
| 6 | Jackson | 72750 | 85600 | | | 290000 | 6500 | 45485 |
| 7 | Main | | 65000 | 8800 | 5000 | | 13300 | 9210 |
| 8 | Plymouth | 31200 | 26500 | 2600 | 5000 | 175000 | 1450 | 24175 |
| 9 | Ypsilanti | 12500 | 57500 | 1800 | | | 1600 | 7340 |
| 10 | Grand Total | 150650 | 234600 | 14400 | 12000 | 615000 | 38450 | 106510 |



| | A | B | C | D |
|---|---|---|---|---|
| 1 | $B$2:$B$4 by | (All) | | |
| 2 | | | | |
| 3 | | Result Cells | | |
| 4 | $B$2:$B$4 | Large_Sale | Points_per_small_sale | Points_per_large_sale |
| 5 | January | 20000 | 4 | 1 |
| 6 | Change large sale points | 20000 | 4 | 1.324970414 |
| 7 | Change minimum for large sale | 32043.37778 | 4 | 1 |
| 8 | Change small sale points | 20000 | 5.247614721 | 1 |

# Task 1

## FILTERING DATA



### Why would I do this?

If you have a lot of data that is mixed together, you can focus on one portion of the data by selecting the characteristics you want and only displaying the rows in the worksheet that meet those criteria.

In the example used in this lesson, you analyze the data from a sales contest at a bank. There are several branch banks and each branch has several employees. There are several different banking services they sell to bank customers for which they are awarded points. The points awarded depend on whether the sale is considered to be above or below a certain size.

In this task, you filter the data by matching names, using *comparison operators* and date ranges.

1. Open **EX1201** from the **Student** folder. Save it as **EX1201-Sort** on your disk.

*The new title appears in the title bar.*

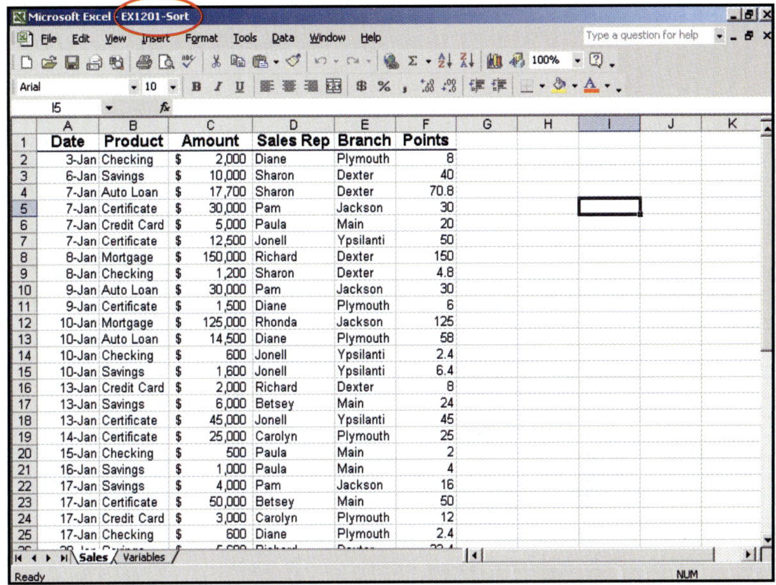

2. Select any cell in the table of data then choose **Data**, **Filter**, **AutoFilter**.

*Arrows are added in the column headings. The arrows display lists of options for filtering the rows based on the contents of the column.*

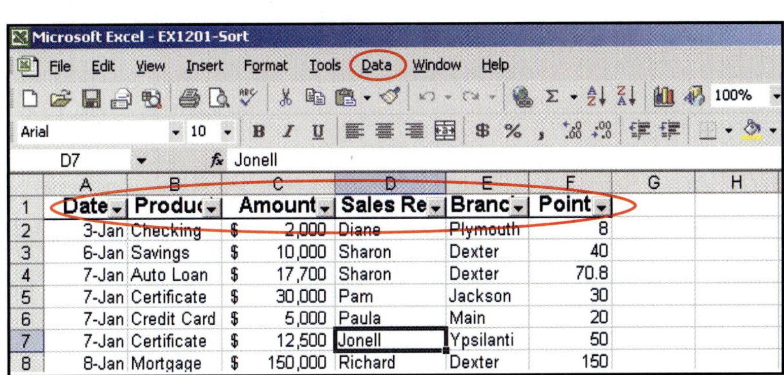

**IN DEPTH**

The program assumes that the first row contains column headings. Do not merge column headings across columns. Keep the headings short and different for each column. Use only one row for column headings. Do not use empty rows or columns for visual spacing. If you ever decide to move an Excel worksheet into an Access database, it will be easier if you use simple rows and columns with simple column headings.

**3** Click the arrow on the **Branch** heading and select **Jackson** from the list.

*The rows for the Jackson branch are displayed. The row numbers change color to draw attention to the fact that all the rows are not displayed, and the small arrow in the heading changes color to show that a filter is active in that column. The cumulative total formulas in the last column still display the totals from all the rows even if they are not displayed.*

|  | A | B | C | D | E | F |
|---|---|---|---|---|---|---|
| 1 | Date | Produc | Amount | Sales Re | Branc | Point |
| 5 | 7-Jan | Certificate | $ 30,000 | Pam | Jackson | 30 |
| 10 | 9-Jan | Auto Loan | $ 30,000 | Pam | Jackson | 30 |
| 12 | 10-Jan | Mortgage | $ 125,000 | Rhonda | Jackson | 125 |
| 22 | 17-Jan | Savings | $ 4,000 | Pam | Jackson | 16 |
| 30 | 22-Jan | Savings | $ 2,500 | Pam | Jackson | 10 |
| 31 | 23-Jan | Certificate | $ 25,000 | Pam | Jackson | 25 |
| 33 | 24-Jan | Auto Loan | $ 17,750 | Rhonda | Jackson | 71 |
| 37 | 28-Jan | Mortgage | $ 165,000 | Pam | Jackson | 165 |
| 38 | 29-Jan | Certificate | $ 15,000 | Rhonda | Jackson | 60 |
| 41 | 31-Jan | Auto Loan | $ 25,000 | Pam | Jackson | 25 |
| 42 | 31-Jan | Certificate | $ 15,600 | Pam | Jackson | 62.4 |
| 46 | | | | | | |

**4** Click the arrow on the **Branch** heading and select **(All)** from the list.

*All the rows are displayed.*

All the rows are displayed again

|  | A | B | C | D | E | F |
|---|---|---|---|---|---|---|
| 1 | Date | Produc | Amount | Sales Re | Branc | Point |
| 2 | 3-Jan | Checking | $ 2,000 | Diane | Plymouth | 8 |
| 3 | 6-Jan | Savings | $ 10,000 | Sharon | Dexter | 40 |
| 4 | 7-Jan | Auto Loan | $ 17,700 | Sharon | Dexter | 70.8 |
| 5 | 7-Jan | Certificate | $ 30,000 | Pam | Jackson | 30 |
| 6 | 7-Jan | Credit Card | $ 5,000 | Paula | Main | 20 |
| 7 | 7-Jan | Certificate | $ 12,500 | Jonell | Ypsilanti | 50 |
| 8 | 8-Jan | Mortgage | $ 150,000 | Richard | Dexter | 150 |
| 9 | 8-Jan | Checking | $ 1,200 | Sharon | Dexter | 4.8 |
| 10 | 9-Jan | Auto Loan | $ 30,000 | Pam | Jackson | 30 |
| 11 | 9-Jan | Certificate | $ 1,500 | Diane | Plymouth | 6 |
| 12 | 10-Jan | Mortgage | $ 125,000 | Rhonda | Jackson | 125 |
| 13 | 10-Jan | Auto Loan | $ 14,500 | Diane | Plymouth | 58 |
| 14 | 10-Jan | Checking | $ 600 | Jonell | Ypsilanti | 2.4 |
| 15 | 10-Jan | Savings | $ 1,600 | Jonell | Ypsilanti | 6.4 |

**5** Click the arrow on the **Amount** heading and choose **Custom**.

*The Custom AutoFilter dialog box opens.*

Click the arrow on the first **Amount** box and choose **is greater than or equal to**. Click in the box to the right and type **50000**.

*The filter limits the rows displayed to those with an amount greater than or equal to $50,000. This is an example of a comparison operator.*

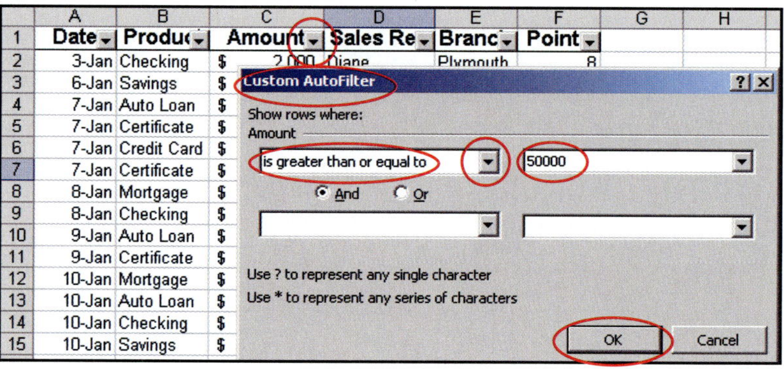

**6** Click **OK**.

*You can add filters to more than one column at the same time. Here, you want to see amounts of $50,000 or more that were sold between January 15, 2002, and January 31, 2002.*

Click the arrow on the **Date** heading and choose **(Custom…)** from the list.

*The Custom AutoFilter dialog box opens.*

Click the arrow on the first box and choose **is greater than or equal to**. Click in the second box and type **January 15, 2002**. Click the arrow on the third box and choose **is less than or equal to**. Click in the fourth box and type **January 31, 2002**.

*The **A**nd option should be checked to require that both conditions are met.*

**7** Click **OK**.

*Three rows meet the combined criteria set in the date and amount columns.*

**8** Select **A50** and enter your name. Include your section number if your instructor requires it. Click the **Print Preview** button.

*The three rows that meet the criteria can be printed with your name.*

Click **Zoom** if necessary to display the top part of the page.

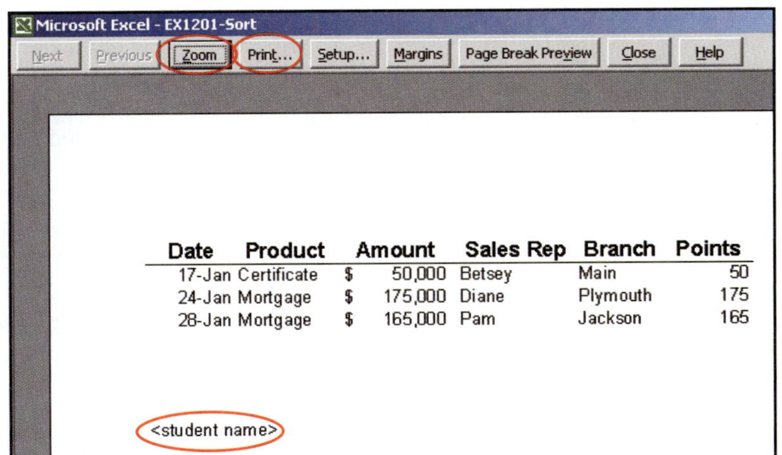

**9** Click **Print**. Select your printer and click **OK**.

*The sheet is printed to display your work.*

Click the **Save** button.

*The filter settings are saved.*

Click the arrow on the **Date** heading and choose **(All)**. Do the same on the **Amount** heading.

*All the rows are displayed.*

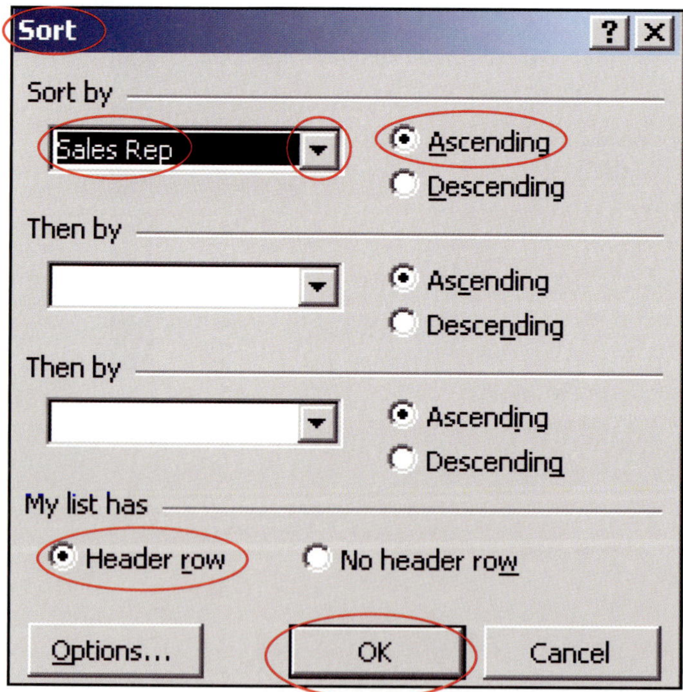

# Task 2

## SORTING, GROUPING, AND SUBTOTALING DATA

### Why would I do this?

The table of data can be sorted, grouped, and subtotaled to provide summaries. You can use such summaries to prepare monthly reports about expenses or other activities. To prepare such reports, it is useful to sort the data by one or more of the columns and then create groups based on that column that can be collapsed to hide the individual records. You can customize reports for different levels of management showing only the data of interest to them. If some of the columns contain numeric values, you can add subtotals at each change in the group. You can also count the number of items in the group and display them in a subtotal.

In this task, you sort the rows by sales representative then group the records by sales representative. You add a subtotal to the Amount and Points columns. This display is useful when you want to see how individual people are doing in the contest.

**1** Select any cell in the data. Choose **Data**, **Sort**.

*The entire table of data is selected and the Sort dialog box opens.*

Select **Header row**, if necessary. Click the arrow on the **Sort by** box and choose **Sales Rep**. Confirm that **Ascending** is chosen.

*The rows will be sorted alphabetically by the sales representative's name.*

**2** Click **OK**.

*The rows are sorted on the Sales Rep field.*

   Select **D2:D5**.

*The cells with Betsey are selected.*

   Choose **Data**, **Group and Outline**, **Group**.

*The Group dialog box opens.*

Sorted on Sales Rep
Selected for a group

| | A | B | C | | D | E | F |
|---|---|---|---|---|---|---|---|
| 1 | Date | Produc | Amount | | Sales Re | Branc | Point |
| 2 | 13-Jan | Savings | $ | 6,000 | Betsey | Main | 24 |
| 3 | 17-Jan | Certificate | $ | 50,000 | Betsey | Main | 50 |
| 4 | 27-Jan | Certificate | $ | 15,000 | Betsey | Main | 60 |
| 5 | 30-Jan | Savings | $ | 6,300 | Betsey | Main | 25.2 |
| 6 | 14-Jan | Certificate | $ | 25,000 | Carolyn | Plymouth | 25 |
| 7 | 17-Jan | Credit Card | $ | 3,000 | Carolyn | Plymouth | 12 |
| 8 | 23-Jan | Credit Card | $ | 2,000 | Carolyn | Plymouth | 8 |
| 9 | 31-Jan | Savings | $ | 1,450 | Carolyn | Plymouth | 5.8 |
| 10 | 3-Jan | Checking | $ | 2,000 | Diane | Plymouth | 8 |
| 11 | 9-Jan | Certificate | $ | 1,500 | Diane | | |
| 12 | 10-Jan | Auto Loan | $ | 14,500 | Diane | | |
| 13 | 17-Jan | Checking | $ | 600 | Diane | | |
| 14 | 20-Jan | Auto Loan | $ | 16,700 | Diane | | |
| 15 | 24-Jan | Mortgage | $ | 175,000 | Diane | | |
| 16 | 7-Jan | Certificate | $ | 12,500 | Jonell | | |
| 17 | 10-Jan | Checking | $ | 600 | Jonell | | |



**3** Confirm that **Rows** is selected and click **OK**.

*An outline pane opens on the left of the screen that displays the group. It is limited to the rows that contain the selected cells.*

Outline pane

| | A | B | C | | D | E | F |
|---|---|---|---|---|---|---|---|
| 1 | Date | Produc | Amount | | Sales Re | Branc | Point |
| 2 | 13-Jan | Savings | $ | 6,000 | Betsey | Main | 24 |
| 3 | 17-Jan | Certificate | $ | 50,000 | Betsey | Main | 50 |
| 4 | 27-Jan | Certificate | $ | 15,000 | Betsey | Main | 60 |
| 5 | 30-Jan | Savings | $ | 6,300 | Betsey | Main | 25.2 |
| 6 | 14-Jan | Certificate | $ | 25,000 | Carolyn | Plymouth | 25 |
| 7 | 17-Jan | Credit Card | $ | 3,000 | Carolyn | Plymouth | 12 |
| 8 | 23-Jan | Credit Card | $ | 2,000 | Carolyn | Plymouth | 8 |

**4** Click the minus sign on the outline box.

*The rows in this group are hidden and the sign on the outline box changes to a plus.*

Rows 2 through 5
are hidden

| | A | B | C | | D | E | F |
|---|---|---|---|---|---|---|---|
| 1 | Date | Produc | Amount | | Sales Re | Branc | Point |
| 6 | 14-Jan | Certificate | $ | 25,000 | Carolyn | Plymouth | 25 |
| 7 | 17-Jan | Credit Card | $ | 3,000 | Carolyn | Plymouth | 12 |
| 8 | 23-Jan | Credit Card | $ | 2,000 | Carolyn | Plymouth | 8 |
| 9 | 31-Jan | Savings | $ | 1,450 | Carolyn | Plymouth | 5.8 |
| 10 | 3-Jan | Checking | $ | 2,000 | Diane | Plymouth | 8 |
| 11 | 9-Jan | Certificate | $ | 1,500 | Diane | Plymouth | 6 |

**QUICK TIP**

You can expand or collapse all the groups at once by using the small numbered buttons at the top of the outline pane.

**5** Click the plus sign on the outline box.
   Choose **Data**, **Group and Outline**, **Ungroup**.

*The Ungroup dialog box opens.*

   Confirm that **Rows** is selected and click **OK**.

*The group is removed. You will use grouping again when you create subtotals.*

Outline pane
removed

Rows displayed

| | A | B | C | | D | E | F |
|---|---|---|---|---|---|---|---|
| 1 | Date | Produc | Amount | | Sales Re | Branc | Point |
| 2 | 13-Jan | Savings | $ | 6,000 | Betsey | Main | 24 |
| 3 | 17-Jan | Certificate | $ | 50,000 | Betsey | Main | 50 |
| 4 | 27-Jan | Certificate | $ | 15,000 | Betsey | Main | 60 |
| 5 | 30-Jan | Savings | $ | 6,300 | Betsey | Main | 25.2 |
| 6 | 14-Jan | Certificate | $ | 25,000 | Carolyn | Plymouth | 25 |

**6** Select a single cell in the table. Choose **Data**, **Subtotals**.

*The Subtotal dialog box opens, and the entire table is automatically selected.*

Click the **At each change in** arrow and choose **Sales Rep**. Confirm that the **Sum** function is selected in the **Use function** box. Select **Amount** and **Points** in the **Add subtotal to** box.

Confirm that **Replace current subtotals** and **Summary below data** are both selected.

*The Amount and Points columns will be subtotaled for each sales representative.*

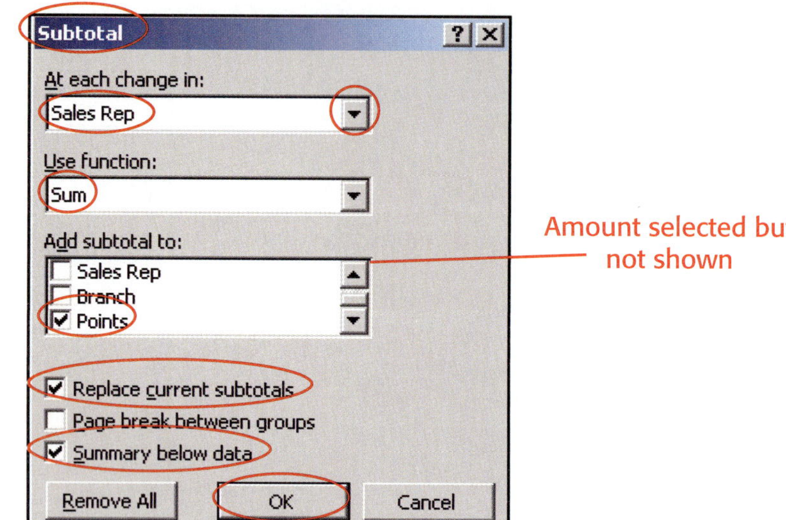

**7** Click **OK**.

*Subtotals for the Amount and Point values are displayed for each Sales Rep. The rows are also grouped automatically, and the outline for the entire group of data appears on the left.*

Outline levels controlled here

Outline pane

Subtotal below change in Sales Rep

| | A | B | C | D | E | F |
|---|---|---|---|---|---|---|
| | Date | Product | Amount | Sales Rep | Branch | Points |
| 2 | 13-Jan | Savings | $ 6,000 | Betsey | Main | 24 |
| 3 | 17-Jan | Certificate | $ 50,000 | Betsey | Main | 50 |
| 4 | 27-Jan | Certificate | $ 15,000 | Betsey | Main | 60 |
| 5 | 30-Jan | Savings | $ 6,300 | Betsey | Main | 25.2 |
| 6 | | | $ 77,300 | **Betsey Total** | | 159.2 |
| 7 | 14-Jan | Certificate | $ 25,000 | Carolyn | Plymouth | 25 |
| 8 | 17-Jan | Credit Card | $ 3,000 | Carolyn | Plymouth | 12 |
| 9 | 23-Jan | Credit Card | $ 2,000 | Carolyn | Plymouth | 8 |
| 10 | 31-Jan | Savings | $ 1,450 | Carolyn | Plymouth | 5.8 |
| 11 | | | $ 31,450 | **Carolyn Total** | | 50.8 |
| 12 | 3-Jan | Checking | $ 2,000 | Diane | Plymouth | 8 |
| 13 | 9-Jan | Certificate | $ 1,500 | Diane | Plymouth | 6 |
| 14 | 10-Jan | Auto Loan | $ 14,500 | Diane | Plymouth | 58 |
| 15 | 17-Jan | Checking | $ 600 | Diane | Plymouth | 2.4 |
| 16 | 20-Jan | Auto Loan | $ 16,700 | Diane | Plymouth | 66.8 |
| 17 | 24-Jan | Mortgage | $ 175,000 | Diane | Plymouth | 175 |
| 18 | | | $ 210,300 | **Diane Total** | | 316.2 |

Level 3 detail collapsed

**8** Click outline level **2**.

*The outline collapses the details in level 3 and displays just the subtotals for each sales representative and the grand total.*

Level 2 shows subtotals and grand totals

| | A | B | C | D | E | F |
|---|---|---|---|---|---|---|
| | Date | Product | Amount | Sales Rep | Branch | Points |
| 6 | | | $ 77,300 | **Betsey Total** | | 159.2 |
| 11 | | | $ 31,450 | **Carolyn Total** | | 50.8 |
| 18 | | | $ 210,300 | **Diane Total** | | 316.2 |
| 25 | | | $ 73,400 | **Jonell Total** | | 158.6 |
| 34 | | | $ 297,100 | **Pam Total** | | 363.4 |
| 41 | | | $ 14,800 | **Paula Total** | | 59.2 |
| 45 | | | $ 157,750 | **Rhonda Total** | | 256 |
| 50 | | | $ 174,100 | **Richard Total** | | 246.4 |
| 54 | | | $ 28,900 | **Sharon Total** | | 115.6 |
| 55 | | | $ 1,065,100 | **Grand Total** | | 1725.4 |

**9** Print this sheet if your instructor requires it.
Save and close the workbook.

Task 3
## CREATING A PIVOTTABLE

### *Why would I do this?*

A PivotTable is a summary table produced by a wizard that allows you to try different columns from the selected data as column and row headings. If you don't like the arrangement of columns and rows, it is easy to switch them or exchange them for other columns from the table.

For example, if you are managing the sales contest at the bank, you may want to know the amount of sales for each product at every branch. You can create a PivotTable with branch names as row headings and product names as column headings. The sales amount is placed in the cells of the table. The PivotTable wizard calculates the total amount for each branch and product and displays it in each cell of the PivotTable.

Many of the data management features of Excel are similar to features found in Microsoft Access, and some of the terms used to describe the data are those used to describe database tables. In a database table, the types of data found in columns are called *fields*. The PivotTable wizard refers to the columns of the table as fields because they are similar to the fields in a database table.

In a PivotTable, you can use fields as row headings, column headings, cell contents, and page headings.

PivotTables produce output similar to sorting and subtotaling. However, you do not need to presort the data to summarize it using a PivotTable.

In this task, you create a PivotTable that summarizes the amount of sales by branch and by product.

**1** Open **EX1202** from the **Student** folder. Save it as **EX1202-Pivot** on your disk.

*The new title appears in the title bar.*

Select any cell in the table. Choose **Data**, **PivotTable and PivotChart Report**.

*The PivotTable and PivotChart Wizard opens. If the Office Assistant opens, close it.*

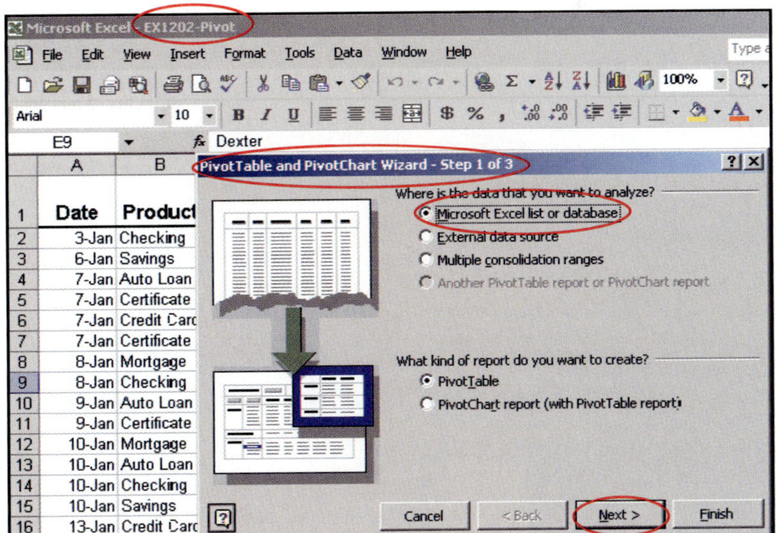

**2** Confirm **Microsoft Excel list or database** and **PivotTable** are selected.

*The table that contains the previously selected cell will be used to create a PivotTable.*

> Click **Next**.

*A marquee displays around the table of data, including column headings in the first row, to indicate the selected area.*

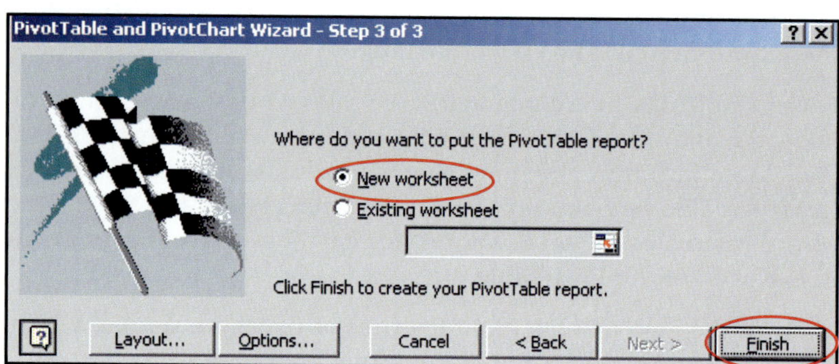

Selected area

**3** Click **Next**.

*The New worksheet option is selected by default.*

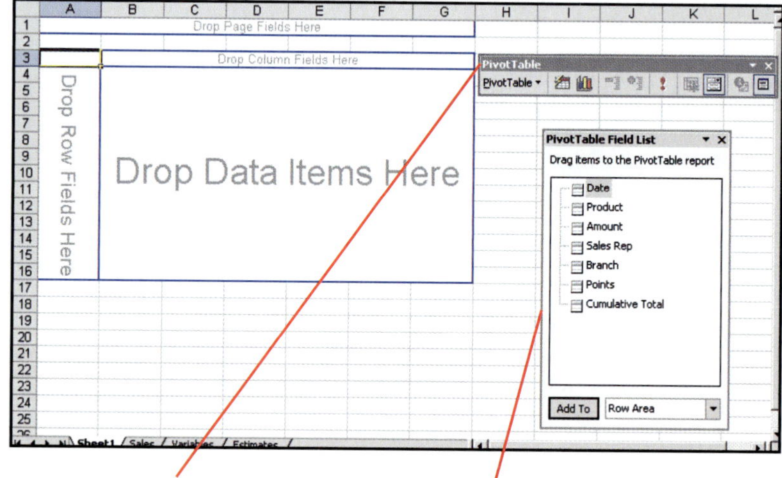

**4** Click **Finish**.

*A new sheet is added to the workbook. The wizard displays a list of fields. The PivotTable toolbar also appears on your screen.*

> If necessary, drag the **PivotTable Field List** box to the right so it is not on top of the PivotTable data area. Do the same for the PivotTable toolbar.

PivotTable toolbar          List of available fields

**5** Drag **Branch** from the list of field names to the section of the PivotTable labeled **Drop Row Fields Here**.

Drag **Product** from the list to the section labeled **Drop Column Fields Here**. Drag **Amount** to the section labeled **Drop Data Items Here**.

*The sales amounts are summarized by branch and by product. The branch and product headings have filter options that allow you to restrict the display to selected products and branches.*

**CAUTION**

If you drag a field to the wrong box, simply drag it back to the PivotTable Field List and try again. Your choices may result in very wide or very long tables that extend across more than one page or screen. If the table is much wider than it is long, switch the fields used for columns and rows to see if you can make the table one page wide and several pages long. This will make it easier to view and print.

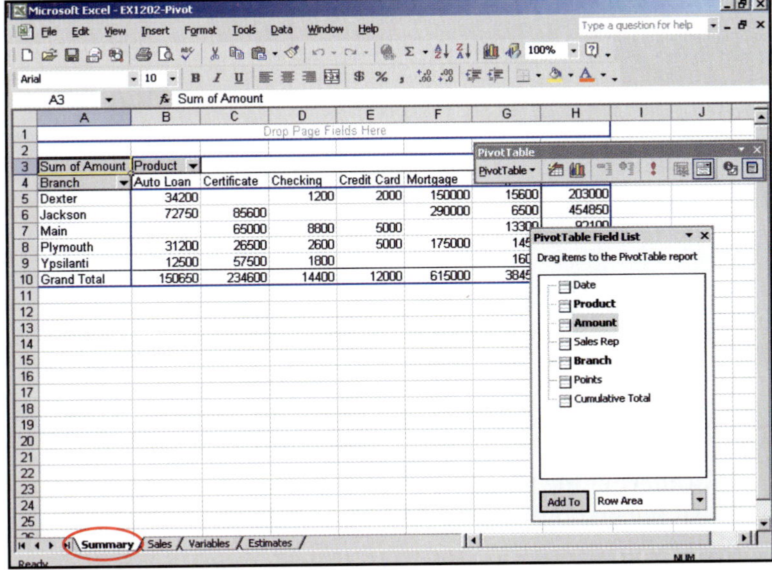

**Branch fields**   **Product fields**

**6** Double-click the **Sheet1** tab and type **Summary**. Press ↵Enter. Save the workbook and leave it open for the next lesson.

# Task 4
## CHARTING A TREND

### Why would I do this?

If you believe that one set of values in your data depends upon another set of values, you can chart them to visualize the relationship between the two. To view this type of relationship correctly, it is important that the labels on the category, or X axis, are equally spaced. To assure that the labels on the X axis are spaced evenly, use an XY Scatter chart, which adjusts the interval between category labels automatically. If the second set of numbers is a simple multiple of the numbers chosen as labels on the category (X) axis, a line drawn between the data points on the chart will be a straight line. Straight lines can be represented by formulas that can be used to estimate new dependent values.

Real data seldom conforms exactly to a simple mathematical formula. If the data points on an XY Scatter chart look like they approximate a straight line, Excel can calculate the line that minimizes the distance between all of the points and the line. This line is called a trend line. The technique for calculating this best-fit line is called *linear regression* and is done automatically. One measure of quality of the fit of the trend line to the data is represented by the R-squared number. A perfect fit has an R-squared value of 1. Data points that do not make an exact straight line produce R-squared values less than 1, such as .94.

For example, as the manager of the sales contest at the bank, you want to predict future sales totals. You chart the cumulative total of the sales against the date of the sales. As the date increases, so does the total sales. You have data for the month of January but you want to predict what that total will be if sales continue at their present rate for another month. A cumulative total column has been added to the worksheet for this purpose.

In this task, you chart the date and the cumulative total, add a trend line, and determine the formula for the trend line that you can use to estimate future total sales.

**1** Click the **Sales** sheet tab. Click the header for column **A**. Hold the Ctrl key and click the header for column **G**.

*Columns A and G are selected.*

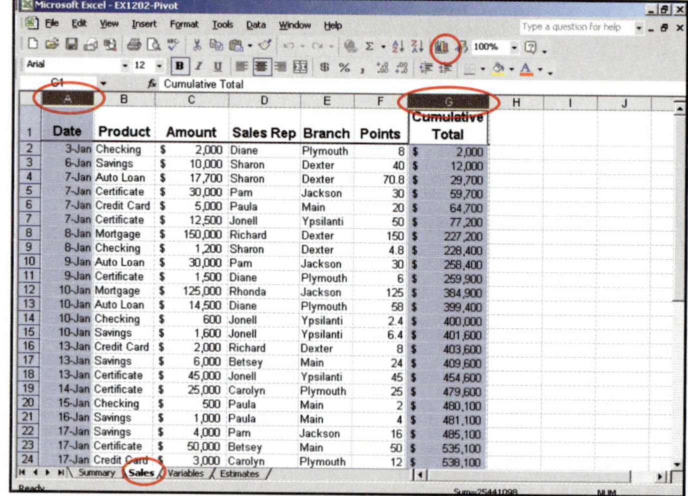

**2** Click the **Chart Wizard** button. Click **XY (Scatter)** in the **Chart type** box. Confirm that the first option in the **Chart sub-type** is selected.

*The data points will be charted without a connecting line. You will add the trend line in a subsequent step.*

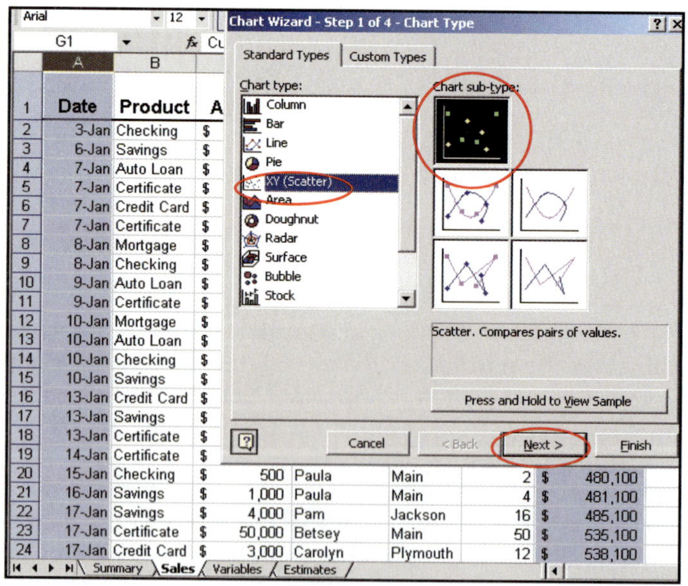

**3** Click **Next**.

*An example of the chart is displayed. The program correctly identified the data as columns.*

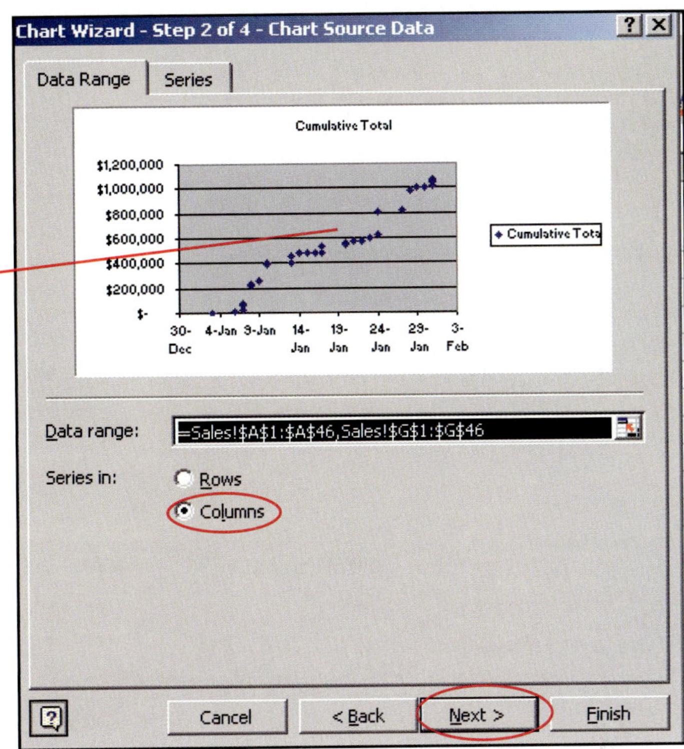


Chart shows total sales related to the passage of time

**4** Click **Next**. Click the **Legend** tab and deselect the **Show legend** option.

*Notice that the data points do not make a perfectly straight line, but that there is a definite trend upwards to the data points.*

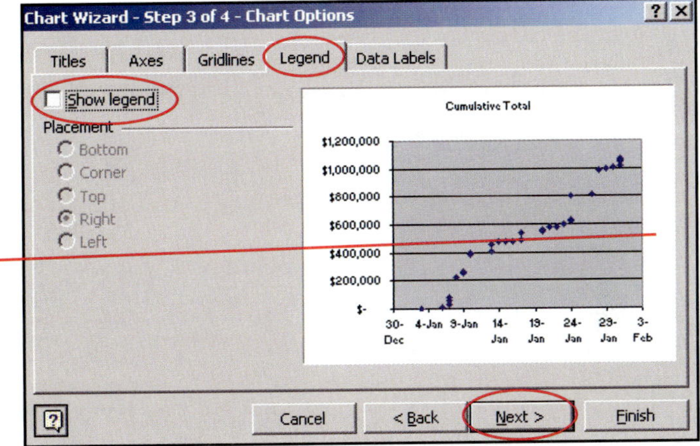


Legend removed

**5** Click **Next**. Click the **As new sheet** option. Select the default sheet name and type **Trend**.

*The chart will be placed on its own sheet labeled Trend.*

**6**  Click **Finish**.

*The chart is displayed on its own sheet. Notice that the interval between dates is uniform on the chart even though the data provided did not have equal intervals.*

Click one of the data points to select them.

*All the data points are selected but all of them are not highlighted. This is normal.*

All data points selected but only
some are highlighted

Equal intervals of time

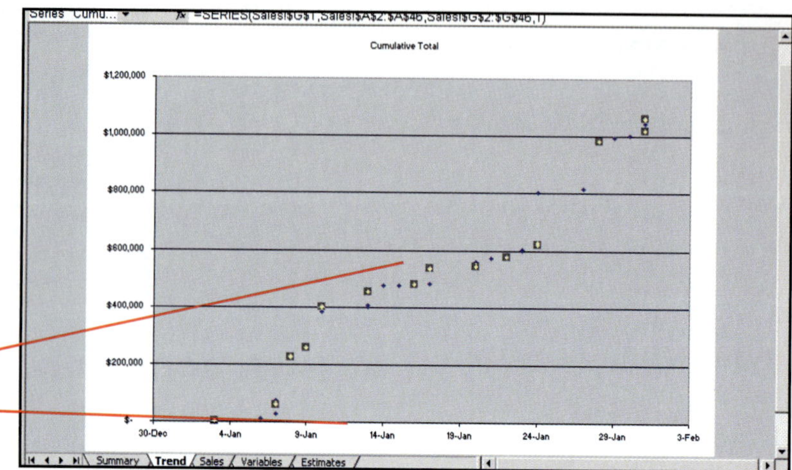

**7**  Choose **Chart**, **Add trendline**. Confirm that **Linear** is selected.

*The data points in this example appear to fit a straight line better than one of the other curves with the possible exception of the polynomial.*

IN DEPTH

> A fourth order polynomial is a slightly better fit than a straight line, but its formula is more complex. The straight line is a reasonable choice in this example if you want to project approximate totals several weeks in advance. Be careful when making predictions about the future by extending a relationship from the past. If the basis for the relationship changes, your predictions might be grossly inaccurate.

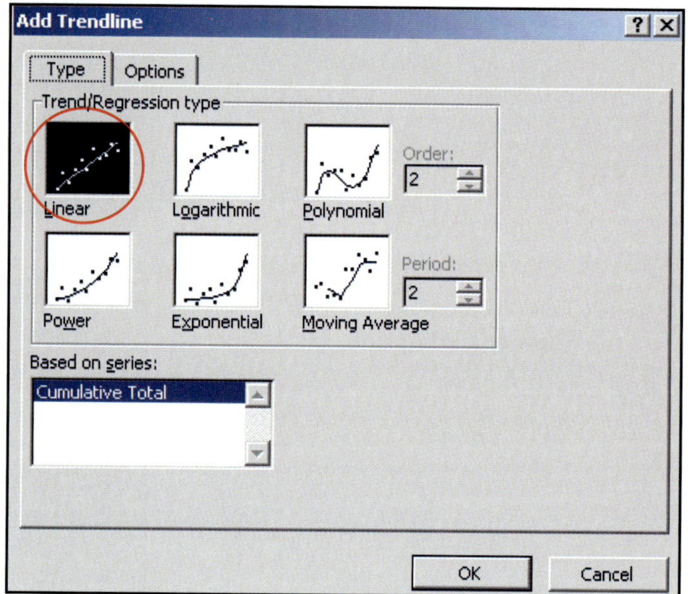


**8**  Click the **Options** tab. Select **Display equation on chart** and **Display R-squared value on chart**.

*The straight trend line will be added along with its formula and the R-squared value.*

IN DEPTH

> The algebraic formula for a straight line is $y = mx + b$ where m is the slope of the line and b is a constant.

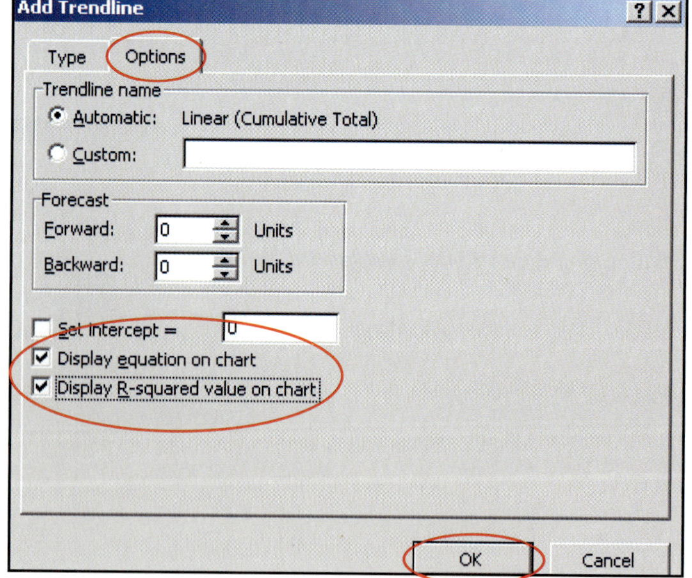

**9** Click **OK**.

*The trend line, its formula, and the R-squared value are added to the chart. The font is too small to read easily, and the numbers in the formula are rounded off too much for accurate use.*

Click the formula.

*A box outlines the formula and the R-squared value.*

Choose **Format**, **Selected Data Labels**. Click the **Font** tab and change the font size to **14**.

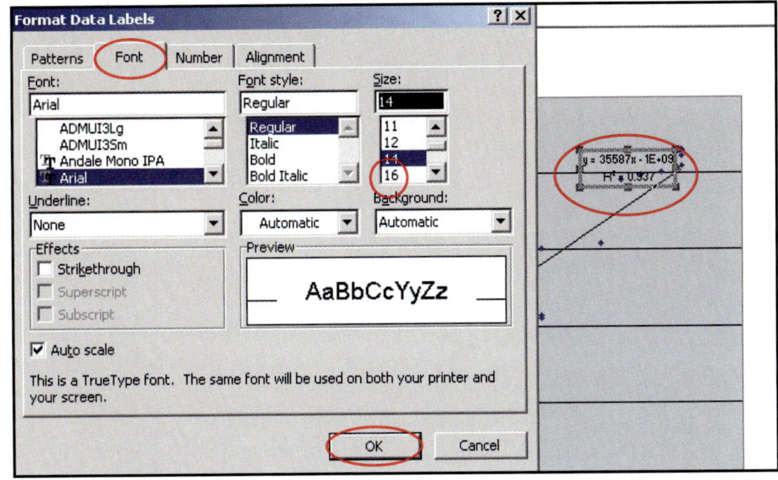

**10** Click the **Number** tab. Change the **Category** to **Number** and the **Decimal places** to **3**.

*The formula and R-squared value will be displayed in a larger font and the numbers will be displayed with sufficient accuracy.*

IN DEPTH

The General format displays the formula constant in scientific notation because it is a large number. You may want to use these numbers to calculate values, in which case they must be displayed with more significant digits.

CAUTION

You may select to use commas in the numbers in this formula. This makes the formula easier to read. However, you have to remove the commas if you want to copy this formula and use it in a cell, which is what you do in the next task.

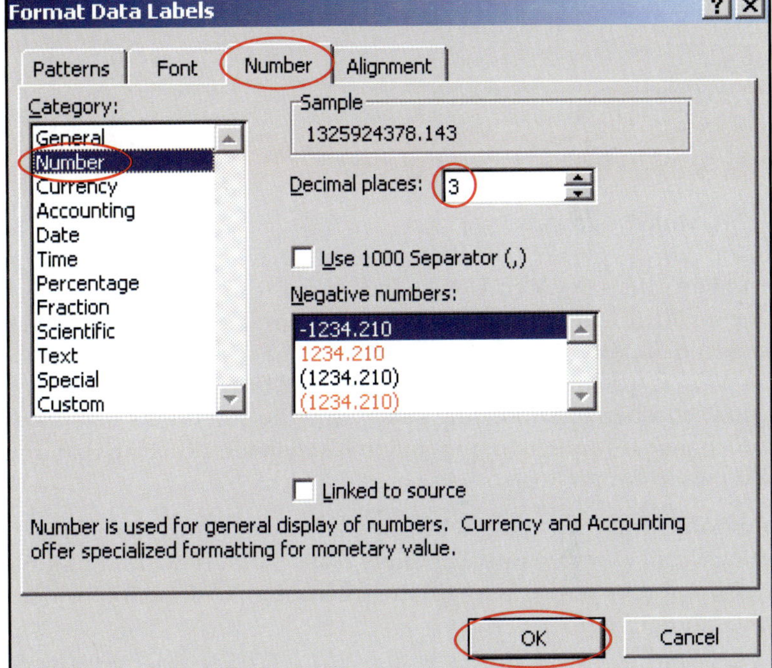

**11** Click **OK**. Drag the box to the left between the grid lines where it is easier to read.

*You can use the formula to predict other sales totals if you pick a date. An R-squared value greater than .9 indicates that the points are fairly close to the trend line.*

Save the workbook and leave it open.

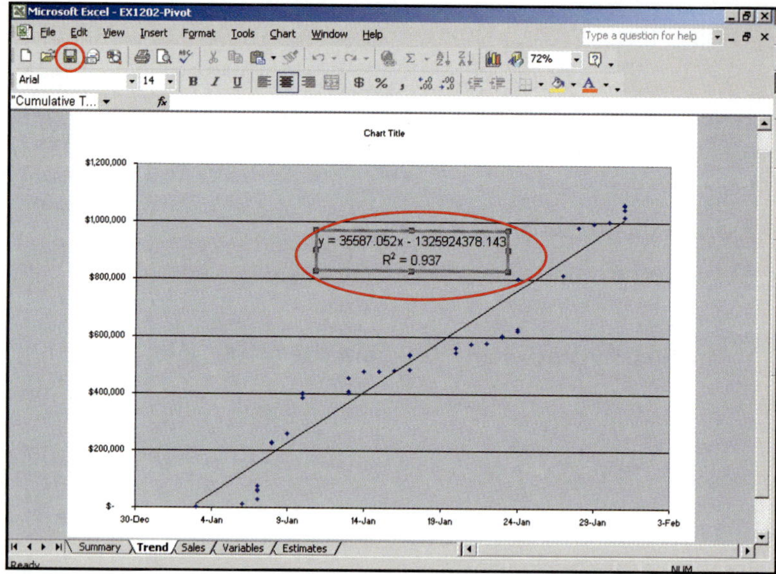



# Task 5

## ESTIMATING VALUES

### Why would I do this?

If you have a chart of data that appears to have a linear relationship, you can estimate values between known data points with confidence. This type of estimation is called *interpolation*. If you try to estimate values beyond either end of the known data, you do so with much less confidence and you need to make assumptions. This type of estimate is called *extrapolation*. The most common assumption used when extrapolating data is that the conditions that produced the data do not change. Although extrapolation is much less accurate than interpolation, it is the most common type of estimate.

You can extrapolate a trend line by using the formula to calculate new dependant values from new category (X) values. This method works for all the trend line types. Another option is to use the *FORECAST* function, which estimates a value in one step.

In this task, you learn how to estimate future total sales using the formula from the trend line. You also learn how to use the FORECAST function.

**1** Select the box containing the formula on the **Trend** sheet. Drag the formula to select it and click the **Copy** button.

*The formula is copied to the Office Clipboard.*

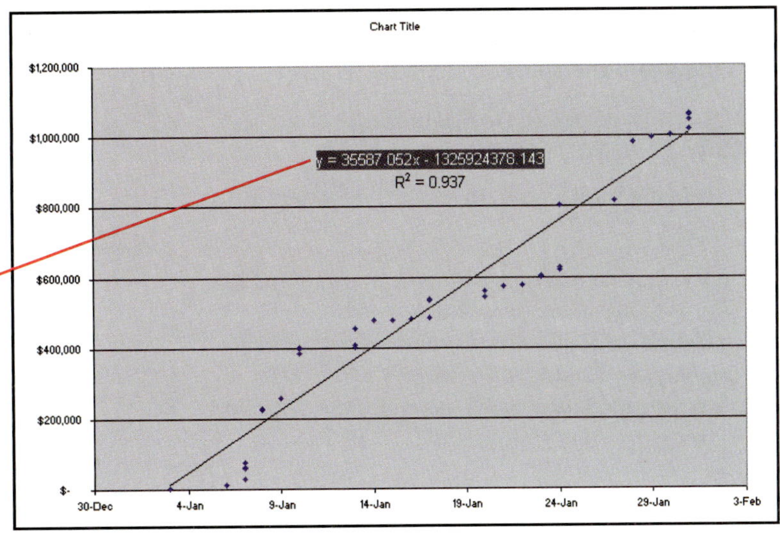



Selected formula

**2** Click the **Estimates** sheet tab and select **B6**. Click the **Paste** button.

*The formula is pasted into the cell. This formula is displayed using standard algebraic conventions. You need to convert it to the conventions used with formulas in a worksheet.*

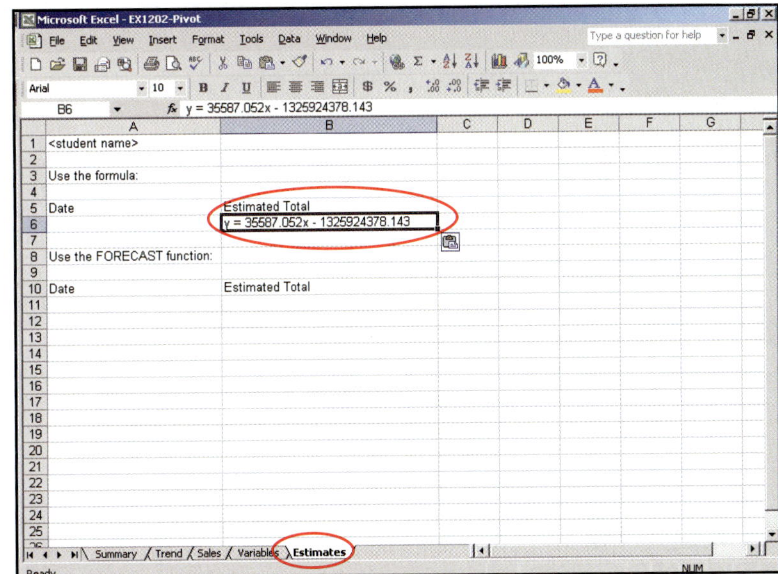

**3** Select **A6**, type **2/28/02**, and then press ⏎Enter.

| | A | B |
|---|---|---|
| 1 | <student name> | |
| 2 | | |
| 3 | Use the formula: | |
| 4 | | |
| 5 | Date | Estimated Total |
| 6 | 2/28/02 | y = 35587.052x - 1325924378.143 |

**4** Double-click **B6** to edit the formula. Delete the **y** and the space.

*The equal sign should be the first character in the formula.*

> Replace **x** with ***A6**. Press ⏎Enter. Select **B6** again.

*The formula takes the date, multiplies by 35587.052, which is the slope of the line, then subtracts 1325924378.143, which is the constant that adjusts the height of the line above the category axis. These numbers were calculated when you added the trend line.*

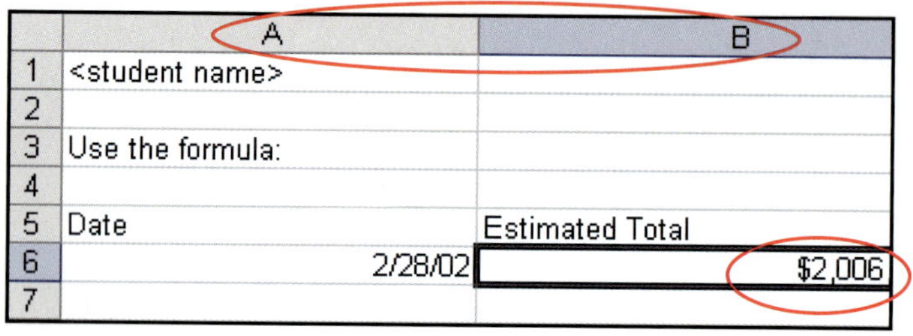


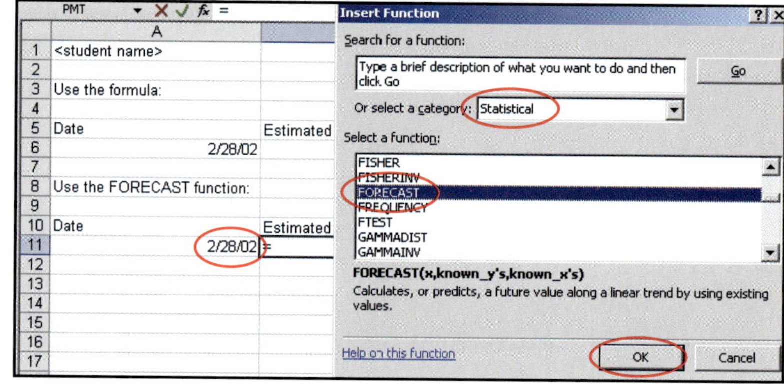


**5** Select cell **A11,** type **2/28/02**, and then press ⏎Enter.

*You will use the same date with the FORECAST function to estimate the value.*

> Select **B11**. Choose **Insert, Function**. Choose the **Statistical** category, scroll down the list, and select **FORECAST**.

*The FORECAST function does all the work of finding the formula for the best-fit straight line and calculating the dependent value.*

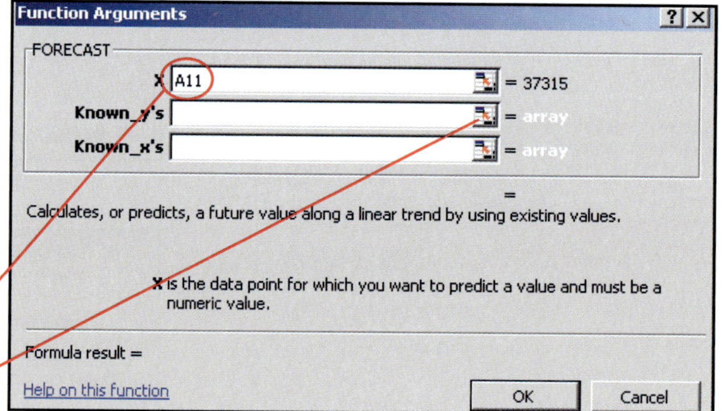


**6** Click **OK**.

*The Function Arguments dialog box opens.*

> Type **A11** to select it as the new value of **X**.

*This is cell A11, not the word All. The FORECAST function estimates the total sales for the date in cell A11, which is February 28, 2002.*

This is the cell in column A, row 11.

Collapse button

**7** Click the **Known_y's** box. Click the **Collapse** button at the end of the box. Click the **Sales** tab and drag cells **G2** through **G45**

*The range of dependent cells is selected. You are assuming that the total amount of sales depends on how long the contest goes on.*

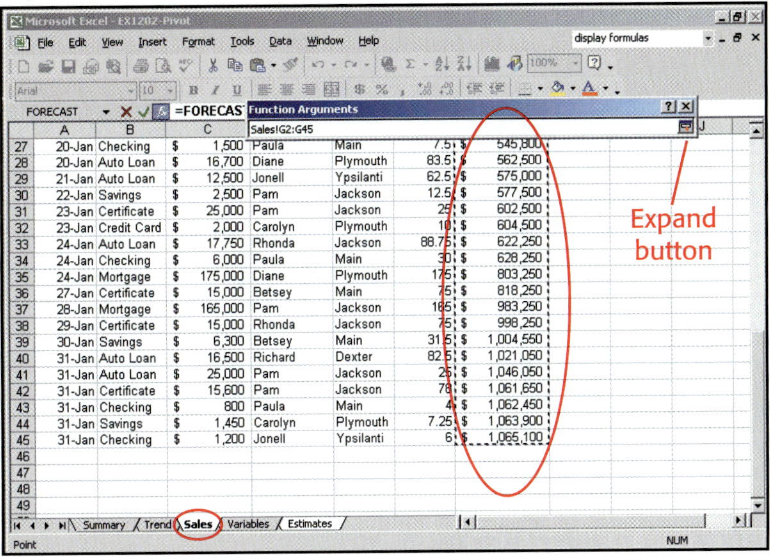


**8** Click the **Expand** button. Click the **Known_x's** box and click the **Collapse** button. Click the **Sales** tab and drag cells **A2** through **A45**.

*The dates are selected and serve as the values along the category (X) axis.*

Click the **Expand** button.

*The date in A11 is used as the category. The FORECAST function will estimate the total amount of sales by that date using the linear regression method.*

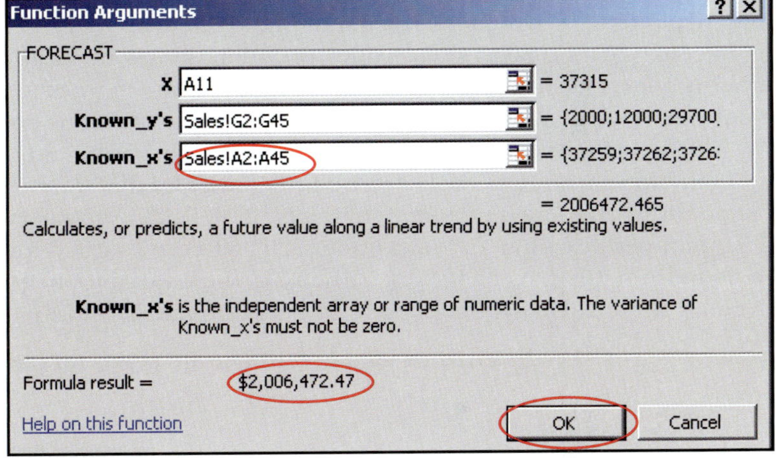


**9** Click **OK**.

*The value calculated by the FORECAST function is slightly different that the one calculated by the formula. The format of the formula did not display the data as accurately as possible. However, they are substantially the same.*

Save the workbook.

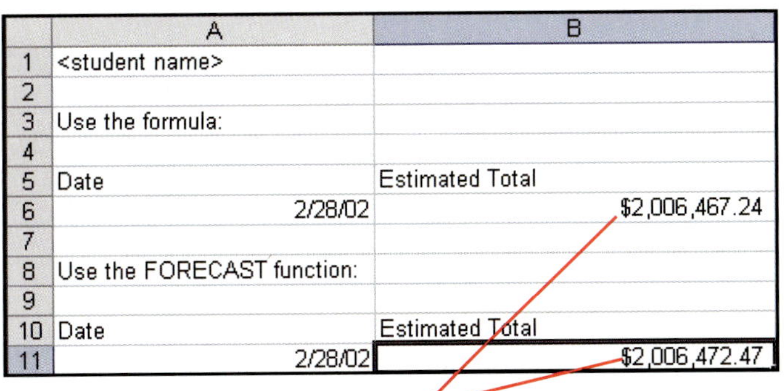


Slightly different answers
due to rounding of the
numbers in the formula

# Task 6
## SAVING SCENARIOS

### Why would I do this?

When the electronic spreadsheet was first invented, users were thrilled by its ability to recalculate complex spreadsheets quickly so they could evaluate different scenarios. The average person is often confronted with making financial decisions that have several variables, such as buying a house or automobile. It is difficult to compare purchases that have different interest rates, closing costs, and monthly payments. You can try different combinations of key variables and save the results of each one as a separate scenario. The scenarios are part of the workbook and can be recalled to make comparisons. You can create a PivotTable that displays the results of the different scenarios.

In the bank sales contest, you decide that in addition to the prizes for first and second place, you want to give each employee a bonus for the points they get in the second month of the contest. You have evaluated the trend and have concluded that the amount and distribution of sales in the second month is likely to match the first month. You have a budget of $2,000 and would like to give a dollar per point to keep it simple. Points are awarded per thousand dollars of product sold, depending on whether the amount of the sale is above or below a certain figure. Sales of mortgages and certificates of deposit involve large sums, while the other products involve smaller amounts but take as much work to sell. Also, some employees are not allowed to sell the larger loans. To make the contest competitive among employees who sell different products, there are fewer points per thousand for the large sales. There are three variables that were used to determine the points given in the first month of the contest. Sales over $20,000 were awarded one point per thousand and sales under $20,000 were awarded four points per thousand. You plan to change one or more of these variables to get the total points to come out to 2,000, so you can give $1 per point and stay within your budget.

In this task, you save the variables used to calculate the points for January as a scenario.

**1** Click the **Sales** sheet tab and select **F2**.

*The formula uses named ranges to calculate the points. These named ranges are found on the Variables sheet.*

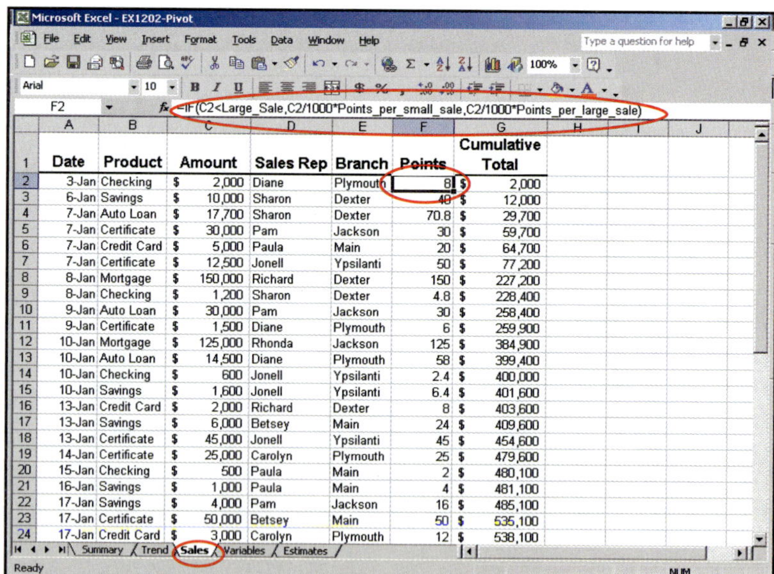

**2** Click the **Variables** sheet tab. Select **B2**.

*The cells in B2, B3, and B4 have defined names that correspond to the labels in column A. The values in these cells are used to calculate the points on the Sales sheet.*

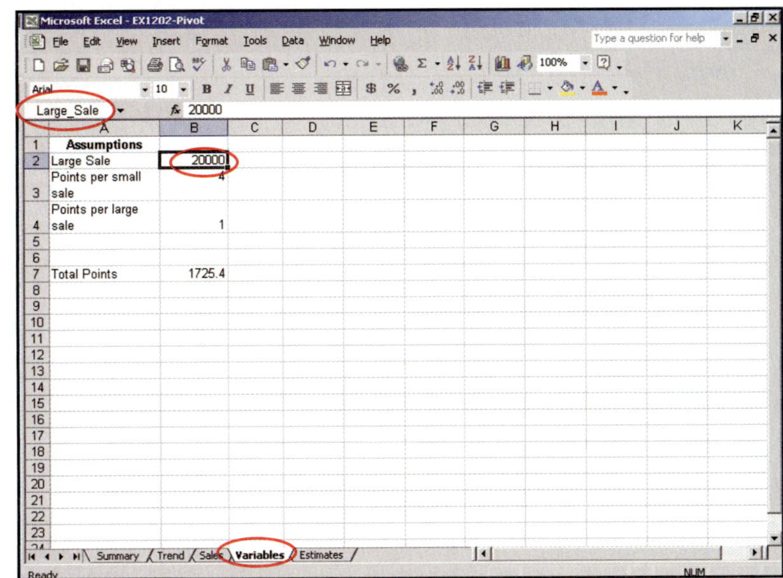

**3** Select **B7**.

*Notice the formula in the formula bar. The Points range includes the cells in the Sales sheet that display the points. Cell B7 displays the total points from the Sales sheet.*

Select **B4**. Type **2** and press ↵Enter.

*All the formulas in the Sales sheet that depend on B4 are recalculated and the value in B7 is updated. Your goal is to change one of the three variables in B2, B3, or B4 to make the total in B7 come out to 2,000.*

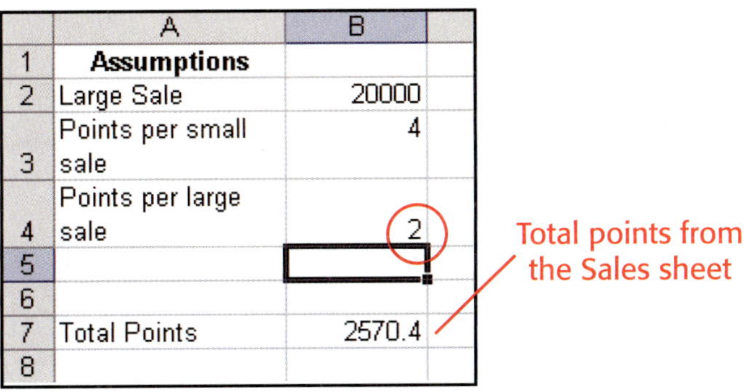


**4** Select **B4**, change it back to **1**, and then press ↵Enter.

*This is the set of variables used to calculate the points for January.*

Choose **Tools**, **Scenarios**.

*The Scenario Manager dialog box opens.*

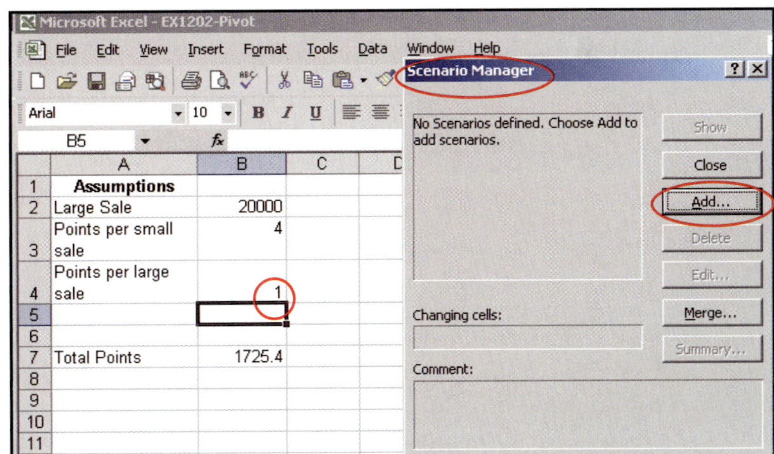

**5** Click the **Add** button. In the **Scenario name** box, type **January**.

*These are the values used to calculate January's points.*

Select the default value in the **Changing cells** box. Drag cells **B2** through **B4**. Add your name and section number to the **Comments** box, if your instructor requires it.

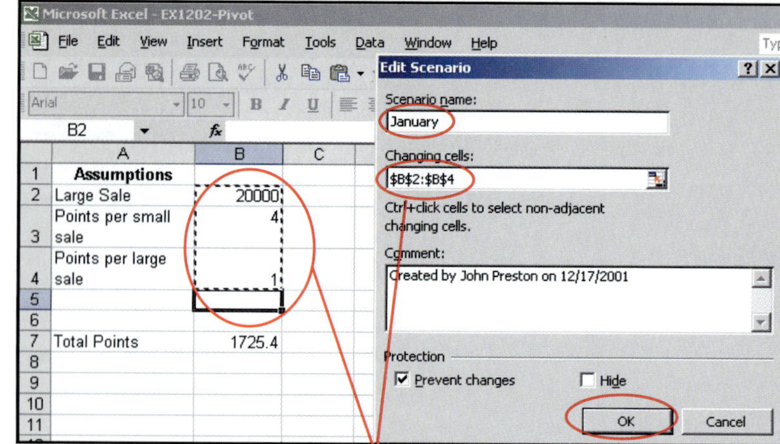

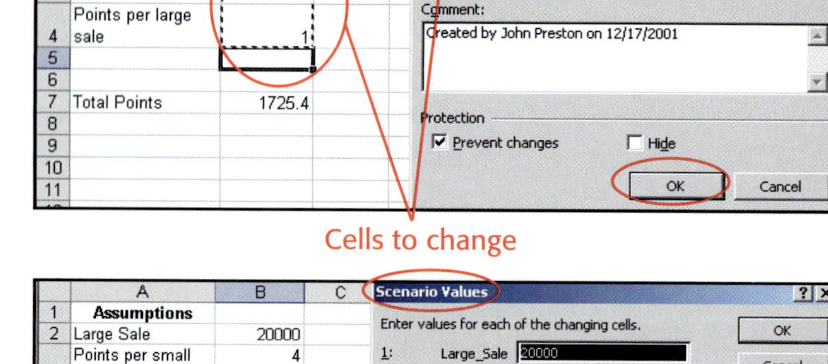

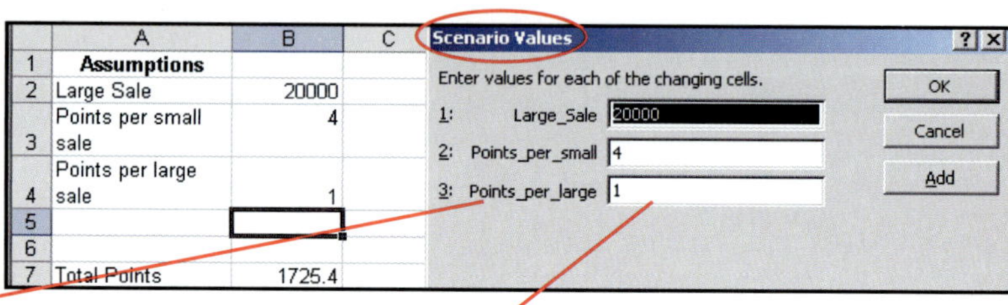

Cells to change

**6** Click **OK**.

*The Scenario Values dialog box opens. It displays the range name and the values.*

Range names created based on cells to the left of each range

Values in each range

The range names for cells B2, B3, and B4 were automatically generated using the Insert, Names, Create, Left commands.

**7** Click **OK**. Click **Close**.

*The original values of the variables are saved as a scenario named January. You use scenarios in the next task to compare several options.*

# Task 7

## USING GOAL SEEK AND USING A PIVOTTABLE TO COMPARE SCENARIOS

### Why would I do this?

You can manually enter different values for the points awarded for a small sale or a large sale, and you can try changing the minimum value considered to be a large sale. However, this is a time consuming process. Excel has a tool called Goal Seek that does this trial-and-error process. With Goal Seek, you specify the cell that contains the goal and what that goal should be. You then pick a cell to change and let the Goal Seek tool try different values in that cell until it gets as close as possible to your goal.

You can use Goal Seek to find the best value for each of the three variables and save each one as a scenario. You can then create a PivotTable to compare the scenarios.

In this task, you use Goal Seek to find the values of each of the three variables that would result in a total of 2,000 points. You save each one as a scenario, then you create a PivotTable to compare the results.

**1** Confirm that the **Variables** sheet is selected. Choose **Tools**, **Goal Seek**. Select the default value in the **Set cell** box and type **B7**.

*This cell contains the value that is your goal. You want this number to be 2000.*

Click the **To value** box and type **2000**. Click the **By changing cell** box and type **B3**.

*In this scenario, you change the points awarded per thousand dollars for each small sale.*

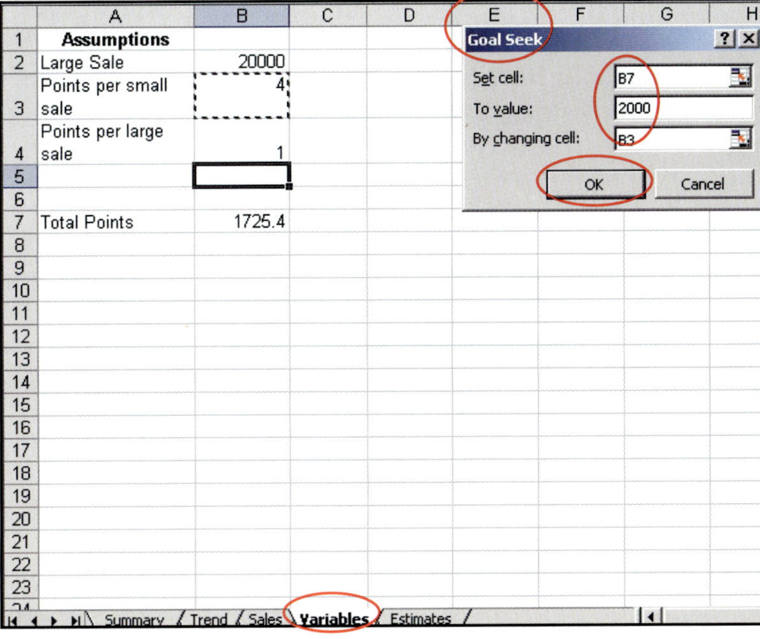

**2** Click **OK**.

*The program quickly tries many values of points for small sales to find the one necessary to produce a total of 2,000 points.*

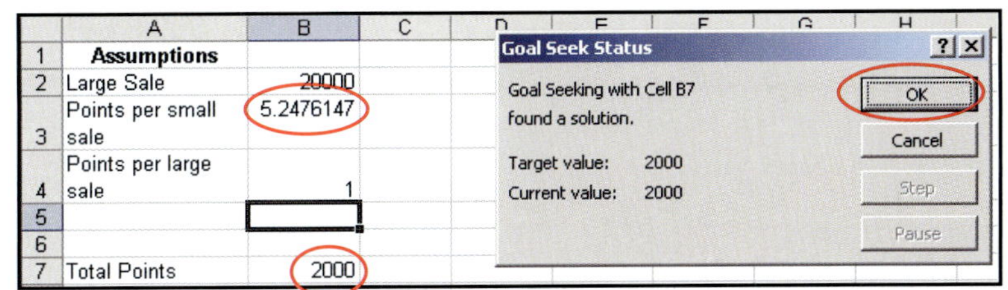

**3** Click **OK**. Choose **Tools**, **Scenarios**. Click the **Add** button. Click the **Scenario name** box and type **Change small sale points**.

*Notice the range of cells, B2 through B4, is still selected from the earlier scenario.*

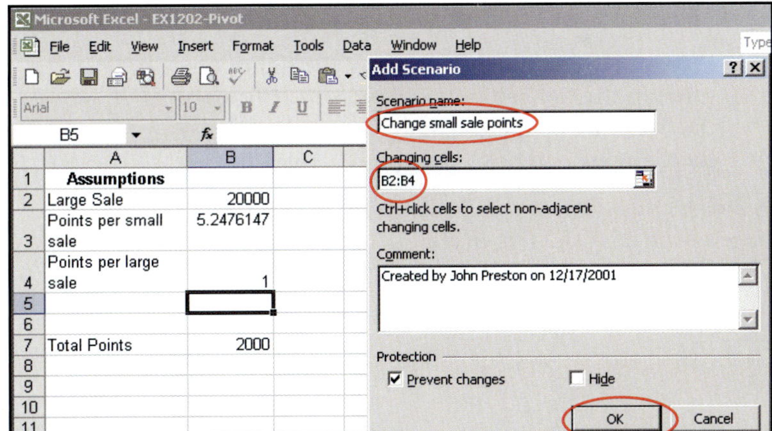

**4** Click **OK**.

*The Scenario Values dialog box opens and displays the values that will be stored for this scenario.*

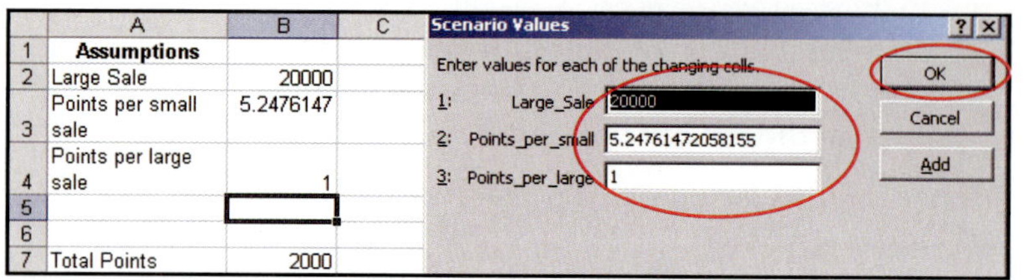

**5** Click **OK**.

*The Scenario Manager dialog box opens and displays the name of the new scenario.*

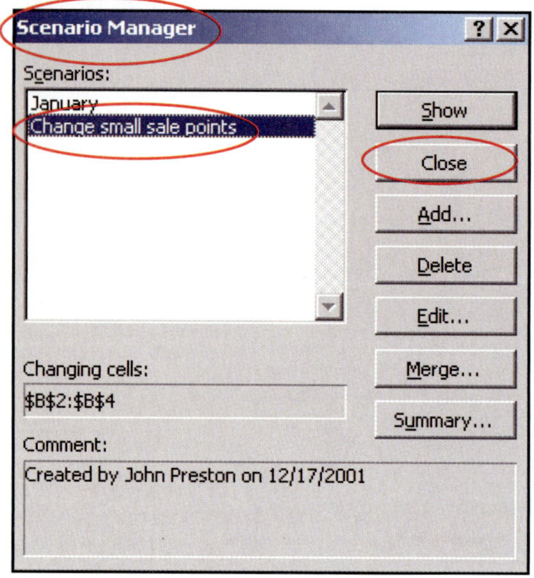

**6** Click **Close**. Select **B3**, type **4**, and then press ↵Enter.

*The value is changed back to the original amount. Next, you try different values of points for large sales.*

> Choose **Tools, Goal Seek**. Select the default value in the **Set cell** box and type **B7**. Click the **To value** box and type **2000**. Click the **By changing cell** box and type **B4**. Click **OK**.

*A value is calculated and displayed in B4 that will produce a point total of 2,000 in B7.*

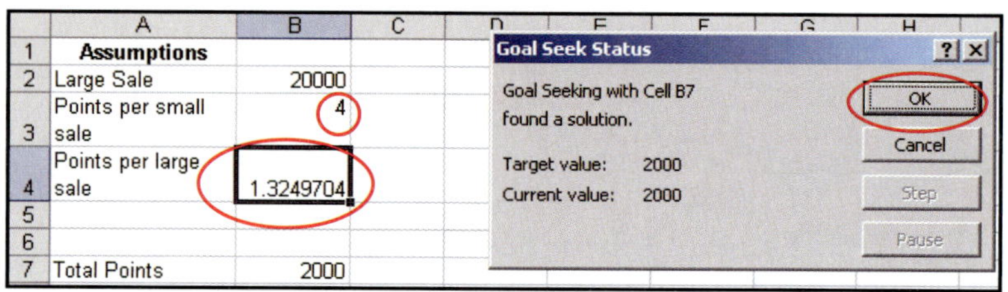

**7** Click **OK**. Choose <u>Tools</u>, <u>Sc</u>enarios. Click the **Add** button. Click the **Scenario name** box and type **Change large sale points**. Click **OK**. Click **OK**. Click **Close**.

*The scenario for changing the points awarded per thousand points of large sales is saved.*

**CAUTION**

Notice that the Undo button is gray. This operation cannot be undone.

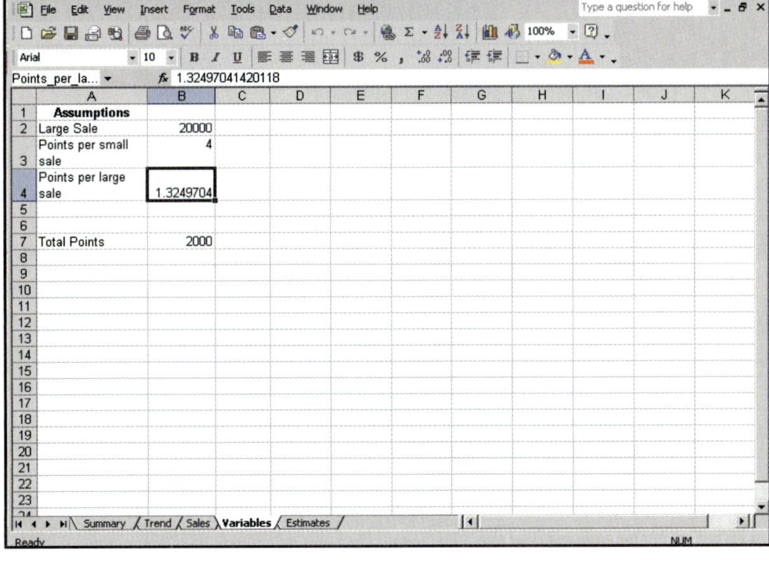

**8** Select **B4**, type **1**, and then press ⏎Enter.

*Next, you try different minimum values that are used to define a large sale.*

Choose <u>Tools</u>, <u>Goal Seek</u>. Select the default value in the **Se<u>t</u> cell** box and type **B7**. Click the **To <u>v</u>alue** box and type **2000**. Click the **By <u>c</u>hanging cell** box and type **B2**. Click **OK**.

*The program tries many options but cannot get any closer than 2130.4. Given the sales that occurred and the point values for large and small sales, this is the best the Goal Seek tool can do.*

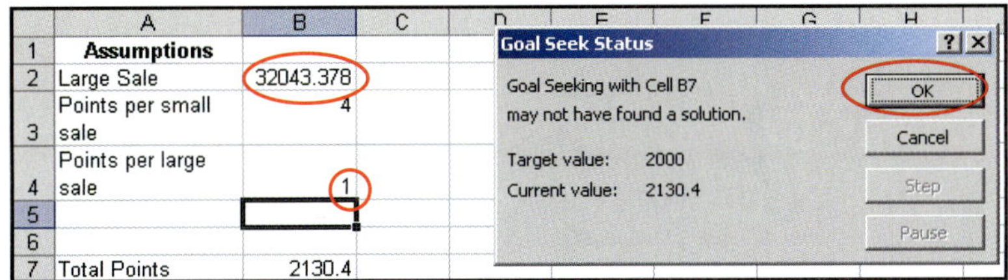

**IN DEPTH**

The number of tries that Goal Seek uses until it gives up is set under Tools, Options, Calculation, Iteration. An *iteration* is a repetition. The default setting is 100. Increasing the number of repetitions in this case will not make a difference due to the constraints of the other variables and the values of sales in the sales table.

**9** Click **OK**. Choose <u>Tools</u>, <u>Sc</u>enarios. Click the **Add** button. Click the **Scenario name** box and type **Change minimum for large sale**. Click **OK**. Click **OK**. Click **Close**.

*The scenario in which you try different values for the minimum large sale is saved.*

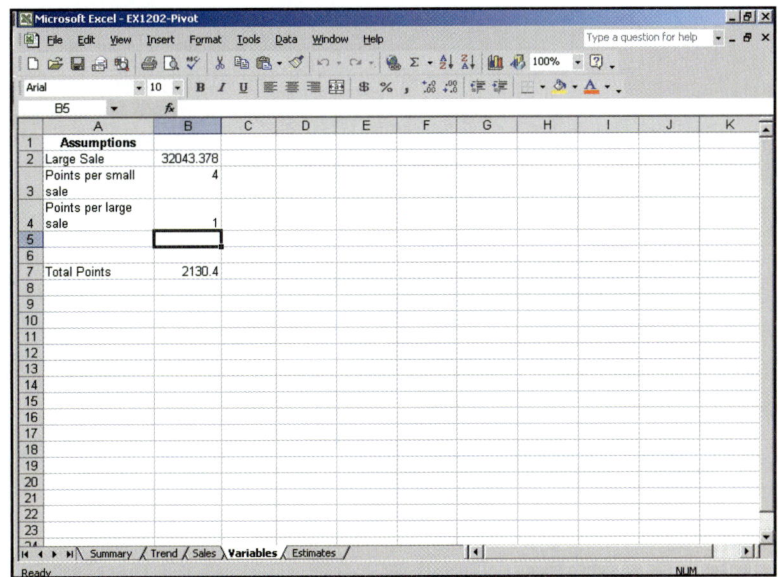

**10** Click **Tools**, **Scenario**, and then click the **Summary** button.

*The Scenario Summary dialog box opens.*

> Select **Scenario PivotTable report**. Select the **Result cells** box and enter **B2:B4**.

*The four scenarios will be summarized in a PivotTable.*

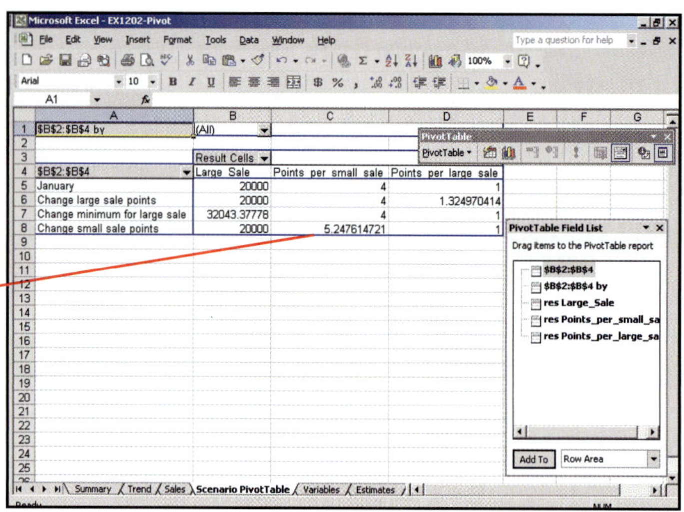

**11** Click **OK**.

*The Scenario PivotTable sheet is created where you can compare the four scenarios. Upon consideration, you decide that it is simplest to increase the points awarded for a small sale from four to five.*

Changing points for a small sale to 5.25 would still yield 2,000 total points so changing it to 5 would stay within the budget and be a simple change.

**CAUTION**

The PivotTable does not update automatically if you change one of the scenarios on which it is based.

**12** Click the **Variables** sheet tab. Select **B3** and enter **5**.

*The total points will be close to 2,000 but slightly under, which will meet the budget consideration.*

> Format **B2** to **Currency** style and format **B7** to **Comma** style.

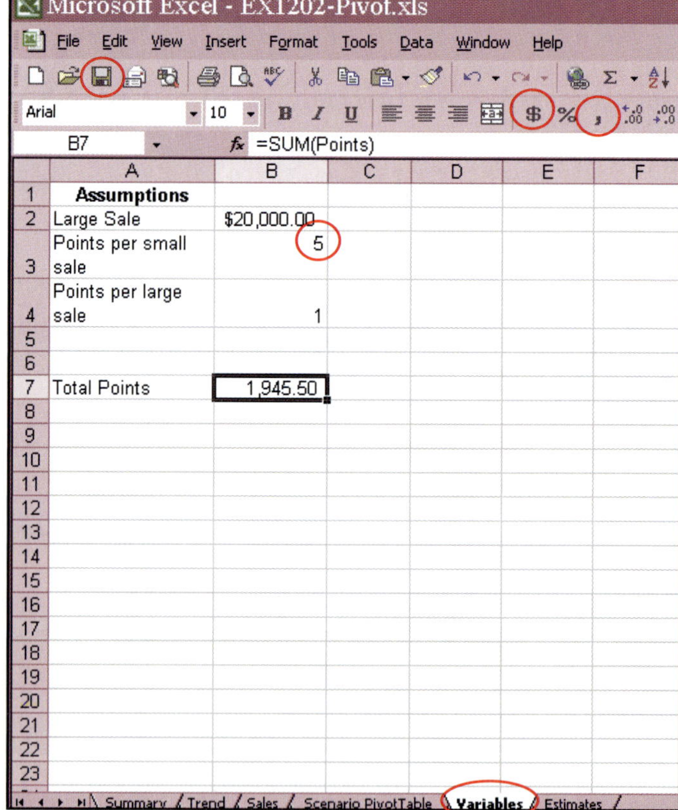

**13** Save and close the workbook.

The exercises that follow are designed for you to review and use what you have learned in this lesson. You also have the opportunity to practice your skills and then expand on them by applying them to new situations.

## COMPREHENSION

Comprehension exercises are designed to check your memory and understanding of the basic concepts in this lesson. You distinguish between true and false statements, identify new screen elements, and match terms with related statements. If you are uncertain of the correct answer, refer to the task number following each item (for example, T4 refers to Task 4) and review that task until you are confident that you can provide a correct response.

## TRUE-FALSE

Circle either T or F.

T  F  **1.** Before you add subtotals, it is a good idea to sort the table if it is not already sorted. **(T2)**

T  F  **2.** Grouping data places each group on a separate worksheet within the workbook and automatically creates a summary sheet. **(T2)**

T  F  **3.** The method used to determine the best-fit straight line for a set of data is called linear progression. **(T5)**

T  F  **4.** Scenarios save sets of values that you can use to recalculate the workbook to show different outcomes. **(T6)**

T  F  **5.** The filter feature works on one column at a time. If you want to filter on a combination of columns, you must use a database program like Access. **(T1)**

T  F  **6.** A PivotTable allows you to try different columns as row or column headings. **(T3)**

T  F  **7.** The Goal Seek function tries different numbers in a cell to get as close as possible to the desired result in another cell. **(T7)**

## MATCHING QUESTIONS

**A.** Pivot  
**B.** Goal Seek  
**C.** Filtering  
**D.** Linear Regression  
**E.** Scenario  
**F.** Subtotal  
**G.** Forecast  

Match the following statements to the word or phrase that is the best match from the list. Write the letter of the matching word or phrase in the space provided next to the number.

**1.** _____ Feature that displays rows of the table that match conditions **(T1)**

**2.** _____ Type of table that summarizes data from another table and allows the designer to choose which columns will be represented as row or column headings **(T3)**

**3.** _____ Allows you to save sets of critical values upon which the rest of the table depends **(T6)**

**4.** _____ Automatically tries different values into a selected cell to produce a desired result in another cell **(T7)**

**5.** _____ Method to find a best-fit straight line for two sets of data, where one set is dependent on the other **(T4)**

**6.** _____ Inserts a row at each change in a selected column **(T2)**

**7.** _____ Function used to predict a value from a trend **(T5)**

# IDENTIFYING PARTS OF THE EXCEL SCREEN

Refer to the figure and identify the numbered parts of the screen. Write the letter of the correct label in the space next to the number.

1. ______________

2. ______________

3. ______________

4. ______________

5. ______________

A. Collapse button  (T2)

B. Filter button  (T2)

C. Subtotal  (T2)

D. Grouping levels  (T2)

E. Sorted column  (T2)

1. ______________

2. ______________

3. ______________

A. Row fields  (T3)

B. Column fields  (T3)

C. Data items  (T3)

1. ______________

2. ______________

3. ______________

4. ______________

A. Trend line  (T4)

B. Data points  (T4)

C. Formula of line  (T4)

D. Measure of the "fit"  (T4)

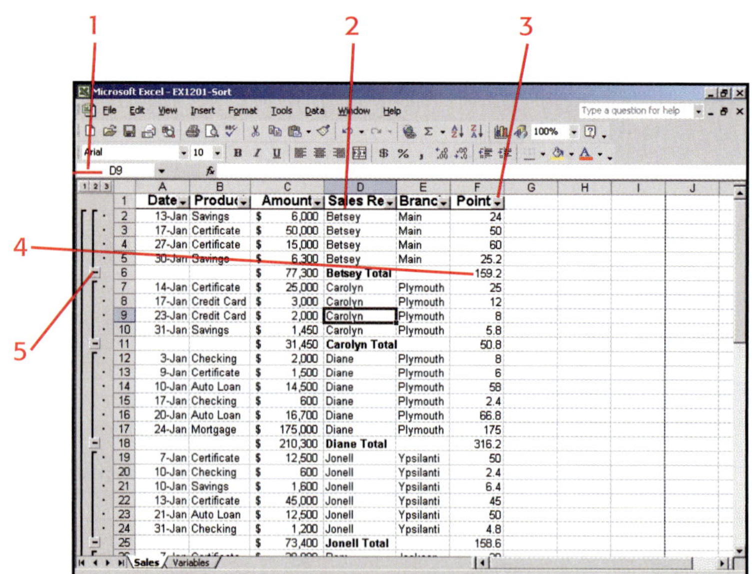

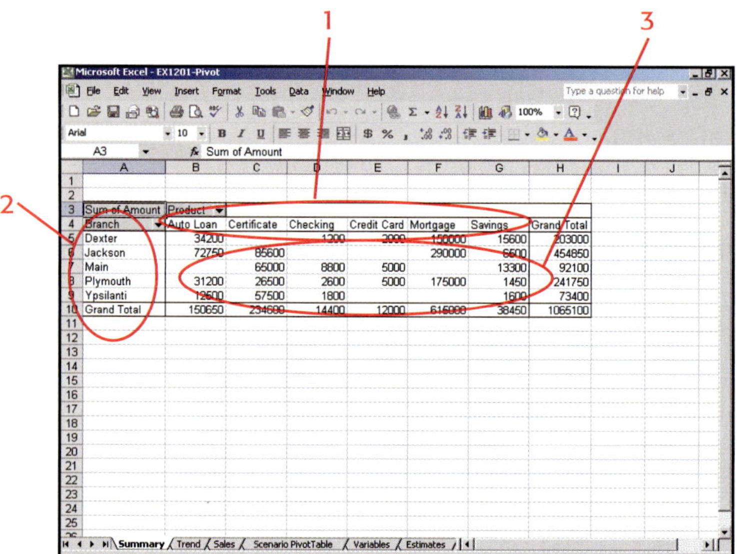

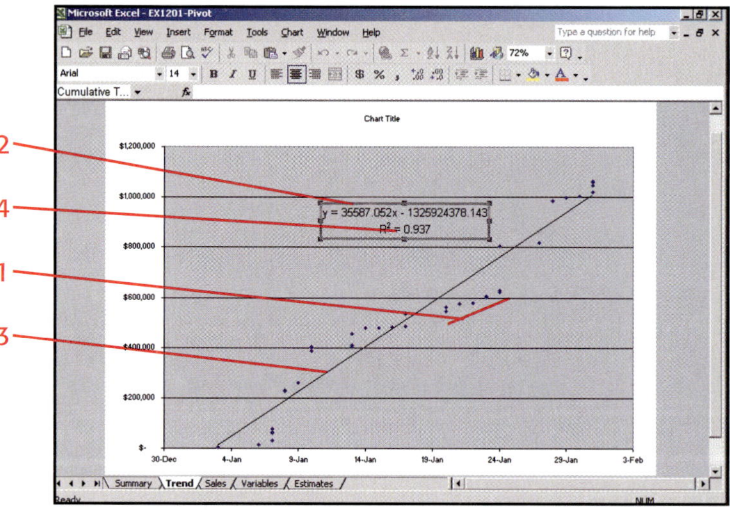

 Reinforcement exercises are designed to reinforce the skills you have learned by applying them to a new situation. Detailed instructions are provided along with a figure, where appropriate, to illustrate the result.

As sales manager of Armstrong Pool, Spa, and Sauna Company, you are reviewing the method by which your salespeople are compensated. Currently they are paid a salary every two weeks without commission on sales. You are considering changing to a system that pays a lower percentage of their current salary plus a commission on sales. In the following reinforcement exercises, you use the analysis tools you have learned in this lesson to evaluate your options.

## R1—Filtering, Sorting, and Subtotaling Sales Data

You have compiled the sales data from all the stores in the company for a two-week period. In this exercise, you sort the data by salesperson and subtotal their sales. You also filter it to look at sales by product description. This exercise gives you a look at the difference in sales by salesperson.

1. Open **EX1203** and save it as **EX1203-Reinforcement** in your folder. Select the **Two-Week Sales** tab, if necessary. Sort the table in ascending order by the **SalesRep** column.

2. Choose **Data, Subtotals**. In the **Subtotal** dialog box, add a subtotal at each change in **SalesRep**, use the **Sum** function, and then add a subtotal to the **Amount** column but not the **City** column.

3. Choose **Data, Filter, AutoFilter**. Click the arrow on the **City** column and select **Southfield**.

4. Enter your name and section number in cell **A95**.

| 1 2 3 | | A | B | C | D | E | F |
|---|---|---|---|---|---|---|---|
| | 1 | OrderDate | SalesRe | FirstNam | LastNam | Description | Amount |
| | 9 | May 14, 2002 | 3 | Margaret | Peacock | 8 person spa | $4,200.00 So |
| | 10 | May 18, 2002 | 3 | Margaret | Peacock | 4 person spa | $2,300.00 So |
| | 11 | May 18, 2002 | 3 | Margaret | Peacock | 12'x24' oval pool | $1,695.00 So |
| | 12 | May 18, 2002 | 3 | Margaret | Peacock | 4'x6' cedar sauna | $3,000.00 So |
| | 13 | May 19, 2002 | 3 | Margaret | Peacock | 6'x10' cedar sauna | $4,750.00 So |
| | 14 | May 19, 2002 | 3 | Margaret | Peacock | 8 person spa | $4,200.00 So |
| | 83 | May 14, 2002 | 24 | Matt | Brinkley | 15'x24' oval pool | $2,450.00 So |
| | 84 | May 16, 2002 | 24 | Matt | Brinkley | 8 person spa | $4,200.00 So |
| | 85 | May 17, 2002 | 24 | Matt | Brinkley | 15'x24' oval pool | $2,450.00 So |
| | 86 | May 17, 2002 | 24 | Matt | Brinkley | 4'x6' cedar sauna | $3,000.00 So |
| | 87 | May 17, 2002 | 24 | Matt | Brinkley | 12'x24' oval pool | $1,695.00 So |
| | 88 | May 19, 2002 | 24 | Matt | Brinkley | 15'x24' oval pool | $2,450.00 So |

5. Print the worksheet if your instructor requires it.

6. Click the arrow on the **City** column and choose **All**. Leave the AutoFilter feature turned on.

7. Choose **Data, Subtotals**. Click the **Remove All** button.

8. Leave the workbook open for the next exercise.

## R2—Creating a PivotTable to Analyze Sales by Person and by Store

Filtering and subtotals provide one method to review sales by individual or by store. You can get a better idea of how they compare by creating a PivotTable.

1. Select a cell in the table on the **Two-Week Sales** sheet. Choose **Data, PivotTable and PivotChart Report**.

2. Click **Finish**. A new sheet is added.

3. Drag **LastName** to the **Drop Row Fields Here** area. Drag **City** to the **Drop Column Fields Here** area. Drag **Amount** to the **Drop Data Items Here** area.

4. Right-click one of the cells in the **Items** area. Choose **Field Settings**. Change the **Summarize by** box to **Sum**, if necessary. Click **OK**.

5. Enter your name and section number in **A2**. Change the sheet name to **Sales by Person** and press **Enter**.

6. Select all the cells in the data items area and in the column and row used for grand totals. Format these numbers to **Currency** with zero decimals.

7. Choose **File, Page Setup**, and then click the **Page** tab. Choose **Landscape** and choose **Fit to**. Choose **1** page wide. Click the **Sheet** tab and turn on the **Gridlines** option.

8. Click the **Print** button and print a copy of the sheet.

9. Leave the workbook open for the next exercise.

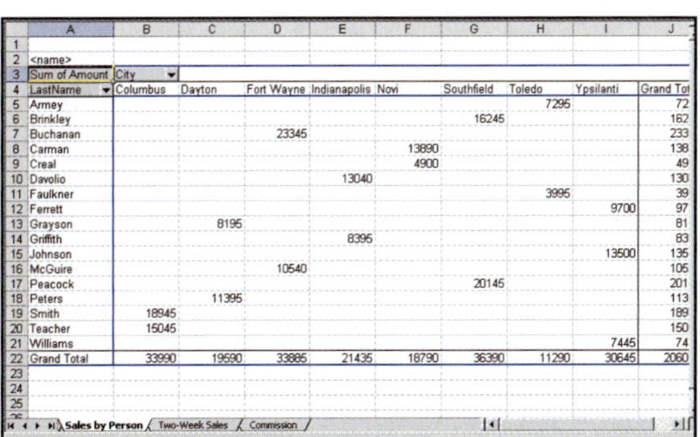

| | A | B | C | D | E | F | G | H | I | J |
|---|---|---|---|---|---|---|---|---|---|---|
| 1 | | | | | | | | | | |
| 2 | <name> | | | | | | | | | |
| 3 | Sum of Amount | City | | | | | | | | |
| 4 | LastName | Columbus | Dayton | Fort Wayne | Indianapolis | Novi | Southfield | Toledo | Ypsilanti | Grand Tot |
| 5 | Armey | | | | | | | 7295 | | 72 |
| 6 | Brinkley | | | | | | 16245 | | | 162 |
| 7 | Buchanan | | | 23345 | | | | | | 233 |
| 8 | Carman | | | | | 13890 | | | | 138 |
| 9 | Creal | | | | | 4900 | | | | 49 |
| 10 | Davolio | | | | 13040 | | | | | 130 |
| 11 | Faulkner | | | | | | | 3995 | | 39 |
| 12 | Ferrett | | | | | | | | 9700 | 97 |
| 13 | Grayson | | 8195 | | | | | | | 81 |
| 14 | Griffith | | | | 8395 | | | | | 83 |
| 15 | Johnson | | | | | | | | 13500 | 135 |
| 16 | McGuire | | | 10540 | | | | | | 105 |
| 17 | Peacock | | | | | | 20145 | | | 201 |
| 18 | Peters | | 11395 | | | | | | | 113 |
| 19 | Smith | 18945 | | | | | | | | 189 |
| 20 | Teacher | 15045 | | | | | | | | 150 |
| 21 | Williams | | | | | | | | 7445 | 74 |
| 22 | Grand Total | 33990 | 19590 | 33885 | 21435 | 18790 | 36390 | 11290 | 30645 | 2060 |

Sales by Person / Two-Week Sales / Commission /

Ready

## R3—Charting Money Paid to Salespeople versus Sales

You want to know if the amount the salespeople sell depends on how much they are paid. You can chart the sales versus the amount their current salary during the two-week period using an XY (Scatter) chart and add a trend line. The R-squared value will tell you how closely the sales relate to the salary. A value close to 1 is a very close relationship and a value close to 0 means the sales do not depend on the salary. Note that the Sales column uses the SUMIF function to add up all the sales by the person with the Rep # found in column D.

1. Click the **Commission** sheet tab. Select **E2** through **E18**. Hold the Ctrl key and select **G2** through **G18**.

2. Click the **Chart Wizard** button. Select the **XY (Scatter)** chart type. Click **Next** for Steps 1 through 3 of the chart wizard.

3. On Step 4 of the chart wizard, click **As new sheet**. Enter **Sales versus Salary**. Click **Finish**.

4. Right-click one of the data points and choose **Add Trendline**. Click the **Options** tab and select **Display R-squared value on the chart**. Click **OK**.

5. Drag the R-squared text to a place above the trendline and between the gridlines where it is easier to read. Change the font size to **18**. This R-squared value is almost 0, which means there is almost no relationship between the amount they sold during this two-week period and the salary they were paid. You could use this chart in a meeting to show that a change in compensation methods is necessary.

6. Leave the workbook open for the next exercise.

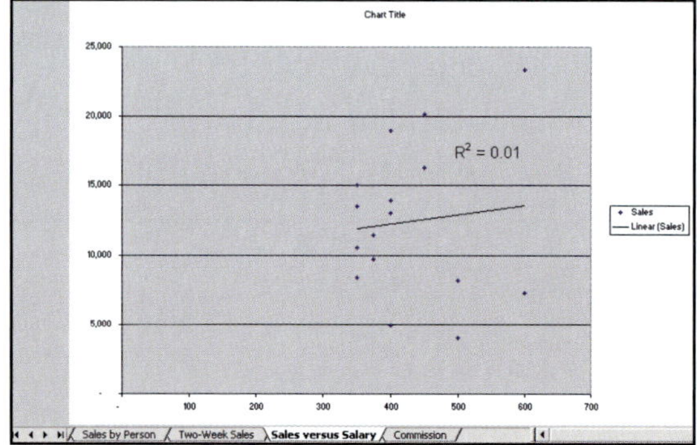


## R4—Comparing Scenarios of Salary and Commission Options

You decide that you need to revamp the method by which the salespeople are compensated, but you don't want to discard completely the difference between their present salaries. A table has been set up to assist with this decision. The sales representative's number is in the first column. The columns to the right contain the current salary, the reduced salary, the sum of sales for that sales representative, the commission, the new total of salary plus commission, and the difference between the old salary and the new combination of reduced salary plus commission. The Sales column uses the SUMIF function and the Salary plus commission column uses a conditional format to display increases.

You use this table to examine different combinations of salary reductions and added commissions.

1. Select the **Commission** sheet. Select **D3**. It has the ID number of one of the sales representatives. Press → to move across the columns and see how formulas have been used to calculate the values in each column. Select **B3**. Press ↓ to move down the column to see how formulas have been used to calculate each of the values in this column.

2. Select **B4**, type **50%**, and then press ↵Enter. Observe the effect (you can use formula auditing arrows if you like).

3. Select **B3**, type **5%**, and then press ↵Enter. Observe the effect. Notice that all the values in column I turned blue. This conditional format shows which people would earn more than their current salary. Notice the total in cell B8 is much larger than the present salary total in cell B5. You want to find a commission rate that exactly offsets the decrease in salary. When that is the case, the total value in cell B8 will match the current salary total of $6,850.

4. Choose **Tools, Goal Seek**. In the **Set cell** box, type **B8**. In the **To value** box, type **6850**. In the **By changing cell** box, type **B3**. Click **OK**. Click **OK** to accept the change.

5. Choose **Tools, Scenarios**. Click the **Add** button. In the **Scenario name** box, type **50 percent**. In the **Changing cells** box, type **B3:B4**. Click **OK**. Click **OK**. Click **Close**.

6. Select **B4** and type **75**. Use Goal Seek to set cell **B8** to **6850** by changing cell **B3**. Save this scenario as **75 percent**.

7. Choose **Tools**, **Scenarios**. Click the **Summary** button. Click the **Scenario PivotTable report** option. Select the default option in the **Result cells** box and type **B3:B9**. Click **OK**.

8. A PivotTable is created that compares the options. You can observe that replacing 50% of the salary with commission can be accomplished with a commission rate of 1.72%, and a commission rate of 2.59% can be used to replace 75% of the current salary. Both methods result in the same total compensation for all employees, but 10 of the 16 salespeople will see increases.

9. Format the cells as shown in the figure. Add your name and section number to **A2**. Print the worksheet if your instructor requires it.

| | A | B | C | D | E | F | G |
|---|---|---|---|---|---|---|---|
| | $B$3:$B$4 by | (All) | | | | | |
| | <name> | | | | | | |
| | | Result Cells | | | | | |
| | $B$3:$B$4 | Commission_Rate | Salary_Reduction | Present_Salary | New_Salary | Commission | Total |
| | 50 percent | 1.72% | 50% | 6,850 | 3,425 | 3,425 | 6,850 |
| | 75 percent | 2.59% | 75% | 6,850 | 1,713 | 5,138 | 6,850 |

## R5—Forecasting What a New Salesperson Would Make

Under the current salary system, the amount the salespeople make is unrelated to the amount they sell. If a prospective employee asked you how much they would make if they sold as much as most of the other salespeople in a recent period, you couldn't answer that question. With the new method that replaces a large percentage of the salary with a commission, the employee's income should be more predictable.

You can generate another XY (Scatter) chart with a trendline to determine how predictable the total salary plus commission rate will be, and then you can use the FORECAST function to predict an income from an average amount of sales.

1. Select the **Commission** sheet. Select cells **H2:H18**. Hold the Ctrl key and select **I2** through **I18**.

2. Click the **Chart Wizard** button. Select the **XY (Scatter)** chart type. Click **Next** for Steps 1 through 3 of the chart wizard.

3. On Step 4 of the chart wizard, click **As new sheet**. Enter **Salary plus Commission Chart**. Click **Finish**.

4. Right-click one of the data points and choose **Add Trendline**. Click the **Options** tab and select **Display R-squared value on the chart**. Click **OK**.

5. Drag the R-squared text to a place above the trendline and between the gridlines where it is easier to read. Change the font size to **18**. This R-squared value is closer to 1 than the Sales versus Salary chart, which means the salary paid to the salespeople is more dependent on the amount they sold during this two-week period. This tells you that the FORECAST function will produce a forecast that won't be too far off.

6. Scroll to the **Commission** tab and click it. Select **B14**. Choose **Insert**, **Function**. Choose the **Statistical** category, scroll down the list, and then select **FORECAST**. Click **OK**. Type **B13** in the **X** box, **I3:I18** in the **Known_y's** box, and **G3:G18** in the **Known_x's** box. Click **OK**. The FORECAST function predicts a biweekly salary that the new person is likely to get if they make an average amount of sales.

7. Enter your name and section in cell **A1**. Format the cells with dollar values to **Currency** with no decimal places. Print this sheet and the **Salary plus Commission Chart** sheet if your instructor requires it.

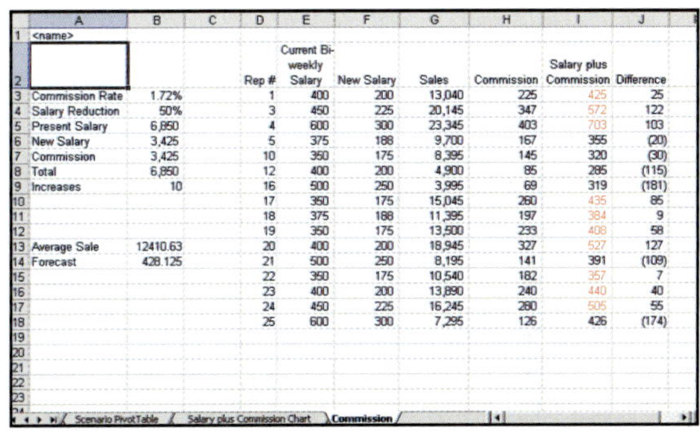

| | A | B | C | D | E | F | G | H | I | J |
|---|---|---|---|---|---|---|---|---|---|---|
| 1 | <name> | | | | | | | | | |
| 2 | | | | Rep # | Current Bi-weekly Salary | New Salary | Sales | Commission | Salary plus Commission | Difference |
| 3 | Commission Rate | 1.72% | | 1 | 400 | 200 | 13,040 | 225 | 425 | 25 |
| 4 | Salary Reduction | 50% | | 3 | 450 | 225 | 20,145 | 347 | 572 | 122 |
| 5 | Present Salary | 6,850 | | 4 | 600 | 300 | 23,345 | 403 | 703 | 103 |
| 6 | New Salary | 3,425 | | 5 | 375 | 188 | 9,700 | 167 | 355 | (20) |
| 7 | Commission | 3,425 | | 10 | 350 | 175 | 8,395 | 145 | 320 | (30) |
| 8 | Total | 6,850 | | 12 | 400 | 200 | 4,900 | 85 | 285 | (115) |
| 9 | Increases | 10 | | 16 | 500 | 250 | 3,995 | 69 | 319 | (181) |
| 10 | | | | 17 | 350 | 175 | 15,045 | 260 | 435 | 85 |
| 11 | | | | 18 | 375 | 188 | 11,395 | 197 | 384 | 9 |
| 12 | | | | 19 | 350 | 175 | 13,500 | 233 | 408 | 58 |
| 13 | Average Sale | 12410.63 | | 20 | 400 | 200 | 18,945 | 327 | 527 | 127 |
| 14 | Forecast | 428.125 | | 21 | 500 | 250 | 8,195 | 141 | 391 | (109) |
| 15 | | | | 22 | 350 | 175 | 10,540 | 182 | 357 | 7 |
| 16 | | | | 23 | 400 | 200 | 13,890 | 240 | 440 | 40 |
| 17 | | | | 24 | 450 | 225 | 16,245 | 280 | 505 | 55 |
| 18 | | | | 25 | 600 | 300 | 7,295 | 126 | 426 | (174) |

8. Save and close the workbook.

Challenge exercises are designed to test your ability to apply your skills to new situations with less detailed instruction. These exercises also challenge you to expand your repertoire of skills by using commands that are similar to those you have already learned. The desired outcome is clearly defined, but you have more freedom to choose the steps needed to achieve the required result.

## C1—Using Pivot Charts

Charts are an excellent tool for making comparisons. You can combine the power of a PivotTable with a chart to analyze patterns and trends.

The file used in this exercise is much larger than most other files you have used. It has almost 38,000 rows and is 2.2 Megabytes in size. The solution file with its pivot table is 5.2 Megabytes. These files are too large to fit on a floppy disk.

*Goal:* Identify how tornadoes in individual states affect the overall pattern of fatalities by year.

Use the following guidelines:

1. Open **EX1204** and save it on your disk as **EX1204-Tornadoes**.

2. Choose **Data, PivotTable and PivotChart Report**. Choose the **PivotChart report (with PivotTable report)** option. Click the **Finish** button.

3. Drag the **Year** field to the **Drop Category Fields Here** area at the bottom of the chart. Drag the **Fatalities** field to the **Drop Data Items Here** area. Drag the **State Name** field to the **Drop Page Fields Here** area. Notice the button at the top left of the chart indicates that this is a count of the records, not a sum of the fatalities.

4. Click the **Sheet2** tab (it may have a different number). Select **B5** through **B50**. Right-click anywhere within the range of selected cells and choose **Field Settings**. Change the **Summarize by** option to **Sum**. Click **OK**.

5. Click the **Chart1** sheet tab. Notice that a few years have far higher numbers of fatalities than most of the others. Click the **Tornadoes** tab. Turn on the **AutoFilter** option. Filter the **Year** column for **74** and sort the table by the **Fatalities** column in descending order.

6. Notice which state has most of the deaths from tornadoes that year. Click the **Chart1** tab. Click the arrow on the **StateName** tab and choose the state with the most deaths from tornado in **74**.

7. Select the title. Change the font size to **18**. Replace **Total** with your name and section number. Right-click the legend and select **Clear**.

8. Print the chart if your instructor requires it.

9. Save and close the workbook.

## C2—Using the Watch Window

Worksheets easily become too large to view all the cells on the screen at once. A cell that is off-screen may contain a formula that is dependent on a cell you are editing. If you want to see the effect of your changes on the dependent formula, you may find yourself scrolling back and forth. You can avoid this problem by using a Watch Window that displays the value of the dependent cell in a small window.

When you arrange a loan for a home, the size of the payments may be based on a long payout, but you are expected to pay off the entire loan after a shorter period. For example, the loan payments may be chosen to pay off the loan in 30 years but you have to pay off the outstanding balance after five years. This is called a *balloon payment*. You can change the terms of the loan at the top of the sheet and use a *Watch Window* to view what effect your changes will have on the balance after five years of payments.

*Goal:* Use the Watch Window to observe changes in an important cell that is off the screen.

Use the following guidelines:

1. Open **EX1205** and save it as **EX1205-Mortgage**.

2. Select **G63**. Choose **Insert, Name, Define**. Type **Five_Year**. Click **OK**.

3. Choose **View, Toolbars, Watch Window**. Click the **Add Watch** button on the toolbar. Click **Add**.

4. Scroll back to the top of the sheet. Move the toolbar to the right side of the screen.

5. You decide that you want to reduce the balance of the loan to approximately $100,000 at the end of five years. Try different values in cell **B6** to get the balance that shows in the Watch Window down to a value that is closest to $100,000. Restrict your choices to whole numbers of years.

6. Enter your name and section number in **A13**. Print the first page of the worksheet.

7. Close the workbook. Close the Watch Window toolbar.

## C3—Using Solver

The Goal Seek function tries different values in one cell to get a target cell to match a given value. *Solver* is similar to Goal Seek except you can vary several cells and you can set the function to match a given value, find a maximum, or find a minimum and display it in the target cell. You can place constraints on the cells as well. The Solver function is an *Add-In* function, which means it is not usually installed on the Tools menu until you specifically choose to do so. It is a very powerful tool for finding optimum solutions to complex problems.

In this exercise, you have a loan amortization statement for a $125,000 loan. The payment is calculated to pay off the loan completely after a given number of years, but you expect to pay the remaining balance on the loan after five years. You want the balance of the loan to be $100,000 after five years. You plan to negotiate the terms of the loan to achieve this. You can vary the number of years on which the payment is calculated, but partial year values are not allowed. You can also vary the interest rate on the loan between 5% and 8%.

*Goal:* Find a combination of integer loan years and an interest rate between 5% and 8% that produces a loan balance of $100,000 after five years.

1. Open **EX1205** and save it as **EX1205-Solver**. Enter your name and section number in **A13**.

2. Choose **Tools**. Expand the menu to determine if the **Solver** option has been installed. If not, click **Add-Ins**. Select **Solver Add-in** and click **OK**.

3. Choose **Tools, Solver**. In the **Set Target Cell,** type **G63**.

4. Click the **Value of** option. Select the box to the right of this option and type **100000**.

5. In the **By Changing Cells** box, type **B4, B6**.

6. Click the **Add** button. In the **Cell Reference** box, type **B4**. Click the arrow on the middle box and select >=. In the **Constraint** box, type **5%**.

7. Click the **Add** button. In the **Cell Reference** box, type **B4**. Click the arrow on the middle box and select <=. In the **Constraint** box, type **8%**.

8. Click the **Add** button. In the **Cell Reference** box, type **B6**. Click the arrow on the middle box and select **int**. Click **OK**. The Solver Parameters dialog box displays the target cell, the value to which you want it set, the cells to be changed, and the three constraints.

9. Click **Solve**. The value is calculated. Click **OK**. Scroll down to **G63** and confirm that it is $100,000. Scroll to the top of the screen. Confirm that the number of years is an integer and the annual percentage rate is between 5% and 8%.

10. Print the first sheet of the loan if your instructor requires it. Save and close the workbook.

## C4—Using Other Types of Trend Lines for Scientific Experiments

Sometimes one set of data is dependent on another, but the relationship is not a simple multiple that produces a straight line on a chart. Excel has several other choices of trendlines that you can use to match the data. You can use the R-squared values and a visual examination of the chart to determine which type of line is the best approximation to the data. There are sophisticated statistical analysis software programs available for detailed, professional analysis, but you can use Excel as a first step.

Radioactive materials lose their activity as time passes, but the relationship is not a simple multiple. For example, if a sample loses half of its activity in 10 years, it isn't gone after another 10 years.

In this exercise, the data represents the radioactivity measured in counts per minute. The first measurement is taken at zero time and then the measurement is taken each hour after that for 30 hours.

*Goal:* Chart the relationship between time and radioactivity of a sample and determine which trendline is the best fit.

1. Open **EX1206** and save it in your folder as **EX1206-Trendlines**. Place your name in **D2**.

2. Select columns **A** and **B**. Click the **Chart Wizard** button. Choose the **XY (Scatter)** chart type. Click **Next** until you get to Step **4** of the chart wizard.

3. Choose **As new sheet** and type **Chart**. Click **Finish**. The relationship between activity and time is clearly not a straight line but some type of curve.

4. Right-click one of the data points and choose **Add Trendline**. Choose **Polynomial** and set the **Order** box to **2**.

5. Click the **Options** tab and select **Display equation on chart** and **Display R-squared value on chart**. Click **OK**.

6. Drag the box with the equation and R-squared value to the left corner of the chart and change the font size to **14**.

7. Right-click one of the data points and choose **Add Trendline**. Choose **Exponential**.

8. Click the **Options** tab and select **Display equation on chart** and **Display R-squared value on chart**. Click **OK**.

9. Drag the box with the equation and R-squared value upward and change the font size to **14**. The exponential trendline has a higher R-squared value and is a better fit to the data points.

10. Select the chart title and type your name. Change the font size of the title to **14**.

11. Print the chart if your instructor requires it.

12. Save and close the workbook.

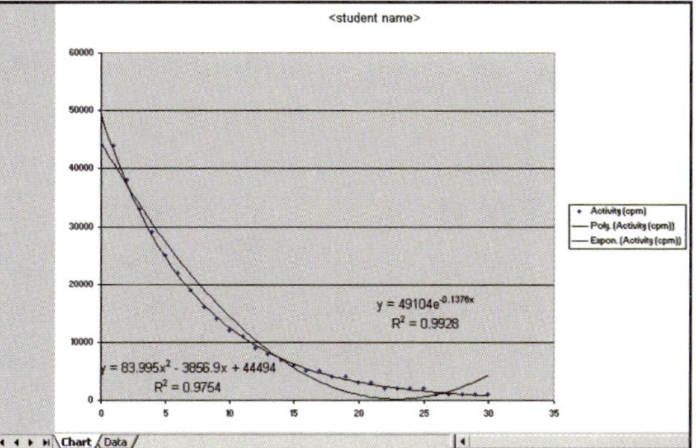

Find a situation where there is data that needs analysis. State your desired outcome. Demonstrate your ability to apply a variety of Excel tools to achieve that outcome.

Criteria for grading will be:

1. Demonstration of the ability to sort, subtotal, and group data.

2. Demonstration of the ability to chart data and estimate values using trendlines and the FORECAST function.

3. Demonstration of the ability to use Goal Seek or Solver to find solutions and to save possible solutions as scenarios.

4. Demonstration of the ability to use PivotTables or pivot charts.

Some examples of features that students have learned to use in previous classes to analyze their data are as follows:

- Use custom filters that define ranges of dates.

- Create two or more PivotTables on the same set of data that show different aspects of the data.

- Combine the use of charts and PivotTables to discover a fact or trend.

- Save several scenarios and create a summary PivotTable to compare them.

1. Identify yourself on at least one of the sheets you print out and place that sheet at the top of the group of papers.

2. To complete the project:

- Save the workbook on your own disk. Name the workbook **EX1207-Own**.

- Check with your instructor to determine if you should submit the project in electronic or printed form. If necessary, print out a copy of the workbook to hand in.

# Lesson 13

## Working with Others



### INTRODUCTION

When you work with others you may find yourself in several different situations. You might have a worksheet you want others to use but with restricted options. For example, you might have a template you want people to use by entering data in a few cells, but you are concerned that they may overwrite the formulas in other cells. In this situation, you need to protect the worksheet from changes with the exception of certain cells.

If you are collaborating on a workbook, your partners may need to have more freedom to make changes but you want to retain control of the final product. For example, you have to prepare an annual report that requires input from other managers. You need to be able to track the changes they make and merge them into a single workbook.

If others have the data you want, you can import it from Web pages or from other data sources such as Access databases.

In this lesson, you learn how protect a template, share a workbook, and retrieve data from Web pages and an Access database using queries.

# VISUAL SUMMARY

By the time you complete this lesson, you will have created a template that is protected from accidental changes, a shared workbook, and an invoice workbook that can be updated from a company Web site:

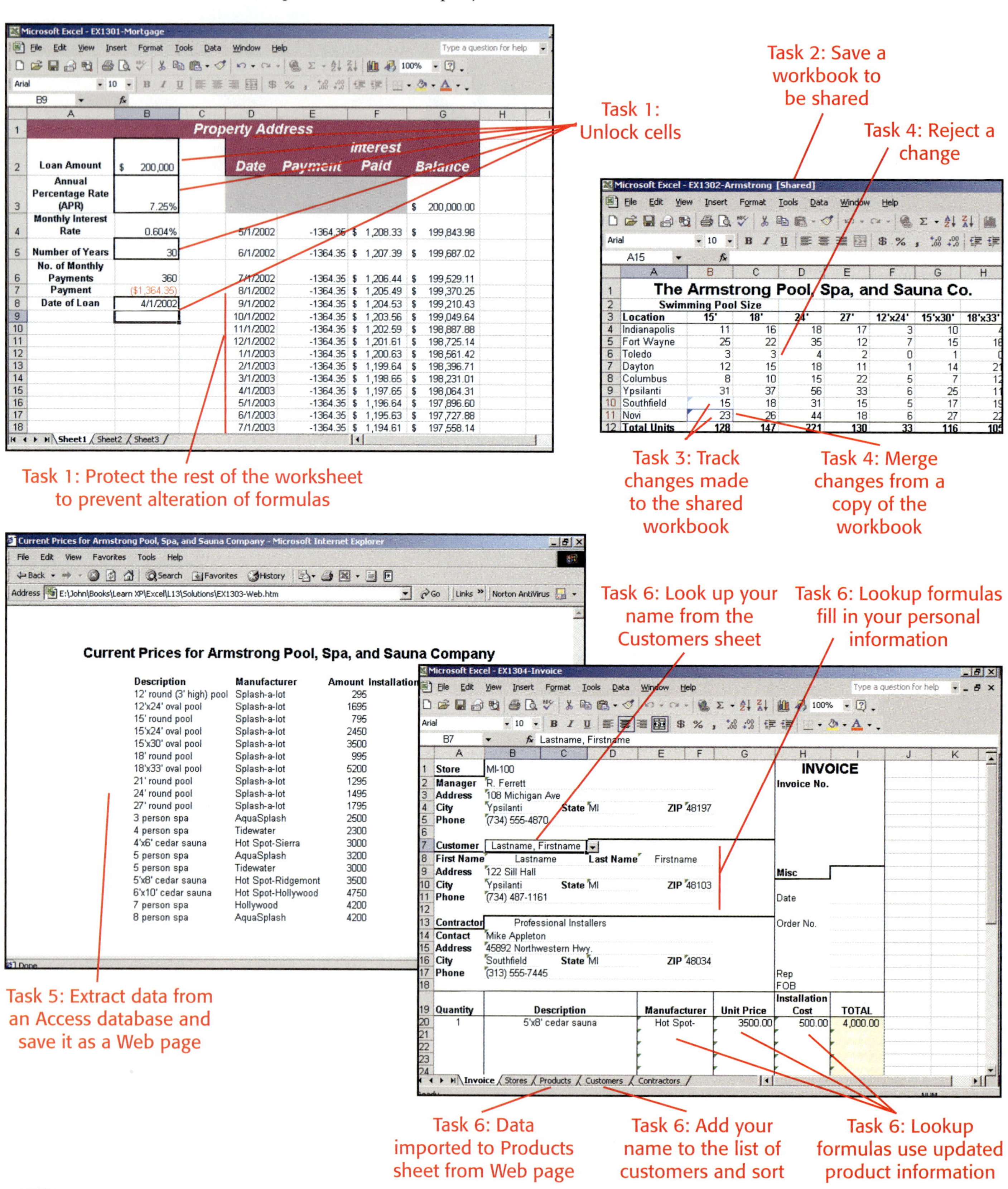

# Task 1
## EDITING AND PROTECTING A TEMPLATE



### Why would I do this?

You have a template that works well but the formulas can be overwritten easily and users who are not familiar with Excel may become confused. You can prevent the user from changing any of the cells in the worksheet except those you choose to make available. This feature is called *protection*. Protecting cells in Excel is a two-step process. First, you choose the cells you want to make available, even when the rest of the cells are protected from change, and *unlock* them. The second step is to protect the entire sheet and give it a password. Users can change the unlocked cells while the rest of the cells in the sheet are protected. A user must know the password to unprotect the sheet and make changes to the *locked* cells. The terms, locked and unlocked, refer to the state of the cell when the sheet is protected and do not apply when the sheet is unprotected.

In this task, you learn how to edit the template. You unlock cells used to input the loan and address information, and protect the rest of the cells in the sheet from change.

**1** Open **EX1301** and save it in your folder as **EX1301-Mortgage**.

*You will protect all the cells in this worksheet except those designed to be altered by the user.*

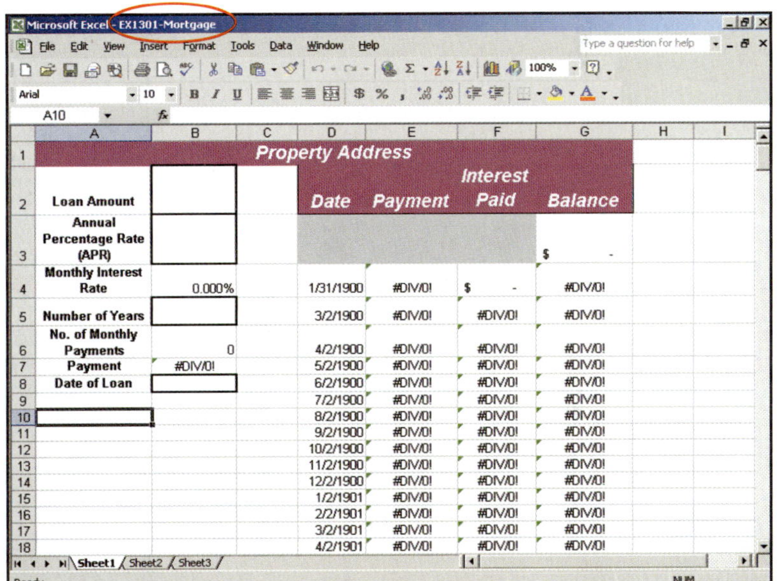

**2** Select the title in **A1** through **G1**. Choose **Format**, **Cells**, and click the **Protection** tab in the **Format Cells** dialog box.

*The selected cells are locked if the sheet is protected.*

Click the **Locked** option to deselect it.

*The user can change this title if the rest of the sheet is protected from change.*

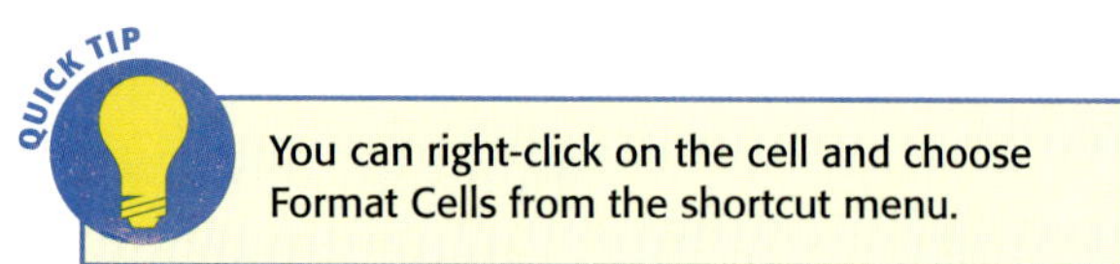


You can right-click on the cell and choose Format Cells from the shortcut menu.

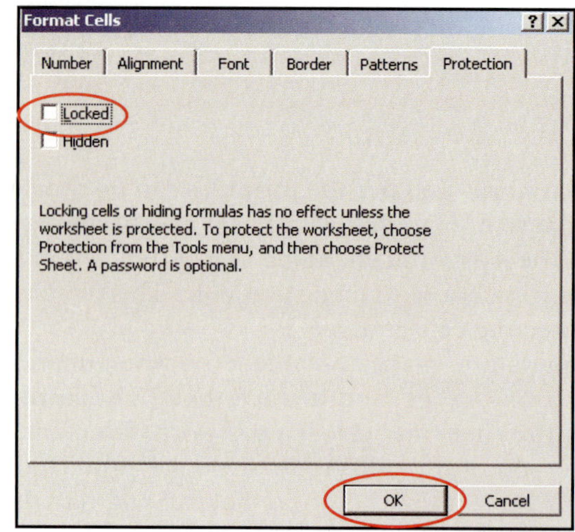


**3** Click **OK**.

*The dialog box closes.*

Select cell **B2**. Hold down the Ctrl key and select cells **B3**, **B5**, and **B8**. Choose **Format**, **Cells**, **Protection**. Click the **Locked** option to deselect it. Click **OK**

*The cells used to describe the loan are unlocked. A user can change the cells after the sheet is protected.*

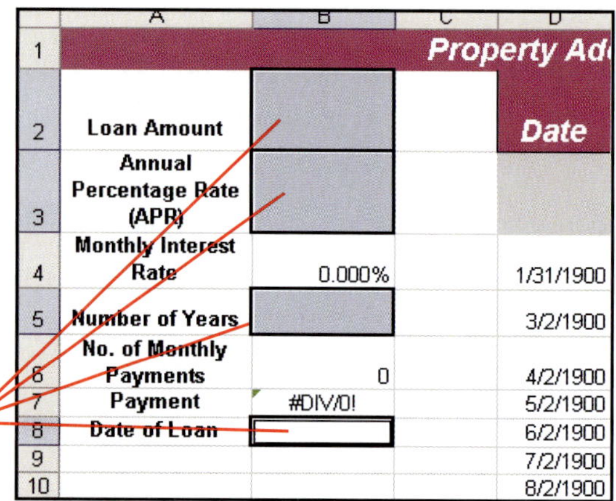


Unlocked cells

**4** Choose **Tools**, **Protection**, **Protect Sheet**.

*The Protect Sheet dialog box opens.*

Select the **Password to unprotect sheet** box and type **Learn**.

*The user must know the password to unprotect the sheet and make changes.*

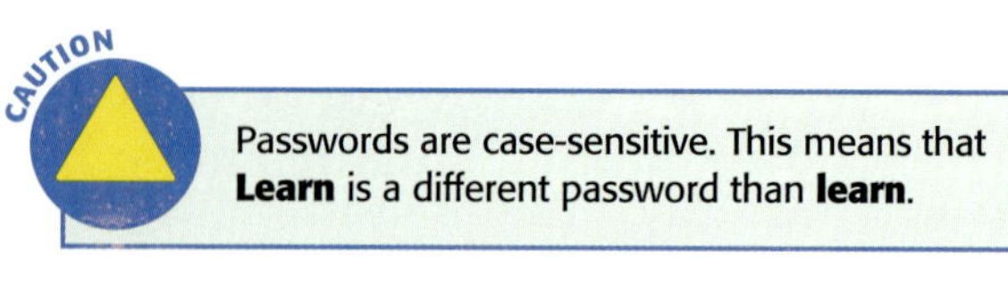


Passwords are case-sensitive. This means that **Learn** is a different password than **learn**.

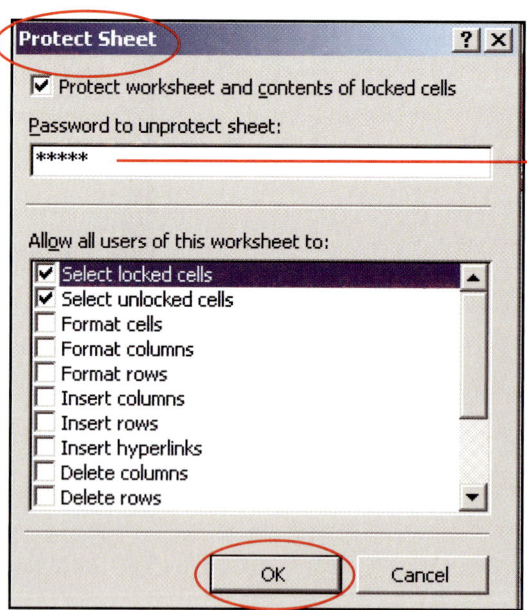


Asterisks displayed to protect password

IN DEPTH

The first two options in the **Allow all users of this worksheet to** box are selected by default. They allow the user to select any of the cells in the worksheet regardless of their locked or unlocked condition. This allows the user to see the formulas in the locked cells, as well as to select and change the unlocked cells.

**5** Click **OK**.

*The Confirm Password dialog box opens.*

Type **Learn** in the **Reenter password to proceed** box. Click **OK**.

*The sheet is protected from changes to all the cells that are still locked, but the unlocked cells can be changed.*

Unlocked cells can be changed

| | A | B | C | D | E | F | G |
|---|---|---|---|---|---|---|---|
| 1 | | | Property Address | | | | |
| 2 | Loan Amount | | | Date | Payment | Interest Paid | Balance |
| 3 | Annual Percentage Rate (APR) | | | | | | $ - |
| 4 | Monthly Interest Rate | 0.000% | | 1/31/1900 | #DIV/0! | $ - | #DIV/0! |
| 5 | Number of Years | | | 3/2/1900 | #DIV/0! | #DIV/0! | #DIV/0! |
| 6 | No. of Monthly Payments | 0 | | 4/2/1900 | #DIV/0! | #DIV/0! | #DIV/0! |
| 7 | Payment | #DIV/0! | | 5/2/1900 | #DIV/0! | #DIV/0! | #DIV/0! |
| 8 | Date of Loan | | | 6/2/1900 | #DIV/0! | #DIV/0! | #DIV/0! |
| 9 | | | | 7/2/1900 | #DIV/0! | #DIV/0! | #DIV/0! |

Formulas protected from change

---

**IN DEPTH**

To make changes to the worksheet, you need to remove the sheet protection. Choose Tools, Protection, Unprotect Sheet, and provide the password. This action does not change the locked/unlocked status of the cells but allows you to make changes to locked cells.

---

**6** Select **B2** and enter **200000**.

*Changes are allowed to the unlocked cells.*

Select **G3** and try to type something.

*A warning is displayed that informs you that you cannot change the contents of this cell without removing the protection from the sheet.*

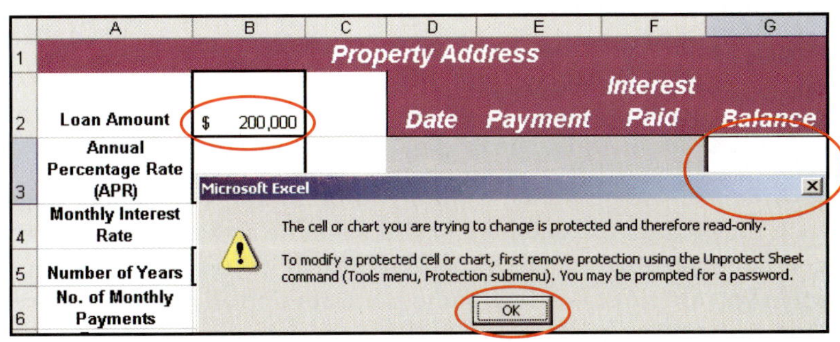



---

**7** Click **OK**. Select **B3**, type **7.25**, and then press Enter.

*The formula in B4 is updated automatically.*

Select **B5**, type **30**, and then press Enter. Select **B8** and enter today's date.

*The worksheet is updated.*

Use current date instead of the example

| | A | B | C | D | E | F | G |
|---|---|---|---|---|---|---|---|
| 1 | | | Property Address | | | | |
| 2 | Loan Amount | $ 200,000 | | Date | Payment | Interest Paid | Balance |
| 3 | Annual Percentage Rate (APR) | 7.25% | | | | | $ 200,000.00 |
| 4 | Monthly Interest Rate | 0.604% | | 5/1/2002 | -1364.35 | $ 1,208.33 | $ 199,843.98 |
| 5 | Number of Years | 30 | | 6/1/2002 | -1364.35 | $ 1,207.39 | $ 199,687.02 |
| 6 | No. of Monthly Payments | 360 | | 7/1/2002 | -1364.35 | $ 1,206.44 | $ 199,529.11 |
| 7 | Payment | ($1,364.35) | | 8/1/2002 | -1364.35 | $ 1,205.49 | $ 199,370.25 |
| 8 | Date of Loan | 4/1/2002 | | 9/1/2002 | -1364.35 | $ 1,204.53 | $ 199,210.43 |

Updated formulas

---

**QUICK TIP**

If the cell is already formatted to display percentages, you do not need to type the percent sign. You have a choice of typing 7.25 or .0725. Excel interprets them both as 7.25%. When you start to type 7.25, Excel automatically adds a percent sign after you type the first number to indicate that it will interpret this number as a percent.

---

**8** Select the title in **A1** through **G1** and enter your name and section number. Print the first sheet of the worksheet if your instructor requires it.

Save and close the workbook.

# Task 2
## SHARING A WORKBOOK AND TRACKING CHANGES

### *Why would I do this?*

You have prepared a summary of sales from each of the stores in the Armstrong Pool, Spa, and Sauna Company and you want to have your store managers check it before you submit it to your supervisor. You can save the workbook in a folder to which most of the store managers have access and allow them to make changes, or you can send individual copies of the workbook and merge the changes into the final version when they return the edited copies. You can also do a combination of sharing and merging.

You play the role of three other store managers who make revisions to the original workbook and then you combine all the revisions into a final version. Two of the store managers are on the company network and can make the changes directly to the worksheet. The manager of the Novi store is not on the company network but has access to the Internet so you send a copy of the worksheet as an e-mail attachment and merge it into the original when it is returned.

To simulate changes made by three different users, you change the user name each time you make a change. If you were the actual store manager, you would not need to make this change. Be sure to return the user name to the original name when you are finished. This name is attached to all documents created by Microsoft Office applications on the computer you are using.

In this task, you open an existing copy of the workbook and save a version of it that can be reviewed. You also make a copy to be sent to the manager of the Novi store.

**1** Open **EX1302** and save it in your folder as **EX1302-Armstrong**.

*This file will be modified. If you get confused and wish to start over, the EX1302 file remains unchanged.*



If this were a real situation, you would save the file in a folder that is shared with the other people who are supposed to make the changes. This folder could exist on a network server. In this exercise, you play the roles of the individual store managers, as well as the owner of the workbook. You store all the files on your own disk.

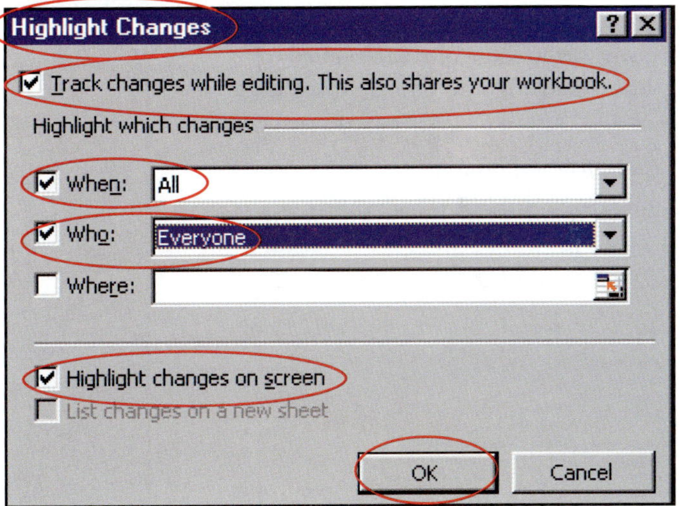



| | A | B | C | D | E | F | G | H |
|---|---|---|---|---|---|---|---|---|
| 1 | The Armstrong Pool, Spa, and Sauna Co. | | | | | | | |
| 2 | Swimming Pool Size | | | | | | | |
| 3 | Location | 15' | 18' | 24' | 27' | 12'x24' | 15'x30' | 18'x33' |
| 4 | Indianapolis | 11 | 16 | 18 | 17 | 3 | 10 | 4 |
| 5 | Fort Wayne | 25 | 22 | 35 | 12 | 7 | 15 | 16 |
| 6 | Toledo | 3 | 3 | 4 | 2 | 0 | 1 | 0 |
| 7 | Dayton | 12 | 15 | 18 | 11 | 1 | 14 | 21 |
| 8 | Columbus | 8 | 10 | 15 | 22 | 5 | 7 | 12 |
| 9 | Ypsilanti | 31 | 37 | 56 | 33 | 6 | 25 | 11 |
| 10 | Southfield | 16 | 18 | 31 | 15 | 5 | 17 | 19 |
| 11 | Novi | 21 | 26 | 44 | 18 | 6 | 27 | 22 |
| 12 | Total Units | 127 | 147 | 221 | 130 | 33 | 116 | 105 |
| 13 | | | | | | | | |



If you are working in a laboratory that does not allow you to change the user name, save the file to a floppy disk. Move to different computers in the lab and make the changes required by the other store managers. You will not be able to use the names as they are shown in the steps but the different names assigned to each computer will be displayed.

**2** Choose **Tools**, **Track Changes**, **Highlight Changes**.

*The Highlight Changes dialog box opens.*

Click **Track changes while editing. This also shares the workbook**. Confirm that **When** and **All** are selected in the **When** box. Click the **Who** box to select it and confirm that **Everyone** is selected, the **Where** box is empty, and **Highlight changes on screen** is selected.

*Other users can open this file if it is located in a folder shared with other users. If they make changes to it, you can see what the changes are and who made them.*





If you do not choose **Highlight changes on screen,** the changes are tracked but not displayed. They can be displayed later by selecting this feature. You can also share the workbook without using the Track Changes option by choosing **Tools**, **Share Workbook**.

**3** Click **OK**.

*A notice is displayed informing you that the workbook will be saved again.*

Click **OK**.

*The workbook is saved and can be shared by others. Notice the change in the title bar. The actual name of the file does not include the [Shared] notation.*

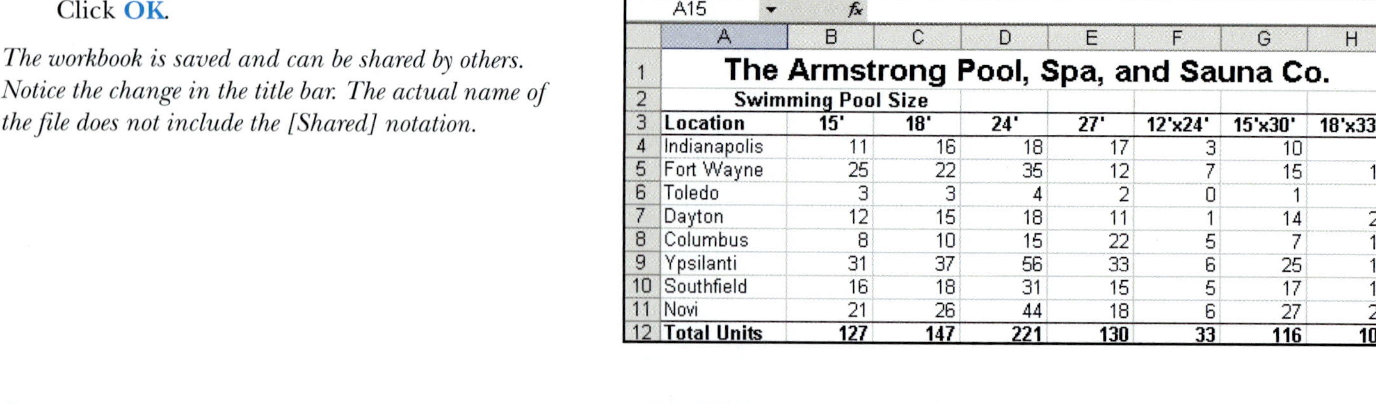

**4** Close the workbook.

*The workbook is available for other users who have access to the folder where the workbook is saved.*

**5** Choose **File, Open**, and locate the folder where you saved your file. Right-click on **EX1302-Armstrong** and choose **Copy** from the shortcut menu

*The file is ready to be duplicated.*

Right-click in an empty space below the list of files in your folder and choose **Paste** from the shortcut menu.

*A copy of the file is created. You can send this file to other store managers.*

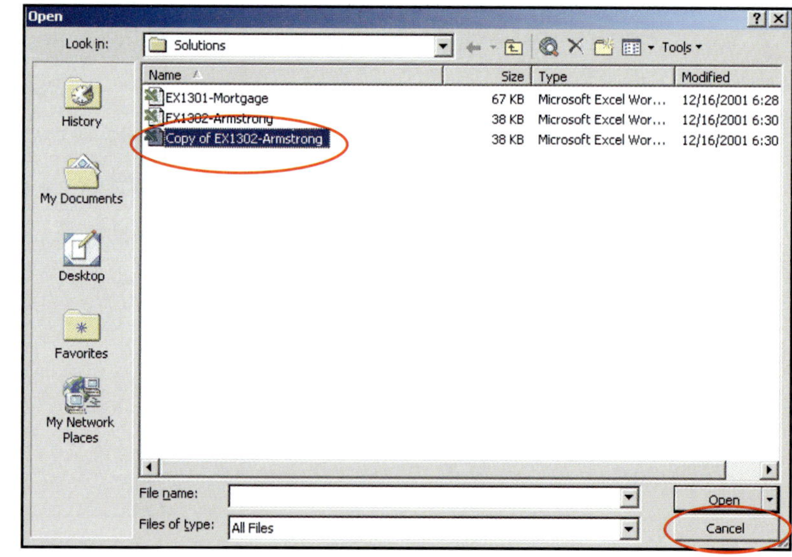

**6** Click **Cancel**.

*The Open dialog box closes. In the next task, you make changes to the workbook as if you are a store manager.*

# Task 3

## MAKING CHANGES TO A SHARED WORKBOOK

### Why would I do this?

You may be the one who is asked to review a workbook and make changes. You can make changes to the workbook as you would normally, but the program tracks your changes so the owner of the workbook can see who made the change. In order for you to simulate the changes made by another user, you must learn how to change the user name.

In this task, you learn how to make changes to a shared workbook as if you had access to the workbook in a shared folder, and as if you received a copy of the workbook as an e-mail attachment. You also learn how to change the user name that identifies who made the changes.

**1** Open **EX1302-Armstrong**. Choose **Tools**, **Options**, and click the **General** tab.

*The User name section displays the name that is shown when a comment is added to the presentation.*

Make note of the name so that you can replace it when you are finished with this task. Type your first name followed by **-Toledo** in the **User name** box.

> **CAUTION**
>
> Be sure to return the user name to the original name when you finish this task. Write down the original user name if you are sharing this computer or using a computer in the laboratory.

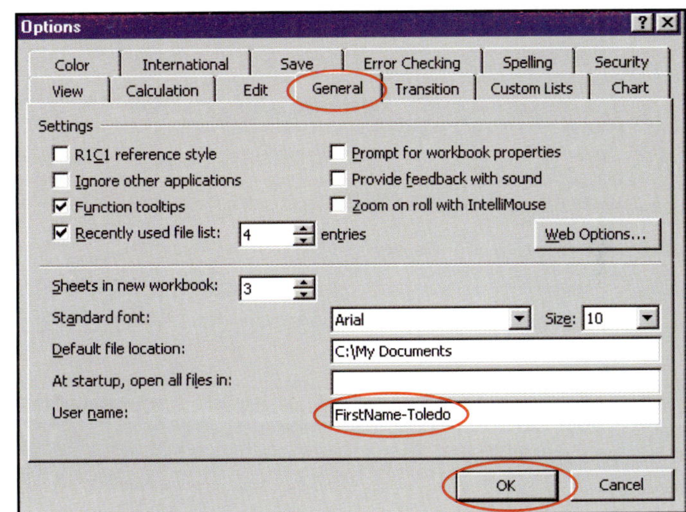


**2** Click **OK**.

*You will make changes to this review version as if you were the manager of the Toledo store.*

Choose the **First Quarter** sheet, select **B6**, type **5**, and then press **←Enter**.



| Location | 15' | 18' | 24' | 27' | 12'x24' | 15'x30' | 18'x33' |
|---|---|---|---|---|---|---|---|
| Indianapolis | 11 | 16 | 18 | 17 | 3 | 10 | 4 |
| Fort Wayne | 25 | 22 | 35 | 12 | 7 | 15 | 16 |
| Toledo | 5 | 3 | 4 | 2 | 0 | 1 | 0 |
| Dayton | 12 | 15 | 18 | 11 | 1 | 14 | 21 |
| Columbus | 8 | 10 | 15 | 22 | 5 | 7 | 12 |
| Ypsilanti | 31 | 37 | 56 | 33 | 6 | 25 | 11 |
| Southfield | 16 | 18 | 31 | 15 | 5 | 17 | 19 |
| Novi | 21 | 26 | 44 | 18 | 6 | 27 | 22 |
| Total Units | 129 | 147 | 221 | 130 | 33 | 116 | 105 |

**3** Choose **Tools**, **Track Changes**, **Highlight Changes**.

*The Highlight Changes dialog box opens.*

Choose **All** in the **When** box. Click **Who** and select **Everyone**.

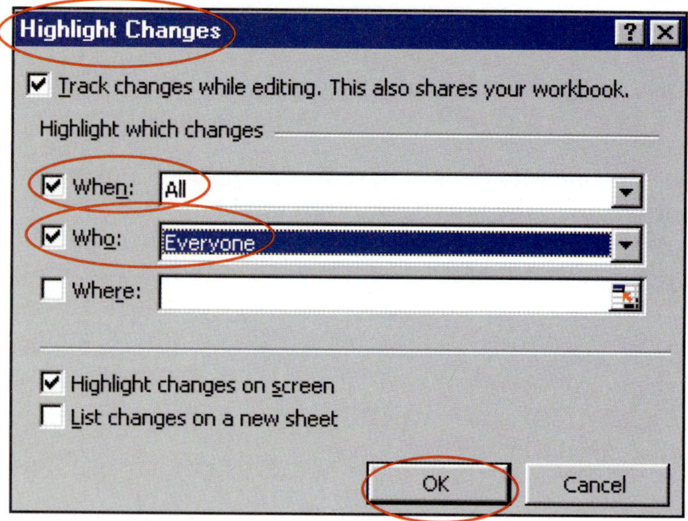


**4** Click **OK**.

*The dialog box closes and leaves a small colored triangle in the corner of the cell.*

Move your mouse pointer onto **B6**.

*The user name and information about the change is displayed.*

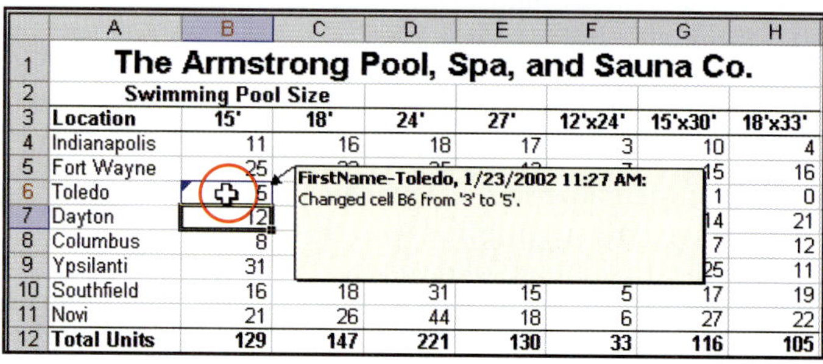

**5** Click the **Close** button on the menu bar to close the workbook. Click **Yes** to save the changes.

*The changes are saved, and the workbook closes. You have simulated a change made by the manager of the Toledo store. The user name is still set to your first name followed by the store name.*

Choose **File**, **Open**. Select **EX1302-Armstrong** from the folder where you saved it and click **Open**.

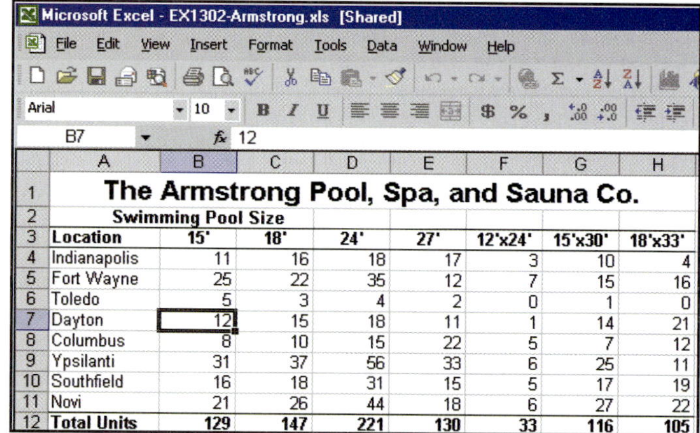

**6** Choose **Tools**, **Options**, and then click the **General** tab.

*You will make changes to this review version as if you were the manager of the Southfield store.*

Select the **User name** box and enter your last name plus **-Southfield**.

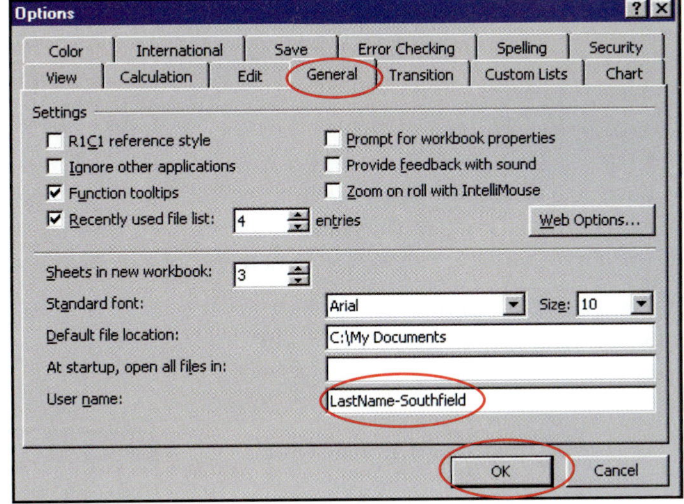

**7** Click **OK**. Select **B10**. Change the value to **15**.

*Track changes records the change but it will not automatically be displayed.*

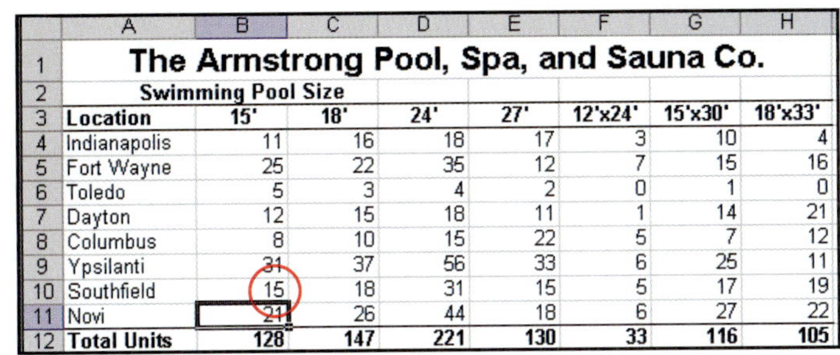

**8** Click the **Close** button on the menu bar to close the workbook. Click **Yes** to save the changes.

*The changes are saved in the shared workbook.*

Open **Copy of EX1302-Armstrong**. Choose **Tools**, **Options**, and then click the **General** tab. Change the **User name** to **John-Novi**.

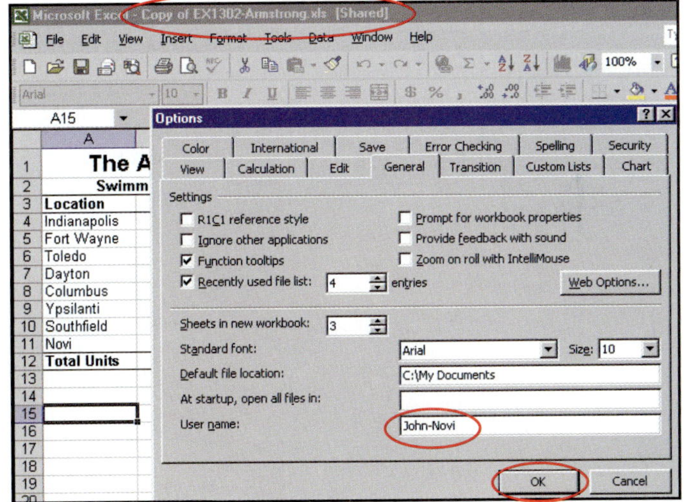

**9** Click **OK**. Change the value of **B11** to **23**. Save the workbook.

*You have made a change as if you were the manager of the Novi store.*

Choose **Tools**, **Options**, and click the **General** tab. Change the **User name** back to the original name. Click **OK**. Close the workbook.

# Task 4
## ACCEPTING CHANGES AND MERGING REVISIONS

### Why would I do this?

You have made two changes to the workbook posing as two different store managers who have access to the shared file in a shared folder on a network. You have also made a change to a copy of the file as if it had been sent to you as an e-mail attachment while identifying yourself as a manager of the Novi store.

In this task, you act as the home office manager and learn how to accept or reject changes and merge a copy of the file with the original file.

**1** Open **EX1302-Armstrong**. Choose **Tools**, **Track Changes**, **Highlight Changes**.

*The Highlight Changes dialog box opens.*

Choose **All** in the **When** box. Click **Who** and select **Everyone**.

*All the changes will be displayed.*

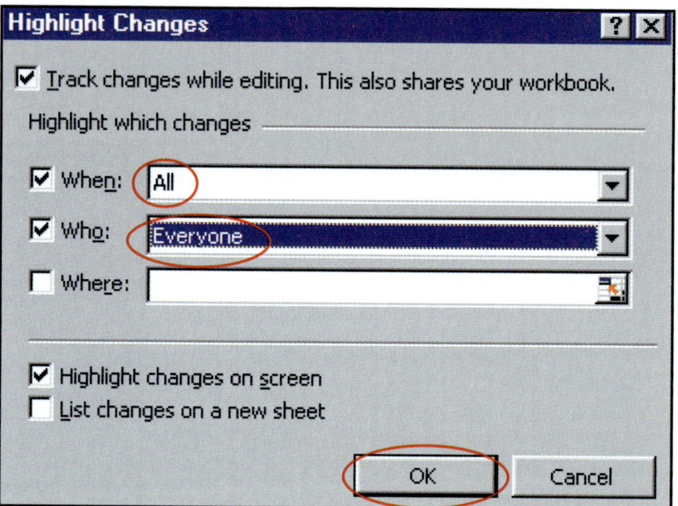


**2** Click **OK**. Move the pointer to **B10**.

*The change made using your last name as store manager is displayed.*

Pointer activates pop-up message

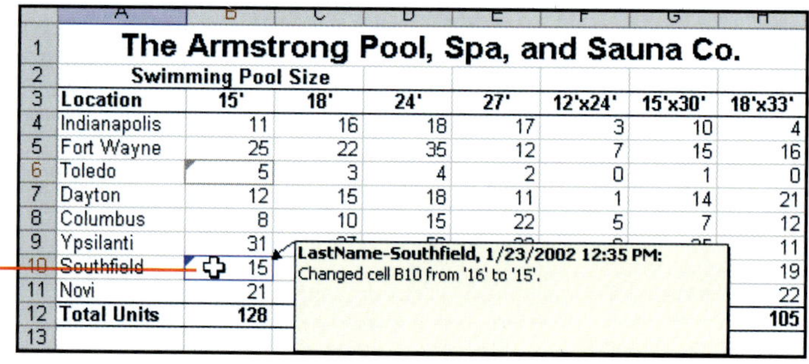


> **CAUTION**
>
> Different users who make changes are represented by different colors, some of which are light colors and not easy to see. The colors used to identify different users are not easily changed in Excel.

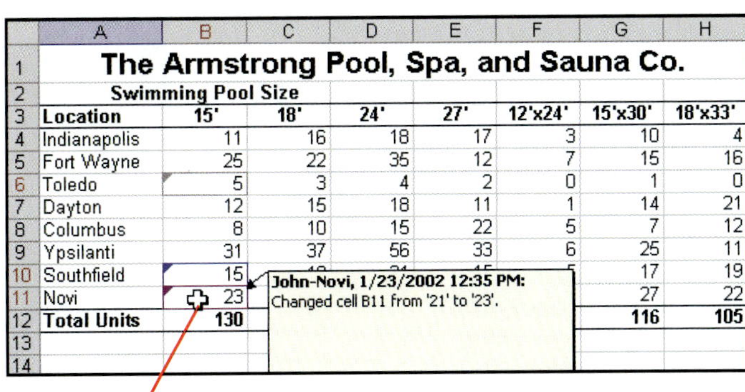



Change from merged file

**3** Choose <u>Tools</u>, <u>Compare and Merge Workbooks</u>.

*The Select Files to Merge Into Current Workbook dialog box opens.*

Locate the **Copy of EX1302-Armstrong** file in the folder where you saved it. Select the file and click **OK**.

*The changes made in the copy are merged into the original.*

Move the mouse pointer onto **B11**.

*The change you made as the manager of the Novi store is displayed.*

**4** Choose <u>Tools</u>, <u>Track Changes</u>, <u>Accept or Reject Changes</u>.

*The Select Changes to Accept or Reject dialog box opens.*

Confirm that **Not yet reviewed** is selected in the **When** box and **Everyone** is selected in the **Who** box.

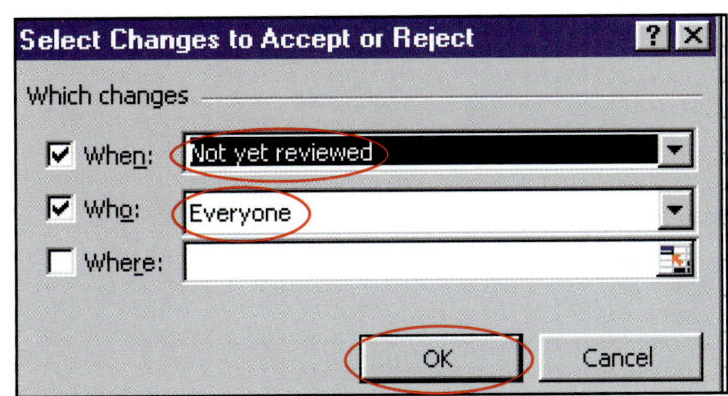



**5** Click **OK**.

*The Accept or Reject Changes dialog box opens and the first change is selected in B6.*

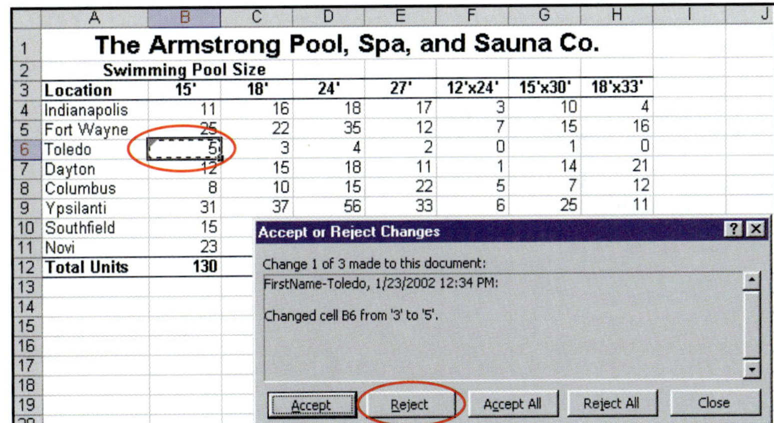

**6** Click **Reject**.

*The change is removed and the selection jumps to the next change in B10.*

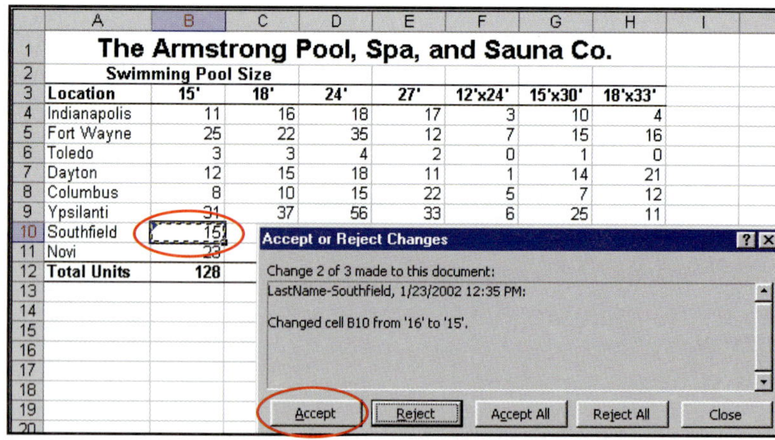

**7** Click **Accept**.

*The change in B10 is accepted and the next change in B11 is selected.*

Click **Accept**.

*The changes for Southfield and Novi were accepted but the change made in B6 was not made.*

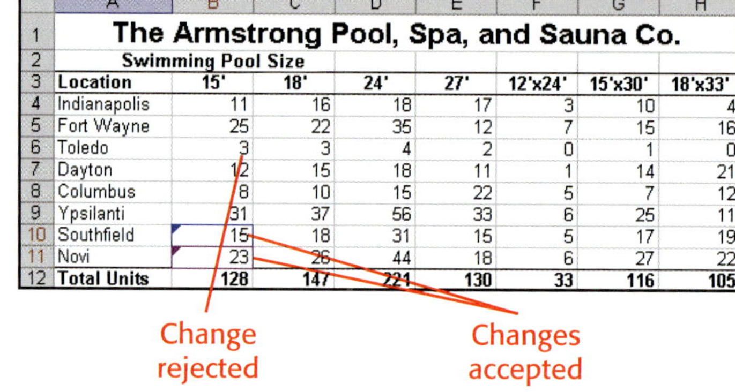


**CAUTION**

If you made any errors while you worked through Tasks 3 or 4 and corrected them, an additional dialog box opens. It asks that you specify which version of the changes should be accepted or rejected. Should this happen, select the correct version by clicking on it and click OK.

**8** Close the file and save the changes. Leave Excel open for the next task.

# Task 5



## Why would I do this?

If your organization keeps detailed records of transactions, prices, customers, vendors, or other facts, they are probably stored in a database such as Microsoft Access. If you are not familiar with Access but want to extract data from a table stored in an Access database, you can do so using a *database query*. A database query allows you to set conditions used to retrieve columns and rows of a table. Once the data is in a worksheet, you can save it as usual or you can save it as a Web page that store managers or salespeople can use.

In this task, you learn to extract a price list from an Access table and save it as a Web page.

**1** Click the **New** button.

*An empty worksheet is displayed.*

> Choose **Data**, **Import External Data**, **New Database Query**.

*The Choose Data Source dialog box opens.*

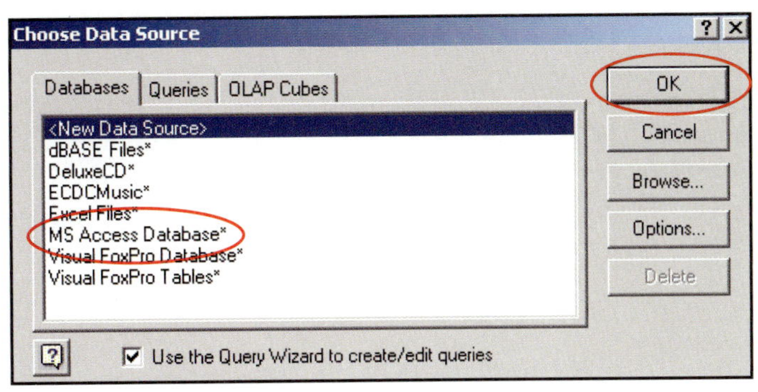

**2** Select **MS Access Database*** and click **OK**.

*The Select Database dialog box opens, and a **Connecting to data source** icon is displayed.*

> Find the folder where the student files are kept in the **Directories** box. Select **EX1303.mdb** in the **Database Name** box.

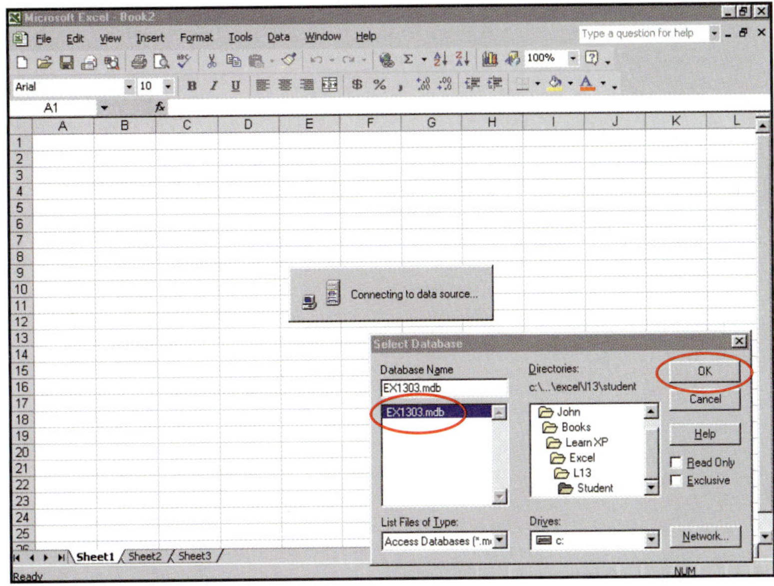

**3** Click **OK**.

*The **Query Wizard-Choose Columns** dialog box opens. This database has several tables.*

> Click the plus sign next to **tblProducts**.

*The column names within the tblProducts table are displayed. You can transfer the columns to the Columns in your query box one at a time or as a group.*

> Click **Description.** Click the **Add** button. Repeat this process to add **Manufacturer**, **Amount**, and **InstallationCost**.

*Four column names are moved into the Columns in your query box.*

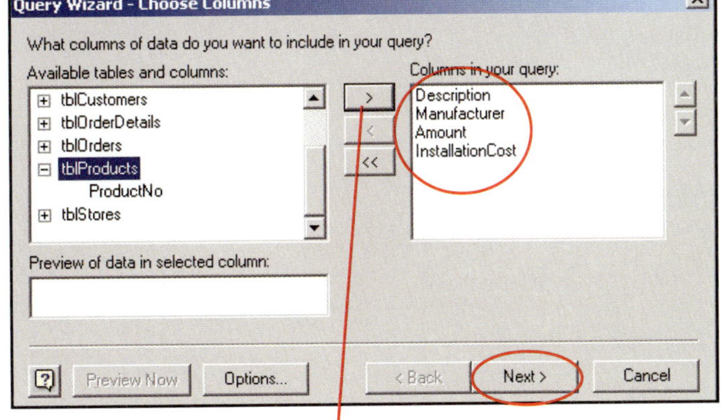

Unless you are familiar with the Access Table relationships, only select columns from a single Access table.

**4**  Click **Next**.

*The Filter Data window of the wizard is displayed. You can use this window to limit the data by matching column contents to conditions specified in the boxes to the right. In this case, you want all the product prices so no restrictions are needed.*

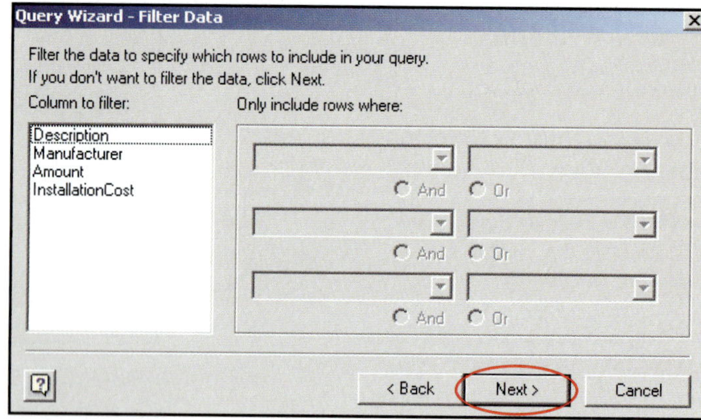

**5**  Click **Next**. Click the arrow on the **Sort by** box and choose **Description**.

*The default sorting method is Ascending.*

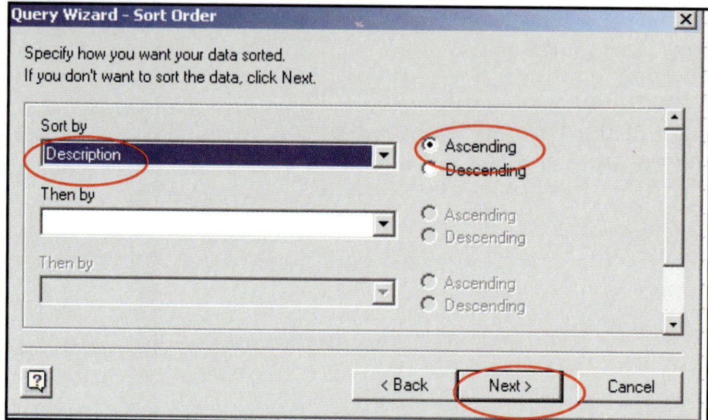

**6**  Click **Next**.

*The last dialog box in the wizard displays.*

Confirm that **Return Data to Microsoft Excel** is selected.

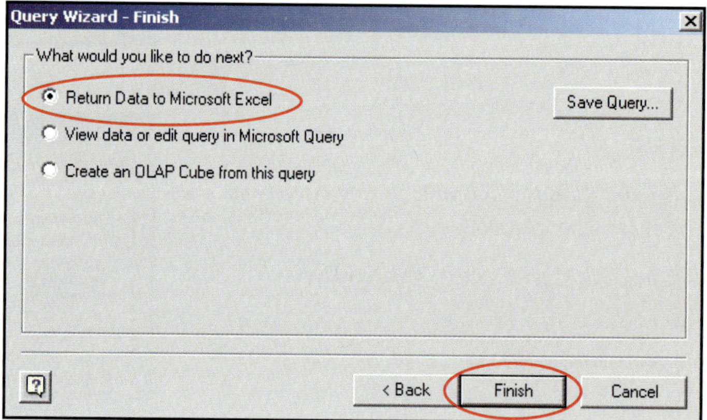

**7** Click **Finish**.

*The Import Data dialog box opens.*

> Confirm that **Existing worksheet** is selected
> and =$A$1 is the selected cell.

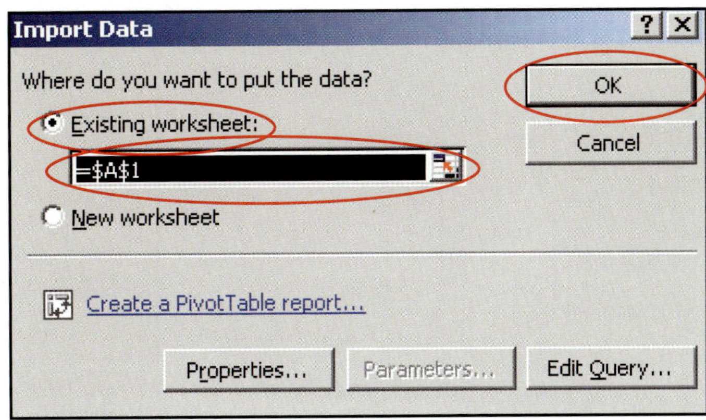

**8** Click **OK**.

*The data from the Access database is placed in the
worksheet. You want to place this information on the
Internet so all your store managers can receive it.*

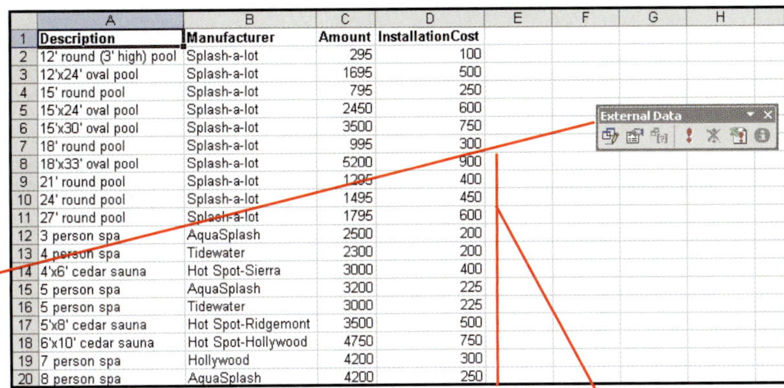

Tool bar used for refreshing
data from the database

Data imported from the database
with the latest product information

**9** Choose **File**, **Save as Web Page**.

*The Save As dialog box displays.*

> Choose **Selection: Sheet**. Select the default
> name in the **File name** box and type
> **EX1303-Web**.

*The worksheet will be saved as a Web page.*

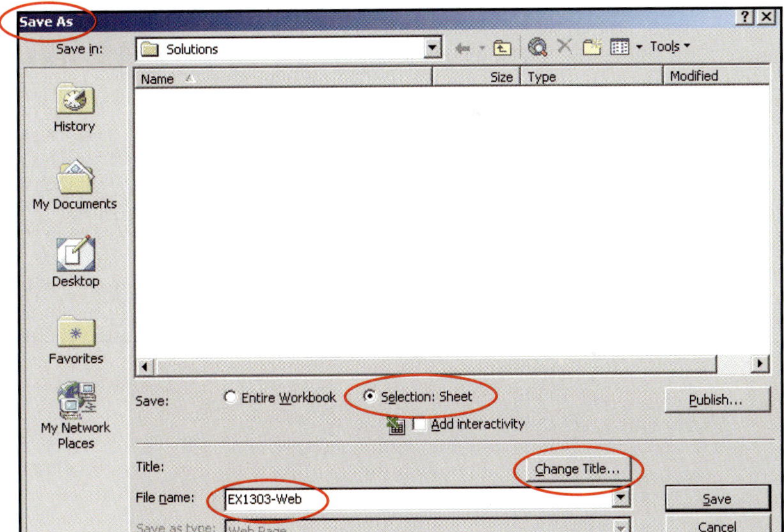

**10**  Click the **Change Title** button.

*The Set Title box displays.*

> Type **Current Prices for Armstrong Pool, Spa, and Sauna Company**.

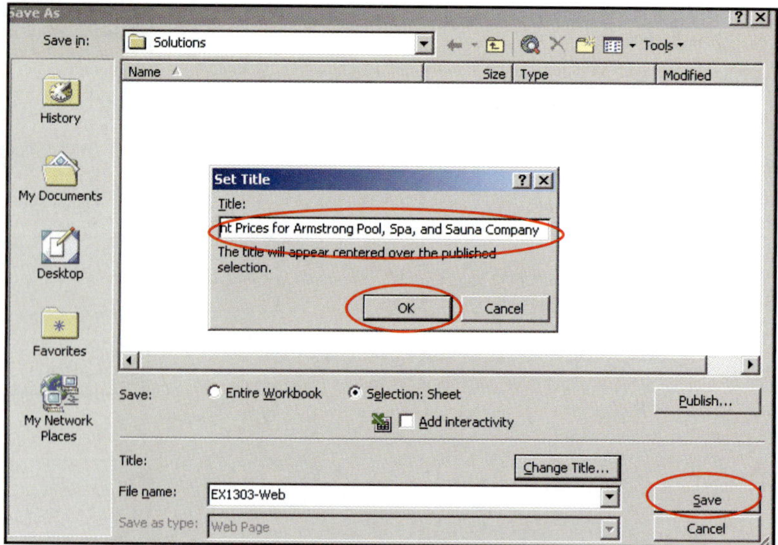

**11**  Click **OK**.

*The Set Title box closes.*

> Click the **Save** button.

*The worksheet is saved as a Web page but the Web page is not opened.*

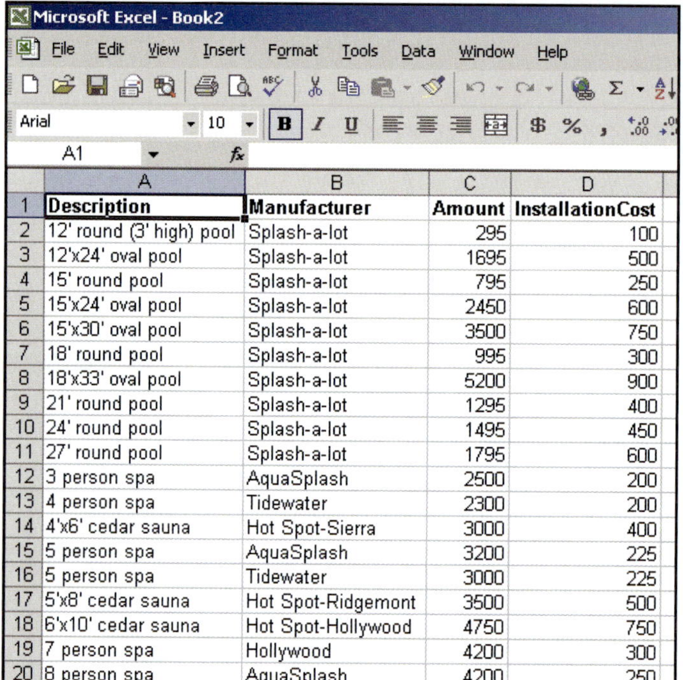

| | A | B | C | D |
|---|---|---|---|---|
| 1 | Description | Manufacturer | Amount | InstallationCost |
| 2 | 12' round (3' high) pool | Splash-a-lot | 295 | 100 |
| 3 | 12'x24' oval pool | Splash-a-lot | 1695 | 500 |
| 4 | 15' round pool | Splash-a-lot | 795 | 250 |
| 5 | 15'x24' oval pool | Splash-a-lot | 2450 | 600 |
| 6 | 15'x30' oval pool | Splash-a-lot | 3500 | 750 |
| 7 | 18' round pool | Splash-a-lot | 995 | 300 |
| 8 | 18'x33' oval pool | Splash-a-lot | 5200 | 900 |
| 9 | 21' round pool | Splash-a-lot | 1295 | 400 |
| 10 | 24' round pool | Splash-a-lot | 1495 | 450 |
| 11 | 27' round pool | Splash-a-lot | 1795 | 600 |
| 12 | 3 person spa | AquaSplash | 2500 | 200 |
| 13 | 4 person spa | Tidewater | 2300 | 200 |
| 14 | 4'x6' cedar sauna | Hot Spot-Sierra | 3000 | 400 |
| 15 | 5 person spa | AquaSplash | 3200 | 225 |
| 16 | 5 person spa | Tidewater | 3000 | 225 |
| 17 | 5'x8' cedar sauna | Hot Spot-Ridgemont | 3500 | 500 |
| 18 | 6'x10' cedar sauna | Hot Spot-Hollywood | 4750 | 750 |
| 19 | 7 person spa | Hollywood | 4200 | 300 |
| 20 | 8 person spa | AquaSplash | 4200 | 250 |

**12**  Close the worksheet. Do not save it.

*This worksheet was created as an interim step and is no longer needed.*

# Task 6
## RETRIEVING DATA FROM WEB PAGES

### *Why would I do this?*

Maintaining current price lists that all the stores use can be a problem when they change rapidly. Instead of sending out updates for price catalogs, you can post the current list of prices as a Web page and then import this page into your workbooks. If the central office makes changes to the price list, you only need to click a button and the price list in your workbooks are updated with the latest values.

In this task, you locate the Web page you created in the previous task and open it in a browser. You copy the address of the file and close the browser, then you import this Web page into a worksheet.

**1** Start Internet Explorer. Choose **File**, **Open**.

*The Open dialog box opens.*

Click **Browse**. Locate **EX1303-Web** in your folder, select it, and then click **Open**.

*The Open box displays the path to the EX1303-Web file on your computer.*

Click **OK**.

*The Web page opens in Internet Explorer.*

**CAUTION**

If Netscape is installed as the default Web browser on the computer you are using, it will start instead of Internet Explorer. This will not affect this step.

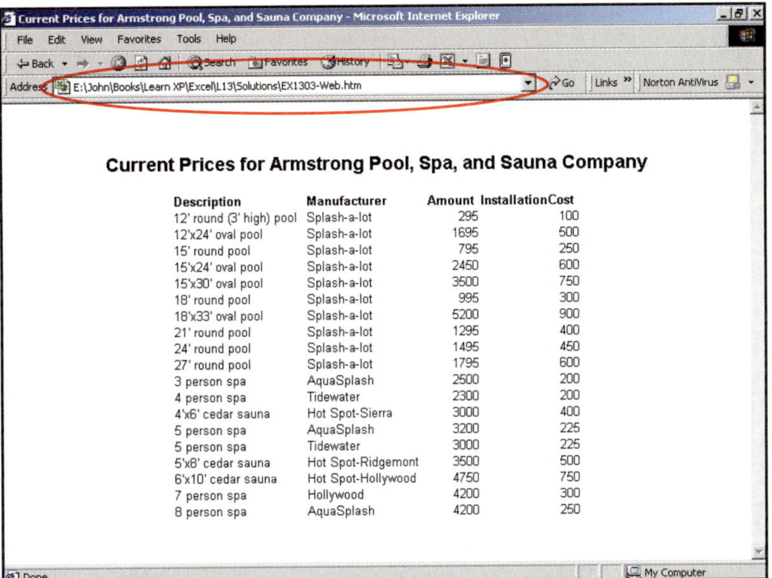


**2** Select the address of the file in the **Address** box. Press Ctrl + **C** to copy the address. Close **Internet Explorer**.

*The address is stored in the Office Clipboard and can be used to locate this Web page.*

Confirm that Excel is open and open **EX1304** from the folder of student files. Save this file as **EX1304-Invoice**.

*An invoice workbook opens that is similar to the one you may have created in the reinforcement exercises in a previous lesson. The formulas in this invoice draw data from the products sheet where the current products and prices are stored.*

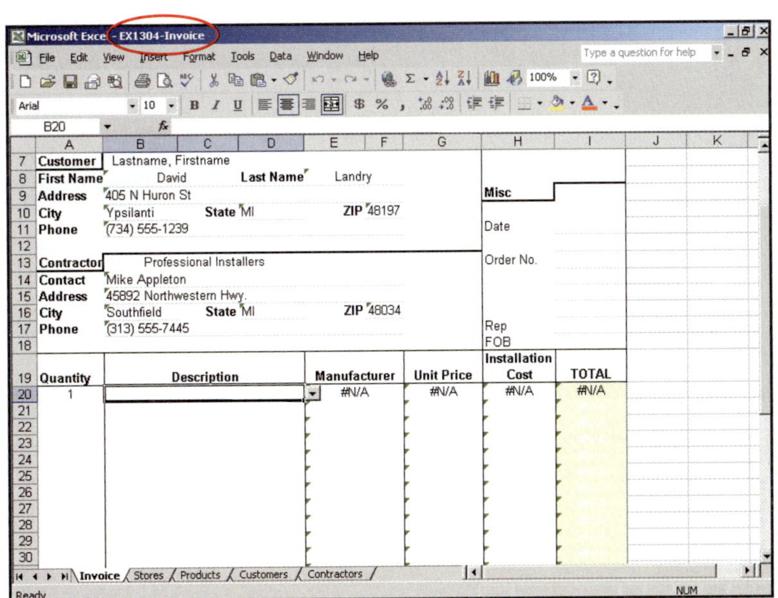

**3** Click the **Products** sheet tab.

*The sheet is empty. Columns A through D have already been defined as a named range called ProductInfo. The lookup formulas in the Invoice sheet will use whatever data you import into this sheet.*

Choose **Data**, **Import External Data**, **New Web Query**.

*The New Web Query window opens and displays the default Web page for your browser. The address line is selected.*

Use **Ctrl** + **V** to paste the address of your Web page in the **Address** box.

*The path to EX1303-Web on your machine differs from the example shown. The Web page displayed in the window is the default home page used by your browser and differs from the example shown.*

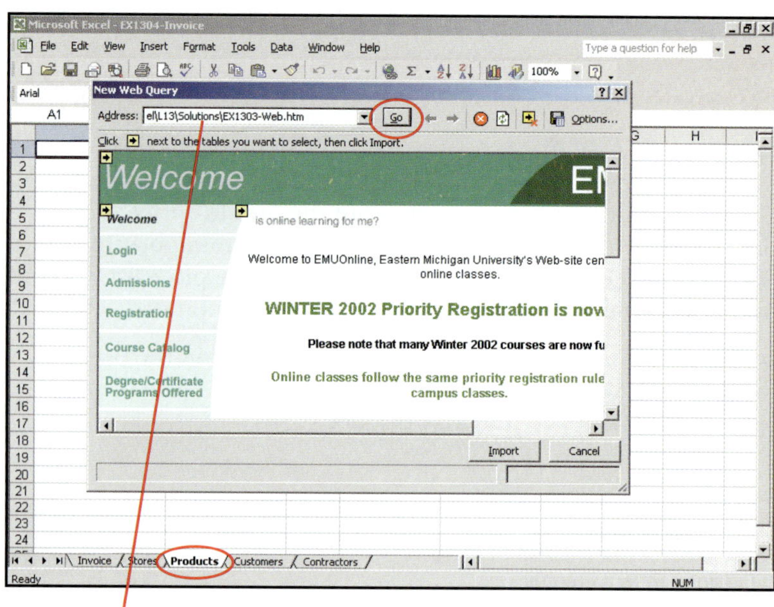

Path to EX1303-Web.htm on your computer

**4** Click the **Go** button.

*The Web page, EX1303-Web, opens in the New Web Query window. Each table in the Web page is identified by a button with a small black arrow on it.*

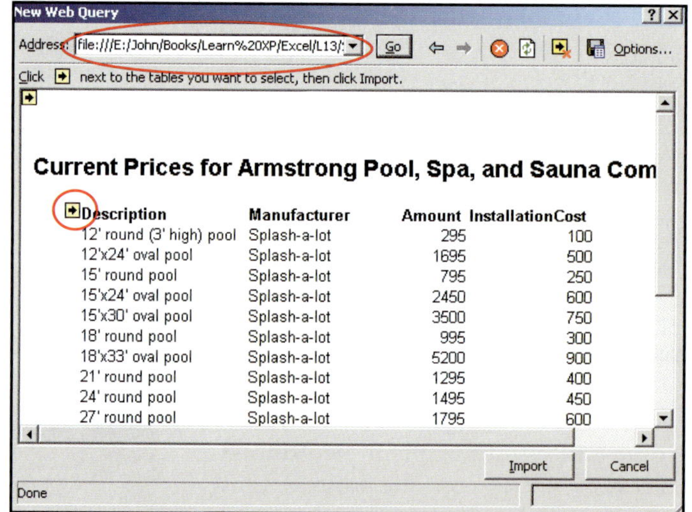

**5** Click the button next to **Description**.

*The button changes to a check box and the table is highlighted to indicate that it is selected.*

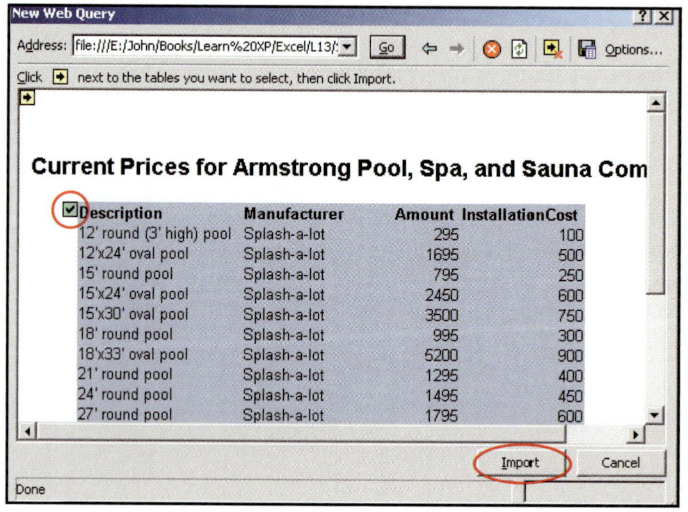

**6** Click **Import**.

*The Import Data dialog box opens.*

Confirm that **Existing worksheet** is selected and that **=$A$1** is chosen as the first cell in the table.

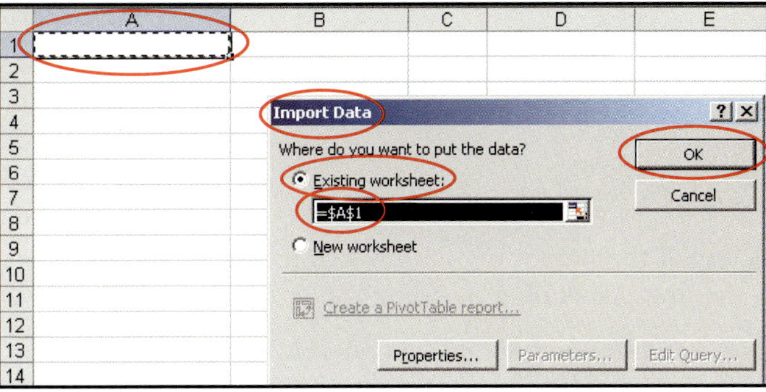

**7** Click **OK**.

*The data is imported into the worksheet and the External Data toolbar is displayed.*

Note the price and installation cost for a 5'x8' cedar sauna. You will add this data to the invoice using lookup functions.

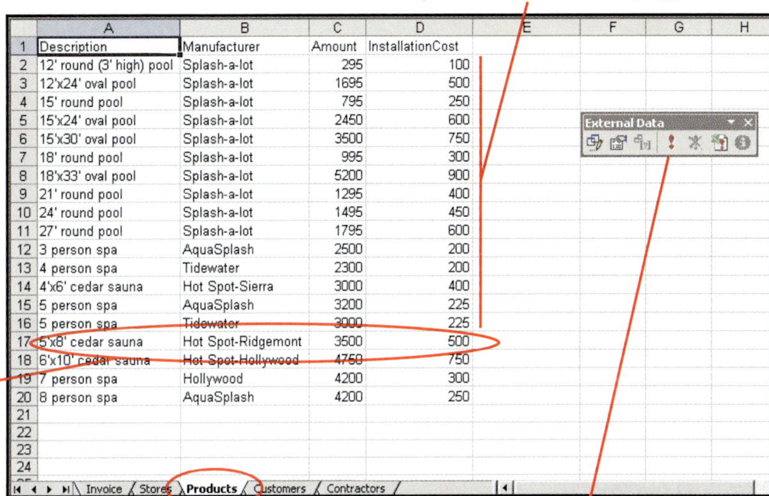

QUICK TIP

To update this sheet with any changes on the company Web page, you can simply click the Refresh Data button on the External Data toolbar.

**8** Click the **Invoice** sheet tab.

*The lookup formulas may use the new data.*

Select cells **B20** through **D20**. Click the arrow next to the box and select **5'x8' cedar sauna** from the list.

*The values used in the Manufacturer, Unit Price, and Installation Cost columns are located on the Products sheet and displayed in the appropriate cells on the Invoice.*

Confirm that the lookup functions in **E20**, **G20**, and **H20** retrieved the correct values from the Products sheet.

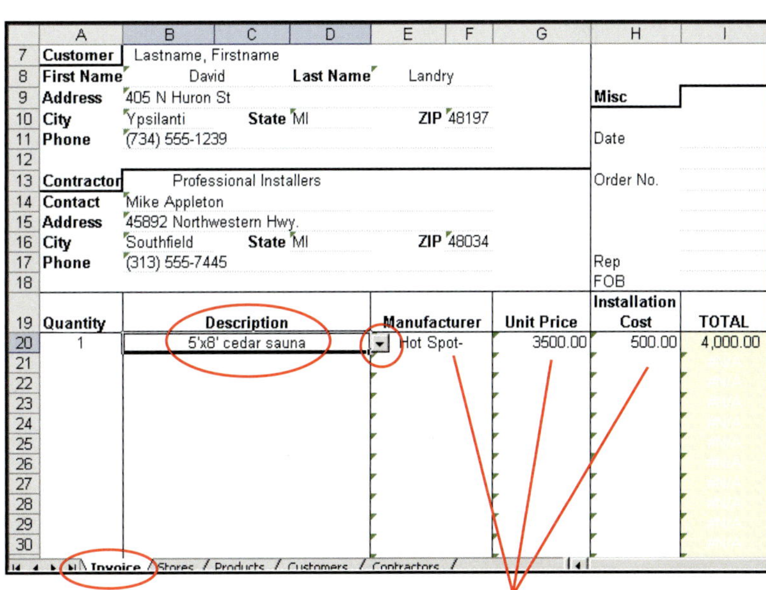

**9** Click the **Customers** sheet tab. Scroll to row **50** and fill in your name and related information. Use **Y-787** as the CustomerNo in column **B**.

*You will create an invoice with your name and address.*

Click any of the names in column **A** and click the **Sort Ascending** button.

*The customer data will be sorted and your name placed in proper alphabetical order. You must sort the list of names so that the lookup functions in the Invoice sheet work properly.*

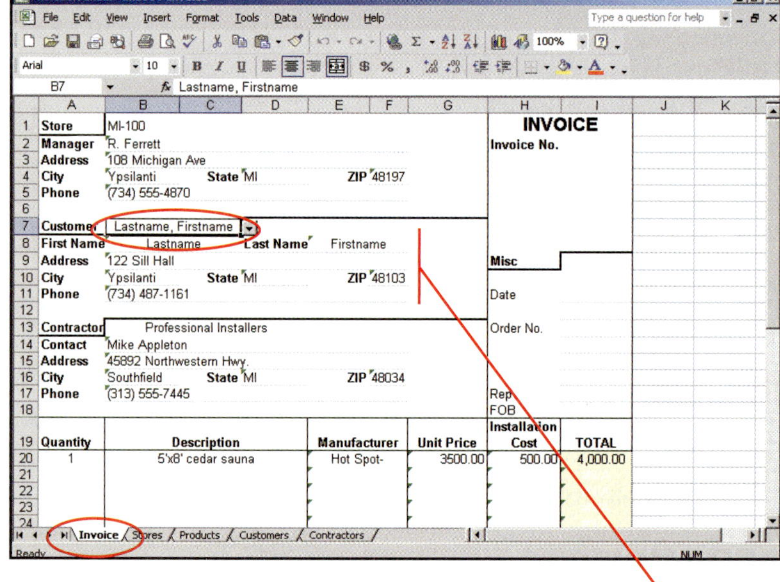


**10** Click the **Invoice** sheet tab. Select **B7** through **B8**. Click the arrow next to the selected cells and choose your name from the list.

*Your information is filled into the Customer information.*

Print this page if your instructor requires it.



**11** Save and close the workbook.

The exercises that follow are designed for you to review and use what you have learned in this lesson. You also have the opportunity to practice your skills and then expand on them by applying them to new situations.

## COMPREHENSION

Comprehension exercises are designed to check your memory and understanding of the basic concepts in this lesson. You distinguish between true and false statements, identify new screen elements, and match terms with related statements. If you are uncertain of the correct answer, refer to the task number following each item (for example, T4 refers to Task 4) and review that task until you are confident that you can provide a correct response.

### TRUE-FALSE

Circle either T or F.

T   F   **1.** To protect worksheet cells from unintended changes, you can select them and choose **Format, Cells, Protection, Enable. (T1)**

T   F   **2.** When you type a password, the text is replaced by asterisks for added security. **(T1)**

T   F   **3.** When you enable the **Track Changes** feature and choose **Highlight Changes,** and the **Highlight changes on screen** option, you can tell what changes have been made to a worksheet. **(T3)**

T   F   **4.** You can accept or reject changes to a whole worksheet but not to individual cells. **(T4)**

T   F   **5.** Excel can import data from Access tables using the **New Database Query** command. **(T5)**

T   F   **6.** Once you import data from a table on a Web page, you can refresh the data by clicking on the **Refresh Data** button on the **External Data** toolbar. **(T6)**

T   F   **7.** When you choose the **Track changes while editing** option, you automatically share the workbook. **(T2)**

### MATCHING QUESTIONS

**A.** [Shared]        **D.** Protect

**B.** Merge          **E.** Track changes

**C.** New Database Query   **F.** New Web Query

Match the following statements to the word or phrase that is the best match from the list. Write the letter of the matching word or phrase in the space provided next to the number.

**1.** _____ Prevent changes to cells **(T1)**

**2.** _____ Displayed next to the file name in the title bar when a workbook is made available to other users **(T2)**

**3.** _____ Combine copies of a shared workbook **(T4)**

**4.** _____ Import data from a Web page **(T6)**

**5.** _____ Import data from a database **(T5)**

**6.** _____ Display changes made to a workbook **(T4)**

Refer to the figure and identify the numbered parts of the screen. Write the letter of the correct label in the space next to the number.

1. _______________

2. _______________

3. _______________

4. _______________

5. _______________

6. _______________

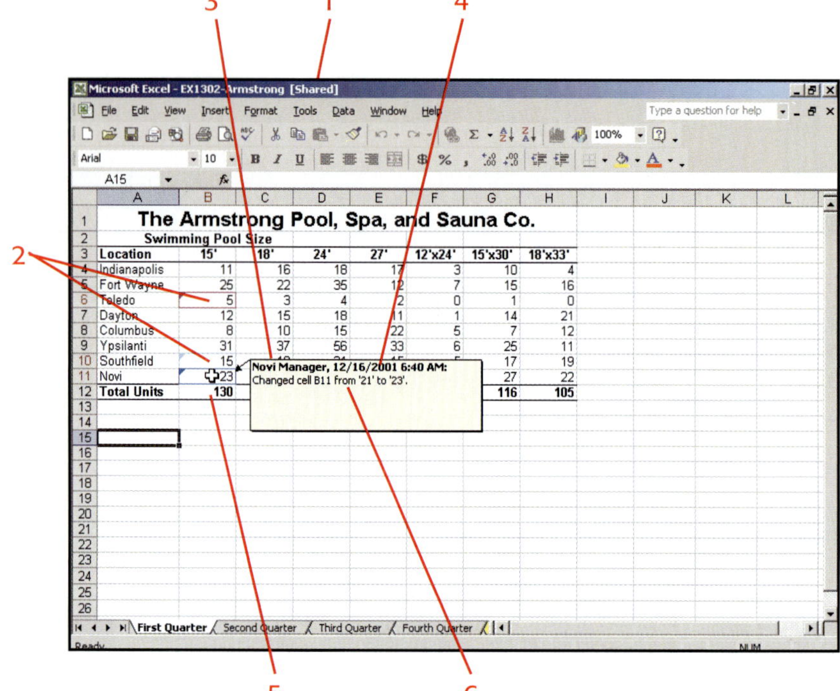


A. Mouse pointer  (T4)

B. Changes made by two different users  (T3)

C. Indicates the workbook is available to multiple users  (T2)

D. Details of a change  (T3)

E. Name of user who made the change  (T4)

F. Date and time of the change  (T4)

Reinforcement exercises are designed to reinforce the skills you have learned by applying them to a new situation. Detailed instructions are provided along with a figure, where appropriate, to illustrate the result. Complete the reinforcement exercises sequentially. Leave the workbook open at the end of each exercise for use in the next exercise until you are specifically directed to close it.

Open **EX1304** and save it as **EX1304-Reinforcement** on your disk for use in the following exercises.

## R1—Importing Data from an Access Database

In this exercise, you import data directly from an Access database into the Contractors sheet of a workbook used to create invoices.

1. Click the **Contractors** sheet tab. Select **A1**.

2. Choose **Data**, **Import External Data**, **New Database Query**. Choose **MS Access Database** and click **OK**.

3. Locate and select **EX1303** in the student files and click **OK**. Click the plus sign next to **tblContractors**. Add all the columns in this table except the first one, ContractorID.

4. Click **Next** twice. Sort the data in ascending order by the **ContractorName** field. Click **Next** and **Finish**.

5. When the **Import Data** dialog box opens, click **Properties**. Select **Overwrite existing cells with new data, clear unused cells**. Click **OK**.

6. Confirm that the data will be placed in the existing worksheet and the cell reference is =$A$1. Click **OK**.

7. Add your name and information as a contractor to the bottom of the list in row **18**. Make up a company name but use your name as the contact person. Sort the table in ascending order on the ContractorName column.

## R2—Protecting a Worksheet

Most of the data on this invoice is looked up from the other sheets. If a user tries to enter data directly in a cell with a formula, the formula could be lost. In this exercise, you unlock the cells intended for user input and protect the sheet with a password. The password in this example is a simple word that is easy to remember. Its purpose is to prevent accidental changes rather than intentional tampering. More secure passwords are collections of letters that cannot be found in the dictionary. The author prefers to take the first letter of each word in a phrase or saying. It is easy to remember but the collection of letters makes no sense by itself.

1. Click the **Invoice** sheet tab. Select **I2**. Choose **Format**, **Cells**, and then click the **Protection** tab. Remove the check mark next to **Locked**. Click **OK**. Repeat this process to unlock **B1**, **B7** through **C7**, **B13** through **D13**, **I11** through **I18**, **A20** through **D36**, and **B41** through **D44**.

2. Choose **Tools**, **Protection**, **Protect Sheet**.

3. Select the **Password to unprotect sheet** box and type **Invoice**. Click **OK**. Enter the password again and click **OK**.

4. Click the arrow next to **D13** and select your company as the contractor. Changes are allowed to this range of cells and your name is retrieved from the Contractors sheet.

5. Try to change your zip code in **F16**. The change is not allowed. Save the workbook.

## R3—Share the Invoice Workbook and Track Changes

You want to make this invoice workbook available to several people in your store and give some of them the option of adding new customers. If anyone makes changes, you want to know who did it and when.

1. Choose **Tools**, **Track Changes**, **Highlight Changes**. Select the option to track changes and share the workbook. Choose **All** and **Everyone**. Click **OK** twice.

2. Click the **Customers** sheet tab. Locate **Daniel Cook**. He moved and changed addresses but kept the same phone number. Change his address to **1316 Glen Leven**.

3. Click the **Invoice** sheet tab. Change the customer to **Daniel Cook**.

4. Print the **Invoice** sheet.

5. Save and close the workbook.

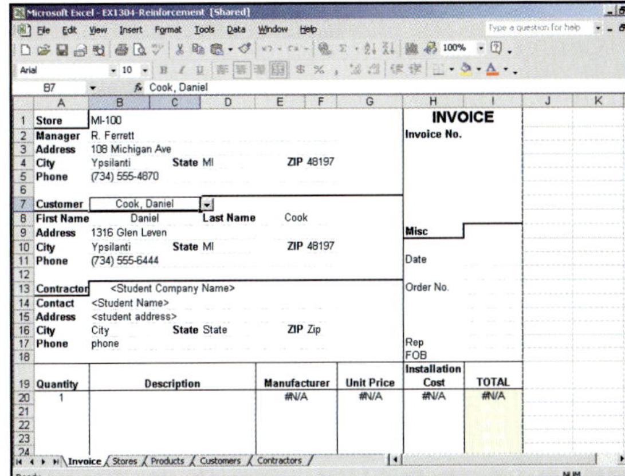

Challenge exercises are designed to test your ability to apply your skills to new situations with less detailed instruction. These exercises also challenge you to expand your repertoire of skills by using commands that are similar to those you have already learned. The desired outcome is clearly defined, but you have more freedom to choose the steps needed to achieve the required result.

## C1—Use a Gantt Chart and Protect the Sheet

Many RFPs (Request for Proposals) require a chart to show the anticipated schedule for completion of the project. One of the most commonly used charts for this purpose is a Gantt chart. A Gantt chart is a method of depicting tasks in a project with horizontal bars that mark the duration of each task and the relationship between them. Diamonds denote milestones. Excel does not have a Gantt chart as one of its charting options but you can create one using the drawing tools. You can use track changes and a Gantt chart in a shared workbook to coordinate a project.

*Goal:* Create a Gantt chart and share the workbook with track changes turned on. Change user names and make changes to the project.

Use the following guidelines:

1. Open a blank worksheet and save it as EX1305-Gantt. Select cell **A1** and type **Term Project for** <your name and section>. Select cell **B3** and enter next Monday's date. Select cell **C3** and enter the date for the following Monday. Select both cells **B3** and **C3**. Use the fill handle to fill in a series of dates to the right. Stop at cell **J3**. You will have a series of dates one week apart.

2. Format row headings and increase row height. Select the row indicators for rows **4** through **9**. Choose **Format**, **Row**, **Height**. Set the row height to **24**. Select cells **A4** through **A10** and choose **Format**, **Cells**. Choose the Alignment tab and check the **Wrap text** option. Choose **Center** for **Horizontal** and **Vertical** text alignment then click **OK**.

3. In cells **A4** through **A10**, type the following row labels: **Develop Idea**, **Get Approval**, **First Draft**, **First Review**, **Make Changes**, and **Due Date**. Center the labels in their respective cells.

4. Draw rectangles, add your name, and use a fill color. Turn on the Drawing toolbar, if necessary. Click the Rectangle drawing tool and drag a long rectangle in row **4** that starts in the middle of cell **B4** and ends in the middle of cell **D4**. Type your name then click the **Center** button on the Formatting toolbar. Click outside the rectangle then click its edge to select it. Click the down-arrow next to the Fill Color button on the Formatting toolbar and choose **yellow**.

5. Draw a diamond to represent a milestone. Click **AutoShapes** on the drawing toolbar, then click **Basic Shapes** and click the diamond at the end of the first row of shapes. Move the pointer to the line between cells **D5** and **E5**. Click and drag to draw a small diamond that is about half the row's height. Fill the diamond with black.

6. Copy and paste the bar and rectangle to finish the chart. Copy the long rectangle and place it in row **6**. Adjust its length and position to start in column **D** and end in column **H**. Copy the black diamond and paste it in row **7** between columns **H** and **I**. Repeat this process to show another task in row **8** and a milestone in row **9**. See the illustration.

7. Choose **Tools**, **Protection**, **Protect Sheet**. Use **Gantt** as the password. Scroll to the bottom of the list of items and select **Edit Objects**. Click **OK**. Reenter **Gantt** and click **OK**.

8. Move the diamond in row **5** to the line between columns **D** and **E**. Adjust the lengths of the bars above and below the diamond so the one above ends at the line between columns **D** and **E** and the one below starts at that line.

9. Try to change one of the cells to confirm that they are protected from change.

10. Print the worksheet. Save and close the workbook.

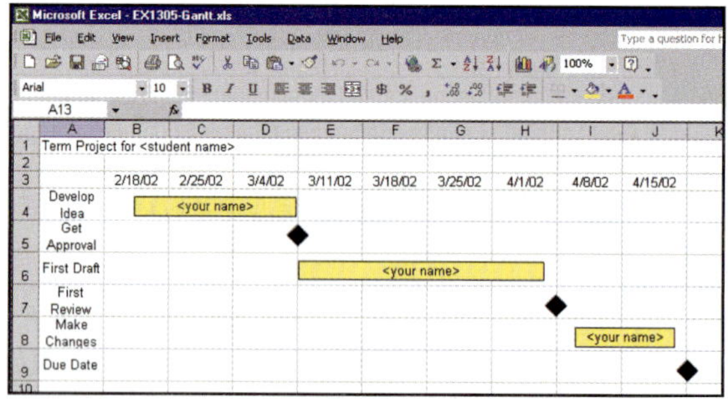

## C2—List Changes on a Separate Sheet

If you need a log of the changes made to a workbook, you can use an option that will list the changes made on a separate sheet and print it.

This exercise uses the file you created doing the tasks in this lesson.

*Goal:* Open EX1302-Armstrong and print a log of the changes made to this file.

Use the following guidelines:

1. Open **EX1302-Armstrong.** Choose Tools, Track Changes, Highlight Changes.

2. Choose **All** in the **When** box and **Everyone** in the **Who** box.

3. Choose **List changes on a new sheet**. Click **OK.** The History sheet appears with a log of all the changes made to the sheet.

4. Print the History sheet.

5. If your instructor requires it, press PrtSc on your keyboard to capture a copy of the screen. Open a blank Word document, type your name, and paste the screen image into the document. Save it as **EX1306-History** and close it.

6. Close the workbook. Do not save the changes.

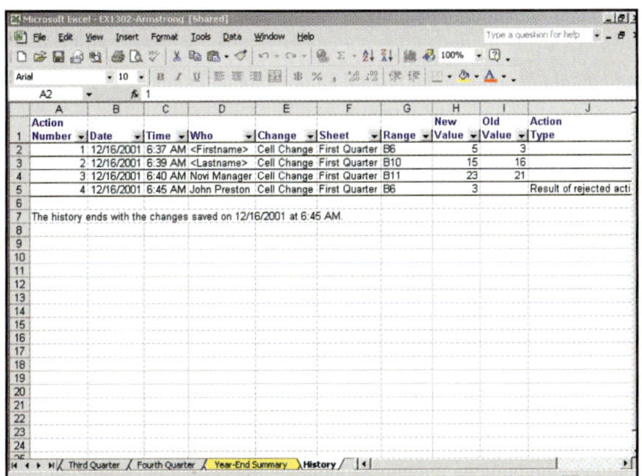

## C3—Import Data from a Government Web Page

Government Web sites are useful for finding information about your own state or county. You can import tables of data from such Web sites.

Open a new workbook in Excel, and save it as **EX1307-Stats**. Choose **Data, Import External Data, New Web Query.** Go to **www.fedstats.gov.** Under **MapStats,** select your state and click the **Submit** button. Choose a table from this site and import it into your workbook. Add your name to cell **A1** on the sheet, and save the file. Print the worksheet or e-mail it to your instructor as directed.

*Goal:* Import data about your state and county.

1. Open a blank workbook and name it **EX1307-Stats.** Rename the **Sheet1** tab **State** and rename the **Sheet2** tab **County.** Select **A1** in the **State** sheet.

2. (Note: If this Web site has changed since publication of this book, check with your instructor. You may need to search for another table of data on a government Web site and use it instead.)

3. Scroll down to the top of the table of data, click the selection button, and import it to the **State** sheet.

4. Select **A1** in the **County** sheet. Choose **Data, Import External Data, New Web Query.** Go to **www.fedstats.gov.** Under the **MapStats** heading, select your state and click the **Submit** button.

5. Select your county from the available list of counties for your state and click **Go.** Scroll down and select the table of county data and import it.

6. Insert your name in **A1** on the **State** and **County** sheets. Format both sheets in **Landscape** orientation and fit the text of each sheet to one page wide.

7. Print both sheets if your instructor requires it. Save and close the workbook.

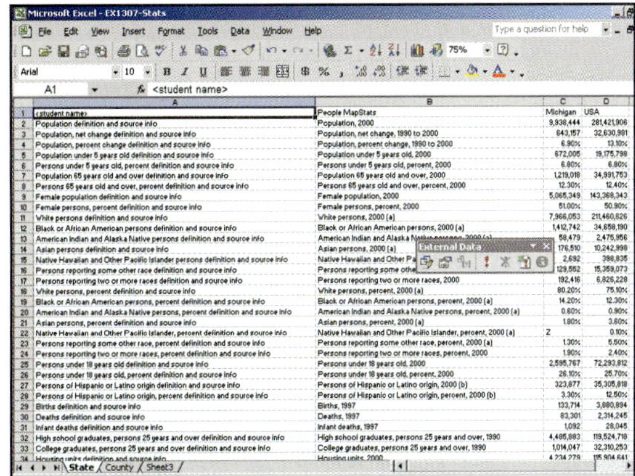

## C4—Collaborating with People Who Have Special Needs

Office XP comes with a full speech recognition program. In Excel 2002, you can use the speech program to have the computer speak the content of the cells to you. This can be helpful if you need to compare data that has been entered with a paper record or if a person is visually impaired. The program can proceed across rows or down columns, and tell you with speech what has been entered in each cell. To do this exercise you must have speakers or headphones connected to your computer and they need to be turned on. Check the volume setting on your speakers before proceeding. The speech software must also be installed.

*Goal:* Use the Speak Cells feature to check accuracy of your entries.

1. Open a blank workbook and save it as **EX1308-Speech**.

2. Choose Tools, Speech, Show Text To Speech Toolbar.

3. Click the **Speak On Enter** button on the right end of the Text To Speech Toolbar.

4. Select **A1.** Type your name and press ↵Enter.

5. Select **A2**. Type **20000000** and press `⏎Enter`. If you typed the correct number of zeros, the program says **twenty million**.

6. Select cell **A4** and enter the following data in cells across this row: **19**, **20-May-02**, **Y-681**, **15x30 pool**, **$4,100.00**, **IN-4**, **01-Jun-02**.

7. Select cells **A6:H20**. Choose **Format**, **Cells**, and then choose the **Alignment** tab. Set **Horizontal** to **General**, **Vertical** to **Top**. Select **Wrap text** and **Merge cells**. Click **OK**.

8. Write a brief essay describing your reaction to this feature. Answer such questions as:

   a) Did you find the Speak On Enter feature helpful?

   b) Did you have any problems getting it to work?

   c) In what circumstances do you think this might be useful?

   d) Do you think this would increase or decrease the speed of entering data?

9. Print this sheet and save it.

10. Click the **Speak On Enter** button on the right end of the Text To Speech Toolbar to turn off this feature. Close the toolbar. Close the workbook.



Create a set of worksheets that use data imported from a Web page to make calculations.

Criteria for grading will be:

1. Demonstration of the use of imported data to keep calculations up to date.

2. Formatting of one of the pages intended for public distribution.

3. Data must be easily updated from the Web page by clicking the refresh button on the Get External Data toolbar.

Some examples of applications that students have used in previous classes to make use of the import data feature are as follows:

- Set up a personal Web page on an Internet portal such as Yahoo.com and display a set of stock prices. The stock prices are imported into a worksheet and then used to calculate the current value of the shares of stock held. The sheet that displays the current status of the user's stock holdings is formatted for printing or may be saved as a Web page.

- Import current population or demographic data from a government site and use that data to make calculations.

- Locate a table of currency exchange rates that is updated daily. Given a mix of currencies that might be in the user's possession, calculate the current total value in U.S. dollars.

1. Place your name in a cell that is clearly visible on the summary worksheet and print it.

2. To complete the project:

   - Save the workbook on your own disk. Name the workbook **EX1309-Import**.

   - Check with your instructor to determine if you should submit the project in electronic or printed form. If necessary, print out a copy of the workbook to hand in.

# Glossary

**Absolute reference**    a cell reference that will not change when copied or filled into other cells.

**Add-In**    tools not usually installed.

**Application**    one of the components of the Microsoft Office XP suite, such as Word, Excel, or Access. An application is often referred to as a program in this book.

**Arguments**    numbers or words used by a function to perform its operation.

**Balloon payment**    a single payment that is made to pay off the balance of a loan.

**Bar chart**    a chart that compares values across categories. The data columns are horizontal.

**Calculations**    mathematical operations involving data in the worksheet cells.

**Cascade**    windows placed on top of each other slightly displaced so you can read the title bar.

**Cell**    a bounded area forming part of a whole that is identified by a column letter and a row number.

**Chart**    a graphic representation of a series of numbers; sometimes referred to as a graph.

**Chart subtype**    a variation on a basic chart type that allows for different emphasis and views of a chart.

**Chart Wizard**    a mini-program that walks you through the steps involved in creating a chart.

**Clipboard**    see Office Clipboard.

**Column chart**    a chart that compares values across categories. The data columns are vertical.

**Column heading**    the letter at the top of each column of an Excel worksheet that identifies the column.

**Comma Separated Values (CSV)**    database values that are separated from each other by a comma.

**Comparison operators**    mathematical operators such as less than and greater than.

**Conditional Formatting**    formatting of the selected cell is applied when a condition is met.

**Customize**    make changes to suit an individual's preferences.

**Database query**    extracts data from a database.

**Delimiters**    characters used to separate values in a database.

**Extrapolation**    estimating values beyond known data points.

**Fields**    types of data in a database.

**Fill handle**    a small box at the lower-right corner of a selected cell that can be used to fill in a series of cells.

**Floating toolbar**    a moveable toolbar that is not located in a specific position on the screen.

**Font**    a typeface style that determines the appearance of text.

**FORECAST**    a function that estimates values from a given set of data.

**Format painter**    a tool that enables you to copy the formatting of one object onto another.

**Formatting toolbar**    a toolbar that contains buttons used to format fonts and alignment. It may share the same row with the standard toolbar.

**Formula**    a representation of the cell locations and the mathematical or logical operations that are performed on the contents of those cells.

**Formula Auditing**    a group of features that may be used to display the relationships between the selected cell and other cells using arrows.

**Formula bar**    the toolbar that displays the contents of the selected cell. If the cell has a formula in it, the formula bar displays the formula rather than the calculated result of executing the formula.

**Freeze panes**    a feature that freezes the rows and columns above and to the left of a selected cell so that they stay on the screen when you scroll through the worksheet.

**Gantt chart**    a chart that uses bars to represent duration and relationships between tasks.

**GDP**    Gross Domestic Product, a measure of a country's economic performance.

**Goal Seek** a tool that determines the value required to produce a desired outcome in a selected cell.

**HLOOKUP** a function that looks up the reference value in the first row of the selected range and then displays the value in a given row. It may be used when the orientation of the table is horizontal.

**Horizontal scrollbar** the bar at the bottom of a window that enables you to move left and right to view information too wide for the screen.

**Hotkey** a letter in a menu or button name that can be used in place of clicking on the menu or button item.

**Hyperlink** a special protocol that is used to connect to another file on your computer or network, to a Web site on the Internet, or between Web pages.

**IF** examines a criteria and then chooses one of two options to perform depending on whether the criteria evaluate as true or false.

**Insertion point** a flashing vertical line that indicates the position where text will be entered. It is sometimes called a cursor.

**Interpolation** estimating a value between known data points.

**ISNA** determines if the selected cell has the #N/A error message.

**Iteration** a synonym for repetition.

**Legend** a list that identifies a pattern or color used in a chart.

**Line chart** a chart that includes a line running through each data point. It is usually used to show trends.

**Linear regression** a statistical method of determining the minimum difference between a line and a set of data points.

**Locked** changes not allowed if the worksheet is protected.

**Macro** an Excel program that is created automatically by recording a sequence of commands.

**Macro virus** an unauthorized program that utilizes the macro options in Microsoft Office.

**Magnifier** displays a panel at the top of the screen that zooms in on the portion of the screen under the mouse pointer.

**Marquee** a box of moving, blinking lines that resembles the flashing lights around the marquee of a theater.

**#N/A** error message displayed when a formula refers to cells that do not have values in them.

**Named range** one or more cells that have been assigned a name. The name may be used in formulas in place of the cell references.

**Normal view** the typical worksheet view.

**Office Assistant** a Microsoft Office help program that enables you to ask questions by typing in sentences or phrases. When you ask a question of the Office Assistant, a series of possible related topics are displayed. You can choose the most appropriate topic for more information.

**Page Break Preview** a view that displays how a large worksheet will be displayed on several pages.

**Pie chart** displays the contribution of each value to the whole.

**PivotTable** an interactive chart that summarizes data by groups and categories.

**Pixel** a unit of screen display.

**Point size** the height of the letters plus the spacing between rows is measured in points. There are 72 points per inch.

**Program** one of the components of the Microsoft Office XP suite, such as Word, Excel, or Access. A program is often referred to as an application in this book.

**Protection** prevents unauthorized changes.

**Range_lookup** an optional argument that may be used with the VLOOKUP or HLOOKUP functions to force exact matches.

**Registered programs** have three letter file extensions associated with files they create.

**Relative reference** a cell reference that will change when the formula is copied, moved, or filled into other cells.

**Remove All Arrows** arrows displayed by the Trace Dependents and Trace Precedents commands may be removed by using the Remove All Arrows command.

**ROUND()** a function that may be used to round the result of the payment or interest calculation to two decimal places, the way it is done at banks.

**Row heading** the number at the left of the row that is used to identify cells in that row.

**R-squared value**   a statistical measurement that describes how well the trend line fits the data.

**Scenario**   a method of saving a set of values.

**Screen area**   the screen area setting controls how many picture elements, or pixels are displayed on the screen.

**Sheet**   a synonym for worksheet, identified by tabs at the bottom of the window.

**Smart Tag**   a small icon with context-sensitive options and advice displayed when the program thinks you have made a mistake or there is a feature you may want to know about.

**Solver**   a tool that is similar to Goal Seek except you can specify several different cells that affect the outcome and place constraints on the values used in the process.

**Standard toolbar**   a toolbar that contains commonly used buttons such as Save, Print, Cut, Copy, and Paste. It may share the same row with the Formatting toolbar.

**Start button**   the button on the left side of the taskbar that is used to run programs, change system settings, get help, or shut down the computer.

**Style**   a combination of font, color, and emphasis.

**SUMIF**   a sum function is combined with criteria to allow the user to sum only those cells in the selected range that meet the criteria in a corresponding range.

**Task pane**   a pane that opens on the right side of the window, which is used to display commonly used tools.

**Template**   a set of standard settings that may be used to reduce the time it takes to create a new worksheet.

**Three-dimensional reference**   references to cells in another worksheet.

**Trace Dependents**   cells that depend on the selected cell for calculations are identified with arrows.

**Trace Precedents**   cells on which the selected cell depends for calculations are identified with arrows.

**Transpose**   axes may be switched when pasting a table using the Transpose option in the Paste Special command.

**Trend line**   a line that displays the general trend of a set of data points.

**Unlock**   allows changes to be made to selected cells when the rest of the worksheet is protected.

**Vertical scrollbar**   the bar at the right side of a window that enables you to move up and down to view information too long for the screen.

**VisiCalc**   the first spreadsheet program for personal computers.

**Visual Basic Editor**   a text editor used for writing or changing a program written in Visual Basic.

**Visual Basic for Applications (VBA)**   a programming language used with Microsoft Office.

**VLOOKUP**   a function that looks up the reference value in the first column of the selected range and then displays the value in a given column.

**Watch Window**   a window that displays the values of selected cells.

**Workbook**   a collection of worksheets saved under one filename.

**Worksheet**   a set of cells that are identified by row and column headings.

**Workspace**   a group of workbooks.

**XML (eXtensible Markup Language)**   an abbreviation for Extensible Markup Language which is a standard for describing data in web pages. The older web page design language, HTML, defines how elements of a web page are displayed while XML defines what those elements contain.

**Zoom**   the percent of screen magnification. It may be set by using a button found on the right side of the standard toolbar.

# Index

 *Clear Formats option*

 *data points*

 *Toolbars option*